FAST TRACK TO A 5

Preparing for the AP® World History Examination

To Accompany

The Earth and Its Peoples

6th and 7th Editions
by Richard W. Bulliet, Pamela Kyle Crossley, Daniel R. Headrick, Steven W. Hirsch, Lyman L. Johnson, and David Northrup

Dawn Bolton
Windermere High School, Orlando, Florida

Christine Custred
Edmond Memorial High School, Edmond, Oklahoma

Rodney Floyd
Alpharetta High School, Alpharetta, Georgia

Eric Hahn
Ladue Horton Watkins High School, St. Louis, Missouri

Jonathan Henderson
West Forsyth High School, Cumming, Georgia

Amie La Porte
Holy Innocents' Episcopal School, Atlanta, Georgia

Kristin Taylor
Plano, Texas

CENGAGE

Australia • Brazil • Mexico • Singapore • United Kingdom • United States

ISBN: 978-1-337-40181-4

Cengage
20 Channel Center Street
Boston, MA 02210
USA

Cengage Learning is a leading provider of customized learning solutions with office locations around the globe, including Singapore, the United Kingdom, Australia, Mexico, Brazil, and Japan. Locate your local office at: **www.cengage.com/global**.

Cengage Learning products are represented in Canada by Nelson Education, Ltd.

To learn more about Cengage Learning Solutions, visit **www.cengage.com**.

AP® is a trademark registered by the College Board, which is not affiliated with, and does not endorse, this product.

Printed in the United States of America
Print Number: 01   Print Year: 2018

CONTENTS

Handwritten notes in margins:

East Asia

10 Terms To know
1. Neo-Confucianism
2. Champa Rice
3. Song Dynasty
4. Khanates
5. Pax Mongolica
6. Sinification
7. Shogunate
8. Shinto
9. Bushido
10. Goryeo

People To know
1. Minamoto Yoritomo
   1147 CE - 1199 CE
   The 1st Shogun

2. Genghis Khan
   1162 CE - 1227 CE
   Founder: Mongol Empire

3. Kublai Khan
   1215 CE - 1294 CE
   Founder: Yuan Dynasty

4. Marco Polo
   1254 CE - 1324 CE
   Italian Traveler

5. Ibn Battuta
   1304 CE - 1369 CE
   Moroccan Islamic Traveler

6. Zhenghe
   1371 CE - 1435 CE
   CHINESE ISLAMIC Navigator

About the Authors

DAWN BOLTON graduated cum laude with a bachelor's degree in history from Emory University. She is entering her 12th year as a history teacher and her 10th year working with the AP program. She teaches both AP World History and AP European History. She currently teaches at Windermere High School in Orlando, Florida. In addition to teaching, she also works for the College Board. She has served as both an exam reader and a table leader for AP World History.

CHRISTINE CUSTRED earned a bachelor's degree from St. Cloud State University and a master's degree from the University of Central Oklahoma. She has taught AP Macro/Microeconomics, AP U.S. History, and AP World History at Edmond Memorial High School in Edmond, Oklahoma. She has been a reader for the AP U.S. History exam and the AP World History exam. She serves as a College Board consultant in AP U.S. History and AP World History and is a National Board Certified Teacher.

RODNEY FLOYD is entering his 32nd year as a World History teacher. He graduated from Auburn University cum laude. He has taught in Florida and Georgia. He has won numerous teaching and coaching awards such as the Nobel Teacher of Excellence, Who's Who Among High School Teachers, and Teacher of the Year in three different schools. He also does training in teacher pedagogy for the Georgia Department of Education and the Fulton County School District. He is also a National AP World History exam reader and table leader.

ERIC HAHN earned his PhD from St. Louis University in Curriculum and Instruction. He has taught AP U.S. History and AP World History. He started the AP World History program at Ladue Horton Watkins High School in St. Louis, Missouri in 2002. In addition to teaching, he has read AP exams for AP U.S. History and then AP World History since 1996. He is a workshop and institute consultant for the College Board for both AP U.S. History and AP World History.

JONATHAN HENDERSON has been teaching AP World History since 2002 and serves as an exam reader and a College Board Consultant in AP World History. He is a question writer for the AP World History test and the SAT subject test in World History. Jonathan studied history at the graduate level at Cambridge University, travelled to Asia as a Fulbright scholar, and taught in Central Asia as a State Department Fellow. He teaches AP World History at West Forsyth High School near Atlanta, Georgia.

AMIE LA PORTE holds a bachelor's degree in history and French literature from Agnes Scott College and a master's degree in education from Walden University. She has been teaching AP World History for 11 years and has served as a reader and table leader scoring exams, in addition to writing content for and presenting about AP Insight—World History. She currently teaches at Holy Innocents' Episcopal School in Atlanta, Georgia, where she started both the AP World History and AP Microeconomics programs.

KRISTIN TAYLOR holds a dual bachelor's degree in English and history from Baylor University and a master's degree in humanities from the University of Dallas. She has taught AP European History, AP World History, and American Studies, a combination of AP U.S. History and AP English Language, in the Plano Independent School District at Jasper High School and Plano West Senior High. She has served in multiple positions with the College Board, acting as a teaching mentor, writing curriculum, and participating since 2006 at the AP World History reading in multiple positions from reader to question leader.

****

PREVIOUS CONTRIBUTORS

ESTHER ADAMS earned a bachelor's degree in history and a master of teaching from the University of Virginia. In addition to AP World History, she has taught AP U.S. History; Global History; Senior Project; U.S. National, State, and Local Government; Latin American Studies; and Model United Nations. She has graded AP World History examinations for four years, two as a reader and two as a table leader. In addition to writing the chapters for the period 600–1450, she served as coordinator for the writing of this book.

BARBARA BRUN-OZUNA holds a bachelor's degree in history from Texas Christian University and a master's degree in history from the University of North Texas. She has taught AP European History, AP Human Geography, and Pre-AP World Geography at Paschal High School in Fort Worth, Texas. She began the AP World History program for the Fort Worth school district in 2001. She serves as a College Board consultant in world history and an AP World History reader and table leader.

THEISEN HEALEY holds a bachelor's degree in history from the University of Michigan and a master of education from George Washington University. Courses he has taught include AP U.S. History; U.S. National, State, and Local Government; AP European History; Philosophy; Peace Studies; and Model United Nations; as well as AP World History. He wrote the Foundations review chapters, covering the period ca. 8000 B. C.E.–600 C.E. He is chairman of the Social Studies Department at Walter Johnson High School.

NATHAN SCHWARTZ has a bachelor's degree in Social Studies/History Education from the University of Maryland and a master of education from Bowie State University. Before joining the Walter Johnson faculty, he was chairman of the Social Studies Department at Surrattsville High School in Prince George's County, Maryland. He has taught both regular and honors sections of every core social studies course, and now teaches AP World History, AP U.S. History, and Model United Nations. His chapters review the period 1750–1914. He began as an AP World History examination reader in 2007.

DAVID UHLER has a bachelor's degree in international affairs from George Washington University and graduate certification in secondary teaching from American University. A book editor before becoming a teacher, he has taught U.S. History, Modern World History, and Model United Nations, along with

AP World History. Author of the chapters covering the period 1450–1750, he started reading AP World History examinations two years ago.

PATRICK WHELAN earned a bachelor's degree in history from Yale University. In addition to AP World History, he has taught AP U.S. History, AP European History, AP Art History, Humanities, Holocaust Studies, and English at Saint Stephen's Episcopal School in Bradenton, Florida. He has scored AP World and European History examinations since 1998 and has served as a College Board institute and workshop consultant for AP World History.

MICHAEL WILLIAMS, a professional soccer player for eight years, has taught for six years. He has a bachelor's degree in political science from Howard University, a master's degree in history from Northwestern University, and a master in the art of teaching from Johns Hopkins University. He teaches both U.S. History and AP World History. He wrote Chapters 21–25, the review of the period from World War I to the present.

ACKNOWLEDGMENTS

The authors of this book would like to dedicate our work to our students, past, present, and future, as well as to our colleagues in the classroom who undertake the journey of world history each year with their own students. We hope you find our work informative and useful, not only as a study tool but more importantly as a window into the past of humankind.

We would like to thank our families and friends who encouraged us through the duration of the project. We would also like to acknowledge the incredible support from Jarrod Massey and Chris Peek, who reviewed the manuscript, as well as the tremendous organization and vision of Karen Ettinger, our project manager.

Dawn Bolton

Christine Custred
Rodney Floyd
Eric Hahn
Jonathan Henderson
Amie La Porte
Kristin Taylor

Part I:

Preparing for the AP® World History Exam

PREPARING FOR THE AP® EXAM

Advanced Placement® is a challenging yet stimulating experience. Whether you are taking an AP® course at your school or you are working on AP® independently, the stage is set for a great intellectual journey. As the school year progresses and you burrow deeper and deeper into the coursework, you can see the broad concepts, events, conflicts, resolutions, and personalities that have shaped the history of our complex world. Examining the cultural, political, and economic developments that have brought great change while acknowledging the continuities that remain throughout world history is a thrilling task. Fleshing out those forces of change and continuity in world history is exciting. More exciting still is recognizing references to those forces in the media and how history has shaped current world events.

But as spring approaches and the College Board examination begins to loom on the horizon, Advanced Placement® can seem quite intimidating, given the enormous scope and extent of the information you need to know. If you are intimidated by the College Board examination, you are certainly not alone.

The best way to approach an AP® examination is to master it, not let it master you. If you manage your time effectively, you will eliminate one major obstacle—learning a considerable amount of factual material along with the analytical skills needed to be a true world historian. In addition, if you can think of these tests as a way to show off how your mind works, you have a leg up: attitude *does* help. If you are not one of those students, there is still a lot you can do to sideline your anxiety. Focused review and practice time will help you master the examination so that you can walk in with confidence and get a 5.

BEFORE THE EXAM

By February, long before the exam, you need to make sure that you are registered to take the test. Many schools take care of the paperwork and handle the fees for their AP® students, but check with your teacher or the AP® coordinator to make sure that you are on the registration list. (This is especially important if you have a documented disability and need test accommodations.) If you are studying AP® independently, call AP® Services at the College Board for the name of the local AP® coordinator, who will help you through the registration process.

AP® is a trademark registered by the College Board, which is not affiliated with, and does not endorse, this product.

The evening before the exam is not a great time for partying. Nor is it a great time for cramming. If you like, look over class notes or drift through your textbook, but concentrate on the broad outlines, not the small details, of the course. You might also want to skim through this book and read the AP® tips. Then relax. Get your things together for the next day. Sharpen a fistful of no. 2 pencils with good erasers for the multiple-choice section of the test, and set out several black or dark-blue ballpoint pens for the free-response questions. You should bring a watch in order to pace yourself since you will not be allowed to use the clock or timer functions on your smartphone. Get a piece of fruit or a snack bar and a bottle of water for the break. Depending on your testing site, you may need your Social Security number, photo identification, and an admission ticket. After you have set aside all of those items, put your mind at ease, go to bed, and get a good night's sleep. An extra hour of sleep is more valuable than an extra hour of study.

On the day of the examination, make certain to eat breakfast—fuel for the brain. Studies show that students who eat a hot breakfast before testing get higher grades. You will be given a 10-minute break between Section I and Section II; the world history exam lasts for over three hours, so be prepared for a long morning. You do not want to be distracted by a growling stomach or hunger pangs. Be sure to wear comfortable clothes, taking along a sweater in case the heating or air-conditioning is erratic. When you get to the testing location, make certain to comply with all security procedures. Cell phones are not allowed, so leave yours at home or in your locker if at all possible. Be careful not to drink a lot of liquids, necessitating trips to the bathroom, which take up valuable test time.

Remember, preparation is key! Best wishes on your journey to success—go out and get that 5.

TAKING THE AP® WORLD HISTORY EXAM

The AP® World History exam consists of four parts in two sections: Section I includes Parts A and B. Section I Part A consists of 55 multiple-choice questions that you will have 55 minutes to answer; all questions will be organized into sets of two to five questions that follow an item of stimulus material (a primary or secondary source). Section I Part B consists of three short-answer questions (SAQs) that you will answer in 40 minutes. Section II includes its own Part A and Part B. Section II Part A is the document-based question (DBQ) assessing your ability to apply your understanding of the documents while using historical reasoning skills. You will be given 60 minutes to read the documents and answer the question. Section II Part B consists of three long-essay questions (LEQs) that focus on the same historical thinking skill as it applies to different time periods; you will choose to respond to one of these in the allotted 40 minutes. Both Part A and Part B of Section II require students to develop a thesis supported by relevant evidence and strengthened with analysis and synthesis. Your proctor will monitor the time, but you need to keep an eye on your watch and pace yourself so you can do your best on all parts of the exam. Remember that smart watches, watch alarms, and smartphones are not allowed.

Here is a chart to help you visualize the breakdown of the exam:

Section	Multiple-Choice Questions	Short-Answer Questions	Document-Based Question (Essay)	Long-Essay Question (Essay)
Weight	40% of exam	20% of exam	25% of exam	15% of exam
Number of Questions	55	3	1	Long-Essay Question: choose one of the three question options
Time Allowed	55 minutes	40 minutes	100 minutes for reading and writing	
Suggested Pace	Approx. 1 minute per question	Approx. 13 minutes per question	15 minutes for reading and planning and 45 minutes to write	40 minutes to plan and write

AP® is a trademark registered by the College Board, which is not affiliated with, and does not endorse, this product.

The Themes, Disciplinary Practice, and Reasoning Skills

In order to be successful on the exam, the AP® World History course requires you to use all of the disciplinary practices and reasoning skills that you have worked all year in class to develop. These skills are essential for any historian, but they are particularly critical in world history because of the large amount of content in the course. The themes and historical reasoning skills were created to provide a framework upon which you can hang all of the information you have learned throughout the year. Additionally, the College Board has developed thematic learning objectives that aid students in identifying broad historical trends and offer students the opportunity to develop historical thinking skills in the process of traversing through the themes. All questions on the AP® World History Exam will require students to apply one or more history reasoning skills to at least one of the thematic learning objectives, so it is a good idea to familiarize yourself with both.

A practical exercise that should become a habit is to ask yourself, "What theme does this piece of historical information fall under?" "What disciplinary practice or reasoning skill am I using right now to process this information and make meaning out of it?" This will help you to see the larger historical trends and global connections that twine through our past and present and into the future.

Following are the themes, disciplinary practices, and reasoning skills for the AP® World History course. Please examine them carefully and use them throughout this review book as an essential reference tool and guideline. A complete list of the Thematic Learning Objectives and Overarching Questions can be found following the overview of the types of questions on the AP® World History Exam.

Themes

1. Interaction Between Humans and the Environment (ENV)
   - Demography and disease
   - Migration
   - Patterns of settlement
   - Technology
   - Use of natural resources

2. Development and Interaction of Cultures (CUL)
   - Religions
   - Belief systems, philosophies, and ideologies
   - Science and technology
   - The arts and architecture

3. State Building, Expansion, and Conflict (SB)
   - Political structures and forms of governance
   - Empires
   - Nations and nationalism
   - Revolts and revolutions
   - Regional, transregional, and global structures and organizations
   - Diplomacy

4. Creation, Expansion, and Interaction of Economic Systems (ECON)
   ▪ Agricultural and pastoral production
   ▪ Trade and commerce
   ▪ Labor systems
   ▪ Industrialization
   ▪ Capitalism and socialism

5. Development and Transformation of Social Structures (SOC)
   ▪ Gender roles and relations
   ▪ Family and kinship
   ▪ Racial and ethnic constructions
   ▪ Social and economic classes

These themes are constant topics throughout the course, and you should be working with them from the beginning of the year. Throughout the course keep asking yourself where you see elements of both continuity and change—in particular societies, across regions, and throughout time—as they relate to each of these themes. It is also a good idea to begin using the themes as a way to make comparisons between societies over the course of human history.

AP® HISTORY DISCIPLINARY PRACTICES AND REASONING SKILLS

One of the broader goals of AP® World History is to train you to think like a historian. That begs the question, "How do historians think?" The answer is found in AP® History Disciplinary Practices and Reasoning Skills. As a student in any rigorous history course, you should be able to do the following:

Disciplinary Practices: Analyzing Historical Evidence and Argument Development
▪ Practice 1—Analyzing Historical Evidence: Make conclusions about the past by using a variety of diverse sources.
▪ Practice 2—Argument Development: Answer a question by making a clear and persuasive argument.

Reasoning Skills: Making Historical Connections and Chronological Reasoning
▪ Skill 1—Contextualization: Connect large historical processes to individual situations in history.
▪ Skill 2—Comparison: View the similarities and differences among societies or among developments within one society.
▪ Skill 3—Causation: Evaluate the causes and effects for what has occurred in the past.
▪ Skill 4—Continuity and Change over Time: Analyze history through an investigation of what has stayed the same and what has changed.

To be successful on the AP® World History exam, you need to master these disciplinary practices and reasoning skills as well as the content. The history reasoning skills are the tools you need to unlock the meaning from the content in the multiple-choice section as well as in the free-response portions of the exam. For example, on the DBQ you will use several different history reasoning skills, from analyzing primary documents to understanding diverse interpretations. Any time you write a thesis you are constructing an argument. LEQs may ask you to demonstrate your ability to assess continuity and change or to compare societies in a variety of ways. In the multiple-choice section, you will apply the disciplinary practice and reasoning skills when you examine graphs, maps, and primary source information, and you will often deal with multiple-choice questions that require an understanding of diverse interpretations or ask you to address an author's point of view.

The history disciplinary practices and reasoning skills are also the tools you use in the classroom every day to think critically about the content of the course. These are the tools of historians that you train with all year; by the time of the exam you should be ready to demonstrate your understanding of these disciplinary practices and reasoning skills as well as the content of the AP® World History course.

STRATEGIES FOR THE MULTIPLE-CHOICE SECTION

As mentioned in the previous chart, the multiple-choice section of the test makes up 40 percent of your total score. Thus, it is important that you spend time learning how to master this section—especially its timing. Here are some rules of thumb to help you work your way through the multiple-choice questions:

- **Read the question carefully.** Pressured for time, many students make the mistake of reading the questions too quickly or merely skimming them. By reading a question carefully, you may already have some idea about the correct answer. You can then look for it in the responses. Careful reading is especially important in EXCEPT or NOT questions because, unlike the typical multiple-choice question, all the answers are right except for one.
- **Eliminate any answer you know is wrong.** You can write on the multiple-choice questions in the test book. As you read through the responses, draw a line through any answer you know is wrong.
- **Read all of the possible answers, then choose the most accurate response.** AP® exams are written to test your precise knowledge of a subject. Sometimes there are a few probable answers but one of them is more accurate.
- **Mark and skip tough questions.** If you are hung up on a question, mark it in the margin of the question book. You can come back to it later if you have time. Make sure you skip that question on your answer sheet too.
- **Apply the history reasoning skills and the course themes to help you answer stimulus-based questions.** All of the multiple-choice questions will ask you to use a primary source, a secondary source, or a historical issue including a document, an image, a map, a graph, or a chart to help answer the question. Examine the wording of the question for clues as to what reasoning skill and theme you should be using.
- **Watch your time carefully!** You can spend too much time pondering potential answers—especially when you have multiple sources to synthesize. Watch the time and don't get bogged down. Instead, mark the best answer and then flag the question for review should you have time remaining at the end.

TYPES OF MULTIPLE-CHOICE QUESTIONS

Although you will encounter various types of multiple-choice questions in Section I Part A of the exam, one characteristic they all have in common is that each question is tied to some type of stimulus. The answer to each question may not come directly from the stimulus, in which case you will need to combine your knowledge of the content of the course (thematic learning objectives and concept outline) with your ability to apply history disciplinary practices and reasoning skills. Additionally, although the stimulus will typically represent one period (or one region or society) in world history, the questions accompanying the stimulus may ask you to make connections to information from a different time period (or region).

Here are some suggestions for how to approach each kind of stimulus you are likely to encounter on the exam.

PHOTOGRAPH/ILLUSTRATION/CARTOON QUESTIONS

These questions require you to interpret a picture in order to answer the question. A good approach is to examine the picture and any given source information before you read the question and possible responses. Look for symbolism in the image; symbols are especially used in cartoons and paintings. Ask yourself what the artist or photographer is trying to convey. After you have read the question, re-examine the image for clues to answer correctly.

41. The author of this cartoon would most likely support which of the following:
    (A) Free market capitalism
    (B) Imperialism
    (C) The development of the factory system
    (D) Workers organizations

ANSWER: D. The cartoon portrays the class divisions that occurred in western Europe during the Second Industrial Revolution. The image shows the lavish lifestyle of the capitalists and the poverty of the labor. The cartoonist is sympathetic to the laborers and would therefore support the formation of labor unions.

History Disciplinary Practice: Analyzing Historical Evidence
Theme: Creation, expansion, and interaction of economic systems; development and transformation of social structures

Chart/Graph Questions

These questions require you to examine the data on a chart or graph. While these questions are not difficult, spending too much time interpreting a chart or graph can slow you down. Therefore, for these kinds of stimuli, it is preferable to read the question and all of the possible answers first so that you know what you are looking for as you look over the stimulus. Often, you can even eliminate obviously incorrect responses quickly by reading the question first, making the final answer selection easier.

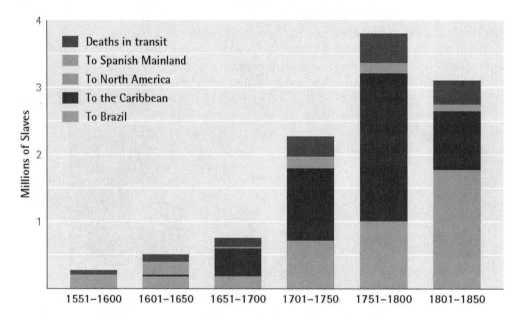

2. Which of the following statements does the above table best support?
   (A) The transatlantic slave trade remained at the same level from 1551 to 1850.
   (B) The period 1801–1850 witnessed the largest forced migration of African slaves.
   (C) Most slaves came from East Africa.
   (D) Beginning in 1651, the majority of slaves were brought to the Caribbean and Brazil.

ANSWER: D. After analyzing the table, Option A can be eliminated because the measurement bars are not level in *any* period. Option B is incorrect because the total number of Africans in transit was highest in the period 1751–1800 and declined some in the period 1801–1850. Option C is incorrect in that there is no way to tell from the table what percentage of the slaves came from a specific region in Africa. Because the bars for transit of slaves to the Caribbean and Brazil are longest beginning in 1651, Option D is the correct answer.

History Disciplinary Practice: Analyzing Historical Evidence
Themes: Interaction between humans and the environment; Creation, expansion, and interaction of economic systems

INTERPRETING A MAP

For history students, maps are used to describe not only geography, but also to convey information about the social, political, cultural, and/or economic organization of human societies. When you are asked to interpret a map, your best bet is to read the title and the key to the map first, to get an idea of what information you will find on the map. Then, read through the questions and the answer choices before going back to the map to find the correct answer.

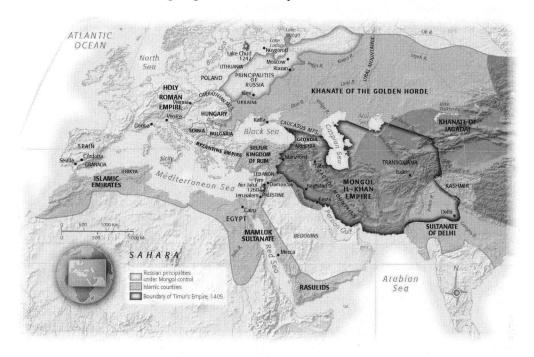

3. This map of western Eurasia in the 1300s shows the
    (A) coexistence of Mongol domains and Islamic sultanates.
    (B) khanate of the Great Khan, which Khubilai Khan ruled.
    (C) Mongol takeover of all of western Eurasia.
    (D) Mongol takeover of all of the Islamic world.

ANSWER: A. The map shows both Mongol khanates and Islamic kingdoms. The answer cannot be B because the domains of the Great Khan were in Central and East Asia. It cannot be C or D because we see other kingdoms that the Mongols did not control, including those of western Europe.

History Disciplinary Practice and Reasoning Skill: Analyzing Historical Evidence; Contextualization

Theme: State building, expansion, and conflict

INTERPRETING A PRIMARY SOURCE

Historians rely on primary sources to gather information about the past. When presented with primary sources on the AP® World History Exam, be sure to note the origin of the source (both time and place) in order to help you situate the source within your knowledge of history. Although authors' names are cited whenever possible, it is likely that you won't be familiar with the author, so attention to the details of time and place in which the source was created can help you better understand the source itself. For these kinds of questions, you should look over the source information first. Next, read through each multiple-choice question before thoroughly reading the entire source carefully. Because textual sources often accompany a longer set of multiple-choice questions (three to five per source), it will save time if you consider the questions first so that you know what information to focus on from the source. Sometimes, you might be presented with two short sources and may be asked to compare or identify the reason for differences between the two.

Code of Nesilim 8. If anyone blind a male or female slave or knock out their teeth, he shall give ten half-shekels of silver, he shall let it go to his home.

—Hittite legal code from c. 1650–1500 B.C.E.

Hammurabi's code 17. If any one find runaway male or female slaves in the open country and bring them to their masters, the master of the slaves shall pay him two shekels of silver.

—Babylonian law code from c. 1750 B.C.E.

http://www.fordham.edu/halsall/ancient

---

4. It appears from the given excerpts of two ancient law codes that
   (A) slaves were considered property.
   (B) male and female slaves were considered equal in value.
   (C) slaves had legal rights.
   (D) silver was a common medium of exchange for slaves.

ANSWER: B. Although answers A, C, and D are also partially evident from the textual evidence, it is evident from the excerpts that both societies viewed the value of male and female slaves equally. Thus, B is the best answer.

History Disciplinary Practice and Reasoning Skills: Analyzing Historical Evidence; Comparison; Contextualization

Theme: Development and transformation of social structures

INTERPRETING A SECONDARY SOURCE

Secondary sources reveal the work historians do to interpret and develop analytical theories about the past. A secondary source presents the historian's argument along with the historical evidence to support it. You might be asked to identify appropriate historical evidence to either support or challenge the argument presented in the source. Sometimes, you will be presented with two short excerpts from two historians that might present opposing views or interpretations of the same topic and then be asked to compare the two and/or identify the differences between the authors' interpretations. As with primary source-based multiple-choice questions, a strategy to help you use your time effectively is to read the questions first to get an idea of what to look for in the source excerpts. Be sure to read the entire excerpt carefully before selecting an answer.

SHORT-ANSWER QUESTIONS (SAQs)

You are required to write responses to a total of three SAQs in 40 minutes for Part B of Section I of the AP® World History Exam. Your score on this portion will count for 20 percent of your final exam score. For the third question, you will have a choice between two options: either from periods 1–3 or from periods 4–6. Each SAQ will have three tasks and the first two questions will require using or interpreting a stimulus (the same types of stimulus material seen in the multiple-choice sections: primary and secondary sources, graphs, charts, maps, images, etc.). You will choose a third question to answer from Question 3 and Question 4. Neither of these will utilize a stimulus. Furthermore, each SAQ will focus on a chronological range using the AP® World History Curriculum Framework as a guide. The following chart will help you visualize the SAQ section of the exam:

Short-Answer Questions	Primary Practice or Skill Assessed	Source Type	Periods Assessed
Questions 1 and 2 are mandatory			
1	Analyzing Secondary Sources	Secondary source	Periods 3–6 (c. 1450 C.E. to present)
2	Comparison or Continuity and Change over Time	Primary source text or visual source	Periods 3–6 (c. 1450 C.E. to present)
Students choose Question 3 or Question 4			
3	Comparison or Continuity and Change over Time (Different skill from SAQ #2)	No stimulus	Periods 1–3 (to c. 1450 C.E. to present)
4			Periods 4–6 (c. 1750 C.E. to present)

As you can see, each SAQ will also directly assess one of the disciplinary practices or reasoning skills. In addition, each question will also assess one or more of the thematic learning objectives.

Although you do not need to develop and defend a thesis for these types of questions, you may not simply write a "bulleted" response. Instead, word your responses to each part of each SAQ in a complete sentence (or a few concise sentences) that respond directly to the question. Take care to also fit your entire response within the indicated space (a lined box) in the response booklet. Be sure to include the correct number of clear and relevant examples as required by the question in your response. The scoring for the SAQs is fairly straightforward: you earn one point for each successfully answered part of each question.

Consider the following example of an SAQ:

3. Answer all parts of the question that follows.
    (A) Identify ONE way in which Christianity influenced the development of Islam in the period 600 C.E. to 1450 C.E.
    (B) Explain ONE similarity between the diffusion of Christianity and the diffusion of Islam in the period 600 C.E. to 1450 C.E.
    (C) Explain ONE difference between the diffusion of Christianity and the diffusion of Islam in the period 600 C.E. to 1450 C.E.

ANSWER: For Part A, there are several ways that Christianity influenced Islam, from monotheism, the incorporation of Jesus of Nazareth as a prophet, or the impact of the Crusades. A good response would not only identify one of these reasons but also directly connect and thoroughly explain how the reason identified actually contributed to the development of Islam.

A good response to Part B could include a discussion of how both Christianity and Islam were adapted by the various cultures that converted to each religion or how both religions were spread in part by the work of missionaries. Regardless of the identified similarity, a good response would need to directly address the similarity and provide specific evidence to bolster the argument.

A good response to part C could include the role of military conquest in the spread of Islam versus Christianity's more gradual spread throughout western Europe, or the role of the Roman Catholic bureaucracy in the spread of Christianity versus the role of the caliphates. Again, the response would need to directly address the difference and provide specific evidence to support it.

STRATEGIES FOR SECTION II

In Section II of the AP® World History exam, you are required to write essays for one DBQ and one LEQ. Part A of Section II is the DBQ, and it represents 25 percent of your final score. For the DBQ, you are given 15 minutes for reading the documents and organizing and outlining your material and 45 minutes for writing the essay. The DBQ is scored out of 7 points.

Part B of Section II is the LEQ, and it represents 15 percent of your final score. For Part B, you will be presented with three questions that assess the same history disciplinary practice or reasoning skill as applied to different time periods, so you will have to choose which question you will answer. You will have 40 minutes to plan and respond to whichever of the three LEQs you choose. The LEQ is scored out of 6 points.

The key to success on each of these essays is understanding and internalizing the components of each type of essay's scoring rubric. That's what we will focus on here.

AP® Tip

For each essay in Section II, the AP® examination has built in time for you to develop an outline. Time spent on an outline is important for a number of reasons:

- ■ It prevents you from writing an essay that is unorganized because you begin writing whatever comes into your head at the moment.
- ■ It allows you to determine your analytical thesis after seeing the evidence you can gather to support your argument.
- ■ It provides you with an opportunity to brainstorm before writing the essay.

Once you have outlined your essay, it is time to put pen to paper. Remember that examination readers are looking for a clear thesis backed up with specifics. Concentrate on setting out accurate information in straightforward, concise prose. You cannot mask vague information with elegant prose.

THE DOCUMENT-BASED QUESTION (DBQ)

As its name implies, the DBQ presents you with a variety of primary-source information in the form of seven documents. Primary sources are original material created during the time period under study, and they include everything from maps, photographs, and illustrations to excerpts of speeches, essays, books, and personal letters. Furthermore, the DBQ will only assess periods 3–6 or c. 1450 C.E. to the present.

All free-response questions require you to utilize your knowledge of the topic, but with the DBQ your essay must additionally be based on the documents provided. Your goal is to link each document to the question and then use that information in an analytical and evaluative essay. Thus, the following are necessary for a quality DBQ essay according to the AP® World History rubric:

- ■ **Thesis/Claim (0–1 point):** One point is earned for the presentation of a thesis that makes a historically defensible claim. The thesis must respond specifically to all parts of the question and must do more than restate or rephrase the question. The thesis must consist of at least one sentence located in either the introduction or conclusion.
- ■ **Contextualization (0–1 point):** One point is earned for relating the topic of the prompt to broader historical events, developments, or processes that occur before, during, or continue after the time frame of the question. Merely a phrase or reference will not count here; you must illustrate a specific relationship.
- ■ **Evidence (0–3 points):** One point is earned for accurately describing the content from at least three of the documents. Quotes are not appropriate and will not be sufficient to earn this point.

  To earn two points, your essay must accurately describe the content from at least six documents. Again, quotes will not be sufficient. In addition, your essay must also use the content of the documents to support an argument in response to the prompt.

  To earn the third point for evidence, you must use at least one piece of specific historical evidence not found in the documents. You will need to describe the evidence and use it to support an argument about the prompt. Furthermore, this piece of evidence may not be the same evidence used to earn the contextualization point.

◾ **Analysis and Reasoning (0–2 points):** One point is earned for explaining how or why the document's point of view, purpose, historical situation, or audience is relevant to an argument about the prompt for at least three documents.

The second point is earned by demonstrating a good understanding of the historical development that is the focus of the prompt and using evidence to corroborate, qualify, or modify an argument that addresses the prompt. There are several ways to demonstrate this, such as:

◾ Explaining nuance of an issue by analyzing multiple variables
◾ Explaining both similarity and difference, or explaining both continuity and change, or explaining multiple causes, or explaining both cause and effect
◾ Explaining relevant and insightful connections within and across periods
◾ Confirming the validity of an argument by corroborating multiple perspectives across themes
◾ Qualifying or modifying an argument by considering diverse or alternative views or evidence

Take a look at this sample DBQ:

1. Using the following documents, analyze the extent to which technology has led to the formation of the global marketplace in the period 1750–1900.

Document 1

Source: *Sketch of the Progress of the Human Mind*, written by the Marquis de Condorcet in 1793. The Marquis de Condorcet was a mathematician, philosopher, and educational reformer in France.

If we were to limit ourselves to showing the benefits derived from the immediate applications of the sciences, or in their application to man-made devices for the well-being of individuals and the prosperity of nations, we would be making known only a slim part of their benefits. The most important, perhaps, is having destroyed prejudices and re-established human intelligence, which until then had been forced to bend down to false instructions instilled in it by absurd beliefs passed down to the children of each generation by terrors of superstition and the fear of tyranny. . . .

Document 2

Source: Joseph Dupleix, Memorandum to the Directors of the French East India Company, written in 1753.

All the Company's commerce in India is shared with the English, Dutch, Portuguese and Danes. The division of trade, or rather this rivalry, has served to raise considerably the price of merchandise here and has contributed quite a little toward cheapening the quality—two unfortunate circumstances which further reduce the price and profits in Europe. . . . Our Company can hope for no monopoly in the Indian trade.

Document 3

Source: Richard Guest, *A Compendious History of the Cotton Manufactory*, published in 1823.

The present age is distinguished beyond all others by the rapid progress of human discovery. . . . One, however, which would seem to merit the attention of the Englishman from its having brought an immense increase of wealth and population to his territory, has obtained comparatively little attention. While admiration has been unboundedly lavish on other triumphs of the mind, the successive inventions and improvements of the Machinery employed in the Cotton Manufacture have [not] obtained the notice . . . their national importance required. . . .

Under the influence of the manufacture of which they have been the promoters, the town of Manchester has, from an unimportant provincial town, become the second in extent and population in England, and Liverpool has become in opulence, magnitude, elegance and commerce, the second Seaport in Europe. . . .

Document 4

Source: Excerpt from a booklet published by the Liverpool and Manchester Railway Company to publicize the opening of its railroad in 1830.

During the last fifty years, the transit of goods between Liverpool and Manchester has taken place on the Mersey and Irwell Navigation or the Duke of Bridgewater's canal. These in their day, were great works . . . but they cease to be adequate to the conveyance of goods . . . it was recommended I 1832 to diminish the distance between these two great towns by the means of a Rail-road. . . .

Speed—despatch—distance—are still relative terms, but their meaning has been totally changed within a few months, what was quick is not slow, what was distant is now near, and this change in our ideas will not be limited to the environs of Liverpool and Manchester—it will pervade society at large.

Document 5

Source: Advertisement for Lipton Teas, published in the *Illustrated London News*, 1890s.

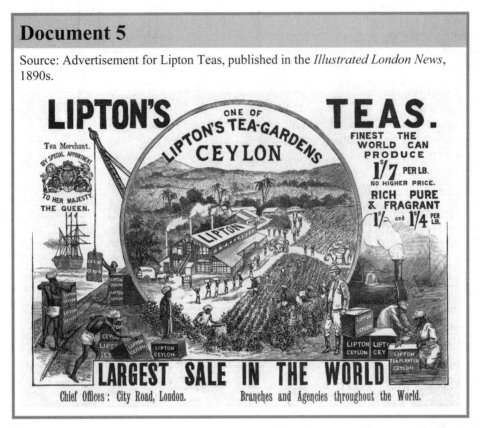

Document 6

Source: Map of the expansion of the United States, 1850–1920.

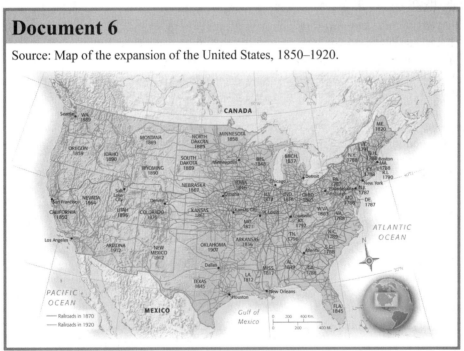

Document 7

Source: Excerpt from a letter by Iwasaki Mitsubishi to his employees in 1876.

Many people have expressed differing opinions concerning the principles and advantages of engaging foreigners or Japanese in the task of coastal trade. . . .

Looking back into the past . . . when we abandoned the policy of seclusion and entered into an era of friendly commerce with foreign nations, we should have been prepared for this very task. However, due to the fact that our people lack knowledge and wealth, we have yet to assemble a fleet sufficient to engage in coastal navigation. Furthermore, we have neither the necessary skills for navigation nor a plan for developing maritime transportation industry. This condition is the cause of attracting foreign shipping companies to occupy our major maritime transportation lines . . . I now propose . . . to recover the right of coastal trade in our hands.

The first step is an analysis of each document in order to come up with evidence in order to create your thesis. What is the meaning of the document? What or who is the source, and how does that affect their point of view? The source provides important clues in the position being put forth in the document. As you analyze the meaning or significance of the document, jot down margin notes—generalizations that relate to the document and the prompt. For example:

- **Margin note for Document 1** *Human intellect should be praised over technology for creating progress.*

- **Margin note for Document 2** *National rivalries drove the need for new technology, which allowed for competition in the global marketplace.*

- **Margin note for Document 3** *Technological advancements in cotton allowed English cities to be prominent in global trade.*

- **Margin note for Document 4** *Railroads increase the speed and volume of trade.*

- **Margin note for Document 5** *Technology allowed easier access to raw materials.*

- **Margin note for Document 6** *Technology increased participation in the global marketplace.*

- **Margin note for Document** *7 Nationalism fueled technological development.*

Once you have done this, you should consider the information you know about the prompt outside of the information presented in the documents. Combine the evidence from the documents with the outside information to create your thesis and the main points you are going to use to prove your thesis (your arguments). Each argument should specifically connect evidence from the document back to your main thesis, while incorporating outside information and analysis of the purpose, intended audience, historical context of the document, and/or author's point of view. For example, your thesis might argue that while technology improved the volume and number of participants in the global marketplace, other factors were also at work. Competition between states was also a driving force behind developing the marketplace between 1750 and 1900. Throughout your essay, you will provide evidence to support this claim. Decide which documents are best for showing your analysis and reasoning skills. You may want to explain that Document 4 is an advertisement—a brochure touting the marvels of the company's product to encourage future investors. Consider mentioning America's arrival in Japan and the subsequent Meiji Restoration as historical context for Document 7. To decide on additional historical examples that would be helpful, look at the sources that are provided. Think about other information you know that could help corroborate your argument that isn't already in any of these sources. Make sure your outside evidence is specific and includes an explanation of how it is relevant to your argument.

As part of your planning, you will also want to consider broader historical events or processes that may have influenced the topic to use for your contextualization. Finally, write your thesis, making sure it answers the prompt and shows your argument. Make sure your thesis has an argument and does not just repeat the prompt. With good planning at the beginning, your DBQ should be in great shape!

There are three DBQs in this book: one in the Diagnostic Test and one in each of the two practice tests. Additional DBQs are provided in the appendix of the textbook. Use these DBQs to practice going through the process of writing a DBQ, and you will feel very comfortable and confident on the exam!

LONG-ESSAY QUESTIONS (LEQS)

The AP® World History Exam concludes with the LEQ. You will be required to respond to one of the three possible prompts. All three prompts assess the same theme and the same reasoning skill but from different time periods. The first prompt deals with periods 1–2, the second with periods 3–4, and the third with periods 5–6. The option you choose really depends on how much accurate, relevant historical evidence you can confidently include in your essay given that you should spend no more than 40 minutes on planning and writing it.

Your essay for this question must come entirely from your knowledge of world history—you will not be provided with any information outside of the prompts themselves. However, the topics of the questions are limited to topics or examples detailed in the concept outline developed by the College Board for AP® World History and available on their site. Again, the prompt will assess your ability to demonstrate one of the reasoning skills, such as comparison, causation, or continuity and change over time. LEQs are scored on a six-point rubric as follows:

■ **Thesis/Claim (0–1 point):** An acceptable thesis must make a historically defensible claim and directly and specifically address all parts of the question. Simply restating or rephrasing the prompt is unacceptable. The thesis must consist of at least one sentence located in either the introduction or the conclusion.

■ **Contextualization (0–1 point):** One point is earned for relating the topic of the prompt to broader historical events, developments, or processes that occur before, during, or continue after the time frame of the question. Merely a phrase or reference will not count here; you must illustrate a specific relationship.

- **Evidence (0–2 points):** In order to earn one point, your essay must contain specific historical examples of evidence relevant to the prompt. To earn the second point, you must use specific historical examples to support an argument in response to the prompt.
- **Analysis and Reasoning (0–2 points):** To earn the first point, you must demonstrate the reasoning skills (comparison, causation, and continuity and change over time) by framing or structuring your argument with them. The skill assessed will be apparent based on the prompt. The second point is earned by demonstrating a good understanding of the historical development that is the focus of the prompt and using evidence to corroborate, qualify, or modify an argument that addresses the prompt. There are several ways to demonstrate this, such as:
  - Explaining nuance of an issue by analyzing multiple variables
  - Explaining both similarity and difference, or explaining both continuity and change, or explaining multiple causes, or explaining both cause and effect
  - Explaining relevant and insightful connections within and across periods
  - Confirming the validity of an argument by corroborating multiple perspectives across themes
  - Qualifying or modifying an argument by considering diverse or alternative views or evidence

Be sure to that in your preparation you practice a few times with each type of skill so that you will feel confident applying any of the skills. You will find practice LEQ prompts in the appendix of the textbook.

To conclude, here are some tips for writing AP® World History essays:

- **Thesis:** Be certain your thesis statement is in either the introduction or conclusion of your essay. You need to present your main argument in the first paragraph or the last paragraph so it is clear what you are proving in your essay. Also, make sure you answer the question asked.
- **Grammar:** You will not lose points for spelling or grammatical errors as AP® exam essays are essentially rough drafts, but it is important to write as coherently as possible. Remember, if the reader is unable to follow your arguments because of excessively poor grammar and/or spelling, it will be harder to get the necessary information across and earn points. It is also important to write as legibly as possible so all of your good ideas can be understood. An illegible essay struggles to earn points.
- **Dates:** Do not panic if you cannot remember a specific date; try to use a broader description such as "early nineteenth century" or "around the sixth century" if you cannot remember an exact date.
- **Quality over Quantity:** Writing a great deal does not mean you are writing what needs to be in your essay. Focus on making sure you are hitting all the rubric points rather than writing long introductions or conclusions. Make your argument, support it with relevant and accurate historical evidence, and wrap up. You want to have time to do both essays well.

THEMATIC LEARNING OBJECTIVES

As mentioned earlier, the College Board has identified five themes present throughout each of the six time periods defined in the concept outline for AP® World History. To further assist students in the study of world history, the College Board has also created thematic learning objectives—a series of tasks students should be able to do with related content, categorized by theme. You should make review of the thematic learning objectives a regular part of your study of world history throughout the school year because every question on the AP® exam serves to measure your understanding of at least one of these objectives. Because all of the learning objectives can be applied to content in multiple time periods, reviewing them can also be a way to trace continuity and change over time. You can use the learning objectives as a way to help you organize and remember content.

Note how many of the thematic learning objectives are embedded within a history reasoning skill, such as comparison, causation, continuity and change over time, and so on. Remember, all questions on the AP® exam are not only based on the following learning objectives, but also require the use of history reasoning skills!

Theme 1: Interaction Between Humans and the Environment (ENV)

Overarching Questions	Learning Objectives—Students are able to . . .
1. How have people used diverse tools and technologies to adapt to and affect the environment over time?	**ENV-1:** Explain how different types of societies have adapted to and affected their environments.
	ENV-2: Explain how environmental factors, disease, and technology affected patterns of human migration and settlement over time.
2. How and to what extent has human migration and settlement been influenced by the environment during different periods in world history?	**ENV-3:** Evaluate the extent to which migration, population, and urbanization affected the environment over time.
	ENV-4: Explain how environmental factors have shaped the development of diverse technologies, industrialization, transportation methods, and exchange and communication networks.
	ENV-5: Evaluate the extent to which the development of diverse technologies, industrialization, transportation methods, and exchange and communication networks have affected the environment over time.

Theme 2: Development and Interaction of Cultures (CUL)

Overarching Questions	Learning Objectives—Students are able to . . .
1. How and why have religions, belief systems, philosophies, and ideologies developed and transformed as they spread from their places of origin to other regions?	**CUL-1:** Explain how religions, belief systems, philosophies, and ideologies originated, developed, and spread as a result of expanding communication and exchange networks.
	CUL-2: Explain how religions, belief systems, philosophies, and ideologies affected political, economic, and social developments over time.
	CUL-3: Explain how cross-cultural interactions resulted in the diffusion of culture, technologies, and scientific knowledge.
2. How have religions, belief systems, philosophies, and ideologies affected the development of societies over time?	**CUL-4:** Explain how technological and scientific innovations affected religions, belief systems, philosophies, and ideologies over time.
	CUL-5: Explain how the arts are shaped by and reflect innovation, adaptation, and creativity of specific societies over time.
3. How were scientific and technological innovations adapted and transformed as they spread from one society or culture to another?	**CUL-6:** Explain how expanding exchange networks shaped the emergence of various forms of transregional culture, including music, literature, and visual art.

Theme 3: State Building, Expansion, and Conflict (SB)

Overarching Questions	Learning Objectives—Students are able to . . .
1. How have different forms of governance been constructed and maintained over time?	**SB-1:** Explain how different forms of governance have been constructed and maintained over time.
	SB-2: Explain how and why different functions and institutions of governance have changed over time.
2. How have economic, social, cultural, and environmental contexts influenced the processes of state building, expansion, and dissolution?	**SB-3:** Explain how and why economic, social, cultural, and geographical factors have influenced the processes of state building, expansion, and dissolution.
	SB-4: Explain how and why internal and external political factors have influenced the process of state building, expansion, and dissolution.
	SB-5: Explain how societies state and stateless societies have interacted over time.
	SB-6: Explain the political and economic interactions between state and non-state actors over time.

Theme 4: Creation, Expansion, and Interaction of Economic Systems (ECON)

Overarching Questions	Learning Objectives—Students are able to . . .
1. How and to what extent have modes of production and commerce changed over time?	**ECON-1:** Explain how technology shaped economic production and globalization over time.
	ECON-2: Explain the causes and effects of economic strategies of different types of communities, states, and empires.
	ECON-3: Explain how different modes and locations of production and commerce have developed and changed over time.
	ECON-4: Explain the causes and effects of labor reform movements.
2. How have different labor systems developed and changed over time?	**ECON-5:** Explain how and why labor systems have developed and changed over time.
	ECON-6: Explain how economic systems and the development of ideologies, values, and institutions have influenced each other.
	ECON-7: Explain how local, regional, and global economic systems and exchange networks have influenced and impacted each other over time.

Theme 5: Development and Transformation of Social Structures (SOC)

Overarching Questions	Learning Objectives—Students are able to . . .
1. How have distinctions based on kinship, ethnicity, class, gender, and race influenced the development and transformations of social hierarchies?	**SOC-1:** Explain how distinctions based on kinship, ethnicity, class, gender, and race influenced the development and transformations of social hierarchies.
	SOC-2: Evaluate the extent to which different ideologies, philosophies, and religions affected social hierarchies.
	SOC-3: Evaluate the extent to which legal systems, colonialism, nationalism, and independence movements have sustained or challenged class, gender, and racial hierarchies over time.
2. How, by whom, and in what ways have social categories, roles, and practices been maintained or challenged over time?	**SOC-4:** Explain how the development of specialized labor systems interacted with the development of social hierarchies.
	SOC-5: Explain how social categories, roles, and practices have been maintained or challenged over time.
	SOC-6: Explain how political, economic, cultural, and demographic factors have affected social structures over time.

A DIAGNOSTIC TEST

The purpose of this diagnostic test is to provide you with an indication of how well you will perform on the AP® World History examination. Keep in mind that the exam changes every year, so it is not possible to predict your score with certainty. The multiple-choice questions here are correlated to key concepts, thematic learning objectives, and historical thinking skills so you can spot areas of weakness quickly. You can use the time-period correlation at the beginning of the answer key for this diagnostic test to identify which periods to concentrate on when preparing for the AP® exam.

AP® WORLD HISTORY EXAMINATION
Section I
Part A: Multiple-Choice Questions
Time: 55 minutes
Number of questions: 55
Percent of examination score: 40%

Note: This examination uses the chronological designations B.C.E. (before the Common Era) and C.E. (Common Era). These correspond to B.C. (before Christ) and A.D. (anno Domini), which are used in some world history textbooks.

DIRECTIONS: The multiple-choice section consists of question sets organized around a stimulus—a primary or secondary source, a historian's argument, or a historical problem. For each question, select the best response.

Questions 1-3 refer to the map below.

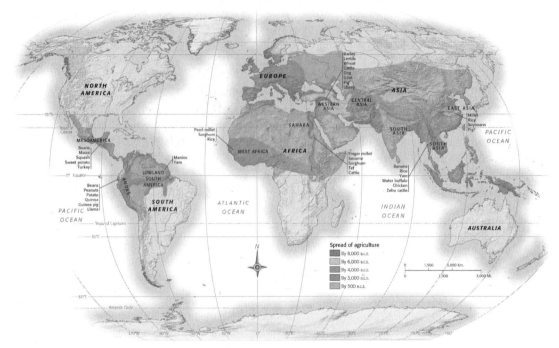

© Cengage Learning

1. Based on the map above, which of the following statements is accurate regarding the development of agriculture?
   (A) Knowledge of agriculture, including domestication of animals, spread rapidly through Eurasia.
   (B) While agriculture widely diffused across the Americas, areas that practice agriculture in Eurasia were relatively isolated.
   (C) The diffusion of agriculture was a gradual process over a period of thousands of years.
   (D) By 500 B.C.E., most human groups had developed sustainable agricultural practices.

2. The development of permanent agricultural villages in many of the areas that developed agriculture illustrated on the map can best be explained by which of the following?
   (A) Climate changes and the suitability of the environment

   (B) The presence of domesticated animals
   (C) The immediate decline of the hunter-forager lifestyle
   (D) The beginning of the last Ice Age

3. Which of the following accurately describes a comparison between the development of agriculture in Mesoamerica and the development of agriculture in the Middle Hast?
   (A) Both regions were able to domesticate animals that could be used as beasts of burden to assist in food production.
   (B) Neither region developed beyond several small, scattered agricultural villages and remained isolated.
   (C) In Mesoamerica, wheat became the primary crop for most farming communities, while the Middle East focused on barley cultivation.
   (D) Agriculture in the Middle East included the domestication of multiple species of animals, which was not the case in Mesoamerica.

Questions 4–8 refer to the following passages.

A woman's duties are to cook the five grains, heat the wine, look after her parents-in-law, make clothes, and that is all! . . . She must follow the "three submissions." When she is young, she must submit to her parents. After her marriage, she must submit to her husband. When she is widowed, she must submit to her son.

> Biography of Mengzi, mother of
> Confucian philosopher Mencius, fourth century B.C.E.

Now examine the gentlemen of the present age. They only know that wives must be controlled, and that the husband's rules of conduct manifesting his authority must be established. . . . But they do not in the least understand that husbands and masters must also be served, and that the proper relationship and the rites should be maintained. Yet only to teach men and not to teach women—is that not ignoring the essential relation between them?

> Ban Zhao, Chinese female writer, "Lessons for Women," first century C.E.

4. The second passage qualifies the first passage by expanding the role of women to include
   (A) education.
   (B) claiming that husbands should not control their wives.
   (C) denying the responsibility of widowed women to submit to their sons.
   (D) adding a fourth submission to the three mentioned by Mengzi.

5. What impact did the writings of Mengzi and Ban Zhao have on Chinese society?
   (A) The ideas described in both passages promoted social harmony through proper behavior and ritual.
   (B) The ideas described in both passages discouraged the development of a powerful merchant class.
   (C) The ideas described in both passages influenced family relationships by advancing the concept of gender equality.
   (D) The ideas described in both passages provided an economic understanding of peasant culture in China.

6. The writings of Mengzi and Ban Zhao in both of the above passages draw upon what Chinese social idea?
   (A) Enlightenment ideas
   (B) Caste duty
   (C) Filial piety
   (D) Mercantilism

7. The ideas in Ban Zhou and Mengzi's writings had an impact on society that is most similar to the influence of which other belief system?
   (A) Daoism's influence on medical practices
   (B) Hinduism's influence on the caste system
   (C) Christianity's influence on monastic life
   (D) Buddhism's influence on Vedic tradition

8. What ideology implemented in twentieth-century China significantly changed the social ideas portrayed in the writings of Ban Zhao and Mengzi?
   (A) Free market capitalism opened China economically to trade with the outside world.
   (B) Totalitarian regimes ruled under fascist ideas in East Asia, such as China and Japan.
   (C) New Age Religions, such as the Falun Gong, shifted social focus away from patriarchy.
   (D) Communism emphasized equality among genders starting in the mid-twentieth century.

GO ON TO NEXT PAGE

Questions 9–13 refer to the following passage.

Yesterday your Ambassador petitioned my Ministers to memorialize me regarding your trade with China, but his proposal is not consistent with our dynastic usage and cannot be entertained. Hitherto, all European nations, including your own country's barbarian merchants, have carried on their trade with our Celestial Empire at Guangzhou. Such has been the procedure for many years, although our Celestial Empire possesses all things in prolific abundance and lacks no product within its own borders.

From "Emperor Qianlong, Edict on Trade with Great Britain,"
Qianlong was a late eighteenth-century Qing emperor of China

9. This quotation from an edict of the Chinese emperor to the king of Great Britain shows China's
   (A) recognition of British naval supremacy.
   (B) resistance to British intervention.
   (C) fear of Christian missionaries.
   (D) acceptance of British imperialism.

10. During the rule of Emperor Qianlong in China, what role did Europeans primarily play in commercial exchange with China?
    (A) European merchants' role was primarily characterized by transporting goods from one Asian country to another in Asia or the Indian Ocean region.
    (B) European merchants controlled large territories in China and throughout the Indian Ocean region in a period of imperialism and exploitation.
    (C) European merchants peacefully partnered with other trading nations and territories to carry on a lucrative trade throughout the Indian Ocean region.
    (D) European merchants had mostly traded with China over extended trade routes across the Silk Road along the Middle East and Central Asia.

11. What economic development of the sixteenth and seventeenth centuries played a significant role in allowing European nations to take a greater economic role in Asian trade?
    (A) The development of the compass and astrolabe, which increased European navigation
    (B) The cooperation among European powers access to foreign trade routes

(C) The discovery and exploitation of cash crops and silver from the Americas
(D) The creation of greater overland trade technology such as caravans and banking

12. What impact did the economic connection between China and European nations described in the passage from 1793 have on domestic Chinese production?
    (A) Chinese peasant production decreased significantly due to the development of factories in China.
    (B) Chinese peasant production was largely replaced by European factory work of expensive cloth.
    (C) Chinese peasant production remained relatively unchanged, as Europeans had little to trade in exchange.
    (D) Chinese peasant production of luxury goods, such as silk, increased significantly due to increased demand for them in Europe.

13. Which of the following events in China was caused by growing European intervention during this time period?
    (A) Increasing cooperation as China opened its doors more and more to free trade with European nations
    (B) Growing resistance concerning political authority and nationalism, such as the Boxer Rebellion
    (C) Chinese efforts to explore beyond their borders to improve trading relations with other nations
    (D) Massive Chinese transitions that successfully saw China transform into a major industrial power

Questions 14–18 refer to the following passage.

The pretended power of suspending of laws or the execution of laws by regal authority without consent of Parliament is illegal; the pretended power of dispensing with laws or the execution of laws by regal authority, as it hath been assumed and exercised of late, is illegal; the levying money for or to the use of the Crown by pretense of prerogative, without grant of Parliament, for longer time, or in other manner than the same is or shall be granted, is illegal.

From "English Bill of Rights," 1689, following the English Civil War

14. This quotation from the English Bill of Rights (1689) indicates that its major political concern was
    (A) between nobles and commoners over voting rights.
    (B) the relationship between the Anglican and Catholic Churches.
    (C) between rival heirs to the British throne.
    (D) the relative power of Parliament versus the monarchy.

15. In which of the following ways did the English Bill of Rights in 1689 most clearly demonstrate a transition in English politics?
    (A) An expansion on the infallibility of the monarchy
    (B) A time of increased religious ideas in government
    (C) A decreasing role of individuals in political life
    (D) A push toward greater representative government

16. The English Bill of Rights was most evidently a part of which of the following European intellectual movements?
    (A) Labor ideas that pushed for socialism and communism
    (B) Environmentalism, which critiqued pollution and waste
    (C) Enlightenment ideas that advocated the idea of a social contract
    (D) Feminism, which pursued greater gender equality

17. What political change experienced by numerous states across Europe in the fifteenth and sixteenth centuries led to greater efforts in the seventeenth and eighteenth centuries to express ideas similar to those described in the passage?
    (A) Imperial strategies of centralization and new forms of legitimacy
    (B) Increased efforts to create cultural diversity and free forms of labor
    (C) Transitions from cottage industries to concentrated factory production
    (D) The beginnings of European exploration and colonization in the Americas

18. The ideas expressed in the passage were most clearly reflected and referenced in which types of documents written later in world history?
    (A) Labor movement manifestos in the nineteenth century
    (B) Arguments for and against total war in the twentieth century
    (C) Decolonization efforts of Africa in the twentieth century
    (D) Artistic ideas expressing individualism in the twentieth century

GO ON TO NEXT PAGE

Questions 19–23 refer to the following data.

Slave Occupations on a Jamaican Sugar Plantation. 1788				
Occupations and Conditions	**Men**	**Women**	**Boys and Girls**	**Total**
Field laborers	62	78		140
Tradesmen	29			29
Field drivers	4			4
Field cooks		4		4
Mule-, cattle-, and stableman	12			12
Watchmen	18			18
Nurse		1		1
Midwife		1		1
Domestics and gardeners		5	3	8
Grass-gang			20	20
Total employed	**125**	**89**	**23**	**237**
Infants			23	23
Invalids (18 with yaws)				32
Absent on roads				5
Superannuated (elderly)				7
Overall total				**304**

© Cengage Learning

19. Which of the following conclusions about slavery in the Caribbean is supported by the table above?
    (A) Female slaves outnumbered male slaves.
    (B) Field labor required the greatest number of workers.
    (C) Most female slaves worked in domestic jobs.
    (D) Elderly and invalid slaves were forced to work in the fields.

20. Which of the following represents the most significant cause for the information presented in the table above?
    (A) Resistance of Native Americans to disease
    (B) Asian interest in purchasing American foods
    (C) European development of racial hierarchies
    (D) Continued European demand for cash crops

21. The information in the table above reveals a coercive labor system that was widespread in European colonial economics. What impact did this coercive labor system have on the development of social hierarchies in the Americas?
    (A) A greater emphasis on creating social equality and removing social divisions
    (B) Increased cooperation among various races in order to share in the profits of the crops
    (C) Increasing gender imbalance in the population as female slaves tended to outnumber males
    (D) The restructuring of racial and political hierarchies favoring those of European descent

22. What impact did the labor systems in the Americas, such as the one depicted in the table on the previous page, have on nineteenth-century ideologies?
    (A) A shift in coercive labor systems from agriculture to factories
    (B) The development of Abolition movements to end or limit coercive labor systems
    (C) Very little change in most coercive labor systems in the Americas
    (D) Change toward small-scale farming and away from plantations

23. Which of the following statements accurately describes a change to labor systems in the Caribbean in the nineteenth century?
    (A) Indentured servants from Asia became a new source of labor as slavery was abolished.
    (B) More women and children arrived on plantations as slave labor.
    (C) Machinery replaced all forms of manual labor as industrialization spread.
    (D) Communist ideology began to shape the relationship between workers and factory owners.

Questions 24–28 refer to the following passage.

It is harder, Montesquieu has written, to release a nation from servitude than to enslave a free nation. This truth is proven by the annals of all times, which reveal that most free nations have been put under the yoke, but very few enslaved nations have recovered their liberty. Despite the convictions of history, South Americans have made efforts to obtain liberal, even perfect, institutions, doubtless out of that instinct to aspire to the greatest possible happiness, which, common to all men, is bound to follow in civil societies founded on the principles of justice, liberty, and equality.

Simón Bolívar, military leader of Latin American independence movements,
from the *Jamaica Letter*, 1815

24. The passage above indicates the influence of which of the following on nineteenth-century revolutionary movements in Latin America?
    (A) The rise of Napoleon in France
    (B) The Abolition movement
    (C) The writings of Enlightenment thinkers
    (D) The defeat and occupation of Spain and Portugal

25. The ideas expressed in Bolívar's Jamaica Letter are most similar to which of the following other documents in world history?
    (A) Women's suffrage documents, such as Mary Wollstonecraft's *A Vindication of the Rights of Women*
    (B) Revolutionary documents such as the French *Declaration of Rights of Man and Citizen*
    (C) Political treatises, such as English King James I *Divine Right of Kings*
    (D) Social and political push for equality, such as Karl Marx, *Communist Manifesto*

26. Which of the following economic policies set the context for the complaints expressed in the writings of Simón Bolívar, prompting him to use phrases like "put under the yoke"?
    (A) Free market capitalism
    (B) Socialism
    (C) Mercantilism
    (D) Feudalism

27. What economic role, referenced in Bolívar's writings, did the colonies in the Americas play in the commercial exchange that developed across the Atlantic Ocean beginning in the sixteenth century?
    (A) Colonies provided raw materials and precious metals for European markets and consumers.
    (B) Colonies provided labor for emerging industrial production of Western European factories.
    (C) Colonies provided cheap manufactured goods, which decreased desire for Asian commodities.
    (D) Colonies provided primarily staple food crops to the Old World, which increased population.

GO ON TO NEXT PAGE

28. Which of the following statements would challenge Bolívar's claims regarding the South Americans' pursuit of "civil societies founded on the principles of justice, liberty, and equality" in the Jamaica Letter?
    (A) The people of the Spanish colonies who were born in the Americas often worked with those of mixed racial descent to improve their social, economic, and political status.
    (B) Spanish and Portuguese colonists actively worked to create a homogeneous society, in which only those of pure European descent could take part in the economy and politics of the colonies.
    (C) Spanish colonial society largely reflected the diversity found in European states at the time, allowing those of mixed racial descent easy entry into higher social classes.
    (D) Spanish colonial society largely placed total political and economic control in the hands of those born in Europe, denying those of mixed race, indigenous, or African descent economic independence.

Questions 29–31 refer to the following passage.

In truth [the Toltecs] invented all the precious and marvelous things. . . . All that now exists was their discovery. . . . And these Toltecs were very wise; they were thinkers, for they originated the year count, the day count. All their discoveries formed the book for interpreting dreams. . . . And so wise were they [that] they understood the stars which were in the heavens.

From an ancient Aztec source about the Toltecs

29. The passage indicates that
    (A) the Toltec people viewed Aztec society as less sophisticated.
    (B) the Aztec were primarily responsible for the decline of Toltec society.
    (C) the Aztec people were familiar with Toltec society and culture.
    (D) the Toltec were primarily responsible for the decline of Aztec society.

30. The inventions mentioned in the passage are most similar to which of the following?
    (A) Mesopotamian cuneiform
    (B) The Mayan calendar
    (C) Greek advances in math
    (D) Egyptian medical practices

31. Which of the following best explains the reason that the Aztec people would have had this information about the Toltec?
    (A) The Aztec people were made to pay tribute to nearby Toltec rulers.
    (B) The Aztec engaged in extensive commerce with both Toltec and Maya peoples.
    (C) The Toltec left extensive written accounts of their civilization at its height.
    (D) The Aztec settled into the area formerly ruled by the Toltec.

Questions 32–36 refer to the following passage.

The descendants of the Spanish conquerors, who knew nothing of labor or thrift, have incessantly resorted to fresh loans in order to fill the gaps in their budgets. Politicians knew of only one solution of the economic disorder—to borrow, so that little by little the Latin American countries became actually the financial colonies of Europe. Economic dependence has a necessary corollary—political servitude. French intervention in Mexico was originally caused by the mass of unsatisfied financial claims; foreigners, the creditors of the State, were in favor of intervention.

Francisco Garcia Calderon, Latin American diplomat, 1912

32. Which of the following types of documents might be used to support Garcia's argument about economic imperialism?
(A) Records of loans by Latin American countries
(B) Journals of Spanish conquistadors
(C) Maps of French military operations in Mexico
(D) Transcripts of U.S. congressional debates

33. Which of the following is one way in which countries in the late twentieth century and early twenty-first century have attempted to prevent economic dependence and, eventually, what Garcia calls "political servitude"?
(A) Formation of numerous regional trade agreements
(B) Conquest and control of neighboring territories
(C) Increasing birth rates to increase productivity
(D) Decreasing global trade to remain self-sufficient

34. Which of the following trends of the twentieth and twenty-first centuries would be an economic effect based on the conclusions drawn by Garcia?
(A) Decreasing power of the United Nations to solve issues
(B) Increasing colonization of poor countries by the wealthy
(C) Increasing economic inequality between countries
(D) Decreasing global commercial exchange between countries

35. To what historical period is Garcia referring when he speaks of the "Spanish conquerors" who came to Latin America and took control?
(A) Prehistoric Latin America
(B) The Colombian Exchange
(C) Neo-colonial Latin America
(D) Twentieth-century revolutionary Latin America

36. What evidence does Garcia use to support the argument in this passage?
(A) French interference in Mexico
(B) Schools built by Europeans
(C) Spanish conquest of Latin America
(D) Politicians guiding economic activity

GO ON TO NEXT PAGE

Questions 37–39 refer to the following passage.

An irrepressible conflict has arisen between two national communities within the narrow bounds of one small country. About 1,000,000 Arabs are in strife, open or latent, with some 400,000 Jews. There is no common ground between them. They differ in religion and in language. Their cultural and social life, their ways of thought and conduct are as incompatible as their national aspirations. The War and its sequel have inspired all Arabs with the hope of reviving in a free and united Arab world the traditions of the Arab golden age. The Jews similarly are inspired by their historic past. They mean to show what the Jewish nation can achieve when restored to the land of its birth.

From an official British report on Palestine, 1937

37. This quotation from an official British report on Palestine would likely lead to what policy recommendation for British-controlled Palestine?
   (A) A return to the boundaries of the ancient Israeli kingdom
   (B) Establishment of Turkish rule over the region
   (C) Separate countries for Arab and Jewish populations
   (D) A single country for all ethnic and religious groups in the area

38. What effect did this report, in addition to later British and United Nations policies, have on the area of the Eastern Mediterranean?
   (A) The expulsion of all Arab populations in the area referred to as Palestine
   (B) Peaceful coexistence of Jews and Arabs in the modern state of Israel
   (C) The reestablishment of the Arab World and the rise of an Arab golden age
   (D) Major population resettlement of Jews and displacement of Palestinians

39. Which of the following most directly led to the migration of the Jewish people to Palestine in the early twentieth century mentioned in this report?
   (A) The discovery of vast amounts of oil reserves in the Middle East
   (B) An increase in anti-Semitism in Europe in the late nineteenth century
   (C) The Treaty of Versailles ending World War I
   (D) Growing anti-imperialist sentiment in the Middle East

Questions 40–42 refer to the following map.

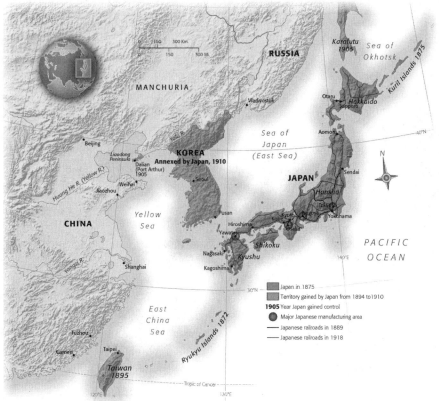

Japan, 1868–1918

© Cengage Learning

40. This map illustrates which of the following historical processes in Japan from 1868 to 1918?
    (A) Expansion of suffrage
    (B) Enlightenment and revolution
    (C) Industrialization
    (D) Exploration and commerce

41. Which of the following led to the developments illustrated in the map?
    (A) Significant political and economic reform in Japan in response to increased foreign presence in East Asia
    (B) Imperial forces from Great Britain and the United States fighting for control over coastal regions
    (C) Slow disengagement from trade in the Pacific and Indian Oceans in order to focus on domestic concerns
    (D) Diffusion of new political ideas from Europe that led to the end of the Japanese imperial system

42. Which of the following is an accurate comparison between China and Japan in the period 1750–1900?
    (A) Both China and Japan engaged foreign powers in direct conflict over unfavorable trade agreements.
    (B) Both China and Japan failed to modernize enough to keep out foreign intervention in their economic development.
    (C) While China successfully industrialized and maintained relative independence from the West, Japan was colonized by Great Britain.
    (D) While Japan eventually adopted Western ideas about governance and manufacture, China continued to resist most reforms.

GO ON TO NEXT PAGE

Questions 43–46 refer to the following map.

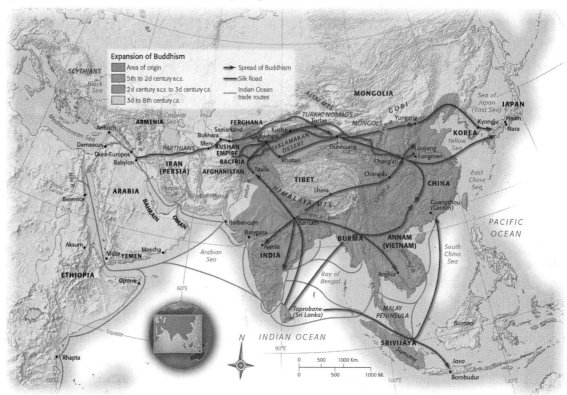

© Cengage Learning

43. The overland trade network featured in the map above connected what two major empires in the period 600 B.C.E. to 600 C.E.?
    (A) The Caliphate and Mughal empires
    (B) The Mongol and Mamluk empires
    (C) The Roman and Han empires
    (D) The Egyptian and Mesopotamian empires

44. Which of the following represents an accurate comparison between the spread of Buddhism, illustrated in the map above, and the spread of Christianity up to 1450 C.E.?
    (A) While Christianity remained practiced only around the Mediterranean basin by 1450, Buddhism had already spread across Asia.
    (B) Trade networks and commercial activities facilitated the spread of both religions.

(C) Buddhism spread as a consequence of increasing commercial activities, while Christianity primarily spread through conquest.
(D) Although knowledge of both religions spread along trade networks, neither religion gained many followers beyond their places of origin.

45. Which of the following accurately describes a change in Chinese society as a result of widespread diffusion of Buddhism through 1450 C.E.?
    (A) Buddhism supplanted Confucianism as the guiding influence in Chinese domestic policy.
    (B) Buddhist beliefs in China allowed for women to have more access to education.

(C) Buddhism blended with Daoist and Confucian practices, leading to the formation of a new priestly class.

(D) Buddhist practices encouraged the development of foot binding among elite Chinese women.

46. Which of the following represents an effect of the resurgence in trade in the 1200s along the network depicted in the map?

(A) The spread of epidemic diseases, such as the Plague, across Eurasia

(B) The collapse of the Roman Empire as a result of an unfavorable trade balance and inflation

(C) The transmission of Confucian ideology into the Middle East and Mediterranean basin

(D) The diffusion of Hellenistic culture across diverse empires

Questions 47–49 refer to the following passage.

Once the various groups within a given community have asserted themselves to the point that mutual respect has to be shown then you have the ingredients for a true and meaningful integration. From this it becomes clear that as long as blacks are suffering from [an] inferiority complex—a result of 300 years of deliberate oppression, denigration and derision—they will be useless as co-architects of a normal society where man is nothing else but man for his own sake. Hence what is necessary as a prelude to anything else that may come is a very strong grassroots build-up of black consciousness such that blacks can learn to assert themselves and state their rightful claim.

Steve Biko, South African thinker and activist and martyr in the struggle against apartheid (1946–1977)

47. Why did Biko write this passage? He wrote it in reaction to

(A) the peace process following World War II.

(B) the incorporation of South Africa in the Atlantic slave trade.

(C) the colonization of South Africa by Great Britain.

(D) the movement to end segregation in South Africa.

48. The "deliberate oppression, denigration, and derision" the author refers to happened as a result of

(A) the growing conflict between the British and the Dutch settlers, known as Boers, in South Africa.

(B) the diffusion worldwide of Enlightenment ideas.

(C) European use of Africans as laborers in their colonies in the Americas and Africa itself.

(D) the spread of industrialization that transformed South African economic activity.

49. The author of this passage is most clearly challenging which of the following ideas?

(A) Armed conflict

(B) Capitalist ideology

(C) Universal suffrage

(D) Racial hierarchies

GO ON TO NEXT PAGE

Questions 50–52 refer to the following passage.

Furthermore, the foundation on which writing is based [is] that only a subordinate should take [it] up and only one who is in a sense a servant [can] master it. We have never seen an important person undertake it for its own sake or share in his secretary's work. . . . A slave is entitled to many complaints against his master. He can request his sale to another if he wishes. The secretary has no way to lay claim to his late back wages or to leave his patron if he acts unfairly. . . .

The most wealthy of them are the least regarded by the ruler. The head of the secretariat who acts as spokesman to the nation earns a tenth of the income of the head of land tax. The scribe whose handwriting lends beauty to the communications of the caliph earns a fraction of the income of the head copyist in the land tax bureau. . . . When the ministers have settled on a course of action and agreed in their appraisal, a note is tossed to him with the gist of the order. . . . He sits as near as anyone to the caliph, in a restricted location away from visitors. Once that task is completed however, there is no difference between those two scribes and the common people.

Jahiz, Arab writer, late eighth to mid-ninth century

50. Which of the following represents how the political structure of the civilization described in this passage differed from political structures of civilizations prior to 600 C.E.?
  (A) The civilization described in this passage required subjects to pay taxes based on land ownership.
  (B) The passage indicates that this civilization had an elaborate bureaucracy, with ministers that specialized in various duties.
  (C) This passage describes a caliphate, ruled by a political leader who also had religious authority in the Islamic world.
  (D) The presence of secretaries in this civilization indicates that a new form of record-keeping emerged for political purposes.

51. Which of the following would serve as a valid argument for why the status of scribes from 600 B.C.E. through 1450 C.E. declined in the Middle East, as implied in the passage?
  (A) An increase in the reliance on scribes to serve in bureaucratic positions

  (B) An increase in literacy rates as a result of the diffusion of papermaking technology from Tang China to the Abbasids
  (C) New forms of governance, such as the caliphate and the city-state
  (D) A decrease in the need for bureaucrats as a result of a decline in interregional trade

52. Which of the following can be inferred about the civilization described in the passage?
  (A) Government officials who served as tax collectors frequently took advantage of their position to enrich themselves.
  (B) People who served as secretaries enjoyed a special status because of their proximity to the caliph.
  (C) The government of this civilization had developed an elaborate bureaucracy to support its political administration.
  (D) The status of women seemed to have improved as patriarchal practices and gender expectations changed.

Questions 53–55 refer to the following image.

© Cengage Learning

53. Based on the map, which of the following statements most accurately reflects world population growth at the end of the twentieth century?
   (A) Because of declining mortality rates, India, Egypt, and the Philippines are experiencing the world's highest rate of population growth.
   (B) Population growth is highest in the United States and western Europe because of greater wealth and the abundance of health facilities.
   (C) Although China has the largest population, its growth rate is slower than that of all other nations except the United States and Nigeria.
   (D) The highest rates of population growth are occurring in nations in Latin America, Africa, and Asia.

54. Which of the following may have allowed for the population growth rates displayed on the map?

   (A) Increasing rate of globalization and economic interdependency
   (B) Improvements in nutrition and innovations in medical practices
   (C) International political organizations, such as the United Nations
   (D) Persistence of diseases related to poverty, such as malaria

55. What might explain the reason for a low or negative population growth rate in nations such as Germany and the United States?
   (A) Declining birth rates in industrialized nations as a result of greater access to birth control
   (B) A shift in global migration patterns away from industrialized nations
   (C) Improvements in communications technology made migration to these areas unnecessary
   (D) Changes in lifestyle that led to new types of diseases, such as diabetes and heart disease

STOP
END OF SECTION I, PART A
IF YOU FINISH BEFORE TIME IS CALLED. YOU MAY CHECK YOUR WORK ON THIS SECTION. DO NOT GO ON TO SECTION I. PART B UNTIL YOU ARE TOLD TO DO SO.

AP® WORLD HISTORY EXAMINATION
Section I
Part B: Short-Answer Questions
Time: 40 minutes
Number of questions: 3
Percent of examination score: 20%

DIRECTIONS: Answer Question 1 **and** Question 2. Answer **either** Question 3 **or** Question 4.
In your responses, be sure to address all parts of the questions you answer. Use complete sentences; an outline or bulleted list alone is not acceptable.

Question 1 refers to the following passage.

The name of Spaniard here has a different meaning from that of Chapitone [*sic*] or European, as properly signifying a person descended from a Spaniard without a mixture of blood. Many Mestizos, from the advantage of a fresh complexion, appear to be Spaniards more than those who are so in reality; and from only this fortuitous advantage are accounted as such. The Whites, according to this construction of the word, may be considered as one sixth part of the inhabitants.

The Mestizos are the descendants of Spaniards and Indians. . . . Some are, however, equally tawny with the Indians themselves, though they are distinguished from them by their beards: while others, on the contrary, have so fine a complexion that they might pass for Whites, were it not for some signs which betray them, when viewed attentively. These marks . . . make it very difficult to conceal the fallacy of their complexion. The Mestizos may be reckoned a third part of the inhabitants.

The next class is the Indians, who form about another third; and the others, who are about one sixth, are the Castes [mixed]. These four classes . . . amount to between 50 and 60,000 persons, of all ages, sexes, and ranks. If among these classes the Spaniards, as is natural to think, are the most eminent for riches, rank, and power, it must at the same time be owned, however melancholy the truth may appear, they are in proportion the most poor, miserable and distressed; for they refuse to apply themselves to any mechanic business, considering it as a disgrace to that quality they so highly value themselves upon, which consists in not being black, brown, or of a copper color. The Mestizos, whose pride is regulated by prudence, readily apply themselves to arts and trades, but chose those of the greatest repute, as painting, sculpture, and the like, leaving the meaner sort to the Indians.

Jorge Juan and Antonio de Ulloa, Spanish naval officers and scientists, mid-eighteenth century

1. Answer all parts of the question that follow.
   A. Explain ONE cause of the historical process described in the passage above.
   B. Explain ONE effect of the historical process illustrated in the passage above. Your response may address effects on cultural characteristics, economic structure, and/or social hierarchy.
   C. Provide ONE ADDITIONAL effect of the historical process illustrated in the passage above. Your response may address effects on cultural characteristics, economic structure, and/or social hierarchy.

Question 2 refers to the following image.

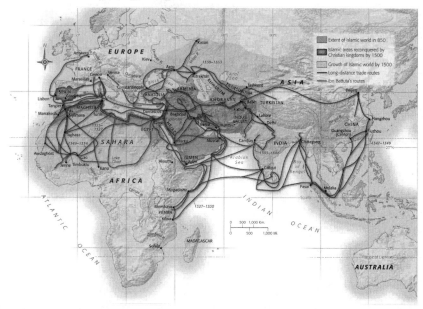

© Cengage Learning

2. Based on the map above, answer Parts A, B, and C.
   A. Describe ONE way that commerce along the networks depicted in the map changed from the period 600 C.E. to 1450 C.E.
   B. Explain ONE continuity in the way commerce was conducted along the trade networks depicted in the map from the period 600 C.E. to 1450 C.E.
   C. Explain ONE historical process that facilitated the change you identified in Part A.

Choose EITHER Question 3 or Question 4.

3. Answer all parts of the question that follow.
   Both the Roman Empire and the first [Han] Chinese Empire arose from relatively small states that, because of their discipline and military toughness, were initially able to subdue their neighbors. Ultimately they unified widespread territories under strong central governments.
   A. Identify ONE way in which both the Han and Roman empires unified their territories.
   B. Explain ONE similar technique both the Roman Empire and the Han Chinese Empire used to establish strong central governments.
   C. Explain ONE difference in techniques the Roman Empire and the Han Chinese Empire used to establish strong central governments.

4. Answer all parts of the question that follows.

   Many historians argue that the Industrial Revolution was a turning point in world history.
   A. Identify ONE piece of evidence that <u>supports</u> this argument.
   B. Explain ONE reason the Industrial Revolution occurred.
   C. Explain ONE technological difference in the Industrial revolution after it occurred.

STOP

END OF SECTION I

IF YOU FINISH BEFORE TIME IS CALLED, YOU MAY CHECK YOUR WORK ON THIS SECTION. DO NOT GO ON TO SECTION II UNTIL YOU ARE TOLD TO DO SO.

AP® WORLD HISTORY EXAMINATION
Section II: Free-Response Essays
Part A: Document-Based Question (DBQ)
Suggested writing time: 60 minutes
Percent of examination score: 25%

It is suggested that you spend 15 minutes reading the documents and 45 minutes writing your response. Note: You may begin writing your response before the reading period is over.

DIRECTIONS: Question 1 is based on the accompanying documents. The documents have been edited for the purpose of this exercise.

In your response you should do the following.
- Respond to the prompt with a historically defensible thesis or claim that establishes a line of reasoning
- Describe a broader historical context relevant to the prompt
- Support an argument in response to the prompt using at least six documents
- Use at least one additional piece of specific historical evidence (beyond that found in the documents) relevant to an argument about the prompt
- For at least three documents, explain how or why the document's point of view, purpose, historical situation, and/or audience is relevant to an argument
- Use evidence to corroborate, qualify, or modify an argument that addresses the prompt

QUESTION 1. Using the documents, analyze the degree of self-determination in the Middle East in the early twentieth century.

Document 1

Source: The Balfour Declaration, written by the British foreign minister to a prominent leader of the Jewish community in Europe.

November 2nd, 1917

Dear Lord Rothschild,

I have much pleasure in conveying to you, on behalf of His Majesty's Government, the following declaration of sympathy with Jewish Zionist aspirations which has been submitted to, and approved by, the Cabinet:

His Majesty's Government view with favour the establishment in Palestine of a national home for the Jewish people, and will use their best endeavours to facilitate the achievement of this object, it being clearly understood that nothing shall be done which may prejudice the civil and religious rights of existing non-Jewish communities in Palestine, or the rights and political status enjoyed by Jews in any other country.

I should be grateful if you would bring this declaration to the knowledge of the Zionist Federation.

Yours,

Arthur James Balfour

Document 2

Source: Woodrow Wilson, President of the United States, from his Fourteen Points, which listed his goals for U.S. involvement in World War I, 1918.

V. A free, open-minded, and absolutely impartial adjustment of all colonial claims, based upon a strict observance of the principle that in determining all such questions of sovereignty the interests of the populations concerned must have equal weight with the equitable claims of the government whose title is to be determined.

XII. The Turkish portion of the present Ottoman Empire should be assured a secure sovereignty, but the other nationalities which are now under Turkish rule should be assured an undoubted security of life and an absolutely unmolested opportunity of autonomous development. . . .

Document 3

Source: The Covenant of the League of Nations, which established European control over non-Turkish parts of the former Ottoman Empire, 1919.

Article 22.

To those colonies and territories which as a consequence of the late war have ceased to be under the sovereignty of the States which formerly governed them and which are inhabited by peoples not yet able to stand by themselves under the strenuous conditions of the modern world, there should be applied the principle that the well-being and development of such peoples form a sacred trust of civilization. . . .

The best method of giving practical effect to this principle is that the tutelage of such peoples should be entrusted to advanced nations who by reason of their resources, their experience or their geographical position can best undertake this responsibility, and who are willing to accept it, and that this tutelage should be exercised by them as Mandatories on behalf of the League.

The character of the mandate must differ according to the stage of the development of the people, the geographical situation of the territory, its economic conditions and other similar circumstances.

Document 4

Source: Memorandum of the General Syrian Congress, 1919.

We the undersigned members of the General Syrian Congress . . . have agreed upon the following statement of the desires of the people of the country who have elected us. . . .

1. We ask absolutely complete political independence for Syria.

2. We ask that the government of this Syrian country should be a democratic civil constitutional Monarchy and that the King be the Emir Feisal, who carried on a glorious struggle in the cause of our liberation and merited our full confidence and entire reliance.

3. Considering the fact that the Arabs inhabiting the Syrian area are not naturally less gifted than other more advanced races . . . we protest against Article 22 of the Covenant of the League of Nations, placing us among the nations in their middle stage of development which stand in need of a mandatory power.

5. In the event of America not finding herself in a position to accept our desire for assistance, we will seek this assistance from Great Britain, also provided that such does not prejudice our complete independence and unity of our country.

6. We do not acknowledge any right claimed by the French Government in any part whatever of our Syrian country.

7. We opposed the pretensions of the Zionists to create a Jewish commonwealth in the southern part of Syria, known as Palestine, and oppose Zionist migration to any part of our country.

Document 5

Source: Map of the mandate system established by the League of Nations, 1920.

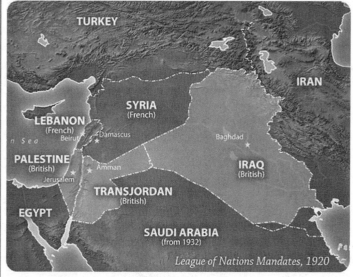

League of Nations Mandates, 1920

© Cengage Learning

Document 6

Source: Mustafa Kemal Atatürk, first president of the Turkish republic, speech to the Turkish Congress of the People's Republican Party, 1927.

In order that our nation should be able to live a happy, strenuous, and permanent life, it is necessary that the State should pursue an exclusively national policy and that this policy should be in perfect agreement with our internal organization and be based on it. When I speak of national policy, I mean it in this sense: To work within our national boundaries for the real happiness and welfare of the nation and the country by, above all, relying on our own strength in order to retain our existence.

Document 7

Source: Photograph of Mustafa Kemal Atatürk teaching the new Turkish alphabet, which was based on the Latin script used in western Europe, 1928.

Fotosearch/Getty Images

END OF DOCUMENTS FOR PART A.
GO ON TO THE NEXT PAGE.

AP® WORLD HISTORY EXAMINATION
Section II: Free-Response Essays
Part B: Long Essay Questions
Suggested planning and writing time: 40 minutes
Percent of examination score: 15%

DIRECTIONS: You are to choose ONE question from the three questions below. Make your selection carefully, choosing the question that you are best prepared to answer thoroughly in the time permitted. You should spend 5 minutes organizing or outlining your answer. Write your answer to the question on the lined pages of the Section II free-response booklet, making sure to indicate the question you are answering by writing the appropriate question number on the top of each page.

In your response you should do the following.

▪ Respond to the prompt with a historically defensible thesis or claim that establishes a line of reasoning
▪ Describe a broader historical context relevant to the prompt
▪ Support an argument in response to the prompt using specific and relevant examples of evidence
▪ Use historical reasoning (e.g., comparison, causation, continuity or change over time) to frame or structure an argument that addresses the prompt
▪ Use evidence to corroborate, qualify, or modify an argument that addresses the prompt

QUESTION 1. Evaluate the effects of the diffusion of Buddhism from its time of origin until c. 600 C.E. on the political and social institutions of the regions to which it spread.

QUESTION 2. Evaluate the effects of the diffusion of Islam from its time of origin until circa 1750 on the political and social institutions of the regions to which it spread.

QUESTION 3. Evaluate the effects of the diffusion of Nationalism from 1750 to the present on political and economic institutions of the regions to which it spread.

END OF EXAMINATION

Answers for Section I, Part A: Multiple-Choice Questions

Answer Key for Part A: Multiple-Choice Questions

1. C	12. D	23. A	34. C	45. B
2. A	13. B	24. C	35. B	46. A
3. D	14. D	25. B	36. A	47. D
4. A	15. D	26. C	37. C	48. C
5. A	16. C	27. A	38. D	49. D
6. C	17. A	28. D	39. B	50. C
7. B	18. C	29. C	40. C	51. B
8. D	19. B	30. B	41. A	52. C
9. B	20. D	31. D	42. D	53. D
10. A	21. D	32. A	43. C	54. B
11. C	22. B	33. A	44. B	55. A

Explanations for the Multiple-Choice Answers

1. ANSWER: C. The map indicates that agriculture gradually spread from areas of independent invention/development to surrounding areas in a process that took thousands of years (*The Earth and Its Peoples*, 6th ed., pp. 9–12/7th ed., pp. 16–19; History Disciplinary Practice—Analyzing Historical Evidence; Learning Objective ENV, ECON; Key Concept 1.2).

2. ANSWER: A. Permanent agricultural villages likely developed as a result of climate changes. Village locations depended on suitability of the land for agricultural practices and access to sources of water (*The Earth and Its Peoples*, 6th ed., pp. 12–14/7th ed., pp. 21–24; History Reasoning Skill—Causation; Learning Objectives ENV, ECON; Key Concept 1.2).

3. ANSWER: D. Relatively fewer species of animals could be domesticated in the Americas, unlike in the Middle East, which had access to pigs, sheep, cattle, and goats (*The Earth and Its Peoples*, 6th ed., pp. 9–11/7th ed., pp. 16–19; History Reasoning Skill—Comparison; Learning Objectives CUL, ECON, SOC; Key Concept 1.2).

4. ANSWER: A. Ban Zhao's "Lessons for Women" conform to traditional expectations such as obeying males and maintaining households, as indicated in the first passage. However, Ban Zhao suggests that these expectations are best realized when proper relationships are maintained and women are provided with at least a basic education (*The Earth and Its Peoples*, 6th ed., pp. 156–157/7th ed., pp. 161–162; History Disciplinary Practice—Argument Development; Learning Objectives ENV; Key Concept 2.1).

5. ANSWER: A. Both passages emphasize appropriate behavior for women, such as obeying males and maintaining households (*The Earth and Its Peoples*, 6th ed., pp. 156–157/7th ed., pp. 161–162; History Reasoning Skill—Contextualization; Learning Objectives CUL, SOC; Key Concept 2.1).

6. ANSWER: C. The concept of filial piety was central to the teachings of Confucius as a guiding principle in the way the people of China should behave toward one another. Filial piety, or obedience and reverence to parents and elders, not only described how children should behave in a family setting, but was also used to describe how wives should behave toward husbands, and how subjects should behave toward rulers (*The Earth and Its Peoples*, 6th ed., p. 81/7th ed., pp. 88–89; History Disciplinary Practice—Analyzing Historical Evidence; Learning Objectives CUL, SOC; Key Concept 2.1).

7. ANSWER: B. These passages by Mengzi and Ban Zhao most clearly reflect Confucian teachings. The teachings of Hinduism most closely resemble the expectations for women described in the two passages, with Hinduism also teaching the subservience of women to males as an expression of virtuous behavior (*The Earth and Its Peoples*, 6th ed., pp. 81, 156–157, 167–168, 171–174/7th ed., pp. 88–89, 161–162, 171–173, 175–178; History Reasoning Skill—Comparison; Learning Objectives CUL, SOC; Key Concept 2.1).

8. ANSWER: D. As communism became the dominant ideology in China by the mid-twentieth century, traditional Confucian conceptions of social order and gender hierarchy changed dramatically. In communist ideology, the division between male and female "spheres" became less severe, as women were allowed to fulfill similar economic, and even political, roles. In addition, traditional views of a distinct social hierarchy changed as communism encouraged the dissolution of socioeconomic elites (*The Earth and Its Peoples*, 6th ed., pp. 824–825, 857–859/7th ed., pp. 768–769, 827–829; History Reasoning Skill—Continuity and Change Over Time; Learning Objectives CUL, SB, SOC; Key Concept 6.3).

9. ANSWER: B. This quotation refers to the idea that China does not need trade items from other countries and can dismiss European diplomatic outreach, thereby illustrating resistance to British attempts to engage in trade (*The Earth and Its Peoples*, 6th ed., p. 565/7th ed., pp. 546–547; History Disciplinary Practice—Argument Development; Learning Objectives SB, ECON; Key Concepts 4.1, 5.1).

10. ANSWER: A. By the mid-eighteenth century, Europeans had cultivated a role in trade in the Indian Ocean similar to that of a "middle man"—they primarily bought goods in one Asian nation to sell in another Asian nation. This role slowly began to evolve in the second half of the eighteenth century as European technological and industrial progress allowed them to increasingly force non-industrialized nations into trade agreements that favored European merchants (*The Earth and Its Peoples*, 6th ed., pp. 418–422, 552–554, 563–566/7th ed., pp. 409–413, 533–536, 546–548; History Reasoning Skill—Contextualization; Learning Objectives SB, ECON; Key Concept 4.1).

11. ANSWER: C. European colonization of the Americas led to the discovery and exploitation of a number of profitable natural resources and cash crops. In particular, Spanish mining of silver in Mexico and South America and European cultivation of sugar allowed Europeans a greater opportunity to establish more favorable commercial connections in East

Asia than in previous periods (*The Earth and Its Peoples*, 6th ed., pp. 404–425, 545–546, 552–554/7th ed., Chapter 16, pp. 533–537; History Reasoning Skill—Contextualization; Learning Objectives ENV, SB, ECON; Key Concept 4.1).

12. ANSWER: D. As Europeans increasingly engaged in trade with nations in the Indian Ocean, demand for products made in the region among European (and European colonial subjects, especially in North America) increased for the goods produced in South and East Asia (*The Earth and Its Peoples*, 6th ed., pp. 444–449, 560–566/7th ed., pp. 434–439, 542–548; History Reasoning Skill—Causation; Learning Objectives ECON; Key Concept 4.2).

13. ANSWER: B. One effect of the increasing presence of Europeans engaging in trade with China was a form of anti–imperial (economic imperialism) nationalism that developed in protest of what many Chinese viewed as submission to European authority. China experienced much social unrest rooted in this nationalistic protest in the nineteenth century (*The Earth and Its Peoples*, 6th ed., pp. 645–654, 746–748/7th ed., pp. 623–629, 722–724; History Reasoning Skill—Causation; Learning Objectives CUL, SB, SOC; Key Concept 5.3).

14. ANSWER: D. Each of the issues addressed in the quotation reflects the notion that the authority of the monarch needs to be contained (*The Earth and Its Peoples*, 6th ed., p. 450/7th ed., p. 440; History Disciplinary Practice—Analyzing Historical Evidence; Learning Objectives CUL, SB; Key Concept 5.3).

15. ANSWER: D. As the issues addressed in the quotation reflect the idea of a monarchy with limited power, the passage simultaneously reflects emerging political ideas in the seventeenth and eighteenth century in Europe: a government in which the people's interests are represented (*The Earth and Its Peoples*, 6th ed., p. 450/7th ed., p. 440; History Reasoning Skill—Continuity and Change Over Time; Learning Objectives CUL, SB; Key Concept 5.3).

16. ANSWER: C. The Enlightenment movement explored new ideas about the role of government, as well as how rulers justified their power and authority to make decisions. The idea of the social contract was a reoccurring one in Enlightenment thought: the government exists to protect the natural rights and property of the people, and any violation should be considered a breach of that contract on the part of the rulers. The English Bill of Rights, written before most major Enlightenment thinkers began publishing their ideas, served as an inspiration for those who sought to limit the power of absolute rulers of the time period (*The Earth and Its Peoples*, 6th ed., pp. 443, 450, 606/7th ed., pp. 433, 440, 586; History Reasoning Skill—Contextualization; Learning Objectives CUL, SB; Key Concept 5.3).

17. ANSWER: A. In the fifteenth and sixteenth centuries, many states in Europe had rulers who worked to consolidate their power by centralizing authority around the ruler's court, as well as introducing new ways of legitimizing power. Historians use the term "absolute rulers" to describe the heads of state who worked to increase the power of the ruler, largely

by diminishing the power of the nobles. As a result of centuries of shifting authority away from nobles into the hands of one person, many intellectuals (as well as the nobles themselves) began to protest the absolute authority of their monarchs in favor of a monarchy limited by some other power, such as a parliament or constitution (*The Earth and Its Peoples*, 6th ed., pp. 443, 450, 606/7th ed., pp. 433, 440, 586; History Reasoning Skill—Contextualization; Learning Objectives CUL, SB; Key Concept 5.3).

18. ANSWER: C. As European colonies in Africa and Asia began pushing for independence in the twentieth century, many independence leaders called upon the ideas of the Enlightenment when developing their arguments in support of independence (*The Earth and Its Peoples*, 6th ed., pp. 799–802/7th ed., pp. 797–799; History Reasoning Skill—Causation; Learning Objectives CUL, SB; Key Concept 6.2).

19. ANSWER: B. While most domestic occupations were assigned exclusively to female slaves, more women than men worked as field laborers on the typical Caribbean plantation, and field laborers formed the bulk of the slave population (*The Earth and Its Peoples*, 6th ed., p. 498/7th ed., p. 485; History Disciplinary Practice—Analyzing Historical Evidence; Learning Objectives ENV, SB, ECON, SOC; Key Concepts 4.2, 5.1).

20. ANSWER: D. Throughout the eighteenth and nineteenth centuries, Europeans continued to demand cash crops, such as sugar cane, tobacco, and cotton grown in their colonies in the Americas. As these cash crops tended to be labor–intensive, producers opted for forms of coercive labor that would keep the costs of production low, such as the use of slaves, in order to maximize profits (*The Earth and Its Peoples*, 6th ed., p. 498/7th ed., p. 485; History Reasoning Skill—Causation; Learning Objectives ENV, SB, ECON, SOC; Key Concepts 4.2, 5.1).

21. ANSWER: D. The coercive labor system used in many of the European colonies in the Americas was a race–based slavery. As a result, the social hierarchy of colonies that used this type of slavery often developed socioeconomic class distinctions also based around race. Those of pure European descent often had the highest social status, accompanied by the most economic and political privileges; those of indigenous or African descent had the lowest social status with almost no economic or political privileges, while those of mixed descent (mestizos, mulattos, etc.) often found themselves with slightly more status and privileges than those at the bottom (*The Earth and Its Peoples*, 6th ed., pp. 472–479, 494–504/7th ed., pp. 485–490, 479–482; History Reasoning Skill—Causation; Learning Objectives SB, ECON, SOC; Key Concept 4.2).

22. ANSWER: B. In the nineteenth century, movements to abolish slavery gradually gained followers in both Europe and the Americas. These movements drew upon Enlightenment ideas of peoples' natural rights to push for expansion of political, economic, and social rights of enslaved peoples (*The Earth and Its Peoples*, 6th ed., pp. 673–675/7th ed., pp. 650–652; History Reasoning Skill—Continuity and Change Over Time; Learning Objectives ECON, SOC; Key Concept 5.3).

23. Answer: A. As slavery was abolished on plantations throughout the Caribbean in the nineteenth century, plantation owners looked for new sources of cheap labor for the labor-intensive cash crops they grew. At the same time, population and economic pressures in Asia, particularly in China and India, led many men to seek opportunities to work abroad in order to support themselves and their families. Indentured servitude became an option that seemingly benefited both parties, although in reality it was a form of semicoercive labor that often took advantage of the worker (*The Earth and Its Peoples*, 6th ed., pp. 728–729/7th ed., pp. 703–705; History Reasoning Skill—Continuity and Change Over Time; Learning Objectives ENV, CUL, ECON, SOC; Key Concept 5.4).

24. Answer: C. In the passage, Simón Bolívar makes several references to Enlightenment ideals. Specifically, he expresses his belief in the idea that people should strive for an ideal government founded on natural rights such as justice, liberty, and equality. Although he does refer to freeing an enslaved nation, here he is not referring to slavery per se, but to political and perhaps economic servitude (*The Earth and Its Peoples*, 6th ed., pp. 660–662/7th ed., pp. 636–638; History Disciplinary Practice—Analyzing Historical Evidence; Learning Objectives CUL, SB, ECON, SOC; Key Concept 5.3).

25. Answer: B. The language used in this particular excerpt of Bolívar's Jamaica Letter are very similar to revolutionary documents, such as the French Declaration of the Rights of Man and Citizen, as well as the American Declaration of Independence (*The Earth and Its Peoples*, 6th ed., pp. 660–662/7th ed., pp. 636–638; History Reasoning Skill—Comparison; Learning Objectives CUL, SB, ECON, SOC; Key Concept 5.3).

26. Answer: C. In this passage, Bolívar is describing the exploitative relationship that developed between European nations and their colonies in the Americas as a result of the implementation of mercantilist economic policies. In mercantilism, nations seek to gain economic, and therefore political, power over other nations by securing a favorable balance of trade. Establishing colonies to ensure a steady supply of natural resources and raw materials to fuel manufacture and export was central to the way many European nations carried out their mercantilist policies (*The Earth and Its Peoples*, 6th ed., pp. 504–505/7th ed., pp. 482–484; History Reasoning Skill—Contextualization; Learning Objectives SB, ECON-3,9; Key Concept 4.1).

27. Answer: A. From the time of early colonization of the Americas by Spain, France, Portugal, and Britain, Europeans began exporting natural resources, such as silver, and raw materials, such as sugar and tobacco from colonial plantations. The primary role of the colonies in the Americas was to provide these resources and materials for European manufacture and export to Africa and Asia, as well as to sell back in the form of finished products in colonial markets (*The Earth and Its Peoples*, 6th ed., pp. 504–505/7th ed., pp. 482–484; History Reasoning Skill—Contextualization; Learning Objectives SB, ECON; Key Concept 4.1).

28. ANSWER: D. Although Bolívar claims that the people of South America have already established a society based around the Enlightenment principles of liberty, justice, and equality; in reality, those of mixed racial descent, as well as those of indigenous Amerindian and African descent, were often excluded from politics, were relegated to lower social status than those of direct/pure European descent, and were often exploited in coercive labor systems (*The Earth and Its Peoples*, 6th ed., pp. 468–479/7th ed., pp. 454–466; History Disciplinary Skill—Argument Development; Learning Objectives CUL, SB, ECON, SOC; Key Concepts 4.2, 5.3).

29. ANSWER: C. The content of the first passage indicates that the Aztec knew about Toltec society. The tone of the source indicates that the Aztec considered the Toltec as marvelous inventors, not understanding that much of what they attributed to Toltec invention was in fact developed in earlier Mesoamerican cultures (*The Earth and Its Peoples*, 6th ed., pp. 201–203/7th ed., pp. 205–207; History Disciplinary Practice—Analyzing Historical Evidence; Learning Objectives CUL, SB; Key Concept 3.2).

30. ANSWER: B. The description of the "day count" and "year count" most closely resemble the Mayan calendar (*The Earth and Its Peoples*, 6th ed., pp. 198–203/7th ed., pp. 201–207; History Reasoning Skill—Comparison; Learning Objectives CUL; Key Concepts 2.1, 3.2).

31. ANSWER: D. The Mexica, later known as the Aztec, settled in central Mexico following the collapse of Toltec power. Building an empire in the same area, the Aztec would have encountered Toltec cities, featuring architecture and décor that would have provided extensive knowledge about Toltec society (*The Earth and Its Peoples*, 6th ed., pp. 201–203/7th ed., pp. 205–207; History Reasoning Skill—Causation; Learning Objectives CUL, SB; Key Concept 3.2).

32. ANSWER: A. According to Garcia, a major cause of the involvement of Europe and the United States in the affairs of Latin America related to the large national debts of Latin American countries. Records of loans might provide insight to the extent of the indebtedness and the nations that were involved (*The Earth and Its Peoples*, 6th ed., pp. 681–683/7th ed., pp. 658–660; History Disciplinary Practice—Analyzing Historical Evidence; Learning Objectives ENV, SB, ECON; Key Concept 5.1).

33. ANSWER: A. One way that many nations protected their economic independence, and therefore by extension preserved sovereignty, was by establishing trade agreements with other nations. These agreements tended to make the economies of the collection of nations that formed them stronger (*The Earth and Its Peoples*, 6th ed., pp. 900–902/7th ed., pp. 877–880; History Reasoning Skill—Causation; Learning Objectives SB, ECON; Key Concept 6.3).

34. ANSWER: C. The growing inequality between wealthy nations and poor nations was facilitated by the conditions that Garcia described in this passage. Economic structures put in place by European colonizers prior to the independence of Latin American nations continued postindependence, leading many nations relying on the export of cash

crops or raw materials. At the same time, attempts at industrialization in these nations were often financed by foreign investments—the loans mentioned in Garcia's passage (*The Earth and Its Peoples*, 6th ed., pp. 660–683, 710–718/7th ed., pp. 636–670, 686–690; History Reasoning Skill—Causation; Learning Objectives SB, ECON; Key Concept 5.1).

35. ANSWER: B. The Spanish conquerors colonized Latin America starting in the 1500s (*The Earth and Its Peoples*, 6th ed., pp. 468–479/7th ed., pp. 454–466; History Reasoning Skill—Contextualization; Learning Objectives ENV, SB, ECON; Key Concept 4.3).

36. ANSWER: A. Garcia draws upon the example of the French attempt at ruling over Mexico in the nineteenth century as evidence to support his argument that financial/economic dependency on Europe led to the struggle for true independence in Latin America (*The Earth and Its Peoples*, 6th ed., pp. 681–683/7th ed., pp. 667–670; History Disciplinary Practice—Analyzing Historical Evidence; Learning Objectives ENV, SB, ECON;Key Concept 5.1).

37. ANSWER: C. This official report discusses what it calls the incompatibility of the Arab and the Jewish people of Palestine. A policy of separate countries for each group was the recommendation of the report (*The Earth and Its Peoples*, 6th ed., p. 773/7th ed., pp. 746–748; History Disciplinary Practice—Analyzing Historical Evidence; Learning Objectives CUL, SB, SOC;Key Concept 6.2).

38. ANSWER: D. The rise of Zionism in the late nineteenth century led to the start of Jewish migration into Palestine. After World War II, Britain, in conjunction with the United Nations, arranged for the creation of an independent Jewish state of Israel. The cultural, religious, and political tensions resulting from the creation of Israel led to the resettlement of thousands of Palestinians, in addition to the mass migration of Jewish people into the new nation (*The Earth and Its Peoples*, 6th ed., p. 773/7th ed., pp. 746–748; History Reasoning Skill—Causation; Learning Objectives CUL, SB, SOC; Key Concept 6.2).

39. ANSWER: B. In the second half of the nineteenth century, many nations in Europe experienced a rise in violence directed against Jewish people, perhaps culminating in the Dreyfus Affair in France following the Franco–Prussian War. These instances led many Jews to want to leave cultures where they were experiencing discrimination and relocate to the place they perceived as their cultural and religious heritage—Palestine (*The Earth and Its Peoples*, 6th ed., pp. 773/7th ed., pp. 746–748; History Reasoning Skill—Causation; Learning Objectives CUL, SB, SOC; Key Concept 6.2).

40. ANSWER: C. The map shows Japan during its first phase of industrialization and modernization following the Meiji Restoration in 1868 (*The Earth and Its Peoples*, 6th ed., pp. 738–742/7th ed., pp. 740–743; History Reasoning Skill—Contextualization; Learning Objectives ENV, SB; Key Concept 5.2).

41. ANSWER: A. Following the arrival of American Mathew Perry to engage Japan in a trade agreement with the United States, Japan underwent significant political and economic changes aimed at strengthening Japan's position relative to European nations and the United States. These changes included reform of the political structure and modernization of the economy through state-sponsored industrialization (*The Earth and Its Peoples*, 6th ed., pp. 738–742/7th ed., pp. 740–743; History Reasoning Skill—Causation; Learning Objectives ENV, SB; Key Concept 5.2).

42. ANSWER: D. In many ways, China and Japan had opposite reactions once faced with interference from Europe and the United States. Whereas China continued to attempt to resist making reforms that would have modernized, industrialized, and Westernized the Chinese economy, Japan set out to strengthen their position by reforming their government and economy to be more like those of the industrialized nations (*The Earth and Its Peoples*, 6th ed., pp. 645–654, 738–742, 746–748/7th ed., pp. 623–631, 740–743; History Reasoning Skill—Comparison; Learning Objectives ENV, SB; Key Concept 5.2).

43. ANSWER: C. The Silk Road was a collection of overland trade routes from East Asia, across Central Asia into the Middle East. During the Classical time period, these routes connected the Roman Empire (Eastern Mediterranean/Middle East) to the Han Empire in China (*The Earth and Its Peoples*, 6th ed., pp. 224–227/7th ed., pp. 226–230; History Reasoning Skill—Contextualization; Learning Objectives ENV, SB, ECON; Key Concept 2.3).

44. ANSWER: B. Commercial connections between diverse societies led to the diffusion of both Christianity and Buddhism along the Silk Road. Both religions were able to spread and gain converts through the efforts of missionaries, as well as an effect of trade (*The Earth and Its Peoples*, 6th ed., pp. 224–227, 328–330/7th ed., pp. 226–230, 322–334; History Reasoning Skill—Comparison; Learning Objectives CUL, SB, ECON; Key Concepts 2.3, 3.3).

45. ANSWER: B. As Buddhism spread into new regions from 600 B.C.E. to 1450 C.E., beliefs and practices of Buddhism blended with and influenced the development of social, cultural, and political practices of the places it spread. In China, one notable way that the arrival of Buddhism changed society and culture is through encouraging women to have greater access to education (*The Earth and Its Peoples*, 6th ed., pp. 298–304/7th ed., pp. 294–301; History Reasoning Skill—Continuity and Change Over Time; Learning Objectives CUL, SB, SOC; Key Concepts 2.3, 3.3).

46. ANSWER: A. In the thirteenth century, at the height of the Mongol empire, trade along the Silk Road experienced a resurgence in activity, following a time of limited contacts after the collapse of the major Eurasian empires at the end of the Classical period. There were numerous consequences to this renewed contact, including the transmission of knowledge and technology and the further diffusion of major religions. In addition, the Black Plague spread across Eurasia, resulting in a

significant decrease in the populations of the places affected (*The Earth and Its Peoples*, 6th ed., pp. 328–330/7th ed., pp. 322–324; History Reasoning Skill—Causation; Learning Objectives ENV, ECON; Key Concept 3.3).

47. ANSWER: D. This passage is discussing the problem of ending segregation under apartheid (*The Earth and Its Peoples*, 6th ed., pp. 850–853/7th ed., pp. 821–824; History Reasoning Skill—Contextualization; Learning Objectives CUL, SB, SOC; Key Concept 6.2).

48. ANSWER: C. The author is referring to the subjugation of many African peoples by Europeans. First, Europeans developed trade agreements with coastal African tribes to acquire slaves for use in the Americas. After the European colonies in the Americas gained their independence, the slave trade across the Atlantic gradually diminished and Abolition movements helped end slavery altogether. In the late 1800s, Europeans began claiming territory in Africa, often using the indigenous people as laborers within their developing African colonies (*The Earth and Its Peoples*, 6th ed., pp. 509–512, 694–702/7th ed., pp. 509–517, 670–676; History Reasoning Skill—Contextualization; Learning Objectives SB, ECON, SOC; Key Concepts 4.3, 5.2).

49. ANSWER: D. The author is challenging existing racial hierarchies in this passage. He states that the black people of South Africa need to overcome the common ideas about race in order to end segregation for themselves, without being "led" or "helped" by white people (*The Earth and Its Peoples*, 6th ed., pp. 850–853/7th ed., pp. 821–824; History Reasoning Skill—Contextualization; Learning Objectives CUL, SB, SOC; Key Concept 6.2).

50. ANSWER: C. The author of this passage, Jahiz, wrote during the time of the Abbasid caliphate. The innovation of the caliphate in the period 600 C.E. to 1450 C.E. was mostly due to its political structure being rooted in the Islamic faith, a new religion in the seventh century. The caliph, the title for the person who ruled over the caliphate, held political power in addition to holding religious authority over his subjects (*The Earth and Its Peoples*, 6th ed., pp. 252–266/7th ed., pp. 252–257; History Reasoning Skill—Contextualization; Learning Objectives CUL, SB; Key Concept 3.2).

51. ANSWER: B. Based on the tone and language choice of the author in this passage, scribes had a low status ("the foundation on which writing is based [is] that only a subordinate should take [it] up and only one who is in a sense a servant [can] master it"). This represents a change from the era of the first civilizations and even the Classical empires, when scribes often benefited from higher social status. One reason why scribes in earlier empires had such a high status was low literacy rates. As written languages evolved and the technology of printing and papermaking spread, literacy rates increased. As the knowledge of how to read and write became more widespread, being a scribe was not as rare, and therefore not as well–paid, as before (*The Earth and Its Peoples*, 6th ed., pp. 391–392/7th ed., pp. 383–384; History Disciplinary Practice—Argument Development; Learning Objectives CUL, SB, ECON; Key Concept 3.2).

52. ANSWER: C. This passage mentions several examples of job titles for people working in the administration of the caliphate (secretary, scribe, tax collector, copyist, minister), which indicates the presence of a bureaucracy. In fact, from 600 B.C.E., many empires used bureaucracies to help rulers manage day-to-day administrative tasks (*The Earth and Its Peoples*, 6th ed., pp. 252–266/7th ed., pp. 252–257; History Disciplinary Practice—Analyzing Historical Evidence; Learning Objectives SB; Key Concept 3.2).

53. ANSWER: D. Industrialized nations of the West are experiencing a decline in fertility rates that is often ascribed to higher levels of female education, employment, and access to contraception. On the other hand, developing nations in Africa, Latin America, and Asia are experiencing rapid population growth. According to the map, 95 percent of the world's population growth will occur in these developing nations. Moreover, calculations suggest that every three years our world will see an increase in population equivalent to the population of the United States (*The Earth and Its Peoples*, 6th ed., p. 883/7th ed., p. 851; History Disciplinary Practice—Analyzing Historical Evidence; Learning Objective SOC; Key Concept 6.1).

54. ANSWER: B. Medical and scientific innovations, such as vaccinations, advances in medicine (antibiotics, etc.), and new agricultural techniques (Green Revolution) all allowed for healthier families, leading to more children surviving through infancy. While many of these nations experiencing high population growth rates still have a relatively young population, more children are surviving into adulthood as a result of the medical advances (*The Earth and Its Peoples*, 6th ed., pp. 879–883/7th ed., pp. 848–851; History Reasoning Skill—Causation; Learning Objectives CUL, SOC; Key Concept 6.1).

55. ANSWER: A. In nations that have been industrialized for more than a century, a common pattern is for the women of these nations to be more educated, be more likely to work outside the home, and have greater access to birth control/contraceptives. As a result of each of these contributing factors, women in these nations tend to wait longer before having children and tend to have fewer children, which leads to the low or declining population growth rates (*The Earth and Its Peoples*, 6th ed., pp. 879–883/7th ed., pp. 848–851; History Reasoning Skill—Causation; Learning Objectives CUL, SOC; Key Concept 6.1).

ANSWERS FOR SECTION I, PART B: SHORT-ANSWER QUESTIONS

QUESTION 1

A. Possible acceptable response: The development of an elaborate social hierarchy featuring European-born white colonists in elite positions, with people of interracial/mixed descent in lower social positions, was largely the result of the exploration and colonization of the Americas by Europeans. Europeans, such as the Spanish referenced in this excerpt, established overseas empires in the Americas in order to guarantee access to valuable resources and raw materials in their quest to maintain a favorable balance of trade under mercantilist economic policy. As a result of sustained contact between Europeans, indigenous Amerindians, and imported African laborers, new ethnic groups emerged, each with a specific place in colonial hierarchies.

B. Possible acceptable response: Significant effects of the creation of new ethnic groups in the Americas following European colonization include the many examples of syncretism (Creole language and cuisine, voodoo, Santería, Cult of Saints, etc.), as well as new conceptions of race.

C. Possible acceptable response: Answers may vary, but the utilization of various labor systems, including mi'ta and encomienda systems emerged. In addition, specific descriptions of how the melding of the Spanish and Amerindian (Latin American) cultures created cultural progressions including new types of music, architecture, OR farming systems would be acceptable.

(*The Earth and Its Peoples*, 6th ed., pp. 475–479/7th ed., pp. 467–474; History Reasoning Skill—Causation; Learning Objectives SOC; Key Concept 4.2)

QUESTION 2

A. Possible acceptable response: One way that commerce along the Indian Ocean, Trans-Saharan, Silk Road, and Mediterranean Sea lane networks changed in the period 600 C.E. to 1450 C.E. was the introduction of new navigational and transportation technologies. For example, by 1450, the use of the compass and astrolabe was widespread along maritime networks, and the use of the horse and camel saddle and stirrups facilitated trade by caravan groups over land. In addition, ship designs, such as the dhow and the junk, facilitated the increase in the transport of luxury goods and commodities.

B. Possible acceptable response: One continuity in trade networks such as the Indian Ocean, Trans-Saharan route, Silk Road, and Mediterranean Sea lanes was that trade continued to facilitate the diffusion of culture (knowledge, technology, religions) as well as germs. As with trade networks prior to 600 C.E. (and after 1450 C.E.), the nature of commercial activity brings people of diverse backgrounds and experiences together for the sake of trade. In the process of engaging in these economic exchanges, religions, ideologies, artistic expressions, and germs spread between merchant groups conducting the trade.

C. Possible acceptable response: One reason for the swift diffusion of navigational and transportation technologies could be the expansion of the Islamic religion. As Islam spread, in part because of the extensive commercial activity of the period, Muslim merchants exchanged not only their wares, but also their knowledge of technological innovations.

(*The Earth and Its Peoples*, 6th ed., pp. 380–393/7th ed., pp. 372–383; History Reasoning Skill—Comparison; Learning Objectives SB; Key Concept 2.2)

Question 3

A. Possible acceptable response: One similarity between the way that the Roman Empire and the Han Dynasty in China established a strong central government was in the use of religious and/or cultural belief systems to justify the authority of the ruler. For example, Roman emperors encouraged the association between themselves and Roman gods in works of art displayed in public, such as statues and relief sculptures on public monuments. Chinese emperors used the belief in the Mandate of Heaven to justify their dynasty's control over China.

B. Possible acceptable response: One difference in the techniques used to create a strong central government between the Roman Empire and the Han Dynasty in China would be the existence of a belief system/ideology in China that reinforced the social hierarchy, as well as the relationship between ruler and subject, that did not exist in Rome. Han Chinese rulers relied on the teachings of Confucianism not only to help justify the emperor's authority, but also to help maintain social order. While some Roman rulers built upon the precedents established by prior emperors, a uniform belief system/ideology did not exist in Roman culture that transcended generations of rulers as Confucianism did in China.

C. Possible acceptable response: Confucianism developed in a time of extreme political and social chaos known as the Period of Warring States. Because a main goal of Confucian teachings is to establish and maintain social and political order throughout the vast Chinese lands, rulers from the Han Dynasty of the Classical era through the Qing Dynasty of the late nineteenth century continued to adhere to Confucian principles as a stabilizing factor in governing China. On the other hand, Roman imperial rule developed out of the conquest of a large amount of territory encompassing diverse peoples, languages, cultures, and religious practices. Whereas Confucian principles dictated social norms at the household and government level, the cultural practices of the Roman family did not necessarily translate to the political arena.

(*The Earth and Its Peoples*, 6th ed., pp. 136–161/7th ed., Chapter 6; History Reasoning Skill—Comparison; Learning Objective 5B; Key Concept 2.2)

Question 4

A. Possible acceptable response: The Industrial Revolution was a turning point in world history for many reasons, including the profound changes in the way humans interacted with the environment (intense extraction of resources, often resulting in pollution; increase in size and number of urban areas in industrialized nations; construction of railroads and canals across landscapes; emergence of new types of diseases, such as cancer, etc.) as well as significant transformations in economic production (mechanized, factory production; wage-labor; mass production; etc.).

B. Possible acceptable response: While there are many causes of the Industrial Revolution, it seems the time was ripe, after many agricultural innovations in the eighteenth century. In addition, newly explored economic systems including capitalism allowed for the building of factories (especially textile factories in England). Although areas of the world that did experience industrialization certainly underwent many changes, many parts of the world did not industrialize at the same time as Western Europe and the United States (China, sub-Saharan Africa, etc.). Also, even in areas that did industrialize, the nature of those that controlled/owned resources exploiting the labor of those that did not possess resources continued (from wealthy land-owners exploiting agricultural laborers—i.e., serfdom, to factory owners exploiting factory workers).

C. Possible acceptable response: Significant technological changes were made in farming (both harvesting and planting), manufacturing (the introduction of the factory, use of water, coal, and oil power) and in modes of transportation such as extensive railroad networks. As a result of railroad innovations, even time itself was monitored in various parts of the world into zones.

(*The Earth and Its Peoples*, 6th ed., pp. 577–601/7th ed., Chapter 22; History Reasoning Skills—Continuity and Change Over Time; Learning Objectives ENV, ECON; Key Concept 5.1)

Answer for Section II, Part A: Document-Based Question (DBQ)

The Documents

Following are short analyses of the documents. The italicized words suggest what your margin notes might include:

Document 1. This document is from the British perspective; it shows support for the Zionist movement while also promising to respect the rights of the Arab peoples already in Palestine. Why does the document promise both, and was that a realistic promise? *This document would seem to show self-determination as a possibility in the Middle East, with both groups co-existing.*

Document 2. This excerpt from Wilson's Fourteen Points shows Wilson's idealist vision for the region and calls for self-determination for all people under the rule of the Ottoman Empire and an opportunity for them—and only them—to determine their future. *This document shows self-determination as a success and real possibility for the Middle East.*

Document 3. Article 22 from the League of Nations calls for the creation of the mandate system and justifies it on the grounds that the Arab peoples were less developed and not ready to determine what their future nations needed. The language used in the document reflects Social Darwinism. *This document is very imperialistic and patronizing in its tone and is a failure for self-determination.*

Document 4. This document, an explicit argument against Document 3, represents the voice of the Syrian people in protest against the mandate system, the French government, and the Zionist movement in Palestine. *This document shows the Syrians' demand for independence and thus shows strong support for the right of self-determination.*

DOCUMENT 5. By 1920, after the fall of the Ottoman Empire, the Middle East is under the control of Europeans. *This map shows the success of the mandate system and the failure of self-determination in the region.*

DOCUMENT 6. After the fall of the Ottoman Empire, Atatürk led a passionate campaign to create a new national identity for the Turks, one that was secular and more reflective of European culture without falling under Europe's control. *This speech by Mustafa Kemal Atatürk shows the failure of the mandate system and success of self-determination.*

DOCUMENT 7. Mustafa Kemal Atatürk taught others the new Turkish alphabet. *This picture of Mustafa Kemal Atatürk shows the success of self-determination.*

A SAMPLE ESSAY

At the end of the nineteenth century, European nations were engaged in a struggle to claim new territories in Africa and Asia. European expansion in the Middle East was hindered by the presence of the Ottoman Empire, although Ottoman power was diminishing by the time World War I began. The lands of the Middle East were attractive to European nations not only because of the wealth of oil deposits, but also because of the strategic location of the Middle East. As World War I ended, and the Ottoman Empire was dismantled by victorious European powers and the United States, the question arose of what the political fate of the formerly Ottoman territories in the Middle East would be. Although some world leaders argued in favor of complete self-determination for these lands, and some European powers presented a plan to support a transition from Ottoman-control to independence, much of the former Ottoman territory in the Middle East continued to be denied self-rule. At the same time, the heartland of the former Ottoman Empire, Turkey, established itself as an independent, modernizing-minded nation.

The initial efforts of some European powers and the United States to develop self-determination in Middle Eastern countries after the collapse of the Ottoman Empire were relatively successful, particularly in the case of Turkey. The self-determination movement was best articulated early on by U.S. President Woodrow Wilson, who spoke directly in his Fourteen Points (Document 2) about the opportunity for all of the nationalities under Turkish rule to be completely free to develop as nations on their own. This document, written while the war was still being fought and a full year before the Treaty of Versailles, reflects Wilson's lofty idealism in its promises that self-determination will be accomplished and that, after the fall of the Ottoman Empire, peoples of the region will finally be given political opportunities that ensure autonomy. The autonomy that was promised to Turkey can be seen in the leadership of Turkey's first president, Mustafa Kemal Ataturk. In his speech to the Turkish Congress of the People's Republican Party (Document 6), Ataturk is clearly using Turkish nationalism to promote greater independence and self-determination for the newly formed Turkish nation. As a new nation, and as its first President, Ataturk will use his speech to further garner support from the Turkish people to help improve the Turkish nation and remain as independent from European influences as possible. Ataturk's leadership and efforts to modernize Turkey without European control are further exemplified by the image of him teaching the new Turkish alphabet (Document 7). This demonstrates both the enduring influence of Europe in the form of the Latin alphabet and the effort of Turkey to control its own destiny. This would allow Turkish businesses and reforms to deal with their European neighbors on better terms. Like the alphabet, Ataturk and other Turkish leaders undertook significant efforts to modernize and transform Turkey from the old Ottoman sultanate, into a western republican style government, including representative government, legal reforms, gender reforms, and other economic reforms. While this represents a great deal of cultural borrowing from European in terms of modernization, it also demonstrates that Turkey was free to determine what it wanted for its future instead of being controlled by European powers, like many other areas of the former Ottoman Empire.

Despite the success of self-determination in Turkey, self-determination in the non-Turkish regions of the former Ottoman Empire was mostly a failure. The Balfour Declaration (Document 1) reflects the British desire to support the Zionist movement in order to gain Jewish-American support for the War. It is not surprising that the British would be careful to address the fears of non-Jewish Palestinians in this declaration. During the war they encouraged Palestinian Arabs to revolt against the Ottoman Empire, an ally of Germany. The promise to establish a national home for Jews in Palestine would certainly offend these Arab Muslims, so the British statement to respect the rights of these non-Jewish communities should not be taken at face value. However, this document still has value. It shows Britain's desire to influence the postwar settlement of the former Ottoman Empire, something that will hinder the self-determination of the people living there. Further limiting self-determination was the League of Nations. Article 22 of the Covenant of the League of Nations (Document 3) authorizes the League to create a Mandate System, which essentially produced British and French colonies in the Middle East. The tone of the document drips of Social Darwinism, an ideology of European imperial nations at that time. Believing themselves to be superior to non-whites, they felt justified in drawing boundaries, breaking promises, and manipulating foreign policy for their own benefit. Syria, who France wanted as a mandate, responded directly to these attitudes in their Memorandum of the General Syrian Congress (Document 4). Here they firmly state that they are just as able as "other races," a clear reference to the prejudice of Europeans. The tone of this document is one of indignation and urgency, both at the thought of being ruled by France and by the prospect of the Zionists getting Palestine, territory the Syrian Congress believed was theirs. Also interesting is that this document is from the Syrian General Congress, a fact that shows they had already begun to form institutions of self-rule. The prospect of being a Mandate of France dashed all hopes of self-determination. This document also demonstrates the failure of self-determination in the Middle East due to the inability of the Syrian government and people to create an independent state. Additionally, it shows the inherent conflict in the documents when comparing this to Wilson's 14 Points. Clearly, if the Syrian people are angry over the lack of political independence and autonomy, then Wilson's efforts and dream of a new international community was not fulfilled.

Finally, the map of the Mandate System (Document 5) demonstrates the blatant disregard for the ideas of self-determinism. This carving up of the Middle East by France and Britain clearly shows the failure of self-determination in much of the Middle East. This policy of Mandates would continue in parts of the Middle East until World War II brought Britain and France to the brink of collapse.

While the speeches of Wilson and other idealists were well intended, the push for self-determination fell short of its intended goals. Turkey was successful in gaining self-determination, but the remainder of the Ottoman Empire was broken up and placed under the control of European powers.

SCORING This essay scores a 7 out of a possible 7 points. 1 point is awarded for the thesis, which can be found at the end of the first paragraph. It addresses both the successes and failures of the self-determination movement. 1 point is awarded for analysis and reasoning by corroborating evidence throughout the essay. Documents 2, 6, and 7 are used together in order to provide corroborating evidence to the success of self-determination in Turkey, while Documents 1, 3, 4, and 5 are used as corroborating evidence to support the argument that self-determination was a failure. Furthermore, Documents 2 and 3 directly contradict Document 4, which is articulated in the second body paragraph. Finally, Document 1 is dealt with in a qualified way, by pointing out how it can be both an argument for the success and the failure of self-determination. 1 point is awarded for utilizing at least six documents as evidence to support the stated thesis. 1 point is also awarded for identifying the Point of View, Purpose, Context, or Audience for at least three of the documents. 1 point is awarded for the Contextualization point, which can be found at the introduction to the paper by situating the self-determination movement in the context of the aftermath of World War I and stating European imperial goals of the period. 1 point is awarded for using evidence beyond the document to support the stated thesis, including discussions of Social Darwinism, Ataturk's modernization movement, discussion of European control of the Middle East until after World War II and the Zionist movement.

(*The Earth and Its Peoples*, 6th ed., pp. 768–775/7th ed., pp. 743–749; History Disciplinary Practices and Reasoning Skills—Analyzing Historical Evidence, Contextualization, Argument Development; Learning Objectives SB; Key Concept 6.2)

ANSWER FOR SECTION II, PART B: LONG ESSAY QUESTION

A SAMPLE ESSAY FOR QUESTION OPTION 2

The spread of religious ideas and belief systems has always had a major impact on the societies and institutions they encounter. This process of diffusion has been an important theme in world history, especially with the development of universalizing religions beginning in the Classical Period. From the time of its origin until circa 1750, the effect of the diffusion of Islam on political institutions was that it provided legitimacy for rulers. However, Islam's impact on social institutions was, initially, an improvement in the treatment of women, while Islam primarily continued to support patriarchal gender roles.

The increase in trade throughout Africa, Europe and Asia that occurred around the same time Islam began helped with its diffusion. The recent domestication of the camel, and use of the camel to traverse the Sahara Desert, allowed Islam to spread along the sand routes into West Africa. Improved technology in the Indian Ocean allowed for the creation of Islamic states on the East Coast of Africa, as well as throughout Southeast Asia. Additionally, the recentralization of government in China allowed for increased use of the Silk Trade Route, which helped the spread of Islam to the East. The later Mongol conquest of this trade route even brought Islam into parts of China.

One effect of the diffusion of Islam from its origin until circa 1750 on political institutions was it provided legitimacy for the rulers of empires and caliphates, which had Muslim leadership. Islam was initially borne out of the Arab conquests led by Muhammad in the seventh century C.E. As Muhammad and his loyal generals expanded their control throughout the Arabian Peninsula, they were eventually able to build the Umayyad Caliphate at the capital of Damascus. The title, caliph, of this empire signified not only the political authority which the caliph had, but also the religious influence the leader of the caliphate had over the cultural affairs of the empire, and as Muhammad was the cultural founder of the religion and its first major political figure, Islam continued to provide a source of political legitimacy to those that would later adopt it or use in their imperial structure. As the Umayyad Caliphate gave way to the Abbasid Caliphate, Islam continued to provide this legitimacy to the leadership of the empire at the new capital of Baghdad. Furthermore, as the caliphates collapsed over time, later empires in the Middle East and South Asia continued to use Islam as a way of legitimizing their rule. The Ottoman Turks who conquered the Middle East in the fourteenth century adopted Islam, as well as the Safavid Empire of Persia and the Mughal Empire of South Asia. In each of these cases, Islam's effect continued to be felt through political institutions, such as the use of Shari'a law, the authority of the Koran and other Islamic texts, and the basis of which rulers' authority were derived. The diffusion of Islam was very rapid and as it was initially tied to the political structure of Muhammad's leadership and the Arab expansion in the Middle East, it provided an important political basis from which later rulers in the area derived legitimacy and authority in their respective empires.

In addition to providing political legitimacy, Islam initially had a large impact on the treatment of women by improving the social standing in those areas, although this change tended to be short lived. Pre-Islamic Arabia tended to be very patriarchal in which women often had very few legal rights, including the right to divorce, inherit property, or marriage consent. With the beginning of Islam in the Middle East, many changes were implemented early on. For one, women were allowed to inherit property, which provided for a more stable economic outlook for women whose husband or father had died. Furthermore, women were afforded the right to consent in marriage, in which marriages became more of a contract rather than a woman becoming the property of her husband. Finally, although it would have been very uncommon, in certain cases, women could obtain divorces under some Islamic law early on. Because early Islamic law allowed women, and especially daughters to inherit property and wealth, it increased the economic and social position of women in society. Combined, these provide for some substantial changes in the relationship between the gender roles, however, over time, these changes would be short-lived, downplayed, or subdued as patriarchal societies continued to dominate sometimes because of and sometimes in spite of the diffusion of Islam.

While there were some significant changes to the role of women due to the diffusion of Islam and its legal teachings, Islam primarily continued to support and justify patriarchal gender roles. While women could inherit property as a result of Islamic law, it was legally less than that of men. Additionally, their court testimonies counted less than men's, making their ability to press legal proceeding more difficult than men's. Furthermore, women were often distrusted in the realm of fidelity and politics. While men were allowed to have polygamous lives, having more than one legal wife, women were not, and suspicions of women's sexual infidelity were a constant point of contention. This coincided with the mistrust of women in the political arena. Men were often suspicious of women who attempted to wield political power, or even women who were just seen as being too influential in political affairs could be demonized for going beyond their assigned gender roles.

Overall, Islam had a tremendous influence not only on the cultural fabric of the areas to which it diffused, but also on the political and social institutions of the societies in which it influenced.

SCORING This essay scores a 6 out of a possible 6 points—1 point for the thesis that is found in the final two sentences of the opening paragraph. It addresses the effect of the diffusion of Islam on political and social institutions. 1 point for the contextualization provided in the second paragraph. 2 points are awarded for analysis and reasoning. The question asks you to deal with effects of the diffusion of Islam, and the response deals with both social and political changes as a result of the spread. Furthermore, it explains the reasons for the stated effects. 2 points were also awarded for evidence as numerous examples are cited to support each part of the thesis as well as that evidence be tied directly back to the stated thesis/argument.

(*The Earth and Its Peoples*, 6th ed., pp. 147–148, 239–241, 248–267, 380–392/7th ed., pp. 153–155, 242–243, 248–266, 372–384; History Disciplinary Practice and Reasoning Skill—Causation, Argument Development; Learning Objectives CUL; Key Concepts 2.1, 3.1)

Part II

A Review of AP® World History

A Note About Geography

Successful students of world history have a solid grasp on basic geography. While you won't face questions on the AP® exam that explicitly test your knowledge of world geography, you are expected to have an awareness of where in the world the societies featured in the course framework developed, as well as a clear understanding of the terminology used to refer to certain world regions. For example, if you are asked to trace continuity and change over time for a society in East Asia in an essay, you would need to know that India is NOT an appropriate choice to write about because India is part of South Asia. Similarly, for an essay that calls for an example from North America or Latin America, it can be advantageous to know that a society originating in Mexico could be used for either region! The following map reflects the way the College Board has identified sub-regions of five major regions: Asia, Europe, Africa, the Americas, and Oceania. You should make a habit of noting the appropriate sub-region(s) of each new society, civilization, nation, and/or empire you learn about as you study world history. Being able to give details about specific historical examples from a region or sub-region that you are asked to write about will certainly give you an advantage on the AP® exam. The layout of this book will help you, as each of the six time periods in world history are divided into chapters discussing developments and patterns by region.

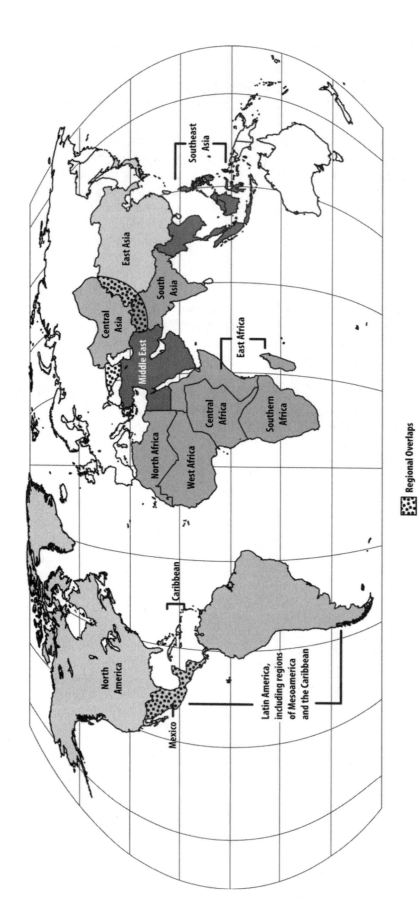

AP World History: World Regions—A Closer Look

Southeast Asia

East Asia

Central Asia

South Asia

Middle East

East Africa

North Africa

West Africa

Central Africa

Southern Africa

North America

Mexico

Caribbean

Latin America, including regions of Mesoamerica and the Caribbean

Regional Overlaps

Period 1: Technological and Environmental Transformations, to c. 600 B.C.E.

Period 1 of the AP® World History framework examines a rather large period of human history: from the origins of human migration to the development of the first urban societies. As human groups migrated during the Paleolithic period, they adapted to the diverse environments they encountered and even developed tools to assist in their daily activities, such as hunting and foraging. Over time, some human groups developed agricultural techniques, such as cultivating plants or raising herds of domesticated animals, or both. The development of agriculture was a very long, slow process that began independently in different parts of the world at different times. As knowledge of these agricultural techniques spread, not all human groups that encountered this form of deliberate food production adopted it for themselves and remained hunter-foragers. Other human groups remained nomadic, while at the same time adopting the herding of animals—we call these groups pastoralists. Settled agricultural, pastoral, and hunter-forager societies coexisted for a long period in human history as the first urban societies developed. As with the start of agriculture, the formation of urban societies happened independently in different parts of the world at different times. These first urban societies laid the framework of cultural, political, social, and economic characteristics for the powerful empires that developed after 600 B.C.E. The following charts outline the learning objectives and topics from the content outline that fit into this period.

Content Review Questions can be found at the end of each chapter.
AP® format questions for Period 1 can be found on page 118. **Document-Based Questions** can be found in the diagnostic test and practice tests.

THEMATIC LEARNING OBJECTIVES FOR PERIOD 1

INTERACTION BETWEEN HUMANS AND THE ENVIRONMENT

Learning Objectives—Students are able to . . .	Relevant Topics in the Concept Outline
ENV-1 Explain how different types of societies have adapted to and affected their environments.	1.1. I—Human migration 1.2. I—Neolithic Revolution 1.2. II—Agriculture and pastoralism 1.3. I—Civilizations formed in a variety of environmental settings 1.3. II—States emerged within civilizations 1.3. III—Iron use; weapons and modes of transportation
ENV-2 Explain how environmental factors, disease, and technology affected patterns of human migration and settlement over time.	1.1. I—Big Geography 1.2. I—Neolithic Revolution 1.2. II—Agriculture and pastoralism 1.3. I—Environmental settings 1.3. II—First States; Transportation and warfare
ENV-3 Evaluate the extent to which migration, population, and urbanization affected the environment over time.	1.2. I, II—Agricultural diversity and abundance

DEVELOPMENT AND INTERACTION OF CULTURES

Learning Objectives—Students are able to . . .	Relevant Topics in the Concept Outline
CUL-1 Explain how religions, belief systems, philosophies, and ideologies originated, developed, and spread as a result of expanding communication and exchange networks.	1.3. III—New religious beliefs
CUL-2 Explain how religions, belief systems, philosophies, and ideologies affected political, economic, and social developments over time.	1.3. III—Early Civilizations
CUL-3 Explain how cross-cultural interactions resulted in the diffusion of culture, technologies, and scientific knowledge.	1.1. I—Human migration and spread of technology 1.3. III—Expanding trade routes, from local to regional
CUL-4 Explain how the arts are shaped by and reflect innovation, adaptation, and creativity of specific societies over time.	1.3. III—Monumental architecture; role of art in unifying early urban cultures
CUL-5 Explain how expanding exchange networks shaped the emergence of various forms of transregional culture, including music, literature, and visual art.	1.3. III—Monumental architecture; role of art in unifying early urban cultures

STATE BUILDING, EXPANSION, AND CONFLICT

Learning Objectives—Students are able to . . .	Relevant Topics in the Concept Outline
SB-1 Explain how different forms of governance have been constructed and maintained over time.	1.2. II—Development of elites 1.3. II—First states emerged 1.3. III—Legal codes developed
SB-2 Explain how and why different functions and institutions of governance have changed over time.	1.3. II, III—Characteristics of first states
SB-3 Explain how and why economic, social, cultural, and geographical factors have influenced the processes of state building, expansion, and dissolution.	1.3. II—Favorable environmental factors; early state and imperial expansion 1.3. III—Monumental architecture
SB-4 Explain how and why internal and external political factors have influenced the process of state building, expansion, and dissolution.	1.2. II—Accumulation of wealth 1.3. II—Competition over land and resources 1.3. III—Regional trade
SB-5 Explain how societies with states and state-less societies interacted over time.	1.2. I, II—Development of elites 1.3. II—Transformation of warfare

CREATION, EXPANSION, AND INTERACTION OF ECONOMIC SYSTEMS

Learning Objectives—Students are able to . . .	Relevant Topics in the Concept Outline
ECON-1 Explain how technology shaped economic production and globalization over time.	1.3. II—Weapons and transportation
ECON-2 Explain the causes and effects of economic strategies of different types of communities, states, and empires.	1.2. I—Neolithic Revolution 1.2. II—Pastoralism and agriculture 1.3. II—First states; record keeping, regional trade
ECON-3 Explain how different modes and locations of production and commerce have developed and changed over time.	1.3. II—First states
ECON-4 Explain how and why labor systems have developed and changed over time.	1.2. II—Agriculture, artisans, specialization 1.3. II—Labor regime in first states
ECON-5 Explain how local, regional, and global economic systems and exchange networks have influenced and impacted each other over time.	1.1. I—Development of pastoralism 1.2. I, II—Diffusion of domesticated plants and animals 1.3. II—Pastoralists as disseminators of technology

DEVELOPMENT AND TRANSFORMATION OF SOCIAL STRUCTURES

Learning Objectives—Students are able to . . .	Relevant Topics in the Concept Outline
SOC-1 Explain how distinctions based on kinship, ethnicity, class, gender, and race influenced the development and transformations of social hierarchies.	1.2. II—Gender hierarchies, including patriarchy; Labor specialization 1.3. II—First states; patriarchy and social hierarchies, intensification of social hierarchies; increasingly unified states
SOC-2 Evaluate the extent to which different ideologies, philosophies, and religions affected social hierarchies.	1.3. III—Increasingly unified states
SOC-3 Evaluate the extent to which legal systems, colonialism, nationalism, and independence movements have sustained or challenged class, gender, and racial hierarchies over time.	1.3. III—State unification
SOC-4 Explain how the development of specialized labor systems interacted with the development of social hierarchies.	1.2. II—Labor specialization 1.3. II—First states
SOC-5 Explain how social categories, roles, and practices have been maintained or challenged over time.	1.3. III—State unification

KEY CONCEPTS FOR PERIOD 1

1.1. Big Geography and the Peopling of the Earth

1.2. The Neolithic Revolution and Early Agricultural Societies

1.3. The Development and Interactions of Early Agricultural, Pastoral, and Urban Societies

1

AFRICA: UP TO C. 600 B.C.E.

KEY CONCEPTS

- The Agricultural Revolutions changed social and gender structures and paved the way for the emergence of civilizations.
- Ancient Egyptian civilization was shaped largely by geographic conditions.
- Ancient Egypt was a male-dominated society centered on the pharaoh.

KEY TERMS

- Agricultural Revolutions
- foragers
- hieroglyphics
- Neolithic
- papyrus
- pastoralists
- pharaoh

Life before and after the Agricultural Revolutions is discussed in *The Earth and Its Peoples*, 6th and 7th editions, Chapter 1. Ancient Egypt and Nubia is covered in 6th edition, Chapters 1, 2, and 3, and 7th edition, Chapters 2, 3, and 4.

THE EARLIEST HUMAN SOCIETIES

Anthropologists and historians theorize that human beings originated in Africa and migrated to other parts of the world over the course of thousands of years. Until approximately 8000 B.C.E., all humans lived in a similar manner: in small nomadic communities defined by marriage and kinship that relied on hunting and gathering in order to meet their needs. This **foraging** lifestyle did not support large numbers of people, and it required all members to participate in the food-gathering process—men were responsible for hunting and women for gathering fruits and plants. These early Paleolithic people migrated out of Africa to areas in Eurasia and eventually the Americas and Oceania.

Approximately 10,000 years ago, the **Agricultural Revolution** ushered in dramatic changes. (These changes are also often referred as the **Neolithic** Revolution.) Over the course of generations, groups of people settled and developed techniques for plant and animal domestication. Because a smaller number of people could meet the nutritional needs of the entire community, this change allowed for specialization of labor and freed members of the community to make important technological and political advances. Those not engaged in food production were able to specialize in other trades and professions. Important technological developments centered on the use of metals—particularly bronze and, later, iron—for farm tools and weapons. The development of civilization also altered gender roles; women were now expected to bear and raise children and tend to the household. Though there are examples of women in prominent political positions, early civilizations were patriarchal systems that limited the rights and power of women.

AP® Tip

For the AP® exam, you should be able to describe the development of the following foundational civilizations: Mesopotamia, Egypt, Indus Valley, Shang dynasty, Mesoamerica, and Andean South America. So, pay careful attention to these details and practice making direct comparisons.

By 3000 B.C.E., major civilizations emerged in Mesopotamia and along the Nile. Later, civilizations emerged in the Indus River Valley, China, Mesoamerica, and South America. River valleys provided means of transportation as well as rich soil in the flood basins. Though farming provided an abundance of food, and thus greater stability from year to year, early civilizations suffered from disease brought on by living among animals and without adequate sewage facilities.

While civilizations emerged along river valleys, **pastoralism** developed in areas not well suited for agriculture. In arid regions, small societies dependent on herds of animals moved their livestock among grazing lands and watering places. Pastoralist communities were small compared with those of agriculturalists, with whom they sometimes came into conflict over land use.

Religion in Neolithic communities continued the pagan beliefs of the foragers. While their predecessors revered geographic features and animals that were no doubt important to their survival, agriculturalists worshiped Mother Earth and gods of the elements such as fire, wind, and rain.

AP® is a trademark registered by the College Board, which is not affiliated with, and does not endorse, this product.

EGYPT: 3100–1070 B.C.E.

Humans first transformed their settled communities into major civilizations in ancient Egypt. Over the course of two millennia, Egypt developed a complex social order and economy, attained scientific and artistic heights, and flexed its military muscle. These achievements, made possible by Egypt's geography, were accomplished through a centralized political system.

Early farming villages appeared in Egypt around 5500 B.C.E. as the people of the region domesticated plants and animals. Between 5000 and 3000 B.C.E., as Egypt's climate became drier, people migrated to the fertile land along the Nile River, which was surrounded by deserts. The geography of ancient Egypt provided the necessary resources for a powerful and self-sufficient empire. Flowing south to north, the river played a key role in agriculture, religion, and transportation. Annual fall flooding irrigated the surrounding land, leaving it fertile for farming. Though the Nile's flood patterns were more consistent than those of the Tigris and Euphrates in Mesopotamia, variations in the amount of water affected food levels, and therefore, political stability. Large floods jeopardized residential areas; small floods decreased the amount of fertile land and thus food levels, which often led to regime change.

Migration and increased food production caused the population along the Nile to increase. Around 3100 B.C.E., the smaller communities along the Nile were unified into a single state led by a pharaoh. Dynasties were established within families and reflected which region along the Nile was most powerful. Egyptian history can also be broken into three kingdoms separated by periods of disunity and decline. The Old Kingdom was centered in Memphis; the Middle and New Kingdoms were based to the south, in Thebes.

Politically, Egypt centered on **pharaoh**, who was viewed as an earthly god. Charged with maintaining order and prosperity, pharaoh was the source of laws. Additionally, pharaoh controlled long-distance trade, which prevented the emergence of a merchant class. Though viewed as all-powerful, pharaoh was supported by a massive bureaucracy that kept records made possible by the development of **hieroglyphics** and the use of **papyrus** and collected taxes. Many pharaohs incorporated a merit-based system for awarding promotions or land grants. That said, pharaoh and his officials enjoyed the wealth and power associated with being at the top of the social hierarchy. Below them were low-level officials and local leaders, priests, and other professionals. At the bottom were peasants, who constituted the majority of the population. Though slavery existed on a limited scale, the prisoners of war, criminals, and others who were enslaved received better treatment and the promise of freedom that slaves in other societies lacked.

Ancient Egypt was a male-dominated society, but women enjoyed legal and economic rights denied to those in other ancient civilizations. For example, women could own and inherit property, and they were able to divorce and retain their dowry if the marriage failed. A few queens and queen mothers also held positions of political power. Additionally, some women were able to exercise authority over some religious cults for female deities.

The importance of the pharaohs is also apparent in the monumental architecture built in their honor after death. The pyramids at Giza, the most famous examples, demonstrate pharaoh's power to assemble workers who, with only simple tools, constructed massive structures, which were often adorned with hieroglyphics indicating the accomplishments of the pharaoh to be buried in the pyramid. This monumental building spurred advances in mathematics, and the Egyptian fascination with the afterlife led to advances in chemistry that allowed for mummification. The Egyptians also used the stars to create an advanced calendar, and they developed efficient transportation methods along the Nile. Additionally, Egyptians developed a cursive written script that was used in early written literature, which included stories of adventure and magic.

During the Old Kingdom (2575–2134 B.C.E.), Egypt was largely self-sufficient and self-interested. Physical isolation prevented mass migration or invasion, and the limited interaction with outsiders was only in the context of trade. During the Middle Kingdom (2040–1640 B.C.E.), Egypt's economic interests led it to invade Nubia to gain control of gold fields. Located along the Nile River south of Egypt, Nubia connected sub-Saharan Africa with North Africa. As a result of its location, Nubian leaders often served as middlemen in the trans-Saharan trade network that slowly developed—a role Egypt sought to destroy with its invasion. Egypt's expansionist tendencies increased during the New Kingdom (1532–1070 B.C.E.) as is evident with its move farther south into the Kingdom of Kush. Egyptian control of Nubia and Kush would last over five hundred years and see the imposition of Egyptian culture on the conquered peoples. In addition to the cultural imprint, children from elite Nubian families were taken to Egypt—hostages to ensure cooperation among their new subjects.

In the last millennium B.C.E., powerful leaders emerged in Nubia and, later, farther south in Meroë. When control shifted south to Nubian kings, Egyptian culture, burial customs, and architecture were actually revitalized. Nubian rule ended with the invasion of the Assyrians in 660 B.C.E. Assyrian rule was broken, in the fourth century B.C.E., when power shifted still farther south, to Meroë, which replaced Egyptian customs with sub-Saharan ones.

Content Review Questions

The transition to agriculture occurred first in the Middle East. By 8000 B.C.E., humans, by selecting the highest-yielding strains, had transformed certain wild grasses into the domesticated grains now known as emmer wheat and barley. They also discovered that alternating the cultivation of grains and *pulses* (plants yielding edible seeds such as lentils and peas) helped maintain soil fertility. Women, the principal gatherers of wild plant foods, had the expertise to play a major role in this transition to plant cultivation, but the heavy work of clearing the fields would have fallen to men.

Bulliet et al., *The Earth and Its Peoples,* 7th edition, Boston: Cengage Learning, 2019, p. 17.

1. Which of the following historical trends emerged as a direct result of the process described in the above passage?
   (A) Patriarchy developed as an organizing principle in both agrarian and pastoral societies.
   (B) Nomadic societies gradually died out as they were replaced by fast-growing agrarian populations.
   (C) Because of the increased availability of food as a result of the spread of agriculture, humans decreased their susceptibility to disease which lengthened human life-spans.
   (D) As agriculturalists learned to control nature through farming, they lost their belief in mystical and supernatural forces connected to natural elements.

2. Details from the above passage can most clearly be used to support which of the following conclusions about the Neolithic Revolution?
   (A) The Neolithic Revolution was a gradual process marked by discovery and experimentation.
   (B) The Neolithic Revolution was the brainchild of the foremost scientists and political leaders of the Middle East, enacted with the goal of rapidly advancing their civilizations to the detriment of their neighbors.
   (C) While the Neolithic Revolution had drastic consequences on the Middle East, it had a relatively minimal impact on other human societies of the same era.
   (D) Although organized and led by women, the Neolithic Revolution actually caused women to lose power in early societies.

3. Based on your knowledge of history, which of the following was most likely the cause of the process described in the above passage?
   (A) People migrated to regions that could finally support agriculture.
   (B) As a response to climate change, some groups of nomads and pastoralists abandoned a lifestyle of continual movement in favor of permanent agricultural villages.
   (C) Foraging groups grew so large that they could no longer function as nomadic societies.
   (D) Major river valleys stopped flooding, which allowed people to settle along their banks.

Michele Burgess/Michele Burgess/Superstock

Pyramids of Menkaure, Khafre, and Khufu at Giza, C. 2500 B.C.E With a width of 755 feet (230 meters) and a height of 480 feet (146 meters), the Great Pyramid of Khufu is the largest stone structure ever built. The construction of these massive edifices depended on relatively simple techniques of stonecutting, transport (the stones were floated downriver on boats and rolled to the site on sledges), and lifting (the stones were dragged up the face of the pyramid on mud-brick ramps). However, the surveying and engineering skills required to level the platform, lay out the measurements, and securely position the blocks were very sophisticated and have withstood the test of time.

4. Which of the following conclusions can best be inferred from the above image?
   (A) The Ancient Egyptian Civilization had a highly developed political system, which allowed them to organize and maintain a large workforce.
   (B) Ancient Egyptian society relied heavily on slave labor in order to build and keep up its monuments and infrastructure.
   (C) Frequent flooding of the Nile prevented Egyptian civilization from rivaling the architectural achievements of contemporary Mesopotamian societies to their north.
   (D) The Egyptians were heavily influenced by their Asian trading partners and often incorporated aspects of both the Tigris–Euphrates River Valley Civilizations and the Indus Valley Civilizations in their artwork.

5. How could a historian best utilize an image like the one above of the Egyptian Pyramids?
   (A) To show the negative impact of overcrowding and poor sanitation in newly urbanized societies
   (B) To prove the existence of unifying culture and monumental architecture in early urban societies
   (C) To demonstrate the impact of interregional trade between early civilizations
   (D) To criticize the authoritarian nature of early state governments

6. Which of the following statements best describes the impact of the geography on the development of early Egyptian Civilization?
   (A) Although Egypt did have limited participation in regional trade routes, the availability of natural resources surrounding the Nile River allowed Egypt to be largely self-sufficient.
   (B) The arid climate of the region made survival a challenge for Egyptians.
   (C) The unpredictable nature of the Nile River made transportation, trade, and agriculture extremely challenging, stunting the growth of Ancient Egypt.
   (D) The harsh nature of the region prevented the establishment of an agricultural foundation.

Answers

1. Answer: A. As men gradually replaced women as the principle suppliers of food in agricultural societies, they also took over the majority of roles occurring outside of the house. Women were, for the most part, relegated to a domestic role as child-bearer and caregiver. (*The Earth and Its Peoples*, 6th ed., p. 8/7th ed., p. 11; History Reasoning Skill—Causation; Learning Objectives ENV-1, SOC-4; Key Concept 1.2).

2. Answer: A. The passage refers to a process of domestication that required humans to select the most useful parts of a plant, propagate them, and repeat the process over many lifecycles of that plant before the plant was permanently transformed. Additionally, most sources agree that farming was discovered accidentally and independently in several places around the world (*The Earth and Its Peoples*, 6th ed., pp. 9–10/7th ed., p. 17; History Disciplinary Practice—Argument Development; Learning Objectives ENV-1,2, ECON-2; Key Concept 1.2).

3. Answer: B. The passage references the transition to farming in the Middle East. Historians believe wide-scale adoption of agriculture after 8000 B.C.E. was likely a response to climate change. While river valleys' flood patterns changing would also be a climate change, this did not happen. In fact, the continual flooding of river valleys like those in Egypt and Mesopotamia kept the soil fertile enough to sustain large-scale agriculture (*The Earth and Its Peoples*, 6th ed., pp. 23–26/7th ed., pp. 38–39; History Reasoning Skill—Causation; History Disciplinary Practice—Argument Development; Learning Objectives ENV-2, SB-1; Key Concept 1.3).

4. Answer: A. Construction of the pyramids required a massive labor force. Workers had to be fed, housed, and managed. Workers also had to followed detailed plans based on advanced Egyptian engineering abilities to keep the pyramids stable. All of this required workers to be organized, which implies a strong state structure to mobilize labor and resources (*The Earth and Its Peoples*, 6th ed., pp. 29–30/7th ed., pp. 42–43; History Reasoning Skill—Causation, History Disciplinary Practice—Analyzing Historical Evidence; Learning Objectives SB-1, ECON-5; Key Concept 1.3).

5. Answer: B. Pyramids are an illustrative example of the existence of state-wide culture and monumental architecture in early urban societies (*The Earth and Its Peoples*, 6th ed., pp. 26–27/7th ed., pp. 40–41; History Disciplinary Practice—Argument Development; Learning Objectives SB-2,3,9,10, ECON-3; Key Concept 1.3).

6. Answer: A. The Nile provided fertile soil and water for irrigation, as well as a means of transportation for local trade. Its regular flooding created fertile lands for Egyptian farmers. As a result of natural resources and geography, Egypt had a more limited reliance on neighbors than the civilizations in Mesopotamia (*The Earth and Its Peoples*, 6th ed., pp. 86–87/7th ed., pp. 93–94; History Reasoning Skill—Causation; Learning Objectives ENV-1,2; ECON-7; Key Concept 1.3).

2

THE MIDDLE EAST: UP TO C. 600 B.C.E.

KEY CONCEPTS

- Civilizations emerged in Mesopotamia with their own distinctive culture and political and social structures.
- City-states and empires in the Middle East engaged in long-distance trade with both Egypt and the Indus Valley civilizations.
- The geographic, political, and economic characteristics of the Middle East gave rise to the first empires.
- Hebrew monotheism originated in the Middle East and had an impact on political events and social structure.

KEY TERMS

- city-state
- cuneiform
- Israelites
- Mesopotamia
- monotheism
- Neo-Assyrian Empire

Early Mesopotamian civilization is covered in the 6th edition of *The Earth and Its Peoples*, Chapters 1 and 2, and in the 7th edition, Chapter 2.

MESOPOTAMIA

The first domestication of plants and animals occurred in the Middle East around 8000 B.C.E. in the Fertile Crescent, which encompasses the area from the Persian Gulf through Iraq to the area around the border between Syria and Turkey. Jericho, located in present-day Palestine, was settled around

8000 B.C.E. It and the ruins of Çatalhöyük (7000–5000 B.C.E.), located in present-day Turkey, provide archaeologists with evidence of early settled communities: mud-brick structures, pottery, metalworking, long-distance trade, religion, and an agriculture-based economy that allowed for division of labor.

By 5000 B.C.E. the Agricultural Revolution had reached **Mesopotamia**, the land between the Tigris and the Euphrates Rivers. The geography of the region allowed such development but offered many challenges. The rivers were important sources of irrigation and offered a means of transportation; however, their unpredictable flood pattern made farming difficult, and it occasionally isolated the fields, people, and towns. Techniques to maximize land use were incorporated beginning around 4000 B.C.E., first with the use of ox-drawn plows and then with the construction of irrigation canals to supply water to fields. Additionally, fields were left fallow every other year so that the soil retained nutrients.

Beginning around 3100 B.C.E., Mesopotamia gave rise to the first complex civilizations and empires, which over time would compete with one another and influence lands beyond the Middle East. The region also saw considerable cultural synthesis as customs, religion, and language were adopted and adapted over time.

Success in agriculture led to the emergence of the city-state—an urban center and the agricultural territory it controlled. Within a **city-state** many worked in the fields while others were craftspeople, religious leaders, or political leaders. Farmers produced food for the city, and city dwellers provided markets, as well as protection for farmers when conflict arose with neighboring city-states. Mesopotamian city-states were centered on two main focal points: the temple and the palace of the king. Religion in Mesopotamia, organized by the state, was a very public affair. Large temples constructed to gods of the elements reflected the geographic challenges of the region and the importance of agriculture. Temples were centrally located and tended by priests, who were important members of society. The importance of religion and the ownership of land—land being a source of wealth—put priests in a prominent political and economic role.

The importance of priests, however, was surpassed by that of the king. Viewed as the gods' representative on earth, he controlled the army, provided protection, built infrastructure, and maintained justice. A good example of strong political leadership is the Babylonian king Hammurabi, who ruled in the eighteenth century B.C.E. Through military campaigns he expanded Babylonian rule and implemented his famous Law Code over the region. Inscribed on a stone pillar, the Law Code established criteria for judicial decisions and clear, often severe punishment for criminals.

The rise of city-states supported long-distance trade by which regions exchanged natural resources native to their land. (The absence of money for most of its history meant that Mesopotamia had a barter economy.) The emergence of city-states also cemented social divisions within society. Rights and privileges differed according to wealth and profession. Hammurabi's Babylonia, with its three main classes, serves as a good example of the divisions within such a society. The highest class was the free landowning class consisting of royalty, high-ranking officials, warriors, priests, and some merchants. As trade flourished, merchants became more prominent members of society, and by the second millennium B.C.E.

guilds—professional organizations—emerged. In the middle were farmers, who made up the agricultural workforce and were often attached to an estate owned privately or by the king or temple. The bottom of the social ladder was occupied by slaves, who worked mostly in a domestic capacity. Slaves were often prisoners of war or people who could not repay debts. Though a presence in society, slaves in Mesopotamia did not play a large role in the economy, unlike slaves in the classical or modern era.

Social distinctions also fell along gender lines. Women's status changed dramatically in the transition from the hunter-gatherer lifestyle to the agriculture-based settled communities. As families grew in size because of a stable food supply and an increased demand for labor, women's main role was bearing and raising children, which left little time for the acquisition of a skill or political influence. That said, women's legal and political rights varied from society to society. In Mesopotamia, women could own property, control their dowry, and engage in trade. Some women did work outside the home but in specific industries at the lower rungs of society. As the city-state emerged in Mesopotamia, women's status deteriorated further with the rise of the middle class. Marriage and divorce laws favored the husband, and marriage was often used as a way to create ties between families and bolster their economic standing. Women were often nothing more than economic objects.

AP® Tip

Pay attention to the social and gender structures of a particular society. This is excellent information to include when making comparisons across time and place.

Writing developed in the Middle East prior to 3300 B.C.E. and likely evolved from a system for documenting property. The system of recording strokes and wedges on a damp clay tablet, which hardened as it dried, **cuneiform**, recorded first the Sumerian language and eventually other languages in the region. In spite of the expansion of cuneiform during the second millennium B.C.E., the number of people who could read and write remained small.

In addition to writing, Mesopotamians developed other important techniques and technologies that helped advance their civilizations. Beasts of burden such as cattle and donkeys were employed as important sources of power and transportation before the domestication of the camel in 1200 B.C.E. Horses, in use by 2000 B.C.E., provided another important mode of transportation. Like archers, horsemen and charioteers revolutionized military strategy. Bronze tools and weapons were made from imported ores, and the effective use of clay in making bricks and pottery was instrumental in constructing housing. Mesopotamians also developed the base-60 system in mathematics and studied astronomy.

Advances by city-states within Mesopotamia often spread through the Middle East. In the second millennium B.C.E., interaction with other regions increased, resulting in a cosmopolitan period. Diplomatic and economic interaction benefited the elite of the societies involved. The peasants, who

AP® is a trademark registered by the College Board, which is not affiliated with, and does not endorse, this product.

continued to constitute the majority of the people, may also have seen some improvements in their lifestyles.

By 1500 B.C.E., Mesopotamia was essentially divided into two political and cultural zones. In the south, Babylonia continued in its position of dominance, gained under Hammurabi's leadership two hundred years earlier. In the north, Assyria, which for centuries had imported ore and textiles, appeared ready to conquer land and expand its economic interests. In contrast to the smaller city-states of the previous millennia, Babylonia and Assyria increased their interaction with Egypt and the Hittites in Anatolia, who provided copper, silver, and iron to much of the Middle East. The coexistence of these large states, however, did not last long. Around 1200 B.C.E., many of the economic and political centers in the region declined as a result of conflict in Anatolia and the subsequent economic collapse of their intertwined economies. For the next three hundred years, Mesopotamia experienced a period of isolation and poverty.

The Neo-Assyrian Empire

The Assyrians rose again to establish what many historians consider the first empire, the **Neo-Assyrian Empire** (911–612 B.C.E.), by conquering and governing diverse peoples inhabiting far-off lands. The Assyrian homeland in northern Mesopotamia, with a more temperate climate and greater rainfall than areas to the south, enabled farmers to support a growing population and expansion. Additionally, experience in defending themselves from invaders to the north served many farmers well when they became foot soldiers for the empire.

The Assyrians succeeded because they had professional soldiers armed with iron weapons and aided by a cavalry and the machinery and techniques for besieging towns. Their expansion, because it followed trade routes, provided immediate economic rewards, and as neighboring kingdoms were conquered, a tribute system was put in place. The Assyrians treated the peoples they conquered harshly. Policies were designed to benefit the imperial center, and the use of terror and forced deportation effectively kept the conquered people in line and discouraged thoughts of rebellion. To administer the empire, regional officials who had sworn their obedience to the king oversaw payment of tribute, enforced laws, built infrastructure, and supplied the army in their region. Though this system proved effective at maintaining order and funneling the wealth of the region to the king, the Neo-Assyrian Empire extended economic prosperity to much of the region and expanded long-distance trade. Assyrian rule lasted until 612 B.C.E., when the empire eroded from the hatred of its conquered peoples and its own increasingly diverse—and less loyal—population.

Israel

On the east coast of the Mediterranean, in about 2000 B.C.E., the **Israelites** were gathering into settled communities and transforming the nature of religion. The Israelites were a relatively small population inhabiting a small region poor in natural resources but strategically located at the crossroads of important trade routes. However, their contributions to history were large.

The story of the Israelites, as documented in the Hebrew Bible, begins with Abraham, who is considered the father of three **monotheistic** religions—Judaism, Christianity, and Islam. Abraham believed that there is only one god, Yahweh, who in a covenant with the Israelites agreed to make them his chosen people and promised them the land of Israel. In exchange, the Israelites would worship only Yahweh as specified by the Ten Commandments. These beliefs in many ways isolated Jews from others, but they also instilled a strong sense of community and identity.

The Israelites reached their political and economic peak in the tenth century B.C.E. under King Solomon. To solidify the position of the Israelites and their religion relative to others in the Middle East, Solomon constructed the First Temple. While the temple helped legitimize Judaism, it also heightened the importance of priests. With the expansion of the city of Jerusalem and the increased economic opportunities of this time, society became more stratified. Others joined the temple priests in setting themselves apart from the relatively homogeneous group that had made the initial transition to a settled community. Gaps between rich and poor emerged, and institutions like marriage took on an economic as well as social significance. Women were respected for the vital role they had played in the early history of Israel, but now they lacked the property and marriage rights of men. Women could not inherit property or initiate divorce, and while some women worked outside the home, most assumed duties in the home and in agriculture.

When the Neo-Assyrian Empire conquered the region around Israel in 721 B.C.E., much of the kingdom was destroyed and its people deported to the east. This destruction and deportation were repeated in 587 B.C.E. when the Neo-Babylonian Empire attacked Jerusalem. Despite these upheavals, Judaism survived the dispersal of Jews from their homeland, known as the Diaspora. The strength of Jewish rituals, rules, and beliefs sustained community and identity.

AP® Tip

Be able to describe the basic features and origins of major religions, and note how they shape society through their rules and expectations for men and women.

The transition from settled communities to vast empires that took place in the Middle East also occurred in Africa, Asia, Europe, and the Americas. All can be easily compared—in many respects the process was much the same, no matter the region. As these civilizations and empires emerged, they were bound together by the trade and interaction that traversed the Middle East.

Content Review Questions

Hammurabi's Code, a collection of Mesopotamian Laws issued by eighteenth-century Babylonian King Hammurabi, was initially carved into a stone pillar and made public for the Mesopotamian people. The pillar also included an image of Hammurabi receiving the code from the gods.

186. If a man has taken a young child to sonship, and when he took him his mother and father rebelled, that nursling shall return to his father's house.
188. If an artisan has taken a son to bring up, and has caused him to learn his handicraft, no one has any claim.
189. If he has not caused him to learn his handicraft, that nursling shall return to his father's house.
200. If a man has made the tooth of a man that is his equal to fall out, one shall make his tooth fall out.
201. If he has made the tooth of a poor man to fall out, he shall pay one-third of a mina of silver.
203. If a man of gentle birth has struck the strength of a man of gentle birth who is like himself, he shall pay one mina of silver.
204. If a poor man has struck the strength of a poor man, he shall pay ten shekels of silver.
205. If a gentleman's servant has struck the strength of a free-man, one shall cut off his ear.

Source: Project Gutenberg, "The Oldest Code of Laws in the World by King of Babylonia Hammurabi," http://www.gutenberg.org/files/17150/17150-h/17150-h.htm.

1. Which of the following historical processes was most significant in allowing for the development of laws like the ones described above from Hammurabi's Code?
   (A) Agricultural societies produced an abundant supply of food, which led to specialization of labor and the creation of social and economic hierarchies.
   (B) Interregional trade networks caused a broader variety of goods and services to become available in Mesopotamia than in other early civilizations.
   (C) Patriarchal societies tended to prefer written law codes rather than relying on the ethical and religious codes to keep order among citizens.
   (D) Early states used monumental building projects as a way to encourage belonging and create cultural unity.

2. All of the following statements about early Mesopotamian society are accurate. Which of the following is most strongly supported by details from this excerpt from Hammurabi's Code?
   (A) The irregular flood patterns of the Tigris and Euphrates Rivers contributed to a greater degree of instability in Mesopotamia than in Egypt.
   (B) Mesopotamia's social hierarchy depended not only upon the status of a child at birth but also upon the skills acquired by that child.
   (C) The Mesopotamian region was invaded and conquered multiple times in part due to their location on major trade routes.
   (D) Mesopotamian law allowed priests to enjoy a privileged position throughout the region.

3. Which of the following best describes the relationship between religion and state in Mesopotamia?
   (A) The leader of the state was seen as a god, and became fully divine upon death. Therefore, laws given by the king were seen as commands issued by the gods.
   (B) The leader of the state was seen as a representative of the gods. Rulers often drew on this divine connection as a way to enforce their authority on earth.
   (C) The leader of the state was seen as a servant of the priests, who were in communication with the gods. Priests created the laws of the state, the leader merely implemented them.
   (D) The leader of the state was often at odds with the religion of the people, causing outbreaks of violence between various sects of Mesopotamian society.

The City of Jerusalem

4. Which of the following was an important long-term effect of the destruction of Solomon's temple in Jerusalem?
   (A) The creation of a Jewish Diaspora into major urban centers and along trade routes, which allowed Jewish faith and culture to be preserved.
   (B) The establishment of a new center of the Jewish faith in East Asia, far from the persecutions of the Babylonians.
   (C) The assimilation of the Jewish faith into Zoroastrianism and later into Christianity, causing Judaism to virtually disappear until a Zionist revival occurred in the nineteenth century.
   (D) The discovery of the ruins of an older, technologically advanced civilization, which had existed underneath Jerusalem. Artisans and engineers used the models from this older civilization to make many of the breakthroughs of the Assyrian and Persian Empires.

5. What conclusion can be drawn from the above image of Solomon's Jerusalem?
   (A) The city of Jerusalem was created near valuable resources, which required them to have an organized system of defense.
   (B) The city of Jerusalem incorporated many of the architectural elements of previously established civilizations.
   (C) The people of Jerusalem placed greater importance on secular state leadership than on religious leadership.
   (D) The city of Jerusalem offered more limited economic opportunities to its residents in comparison to other urban centers of the same period.

6. Major urban centers, like Jerusalem, from the period before 600 B.C.E. share the same characteristics EXCEPT
   (A) evidence of urban planning like defensive walls.
   (B) monumental architecture that is often connected to religion.
   (C) large-scale irrigation from nearby water sources.
   (D) multiple tiers constructed at different heights to reflect social hierarchies.

Answers

1. ANSWER: A. The passage refers to different penalties accruing for members of different social classes, showing that social structure weighted heavily on the creation of Hammurabi's Code. The Neolithic Revolution transformed more equal nomadic societies into hierarchical societies by creating a surplus of food, allowing some people to develop specialized skills and to therefore accumulate wealth for using those skills (*The Earth and Its Peoples*, 6th ed., p. 19/7th ed., p. 32; History Reasoning Skill—Causation; Key Concept 1.3.III.C; Learning Objectives CUL-2, SB-1, SOC-3).

2. ANSWER: B. By using the terms gentleman and poor, the law code demonstrates that Mesopotamians were born into different social ranks. However, the last lines from the excerpt show that Mesopotamians saw value in the skills learned by children, not just the lineage of a child. Mesopotamian social structure was divided into three general groups, and some skilled merchants and craftsmen were considered part of the top rung of Mesopotamian society (*The Earth and Its Peoples*, 6th ed., p. 19/7th ed., p. 32; History Disciplinary Practice—Analyzing Historical Evidence; Key Concept 1.3.III.F; Learning Objectives SOC-2,3).

3. ANSWER: B. Hammurabi's Code shows an image of Hammurabi getting the Code from the gods, demonstrating that while Hammurabi is favored by and respects the gods, he himself was not a god (*The Earth and Its Peoples*, 6th ed., pp. 18–19/7th ed., p. 34; History Disciplinary Practice—Analyzing Historical Evidence; Key Concept 1.3.II.A; Learning Objectives SB-1,2,3).

4. ANSWER: A. The destruction of the city of Jerusalem by the Babylonians, and later by the Romans caused the creation of a Jewish Diaspora. The Jewish faith and culture has been kept alive by the scattered believers up to present day (*The Earth and Its Peoples*, 6th ed., p. 19/7th ed., pp. 33–34; History Reasoning Skill—Causation; Key Concept 1.3.III.D; Learning Objectives CUL-3, SB-3,4).

5. ANSWER: A. Most urban centers from this period had some defensive capabilities, such as defensive walls. Walls are clearly shown surrounding the city of Jerusalem in the above image (*The Earth and Its Peoples*, 6th ed., p. 53/7th ed., pp. 62–63; History Reasoning Skill—Contextualization; Key Concept 1.3.III.A; Learning Objectives ENV-1, CUL-3).

6. ANSWER: D. The tiers shown in the image are reflective of an expanding city, not purposefully constructed to divide different social hierarchies (*The Earth and Its Peoples*, 6th ed., p. 56/7th ed., p. 65; History Reasoning Skill—Contextualization; Key Concept 1.3.III.A; Learning Objectives CUL-2, SOC-2,3).

3

ASIA:
UP TO C. 600 B.C.E.

KEY CONCEPTS

- Both China and India experienced major political developments that gave rise to early civilizations.
- The Shang and Zhou dynasties established the political and social foundation for future Chinese dynasties.
- City-states developed in the Indus Valley.

KEY TERMS

- caste
- Confucianism
- karma
- Legalism
- Mandate of Heaven
- varna

Information on Asia up to c. 600 B.C.E. can be found in *The Earth and Its Peoples*, 5th edition, Chapters 1, 2, and 6; 6th edition, Chapters 1, 3, and 6; and 7th edition Chapters 2, 3 and 7.

EAST ASIA

The transition to settled agricultural communities began along the Yellow River in China around 8000 B.C.E. By the second millennium B.C.E., the first Chinese dynasty emerged, and the foundation for two thousand years of Chinese history was established. Over that time, China became an economic and political force that was often the envy of peoples near and far.

Like river valley civilizations elsewhere, early Chinese settlements took advantage of the rich, fertile land along the Yellow and Yangzi Rivers. The geography of eastern Asia, however, kept Chinese civilizations isolated from those in the Middle East and the Indus River Valley. The climate of the southern region was well suited for growing rice, which produces a very high yield but requires substantial time and labor. As a result, the population and importance of the southern region eventually exceeded that of the northern region. Early civilizations in China exhibited many of the same characteristics as those elsewhere. Plants and animals were domesticated, stone and eventually bronze tools were used, and pottery was produced on a wheel and fired in a kiln. Labor was divided, and political and social structures took shape.

In 1750 B.C.E. the history of China truly began when the Shang clan rose to power. Originating in the Yellow River Valley, the Shang extended their control by means of their military strength and strategy. The Shang were ruled by a king, who was seen as an intermediary between the gods and the people. To expand and manage the land, the king was aided by an aristocracy that acted as generals, ambassadors, and public servants. Conquered territory was governed by members of the royal family, and far-off lands were left to native rulers who swore their allegiance to the king. Many of the conquered people were taken as prisoners of war and enslaved by the Shang rulers.

Shang cities grew into political and social centers. Surrounded by agricultural areas, cities were laid out on a grid and served as hubs for a far-reaching trade network. Jade, ivory, silk, and bronze weapons and vessels were prized by outsiders, who carried them perhaps as far as Mesopotamia. Writing developed under the Shang and facilitated administration, even though only a small number of the elite had time to master this skill.

In 1027 B.C.E. the last Shang king was defeated by the Zhou, who established the longest-lasting dynasty in Chinese history and introduced the concept of the Mandate of Heaven, the key to the dynastic cycle that would last nearly three thousand years. To justify the overthrow of the Shang king, Zhou rulers claimed that the new ruler had been chosen by "Heaven" and should be seen as the "Son of Heaven." As long as the king was a moral servant of the people, he would retain the Mandate of Heaven and China would prosper. If the king became corrupt, then he would lose the **Mandate of Heaven**, justifying his replacement. The end of the Shang was marked by corruption, violence, greed, and arrogance; therefore, according to the Zhou, the overthrow was justified.

The Zhou dynasty retained many of the traditions and rituals of the Shang and was similarly decentralized. The dynasty was divided into over one hundred territories, each ruled by allies or relations of the king. Government officials were expected to rule in a fair and moral fashion. This system worked well for a time, but around 800 B.C.E., territories began to compete with one another for power until 480 B.C.E., when China entered a two-hundred-year phase known as the Warring States Period. In many states, rulers imposed an authoritarian system known as **Legalism** in order to keep their subjects under control and promote the state above the individual. Legalism was based on the view that because human nature is evil, order is maintained with laws and punishment.

It was during the Zhou dynasty that the roots of another, more important philosophical and managerial approach were established. Though his influence would not be felt until after his death, Confucius (551–479 B.C.E.)

established his teachings based on the culture and practices of the Zhou dynasty. Confucius drew parallels between the family and the state, with the king serving as a father figure to his people and ruling with their interests at heart. Coincidentally, social structure of the later Zhou period moved from the clan-based system to the smaller family model that included grandparents, parents, and children. With the help of its followers, **Confucianism** would eventually become the philosophy that future dynasties embraced as a means to establish clear social structure.

Throughout the Shang and Zhou dynasties, China's patriarchal nature resembled that of many other early civilizations and empires: the father was the head of the family, and women were expected to tend to the household. Marriage was often an economic and political tool to promote power among elite families. Any land the family owned belonged to the father and was divided among his sons upon his death.

SOUTH ASIA

The diversity and culture of the Indian subcontinent developed because of its geographic isolation from the rest of Asia, as well as a combination of political forces. India is separated from the rest of Asia by the Himalayas to the north and the Indian Ocean on the other three sides. The most accessible land route to India is to the northwest, but it requires passing over the Hindu Kush Mountains and traversing the Thar Desert. Despite its diversity and relative isolation, the region would achieve cultural and economic influence throughout Asia.

Civilization developed in South Asia along the Indus River shortly after it did in Mesopotamia and Egypt. While archaeologists have located hundreds of communities, the high water table in the region has limited excavation—and therefore knowledge—of these early civilizations. The extensive urban planning and construction of the cities of Harappa and Mohenjo-Daro, for example, suggest that a strong central authority ruled. A strong central authority combined with the use of technologies such as irrigation techniques, the potter's wheel, and metalworking lead us to believe that the people in the Indus River Valley had attained a high level of knowledge and skills. Long-distance trade existed, as evidenced by the presence of Indus River Valley artifacts in Mesopotamia. Cities in the valley were abandoned after 1900 B.C.E., perhaps because of political, economic, and social failures brought on by natural disasters such as earthquake or flood. Urban centers in the area were replaced by patriarchal villages that relied on herds of animals and limited farming.

> ### AP® Tip
>
> Belief systems can profoundly affect a time and place because they often impact political, social, and gender structures. With that in mind, it is important to study not only the basic tenets of different belief systems but also the impact they have on government, social structure, and gender roles.

AP® is a trademark registered by the College Board, which is not affiliated with, and does not endorse, this product.

The next important phase in Indian history began in 1500 B.C.E. when nomadic warriors from the northwest migrated to India. The Vedic Age—so called because the Vedas, the religious texts, provide the main source of information—saw the rise to dominance of Indo-European groups. After 1000 B.C.E., the lighter-skinned Aryas, who spoke Indo-European languages, competed with the darker-skinned Dasas, who spoke Dravidian languages. Over time the Aryas pushed the Dasas south, and skin color became a basis for making sharp social divisions based on **varna**, the four major social classes: priests and scholars (Brahmin); warriors and government officials (Kshatriya); merchants, artisans, and landowners (Vaishya); and peasants or workers (Shudra). Installed by the Aryas, the system naturally restricted the Dasas to the lowest class. Eventually a fifth group was added, the Untouchables, who were excluded from the system, isolated from the others, and given the most demeaning jobs such as leather-tanning, which required contact with dead animals. These classes within the varna system were further broken down into different jati, or castes. Born into a **caste**, a person was expected to live, marry, and interact with his or her caste members. The belief in reincarnation helped entrench people in their caste. It was thought that when the soul is separated from the body at death, it is reborn in another form according to the karma of the individual. If a person accepted his role and did his duty, then he built up good **karma** that would be rewarded in his next life. In this way, the varna and the belief in reincarnation cemented a rigid social hierarchy in India. Despite the arrival of the Aryas, India remained politically fragmented, resulting in linguistic, cultural, and economic diversity until the rise of the Mauryan Empire.

Content Review Questions

Scholars' debates about the existence and impact of changes in the climate and landscape of the Indus Valley illuminate some of the possible factors at work, as well as the difficulties of verifying and interpreting such long-ago changes.

One of the points at issue is climate change. Earlier scholars believed the climate of the Indus Valley was considerably wetter during the height of that civilization than it is now. They pointed to the enormous quantities of timber needed to bake the millions of mud bricks used to construct the cities, the distribution of human settlements on land now unfavorable for agriculture, and the representation of jungle and marsh animals on decorated seals. They maintained that the growth of population, prosperity, and complexity in the Indus Valley in the third millennium B.C.E. required wet conditions, and they concluded that the change to a drier climate in the early second millennium B.C.E. pushed this civilization into decline.

Other experts, skeptical about radical climate change, offered alternative calculations of the amount of timber needed and pointed to the evidence of plant remains—particularly barley, a grain that is tolerant in dry conditions. However, recent studies of the stabilization of sand dunes, which occurs in periods of heavy rainfall, and analysis of the sediment deposited by rivers and winds have strengthened the view that the Indus Valley used to be wetter and that in early- to mid-second millennium B.C.E. it entered a period of relatively dry conditions that have persisted to the present.

Bulliet et al., *The Earth and Its Peoples*, 7th edition, Boston: Cengage Learning, 2018, p. 47.

1. Based on the above passage, which of the following pieces of evidence best supports the idea that climate change occurred in the Indus Valley and likely had detrimental effects on the inhabitants?
   (A) Evidence suggests that residents of the Indus Valley civilization used lots of timber in creating the materials necessary to build their city, suggesting the region once had sufficient access to water to grow large quantities of trees.
   (B) The Indus River no longer flows through the location of the current archeological site for the Indus Valley civilization.
   (C) The Indus Valley inhabitants were skilled at creating irrigation in order to get access to water in their arid environment.
   (D) Archeological evidence suggests that the diet of Indus Valley inhabitants consisted mostly of animals that live on or near wetlands.

2. Based on the above passage, which of the following pieces of evidence could best be used by historians to refute the claim that climate change was a significant factor causing change in the Indus Valley Civilization?
   (A) The Indus Valley region shows signs of heavy population growth, proving the people adapted to the arid conditions.
   (B) The people of the Indus Valley grew large quantities of barley, a drought-tolerant crop, suggesting that their climate has always been arid.
   (C) The people of the Indus Valley portrayed marsh and jungle animals in their artwork, suggesting these creatures were rare and therefore held some fascination for them.
   (D) Because the civilization of the Indus Valley occurred so long ago and left an extremely limited quantity of evidence, it is safest for historians to assume that the climate of the Indus Valley in the second millennium was the same as the climate of the Indus Valley in present times.

3. Which of the following provides the best historical context that likely inspired the creation of the above passage?
   (A) Twenty-first century debates about the nature and causes of climate change
   (B) Twentieth century growth in the population of India
   (C) Eighteenth century ideas that science should be based on empirical data
   (D) The end of the Indus Valley Civilization in the first millennium

Covered ritual 'Fang-yi' wine vessel with 'Tao-tie' motif, Shang Dynasty (cast bronze with grey patina), Chinese School, (12th century B.C.)/Arthur M. Sackler Museum, Harvard University Art Museums, USA/Bequest of Grenville L. Winthrop/The Bridgeman Art Library

Shang Period Bronze Vessel Vessels such as this large wine jar were used in rituals by the Shang ruling class to make contact with their ancestors. As both the source and the proof of the elite's authority, these vessels were often buried in Shang tombs. The complex shapes and elaborate decorations testify to the artisans' skill.

4. Based on the above object from Shang China, which of the following can be proven about Confucianism?
   (A) It conformed to an already existing sense of respect for elderly family members in Chinese society.
   (B) It rejected a previously existing rigid social hierarchy in China.
   (C) It introduced China to the ideas of hierarchical social structures.
   (D) It was heavily influenced by foreign ideas brought into China along long-distance trade routes.

5. Which of the following most accurately compares the source of authority for Chinese rulers to that of Mesopotamian and Egyptian rulers?
   (A) Leaders from all three places used a connection with the gods to legitimize their position as rulers of the state.
   (B) Chinese rulers relied most heavily on military expansion to justify their leadership, while Egyptian and Mesopotamian leaders instead emphasized successful economic policies as the reason they should remain in power.
   (C) Egyptian, Chinese, and Mesopotamian leaders all claimed to be directly descendants from the gods and relied on this familial connection to cement their place of power.
   (D) Mesopotamian rulers used positive readings of omens and oracles to convince the people of their leadership, while Chinese and Egyptian rulers claimed ascendancy over supernatural forces as a reason they should hold onto power.

6. The above object could be used as evidence supporting which of the following historical trends?
   (A) Culture helped unify the people within a state by providing common literature, religion, myths, and art.
   (B) Expanding networks of trade led to interregional cultural exchanges.
   (C) Patriarchy expanded as settled agricultural societies expanded.
   (D) States practiced urban planning to create an ordered allocation of limited resources.

Answers

1. ANSWER: A. In the second paragraph, the passage states that residents of the Indus Valley used to use timber to bake mud bricks to construct their cities. This section is included to prove that the Indus Valley civilization used to have access to timber, and wetter climates to grow trees (*The Earth and Its Peoples*, 6th ed., pp. 78–79/7th ed., pp. 45–49 and pp. 171–178; History Disciplinary Practice—Argument Development; Key Concept 1.3.III ; Learning Objective ENV-1).

2. ANSWER: B. In the third paragraph, the passage counters the argument of climate change, using barley as evidence (*The Earth and Its Peoples*, 6th ed., p. 81/7th ed., pp. 45–49 and pp. 171–178; History Disciplinary Practice—Argument Development; Key Concept 1.3.III; Learning Objective ENV-1).

3. ANSWER: A. This article is included in a twenty-first century edition of a World History textbook. Historical context refers to the conditions surrounding the creation of the article, not the period the article is written about (*The Earth and Its Peoples*, 6th ed., p. 174/7th ed., pp. 45–49 and pp. 171–178; History Reasoning Skill—Contextualization; Key Concept 1.3.III ; Learning Objective ENV-1).

4. ANSWER: A. Confucianism's five relationships include children respecting their elders. This image, produced centuries before Confucius was alive, was used in rituals to contact ancestors suggesting an already present sense of respect for elder family members (*The Earth and Its Peoples*, 6th ed., p. 169/7th ed., pp. 83–93; History Disciplinary Practice—Analyzing Historical Evidence; Key Concept 2.1.II.B; Learning Objective CUL-2,5).

5. ANSWER: A. Chinese rulers used the Mandate of Heaven, Mesopotamian rulers like Gilgamesh and Hammurabi were believed to have the approval of the gods, and Egyptian Pharaohs were seen as gods (*The Earth and Its Peoples*, 6th ed., pp. 32–33 and pp. 75–78/7th ed., pp. 48–49 and pp. 83–93; History Reasoning Skill—Comparison; Key Concept 1.3.II.A; Learning Objective SB-1).

6. ANSWER: A. The image is an example of Chinese culture, used for religion and to symbolize authority. This shows that the Chinese, like more other ancient civilizations, used culture as a way of unifying their people (*The Earth and Its Peoples*, 6th ed., p. 74/7th ed., pp. 83–93; History Reasoning Skill—Comparison; Key Concept 1.3.II.A; Learning Objective SB-1).

4

EUROPE:
UP TO C. 600 B.C.E.

KEY CONCEPTS

- ▦ Agriculture emerged in mainland Europe and the Mediterranean following similar patterns as other regions in the world.
- ▦ The Phoenicians developed an alphabet that was adopted by other civilizations in the Mediterranean region.
- ▦ Greek civilization began to take shape with the rise of several city-states.

KEY TERMS

- ▦ Celtic Europe
- ▦ hoplite
- ▦ Linear B
- ▦ Minoans
- ▦ Mycenaeans
- ▦ Phoenicians
- ▦ polis

Information on Europe up to c. 600 B.C.E. can be found in *The Earth and Its Peoples*, 6th edition, Chapters 2, 3, and 4, and 7th edition, Chapters 3, 4, 5, and 6.

EARLY CIVILIZATIONS OF EUROPE AND THE MEDITERRANEAN

Farming communities emerged in southern Europe by 6000 B.C.E., years after similar developments in Africa, the Middle East, and East Asia. By 3500 B.C.E. agricultural communities existed throughout Europe, and the population density of the region increased as food sources became more reliable. Although European development of civilizations and empires was similarly delayed relative to its counterparts elsewhere in the world, when European civilizations did finally emerge, a cultural and intellectual foundation was established for the Western world.

The first complex civilizations in Europe developed on the Mediterranean island of Crete and on the Greek peninsula. With natural resources such as arable land and metal deposits in short supply, the people of these lands took to the sea and created trade-based societies with close commercial and political ties to their neighbors. By 2000 B.C.E. the **Minoan** civilization had emerged on the island of Crete. Its centralized government, grand architecture, metal use, writing, and recordkeeping resembled the civilizations of Mesopotamia and Egypt. The similarities are best explained by the Minoans' proximity to Western Asia and North Africa and a trade-based economy that allowed them to compensate for the geographic shortcomings of their homeland.

Around 1450 B.C.E. the **Mycenaean** Greeks destroyed much of the Minoan civilization and became the next significant civilization in the region. Borrowing the architectural, economic, and political components of their predecessors, the Mycenaeans were centered on the Greek peninsula and the islands in the Aegean Sea. They also used the Minoan writing system as the basis of their own, **Linear B**, which endured as an early form of Greek. Highly skilled sailors, the Mycenaeans built a trade-based economy, evidence of which is seen in the clay pots found throughout the Mediterranean and Middle East that once contained wine and olive oil, and were traded for metals, grain, amber, and ivory. The accomplishments of the tough, warlike Mycenaeans were undone around 1200 B.C.E. by the economic and political collapse of their trading partners. Just one example of this is the destruction of the Hittite kingdom of Anatolia. The Middle East was destabilized, key relationships were lost, and soon the Mycenaean civilization declined. The cosmopolitan nature of the Middle East and the eastern Mediterranean that existed from approximately 1700–1100 B.C.E. gave way to a three-hundred-year period of poverty and isolation.

In this period of instability a group of small city-states arose on the east coast of the Mediterranean. While power shifted from one to another, as a group the Phoenician city-states prospered economically and politically by trading natural resources, food, and luxury items. Perhaps the most lasting contribution of the **Phoenicians** was their development of an alphabetic system of writing in which symbols represented sounds that could then be used to construct words. In the ninth century B.C.E., the Phoenicians established a trade network around the entire Mediterranean and colonized the region as their population grew. One of the most significant such colonies was Carthage. Located in present-day Tunisia, it was strategically positioned to control the middle portion of the Mediterranean. By 500 B.C.E., Carthage was one of the world's largest and most ethnically diverse cities. Though Carthage did not rule over a large territory, its strong navy and army of mercenaries protected its access to sea trade and made it influential in setting policies in the region until it was destroyed by the Romans in 202 B.C.E.

The geography, climate, and soil of continental Europe, as well as the rich natural resources, supported agriculture and herding animals. While humans lived in this region for thousands of years, little is known of the earliest societies because of a lack of writing. By 300 B.C.E., the Celts had significantly influenced the language and culture of Europe by migrating from central Europe and settling across much of the continent. This expansion across Europe was not a coherent movement or empire because, politically, the Celts were organized around kinship and it is unlikely there was a sense of a greater **Celtic** civilization. Socially, the Celts were divided into warriors, priests, and commoners. Wealth and power were concentrated among the landowning warriors, while the priests performed religious rituals and supported education and the judiciary and the commoners worked the land. Women focused on domestic tasks like raising children, though they did possess marriage and property rights better than their counterparts' in Greece and Rome. Marriage was viewed as a partnership.

AP® Tip

Pay attention to geographic characteristics of regions, which can help explain political and economic characteristics. Remembering whether an area is rich in natural resources or a certain people come from a landlocked homeland can help you recall political and economic characteristics of that region or people.

THE GREEK CITY-STATES

The first European empire grew out of the resource-poor region of Greece. The Dark Age that had settled in after the fall of the Mycenaean civilization lifted when Phoenician merchants helped reconnect the Greek peninsula to the regional trade network. By 800 B.C.E. Greek sailors were bringing goods and ideas home, and the Archaic period of Greek history had begun. A notable import was the Phoenician alphabet, to which the Greeks added symbols for vowels. The Greek alphabet was easier to learn than other forms of writing such as cuneiform or hieroglyphics and thus promoted more widespread literacy. However, Greek culture was still largely preserved through the oral tradition and the use of storytelling, theater, and philosophical dialogues.

Shortly into the Archaic period, Greece saw a population explosion likely caused by more effective farming and increased prosperity, thanks to its renewed role in the regional economy. As the population increased, villages expanded, and Greece became a collection of city-states. Each city-state, or **polis**, cherished its independence, and as a result, conflict among the heavily armed infantries of neighboring city-states was common. These infantrymen, known as **hoplites**, were not professional soldiers but rather citizens called upon in times of crisis. The military techniques employed by the Greeks did not require extensive training; the priorities were courage and strength to bear arms. Battles and campaigns were typically quick, which allowed the soldiers, most of whom were farmers, to return to their land.

While the population increase of the eighth century B.C.E. sparked urbanization and conflict, it also set off a period of colonization. From approximately 750 to 550 B.C.E., Greek people and culture spread around the Black Sea, across North Africa, and through southern Italy and Sicily. As they encountered new people and lands, the Greeks took on an air of superiority and reinforced their bonds among themselves. Their language and customs made them unique in these new lands. They referred to themselves as Hellenes, to non-Greeks as barbaroi (the root of the word "barbarian"). With a Greek presence throughout the region, the transfer of technology was facilitated. For example, the use of coins began in western Anatolia (modern-day Turkey) in the sixth century B.C.E. and quickly spread through the Greek world. Though hindered by the various weights and measures used by different states, coinage expedited trade and recordkeeping.

Greek society and politics evolved during the Archaic period and eventually resembled the democratic society for which ancient Greece is known. Early on, councils of nobles challenged and eventually surpassed Greek kings. Such nobles gained their wealth and status from owning large amounts of land. Peasants worked the land and kept only a portion of what they grew for themselves. Working alongside the peasants were debt slaves, who had defaulted on loans from the landowner and subsequently lost their freedom. Owners of small farms, merchants, and craftsmen made up a small middle class. In the mid-seventh and sixth centuries B.C.E., city-states saw the rise of tyrants. Typically ambitious and aggressive members of the nobility, these tyrants often seized control with the support of the middle class, which sought greater rights and power. While some tyrants were able to remain in power and even pass it on to an heir, eventually these leaders were removed, and communities reacted by installing an oligarchy (rule by a small group) or a democracy, in which all free adult males participated.

Greek culture saw important developments during this early period and laid the foundation for the empire to come. Religion was based on a pantheon of anthropomorphic gods representing the power of nature. Altars and temples were constructed so that sacrifices could be made to these gods, and seers were employed to communicate with the gods and provide advice and insight. During the Archaic period, the role and value of the individual grew in importance. Colonists were valued for their efforts, and clearly the tyrants who assumed power believed in the strength and ability of the individual.

Content Review Questions

1. The above image of the Acropolis at Athens could best be used by historians to demonstrate the existence of which of the following general trends of World History?
   (A) Religions and cultural traditions transformed as they spread.
   (B) Patriarchy persisted.
   (C) A range of methods existed to provide rewards for the loyalty of the elites.
   (D) Urban areas served as centers of religious rituals, political and state administration.

2. Which of the following was a result of the use of maritime technology by the Greeks before the year 600 B.C.E?
   (A) Similar patterns in architecture can be found across the Mediterranean region.
   (B) Early Greek colonies sprouted up in the Americas.
   (C) Greek scientists discovered and used monsoon winds.
   (D) The development of a Greek Empire stretching from Northwest Africa to the Anatolian Peninsula.

3. After the eighth century B.C.E. the Greek political system was based on the polis, or city-state. All of the following are aspects of the Greek polis system EXCEPT
   (A) each polis consisted of an urban center and the surrounding rural territory.
   (B) each polis used democratic elections to select their leadership.
   (C) each polis was fiercely independent, and as a result they often fought with one another to preserve their autonomy.
   (D) most urban centers were designed in similar fashion so as to meet the political and security needs of the people.

ARCÉSILAS II, ROI DE CYRÈNE, ASSISTE

4. Historians can best use the image above as evidence of which of the following from Greece by 600 B.C.E?
   (A) The existence of the development of social hierarchies
   (B) A preference for Greek rationalism over nature-based religions
   (C) The existence of conflict between Greek city-states
   (D) The development of a trans-regional trade network

5. The above image demonstrates the existence of which of the following trends in Greece by 600 B.C.E?
   (A) Political leaders maintaining economic success through standardization of weights and coinage
   (B) Slavery
   (C) Continuation of shamanistic religions in Africa
   (D) Respect for nature

6. Which other leader similarly gained control over China in part by creating economic unity?
   (A) Shi Huangdi
   (B) Laozi
   (C) Liu Bang
   (D) Ashoka

Answers

1. ANSWER: D. The Acropolis shows an urban center for Athens—it includes a temple, a government center and an economic center. This shows that Athens fit the pattern of urban centers functioning as centers of religion, politics, and economics for early civilizations (*The Earth and Its Peoples*, 6th ed., pp. 116–117 /7th ed., pp. 121–122; History Disciplinary Practice—Analyzing Historical Evidence; Learning Objectives CUL-2; Key Concept 1.3.III.A).

2. ANSWER: A. Temples built in a similar pattern to the one shown in the picture, rectangular with columns and friezes, can be found throughout the Mediterranean, suggesting the Greeks spread their architectural style as they colonized the region (*The Earth and Its Peoples*, 6th ed., pp. 122–124 /7th ed., pp. 124–125; History Reasoning Skill—Comparison; Learning Objectives CUL-1; Key Concept 1.3.III.E).

3. ANSWER: B. While Athens did in fact have a democracy, Athens was unique. Most Greek city-states had more traditional forms of government. Sparta, for example, had an oligarchy (*The Earth and Its Peoples*, 6th ed., p. 116 /7th ed., pp. 128–130; History Reasoning Skill—Comparison; Learning Objectives CUL-2; Key Concept 1.3.III.C).

4. ANSWER: A. While all of those things existed in Ancient Greece, only one can be tied back to the image—social hierarchy. The image clearly shows a status difference between the figure on the left and those on the right (*The Earth and Its Peoples*, 6th ed., pp. 124–125 /7th ed., p. 113; History Disciplinary Practice—Analyzing Historical Evidence; Learning Objectives CUL-2, SB-2; Key Concept 1.3.III.C).

5. ANSWER: A. This answer comes from the source line on the image which explains that valuables are weighed before they are exported, showing the existence of a standard set of weights. While it is possible that some of the figures in the image are slaves, it is not conclusive based on just this image and caption (*The Earth and Its Peoples*, 7th ed., p. 113; History Disciplinary Practice—Analyzing Historical Evidence; Learning Objectives CUL-6; Key Concept 1.3.III.B).

6. ANSWER: A. Shi Huangdi of the Qin Empire also helped bring his powerful, if short-lived, dynasty together by standardizing the weights and measures (*The Earth and Its Peoples*, 6th ed., p. 152 /7th ed., p. 158; History Reasoning Skill—Comparison; Learning Objectives CUL-6; Key Concept 1.3.III.B).

5

THE AMERICAS: UP TO C. 600 B.C.E.

A major focus of the first unit of the AP® World History course is the development and characteristics of civilizations and empires. The development of complex civilizations in the Americas occurred later than in the Middle East, Indus Valley, and China. The first empires of the Americas do not arise until around 600 C.E. As a result of these curriculum choices and historical facts, this chapter is shorter than most of the other chapters. That said, key aspects of the early history of the Americas outlined in the AP® World History course description are included.

KEY CONCEPTS

▪ The development of civilization in the Western Hemisphere differed from that in the Eastern Hemisphere because of environmental factors and relative isolation.
▪ Societies with complex political, economic, and social structures did emerge in the Western Hemisphere.

KEY TERMS

▪ Olmec
▪ Chavín
▪ Mesoamerica

Information on the Americas from up to c. 600 C.E. can be found in *The Earth and Its Peoples*, 6th edition, Chapter 7, and 7th edition, Chapter 8.

AP® is a trademark registered by the College Board, which is not affiliated with, and does not endorse, this product.

THE WESTERN HEMISPHERE

Human beings had migrated to the Western Hemisphere from Asia by 13,000 B.C.E. and would remain isolated from the rest of the world for thousands of years. This isolation and the geographic characteristics of the Western Hemisphere resulted in different patterns of development among its early civilizations compared with those of the Eastern Hemisphere. The political and social structures of the Olmec and the Chavín societies, however, were similar to their counterparts in early Mesopotamia, Egypt, China, and the Indus Valley. These early American civilizations established a foundation for the classical age of the Maya, Aztecs, and the Inca.

By 3000 B.C.E. people in **Mesoamerica** (Mexico and northern Central America) had developed an agricultural system based on maize, tomatoes, peppers, and squash. Similarly, by 1500 B.C.E. people of South America relied on quinoa, corn, and potatoes. While the settling of farming societies may have begun later in the Americas, the domestication of dogs, which helped hunters find prey, likely began prior to the Neolithic age. In addition to dogs, people of the Americas eventually domesticated llamas, guinea pigs, and turkeys. The smaller number of species available for domestication and the absence of a true beast of burden (except for the llama) help explain some of the developmental differences in the Americas. While the Agricultural Revolution transformed much of the Americas, the Amerindians of the Great Plains hunted bison, and groups in the Pacific Northwest relied on fishing for sustenance. Following the Agricultural Revolution in the Americas came the emergence of the Olmec and the Chavín, both of whom developed important and complex civilizations.

THE OLMEC

The **Olmec** flourished in Mesoamerica between 1200 and 400 B.C.E. and in that time greatly influenced much of modern-day Mexico. Though Mesoamerica was never unified politically, the civilizations there had clear similarities in their political and social characteristics. This can likely be accounted for by trade and cultural exchange. As agricultural production and efficiency increased, specialization allowed for the rise of religious and political figures. These people gained status from their role in religious and political rituals, and they used this status to organize the labor of the people. As a result, Olmec urban centers included large-scale religious and civic buildings, and irrigation and canal projects were completed. Historians speculate that the Olmec were led by a king who had religious and secular duties. It was perhaps these rulers, famous athletes, and warriors who are commemorated in the famous large stone heads found in Olmec territory. In addition to efficient organization and direction of labor, the Olmec had elaborate religious rituals dedicated to their many deities, most of whom had a male and female nature. In addition to a political and religious foundation, the Olmec developed a writing system that influenced the Maya and a calendar based on astronomical observations, and they were probably the originators of a ritual ball game that became a fixture in Mesoamerican societies. Although the Olmec never physically dominated their neighbors, their cultural influence can be seen in a wide area and in succeeding civilizations.

THE CHAVÍN

In South America, the **Chavín** prospered between 900 and 250 B.C.E. Their society was built on the foundation of coastal societies, which relied on seafood to sustain their early cities, and the people of the foothills, who relied on corn and other foods. The Chavín emerged in part because of their strategic location between the coast and the Andes Mountains, and they preserved many of the cultural and economic characteristics of their predecessors, including irrigation networks, ceremonial plazas, and pyramids. Chavín growth was enabled by their location along trade routes and the increase in food production that came with the introduction of maize from Mesoamerica. As their society grew, the Chavín developed a reciprocal labor system that constructed the irrigation networks, roads, and bridges. The details of this system are not known, but the example would be adopted by later civilizations, including the Inca. Also crucial to the Chavín success and development was the domestication of the llama. Llamas provided meat, wool, and transportation that increased the efficiency and effectiveness of trade. Chavín artifacts, like those of the Olmec, were dispersed over a wide area and suggest cultural and economic influence rather than political control of neighbors. It is thought that regional wars disrupted this economic and cultural exchange, weakened the ruling class, and led to the collapse of Chavín society. Despite the society's collapse, Chavín architecture, urban planning, and culture, would influence people of the Andes for centuries.

Content Review Questions

Within each of these ecological niches, Amerindian peoples developed specialized technologies that exploited indigenous plants and animals, as well as minerals like obsidian, quartz, and jade. The ability of farmers to produce dependable surpluses of maize, beans, squash, and other locally domesticated plants permitted the first stages of craft specialization and urbanization. Eventually, human contacts across environmental boundaries led to trade and cultural exchange with emerging centers across the region and ultimately with Central and South America. Enhanced trade, increasing agricultural productivity, and rising population created the conditions for urbanization and social stratification.

Bulliet et al., *The Earth and Its Peoples*, 7th edition, Boston: Cengage Learning, 2018, p. 194.

1. Based on your knowledge of history, what is the most likely method by which the Olmec acquired the skills described in the passage?
   (A) From trade ventures with Mesopotamia
   (B) By conquering pre-existing, established urban and agricultural societies
   (C) Independent development through accidental experimentation and observation
   (D) By enslaving local Mayans to do their labor and teach them local customs

2. Which civilization's development can best be compared to that of the Olmec as described in the passage?
   (A) Sumerians in Mesopotamia
   (B) Xiongnu near China
   (C) Phoenicians in the Mediterranean
   (D) Mauryans in India

3. Which of the following was a likely result of the process described in the earlier passage?
   (A) An increased competition for land and resources
   (B) The development of nature-based religions
   (C) Sea exploration to find more colonies
   (D) Class revolution as lower classes became more aware of their subjugation

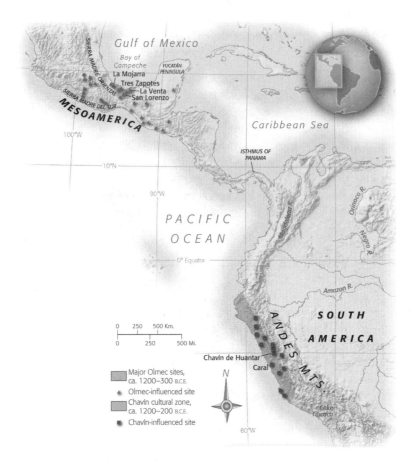

4. Based on the map and your knowledge of history, which of the following conclusions can be reached?
   (A) The Maya were most heavily influenced by the Chavín.
   (B) The Chavín's isolation kept their culture from surviving long enough to impact other civilizations.
   (C) The Chavín derived agricultural techniques from long-distance trade with the Pacific Islanders.
   (D) The Chavín's techniques for farming and traversing mountains inspired the Inca.

5. Which of the following was likely MOST essential in the development of the Olmec and Chavín as depicted in the map?
   (A) Access to mountains for protection
   (B) Access to water for irrigation
   (C) Animals that could be domesticated
   (D) Access to trade routes

6. What was the likely purpose for the creation of this map?
   (A) To demonstrate that the Olmec and Chavín influenced later Meso and South American civilizations
   (B) To show change over time within the Olmec and Chavín civilizations
   (C) To show the disconnectedness and relative unimportance of the Olmec and Chavín
   (D) To illustrate major battles fought between the Olmec and Chavín

Answers

1. ANSWER: C. Early agricultural civilizations, including those in the Americas, independently developed the ability to farm over a gradual process. They likely started to realize seeds grew into plants, that they could plant them, and for various reasons began to settle down into river valleys (*The Earth and Its Peoples*, 6th ed., p. 192/7th ed., p. 194; History Disciplinary Practice—Analyzing Historical Evidence; Learning Objectives ENV-1; Key Concept 1.3.I).

2. ANSWER: A. The Sumerians also gradually developed agriculture, then slowly established urban centers and civilization. The Xiongnu remained nomadic, and both the Phoenicians and the Mauryans got their skills from earlier river valley civilizations (*The Earth and Its Peoples*, 6th ed., p. 17–20/7th ed., pp. 29–30, 69, 99, 194; History Reasoning Skill—Comparison; Learning Objectives ENV-1,2; Key Concept 1.3.1).

3. ANSWER: A. The passage describes the transition to farming. This transition followed a similar pattern in the Americas as it did in the rest of the world—farming led to population growth, which led to competition over land and resources. Nature-based religions instead often preceded farming (*The Earth and Its Peoples*, 6th ed., p. 192/7th ed., p. 194; History Reasoning Skill—Causation; Learning Objectives SB-3; Key Concept 1.3.II.B).

4. ANSWER: D. Both the Chavín and the Inca were located in the Andes Mountain region of South America and share some cultural similarities leading historians to believe the Chavín influenced the later Incan civilization (*The Earth and Its Peoples*, 6th ed., pp. 195–196/7th ed., pp. 196–199; History Disciplinary Practice—Analyzing Historical Evidence; Learning Objectives ECON-7; Key Concept 1.3.II).

5. ANSWER: B. All early agricultural civilizations depended on water for irrigation. While the other choices could certainly be useful, none were as essential (*The Earth and Its Peoples*, 6th ed., pp. 194–195/7th ed., p. 196; History Disciplinary Practice—Argument Development; Learning Objectives ENV-1,2; Key Concept 1.3.I).

6. ANSWER: A. Since the map includes not just the location of the Olmec and Chavín civilizations, but also areas where they were influential to later civilizations, this is likely the reason for the creation of the map (*The Earth and Its Peoples*, 6th ed., pp. 194–197/7th ed., p. 196; History Disciplinary Practice—Analyzing Historical Evidence; Learning Objectives SB-4; Key Concept 1.3.II.B).

AP® FORMAT QUESTIONS FOR PERIOD 1

Multiple-Choice Questions

Questions 1–3 refer to the following passage.

> Wives of a man, or (widows), or any women who go out into the main thoroughfare (shall not have) their heads (bare). Daughters of a man . . . shall be veiled. When they go about in the main thoroughfare during the daytime, they shall be veiled. A prostitute shall not be veiled, her head shall be bare. And if a man should see a veiled prostitute and release her, and does not bring her to the palace entrance, they shall strike the man 50 blows with rods. Slave women shall not be veiled, and he should see a veiled woman shall seize her and bring her to the palace entrance; they shall cut off her ears.
>
> Assyrian Law, 1100 B.C.E.

1. Which of the following is evidenced in this passage?
   (A) People domesticated locally available plants and animals.
   (B) Diverse and sophisticated tools were developed.
   (C) New religious beliefs developed in this period.
   (D) Social hierarchies, including patriarchy, intensified as states expanded and cities multiplied.

2. Which of the following can be inferred about the Assyrian civilization from the passage?
   (A) The Assyrians had a strict social hierarchy.
   (B) The Assyrians were pastoralists.
   (C) The Assyrians lived in small groups.
   (D) The Assyrians did not have religious beliefs.

3. Which of the following conclusions about the first states is most directly supported by the passage?
   (A) It is evidence of hunting and foraging.
   (B) It is evidence of the development of fire.
   (C) It is evidence of states developing legal codes.
   (D) It is evidence of the development of sophisticated tools.

AP® is a trademark registered by the College Board, which is not affiliated with, and does not endorse, this product.

Questions 4–6 refer to the following chart.

CHRONOLOGY		
Mesopotamia	**Egypt**	**Indus Valley**
8000 B.C.E. 8000–2000 B.C.E. Neolithic (New Stone Age); earliest agriculture		
3000 B.C.E. 3000–2350 B.C.E. Early Dynastic (Sumerian)	3100–2575 B.C.E. Early Dynastic	
2500 B.C.E.	2575–2134 B.C.E. Old Kingdom	2600 B.C.E. Beginning of Indus Valley civilization
2350–2230 B.C.E. Akkadian (Semitic)	2134–2040 B.C.E. First Intermediate Period	
2112–2004 B.C.E. Third Dynasty of Ur (Sumerian)	2040–1640 B.C.E. Middle Kingdom	
2000 B.C.E.		
1900–1600 B.C.E. Old Babylonian (Semitic)	1640–1532 B.C.E. Second Intermediate Period	1900 B.C.E. End of Indus Valley civilization
	1532–1070 B.C.E. New Kingdom	
1500 B.C.E. 1500–1150 B.C.E. Kassite		

The Earth and Its Peoples, 5th ed., p. 7

4. Which of the following can be inferred from this chart?
   (A) Early civilizations developed from intricate trade networks.
   (B) Early civilizations arose near rivers.
   (C) Early civilizations were nomadic.
   (D) Early civilizations were hunters and foragers.

5. Which of the following did these civilizations have in common?
   (A) The people in each region domesticated locally available plants and animals.
   (B) They all had the same religion.
   (C) They all were located between the Tigris and Euphrates river valleys.
   (D) They all had contact with the Olmecs.

6. All of the following are tied to the growth of civilizations. Which of the following was the cause of the development of the other three?
   (A) Irrigation systems
   (B) Writing systems
   (C) Large-scale architecture
   (D) Urban planning

Questions 7–9 refer to the following image.

Public domain

7. The structure was most likely used for which of the following?
   (A) To develop iron weapons
   (B) To irrigate crops
   (C) To practice religious beliefs
   (D) To encourage pastoralism

8. This structure gives evidence to which of the following?
   (A) Early civilizations developed monumental architecture.
   (B) Early civilizations transformed warfare.
   (C) Early civilizations had rulers that used human sacrifice as a method of population control.
   (D) Early civilizations lived in small bands of people.

9. This structure could not have been built without which of the following?
   (A) Foraging
   (B) Economic exchange between civilizations
   (C) Specialization of labor
   (D) Hunting

Questions 10–12 refer to the following map.

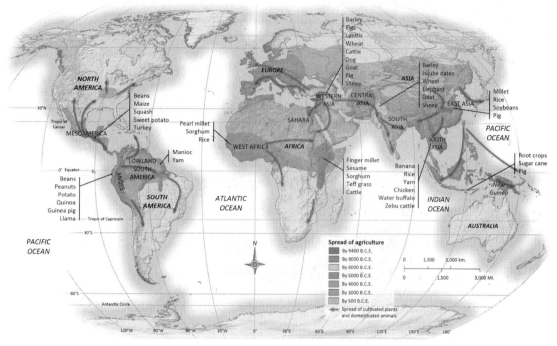

© Cengage Learning

10. Which of the following is evidenced in the map?
    (A) The Paleolithic period lasted until 600 B.C.E.
    (B) Warfare led to the development of early agricultural societies.
    (C) Hunting and foraging ceased to exist.
    (D) Agriculture developed independently.

11. According to your knowledge of history and the information provided on
    the map, which of the following is accurate?
    (A) Early agricultural societies did not have a diversified food supply.
    (B) The Ice Age was still occurring.
    (C) Humans did not develop sophisticated technologies.
    (D) Plants had been domesticated but not animals.

12. The civilizations highlighted on the map had, most likely, developed
    which of the following?
    (A) Gunpowder
    (B) Compass
    (C) Systems of record keeping
    (D) Democratic governing systems

Questions 13–15 refer to the following passage.

> When the species Homo sapiens sapiens, anatomically modern humans, first appeared in central and southern Africa some 150,000 years ago, they lived side by side with other animals and other hominins. . . . But in important respects they were totally different from their neighbors, for they learned to change their environment with radically new tools and skills. Their departure from Africa, their first art works, their hunting prowess, and their trade networks are all signs of recognizably human behavior.

Voyages in World History, 3rd ed., p. 4

13. How were the humans described in the passage different from those that lived around 10,000 years ago?
    (A) The humans described in the passage were artisans but later humans excelled in urban planning.
    (B) The humans described in the passage developed social hierarchies but later humans did not.
    (C) The humans described in the passage were not agriculturalists but later humans were.
    (D) The humans described in the passage did not live in small groups, where later humans did.

14. In addition to the methods mentioned in the passage, how else did the first groups of humans change their environment to better meet their needs?
    (A) Domestication of animals
    (B) Multiple uses of fire
    (C) Access to iron
    (D) Surplus labor

15. The period summarized in the passage is referred to by which of the following terms?
    (A) Paleolithic Era
    (B) Neolithic Era
    (C) Little Ice Age
    (D) Big Geography

Short-Answer Questions

Question 1 refers to the following passage.

> Fossilized animal bones bearing the marks of butchering tools testify to the scavenging and hunting activities of Stone Age peoples, but anthropologists do not believe that early humans depended primarily on meat for their food. The few surviving present-day foragers in Africa derive the bulk of their day-to-day nourishment from wild vegetable foods, with meat reserved for feasts. The same was probably true for Stone Age peoples, even though tools for gathering and processing vegetable foods have left few traces because they were made of perishable materials.
>
> *The Earth and Its Peoples*, 6th ed., p. 8

1. Answer Parts A, B, and C.
   A. Identify the central argument in this passage.
   B. Explain the evidence the author of this passage uses to support the central argument.
   C. Explain ONE disadvantage of studying modern-day foragers to understand foragers of the Stone Age.

2. Answer Parts A, B, and C.
   A. Identify ONE similarity in the cultural characteristics of Mesopotamia and the Nile Valley.
   B. Identify a difference in the cultural characteristics of Mesopotamia and the Nile Valley.
   C. Explain one reason for the development of different cultural characteristics in Mesopotamia and the Nile Valley.

Question 3 refers to the following map.

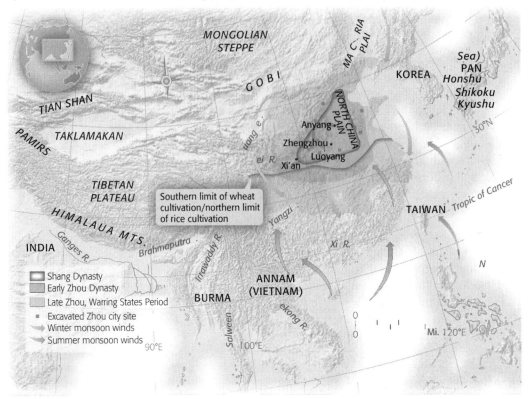

3. Answer Parts A, B, and C.
   A. Identify ONE historical claim about the Shang dynasty that can be drawn directly from the information in the map.
   B. Identify ONE historical claim about the Zhou dynasty that can be drawn directly from the information in the map.
   C. Explain ONE way in which Zhou dynasty rulers legitimized their power.

4. Answer Parts A, B, and C.
   A. Identify ONE cause for the development of writing in the Mediterranean region prior to 600 B.C.E.
   B. Explain ONE effect of the development of writing in the Mediterranean region prior to 600 B.C.E.
   C. Analyze the impact of differences between writing systems used in the Mediterranean region and writing systems used in Asia prior to 600 B.C.E.

Question 5 refers to the following passage.

> Little is known about Olmec political structure, but it seems likely that the rise of major urban centers coincided with the appearance of a form of kingship that combined religious and secular roles. The authority of the rulers and their kin groups is suggested by a series of colossal carved stone heads, some as large as 11 feet high. Since each head is unique, most archaeologists believe they were portraits carved to memorialize individual rulers. This theory is reinforced by the location of the heads close to the major urban centers, especially San Lorenzo.

The Earth and Its Peoples, 6th ed., pp. 193–194

5. Answer Parts A, B, and C.
   A. Identify one way the developments hypothesized in the passage would have influenced Olmec civilization.
   B. Explain the evidence given to support the central argument of this passage.
   C. Provide ONE additional example of this political development in a civilization prior to 600 B.C.E. outside of the Americas.

Long Essay Questions

1. Analyze the factors that contributed to the rise of settled (permanent) civilizations prior to 600 B.C.E.

2. Analyze changes and continuities in legal systems from the rise of settled civilizations to 600 B.C.E.

3. Using specific examples, analyze continuities and changes in India up to 600 B.C.E.

4. Evaluate the extent to which pastoralists and nomads influenced the development of settled agricultural societies prior to 600 B.C.E.

5. Analyze the similarities and differences in the development of settled agricultural societies in the Americas to the development of settled agricultural societies in the Middle East prior to 600 B.C.E.

Answers

MULTIPLE-CHOICE QUESTIONS

1. ANSWER: D. The passage refers to differing punishments and regulations based on social standing, which is evidence of social hierarchies and elite classes (*The Earth and Its Peoples*, 6th ed., p. 443/7th ed., pp. 31–34; History Disciplinary Practice—Analyzing Historical Evidence: Content and Sourcing; Learning Objectives CUL; Key Concept 1.2 IIA,1.3 IIIF).

2. ANSWER: A. The passage makes very clear distinctions between men and women, showing the existence of patriarchy, and very clear distinctions between free women and slaves. The passage thus makes it clear that the Assyrians had a social hierarchy (*The Earth and Its Peoples*, 6th ed., p. 18/7th ed., pp. 31–34; History Disciplinary Practice—Analyzing Historical Evidence: Content and Sourcing; Learning Objectives SOC; Key Concept 1.2 IIA,1.3 IIIF).

3. ANSWER: C. Besides specialization of labor, historians identify early civilizations as those that developed legal codes (*The Earth and Its Peoples*, 6th ed., p. 18/7th ed., pp. 31–34; History Disciplinary Practice—Analyzing Historical Evidence; Learning Objectives SB; Key Concept 1.3 IIIC).

4. ANSWER: B. The chart details civilizations that developed along the Nile River Valley, between the Tigris and Euphrates, and the Indus River Valley. Early civilizations were located near a source of irrigation (*The Earth and Its Peoples*, 6th ed., p. 85/7th ed., pp. 39–49; History Disciplinary Practice—Analyzing Historical Evidence; Learning Objectives CUL; Key Concept 1.2 IA, 1.3 I).

5. ANSWER: A. Early civilizations had settled agriculture and had learned how to herd and raise animals for food (*The Earth and Its Peoples*, 6th ed., p. 15/7th ed., pp. 19–22; History Reasoning Skill—Comparison; Learning Objectives ECON, CUL; Key Concept 1.2).

6. ANSWER: A. Irrigation systems were necessary for any group of peoples to transfer from a pastoral or nomadic lifestyle to a settled agricultural lifestyle. After developing farming and irrigation, the population grew, developed a specialization of labor, and began focusing on the other characteristics of civilizations like architecture and writing (*The Earth and Its Peoples*, 6th ed., p. 15/7th ed., pp. 19–23; History Reasoning Skill—Causation; Learning Objectives CUL; Key Concept 1.2).

7. ANSWER: C. The Ziggurat in the image was found in Mesopotamia and was used for religious purposes (*The Earth and Its Peoples*, 6th ed., p. 20/7th ed., pp. 34–35; History Disciplinary Practice—Analyzing Historical Evidence; Learning Objectives CUL; Key Concept 1.3 IIID).

8. ANSWER: A. Early civilizations were able to build massive buildings because they were able to specialize their labor. Early civilizations developed monumental architecture and urban planning (*The Earth and Its Peoples*, 6th ed., p. 26/7th ed., pp. 48–49; History Disciplinary Practice—Analyzing Historical Evidence; Learning Objectives CUL; Key Concept 1.3 IIIA).

9. ANSWER: C. Early civilizations were able to have specialized labor because they had a surplus of food and did not need to constantly search for food (*The Earth and Its Peoples*, 6th ed., p. 17/7th ed., pp. 48–49; History Disciplinary Practice—Analyzing Historical Evidence; Learning Objectives SB, ECON; Key Concept 1.2 IIA).

10. ANSWER: D. The map shows that civilizations that had no contact with one another developed agriculture; therefore, they developed agriculture independently (*The Earth and Its Peoples*, 6th ed., p. 17/7th ed., pp. 17–19; History Disciplinary Practice—Analyzing Historical Evidence; Learning Objectives ENV; Key Concept 1.2 IA).

11. ANSWER: A. Early civilizations were able to create a more reliable food source, but they domesticated locally available plants and did not have a diversified food source (*The Earth and Its Peoples*, 6th ed., p. 26/7th ed., pp. 19–21; History Disciplinary Practice—Analyzing Evidence: Content and Sourcing; Learning Objectives ENV; Key Concept 1.2 IB).

12. ANSWER: C. Early civilizations developed language, writing, and a method of record keeping. The other possible answers were developed much later (*The Earth and Its Peoples*, 6th ed., p. 28/7th ed., pp. 41–42; History Disciplinary Practice—Analyzing Historical Evidence; Learning Objectives CUL; Key Concept 1.3 IIIB).

13. ANSWER: C. The first humans were hunters and foragers and had not yet developed agriculture (*The Earth and Its Peoples*, 6th ed., p. 26/7th ed., pp. 11–15; History Disciplinary Practice—Analyzing Historical Evidence; Learning Objective CUL, ENV; Key Concept 1.1 I).

14. ANSWER: B. Early humans used fire to help adapt to their environments; the other possible answers coincide with the development of agriculture (*The Earth and Its Peoples*, 6th ed., p. 8/7th ed., pp. 11–14; History Disciplinary Practice—Analyzing Historical Evidence; Learning Objectives ENV; Key Concept 1.1 IA).

15. ANSWER: A. The Paleolithic Age identifies the age in which humans were nomadic hunters and foragers, before settled civilizations developed (*The Earth and Its Peoples*, 6th ed., p. 8/7th ed., pp. 11–14; History Disciplinary Practice—Analyzing Historical Evidence; Learning Objectives ENV; Key Concept 1.1 I).

SHORT-ANSWER QUESTIONS

1. A. The central argument in the passage is that the diets of hunter-forager groups of the Paleolithic Age largely consisted of vegetables, with meat making up only a small percentage of the diet (*The Earth and Its Peoples*, 6th ed., pp. 7–9/7th ed., pp. 11–14; History Disciplinary Practice—Argument Development; Key Concepts 1.1,1.2; Learning Objective ENV-2,5, ECON-1).

   B. The author references studies of the practices of modern-day foraging groups in Africa as evidence. These groups eat mostly vegetables and reserve meat for special occasions (*The Earth and Its Peoples*, 6th ed., pp. 7–9/7th ed., pp. 11–14; History Disciplinary Practice—Analyzing Historical Evidence; Key Concepts 1.1,1.2; Learning Objective ENV-2,5, ECON-1).

C. One disadvantage of drawing conclusions about hunter-foragers who lived before the first civilizations based on observations of modern hunter-forager groups is that there is no absolute way of knowing that practices in the present day reflect what was done in the past. As the author indicates, tools that would have been used for gathering and preparing vegetables and plant-based foods have not survived, nor do we have written records of hunter-forager society. The diets of contemporary hunter-forager groups may be different for a number of reasons, such as different climates and available sources of food, as well as greater likelihood of interactions with settled societies now than in the Paleolithic Age (*The Earth and Its Peoples*, 6th ed., pp. 7–9/7th ed., pp. 11–14; History Disciplinary Practice—Analyzing Historical Evidence; Key Concepts 1.1,1.2; Learning Objective ENV-2,5, ECON-1).

2. A. Acceptable responses could include discussion of the development of record keeping/writing systems (cuneiform and hieroglyphics), polytheistic religious beliefs/practices, and construction of large, public monuments (ziggurats and pyramids) (*The Earth and Its Peoples*, 6th ed., pp. 15–32/7th ed., pp. 17–45; History Reasoning Skill—Comparison; Key Concept 1.3; Learning Objectives CUL-1,8, ECON-11).

   B. Acceptable responses could include discussion of the differences in the way people viewed the afterlife and burial practices. While the Mesopotamians had a pessimistic view of what happened in the afterlife, Egyptians, particularly those with elite social status, looked forward to a pleasant afterlife (*The Earth and Its Peoples*, 6th ed., pp. 15–32/7th ed., pp. 17–45; History Reasoning Skill—Comparison; Key Concept 1.3; Learning Objective CUL-1).

   C. Acceptable responses could include differences in river flooding patterns, Mesopotamia's location as less defensible and more central to trade routes or Mesopotamia's origin as independent city-states among others (*The Earth and Its Peoples*, 6th ed., pp. 15–32/7th ed., pp. 17–45; History Reasoning Skill—Comparison; Key Concept 1.3; Learning Objective CUL).

3. A. Conclusions from this map about China during the Shang dynasty include Shang rulers controlled a smaller area than the later Zhou dynasty, people cultivated wheat in Shang-controlled areas, and Shang China was likely located on fertile lands (rivers, North China Plain) (*The Earth and Its Peoples*, 6th ed., pp. 74–81/7th ed., pp. 85–88; History Disciplinary Practice—Argument Development; Key Concept 1.3; Learning Objectives ENV-2, SB-1).

   B. Conclusions from this map about China during the Zhou include Zhou rulers controlled a larger area than the earlier Shang dynasty, people cultivated both wheat and rice in Zhou-controlled areas, and there were many urban areas in Zhou-controlled lands (*The Earth and Its Peoples*, 6th ed., pp. 74–81/7th ed., pp. 85–88; History Disciplinary Practice—Argument Development; Key Concept 1.3; Learning Objectives ENV-2, SB-1).

C. Zhou rulers used the Mandate of Heaven, or the belief that the ruling family had been specially chosen by "Heaven" to rule, to legitimize their power and justify their authority over the people (*The Earth and Its Peoples*, 6th ed., pp. 74–81/7th ed., p. 85; History Reasoning Skill—Contextualization; Key Concept 1.3; Learning Objectives CUL-4, SB-1,4).

4. A. One common factor contributing to the development of writing and record keeping was the expansion of commerce and trade networks that accompanied the rise of the early civilizations. Merchants used writing systems to keep track of important commercial records. Specifically in the Mediterranean region, we see the rise of phonetic alphabets, initially developed by the Phoenicians and eventually adopted by many Mediterranean civilizations (*The Earth and Its Peoples*, 6th ed., pp. 48–52, 59–67/7th ed., pp. 53–57, 72–73; History Reasoning Skill—Causation; Key Concept 1.3; Learning Objectives ECON-11).

   B. One effect of the development of the phonetic alphabet in the Mediterranean region was its diffusion to other civilizations, such as the Greeks, for use not only in commerce but also for administrative and cultural purposes. The phonetic alphabet is the basis of the alphabet used today in much of the world (Western Europe, North, and South America, and much of Africa) (*The Earth and Its Peoples*, 6th ed., pp. 48–52, 59–67/7th ed., pp. 53–57, 72–73; History Reasoning Skill—Causation; Key Concept 1.3; Learning Objectives CUL-6,9, ECON-11).

   C. A major difference between the phonetic alphabet developed by the Phoenicians in the Mediterranean region and writing systems used in Asia was that those used in Asia tended to be pictographic systems— pictures and symbols represented words. Therefore, the pictographic systems of China and the Indus River valley city-states were more complex and harder to learn compared to the phonetic alphabet, which has a symbol to represent sounds. Phonetic alphabets are simpler and easier to learn, allowing literacy to be more accessible for the people (*The Earth and Its Peoples*, 6th ed., pp. 48–52, 59–67/7th ed., pp. 41–42, 72–73; History Reasoning Skill— Comparison; Key Concept 1.3; Learning Objectives ECON-11).

5. A. The political development the passage describes is the use of monumental architecture by elites to reinforce their power. Often political elites mobilized resources and labor for the construction of large public works, such as the big head statues described in the passage. These projects often served to glorify the ruler and help legitimize his authority over the people (*The Earth and Its Peoples*, 6th ed., pp. 192–195/7th ed., pp. 194–197; History Reasoning Skill—Contextualization; Key Concept 1.3; Learning Objectives CUL-8, SB-1,4).

   B. The central argument in the passage is that Olmec society developed some form of ruler with extensive power. The evidence to support this claim is the construction of the big heads located close to urban areas with ceremonial significance in Olmec society (*The Earth and Its Peoples*, 6th ed., pp. 192–195/7th ed., pp. 194–197; History Disciplinary Practice—Analyzing Historical Evidence; Key Concept 1.3; Learning Objectives CUL-8, SB-1,4).

C. Another example of rulers using monumental architecture to legitimize rule includes the construction of the pyramids in Egypt that served as tombs to supply the royal family with possessions and companions into the afterlife. These pyramids also served as giant reminders of the power each ruler had in life (*The Earth and Its Peoples*, 6th ed., pp. 23–32, 192–195/7th ed., pp. 40–41, 194–197; History Disciplinary Practice—Argument Development; Key Concept 1.3; Learning Objectives CUL-8, SB-1,4).

LONG ESSAY QUESTIONS

1. A good response to this long essay question would center around discussion of the development of agriculture (cultivation of plants and domestication of animals). Following climate changes at the end of the last Ice Age, some human groups found new ways to adapt to the environment, including discovering ways to favor some types of crops over others, as well as using selective breeding techniques to domesticate animals. As these groups shifted to food production over hunting and foraging, they were able to remain in one place for longer amounts of time, typically in river valleys or places with abundant rain for agriculture. Experimentation with irrigation techniques facilitated the further expansion of food production, allowing for larger (in terms of population count and density) settlements to develop (*The Earth and Its Peoples*, 6th ed., pp. 9–15/7th ed., pp. 16–21; History Reasoning Skill—Causation; Key Concepts 1.2; Learning Objective ENV-1,2,4,6, ECON-1).

2. A good response will include changes like written laws and the codification of customs to keep societies unified, as well as continuities like preserving patriarchy, social classes, and using religion to legitimize authority. Evidence for changes can be found in Babylonian and Hebrew kingdoms. Hammurabi collected and codified the various laws of his state, then published them in stone. Evidence for continuities in terms of patriarchy could come from the existence of many laws about family and paternity. Evidence for continuities in terms of social class can come from Hammurabi's famous "eye for an eye" idea, which includes different punishments if the two people involved are from different classes. Evidence for using religion could come from the fact that Egyptian leaders didn't feel the need to publish their laws in part because they were gods, while Hammurabi shows the gods giving laws to him (*The Earth and Its Peoples*, 6th ed., pp. 16–18/7th ed., pp. 30–33; History Reasoning Skill—Continuity and Change over Time; Key Concept 1.3; Learning Objectives SB-1,2, SOC-4).

3. For this essay, students could successfully discuss changes and continuities from each of the five themes. In terms of interactions between humans and the environment, humans altering the environment through agricultural practices remained a continuity. Sometime around 1900 B.C.E., patterns of settlement changed as people began to abandon the once-prosperous city-states. Politically, India saw the rise and eventual collapse of city-states along the Indus River, followed by the arrival of the Aryans who eventually established political authority over

much of the subcontinent. Culturally, India experienced many changes, mostly as a result of Aryan influence. The form of writing changed from a pictographic system to Sanskrit, and the Vedas introduced new ideas about religion and social hierarchy. Again, as a result of the increased power of the Aryans, the social hierarchy of India transformed into one with a fairly rigid caste system, rooted not only in ethnic differences, but also in religious (Vedic) beliefs. Economic developments in this period included the establishment of long-distance commercial connections to the Middle East, at least until the collapse of the city-states. Farming and the herding of animals remained the prominent economic activity (*The Earth and Its Peoples*, 6th ed., pp. 32–35/7th ed., pp. 45–49, 170–178, 166–169; History Reasoning Skill—Continuity and Change over Time; Key Concept 1.3; Learning Objectives ENV-2,4, CUL1,4,5, SB-1,2, ECON-1,3,8,11,12, SOC-1,3).

4. A good response would say pastoralists and nomads continued to influence settled societies by trading between them and spreading technologies. It could also mention that the threat of nomadic invasion made fortifications a priority for settled societies. However, it should also say that many significant facets of settled society like patriarchy and social hierarchy developed independent of interactions with pastoralists or nomads. Evidence for spreading technologies could come from the spread of chariots. Evidence for fortifications could come from the walls surrounding Jerusalem or the importance of military in later Mesopotamian societies. Evidence for patriarchy could come from the persistence of male rulers and priests, and evidence of a new social class structure could come from Hammurabi's Code (*The Earth and Its Peoples*, 6th ed., pp. 16–20, 42–65/7th ed., pp. 30–34, 51–73; History Reasoning Skill—Causation; Key Concept 1.3; Learning Objectives SB-1,2,3,4,9).

5. Similarities in the development of settled agricultural societies in the Americas and the Middle East include the human impact on the environment as a result of agricultural practices (irrigation, selecting certain crops over others, etc.) as well as the changes to society that accompanied agriculture, such as accumulation of wealth and social stratification, the development of specialized workers, and the emergence of a political and social elite class that governed the civilization and mobilized resources and workers for large public works. Differences would include the fact that no large animals were ever domesticated in the Americas as were in the Middle East and the fact that settled society in the Middle East evolved as the first empires were established there, while in the Americas, no central, unifying authority developed prior to 600 B.C.E. (*The Earth and Its Peoples*, 6th ed., pp. 15–23, 192–197/7th ed., pp. 29–34, 294–299; History Reasoning Skill—Comparison; Key Concept 1.3; Learning Objectives ENV-1,2,4, SB-1,2,3,4).

Period 2: Organization and Reorganization of Human Societies, c. 600 B.C.E. to c. 600 C.E.

Period 2 of the AP® World History framework examines a time when several substantial and influential empires developed in multiple regions of the world. In this period, which many historians refer to as the "Classical Age," major empires developed in the Middle East (Southwest Asia), South Asia, East Asia, the Mediterranean region, and the Americas (Mesoamerica, Andean South America, and North America). The rulers of each of these empires had to develop sophisticated bureaucracies to assist in the organization, integration, and administration of vast territories. Many of these empires encompassed a diverse array of people with different cultures, religions, languages, traditions, etc. In studying the empires featured in this section of the concept outline, you will need to take note of how rulers not only established and expanded their empires, but also how they maintained control, supported growing economic activity, secured essential resources, supported the arts, organized labor for agricultural and artisanal production, and engaged with neighboring empires and nomadic peoples.

Additionally, the period 600 B.C.E. to 600 C.E. saw the continuation of religious beliefs and practices from before 600 B.C.E. as well as the development of new religions. Many of the modern world's major religions trace their origins and early expansion to this period, including Buddhism, Hinduism, and Christianity. Other significant belief systems that developed in this period include Daoism, Confucianism, and Greco-Roman philosophy. Regardless of the belief system, religion, or philosophy of the rulers of Classical societies, a pattern of these beliefs shaping political and social structures clearly emerged.

Furthermore, a major transregional commercial network developed that facilitated the exchange of luxury goods, as well as biological transfers, across Eurasia. The Silk Road network stretched from China to the Middle East, where Mediterranean and Indian Ocean sea-lanes facilitated the movement of goods, people, culture, technology, plants, animals, and germs to Europe and Africa. A major connection developed particularly between the Han Empire in China and the Roman Empire of the Mediterranean basin. As with later periods, extensive commercial activity fostered the diffusion of religion, artistic styles, and technical knowledge. Another common side effect of long-distance trade was the transfer of diseases.

The following charts outline the learning objectives and topics from the content outline that fit into this period.

Content Review Questions can be found at the end of each chapter. **AP® format questions** for Period 2 can be found on page 173. **Document-Based Questions** can be found in the diagnostic test and practice tests.

THEMATIC LEARNING OBJECTIVES FOR PERIOD 2

INTERACTION BETWEEN HUMANS AND THE ENVIRONMENT

Learning Objectives—Students are able to . . .	Relevant Topics in the Concept Outline
ENV-1 Explain how different types of societies have adapted to and affected their environments.	2.1. II—Architecture 2.1. IV—Daoism 2.2. II—Shamanism 2.2. IV—Walls and roads 2.3. I—Mobilization of resources 2.3. II—Emerging trade routes shaped by climate and geography 2.3. III—Long-distance trade and communication
ENV-2 Explain how environmental factors, disease, and technology affected patterns of human migration and settlement over time.	2.2. I—Expansion of empire 2.2. II—Walls and roads 2.2. IV—Mobilization of resources; expansion of empire 2.3. I—Climate and geography shape emerging trade routes 2.3. II—Long-distance trade and communication 2.3. III—Farming and irrigation
ENV-3 Evaluate the extent to which migration, population, and urbanization affected the environment over time.	2.2. II—Imperial government 2.2. IV—Environmental change 2.3. I—Establishment of interregional land and water routes 2.3. III—Exchange of disease pathogens; urban and imperial decline
ENV-4 Evaluate the extent to which the development of diverse technologies, industrialization, transportation methods, and exchange and communication networks have affected the environment over time.	2.2. II—Imperial government 2.2. IV—Environmental change 2.3. III—Urban and imperial decline

DEVELOPMENT AND INTERACTION OF CULTURES

Learning Objectives—Students are able to . . .	Relevant Topics in the Concept Outline
CUL-1 Explain how religions, belief systems, philosophies, and ideologies originated, developed, and spread as a result of expanding communication and exchange networks.	2.1. I—Early codification of religious beliefs; the development of monotheistic Judaism 2.1. II, III—Assertion of universal truths; religious practice and gender roles; Buddhism, Confucianism, Daoism, Christianity 2.3. III—Cultures changed when spread; Hinduism, Christianity, Buddhism
CUL-2 Explain how religions, belief systems, philosophies, and ideologies affected political, economic, and social developments over time.	2.1.I—Early codification of religious beliefs; caste-, 2.1.II —Vedic-, Confucian Daoist , Christian-, Greco-Roman-influenced institutions 2.1.III— Buddhism, Christianity, Confucianism
CUL-3 Explain how cross-cultural interactions resulted in the diffusion of culture, technologies, and scientific knowledge.	2.3. II—New technology facilitated long-distance trade 2.3. III—Technologies and other ideas spread along trade routes

CUL-4 Explain how the arts are shaped by and reflect innovation, adaptation, and creativity of specific societies over time.	2.1. II—Art and architecture reflected religious beliefs; art and religious systems 2.2. III—Imperial cities and public performance
CUL-5 Explain how expanding exchange networks shaped the emergence of various forms of transregional culture, including music, literature, and visual art.	2.1. I—Art and architecture reflected religious beliefs and religious systems

STATE BUILDING, EXPANSION, AND CONFLICT

Learning Objectives—Students are able to . . .	Relevant Topics in the Concept Outline
SB-1 Explain how different forms of governance have been constructed and maintained over time.	2.2. II—Imperial governments 2.2. III—Labor organization and food production
SB-2 Explain how and why different functions and institutions of governance have changed over time.	2.1. II—Role of religion in the state 2.2. I–IV—First major empires
SB-3 Explain how and why economic, social, cultural, and geographical factors have influenced the processes of state building, expansion, and dissolution.	2.1. II—Belief systems and empire 2.2. I—City-states 2.2. II—Techniques of administration 2.2. III—Urbanization, labor organization, gender roles; growing commercial and administrative centers 2.2. IV—Imperial decline and collapse 2.3. III—Exchange of disease pathogens
SB-4 Explain how and why internal and external political factors have influenced the process of state building, expansion, and dissolution.	2.1. I—Conquest of Jewish states 2.2. II—Roads and currencies 2.2. III—Rise of cities as centers of trade 2.2. IV—Mobilization of resources
SB-5 Explain how societies with states and state-less societies interacted over time.	2.2. I—Consequences of expanding states and empires 2.2. II—Administrative techniques, diplomacy, military, roads 2.2. III—Cities as administrative centers 2.2. IV—Xiongnu, Huns
SB-6 Explain the political and economic interactions between states and non-state actors over time.	2.2. I—Consequences of expanding states and empires 2.2. II—Administrative techniques, diplomacy, military, roads 2.2. III—Cities as administrative centers 2.3. I, II—Emergence of interregional networks

CREATION, EXPANSION, AND INTERACTION OF ECONOMIC SYSTEMS

Learning Objectives—Students are able to . . .	Relevant Topics in the Concept Outline
ECON-1 Explain how technology shaped economic production and globalization over time.	2.3. II—New and maritime technologies
ECON-2 Explain the causes and effects of economic strategies of different types of communities, states, and empires.	2.2. II—Roads, currency 2.2. III—Administrative cities, social hierarchies 2.3. III—Trade route exchanges
ECON-3 Explain how different modes and locations of production and commerce have developed and changed over time.	2.2. II—Roads, currency 2.2. III—Administrative cities, social hierarchies
ECON-4 Explain how and why labor systems have developed and changed over time.	2.2. III—Patriarchy, imperial economies; slavery, corvée labor
ECON-5 Explain how economic systems and the development of ideologies, values, and institutions have influenced each other.	2.1. II—Buddhism, Christianity spread through merchants 2.3. III—Religions spread along trade routes
ECON-6 Explain how local, regional, and global economic systems and exchange networks have influenced and impacted each other over time.	2.3. III—Development of trade routes
ECON-7 Evaluate how and to what extent networks of exchange have expanded, contracted, or changed over time.	2.3. I,—Mobilization of resources 2.3. II—Technological innovations 2.3. III—Development of trade routes, new trade networks in Afro-Eurasia

DEVELOPMENT AND TRANSFORMATION OF SOCIAL STRUCTURES

Learning Objectives—Students are able to . . .	Relevant Topics in the Concept Outline
SOC-1 Explain how distinctions based on kinship, ethnicity, class, gender, and race influenced the development and transformations of social hierarchies.	2.1. I—Confucian and Christian ideologies 2.1. II—Belief systems and gender roles 2.1. III—Patriarchy and gender in imperial society, labor regimes 2.2. III—Legitimizing imperial rule; Islam and conquest
SOC-2 Evaluate the extent to which different ideologies, philosophies, and religions affected social hierarchies.	2.1. I—Caste 2.1. II—Confucian and Christian ideologies 2.2. III—Imperial social structures
SOC-3 Evaluate the extent to which legal systems, colonialism, nationalism, and independence movements have sustained or challenged class, gender, and racial hierarchies over time.	2.1. II—Confucian and Christian ideologies 2.2. III, IV—Imperial social structures
SOC-4 Explain how the development of specialized labor systems interacted with the development of social hierarchies.	2.2. III—Labor regimes
SOC-5 Explain how social categories, roles, and practices have been maintained or challenged over time.	2.1. I—Caste, Judaism 2.1. II—Greco-Roman philosophy; Confucianism, Christianity, Buddhism 2.1. III—Monasticism 2.3. III, IV—Imperial societies

KEY CONCEPTS FOR PERIOD 2

2.1. The Development and Codification of Religious and Cultural Traditions

2.2. The Development of States and Empires

2.3. Emergence of Interregional Networks of Communication and Exchange

6

AFRICA: C. 600 B.C.E. TO C. 600 C.E.

A major focus of the second unit of the AP® World History course is the development and characteristics of civilizations and empires. In this period, many parts of northern Africa were incorporated into various major empires discussed in the chapters about Europe and the Middle East for this unit. Although there were civilizations and societies that practiced agriculture in sub-Saharan Africa during this period, a major empire did not develop there between 600 B.C.E. and 600 C.E. As a result of these curriculum choices and historical facts, this chapter is shorter than most of the other chapters. That said, key aspects of the early history of Africa outlined in the AP® World History course description are included.

KEY CONCEPTS

- Sub-Saharan Africa was an isolated region with many separate societies, each with its own political and social characteristics, until the migration of the Bantu people provided cultural unity.

KEY TERMS

- Bantu
- trans-Saharan trade

Sub-Saharan Africa and the trans-Saharan trade network are discussed in *The Earth and Its Peoples*, Chapter 8 of the 6th edition and Chapter 9 of the 7th edition.

AP® is a trademark registered by the College Board, which is not affiliated with, and does not endorse, this product.

SUB-SAHARAN AFRICA

Prior to the development of **trans-Saharan trade** and the rise of the Indian Ocean trade network, sub-Saharan Africa was an isolated region. Because of the scarcity of water, low population density, and the massive size of the Sahara Desert, sub-Saharan Africa was a complex mix of cultures having their own languages and political and social characteristics. Nonetheless, there were some common characteristics: all were monarchies with a clear social structure that grouped people according to age, kinship, gender, and occupation.

Though there had been some trade, exchange did not expand significantly until the domesticated camel was introduced in the first millennium B.C.E. Salt from the southern region of the desert was traded for palm oil and forest products from the forest zone near the equator. When the Roman Empire dominated North Africa, products from that region were incorporated into the Mediterranean until Rome's decline in the third century C.E.

AP® Tip

When looking at a long period of time, you should be able to identify significant developments and explain how they initiated periods in regional or world history. For example, the development of settled agricultural communities, the use of bronze and iron, and the introduction of the domesticated camel to the Sahara Desert represent events that mark the beginning of new eras in history.

The **Bantu** people provided unity in sub-Saharan Africa in the first millennium C.E. when they slowly migrated from the equatorial region to southern Africa. As they migrated, they spread the Bantu family of languages—over three hundred languages of southern Africa belong to the Bantu family, the origins of which can be traced to the Niger–Congo region. The Bantu also spread the use of iron. Iron tools improved farming techniques and agricultural efficiency, and the greater food supply sparked economic development and population growth. The changes instigated by the Bantu migration increased the vitality of sub-Saharan Africa, which played a key role in the Indian Ocean's large and prosperous trade network.

Content Review Questions

The windswept Sahara, a desert stretching from the Red Sea to the Atlantic Ocean and broken only by the Nile River, isolates sub-Saharan Africa from the Mediterranean world. The current dryness of the Sahara dates only to about 2500 BCE. The period of drying out that preceded that date lasted twenty-five centuries and encompassed several cultural changes. To begin with, travel between a slowly shrinking number of grassy areas was comparatively easy. However, by 300 BCE, scarcity of water was restricting travel to a few difficult routes initially known only to desert nomads. Trade over trans-Saharan caravan routes, at first only a trickle, eventually expanded into a significant stream.

Bulliet et al., *The Earth and Its Peoples*, 7th edition., Boston: Cengage Learning, 2019, p. 234.

1. Which event preceded and was most responsible in allowing for the expansion of trade networks as described in the aforementioned passage?
    (A) The creation of postal-stations at Saharan oases to allow information to travel quickly
    (B) The domestication of the camel
    (C) The invention of the saddle
    (D) The construction of a Royal Road connecting North Africa to sub-Saharan Africa

2. Which event can best be compared to the historical process alluded to at the end of the passage?
    (A) The collapse of the civilizations at Harappa and Mohenjo-Daro
    (B) The discovery of the monsoon winds
    (C) The adoption of the Arabic alphabet on the Swahili Coast of East Africa
    (D) The trade connections between the Aztec and Inca in the Americas

3. What was the most likely cause of cultural similarities in sub-Saharan Africa before 600 C.E.?
    (A) The Bantu Migrations
    (B) Similar environmental conditions across sub-Saharan Africa
    (C) Trans-Saharan Trade
    (D) Colonization by the Phoenicians

Many historians believe that the secret of smelting iron, which requires very high temperatures, was discovered only once, by the Hittites of Anatolia (Modern Turkey) around 1500 B.C.E. If that is the case, it is hard to explain how iron smelting reached sub-Saharan Africa. The earliest evidence of ironworking from the kingdom of Meroe, situated on the upper Nile and in cultural contact with Egypt, is no earlier than the evidence from West Africa (northern Nigeria). Even less plausible than the Nile Valley as a route of technological diffusion is the idea of a spread southward from Phoenician settlements in North Africa, since archeological evidence has failed to substantiate the vague Greek and Latin accounts of Phoenician excursions to the south.

From Bulliet et al., *The Earth and Its Peoples*, 3rd ed., p. 187

4. What evidence does the author of the aforementioned passage give to refute the claim that sub-Saharan Africa learned ironworking from the Hittites?
    (A) The author points out a large chronological gap between the existence of the Hittites and the earliest evidence of ironworking in sub-Saharan Africa.
    (B) The author suggests that Meroe, not the Hittites, spread ironworking to sub-Saharan Africa.
    (C) The author suggests sub-Saharan Africa did not participate in ironworking.
    (D) The author fails to provide evidence for how iron technology spread from Turkey to sub-Saharan Africa.

5. What evidence does the author of the aforementioned passage give to refute the idea that sub-Saharan Africa learned ironworking from the Phoenicians?
    (A) There is little archeological evidence to prove that the Phoenicians were skilled ironworkers.
    (B) Archeological evidence that shows a connection between the Phoenicians and sub-Saharan Africa does not exist.
    (C) Archeological evidence suggests sub-Saharan Africa learned ironworking from Meroe before coming into contact with the Phoenicians.
    (D) Archeological evidence instead suggests that the Greeks and Romans spread ironworking to sub-Saharan Africa.

6. Based on the aforementioned passage, what alternative might this historian be suggesting to explain the existence of ironworking in sub-Saharan Africa?
    (A) The historian is likely suggesting both the Hittites and Phoenicians were equally responsible for bringing ironworking to sub-Saharan Africa.
    (B) The historian is likely suggesting that, since iron is scarce in sub-Saharan Africa, people saw no need to learn how to work with it.
    (C) The historian is likely suggesting that iron developed independently in sub-Saharan Africa rather than originating from an outside source.
    (D) The historian is likely suggesting that sub-Saharan Africa failed to develop the necessary knowledge to work with iron.

Answers

1. ANSWER: B. While horses were initially used in trans-Saharan trade, camels proved to be far more suitable to the conditions of the desert. The domestication of the camel allowed for a huge increase in the volume of trade moving across the Sahara (*The Earth and Its Peoples*, 6th ed., p. 231/7th ed., p. 234; History Reasoning Skill—Causation; Learning Objectives ENV-1,2; Key Concept 2.3.II.A).

2. ANSWER: B. The end of the passage describes a period where trade expanded—gradually at first and then rapidly to achieve a high volume of exchange. The discovery of the patterns of the monsoon winds similarly expanded trade possibilities for Indian Ocean routes (*The Earth and Its Peoples*, 6th ed., p. 231/7th ed., p. 234; History Reasoning Skill—Comparison; Learning Objectives CUL-3 ENV-1,2; Key Concept 2.3.II.B).

3. ANSWER: A. The Bantu migrations likely spread ironworking and agricultural techniques, as well as created a common language family throughout sub-Saharan Africa. Trans-Saharan trade was extremely limited before 600 C.E. and would not have as much of an impact as the Bantu (*The Earth and Its Peoples*, 6th ed., pp. 231–236/7th ed., pp. 234–238; History Reasoning Skill—Causation; Learning Objectives CUL-3 ENV-2; Key Concept 2.3.II.A).

4. ANSWER: A. The passage states that the Hittites existed around 1500 B.C.E., while Meroe instead grew strong only in the fourth century B.C.E. (*The Earth and Its Peoples*, 6th ed., pp. 236–237/7th ed., pp. 239–240; History Disciplinary Practice—Argument Development; Learning Objectives SB-1; Key Concept 1.3.II).

5. ANSWER: B. The passage refutes its second suggestion, that the Phoenicians spread ironworking, by noting a lack of archeological evidence to support Greek and Roman accounts of a connection between the Phoenicians and sub-Saharan Africa (*The Earth and Its Peoples*, 6th ed., pp. 236–237/7th ed., pp. 239–240; History Disciplinary Practice—Argument Development; Learning Objectives CUL-3 ENV-1; Key Concept 2.3.II.B).

6. ANSWER: C. This passage is part of a piece of revisionist history. The author begins by refuting previous claims in order to set up their proposed alternative. After rebuking the idea that iron came from the two most likely outside sources, the most logical next step would be to argue that ironworking developed internally. Sub-Saharan Africa must have had ironworking since the techniques were spread throughout the region during the Bantu migrations (*The Earth and Its Peoples*, 6th ed., pp. 236–237/7th ed., pp. 239–240; History Disciplinary Practice—Argument Development; Learning Objectives ENV-1,2 CUL-3; Key Concept 2.3.II.B).

7

THE MIDDLE EAST:
C. 600 B.C.E. TO C. 600 C.E.

KEY CONCEPTS

- Empires in the Middle East sat at the crossroads of major trade routes, such as the Silk Road and sea routes through the Mediterranean Sea and Indian Ocean, along which both products and culture traveled.
- Judaism and Christianity originated in the Middle East and had an impact on political events and social structure.

KEY TERMS

- Christianity
- Hellenism/Hellenistic Age
- Judaism
- Persian Empire
- polytheism
- Zoroastrianism

The Persian Empire is covered in detail in *The Earth and Its Peoples*, 6th edition, Chapter 4, and 7th edition, Chapter 5. The Roman presence in the region and the rise of Christianity can be found in 6th edition, Chapter 5, and 7th edition, Chapter 6.

THE PERSIAN EMPIRE

The Neo-Assyrian Empire was followed by the rise of the **Persian Empire**. Bound by language and culture, various groups that made their homeland in modern-day Iran joined to form the largest empire the world had yet seen. One group, the Medes, took the lead in challenging the Assyrian Empire and precipitating its collapse. Beginning about 550 B.C.E., the Persians, led by Cyrus, put together an empire of staggering size, stretching from Greece to India and from the Caucasus Mountains to North Africa. To administer such an expansive territory, Darius I created a unique organizational structure. He, like Cyrus before him, divided the empire into twenty provinces, each controlled by a *satrap*, or governor. Typically related to the royal family, satraps oversaw their territory and, most importantly, collected taxes and tribute to send to the king. Though roads were well maintained and patrolled, information traveled slowly, so satraps farther from the capital enjoyed some autonomy. Darius is also remembered as a lawgiver, and building on the decentralized nature of the provincial system, he allowed people within the empire to live according to their own traditions and rules. Darius and his followers also practiced **Zoroastrianism**. A unique religion that may have influenced **Judaism**, and later Christianity and Islam, Zoroastrianism preached the belief in one supreme god, introduced the notions of Heaven and Hell, reward and punishment, and the Messiah—a savior sent by God.

After ongoing conflict with the Greeks in the fifth and fourth centuries B.C.E, the Persian Empire eventually succumbed to the armies of Alexander the Great in 330 B.C.E. The Greek Empire then controlled virtually the same territory as the Persians had and, after the death of Alexander, for the next three hundred years the region experienced the influence of Greek culture known as the **Hellenistic Age**.

The Hellenistic Age ended with the rise of the Roman Empire. Though centered more on the Mediterranean, Roman rule did extend through Anatolia, and by 6 C.E. had reached present-day Israel and Palestine. Occupying the eastern Mediterranean region, the Roman Empire sat at the end of the Silk Road, which brought goods from as far away as China.

The **polytheistic** and pagan nature of Roman religion did not blend well with the tenets of Judaism, and in this tense environment Jesus and **Christianity** emerged. That Judaism and Christianity emerged in the same geographic area and that Jesus was a Jew help explain many of the similarities between these two religions. Both are monotheistic; further, both believe in the same god. The Five Books of Moses that constitute the Hebrew Torah are the first five books of the Bible. The Ten Commandments apply to both religions. Christians, however, believe Jesus was the Messiah, and their Bible also contains the New Testament, which tells of the life and teachings of Jesus. After Jesus' crucifixion, Paul and other followers spread Christianity in spite of Roman opposition. In the face of hostility, many of the early converts were women, slaves, or the urban poor—groups oppressed by Roman rule.

The transition from settled communities to vast empires that took place in the Middle East also occurred in Africa, Asia, Europe, and the Americas. All can be easily compared—in many respects the process was much the same, no matter the region. As these civilizations and empires emerged, they were bound together by the trade and interaction that traversed the Middle East.

Content Review Questions

> In 312 Constantine won a key battle at the Milvian Bridge near Rome. He later claimed that he had seen a cross—the sign of the Christian God—superimposed on the sun before the battle. Believing that the Christian God had helped him achieve the victory, in the following year Constantine issued the Edict of Milan, ending the persecution of Christianity and guaranteeing freedom of worship to Christians and all others. Throughout his reign he supported the Christian church, although he tolerated other beliefs as well.
>
> *The Earth and Its Peoples*, 7th edition, p. 157.

1. Which of the following was a result of the religious changes discussed in the passage?
   (A) High-ranking members in the Christian social structure gained and maintained political power as the Roman Empire fell.
   (B) A strong reaction against Christianity occurred when Rome fell because people associated it with the failing state.
   (C) While the Eastern Roman Empire readily adopted Christianity, it didn't take hold in the west for several more centuries.
   (D) Leaders of the Christian church gained enough political power that they were able to overthrow the Emperor and create a theocracy.

2. Which of the following leaders had a religious policy that can best be compared to that of Constantine as described in the passage?
   (A) Octavian Augustus
   (B) Ashoka
   (C) Shi Huangdi
   (D) Alexander the Great

3. Which of the following was NOT a common characteristic of Christianity, Judaism, and Zoroastrianism?
   (A) The existence of a network of believers dispersed over trade routes in multiple different regions
   (B) The belief in a single, all-powerful god
   (C) The existence of a state whose leaders expressed preference for the religion during the period from 600 B.C.E. to 600 C.E.
   (D) The belief in dual forces of good and evil

"I am the Lord, who made all things,
who stretched out the heavens alone. . .
who says of Jerusalem, 'She shall be inhabited.'
and of the cities of Judah, "They shall be built,
and I will raise up their ruins,'. . .
who says of Cyrus, 'He is my shepherd.
and he shall fulfill all my purpose';
saying of Jerusalem, 'She shall be built,'
and of the temple, 'Your foundation shall be laid.' "
Thus says the Lord to his anointed, to Cyrus,
whose right hand I have grasped,
to subdue nations before him
and ungird the loins of kings,
to open doors before him
that gates may not be closed:

Excerpt from The Book of Isaiah

The Human Record: *Sources of Global History*, 8th edition, volume 1, p. 85.

4. What led to the "ruins" referenced in the passage?
    (A) The Assyrian and Babylonian Empires conquered the Jewish states
    (B) War between the Kingdom of Israel and the Kingdom of Judah
    (C) A Jewish diaspora created by the expansion of the Persian Empire
    (D) A series of holy wars between the Jewish community and the emerging Christian community

5. Which trend explains the historical context behind the Jewish perspective on Cyrus, as mentioned in the passage?
    (A) Some imperial governments imposed cultural uniformity to instill a sense of belonging in their subjects.
    (B) Some imperial governments chose religious toleration allowing them to diminish resistance and rebellion.
    (C) Some imperial governments adopted the religions of neighboring regions as they expanded.
    (D) Some imperial governments took little to no interest in religion, which provided religious freedom to the people.

6. How did the Roman state's initial behavior toward Christianity differ from the Persian state's behavior toward Judaism as stated in the passage?
    (A) Rome was openly hostile toward Christianity, viewing it as a threat to Roman authority.
    (B) Rome adopted Christianity, seeing it as a way to unify the Roman people.
    (C) Rome added the Christian God to the Roman pantheon of gods, giving religious freedom to the Roman people.
    (D) Rome promoted Christianity as a religion acceptable for the barbarians on its borders, but allowed only religions connected to Greek traditions to be practiced by Roman citizens.

Answers

1. ANSWER: A. As the Roman Empire fell, the Christian church took on many of the responsibilities of the Empire. Thus priests and bishops took on the positions of landlords and magistrates, settling local disputes. The religious hierarchy held elite social status, similar to Roman patricians during the Empire (*The Earth and Its Peoples*, 6th ed., p. 151/7th ed., p. 157; History Reasoning Skill—Causation; Learning Objectives CUL-1-2; Key Concept 2.1.II.D).

2. ANSWER: D. The passage mentions that while Constantine personally adopted Christianity, he created a spirit of tolerance in the Empire by legalizing Christianity. Christianity did not become the official religion of the Roman Empire until the rule of Theodosius at the end of the fourth century (*The Earth and Its Peoples*, 6th ed., pp. 151, 161/7th ed., pp. 157, 167; History Reasoning Skill—Comparison; Learning Objectives CUL-2; Key Concept 2.1.II.C,D).

3. ANSWER: A. A network of believers dispersed over trade routes refers only to the Jewish religion during the classical era. Zoroastrianism didn't really spread outside of Persia, and only a small number of Christians ventured east along trade routes. Those who did often did not stay connected to Christian communities back in Europe (*The Earth and Its Peoples*, 6th ed., pp. 58–59/7th ed., p. 68; History Reasoning Skill—Comparison; Learning Objectives CUL-1,2; Key Concept 2.1.I.A).

4. ANSWER: A. The passage is referring to the rebuilding of the temple of Jerusalem with the consent of Cyrus as a result of the destruction of the previous Temple of Solomon when the Jewish States were conquered by the Assyrians, then the Babylonians in the sixth century B.C.E (*The Earth and Its Peoples*, 6th ed., pp. 48–50/7th ed., pp. 58–59; History Disciplinary Practice—; Learning Objective; Key Concept).

5. ANSWER: B. The passage takes a positive outlook on Cyrus, praising him as the "anointed." This outlook was likely inspired by the religious tolerance the Persians showed toward the Jewish population—they ended the persecution that had existed under the Babylonians and allowed the Jewish people to rebuild their temple in Jerusalem (*The Earth and Its Peoples*, 6th ed., pp. 48–50/7th ed., pp. 58–59; History Disciplinary Practice—Analyzing Historical Evidence; Learning Objectives CUL-1,2; Key Concept 2.1.I.A).

6. ANSWER: A. While the Persians showed religious tolerance toward the Jewish population, Rome persecuted the early Christians. Augustus was establishing the tradition of emperor worship and saw the Christians as a potentially subversive group within his new state. Persecution of the Christians continued with varying severity until the reign of Constantine (*The Earth and Its Peoples*, 6th ed., pp. 48–50/7th ed., pp. 58–59; History Reasoning Skill—Comparison; Learning Objectives CUL-1,2, SOC-3; Key Concept 2.1.I.A, 2.1.II.D).

8

ASIA:
C. 600 B.C.E. TO C. 600 C.E.

KEY CONCEPTS

- Both China and India experienced major political developments that gave rise to powerful empires.
- Buddhism, Confucianism, Hinduism, and Daoism are all important belief systems that impacted social and gender structures.
- Across Asia there emerged land and sea trade networks that fostered the transfer of goods and ideas.

KEY TERMS

- Buddhism
- Daoism
- Hinduism
- nirvana
- sati

Information on Asia from 600 B.C.E. to 600 C.E. can be found in *The Earth and Its Peoples*, 6th edition, Chapters 5 and 6, and 7th edition, Chapter 4, 6, and 9.

EAST ASIA

The Warring States Period inspired an important Chinese philosopher, Laozi (believed to have lived in the sixth century B.C.E.), who conceived Daoism as an alternative to the authoritarian nature of Legalism and the rigid hierarchy of Confucianism. **Daoism** promoted an end to conflict by teaching people to follow the path (Dao) and to accept the world instead of seeking to change it.

The Warring States Period ended in the third century B.C.E. when the Qin, led by Shi Huangdi, defeated their rivals and created China's first empire. The Qin was a totalitarian regime that promoted Legalism and enacted laws to prevent the rise of a rival power that might challenge Shi Huangdi's authority. For example, upon the death of an owner, land was divided among several heirs, and slavery was abolished to create a free labor force that would pay taxes and provide labor and military service. Shi Huangdi standardized coinage and laws and built thousands of miles of roads, canals, and walls to secure China. Upon his death, people rose up against the oppressive rule; when the rebellion ended, the Han dynasty was established.

The Han dynasty (206 B.C.E.–220 C.E.) was the classical period in Chinese history, and its cultural and political characteristics greatly influenced all subsequent dynasties. Like previous dynasties, the Han dynasty was centered on the river valleys in the eastern portion of the country. This fertile region produced crops that supported the population and was the basis of the tax system. To build the infrastructure, the government required able-bodied men to donate one month's worth of labor each year for the construction of palaces, temples, and roads and required two years of military service.

As the Han expanded, Chinese culture and social structure spread. The tenets of Confucianism established a clear hierarchy in which individuals saw themselves as having a particular role in the family and society. Fathers were the head of the family; a woman was to submit to her parents while she was young, her husband while married, and her son if widowed. As in the Zhou, the emperor was the "Son of Heaven" who was to rule in a paternal fashion so as to retain the Mandate of Heaven. Throughout the empire, peasants, soldiers, and administrators had their own particular role under the rule of the emperor, and they followed his word as law.

To administer the vast empire, Han emperors relied on local leaders to collect taxes, organize labor, and defend the empire. In order to get a prestigious government position, young men attended universities located around the country. Theoretically, this was a meritocracy that provided an opportunity for anyone to rise through the hierarchy, but in reality it was the sons of the wealthy and privileged classes who had the time and resources to study the Confucian classics and attend the universities. In part because of this, a large number of peasants turned to Daoism, which questioned the hierarchy, rules, and rituals of Confucianism that kept most peasants on the bottom rung of the social ladder.

The Han dynasty achieved many advances in technology that sustained the empire and eventually reached Europe. The crossbow and the use of cavalry helped the Han withstand challenges from nomadic people of Central Asia. Military forces, people, and goods traveled the extensive road system begun under the Qin and expanded by Han rulers. The watermill harnessed the power of running water to turn a grindstone, and the Han developed a horse collar that improved the use of animals in agriculture. These developments, along with paper, eventually made their way to Europe and the Middle East. But China's most valuable innovation was the production of silk. Silk was in high demand elsewhere in the world, and China maintained a monopoly on its production for centuries.

> ## AP® Tip
>
> When asked to make comparisons, you will often be given several items and asked to choose two to compare. Many times there will be natural pairs among the choices given. If you can identify those, you will have an easier time making direct comparisons. For example, if asked to compare how belief systems impacted society or government, Confucianism and Daoism have historical connections, as do Hinduism and Buddhism. While other combinations are certainly possible, these pairings allow for more substantial analysis.

Unable to maintain a large empire over vast territories, the Han dynasty ended in 220 C.E. The cost of maintaining a military presence on the frontier, coupled with corruption within the government, peasant rebellions, and the rise of regional warlords, returned China to a period of political, economic, and cultural fragmentation that lasted until the Sui unification of the late sixth century C.E.

SOUTH ASIA

The rigid social system, known as the caste system, that had developed in India following the arrival of the Aryans began to spark opposing movements in the eighth century B.C.E. The most serious threats to the Vedic religion and the power of the Brahmin class were Jainism and Buddhism. Jainism emphasized the value of all living creatures and promoted self-denial and nonviolence, but its influence and impact paled in comparison to **Buddhism**, which was founded by Siddhartha, a prince from the Kshatriya class, who gave up his wealthy lifestyle to pursue spiritual insight. Eventually he settled on the Middle Path of moderation and identified the Four Noble Truths about life: life is suffering; suffering comes from desire; suffering will end if desire ends; the way to end desire is to follow the Eightfold Path that outlines proper conduct. Followers of the Buddha sought **nirvana**, which was the ultimate reward of tranquility at the end of the cycle of reincarnation.

Buddhism became more popular than Jainism and had much greater influence in India and throughout Asia. After the death of the Buddha in 483 B.C.E., Buddhism spread throughout India and, via trade routes, to much of Asia. Without clear instructions left by the Buddha, the religion evolved as it spread. Those who began to worship Buddha as a god and produced images of him became known as Mahayana Buddhists. Mahayana Buddhists also revered bodhisattvas, who were enlightened men and women who forsook nirvana in order to help others live the proper life. Conversely, those bound to the original teachings that prohibited worship of a divine Buddha and depictions of him were Theravada Buddhists.

The popularity of Buddhism in India forced the Vedic religion to evolve into what is known as **Hinduism**. Though Brahmins retained their lofty position, they adopted the accessibility of Buddhism and allowed for more

---

individual and personal interaction with the gods. Hinduism emphasized one's personal relationship with one of the gods, all of whom manifest the same universal force. Adopting key aspects of Buddhism allowed Hinduism to sustain its popularity; in fact, it drove Buddhism from the land of its origin. Though it would have a resurgence under Ashoka during the Mauryan Empire, Buddhism's popularity in East and Southeast Asia would exceed its popularity in India.

The diversity, geography, and social structure of the subcontinent made political unification rare in its early history. Language and customs differed across India, as did the organization and economic nature of each region. A stronger deterrent to political unity was the complicated social hierarchy and its promotion of caste identification over loyalty to a centralized political power. In spite of these factors promoting decentralization, the Mauryan and Gupta Empires emerged and helped create a unified civilization in India.

In 324 B.C.E., the Mauryan Empire rose out of a landscape of competing kinship groups and independent states. Its reign would extend over the entire subcontinent save the southernmost tip. A quarter of agricultural production was paid to the king, who also controlled mines, issued coinage, and oversaw a large and powerful army. He also appointed relatives and allies in each district to tend to administrative affairs. The most famous Mauryan king was Ashoka, the founder's grandson. After extensive and brutal military campaigns to extend the borders of the empire, Ashoka converted to Buddhism and began preaching nonviolence and tolerance. He famously inscribed his moral codes on large pillars throughout the empire. The Mauryan Empire constructed roads and towns that increased their role in land and sea trade networks that connected East and Southeast Asia with the Middle East and Europe. This key role continued even after the Mauryan Empire, attacked by outsiders, collapsed in 184 B.C.E.

After some five hundred years of political rivalry within India, the Gupta Empire came to power in much the same way the Mauryan Empire had. Gupta leaders controlled both agriculture and mining and required that their subjects donate labor to construction projects. The Gupta Empire, however, was not as centralized as the Mauryan Empire. A strong army helped the Gupta retain control, but as distance from the center increased, so too did the autonomy of the local leaders. By sharing profits from trade with the local leaders, Gupta kings were able to provide those with greater autonomy with an incentive to remain part of the empire. In addition to maintaining an influential role in regional trade, Indians were interested in the arts and sciences; mathematicians invented the concept of zero and developed the "Arabic" numerals that are used in much of the world today.

The role of women in India changed as the economy of South Asia developed. Increased trade created an urban middle class that valued property and undermined women's rights to own or inherit it. Opportunities for influence outside of the home were limited, and women in India, like their counterparts in China under Confucianism, were expected to obey their fathers, husbands, and sons. In parts of India, a woman was expected to commit **sati**—throwing herself on her husband's funeral pyre—or else be shunned by the community. Buddhism and Jainism did provide women with some freedom from male domination in the Hindu empire. Additionally, upper-class women had access to education and enjoyed more freedom than the poor. The Gupta Empire collapsed in 550 C.E. when it was attacked by the Huns of Central Asia.

Southeast Asia

Southeast Asia includes Indochina, Malaysia, and the many islands extending out into the Pacific Ocean. Vast amounts of fertile land and a climate that enables multiple growing seasons promoted population growth and produced plants and animals that would eventually be exported to other regions—among them wet rice, soybeans, sugarcane, chickens, and pigs. Periodic disruptions to overland trade across Asia increased the role and power of Southeast Asia as sea trade expanded to meet demand. Trade routes also brought Hinduism and Buddhism to the area as Indian missionaries and East Asian pilgrims passed through on their way to and from India.

Content Review Questions

Source: *The Earth and Its Peoples*, 7th ed., p. 175.

1. What was the most likely cause of the cultural syncretism found in the image of the Buddha?
   (A) The creation of the Hellenistic Empire of Alexander the Great
   (B) The extensive trade networks that existed between India and Classical Greece
   (C) Pilgrimages made by Buddha's followers into Eastern Europe
   (D) Missionaries sent West by Mauryan Emperor Ashoka

2. What was the most significant difference between the religion depicted in the image and previous religious tradition in the same region?
   (A) The religion was heavily influenced by foreign ideas, while previous religious traditions were indigenous to the region.
   (B) The religion rejected a formal social class structure, while previous religious traditions embraced one.
   (C) The religion sanctified poverty, while previous religious traditions condoned wealth accumulation.
   (D) The religion is based off a singular holy text, while previous religious traditions have many texts contributing to the beliefs.

3. Which of the following conclusions could best be supported by using the image as evidence?
    (A) During his lifetime, the Buddha had an imposing physical stature and often towered above other men.
    (B) Although Buddhism declined in popularity in India, it still retained followers throughout the classical era.
    (C) Buddhism supported a centralized political structure with a divine king at the center.
    (D) Buddha inspired the idea of rational knowledge popular in Classical Greece.

4. Buddhism's incorporation of bodhisattvas and divine variations of Buddha illustrate which of the following trends about classical era religions?
    (A) They often started independently, in multiple regions, then blended together.
    (B) They often incorporated local beliefs and adapted as they spread.
    (C) The further they got from their origin, the more orthodox they became.
    (D) They were most popular immediately after the death of their founder and gradually lost followers over time.

A woman's duties are to cook the five grains, heat the wine, look after her parents-in-law, make clothes, and that is all! [She] has no ambition to manage affairs outside the house. . . . She must follow the "three submissions." When she is young, she must submit to her parents. After her marriage, she must submit to her husband. When she is widowed, she must submit to her son."

-Excerpt from the biography of the mother of Chinese philosopher Mencius (Mengzi)

Source: *The Earth and Its Peoples*, 7th ed., p. 162.

5. Which philosophy is reflected best by the ideas expressed in the passage?
    (A) Daoism
    (B) Confucianism
    (C) Legalism
    (D) Jainism

6. The ideas in the passage most likely came as a result of which of the following developments?
    (A) The centralization of the Chinese state
    (B) The implementation of Bronze tools and technology
    (C) The transition from nomadic and pastoral lifestyles to sedentary farming
    (D) The widespread adoption of Confucian ideas by the Chinese government

7. Which of the following developments in China was seen as the greatest challenge to the ideas expressed in the passage?
   (A) The Warring States Period, which saw the absence of a centralized Chinese state to control the position of women
   (B) The nomadic invasions of the Xiongnu when women were encouraged to take up arms to defend China
   (C) The Qin Dynasty's preference for Legalism, which held that both genders were equally disruptive without laws to guide and punish them
   (D) The development of Buddhist monasteries and convents after the fall of the Han Empire, which offered men and women an alternative to married domestic life

Answers

1. ANSWER: A. Alexander's Empire collapsed as he reached the Indian border, but the Hellenistic cultural ideas spread by his expanding army still influenced Classical India. It is likely because of Alexander's influence that Buddha is shown pictured in a toga in the image provided (*The Earth and Its Peoples*, 6th ed., pp. 169–171, 174–175/7th ed., pp. 173–175, 178–179; History Reasoning Skill—Causation; Learning Objectives CUL-1,2,5; Key Concept 2.1.II.A).

2. ANSWER: B. Buddha rejected the caste structure of Hinduism. According to Buddhism, all could achieve Enlightenment by following the Eightfold Path, regardless of what caste they were born into (*The Earth and Its Peoples*, 6th ed., pp. 169–171/7th ed., pp. 173–175; History Reasoning Skill—Comparison; Learning Objectives CUL-1,2,5; Key Concept 2.1.II.A).

3. ANSWER: B. Buddhism did lose followers in India, but the existence of the relief, from almost 800 years after the life of Buddha, proves that the religion was still practiced in the region (*The Earth and Its Peoples*, 6th ed., pp. 174–177/7th ed., pp. 178–180; History Reasoning Skill—Causation; Learning Objectives CUL-1,2,5; Key Concept 2.1.II.A).

4. ANSWER: B. Buddhism, Christianity, and many classical era religions incorporated new ideas as they spread. Buddhism incorporated bodhisattvas, possibly to correspond to the many gods of Hinduism. Christian saints similarly began to represent many of the causes for which people used to turn to pagan gods (*The Earth and Its Peoples*, 6th ed., p. 171/7th ed., p. 175; History Reasoning Skill—Contextualization; Learning Objectives CUL-1,2,5; Key Concept 2.1.II).

5. ANSWER: B. The passage expresses ideas of patriarchy and duty, which are essential to Confucianism (*The Earth and Its Peoples*, 6th ed., p. 156/7th ed., p. 162; History Disciplinary Practice—Analyzing Historical Evidence; Learning Objectives CUL-2, SOC-2; Key Concept 2.1.II.B).

6. ANSWER: C. Confucianism was codifying an already present tradition—patriarchy. Patriarchy likely became prominent in China during the transition to agriculture as women lost the role of principle food supplier (*The Earth and Its Peoples*, 6th ed., p. 13/7th ed., p. 21; History Reasoning Skill—Causation; Learning Objectives CUL-2; Key Concept 2.1.II.B).

7. ANSWER: D. Buddhism became popular in China as the Han Dynasty collapsed—partly because it was popular with the nomads who were invading China and partly because it offered a sense of hope during chaotic times. Buddhism didn't have the strong patriarchal tones found in Confucianism, and instead offered both men and women an alternative to married life. These alternatives were attacked and banned when China transitioned back to Confucianism under the later Tang Dynasty (*The Earth and Its Peoples*, 6th ed., p. 156/7th ed., p. 164; History Disciplinary Practice—Argument Development; Learning Objectives CUL-2; Key Concept 2.1.II.B).

9

EUROPE:
C. 600 B.C.E. TO C. 600 C.E.

KEY CONCEPTS

- The foundation of the Western world was established by the classical empires of Greece and Rome.
- The uneven collapse of the Roman Empire set Europe on two divergent paths for the following centuries.
- Christianity arose under Roman rule, and although initially reviled, it eventually flourished, in large part as a result of the policies of Emperor Constantine.

KEY TERMS

- Byzantine Empire
- Celtic Europe
- Hellenistic Age
- Pax Romana
- Roman Republic
- Romanization
- third-century crisis

Information on Europe 600 B.C.E. to 600 C.E. can be found in *The Earth and Its Peoples*, 6th edition, Chapters 4 and 5, and 7th edition, Chapters 5 and 6.

GREEK CITY-STATES AND EMPIRE

During the Archaic period, Greek culture developed significantly, laying the foundation for many traditions that would establish themselves in the Classical era. As colonization spread Greek peoples and culture around the Mediterranean, p there was a growing importance placed on the individual in Greek culture. The celebration of the individual became known as humanism, which remains a guiding principle in the Western world. In addition to rethinking the role and view of the individual, early Greeks challenged the traditional approach to knowledge. Pre-Socratic philosophers sought rational explanations for the origins and workings of the world. Later, Socrates (470–399 B.C.E.), his disciple Plato, and Plato's student Aristotle would lay the foundation of Western philosophy by asking probing questions about such topics as truth, knowledge, and ethics.

By the end of the Archaic period in 480 B.C.E., Athens and Sparta were the two dominant Greek city-states. Sparta's strength came from its army of highly trained and well-armed professional soldiers. The individual existed to support the state; in an effort to maintain internal peace, coinage and trade were banned for their potential to promote inequality. The Spartans formed cautious alliances with their neighbors and tried to remain as isolated as possible. Athens, on the other hand, had a clear social structure that made connections between wealth and power. Those in the top three classes could hold office; those with little or no property, who constituted the fourth class, could participate in meetings but not hold office. Although not the direct democracy that is often romantically associated with Athens, it broke the mold of rule by one or few that existed throughout much of the world at this time. In 450 B.C.E., Pericles altered the system so as to allow even those with little land to hold office and participate in government.

The rival city-states of Athens and Sparta each played a significant role in the next phase of Greek history, the fight against the Persian Empire in the fifth and fourth centuries B.C.E. Initially, Persian control of Greek city-states in western Anatolia was met with a revolt that the Persians eventually put down. These revolts inspired the Persian leader Darius to punish those city-states that supported the revolt, a group that included Athens. Many Greek city-states suffered harsh defeats in what is known as the Persian Wars, though Athens was able to fend off the Persians' initial attempts. Darius' son Xerxes would stage a larger invasion of Greece in 480 B.C.E. and succeed in attacking Athens. To halt this invasion, southern Greek communities aligned under Spartan rule, forming the Delian League, and though the first efforts failed, by the middle of the fifth century B.C.E., the Persians were expelled from Greek lands. The classical era of Greek history, which would last until 323 B.C.E., had begun.

During the classical age, Athens used its strong navy and economic strength to subjugate members of the Delian League. Neighboring city-states were required to make yearly payments to Athens, which funded further military spending and accomplishments in theater, philosophy, art, and science. Politically, classical Greece was a democracy limited to the 10–15 percent of the population that were free adult males. Foreign-born slaves made up 30 percent of the population; the typical Athenian family owned one or more. Most slaves served in a domestic capacity and developed relationships with their owners by working in close proximity to them. In spite of such relations, the Greeks viewed slaves as inferior beings who, unable to reason, were better off under Greek rule. Women's roles in the classical era varied depending on where they lived. In Sparta, they had the important role of raising strong children, and their presence and voices were welcomed in public. In Athens, however, women lacked access to education, had limited legal protection, and were confined to their homes, where they were expected to produce children. Women's treatment in Athens resembled that of slaves and was rationalized by males, who asserted that women were by nature promiscuous and that promiscuity could destabilize society.

In 431 B.C.E. the Peloponnesian War began between city-states aligned with Athens and those aligned with Sparta. After nearly thirty years, the Spartans, with financial help from Persia for their navy, defeated the Athenians and temporarily assumed a leadership role in Greece. Soon Greek city-states got tired of strict Spartan rule, and unrest continued. While southern Greece endured the Peloponnesian War and Spartan rule, the kingdom of Macedonia in northern Greece was growing into a military power. Philip II (359–336 B.C.E.) had improved his military's technology and techniques with longer spears, catapults, and the use of cavalry to support infantry. These changes proved effective in defeating southern Greek states and led to an all-Greek attack on the Persian Empire. Though Philip II did not live to see the outcome of the campaign against the Persians, his son Alexander (356–323 B.C.E.) avenged Persia's attacks on Greece by defeating the forces of King Darius III.

Alexander the Great's ambitious efforts resulted in Greek control of a territory similar in size and shape to the Persian Empire. To administer this vast empire, Alexander initially placed loyal Macedonian and Greek aides in charge of city-states. Later, he left Persian officials in place, allowed for Persian soldiers in his military, and adopted aspects of Persian culture. When Alexander died suddenly at the age of thirty-two, his empire fell into a period of chaos. Without a plan for succession, the empire was broken into three kingdoms ruled by Macedonians.

This next period in Greek history is known as the **Hellenistic Age** (323–30 B.C.E.). In this era, land from northern Egypt to nearly the Indus Valley was influenced by Greek culture. Long-distance trade and the growth of libraries, universities, literature, and art made Greek culture available; local populations accepted Greek culture because doing so brought political and economic advantages. The three Hellenistic kingdoms had the same difficulties defending a long frontier experienced by the Persians. In the face of this challenge, the Persian system of local control was maintained along with Alexander's policy of establishing city-states as administrative centers. The classical era in Greek history ushered in new intellectual and political approaches that would stand the test of time and, with the creation of a Hellenistic empire, would spread through a vast territory.

AP® Tip

Having a sense of chronology (as opposed to memorizing specific dates) can be very helpful in answering multiple-choice and free-response questions on the AP® exam. For example, in a continuity and change over time essay, the dates should give you an early clue about how you will start and end your essay. They often correspond to the beginning and/or end of a period in world or regional history. Knowing the order of events can help you see this.

ROME: REPUBLIC TO EMPIRE

While the Greeks established a foundation for the modern Western world, their legacy was cemented by their European successors, the Romans. Located in central Italy, Rome had many geographic advantages that the Greeks lacked. The fertile soil, long growing season, vast forests, and iron deposits on the Italian peninsula would be vital to their expansion through Europe and North Africa. The **Roman Republic** (507–31 B.C.E.) was largely a society of small, independent farms. In time some individuals acquired large portions of land, and as a group these wealthy men constituted the Senate, which dominated Roman politics. Although all male citizens were allowed to attend Senate meetings, votes of the wealthy were weighted more than those of the poor, and society was governed by the elite. Such inequality caused tensions in the Roman Republic, and periodic strikes by the working class were held in hopes of gaining more political rights.

In the fifth century B.C.E. Rome assumed a leadership position among central Italian cities that had formed a group for defense. By the third century B.C.E., Roman expansion accelerated as its highly trained and disciplined armies conquered new land in a never-ending effort to provide a buffer zone against enemies on the frontier. As Rome expanded its control, it granted citizenship to conquered peoples and required men from these lands to join the army. When the Romans finally defeated the Carthaginians in 202 B.C.E., they were the supreme power in the western Mediterranean region.

The vast Roman Republic was governed by senators, who served one-year posts as governors of the Roman provinces. Chosen for their connections rather than their ability, many governors were corrupt and ineffective. Local people cooperated with Roman rule because, as in the Hellenistic kingdoms, political and economic advantages came with adopting the customs of the ruling class. The adoption of the Roman lifestyle (**Romanization**) was a significant legacy of Roman expansion, although the eastern Mediterranean region continued to be dominated by the Greek language and culture. The expansion of the Roman Republic put strains on the system that would eventually lead to its failure. Italian peasant farmers, who constituted the backbone of the military, spent long periods away from their land. In their absence, land was purchased or obtained by wealthy individuals and consolidated into large tracts of land that were often used for the more profitable purpose of grazing than growing grain. These changes forced parts of Italy to rely on imported grain and left a now landless population to compete against the cheap slave labor provided by war prisoners. The Republic had obligated landowning men to serve in the military; as the number of landowning men decreased, so too did the population of its soldiers. The poor, landless population had difficulty finding work on farms and in cities. Eventually they turned their allegiance from the Republic to ambitious military leaders who would battle one another for power.

By the dawn of the Common Era, Roman rule was transformed from a republic to an empire built on an agricultural foundation and controlled through a network of cities. Octavian Caesar emerged in 31 B.C.E. as a military dictator disguised in the trappings of a republican ruler. Adding Egypt, portions of the Middle East, and central Europe, Octavian became known by the title Augustus. He and his successors ruled with the approval of the Senate and ultimately became the source of laws and even viewed as gods after their death. In the cities, a large economic and physical gap existed between the rich and the poor. The wealth of the urban upper class came from a large and productive agricultural foundation or from manufacture and trade that prospered during the **Pax Romana** (Roman Peace). The poor in the cities inhabited crowded, low-lying slums; in rural areas they became tenant farmers as the source of slaves diminished when Roman expansion reached its limits.

Roman society was based on the family and the patron/client relationship. The oldest male headed the family and its slaves. The heads of wealthy families served as patrons for the dozens or hundreds of clients who worked and defended their land. In return for this service, clients received legal protection and financial aid from their patrons. In general, women in the Roman Republic could not own property or represent themselves in legal proceedings. That said, some upper-class women were able to influence their husbands or eldest sons and unmarried women could hold, inherit, and dispose of property. Religion was greatly influenced by the Romans' contact with the Greeks. Sacrifices were made to ensure protection of the gods, whose myths and identities were taken from the Greeks although given Roman names. When Christianity was born in Roman-controlled Palestine, early Christians were persecuted. In time, the Roman Empire's disenfranchised—the poor, women, slaves—were drawn to the teachings of Jesus.

Successful Roman control over a huge empire can be attributed in large part to technological innovations such as arches, aqueducts, roads, and concrete. But the empire endured a "**third-century crisis**" from 235 to 284 C.E. High turnover of rulers, economic problems, and the infiltration of the Germanic tribes in the central European frontier destabilized the empire. Trade declined to the point where a barter system replaced coinage, and the wealth of cities that served as administrative centers declined dramatically. Diocletian became emperor in 284 C.E. and, in an effort to stabilize the economy of the empire, fixed prices and forced workers in key industries to stay in their professions. Any stability that came about was offset by the resentment among the people at a government that became more intrusive and regimented.

Diocletian's successor, Constantine, is notable for his religious tolerance and his decision to move the capital of the Roman Empire east to Byzantium, which he renamed Constantinople. By the late third century C.E., Christian converts included educated and wealthy people, and the movement had a strong foothold in the Roman Empire. It would eventually become the religion of the empire. When Constantine had a vision of a cross prior to a military victory, he attributed his success to the Christian God and ended persecution of Christians, supported the church, and guaranteed freedom of religion for all others. Seeing the political and economic advantages of being Christian, more and more converted to the faith. The eastern portion of the Roman Empire, now centered in Constantinople, retained wealth better than the west during the third-century crisis and contained more educated people and Christians.

In 395 C.E. the Roman Empire officially split into an eastern and western portion. Rome was sacked in 410 C.E., and by 476 C.E. the western portion of the Roman Empire had disintegrated into a collection of kingdoms under Germanic rulers and entered the medieval era. No longer the political center of an empire, Rome nonetheless remained important because it was the home of the patriarch of Rome, the position that would eventually be called Pope.

Culturally, the medieval era saw a decline in literacy and the emergence of local dialects that would evolve into modern Romance languages such as Portuguese, Spanish, French, Italian, and Romanian. Meanwhile, to the east, the Byzantine Empire continued the legacy of the Greek and Roman Empires. Tensions arose between the east and west over doctrinal disputes and eventually led to a division in Christianity. Under the rule (527–565 C.E.) of Justinian, the **Byzantine Empire** recaptured parts of North Africa and Italy. More important, Justinian established a collection of laws that would become the basis of European legal systems in the coming centuries.

Content Review Questions

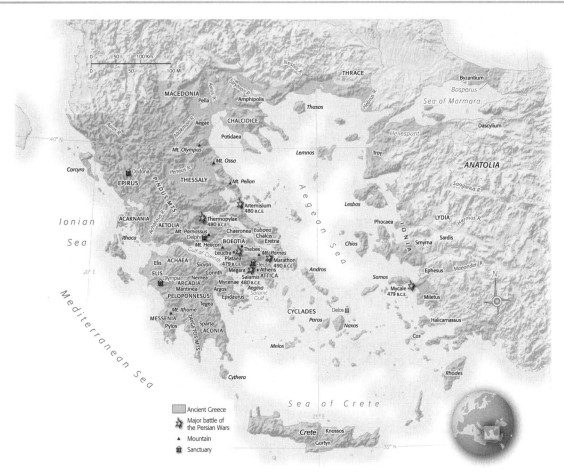

1. Based on the map and your knowledge of history, which of the following best explains the reason for the long-lasting influence of Greek Civilization?
   (A) The large extent of the Greek Empire
   (B) The diaspora of Greek colonies
   (C) The incorporation of Greek territory and many Greek ideas into the larger Roman Empire
   (D) The widespread trading empire of the Phoenicians

2. What additional source would be most useful for a historian trying to understand the interactions between the Greeks and Persians?
   (A) A treatise on Greek philosophy and rational knowledge
   (B) Records of imports and exports from the port of Athens
   (C) Literature from pre-classical Greek writers including the tales of Homer
   (D) A historical account written by the biographer of Alexander the Great during the expansion of his Empire

3. Within just over a century of the battles shown on the map, which empire expanded into the territory shown on the map?
   (A) The Roman Empire
   (B) The Persian Empire
   (C) The Hellenistic Empire of Alexander the Great
   (D) The Mauryan Empire

4. Which of the following methods was employed by Imperial Rome to maintain control over the frontiers of the Empire?
   (A) Conquered people were forced to convert to the Roman religion to create cultural homogeneity.
   (B) Urban centers in conquered areas retained the architecture and lifestyle of their indigenous populations allowing people to feel at home.
   (C) Rome pulled men from newly conquered areas to join the Roman military providing employment and unity.
   (D) Rome shuffled skilled craftsmen from conquered areas into state-run industries throughout the Empire allowing conquered peoples to feel respected in Roman society.

5. Based on the map and your knowledge of history, all of the following were important to the Roman Empire EXCEPT
   (A) road maintenance.
   (B) missionaries to spread Roman religion.
   (C) urban centers to promote economic exchange.
   (D) a developed bureaucracy to spread and maintain control from a centralized government.

6. All of the following played a significant role in the collapse of the Roman Empire EXCEPT
   (A) decline of trade with China as a result of the collapse of the Han Empire.
   (B) pressure from nomadic groups north and east of Rome.
   (C) bureaucratic corruption tied to difficulties with maintaining such a large empire.
   (D) a gap in social hierarchy as an increasing amount of wealth became concentrated in the hands of the elites.

Answers

1. ANSWER: C. The Roman Empire expanded into Greece and parts of Persia. The Romans believed they had a cultural connection with the Greeks and adopted many parts of Greek culture including the pantheon of gods and architectural styles. This helped preserve the culture of the relatively small Greek region and gave it a larger influence over later civilizations (*The Earth and Its Peoples*, 6th ed., pp. 113–116 /7th ed., p. 121; History Reasoning Skill—Causation; Learning Objectives ENV-5 SB-1,3; Key Concept 2.2.II A).

2. ANSWER: B. Although Greece and Persia fought, they were also trading partners. The map details battle sites, and an account from the port of Athens would explain the economic side of their relationship (*The Earth and Its Peoples*, 6th ed., pp. 115 and 128–133/7th ed., pp. 121, 134–135; History Disciplinary Practice—Argument Development; Learning Objectives SB-3; Key Concept 2.2.II.B).

3. ANSWER: C. Alexander's Empire included both the former Greek city-states and the Persian Empire. It is in part because Persia was weakened by the wars with Greece shown on the map that Alexander was able to conquer the Persian Empire. Alexander created his Empire between 336 and 323 B.C.E. (*The Earth and Its Peoples*, 6th ed., pp. 115 and 128–133/7th ed., pp. 121, 134–135; History Reasoning Skill—Causation; Learning Objectives SB-4; Key Concept 2.2.II.B).

4. ANSWER: C. Rome regularly used the men of conquered people, for example, the Gauls of Northern Europe, to supply their growing army. This pulled men from their home region where they might have had a chance to organize rebellion and gave them a position in the Roman state to feel more connected. In terms of religion, conquered people were allowed to keep their religious preferences, and some of their gods were incorporated into the Roman pantheon. Urban centers tended to resemble Rome with aqueducts, public fountains, theaters, and forums. Rome had a limited number of state-run industries (*The Earth and Its Peoples*, 6th ed., pp. 138–141/ 7th ed., pp. 149–153; History Reasoning Skill—Causation; Learning Objectives SB-2,3; Key Concept 2.2.II.B).

5. ANSWER: B. Rome had no interest in spreading the Roman religion, although it was often incorporated into the religions of conquered people. There was no sense of religious merit of helping to save others for converting them to the Roman religion. Road maintenance, however, was essential to the Empire to allow communication across its enormous territory, as was an established bureaucracy. Additionally, cities were needed for economic growth (*The Earth and Its Peoples*, 6th ed., pp. 138–141/7th ed., pp. 149–153; History Disciplinary Practice—Analyzing Historical Evidence; Learning Objectives ECON-2, SB-3; Key Concept 2.2.II.B).

6. ANSWER: A. Han China collapsed almost two hundred years before the Roman Empire. While Rome and China had exchanged luxury goods, this market was not the principle source of income for the Roman Empire. Other reasons, such as invasion, corruption, and a gap in wealth, were far more prominent in Rome's fall (*The Earth and Its Peoples*, 6th ed., pp. 158–159/7th ed., pp. 164–165; History Reasoning Skill—Causation; Learning Objectives SB-3,4; Key Concept 2.2.II.B).

10

THE AMERICAS: C. 600 B.C.E. TO C. 600 C.E.

A major focus of the second unit of the AP® World History course is the development and characteristics of civilizations and empires. The development of complex civilizations in the Americas occurred later than in the Middle East, Indus Valley, and China. The first empires of the Americas do not arise until around 600 C.E. As a result of these curriculum choices and historical facts, this chapter is shorter than most of the other chapters. That said, key aspects of the early history of the Americas outlined in the AP® World History course description are included.

KEY CONCEPTS

- The city of Teotihuacan emerged as a center for economic activity, as well as for the celebration of cultural rituals.
- The Maya civilization began to develop in Mesoamerica, with multiple cultural centers constructed throughout the Yucatan region of modern day Mexico.

KEY TERMS

- chinampas
- Maya
- Teotihuacan

Information on the Americas from 600 B.C.E. to 600 C.E. can be found in *The Earth and Its Peoples*, 6th edition, Chapter 7 and 7th edition Chapter 8.

AP® is a trademark registered by the College Board, which is not affiliated with, and does not endorse, this product.

CLASSIC-ERA CULTURE AND SOCIETY IN MESOAMERICA

Although never under one central rule, the peoples of Mesoamerica developed similar religious, social, and cultural practices. Mesoamericans also made strides in agriculture, astronomy, math, and political organization, building on the work of earlier civilizations like the Olmec. Population growth and the rise of long-distance trade led to the development of large urban centers with both religious and political significance. These cities had many architectural features, including pyramid structures, designed for elaborate religious ceremony. Thousand-year-old agricultural practices like terraced farming and irrigation continued to serve as the economic foundation for Mesoamerican society in the classic period; the distinctive feature of the classic period in Mesoamerican society was not agricultural advances but rather social changes. These changes created a new political elite that controlled larger numbers of laborers and soldiers, grew in power, and extended its political reach over larger areas of Mesoamerica. Two civilizations that exemplify the classic period are the people of Teotihuacan in Mexico and the Maya in the Yucatan peninsula.

TEOTIHUACAN

Located just north of modern-day Mexico City, the city of **Teotihuacan** reached its zenith in 600 C.E. The largest city in the Americas at the time, it had well over 100,000 inhabitants, perhaps as many as 200,000, and was one of the largest cities in the world as well. Teotihuacan was also a religious center that drew people from neighboring areas; priests were highly regarded and played a central role in society. The elite status of priests was common in other Mesoamerican societies as well. The people of Teotihuacan were polytheistic, and much of their religious architecture focused on pyramid-like structures dedicated to worshiping the sun, moon, and the god Quetzalcoatl, who was believed to be the source of agriculture and the arts. The people of Teotihuacan practiced human sacrifice, which they considered a sacred duty necessary for the maintenance of human society.

As the city grew, the governing elite developed the surrounding lands for agricultural production. In addition to irrigation and terraced farming on hillsides, the use of chinampas increased. **Chinampas**, man-made islands constructed out of materials found in the lake environment, allowed for agricultural production year-round, which provided a constant food supply for the growing population. A reliable food supply permitted specialization of labor in architecture as well as trade and art pottery, and obsidian tools were key goods in long-distance trade.

Other Mesoamerican societies had one central ruler. Historical evidence suggests that in Teotihuacan, an alliance of aristocratic families had political authority. Scholars also debate the role of Teotihuacan's military; archaeological evidence suggests that soldiers were used both to secure long-distance trade and to ensure that agricultural surpluses were used to the city's benefit. Why Teotihuacan was destroyed is not clear, but there is evidence that the final decades were violent and that disagreements among the elites as well as mishandling of resources led to disorder and mass conflict, resulting in the destruction of much of the city by 650 C.E.

THE MAYA

The **Maya** civilization covered modern-day Guatemala, Honduras, Belize, and southern Mexico. The Maya were never politically unified but shared a single culture. Rulers of the various city-states competed with one another for territorial supremacy. As in Teotihuacan, feeding the large populations in Maya urban centers necessitated planned agricultural strategies like terraced farming and irrigation. Strong Maya cities featured elaborately decorated and colorful religious palaces, pyramids, and temples—all designed to express the political and religious authority of the king. Pyramids like Tikal in Guatemala, which rose above the trees, represented the access point to both the heavens and the underworld, and they were visible from large plazas where people gathered to witness the elaborate ceremonies of sacrifice and ritual that awed them. Amazingly, the Maya and other Amerindian societies were able to construct such incredible buildings without the use of the wheel or metal tools; stone tools and levers were the only technology used by the thousands of men and women who built these structures.

The role of religious ritual cannot be overstated. The elite had both secular and religious responsibilities and acted as intermediaries between the spirit world and the material world. Both bloodletting and sacrifice were considered essential to succeed in life and in war. Kings and other members of the elite led their soldiers in war, and their captives were sacrificed. Women of the ruling families also had important religious and political roles and participated in ritual bloodletting ceremonies. Two kingdoms are known to have been ruled by women. Although less is known about lower-class women, scholars believe women played important religious roles in their homes, wove cloth, managed their households, and directed family life.

Some of the most important intellectual contributions of the Maya were in the areas of astronomical observation, hieroglyphic writing, and math, which included a concept of zero. These intellectual accomplishments allowed for the development of elaborate calendars that represent the best of Mesoamerican culture. The Maya had three calendars: one tracked a ritual cycle of 260 days; one was a solar calendar of 365 days; the third, a long-count calendar, began on a set date in 3114 B.C.E., the Maya date of creation, and was continual.

There is much speculation about how the classic period of the Maya ended. Although a few Maya urban centers lasted far beyond the classic period, it is clear that between 800 and 900 C.E many centers were destroyed or abandoned. Of the many reasons suggested, the strongest is that the combination of expansion and lack of agricultural productivity caused social tension that degenerated into warfare.

Content Review Questions

1. Which of the following was a necessary precondition for the creation of the structures shown in the picture?
   (A) Frequent, successful wars to establish a base of prisoners of war to use as slave labor
   (B) The development of multiple competing city-state style governments
   (C) The growth of trade networks between inland areas and the coast
   (D) The establishment of irrigation and sedentary agriculture

2. Which of the following conclusions could a modern-day historian draw about the Maya from studying the structures shown in the picture?
   (A) The Maya had contact with the Egyptians.
   (B) Mayan religious figures had a more prominent place in society than political figures.
   (C) The Maya had advanced skills in math and engineering.
   (D) The Maya sacrificed humans to their gods.

3. All of the following are cultural developments of the Maya EXCEPT
   (A) the development of an accurate calendar.
   (B) the use of the concept of zero in math.
   (C) the construction of large, pyramid-like temples.
   (D) the development of wheeled vehicles for transport.

The rapid growth in urban population at Teotihuacan initially resulted from a series of nearby volcanic eruptions that disrupted agriculture and forced rural villagers to relocate to the city. Later, as the city elite increased their power, they forced additional farm families from the smaller villages in the region to relocate closer to the urban core. The elite organized these new labor resources to bring marginal lands into production, drain swamps, construct irrigation canals, and build terraces into hillsides. They also expanded the use of chinampas, sometimes called "floating gardens."

Bulliet et al., *The Earth and Its Peoples*, Boston: Cengage Learning, 2018, p. 200.

4. Which of the following civilizations is most comparable to the people of Teotihuacan when it comes to methods of environmental control?
   (A) The Maya
   (B) The Aztecs
   (C) The Inca
   (D) The Anasazi

5. Based on the passage, which of the following was most likely true of Teotihuacan?
   (A) The elite likely lived in the countryside and occasionally travelled into the city to segregate themselves from their sources of labor.
   (B) The city likely crumbled and disappeared due to a limited food supply, diminishing its influence on later civilizations.
   (C) In addition to a major food production area, the city likely served as a center of trade, public performance, and religious ritual.
   (D) The city likely saw many uprisings as the laboring class grew and gained awareness of their subjection to the elites.

6. Which of the following is an accurate comparison of the Maya and the people of Teotihuacan?
   (A) Only the people of Teotihuacan were able to construct elaborate buildings to use for religious and political purposes.
   (B) Both the Maya and the people of Teotihuacan developed monotheistic religions that promoted monasticism for priests.
   (C) The Maya were involved in an intricate commercial exchange network, unlike the city of Teotihuacan.
   (D) In both societies, the development of urbanized areas required planned agricultural strategies.

Answers

1. Answer: D. In order to create monumental buildings, the Maya needed a surplus of food and labor. Both of those are results of the switch from pastoralism and nomadism to sedentary farming. While the Mayans did have several of the other options, such as multiple city-states that were competing, none of these were preconditions for creating monumental architecture (*The Earth and Its Peoples*, 6th ed., pp. 198–201/7th ed., pp. 202–204; History Disciplinary Practice—Analyzing Historical Evidence; Learning Objectives CUL-5, SB-1; Key Concept 2.2.III.A).

2. Answer: C. A historian could draw the conclusion that the Maya had advanced skills with math and engineering based on the size of the structures and the fact that they are still standing. In fact, the Maya had an elaborate writing system and a mathematical system that incorporated the number 0 (*The Earth and Its Peoples*, 6th ed., pp. 198–201/7th ed., pp. 203–204; History Disciplinary Practice—Analyzing Historical Evidence; Learning Objectives CUL-5, SB-1; Key Concept 2.2.III.A).

3. Answer: D. The Maya constructed large, elaborately decorated pyramid-like temple structures in their religious and ceremonial centers. They developed a surprisingly accurate calendar based on astronomical observations, and they used the concept of zero in their mathematical calculations, unlike many other civilizations seemingly more advanced at the time. One innovation the Maya did not have was the wheel or wheeled vehicles. Many historians speculate that wheeled vehicles were impractical given the absence of beasts of burden or pack animals in Mesoamerica that would have pulled the vehicles (*The Earth and Its Peoples*, 6th ed., pp. 198–201/7th ed., pp. 202–203; Learning Objectives CUL-5, SB-1; Key Concept 2.2.III.A).

4. Answer: B. The passage describes the people of Teotihuacan using elaborate procedures to turn marshy territory into land suitable for farming by building chinampas. This is most comparable to the Aztecs, who also reclaimed marshy territory by building chinampas (*The Earth and Its Peoples*, 6th ed., pp. 197–203/7th ed., pp. 199–201; History Disciplinary Practice—Analyzing Historical Evidence; Learning Objectives ECON-2,3; Key Concept 2.2.III.C).

5. Answer: C. This fits a pattern for imperial cities during the classical age. Imperial cities generally served multiple purposes—both as areas of economic production and as areas of cultural and religious activity (*The Earth and Its Peoples*, 6th ed., pp. 197–203/7th ed., pp. 199–201; History Disciplinary Practice—Analyzing Historical Evidence; Learning Objectives CUL-5, SB-1; Key Concept 2.2.III.A).

6. Answer: D. The urban nature of the Maya society and the city of Teotihuacan meant that the elites needed to employ agricultural strategies, such as terraced farming, chinampas, and irrigation networks in order to ensure the food supply could support the populations of the urban areas (*The Earth and Its Peoples*, 6th ed., pp. 197–203/7th ed., pp. 199–201; History Reasoning Skill—Comparison; Learning Objectives CUL-5, SB-1; Key Concept 2.2.III.A).

AP® FORMAT QUESTIONS FOR PERIOD 2

Multiple-Choice Questions

Questions 1–3 refer to the following passage.

> Let a woman modestly yield to others; let her respect others; let her put others first, herself last. Let a woman retire late to bed, but rise early to her duties. Let her not refuse to perform domestic duties whether easy or difficult. Let her live in purity and quietness. To guard carefully her chastity; in every motion to exhibit modesty, this is womanly virtue.
>
> Ban Zhao, unofficial imperial historian to Emperor He (89–105 C.E.), *Lessons for Women*

> In childhood a female must be subject to her father, in youth to her husband, and when her lord is dead, to her sons; a woman must never be independent. A virtuous wife who after the death of her husband constantly remains chaste, reaches heaven, though she have no son. But a woman who from a desire to have offspring violates her duty toward her dead husband, brings on herself disgrace in this world, and loses her place with her husband in heaven. By violating her duty towards her husband, a wife is disgraced in this world, after death she enters the womb of a jackal.
>
> *The Laws of Manu*, India, 100 B.C.E.–200 C.E.

1. The messages of both of these passages reinforce which of the following?
   (A) The universalizing effect of Buddhism
   (B) Monotheism
   (C) Daoist teachings of balance
   (D) Patriarchy

2. The second passage references which of the following Hindu beliefs?
   (A) Reincarnation
   (B) Monotheism
   (C) The divinity of Jesus
   (D) Animism

3. The first passage supports which of the following ideals of Confucianism?
   (A) Enforcement of Vedic beliefs
   (B) Ancestor veneration
   (C) Filial piety
   (D) A centralized government supported by a bureaucracy

Questions 4–6 refer to the following image.

THE GREAT WALL

The Great Wall, China, 221–207 B.C.E.

4. Which of the following caused the emperor of China to order the construction of the object in the image?
   (A) Religious beliefs
   (B) Increased trade along the Silk Road
   (C) Security issues along China's frontiers
   (D) The spread of Buddhism

5. Which of the following empires built the object in the image?
   (A) Han
   (B) Zhou
   (C) Gupta
   (D) Qin

6. Which of the following was necessary to build this object?
   (A) A strong imperial government
   (B) Monotheistic religious beliefs
   (C) Trans-Saharan caravan routes
   (D) Innovations in maritime technologies

Questions 7–9 refer to the following map.

Map of the Roman Empire at its greatest extent

7. Which of the following was most viewed as a threat by the Empire pictured in the map?
   (A) Buddhism
   (B) Christianity
   (C) Judaism
   (D) Confucianism

8. Which of the following trade routes connected the empire, shown in the map, to the East?
   (A) Eurasian Silk Road
   (B) Trans-Saharan caravan routes
   (C) The Triangle Trade Route
   (D) Mediterranean sea lanes

9. Which of the following was a contributing factor in the decline of the empire depicted in the map?
   (A) Climate change
   (B) The failure of the Roman Republic
   (C) A challenge from the Gupta Empire
   (D) Administrative difficulties

Questions 10–12 refer to the following passage.

> The varna system was just one of the mechanisms developed to regulate relations between different groups. Within the broad class divisions, the population was further subdivided into numerous jati, or birth groups. Each jati had its proper occupation, duties, and rituals. Individuals who belonged to a given jati lived with members of their group, married within the group, and ate only with members of the group. Elaborate rules governed their interactions with members of other groups. Members of higher status groups feared pollution from contact with lower individuals and had to undergo elaborate rituals of purification to remove any taint.

> *The Earth and Its Peoples*, 6th ed., pp. 168–169

10. The social system described in this passage was central to which of the following religions?
    (A) Vedic religions
    (B) Buddhism
    (C) Judaism
    (D) Shamanism

11. Which of the following challenged the social system described in the passage?
    (A) Nomadic invaders
    (B) High taxes on the peasantry
    (C) Buddhism
    (D) Daoist beliefs about balance and nature

12. Which of the following was the consequence of the divisions described in the passage?
    (A) An increase in trade along Indian Ocean sea routes
    (B) A monastic life for Brahmans
    (C) The development of a rigid caste system that contributed to political roles in India
    (D) The spread of Confucianism into India via the Silk Road

Questions 13–15 refer to the following chart.

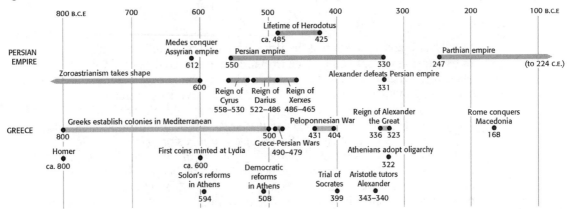

13. The empires in the chart shaped which distinctive trade route?
    (A) Trans-Atlantic
    (B) Indian Ocean
    (C) Mediterranean Sea
    (D) Baltic Sea

14. Which of the following empires borrowed heavily from the empires in
    the chart?
    (A) Han
    (B) Roman
    (C) Mauryan
    (D) Gupta

15. Which of the following is evidenced in the chart?
    (A) Early empires did not stress education.
    (B) The Persian and Greek empires did not have contact with each other.
    (C) Greece only focused on democracy.
    (D) Early empires built powerful military machines.

Short-Answer Questions

Question 1 refers to the following passage.

> Some historians maintain that the Romans inaugurated an important trans-Saharan trade, but they lack firm archaeological evidence. More plausibly, Saharan trade relates to the spread of camel domestication. Supporting evidence comes from rock art, where overlaps of images imply that camel riders in desert costume constitute the latest Saharan population. . . . Since the native camels of Africa probably died out before the era of domestication, the domestic animals probably reached the Sahara from Arabia, probably by way of Egypt in the first millennium B.C.E. They could have been adopted by peoples farther and farther to the west, from one central Saharan highland to the next, only much later spreading northward and coming to the attention of the Romans. Camel herding made it easier for people to move away from the Saharan highlands and roam the deep desert.
>
> *The Earth and Its Peoples*, 6th ed., pp. 232–233

1. Answer Parts A, B, and C.
   A. Explain a transformation in trans-Saharan trade prior to 600 C.E.
   B. Identify ONE other example of an innovation in technology used for commerce along a trade network in the period 600 B.C.E. to 600 C.E.
   C. Explain how the innovation you described in Part B transformed the trade network for which it was used prior to 600 C.E.

Question 2 refers to the following passage.

> I am Darius, the great king, king of kings, the king of Persia, the king of countries, the son of Hystaspes, the grandson of Arsames, the Achaemenid . . . from antiquity we have been noble; from antiquity has our dynasty been royal. . . .
>
> King Darius says: By the grace of Ahuramazda am I king; Ahuramazda has granted me the kingdom.
>
> King Darius says: These are the countries which are subject unto me, and by the grace of Ahuramazda I became king of them: Persia, Elam, Babylonia, Assyria, Arabia, Egypt, the countries by the Sea, Lydia, the Greeks, Media, Armenia, Cappadocia, Parthia, Drangiana, Aria, Chorasmia, Bactria, Sogdiana, Gandara, Scythia, Sattagydia, Arachosia and Maka; twenty-three lands in all.
>
> King Darius says: These are the countries which are subject to me; by the grace of Ahuramazda they became subject to me; they brought tribute unto me. Whatsoever commands have been laid on them by me, by night or by day, have been performed by them.
>
> King Darius says: Within these lands, whosoever was a friend, him have I surely protected; whosoever was hostile, him have I utterly destroyed. . . .
>
> King Darius says: As to these provinces which revolted, lies made them revolt, so that they deceived the people. Then Ahuramazda delivered them into my hand; and I did unto them according to my will.
>
> Inscriptions on a cliff at Behistun commissioned by King Darius, sixth century B.C.E.

2. Answer Parts A, B, and C.
   A. Identify one way (not referenced in the passage) Persian rulers enforced their leadership.
   B. Identify the way that ONE ruler of another empire in the period 600 B.C.E. to 600 C.E. used religion to reinforce political authority.
   C. Provide an example of ONE additional technique a ruler of an empire in the period 600 B.C.E. to 600 C.E. used to reinforce political authority.

Question 3 refers to the following passage.

The towns and villages have inner gates, the walls are wide and high, the streets and lanes are tortuous, and the roads winding. The thoroughfares are dirty and the stalls arranged on both sides of the road with appropriate signs. Butchers, fishers, dancers, executioners, and scavengers, and so on, have their abodes without the city. In coming and going these persons are bound to keep on the left side of the road till they arrive at their homes. Their houses are surrounded by low walls, and form the suburbs. The earth being soft and muddy, the walls of the town are mostly built of brick or tiles. The towers on the walls are constructed of wood or bamboo; the houses have balconies and belvederes [turrets], which are made of wood, with a coating of lime or mortar, and covered with tiles. The different buildings have the same form as those in China: rushes [a dried, grass-like plant], or dry branches, or tiles, or boards are used for covering them. The walls are covered with lime and mud, mixed with cow's dung for purity. At different seasons they scatter flowers about. Such are some of their different customs.

Xuanzang, Chinese traveler writing about South Asia, seventh century C.E.

3. Answer Parts A, B, and C.
   A. Identify, based on the description of the passage, ONE function imperial cities fulfilled in Indian civilization in the seventh century C.E.
   B. Identify from your knowledge of history, ONE additional function of imperial cities, different from the function you identified in Part A, in the period 600 B.C.E. to 600 C.E.
   C. Explain the connection between the development of imperial cities and the process of empire building in the period 600 B.C.E. to 600 C.E.

4. Answer Parts A, B, and C.
   A. Identify and explain ONE cause of the conflict between Persians and Greeks.
   B. Identify and explain ONE short-term effect of the conflict between Persians and Greeks.
   C. Identify and explain ONE long-term effect of the conflict between Persians and Greeks.

Question 5 refers to the following map.

© Cengage Learning

5. Answer Parts A, B, and C.
   A. Describe a feature of the religious and ceremonial centers in Mayan civilization.
   B. Identify and explain ONE continuity in Mesoamerican civilization up to 600 C.E.
   C. Identify and explain ONE change in Mesoamerican civilization up to 600 C.E.

Long Essay Questions

1. Analyze the effects of the Bantu migrations in sub-Saharan Africa to 600 C.E.

2. Analyze cultural continuities and changes in the Middle East from c. 600 B.C.E. to c. 600 C.E.

3. Compare the impact of TWO of the following religious and philosophical systems on political and social structures in Asia in the period 600 B.C.E. to 600 C.E.
   - Buddhism
   - Confucianism
   - Hinduism

4. Analyze the continuities and changes in European involvement in interregional trade from c. 2000 B.C.E. to c. 600 C.E.

5. Analyze the similarities and differences in the function of the city of Teotihuacan to the function of ONE of the following cities:
   - Alexandria
   - Persepolis
   - Chang'an

Answers

MULTIPLE-CHOICE QUESTIONS

1. ANSWER: D. Both passages reflect the patriarchal societies that existed in classical China and India. A patriarchy is a system of society or government in which men hold the power and women are largely excluded (*The Earth and Its Peoples*, 6th ed., pp. 157, 177/7th ed., pp. 162–163, 181–182; History Disciplinary Practice—Analyzing Historical Evidence; Learning Objectives CUL; Key Concept 2.2 III D).

2. ANSWER: A. The second passage references a woman being reborn in the womb of a jackal. This is evidence of the Hindu belief in karma and reincarnation. If a person did not behave in an acceptable manner, he or she would move down a caste after death; animals were lower than the lowest caste (*The Earth and Its Peoples*, 6th ed., p. 169/7th ed., pp. 171–172; History Disciplinary Practice—Analyzing Historical Evidence; Learning Objective CUL; Key Concept 2.1 I B).

3. ANSWER: C. Filial piety is a Chinese belief that it is virtuous to respect one's father, elders, and ancestors. One of the relationships that is central to filial piety and Confucianism is that of a woman being obedient to her husband (*The Earth and Its Peoples*, 6th ed., p. 81/7th ed., pp. 88–92; History Disciplinary Practice—Analyzing Historical Evidence; Learning Objective CUL; Key Concept 2.1 III).

4. ANSWER: C. The Great Wall was started in an effort to keep the nomadic groups of the Eurasian Steppes from invading China (*The Earth and Its Peoples*, 6th ed., p. 18/7th ed., p. 159; History Reasoning Skill—Causation; Learning Objective SB; Key Concept 2.2 IV B).

5. ANSWER: D. The Qin dynasty (221–206 B.C.E.) was led by Qin Shi Huang and was based on the philosophy of Legalism. The Emperor was constantly vigilant with regard to protecting his empire from threats from outside the borders, as well as threats from inside the borders (*The Earth and Its Peoples*, 6th ed., p. 152/7th ed., pp. 89, 158; History Disciplinary Practice—Analyzing Historical Evidence; Learning Objective SB; Key Concept 2.2 I).

6. ANSWER: A. The Qin dynasty utilized conscripted labor in order to complete the wall, which required a strong, centralized, and imperial government (*The Earth and Its Peoples*, 6th ed., p. 152/7th ed., p. 158; History Disciplinary Practice—Analyzing Historical Evidence; Learning Objective SB; Key Concept 2.2 II B).

7. ANSWER: B. The map shows the Roman Empire at its height. The development of Christianity threatened to undermine the power and appeal of the emperor, therefore, many Roman emperors were hostile to Christianity and often persecuted Christians. It was not until the fourth century C.E. that Rome had its first Christian emperor, Constantine (*The*

Earth and Its Peoples, 6th ed., p. 151/7th ed., p. 146; History
Disciplinary Practice—Analyzing Historical Evidence; Learning
Objective SB, CUL; Key Concept 2.1 II D).

8. ANSWER: A. The Eurasian Silk Road connected Rome to India and
China. There were numerous roads included in the Silk Road (*The Earth
and Its Peoples*, 6th ed., p. 224/7th ed., pp. 226–230; History
Disciplinary Practice—Analyzing Historical Evidence; Learning
Objective ECON; Key Concept 2.3 I A).

9. ANSWER: D. The Roman Empire expanded to a size that was difficult for
the Imperial leader to maintain. The late Roman Emperors began taxing
the citizens at a high rate and could not manage the military; these
internal administrative difficulties contributed to the fall of the Roman
Empire (*The Earth and Its Peoples*, 6th ed., p. 142/7th ed., pp. 156–157;
History Disciplinary Practice—Analyzing Historical Evidence; Learning
Objective SB; Key Concept 2.2 IV).

10. ANSWER: A. The passage describes the rigidity of the Hindu caste
system. Hinduism stems from the Vedic religions (*The Earth and Its
Peoples*, 6th ed., p. 169/7th ed., pp. 172–173; History Disciplinary
Practice—Analyzing Historical Evidence; Learning Objective CUL; Key
Concept 2.1 I B).

11. ANSWER: C. One of the main tenets of Buddhism is that all people can
achieve enlightenment; Buddhism rejected the Hindu caste system that is
why the Brahmans in India were threatened by Buddhism. Buddhism
originated in India but did not become the dominant religion there (*The
Earth and Its Peoples*, 6th ed., p. 170/7th ed., pp. 173–174; History
Disciplinary Practice—Analyzing Evidence: Content and Sourcing;
Learning Objective CUL, SB; Key Concept 2.1 II A).

12. ANSWER: C. The caste system in India was an extremely rigid social
hierarchy. The only way to move up to a higher caste was to live a good
life (have good karma) and be reincarnated into a high caste after death
(*The Earth and Its Peoples*, 6th ed., p. 169/7th ed., pp. 172–173; History
Disciplinary Practice—Argument Development; Learning Objective
CUL; Key Concept 2.1 I B).

13. ANSWER: C. The Greeks perfected trade along Mediterranean sea lanes
(*The Earth and Its Peoples*, 6th ed., p. 123/7th ed., pp. 120–122; History
Disciplinary Practice—Analyzing Historical Evidence; Learning
Objective ECON; Key Concept 2.3 I A).

14. ANSWER: B. The Roman Republic and later the Roman Empire borrowed
heavily from the Greeks. Greco-Roman philosophy, science, and
architecture are examples of this (*The Earth and Its Peoples*, 6th ed.,
p. 88/7th ed., pp. 145–152; History Disciplinary Practice—Analyzing
Historical Evidence; Learning Objective CUL; Key Concept 2.1 II E).

15. ANSWER: D. The chart shows that both the Persian Empire and the Greek city-states waged war against each other and other enemies. In an effort to gain power and expand territorially, early empires often built powerful military machines (*The Earth and Its Peoples*, 6th ed., p. 118/7th ed., p. 115; History Disciplinary Practice—Analyzing Historical Evidence; Learning Objective SB; Key Concept 2.2).

SHORT-ANSWER QUESTIONS

1. A. Camel domestication, as the passage indicates, allowed for more extensive commercial connections across the Sahara, because the camel was more suited to travel in the desert than other pack animals. Therefore, the domestication and use of the camel transformed trade by allowing for more products to be exchanged more efficiently (*The Earth and Its Peoples*, 6th ed., pp. 231–234/7th ed., pp. 226–230; History Reasoning Skill—Causation; Key Concept 2.3; Learning Objectives ENV-1,2,3,5, ECON-7).

   B. A major innovation in technology used for trade in the classical period was the invention of the compass by the Chinese. The use of the compass spread along trade networks in the Indian Ocean and therefore helped increase trade there (*The Earth and Its Peoples*, 6th ed., pp. 305–306/7th ed., pp. 230–234, 302; Historical Thinking Skill—Contextualization; Key Concept 2.3; Learning Objectives ENV-1,2,3,5, ECON-7).

   C. The innovation of the compass was that it was a more efficient navigational technology that allowed for more long-distance trade along maritime networks, such as the Indian Ocean. The compass allowed merchants to not have to rely strictly on maps and risk more direct routes across open waters (*The Earth and Its Peoples*, 6th ed., pp. 305–306/7th ed., p. 302; History Reasoning Skill—Causation; Key Concept 2.3; Learning Objectives ENV-1,2,3,5, ECON-7).

2. A. Persian rulers also organized their people to create massive public works projects, such as the Royal Roads (*The Earth and Its Peoples*, 6th ed., pp. 107–112/7th ed., pp. 115–120; History Disciplinary Practice—Analyzing Historical Evidence; Key Concept 2.2; Learning Objectives CUL-5, SB-1-6).

   B. Many rulers of the classical empires in the time 600 B.C.E. to 600 C.E. used religious beliefs to legitimize power. By claiming some kind of connection to a divine figure, rulers could use the beliefs their subjects already had as a way to increase their power over the people. Rule through divine right, in other words, by permission of a god or gods, was a powerful way to gain and maintain political authority. Examples of rulers that used religion to legitimize power: Alexander the Great, Ashoka (Buddhism), and several Roman emperors (cult of the emperor, then later Christianity with Constantine) (*The Earth and Its Peoples*, 6th ed., pp. 107–112, 125–132, 143–156, 174–182/7th ed., pp. 115–120, 134–135, 153–155, 178–180; History Disciplinary Practice—Argument Development; Key Concept 2.2; Learning Objectives CUL-5, SB-1-6).

C. Examples of other techniques rulers of the classical era used to legitimize rule include the sponsorship of the construction of large public works, glorifying the ruler and/or imperial victories. Examples of this technique could include Roman and Chinese emperors commissioning statues and, in the case of Qin emperor Shi Huangdi, an elaborate tomb (*The Earth and Its Peoples*, 6th ed., pp. 107–112, 125–132, 143–156, 174–182/7th ed., pp. 149–151, 159–160, 178–180; History Reasoning Skill—Contextualization; Key Concept 2.2; Learning Objectives CUL-5, SB-1-6).

3. A. From the passage, the towns and villages in India, as described by the author, appear to have an economic role (description of specific artisans and tradesmen, such as butchers, as well as people coming in and out of the city for their trade) and also a political role (description of defensive fortifications, such as the walls, and executioners) (*The Earth and Its Peoples*, 6th ed., pp. 174–182, 228–229/7th ed., pp. 178–186, 230–231; History Disciplinary Practice—Analyzing Historical Evidence; Key Concept 2.2; Learning Objectives CUL-5, SB-1-6, ECON-2-5).

B. Imperial cities in the period 600 B.C.E. to 600 C.E. served as centers of trade, public performance of religious rituals, and political administration. Examples of acceptable responses would address one or more of these roles. Cities are a natural location for commercial connections to be made—in fact, cities often develop along trade networks and where multiple networks converge. Cities are often where artisans live and the manufacture of goods takes place. Cities also served an administrative role as centralized governments of the period developed increasingly elaborate bureaucracies. More people moved to capital cities to serve as bureaucrats, and political decisions and policies increasingly radiated out to the rest of the empire from these administrative cities. Cities, with larger population density than rural areas, were also better suited to host important public rituals that helped glorify the empire as well as legitimize a ruler's power (*The Earth and Its Peoples*, 6th ed., pp. 144–152, 152–156, 174–182, 228–229/7th ed., pp. 149–162, 178–186, 230–234; History Reasoning Skill—Contextualization; Key Concept 2.2; Learning Objectives CUL-5, SB-1-6, ECON-2-5).

C. The development of imperial cities with administrative, cultural, and economic roles facilitates the process of empire building. Through economic functions, cities help ensure access to essential resources needed to expand and often helped determine the path of expansion (along commercial networks to access more economic centers). Because of their larger population density, cities were often targeted for propaganda to glorify the empire and encourage a sense of pride, which in turn fostered support for military campaigns. (*The Earth and Its Peoples*, 6th ed., pp. 144–152, 152–156, 174–182, 228–229/7th ed., pp. 149–162, 178–186, 230–234; History Disciplinary Practice—Argument Development; Key Concept 2.2; Learning Objectives ENV-1, CUL-5, SB-1-6, ECON-2-5).

4. A. Initial conflict between Greeks and Persians happened when Greek city-states in Anatolia resisted Persian expansion and control over the region. Greek city-states, such as Athens, supported the rebellion, prompting Persian ruler Darius to attack the Greek mainland as punishment for supporting the rebellious city-states in Anatolia (*The Earth and Its Peoples*, 6th ed., pp. 121–124/7th ed., pp. 130–133; History Reasoning Skill—Causation; Key Concept 2.2; Learning Objectives SB-4).

    B. In fighting the Persians, one significant short-term effect of the Persian wars was that the city-states of Athens and Sparta rose to prominence, each leading efforts to repel the Persians. Eventually, rivalry between these two cities led to the Peloponnesian War, pitting Greek city-state against Greek city-state (*The Earth and Its Peoples*, 6th ed., pp. 121–126/7th ed., pp. 130–133; History Reasoning Skill—Causation; Key Concept 2.2; Learning Objectives SB-4).

    C. A long-term effect of the Persian wars could be that the rivalry and eventual conflict between Athens and Sparta that emerged following the Greek victory contributed to each city's decline, creating a power vacuum that allowed Macedonian rulers (Philip then Alexander) to exert power and influence over Greece. Alexander used this power base to create, through conquest, a large empire spanning from the eastern Mediterranean to central and south Asia (*The Earth and Its Peoples*, 6th ed., pp. 125–132/7th ed., pp. 134–135; History Disciplinary Practice—Analyzing Historical Evidence; Key Concept 2.2; Learning Objectives SB-4).

5. A. The religious and ceremonial centers of the Maya typically included large, pyramid-like temples adorned with carvings of pictographs. The temples were likely used for important religious and political ceremonies. Many of these centers also included a ball court for ceremonial games (*The Earth and Its Peoples*, 6th ed., pp. 198–201/7th ed., pp. 201–204; History Reasoning Skill—Contextualization; Key Concept 2.1; Learning Objectives CUL-5).

    B. Continuities in Mesoamerican civilization to 600 C.E. include agriculture, persistent use of trade networks throughout the region, construction of monumental architecture for political and/or religious purposes, the development of urban areas for religious/ceremonial purposes, and a social hierarchy placing political and religious elites at the top (*The Earth and Its Peoples*, 6th ed., pp. 192–195, 197–201/7th ed., pp. 194–199, 201–204; Historical Thinking Skill—Patterns of Continuity and Change over Time; Key Concepts 1.3,2.1,2.2; Learning Objectives ENV-1,3,5, CUL-5, SB-1,2,3,4,5, ECON-2,3,5, SOC-1,2,3,5).

    C. Changes in Mesoamerican civilization to 600 C.E. include the collapse of the Olmec civilization and the rise of the Maya civilization, as well as the development of independent Teotihuacan, with its innovative chinampa farming technique (*The Earth and Its Peoples*, 6th ed., pp. 192–195, 197–201/7th ed., pp. 194–199, 201–204; History Reasoning Skill—Continuity and Change over Time; Key Concepts 1.3,2.1,2.2; Learning Objectives ENV-1,3,5, CUL-5, SB-1,2,3,4,5, ECON-2,3,5, SOC-1,2,3,5).

Long Essay Questions

1. A good response would center on discussion of the transmission of several aspects of Bantu society to the sub-Saharan groups they encountered in the process of migration. Primary among these aspects would be the knowledge of iron metallurgy and agriculture. The Bantu had already developed agriculture and made tools with iron before they left their homelands near modern-day Nigeria. As they migrated over a period of thousands of years, they introduced iron metallurgy and their agricultural practices in the places they settled, often adapting original practices to fit new environments. They also transmitted their language to the people they encountered and settled with throughout the process of migration. Today, many areas of sub-Saharan Africa speak a language related to Bantu (*The Earth and Its Peoples*, 6th ed., pp. 236–237/7th ed., pp. 234–240; History Reasoning Skill—Causation; Key Concepts 2.3, 3.1; Learning Objectives ENV-1,2,3,5, CUL-1,3, ECON-2,6,7).

2. A good response will identify the continued practice of Zoroastrianism and Hebrew monotheism (Judaism) as cultural continuities, as well as the continued use of monumental architecture to demonstrate the power of ruling elites. Both Hebrew monotheism and Zoroastrianism developed prior to 600 B.C.E. and continued to be practiced throughout the classical period. Although the Israelites experienced persecution and even exile, the people largely remained faithful and continued to practice their religion. Zoroastrianism maintained its largest influence in Persia, although there is some evidence that its beliefs influenced Middle Eastern cultures outside of the religion's hearth. Changes include the development and spread of Hellenistic culture, as well as the emergence of Christianity. As a result of Alexander the Great's conquests, several different cultures of the world came into direct, sustained contact, resulting in a transfer and blending of Greek, Egyptian, Persian, and Indian cultures. Christianity emerged in the middle of the period and slowly gained influence and followers as it spread around the Mediterranean basin and along trade networks (*The Earth and Its Peoples*, 6th ed., pp. 105–132, 147–148/7th ed., pp. 64–68, 113–119; History Reasoning Skill—Comparison; Key Concept 2.1; Learning Objectives CUL-1,2,5,6).

3. Acceptable examples of comparisons for this essay prompt would depend on which two religions/belief systems are selected. The Mauryan emperor Ashoka converted to Buddhism and infused Buddhist beliefs into his Rock and Pillar Edicts constructed around the empire. These edicts reflect the influence of Buddhism in Ashoka's governing policies. Buddhism developed in part as a rejection of many Vedic beliefs, and therefore the rigid caste system was less important and influential in the lives of Buddhist followers. Confucianism had a dramatic impact on the political structure of China as Han rulers developed the civil service exam, testing potential bureaucrats' knowledge of Confucian teachings in order to select qualified candidates. Confucian teachings continued to shape governing policies for a long time after the collapse of the Han dynasty. The emphasis on respecting certain social relationships not only

ensured social harmony (according to Confucius) but also guaranteed patriarchal influence on gender roles and expectations. Hindu beliefs are centered around the idea of accumulating good karma by fulfilling the appropriate caste duties (dharma). These beliefs therefore shape the social hierarchy, known as the caste system, as well as lend justification for social elites also holding political power (*The Earth and Its Peoples*, 6th ed., pp. 81–85, 152–159, 169–182/7th ed., pp. 160–165, 178–180, 181–186; History Reasoning Skill—Comparison; Key Concept 2.1; Learning Objectives CUL-1,2).

4. Think about the dates given and what you know about the region at that time. In the case of 2000 B.C.E., the Minoan civilization emerged and created a trade-based society in order to make up for the geographic shortcomings of their homeland. By 600 C.E., western Europe was headed into the medieval era, a period with little long-distance trade, while the eastern portion (Byzantine Empire) is strategically located at the crossroads of key trade routes. In between, you need to decide what period helps illustrate the changes and continuities of the region's role in international trade. You might choose to look at the economic activity during the Hellenistic Age and perhaps discuss long-distance trade and communication caused by the Pax Romana. In any case, choose information that matches the parameters established in your thesis, which must include both continuities and changes (*The Earth and Its Peoples*, 6th ed., pp. 48–52, 59–65, 112–120/7th ed., pp. 57–61, 149–155, 270–273; History Reasoning Skill—Continuity and Change over Time; Key Concepts 1.3,2.3; Learning Objectives ENV-1,2,3,5).

5. Cities of the classical era tended to fulfill many functions, including administrative, economic, and cultural. Each of the cities for this prompt served economic and cultural roles, but Teotihuacan is the only city in this list that did not serve as a capital city for a larger empire. A good response for this prompt would include discussion of the functions of Teotihuacan and the other city selected, citing specific examples of how the city fulfilled economic and cultural roles for the wider civilization. Also, discussion should include examples of the selected city's political role in contrast to the fact that Teotihuacan was not a capital city for a larger empire (*The Earth and Its Peoples*, 6th ed., pp. 107–110, 128–132, 156–157, 197–198/7th ed., pp. 194–197, 199–204, 205–207; History Reasoning Skill—Comparison; Key Concept 2.2; Learning Objectives ECON-2).

Period 3: Regional and Interregional Interactions, c. 600 C.E. to c. 1450

Period 3 of the AP® World History framework continues to examine changes to and continuities in the building and governance of empires and states from the previous period. While some societies attempted to blend traditional methods with innovation, other societies developed new forms of political organization (or at least forms new to that area!). Indeed, in Period 3, we see "successor states"—empires or nations that built upon what was left of a former, powerful state, often using the political ideologies and strategies of those former states to justify the new state's power. For example, the Byzantine Empire and the Sui, Tang, and Song Dynasties of China each actively sought to use the strong reputation of past empires (Roman and Han, respectively) in order to bolster the power and prestige of the rulers of the new empires, as well as to foster a sense of cultural and political unity and continuity for their subjects. As with Period 2, religions, belief systems, and philosophy continued to influence political and economic policies, as well as social structures in the societies of Period 3.

The rise of Islam counts as one of the most significant developments at the beginning of this period (in the wake of the collapse of many Classical empires), with major cultural, economic, social, and political implications. Islam gradually spread first through conquest and commerce, and later through the efforts of missionaries. By 1450, Islam was practiced across a broad stretch of Afro-Eurasia outside of the Middle East, including West Africa, the Iberian Peninsula in Europe, the Swahili Coast in East Africa, South Asia, Central Asia, Southeast Asia, and East Asia. Just as trade networks helped diffuse the religion in these areas, the cultural ties that connected Muslims in these diverse areas facilitated the growth of significant trade networks across the Sahara Desert, over the Indian Ocean, and along the Silk Road.

Another major development making this period distinct in world history was the rise of the Mongol Empire, one of the largest empires you will learn about in this course. The Mongols swept across Central Asia, conquering lands from the Middle East and the northern part of the Indian subcontinent to the south, Eastern Europe to the west, and China and Korea to the east. Consequences for the conquered societies were often a mix of positive and negative: conquered peoples were often introduced to technologies, cultural ideas (religions, artistic styles, etc.), and luxury goods as a result of the Mongols' attentiveness to keeping trade networks active and safe. However,

---

the increase in commerce along the major trade networks also ushered waves of plague, stretching from China to Europe, which devastated populations.

The following charts outline the learning objectives and topics from the content outline that fit into this period.

Content Review Questions can be found at the end of each chapter. **AP®** **format questions** for Period 3 can be found on page 250. **Document-Based Questions** can be found in the diagnostic test and practice tests.

THEMATIC LEARNING OBJECTIVES FOR PERIOD 3

INTERACTION BETWEEN HUMANS AND THE ENVIRONMENT

Learning Objectives—Students are able to . . .	Relevant Topics in the Concept Outline
ENV-1 Explain how environmental factors, disease, and technology affected patterns of human migration and settlement over time.	3.1. I—Interregional trade 3.1. II—Migration 3.1. IV—Disease; bubonic plague 3.3. II—Fate of cities
ENV-2 Evaluate the extent to which migration, population, and urbanization affected the environment over time.	3.1. I, II—Expansion of long-distance trade routes 3.1. II—Migration 3.1. IV—Bubonic plague; crop diffusion; effects of migration 3.3. I—Increasing agricultural productivity 3.3. II—Urban decline
ENV-3 Explain how environmental factors have shaped the development of diverse technologies, industrialization, transportation methods, and exchange and communication networks.	3.3. I—Technological innovations
ENV-4 Evaluate the extent to which the development of diverse technologies, industrialization, transportation methods, and exchange and communication networks have affected the environment over time.	3.1. I—Intensification of trade 3.1. IV—Crop diffusion 3.1. II, IV—Effects of migration 3.1. IV—Bubonic plague 3.3. I—Increasing agricultural productivity 3.3. II—Declines of urban areas

DEVELOPMENT AND INTERACTION OF CULTURES

Learning Objectives—Students are able to . . .	Relevant Topics in the Concept Outline
CUL-1 Explain how religions, belief systems, philosophies, and ideologies originated, developed, and spread as a result of expanding communication and exchange networks.	3.1. III—Islam 3.2. I—Collapse of empires
CUL-2 Explain how religions, belief systems, philosophies, and ideologies affected political, economic, and social developments over time.	3.1. III—Spread of trade, religions, and diasporic communities 3.2. I—Influence of belief systems on new forms of governance; traditional sources of power and legitimacy 3.3. III—Changes in gender and family structures; Buddhism, Christianity, Islam, Neo-Confucianism
CUL-3 Explain how cross-cultural interactions resulted in the diffusion of culture, technologies, and scientific knowledge.	3.1. I—Growth of existing and new trade routes 3.1. II—Spread of language and technology by Bantu and Polynesian migrations 3.1. III—Intensification of trade networks 3.2. II—Technological transfer
CUL-4 Explain how technological and scientific innovations affected religions, belief systems, philosophies, and ideologies over time.	3.1. III—Cross-cultural exchange; transportation technologies facilitated cultural diffusion
CUL-5 Explain how the arts are shaped by and reflect innovation, adaptation, and creativity of specific societies over time.	3.1. III—Diffusion of artistic traditions; diasporic communities
CUL-6 Explain how expanding exchange networks shaped the emergence of various forms of transregional culture, including music, literature, and visual art.	3.1. III— Diffusion of artistic traditions; diasporic communities

STATE BUILDING, EXPANSION, AND CONFLICT

Learning Objectives—Students are able to . . .	Relevant Topics in the Concept Outline
SB-1 Explain how different forms of governance have been constructed and maintained over time.	3.1. I—State involvement in economic activity 3.2. I—Synthesized, borrowed, and new state structures emerged
SB-2 Explain how and why different functions and institutions of governance have changed over time.	3.1. I—New trading cities, state-sponsored commerce, expansion 3.2. I—Reconstitution and new forms of governance 3.3. II—Fate of cities 3.3. III—Women rulers
SB-3 Explain how and why economic, social, cultural, and geographical factors have influenced the processes of state building, expansion, and dissolution.	3.1. I—Growth of trade and new cities 3.1. II—Cultural and environmental impacts of migration 3.1. III—Cross-cultural exchanges 3.2. I—City-states 3.2. I, II—Continuities and innovations of state forms; Dar al Islam, khanates, feudalism 3.3. II—Fates of cities; urban decline and renewal 3.3. III—Globalizing networks
SB-4 Explain how and why internal and external political factors have influenced the process of state building, expansion, and dissolution.	3.1. I—Cities and increased trade, state practices that facilitated trade 3.2. I—Collapse and reconstitution of empires 3.3. II—Rise and fall of cities 3.3. III—Peasant revolts
SB-5 Explain how societies with states and state-less societies interacted over time.	3.1. I—Empire expansion 3.1. III—Arab expansion 3.2. I—Conquests, tributary empires, new forms of government; Mongol expansion, Aztec/Mexica 3.2. II—Interregional conflicts; technological and cultural transfers 3.3. III—Nomadic pastoralism: changes in labor organization, military obligations, POW/slaves
SB-6 Explain the political and economic interactions between states and non-state actors over time.	3.1. III—Arab expansion 3.2. I—Conquests, tributary empires, new forms of government 3.2. II—Interregional conflicts 3.3. III—Changes in labor organization, military obligations, POW/slaves

CREATION, EXPANSION, AND INTERACTION OF ECONOMIC SYSTEMS

Learning Objectives—Students are able to . . .	Relevant Topics in the Concept Outline
ECON-1 Explain how technology shaped economic production and globalization over time.	3.1. I—Transportation and commercial technology
ECON-2 Explain the causes and effects of economic strategies of different types of communities, states, and empires.	3.2. I—Imperial innovations 3.3. I–III—Imperial support for production and trade
ECON-3 Explain how different modes and locations of production and commerce have developed and changed over time.	3.2. I—Imperial innovations 3.3. I–III—Imperial support for production and trade
ECON-4 Explain how and why labor systems have developed and changed over time.	3.1. I—Caravan organization 3.3. I—Artisans expand production 3.3. II—Urban decline and revival 3.3. III—Labor organization, family life; military and household slaves, *mit'a,* serfdom
ECON-5 Explain how economic systems and the development of ideologies, values, and institutions have influenced each other.	3.1. I—Islam
ECON-6 Explain how local, regional, and global economic systems and exchange networks have influenced and impacted each other over time.	3.1. I—Ship design 3.1. III—Diffusion of scientific ideas and technology; cross-cultural exchanges 3.1. IV—Spread of crops and diseases in Afro-Eurasia; Eastern Hemisphere diffusion 3.2. I—Changing imperial rule affected trade 3.2. II—Technology transfer 3.3. I—Afro-Eurasian exchanges of crops; demand for luxury goods 3.3. II— Changing urbanization; safe and reliable transport

DEVELOPMENT AND TRANSFORMATION OF SOCIAL STRUCTURES

Learning Objectives—Students are able to . . .	Relevant Topics in the Concept Outline
SOC-1 Explain how distinctions based on kinship, ethnicity, class, gender, and race influenced the development and transformations of social hierarchies.	3.1. III—Patriarchy and power 3.2. I—Continuities of patriarchy, religious influence on gender 3.3. III—Diversification of labor organization, new labor coercion
SOC-2 Evaluate the extent to which different ideologies, philosophies, and religions affected social hierarchies.	3.1. III—Cross-cultural exchanges of social systems; Islam and conquest
SOC-3 Evaluate the extent to which legal systems, colonialism, nationalism, and independence movements have sustained or challenged class, gender, and racial hierarchies over time.	3.2. I—Sources of power and legitimacy 3.3. III—Postclassical legal systems
SOC-4 Explain how the development of specialized labor systems interacted with the development of social hierarchies.	3.3. III—Diversification of labor organization; new labor coercion
SOC-5 Explain how social categories, roles, and practices have been maintained or challenged over time.	3.1. III—Islam 3.3. III—Postclassical social organization; changes and continuities in the wake of economic growth
SOC-6 Explain how political, economic, cultural, and demographic factors have affected social structures over time.	3.1. III—Diasporic communities 3.3. III—Changes to labor structures

KEY CONCEPTS FOR PERIOD 3

3.1. Expansion and Intensification of Communication and Exchange Networks

3.2. Continuity and Innovation of State Forms and Their Interactions

3.3. Increased Economic Productive Capacity and Its Consequences

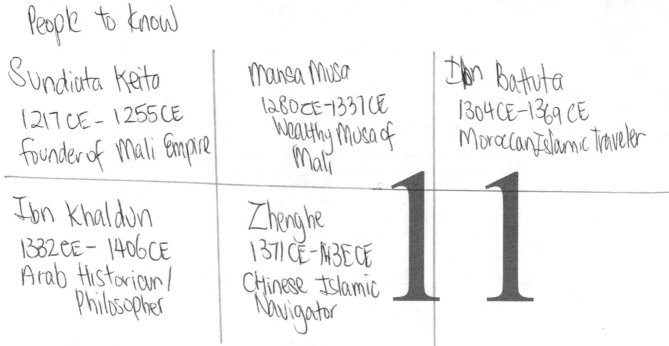

People to know

Sundiata Keita
1217 CE - 1255 CE
founder of Mali Empire

Mansa Musa
1280 CE - 1337 CE
Wealthy Musa of Mali

Ibn Battuta
1304 CE - 1369 CE
Moroccan Islamic traveler

Ibn Khaldun
1382 CE - 1406 CE
Arab Historian/Philosopher

Zhenghe
1371 CE - 1433 CE
Chinese Islamic Navigator

11

AFRICA: C. 600 C.E. TO C. 1450 C.E.

KEY CONCEPTS

- ▪ The varied environments of different African regions had an important influence on the cultural and economic developments of societies.
- ▪ Regional and long-distance interactions among African societies and with outsiders helped create the cultural diversity that characterized the period.
- ▪ Various African societies played a major role in the larger networks of trade, including both the trans-Saharan and Indian Ocean trade networks.
- ▪ Islam's spread to Africa had a significant impact in terms of religious and economic influence in the period of c. 600 to c. 1450.

KEY TERMS

- ▪ Ethiopia
- ▪ Ghana
- ▪ Great Zimbabwe
- ▪ Ibn Battuta
- ▪ Mali
- ▪ Mansa Kankan Musa
- ▪ Swahili Coast
- ▪ Timbuktu

Caravanserai = roadside inn where travelers could rest and recover from the days journey
Sundiata = epic poem of the Malinke people
Berbers = ethnic group of several nations
Bantu Migrations = major series of migration
Hausa = collections of states started by the Hausa people

Africa is discussed in depth in *The Earth and Its Peoples*, Chapters 8 and 14 of the 6th edition and Chapters 9 and 15 of the 7th edition.

AFRICAN ENVIRONMENTS

The vast and diverse continent of Africa is home to many different cultures. During the period 600–1450, these cultures forged Africa's social, religious, and economic relationships with other cultures both within the continent and beyond. Africa cannot be looked at monolithically. Throughout the continent similarities and differences abound. Likewise, dramatic changes brought about by trade are as visible as the cultural continuities.

Building on generations of experience, the peoples of Africa used various techniques to adapt to the differing environments and climates of the continent, which produced incredible diversity among societies by 1200. Africa is almost entirely in the tropical zone of the earth, and its cycles are rainy and dry seasons rather than hot and cold seasons. Whether their environment was grassland, the dense tropical rain forests of West and Central Africa, or desert—the Sahara Desert in the north is the largest desert in the world—Africans could produce food. Because desert zones lie in both the north (Sahara) and southwest (Kalahari), most Africans lived in the moderate areas where some rainfall would be expected. (This is still the case today.) Some lived in settled agricultural societies; some formed pastoral societies; others hunted, gathered, and fished.

Africans also used irrigation. The importance of Africa's rivers cannot be overstated. The Nile, which flows from central Africa to the north; the Niger in West Africa; and the Zambezi in the south and the central African Congo are some of the crucial bodies of water that give life to trading cities and smaller communities. By 1200, agriculture had been the dominant enterprise for centuries. Regional exchange of plants, fruits, and crops occurred thanks in part to the Bantu migrations, which brought grains and other plants south from West Africa. A larger network of trade brought products like bananas and yams to Africa from Southeast Asia and carried African exports to other regions—for example, Ethiopian coffee to the Middle East.

Another great strength of the African tropical regions was the mining of precious metals. Skillful craftsmen worked metal into a variety of objects. Copper and gold were the most valuable metals, but iron, the most plentiful metal in tropical Africa, was especially important: iron was made into hoes, axes, and knives for farming; spears and arrows for hunting; and needles and nails for day-to-day life. Copper, plentiful in southeastern Africa, was used to make copper wire and decorative objects. The copper and brass statues coming out of West Africa were some of the most famous art of the period dating to 1500. Gold became incredibly profitable as an export, particularly to India. Important sources of gold were the Niger River and the hills south of the Zambezi River, where archaeologists have found thousands of mine shafts used for mining gold.

NEW ISLAMIC EMPIRES IN AFRICA

The spread of Islam across North Africa and down into sub-Saharan Africa is one of the key developments of the period, both culturally and economically. North Africa was under Muslim rule by the eighth century. Only gradually did Islam spread to sub-Saharan Africa, the land south of the Sahara Desert known to the Arabs as *bilad al-sudan*, "land of the blacks." Muslim Berbers conquered **Ghana** in 1076; the subsequent empire of Mali, which flourished from 1200 to 1500, was one of the richest and largest Muslim states, rivaled only by the Delhi Sultanate in India.

Other religions had influence as well; in East Africa, Christianity maintained a stronghold in **Ethiopia** although the Christian Nubian kingdoms along the upper Nile were conquered in the name of Islam. However, throughout the whole sub-Saharan region, and the east coast of Africa in particular, most Africans were introduced to Islam peacefully. Economic interaction produced personal relationships that in turn provided opportunities for conversion. The teachings of Islam and Islamic methods of managing empires and cities appealed to African merchants and political leaders.

The first sub-Saharan place where Islam was adopted was Takrur, in 1030. By 1200, King Sumanguru had increased the status of Takrur, and in 1240, Sundiata of the Malinke people defeated Sumanguru. Both Sumanguru and Sundiata were Muslims who had peacefully converted to Islam before the empire was established. Sundiata's continued conquests brought about the birth of the **Mali** Empire.

Like many other earlier and contemporaneous Muslim empires, Mali's wealth derived largely from trade—not only from the sale of goods but also from the strategic control of the actual routes. As in Ghana, agriculture met basic needs; again, a river was the source of both physical and economic life. But Mali, with the trading area of the upper Niger as well as the gold fields of the Niger, controlled even more precious territory than Ghana did. Mali also had strong Muslim political and merchant classes that interacted well with North African Muslim traders. This combination of strategic control of key economic resources and established trading relationships brought astronomical wealth to the empire. **Mansa Kankan Musa**, who ruled Mali from 1312 to 1337, took so much gold with him on a pilgrimage to Mecca in 1324 that the value of gold in Cairo was reduced for years to come.

Mansa Kankan Musa's rule illustrates both Mali's wealth and the extent to which Islam permeated all aspects of administrative life, from law to military systems. Upon return from his pilgrimage, Musa sponsored the building of schools in many of the cities of the empire, and his successors ran a government that was praised for its effectiveness. One of the reasons historians know so much about Mali is because of the journals of **Ibn Battuta** (1304–1369), a Muslim scholar from Morocco. He journeyed to Mecca to complete the hajj and went on to explore the Muslim world in the Middle East, Africa, and Asia, traveling 75,000 miles (120,000 kilometers) in twenty-nine years. His insights as the most traveled man of his time are invaluable in describing the Muslim world. When Ibn Battuta visited Mali, he credited the leadership of Mansa Suleiman, Mansa Kankan Musa's successor, with the peace that permeated all the territories of the empire.

Unfortunately that peace did not last. The rule of Suleiman's successors opened the way for revolt by the various peoples who resented the domination of the Malinke. The Tuareg people took back the great city of Timbuktu in 1433, and by 1500, Mali was reduced to the home territory of the Malinke.

The spread of Islam continued into central Africa despite the end of Mali. For example, the leaders of the Hausa city-states in central Sudan converted and made Islam their official religion. Kanem-Bornu, also in central Sudan, was another huge empire that continued to spread Islam in the late fifteenth century.

AP® Tip

The Islamic world expanded into the continents of Europe, Asia, and Africa during the period 600–1450. The ability to compare the spread of Islam and the nature of Islam on various continents is an important issue for AP® World History and the exam. How could you analyze the similarities and differences in the cultures that spanned the Islamic world?

AFRICA AND INDIAN OCEAN TRADE

Between 1200 and 1500, the Indian Ocean trade network was the richest of the maritime trading routes. Much of this growth was spurred by the development of wealthy states in Europe, Asia, and Africa at the time. In addition, the Indian Ocean trade network grew in prominence with the end of the Mongol Empire. Once Mongol control was gone, and with it the guarantee of a smooth overland flow of goods, the maritime trade routes became more important. The Indian Ocean trade network connected Africa, Europe, Asia, and the Middle East in layers of communication that brought a large part of the world together on an unprecedented scale, and it fostered the spread of Islam.

Africa played a major role in this trade network. By 1500, between thirty and forty city-states—among them Kilwa, Mombasa, and Mogadishu—grew up along the east coast thanks to Indian Ocean trade. Ibn Battuta visited Kilwa and marveled at its beauty as well as the devotion to Islam. This thriving trade coast became known as the **Swahili Coast**; Arabs and Persians called the people there "Swahili" after the Arabic *sawahil al-sudan*, which means "shores of the blacks." This name is a great example of the interaction among different peoples that occurred along the Indian Ocean basin.

Cities on the Swahili Coast prospered in part because of the trade in gold, which came from farther inland, in southern portions of the continent. A state known as **Great Zimbabwe**, after the name of the capital city, relied on farming and cattle herding, but it also had considerable control of the gold trade south of the Zambezi River. Trade, first regional and then as part of the larger Indian Ocean trade network, brought real economic prosperity to Great Zimbabwe. Zimbabwe is known for massive stone structures built for the elite and to enclose the king's court. Zimbabwe declined in the fifteenth century.

SOCIAL AND CULTURAL CHANGE IN AFRICA FROM 1200 TO 1500

Although Islamic beliefs had a significant impact on society and culture in Africa, local cultures continued to thrive and sustain the diversity of dynamic sub-Saharan Africa. Local cultures also influenced the way outside religions were adapted in various regions and states. For example, mosques in Africa were based on Middle Eastern designs but used materials local to the region; a mosque in West Africa did not look like a mosque on the Swahili Coast. Christian churches also reflected diverse building styles. Mosques and churches were both houses of worship and centers of education. The spread of Islam in sub-Saharan Africa went hand in hand with an increase in literacy, first in Arabic and then in local languages written in Arabic characters. Islamic scholarship flourished in sub-Saharan Africa. In the West African city of **Timbuktu**, learning was so valued that books were among the hottest trading commodities.

With the increase in wealth came the growth of elite classes—and the demand for those to serve the elites. Mali, Bornu, and Ethiopia all participated in selling and transporting slaves across Africa and into the Middle East, India, and even China. It is estimated that some 2.5 million Africans crossed the Sahara and Red Sea as slaves between 1200 and 1500. The slavery that these Africans experienced was different from the slavery experienced under Europeans in later centuries. These slaves had some opportunities to advance. Although some slaves were used for jobs like mining, most were trained to specialize in a service. As a result, some slaves became powerful and wealthy because of their military ability or other skills—for example, a slave general took power in the Songhai Empire, which succeeded the Mali Empire. Female slaves were household servants or concubines, and some male slaves became eunuchs.

Women in tropical Africa had many roles. They farmed; transported food, water, and other materials needed for cooking; made clay vessels for household purposes; and bought and sold food and crafts at markets. The impact of Islam on women in sub-Saharan Africa varied, reflecting the influence of local traditions and customs. Traveling in Mali, Ibn Battuta was startled to see that women did not completely cover their bodies and veil their faces when in public and interacted with men who were not their husbands or family members.

AP® Tip

The role of the trade networks in the period of 600–1450 was crucial in establishing a thriving, multifaceted Islamic world while allowing for the preservation of local cultures. Understanding the dynamics of the exchange of goods and ideas along these cross-regional trade routes is key to understanding this period.

Content Review Questions

We arrived at the capital, Fas [Fez], God Most High Guard it. There I said farewell to our master, God strengthen him, and set out on a journey to the country of the blacks. I reached the city of Sijilmasa, a very beautiful city. After twenty-five days we reached Taghaza. It is a village with no attractions. A strange thing about it is that its houses and mosque are built of blocks of salt and roofed with camel skins. There are no trees, only sand in which is a salt mine. They dig the ground and thick slaves are found in it. A camel carries two slabs.

From *The Travels of Ibn Battuta, A.D. 1325–1354*

The Human Record: Sources of Global History, 8th edition, volume 1, p. 347.

1. Which of the following explorers can best be compared to Ibn Battuta?
   (A) Vasco da Gama
   (B) Marco Polo
   (C) Zheng He
   (D) Faxian

2. Ibn Battuta describes northern cities located on which of the following trade networks?
   (A) The Mediterranean Sea
   (B) Indian Ocean basin
   (C) Silk Roads
   (D) Trans-Saharan routes

3. Which of the following had the least impact on the events described in the passage?
   (A) The collapse of imperial states in the wake of the expansion of the Mongol Khanates
   (B) The domestication of the camel and creation of new related technology like camel saddles
   (C) The expansion of Islam due to the activities of merchants and missionaries
   (D) The rise of the Islamic gunpowder empires including the Ottoman Sultanate

In the lands around the Indian Ocean, the rainy and dry seasons reflect the influence of alternating winds known as monsoons. A gigantic high-pressure zone over the Himalaya Mountains that peaks from December to March produces southern Asia's dry season by forcing strong ocean winds in the western Indian Ocean to blow toward southward and westward toward Africa. This is the northeast monsoon. Between April and August, a low-pressure zone over India reverses the process by drawing moist oceanic air from the south and west to form the southwest monsoon. This brings southern Asia the heavy rains of its wet season, usually called the monsoon season.

Bulliet et al., *The Earth and Its Peoples*, 7th edition, Boston: Cengage Learning, 2018, p. 350.

4. How did human adaptation to the environmental patterns described in the passage impact the development of Eastern Africa during the period 600–1450?
   (A) Eastern Africa became a major trade center on the Indian Ocean trade route.
   (B) East Africa remained sparsely populated due to difficulties travelling to and from the region.
   (C) East Africa developed a homogenous culture because they remained cut off from major avenues of cultural interaction.
   (D) East Africa became a center of maritime innovation.

5. Which of the following is an accurate comparison between the eastern and western regions of Africa during the period 600–1450?
   (A) Both regions rejected their African cultural heritage in favor of new technology and ideas spread by Asian traders.
   (B) Islam spread to both regions mostly due to the activities of merchants.
   (C) Both regions developed centralized imperial governments to regulate and protect merchants.
   (D) In addition to participating in trade routes connecting to the exterior of Africa, both also traded regularly with each other through the interior of Africa.

6. Which of the following emerged in East Africa as a result of the migrations and commercial contacts made possible by the environmental conditions described in the passage?
   (A) The domestication of the camel for travel through the interior of Africa
   (B) The emergence of the new Swahili language
   (C) De-urbanization as people preferred temporary structures to permanent ones due to the destruction caused by coastal storms
   (D) A sense of curiosity about science and nature that led to state-sponsored voyages of exploration and scientific discovery

Answers

1. ANSWER: B. During the period 600–1450, trade routes expanded and more people travelled these routes to study and record what they found along the way. Both Ibn Battuta and Marco Polo fit this trend. Marco Polo went to China and kept a travel journal of his experiences in the Yuan Kingdom (*The Earth and Its Peoples*, 6th ed., pp. 327, 329, 380, and 387– 389/7th ed., pp. 327–329, 372–374; History Reasoning Skill—Comparison; Learning Objectives CUL-3,6; Key Concept 3.1.III.C).

2. ANSWER: D. Fez as well as the other cities mentioned are located along the northwestern edge of the Sahara Desert. All are therefore part of the trans-Saharan routes. In addition, Battuta references some of the major products traded on this route (salt) as well as the method of travel used in the Saharan Desert (camels) (*The Earth and Its Peoples*, 6th ed., pp. 380, 385, 387–389, and 392 /7th ed., pp. 372–374, 381; History Disciplinary Practice—Analyzing Historical Evidence; Learning Objectives ENV-2,3,5; Key Concept 3.1.II.A).

3. ANSWER: D. Ibn Battuta's travels occur before the height of the gunpowder Empires. While the Mongols had limited impact in North Africa, the decline of the Mongols influenced Ibn Battuta's ability and decision to travel in the first place. Camels and the spread of Islam both had a strong influence on Ibn Battuta's travels. (*The Earth and Its Peoples*, 6th ed., pp. 379 and 382 /7th ed., pp. 323, 372–374; History Disciplinary Practice—Analyzing Historical Evidence; Learning Objectives CUL-5, SB-1; Key Concept 2.2.III.A).

4. ANSWER: A. The passage describes the monsoon patterns. Once travelers learned these patterns, trade on the Indian Ocean became easier. This increased the volume of trade and size of the trade route. The trade route grew to more regularly include East Africa (*The Earth and Its Peoples*, 6th ed., pp. 377–380/7th ed., pp. 370, 378–380; History Reasoning Skill—Contextualization; Learning Objectives ENV-2,3,5; Key Concept 3.1.I.A).

5. ANSWER: B. Merchants on the trans-Saharan routes brought Islam to West Africa. Merchants on the Indian Ocean route brought Islam to the Swahili Coast of East Africa (*The Earth and Its Peoples*, 6th ed., pp. 377–382/7th ed., pp. 372–374; History Reasoning Skill—Comparison; Learning Objectives ENV-2,3,5, CUL-3; Key Concept 3.1.I.A).

6. ANSWER: C. Bantu language groups were present in East Africa as the region became more connected to the Indian Ocean trade, but there was no written language. Merchants needed a system to tabulate economic data. Thus the Arabic script combined with the existing Bantu languages to create the Swahili language, after which the region is named (*The Earth and Its Peoples*, 6th ed., pp. 380–383 /7th ed., pp. 380–381; Reasoning Skill—Causation; Learning Objectives ENV-2,3,5; Key Concept 3.1.I.A).

People

Rumi
1207 CE to 1273 CE
Persian Sufi mystic/Poet

Ibn Battuta
1304 CE - 1369 CE
Moroccan Islamic
Traveler

Ibn Khaldun
1332 CE - 1406 CE
Arab Historian/Philosopher

A'ishah Bint Yusuf Al-Bauniyah
c. 1465 CE - 1517 CE
Female Sufi Writer / Poet

12

THE MIDDLE EAST:
C. 600 C.E. TO C. 1450 C.E.

KEY CONCEPTS

- The world of Islam represents peoples of different ethnicities, cultures, and languages throughout the Middle East, Africa, Asia, and parts of Europe who were unified through the religion of Islam while still maintaining regional diversity.
- The Islamic world made tremendous contributions to art, science, and technology that would have a huge impact on cultural and economic developments in Asia, Africa, and Europe.
- The Mongols had a significant impact on the spread of Islam and also preserved and built upon Islamic intellectual discoveries.
- The Mongols affected the Middle East in both positive and negative ways in terms of social, political, and economic stability.

KEY TERMS

- Abbasid Caliphate
- bubonic plague
- caliphate   *expansion & effects of the control*
- Five Pillars
- hajj
- Il-khan
- Islam
- mamluks
- Mongols
- Ottomans
- Quran
- Seljuk Turks

196

- Shari'a
- Shi'ite
- Sufism
- Sunni
- ulama
- Umayyad Caliphate
- umma

Handwritten notes:

Trans saharan Trade = across the Sahara to reach sub-Saharan Africa from the North African coast, Eur-Levant

Karavanseral = roadside inn where travelers could rest and recover from the days journey

Diaspora = scattered population whose origin lies in a seperate geo. loc.

Dar House of Wisdom = a major Abbasid public academy and intellectual center in Baghdad or to a large private library belonging to the Abbasid Caliphs during the Islamic Golden Age.

Sultanate = position with several historic meanings including "strength", "authority", "rulership", & "power".

Islam is discussed in depth in *The Earth and Its Peoples*, 6th edition, Chapter 9 and in the 7th edition, Chapter 10. The Crusades are discussed in Chapter 10 of the 6th edition and in Chapter 11 of the 7th edition; the Mongols are discussed in Chapter 12 of the 6th edition and in Chapter 13 of the 7th edition; the Ottoman Turks are discussed in Chapter 19 of the 6th edition and Chapter 20 of the 7th edition.

THE ORIGINS OF ISLAM

Islam, the youngest of the monotheistic religions, began on the Arabian peninsula. The founding prophet of the faith, Muhammad, was born in the trading town of Mecca in 570. Mecca was important in pre-Islamic history not only as an economic center but also as a holy site. Pilgrims went to Mecca to visit the Ka'ba, a shrine believed to have been built by the patriarch Abraham. Muhammad was raised as an orphan by his uncle, chief of his clan, and grew up to be a successful trading merchant. About 610, Muhammad began to meditate and had visions in which he came to believe that God—Allah, in Arabic—was revealing himself. Sharing his revelations, he began to gather a following that embraced his belief that there is only one true god, who was responsible for all of creation, and that people must submit to the authority of God. The word *Islam* means submission; a Muslim is one who submits to the will of Allah.

AP® Tip

The basic tenets of the Muslim faith, called the Five Pillars of Islam, are based on the practices of Muhammad and affirmed by the first caliph, Abu Bakr. The **Five Pillars** are

- the statement of faith in one God and Muhammad as his messenger,
- prayer five times a day,
- fasting during Ramadan,
- charity through giving to the poor, and
- completion of a pilgrimage to Mecca, known in Arabic as the hajj.

The tribal leaders in Mecca came to fear that Muhammad's belief in one god threatened their power and security as well as the polytheistic traditions

---

AP® is a trademark registered by the College Board, which is not affiliated with, and does not endorse, this product.

of their communities. Muhammad was therefore forced to flee to Medina in 622, a journey that is known as the Hijra, meaning the migration or flight of Muhammad from Mecca to Medina. This date, considered to be the beginning of the Islamic faith, marks the start of the Muslim calendar. It was in Medina that the Islamic community, or **umma**, solidified and ultimately was able to win over Mecca in 630. After completing a pilgrimage to the Ka'ba, a tradition that lives on as the **hajj**, Muhammad returned to Medina to manage both the political and religious affairs of this reinvigorated city-state, until his death two years later, in 632.

Muhammad's death immediately raised the question of who would be Muhammad's successor, or caliph, which provoked the first major split in the Islamic umma. This split ultimately divided Muslims into two major sects, the Sunnis and the Shi'ites. **Shi'ite** Muslims believe that succession should be traced through the bloodline of Muhammad; therefore, Muhammad's cousin Ali should have been the caliph and only Ali's descendants should be imams, or religious leaders of the Muslim community as a whole. To Shi'ites, the caliph is more of a secular leader. **Sunni** Muslims, believing that the caliph is to be chosen by the community, regard the first three caliphs who succeeded Muhammad as properly selected. Sunnis see the caliph as a secular and religious leader; therefore, the caliph is an imam as well. While the concept of the **caliphate** was a unifying factor, in reality the caliphate was quite fragmented by the late ninth century.

ISLAMIC CALIPHATES

One of the first tasks of Abu Bakr, the first caliph, was to collect and organize Muhammad's revelations into a book. Muslims, like Jews and Christians, are considered to be people of the book; the Muslim holy book is the **Quran**. Unlike the Hebrew and Christian Bibles, the Quran is believed by Muslims to be the literal words of God as given to Muhammad, not a collection of writings by many authors over a long period. The Quran was revealed in Arabic, is written in Arabic, and is to be read in Arabic. As the Muslim world grew to non-Arabic-speaking regions, the need to read the Quran in Arabic encouraged the growth of schools to teach the language and to interpret the Quran. Out of this holy book and the traditions of Muhammad slowly came Muslim law, **Shari'a** in Arabic, as well as the practices and traditions that are essential to the religion.

As the dominant sect, Sunni Muslims established the **Umayyad Caliphate** in 661, with its capital in Damascus, Syria. The peoples living under the control of the Umayyad caliph were predominately Arab. By 732 Arab Muslims had conquered Syria, Palestine, and North Africa; they gained control of a part of southern Spain—referred to as al-Andalus—in the early eighth century. Under Muslim rule, Spanish cities like Seville and Cordoba flourished as centers of government, where Muslims, Christians, and Jews created a unique culture known for its literature, art, architecture, and agricultural accomplishments.

After a period of increasing conflict, the **Abbasid Caliphate** was established in 750 and ruled until 1258 from its capital in Baghdad. Effective rule over such a large empire proved challenging for the Abbasids, particularly in terms of holding territory. The empire also became more diverse as more non-Arabs converted to Islam. Baghdad, the capital, became a thriving center for learning, culture, and technological advancements despite the political and territorial fragmentation of the ninth century and, later, the Crusades. Islam continued to spread despite territorial loss. Scholars from all over Eurasia came to Baghdad to learn about Islam and exchange information. Thanks to the transmission of papermaking from China, literature and books were much more available in the Middle East than in Europe. Unlike Christianity at this time, in particular the Catholic Church, Islam looked to many different sources for knowledge. Much of the great knowledge of antiquity, including the Greek classics, which would prove so important for the European Renaissance, as well as works from Persia and India, had been copied into Arabic, allowing the ideas to be shared across the Muslim world. Many of the works from the Hellenistic past helped Muslims to excel in science and technology. Astronomical observations, medicinal studies, and mathematics from the Greek past were reexamined, and Muslim scholars built on these studies.

Cities like Baghdad and Cordoba were essential for the Muslim empire, both as ways of spreading the faith and as governing centers. New converts, many of whom were not Arab, could count on the cities as places to learn the language and traditions of their new faith free of discrimination. The mosque, the Muslim house of worship, became a central architectural landmark that newcomers of the faith could recognize because of its distinctive features.

One social group that rose in cities was the **ulama**, an Arabic word for people with religious knowledge. As the Muslim empire grew in cultural diversity under the Abbasid Caliphate, the ulama sought to preserve central teachings and tenets of the faith. Two examples, both originating with Persians, are the madrasa, or religious college, and **Sufi** brotherhoods, mystic religious groups, widespread in the Muslim world, which began to form in the early days of Islam.

Cities were also essential as places of trade. Since the time of the Umayyad Caliphate, a coinage system allowed for both local and long-distance trade that linked the more isolated portions of the Islamic empire and encouraged the burgeoning textile industry as well as other crafts. The Islamic world stood at the western end of the Silk Road, the most important overland trade route of the period 600–1450.

AP® Tip

Women in the Islamic world had greater legal freedoms than Jewish or Christian women in post-classic times. Although seclusion of women and veiling are practices that are believed by many to have originated with Islam, they actually date to Byzantine and Sassanid times and later came to be a part of the Islamic tradition. Although Muslim women were not considered the equals of men, which was also true in the Byzantine Empire and western Europe, they were influential in family life; could own and inherit property; divorce; remarry; and testify in court.

The Islamic faith spread through Muslim merchants who traveled along the Silk Road, allowing the religion to spread from Spain to China, at the eastern end of the Silk Road.

By the middle of the ninth century, several provinces had broken away and established their own caliphates, such as the Fatimid caliphate in Egypt. Another example was the Samanid caliphate, a Persian dynasty that brought many Persian influences to the art and literature of the Islamic world. Because of territorial fragmentation, the Abbasid leaders came to rely on the **mamluks**, Turkish slaves from central Asia with exceptional skill in warfare. They became a powerful military presence in the Middle East during Islamic rule, and by the eleventh century, Turkish groups had significantly diminished the territory and political power of the Abbasid Caliphate. For example, in the early eleventh century the **Seljuk Turks** created a Turkish Muslim state that controlled territory from Baghdad up through Syria and into Anatolia and Byzantine areas. Christians viewed the Seljuk Turks as a tremendous threat, and they set out to take the Holy Land back from Turkish Muslims.

The Crusades

The Crusades were a series of battles initiated by one monotheistic faith, Christianity, against another monotheistic faith, Islam. Study of the Crusades offers a wealth of fascinating ideas and details, but for AP® students, the causes of the Crusades and their impact are of fundamental importance. The causes are discussed later, but the impact of the Crusades on the Middle East is discussed here.

By the eleventh century, Muslim leaders were in control of many cities that were considered sacred by Christians, among them Jerusalem, Antioch, and Alexandria. Christians had been allowed to make pilgrimage to these places, but as Muslims continued to eat away at the Byzantine Empire and conquer more territory deemed precious to Christendom, a campaign against the Muslims began to form in both western Europe and the Byzantine Empire.

Jerusalem, a city of particular significance to Christians, Muslims, and Jews, was in the hands of the Seljuk Turks, who at the time of the First Crusade were going through a period of internal dispute. Even though Christian crusaders had wrested Jerusalem from the Seljuk Turks in 1099, Islamic military forces under the dynamic leader Saladin were able to take back the city in 1187. The Islamic world in the Middle East continued to thrive despite the Crusaders' unsuccessful attempt to take land permanently, and the Crusades had very little long-term effects on Muslim territory.

The greatest impact of the Crusades was therefore not on the Muslims themselves. Instead, European life, which was far less sophisticated than Muslims', was dramatically improved. The incredible amount of information, ideas, goods, and resources that the Crusaders were exposed to in their encounter with the Muslim world was remarkable. Over time, the Crusaders brought back paper and sugar, and they learned how to make many of the goods they previously could only import. The establishment of trading ports in Italian cities like Venice and Genoa helped open Europe to the diverse Muslim world of the Middle East. Demand for goods from the Middle East stimulated the markets of late medieval Europe and also encouraged trade between the Muslim world, western Europe, and the Byzantine Empire. Muslims also made enormous intellectual contributions to Europe in two ways: their Arabic translations of works by ancient Greek scientists and philosophers such as Aristotle allowed for the restoration of ideas that had long been buried during the Middle Ages. Second, Arabs and Persians, building on the work of the ancient philosophers, had added their own insights to give rise to new and innovative ideas. This double gift of knowledge by the Muslim world was essential in laying the groundwork for the Renaissance.

AP® Tip

Women in the Islamic world had greater legal freedoms than Jewish or Christian women in post-classic times. Although seclusion of women and veiling are practices that are believed by many to have originated with Islam, they actually date to Byzantine and Sassanid times and later came to be a part of the Islamic tradition. Although Muslim women were not considered the equals of men, which was also true in the Byzantine Empire and western Europe, they were influential in family life; could own and inherit property; divorce; remarry; and testify in court.

THE MONGOLS IN THE MIDDLE EAST

Migrating from the Central Asian steppes as a nomadic group, the **Mongols** were able to do what Europeans had failed to in the Crusades: they shattered what had once been the heart of the Muslim empire. The weakened and fragmented Abbasid Caliphate was destroyed when Baghdad was sacked in 1258. This event appalled the Islamic world, which did not expect a catastrophe of this magnitude. Rather than destroy all that Islam had contributed to the world, however, the Mongols became ardent patrons of Islamic culture, including art, literature, and architecture. Many of the Mongol leaders, known as khans, eventually converted to Islam and came to appreciate the urban infrastructure of the Islamic world. Still, tensions between Mongols and Muslims continued, much of it because of differences in cultural practices.

The Mongols set up four khanates in Eurasia. The **Il-khan** Empire in the Middle East was established in 1256 by the grandson of Genghis. Mongol nobles were placed in positions of power. Borrowing from an earlier Middle Eastern economic practice, the Mongols used tax farming—giving out private contracts to merchants to collect taxes by whatever means served them best. To foster the collection of as much money as possible, these merchants were allowed to keep any money above what was due to the government. Although this method was initially successful, tax farming coupled with an experiment using paper money from China eventually brought about an economic depression that outlived the Il-khan Empire.

Baghad House

The Islamic world had served as a major conduit for ideas and goods in its position at the western end of the Silk Road, and that continued under Mongol rule. Fine products from the East such as silk and porcelain flowed into the Middle East and from there to Europe. Scholars, merchants, and missionaries traveled to the courts of the Mongols and recorded what they saw there. In addition, scholars such as Rashid al-Din were patronized by the Il-khans and wrote histories describing the greatness of the world controlled by the Mongols as well as histories of such faraway places as China and Europe. The Mongols were also fascinated by the scientific and mathematical innovations of the Muslim world. Algebra and trigonometry, as well as astronomical work that would one day be used by Europeans such as Copernicus, were all preserved and supplemented under both the Il-khans and their successors, the Timurids. This knowledge spread across the world of the Mongols and Turks and eventually through translation reached Europe. In addition, trade also brought disease, specifically the **bubonic plague**, which made its way through the Middle East and into Europe during Mongol rule. Far more than any attack or conquest, the plague would be the Mongols' most devastating impact.

By the fourteenth century, the Middle East was in the control of Turkish sultans and the Mongol khans. The Seljuk Turks still had a small kingdom that stood between the Byzantine Empire and the Mongols. The Mamluk Sultanate controlled Egypt and had successfully resisted a Mongol takeover to become a major player in shifting alliances with various khans to keep both Il-khan power at bay and the Crusaders from gaining any ground. The Il-khan Empire, which controlled territory from Syria to the Indus River, gave way to the Timurid Empire when the Central Asian Turkic leader Timur rose to take much of the Middle East before his death in 1405.

The Timurid Empire was short-lived. The **Ottoman** Empire would be the next great Turkish presence in the Middle East. Like the Seljuk Turks and the mamluks, the Ottomans were exceptionally skilled in warfare and conquest. As Mongol power began to decline, the Ottomans tightened their political organization and began their political ascent, establishing Turkic principalities in western Anatolia. Despite a defeat by Timur in 1402, the Ottoman sultans would take over the Byzantine Empire in 1453 and create a Muslim empire that would endure until the twentieth century.

Content Review Questions

1. Which of the following was a significant difference between the beliefs of the people in the image and the beliefs of earlier communities of Muslims?

    (A) Earlier communities focused on reading the Quran and following the Prophet Muhammad's example, while the group pictured also emphasized using ritual to focus on interior spirituality.

    (B) Earlier groups of Muslims believed Muhammad was a prophet, while the group pictured believed he was the son of god.

    (C) Earlier communities of Muslims believed dance and music were useful methods to spread the Islamic religion, while the group pictured believed dance and music should not be celebrated with outsiders.

    (D) Earlier groups mostly spread the religion through military conquest, while the group pictured also used ritual and ceremony.

2. How did the pictured group most contribute to the spread of Islam?
 (A) By invading neighboring states
 (B) Through the use of missionaries
 (C) With diasporic merchant communities
 (D) By controlling major centers of printing

3. How does the image differ from most forms of Islamic art?
 (A) The image includes color, while most forms of Islamic art used black calligraphy on a white background.
 (B) The image includes people, while most forms of Islamic art used geometric shapes and script.
 (C) The image includes Arabic script, while most Islamic art used Turkish.
 (D) The image is not signed by an artist, while most Islamic art is signed by the artist as a celebration of his individuality.

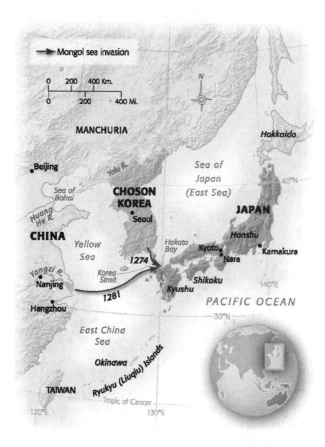

4. In addition to those indicated on the map, which of the following was NOT conquered by the Mongols?
 (A) Japan
 (B) Song China
 (C) The territory bordering China to the North
 (D) Korea

5. Which of the following was a short-term effect of the creation of the Mongol states shown in the map?
   (A) Rapid urbanization into centers of Mongol culture
   (B) An increase in the volume of long-distance commerce due to Mongol protection provided for trade routes
   (C) Population growth due to Mongol rejection of traditional monogamous marriages
   (D) A decline in the number of people practicing Islam as people converted to Mongol polytheism for political favors

6. Which of the following was NOT a long-term effect of the creation of the Mongol states shown in the map?
   (A) A negative demographic impact resulting from the spread of disease from east Asia to west Asia and Europe
   (B) The spread of Islam from its heartland in the Middle East to the Indian Ocean region
   (C) The widespread adoption of firearms by states in the Middle East and Western Europe
   (D) Environmental degradation caused by the destruction of farmland and forests

Answers

1. ANSWER: A. The image shows a Sufi ritual. Sufis shared most beliefs and practices with other communities of Muslims including reading the Quran and following the example set by Muhammad. However, Sufis also believed dancing, music, trance, and other rituals were also an important part of their religious practice (*The Earth and Its Peoples*, 6th ed., pp. 264–266 and p. 391/7th ed., pp. 265–266. ; History Reasoning Skill—Comparison; Learning Objectives CUL-1,2,5; Key Concept 3.1.III.A).

2. ANSWER: B. Sufis spread their ideas throughout Asia and East Africa through the use of missionaries. The Sufis did not control an army to carry out invasions, nor did they control major urban centers that would house early versions of printing. While they did spread out from their origin, they were more often wandering mystics and scholars than merchants (*The Earth and Its Peoples*, 6th ed., pp. 264–266 and p. 391/7th ed., pp. 265–266; History Reasoning Skill—Causation; Learning Objectives CUL-1,2,5; Key Concept 3.1.III.A).

3. ANSWER: B. Most forms of Islamic art didn't allow the use of people, instead preferring calligraphy and geometric design. However, the image shows a blending between Islamic and Persian traditions, and Persian art typically included people (*The Earth and Its Peoples*, 6th ed., pp. 258–264/7th ed., pp. 261–265; History Reasoning Skill—Comparison; Learning Objectives CUL-1,2,5; Key Concept 3.1.III.A).

4. ANSWER: A. While the Mongols attempted to conquer Japan, they ultimately failed in part due to the fact that Japan is an island, and in part due to some disorganization. The Mongols conquered Song China to set up the Yuan Dynasty, launched their intended invasion of Japan from Korea, and started from the area north of China (*The Earth and Its Peoples*, 6th ed., p. 327/7th ed., p. 323; History Disciplinary Practice—Analyzing Historical Evidence; Learning Objectives SB-1,3,4; Key Concept 3.2.I.B).

5. ANSWER: B. The Mongols maintained and protected trade routes, which also served as ways to send messages across their vast empire. They set up rest stations for merchants and messengers and places to switch out for fresh horses for their messengers. Mongol law also protected merchants with strict punishments for thieves (*The Earth and Its Peoples*, 6th ed., pp. 327–330/7th ed., pp. 323–326; History Reasoning Skill—Causation; Learning Objectives ECON-2; Key Concept 3.1.I.E).

6. ANSWER: B. By the time the Mongols established the Khanates shown in the map, Islam had already spread throughout the Indian Ocean due to the travels of Middle Eastern merchants. Ibn Battuta, travelling shortly after the period shown on the map, describes flourishing, established, Islamic communities throughout Southeast Asia (*The Earth and Its Peoples*, 6th ed., pp. 324–330/7th ed., pp. 319–322; History Reasoning Skill—Contextualization; Learning Objectives CUL-3; Key Concept 3.1.I.E).

People

Marco Polo
1254 CE - 1324 CE
Italian Traveler

Ibn Battuta
1304 CE - 1369 CE
Moroccan Islamic
Traveler

Tamerlane
1336 CE - 1405 CE
Turco - Mongol
Conqueror

Zhenghe
1371 CE - 1435 CE
Chinese Islamic
Navigator

13

ASIA: C. 600 C.E. TO C. 1450 C.E.

KEY CONCEPTS

- During the period 600–1450, China rose as the most influential state in East Asia in terms of economic and political dominance.
- Japan, Korea, and Vietnam accepted some aspects of Chinese culture and rejected others, carving out their own unique cultural and political identities.
- The impact of Mongol rule in Central, East, and Southeast Asia varied, depending on whether the Mongols had direct or peripheral control of a given area. Mongol presence in Asia had long-lasting consequences on the development of East Asia in particular.
- The Silk Road, an overland trade route, and the Indian Ocean trade network were the dominant trading networks of the period 600–1450 and allowed for important cultural and economic interactions among Africa, the Middle East, Europe, and Asia.
- Mahayana Buddhism exerted significant social, cultural, and political influence in China, Japan, Korea, and Vietnam during this period.
- While India experienced great political and religious turmoil as the Muslim Delhi Sultanate came to power, it also experienced economic prosperity because of its central location in the Indian Ocean trade network.

KEY TERMS

- bubonic plague
- Delhi Sultanate
- dhow
- footbinding
- Grand Canal

Sultanate = position   Urdu = Persianized standard register   Zhenghe = Chinese mariner

Angkor Wat = Buddest temple   Tamerlane = TMP Conqueror   Maharaja = Sanskrit title for "great ruler"

Qilin = mythical hooved chimerical creature   Battle of Bach Dang = one of the greatest victories in Vietnamese military history.

207

People

- Jagadai Khanate
- junk
- Kamakura Shogunate
- Koryo
- Malacca
- movable type
- neo-Confucianism
- nomadism
- tributary system
- tribute state
- Yuan Empire

Asia is discussed in depth in *The Earth and Its Peoples*, 6th edition, Chapters 11, 12, and 14, and 7th edition, Chapters 12, 13, and 15.

CHINA

After a three-hundred-year period of disunity following the collapse of the Han dynasty in 220 C.E., the Sui family reunited China in a short forty years. The Sui dynasty was short-lived, but it set the stage for China's growth into a powerful society that dominated Asia up through the twentieth century and affected the evolving cultures of Korea, Japan, and Vietnam. The Sui laid the groundwork for many of the practices of the Tang Empire, which would come to power in 618. Under the Sui, Confucianism was reestablished as the philosophy of the state, and the examination system was revived. By the time of the Sui, Mahayana Buddhism had grown to be very influential in China and would be a defining characteristic of the Tang dynasty. The Sui placed their capital in Chang'an and built several canals to link the capital to the coast of southern China. The most important, the **Grand Canal**, linked the Yellow and Yangzi Rivers and would be a key part of the Tang's economic success.

THE TANG EMPIRE: 618–907

The Li family, whose roots were both Turkish and Chinese, established the Tang Empire in 618. The Tang established a large empire, giving a great deal of power to local nobility in order to ensure control. They expanded westward into Central Asia until Muslim Arabs and Turks stopped their advance. The Tang had ethnic ties to the areas of Central Asia where Buddhism had proved politically useful, and as they extended their empire into areas where Buddhism was popular among people of all classes, they continued to use it as a political tool. For this reason, Tang princes rewarded Buddhist monasteries that supported their rule with monetary gifts, tax exemptions, and land grants. The Tang also reinstituted the **tributary system**, first used by the Han dynasty, by which independent states gave gifts to the Chinese emperor. Both Japan and Korea paid tribute to the Tang and in doing so acknowledged China's regional power.

The Tang Empire quickly attracted people from all over Asia, who flocked especially to the Tang capital at Chang'an, a trading center, where Muslims, Christians, and Buddhists could all be found worshiping. With more than one million people in the city and its suburbs, Chang'an was a

Handwritten annotations:

East Asia 1200–1450 CE

neo-Confucianism

Song Dynasty = imperial dynasty of China

Champa Rice = quick maturing, drought resistant rice

Khanates = political entity ruled by khanor khagan

Pax Mongolica = historiographical term

Sinification = process whereby ___ influence culture & position

Shogunate = position

Shinto = religion from Japan

Bushido = Japanese collective term for honor

Goryeo = Korean kingdom founded in 918

People
1. Minamoto Yoritomo 1147 CE – 1199 CE 1st Shogun
2. Genghis Khan 1162 CE to 1227 CE Founder = Mongol Empire
3. Kublai Khan 1215 CE – 1294 CE Founder of Yuan Dynasty
4. Marco Polo 1254 CE – 1324 CE Italian Traveler
5. Ibn Battuta 1304 CE – 1369 CE Moroccan Islamic
6. Zhenghe 1371 CE – 1435 CE Chinese Islamic Navig___

center for cultural exchange in the arts, textiles, and music. This cultural exchange was possible in part because the Tang, with control of the coast of southern China, participated in Indian Ocean trade. Chinese maritime technology included the compass and the ability to make oceangoing vessels that could transport all kinds of goods up through the Grand Canal. The Chinese also began to master new kinds of skills, such as cotton production, and increasing competition with the textile industry in western Asia spurred them to increase their expertise in silk production.

In the eighth century, the power of the Tang began to be threatened by rival states, including the Uighur and Tibetan Empires. These external threats, combined with internal rebellion and overexpansion, signaled the decline and eventual destruction of the Tang Empire. Buddhism, because it had come to China from India, became a scapegoat for many of the problems the Tang faced. Buddhist monasteries were accused of being a foreign evil that drained money from the state because they were tax exempt. Monasteries were also blamed for causing the breakdown of the family because elite sons and daughters were entering monasteries rather than getting married and producing heirs.

THE SONG EMPIRE: 960–1279

After the fall of the Tang dynasty, three smaller empires controlled territory in China. The Song Empire, based in central China, had a large army but never grew as large as the Tang, primarily because of the strength of the rival Tanggut and Liao Empires in northern China. These three empires had different religious and ethnic identities and competed for resources. The Song fought against these "barbarians" in the north and focused on advancing their maritime expertise in order to build relationships with other states by sea. The Jin, who defeated the Liao in 1115, captured the Song emperor two years later in the capital city of Kaifeng and forced the Song south of the Yellow River, where they established a new capital at Hangzhou. From this point on, historians refer to the Song Empire as the Southern Song.

Although never as large as the Tang, the Song made outstanding scientific and technological contributions by building on the mathematical and engineering skills that had come to the far-flung Tang Empire. For example, they used their knowledge of astronomy to build a mechanical celestial clock and to improve the compass and the junk, the main Chinese seafaring ship. The **junk** navigated the oceans with ease and had special features, such as watertight compartments that allowed it to preserve all kinds of goods. Military technologies were also essential because the Song military commanded more than one million men. Improvements in iron and steel production and experiments with gunpowder produced innovative and effective weapons.

The Song also had many economic accomplishments. Paper money, possibly thanks to printing techniques such as **movable type**, was a tremendous technological contribution that would spread across Asia, into Europe, and beyond. Printing also allowed for the dissemination of agricultural techniques, educational resources, and public-health materials in cities and villages across China, improving production and health conditions in areas by combating malaria and the plague. Another economic tool was credit, which could be used across the region.

Although the religious influence of Buddhism remained strong, Confucianism reemerged as the philosophical and ethical basis for Song society. **Neo-Confucianism**—Confucian ideas that emerged in the Song period and thereafter—reflected Buddhist influence and incorporated new understandings of Confucian teachings. Mastery of the Confucian classics was required under the scholar examination system, and merit-based appointments gave new prominence to the role of the scholar-official in Chinese society. Confucianism's patriarchal tradition, coupled with the backlash against Buddhism dating from the end of the Tang period, meant that expectations for women were closely regulated in China and subsequently in all East Asian states. In China, women did not have property rights or the ability to remarry, and rarely had educational opportunities comparable to those of men. **Footbinding**, a practice unique to China, came to embody the restrictions on women in Song China. Women's feet were tightly wrapped and subsequently broke; when the feet healed, they appeared smaller—and made the woman unable to work. Footbinding became a status symbol among the elite in China.

AP® Tip

The cities of Song China, such as Chang'an, Kaifeng, and Hangzhou, were thriving economic and cultural centers and were among the largest cities in the world at this time. You should be able to make comparisons between these cities and other city centers in the world during this period. For example, the AP® exam could ask you to compare the economic role of cities in China with the economic role of the cities of the Islamic empires or the cities of the Americas.

THE MONGOLS

The Mongols, a **nomadic** group that originated in Central Asia in what is now Mongolia, were self-sufficient pastoralists; families moved quickly, and from the earliest ages, children learned the skills necessary to thrive in the steppes of Central Asia. The Mongols had many traditional practices and beliefs centered on shamanism. A shaman could move between the physical and spiritual worlds and influence events in both worlds. The Mongols often adopted other faiths that spread along the Silk Road, such as Buddhism, Islam, and Christianity, but still maintained their shamanistic traditions. They believed the tribal leader, or khan, and his shamans could speak for the god of the universe, known as Sky or Heaven. The most powerful families could voice their opinions to the khan, and they grew even more powerful through intermarriage and warfare.

Genghis Khan rose to power as the supreme leader of the Mongols, a title known as the Great Khan. In 1206, he set out to conquer Eurasia and force

---

AP® is a trademark registered by the College Board, which is not affiliated with, and does not endorse, this product.

rival kingdoms to pay tribute. By 1215, he had captured Beijing, then the capital of the Jin Empire. By 1221, he had control of Persia, and his first attacks on Russia had begun. Genghis Khan died in 1227, but conquest of the north of China continued with his son, the Great Khan Ögödei. By 1234, the Mongols were positioned to take the Southern Song Empire in China. The Middle East came under Mongol control in 1258 with the sacking of Baghdad, the capital of the Abbasid Caliphate.

What made the Mongols able to conquer Eurasia relatively quickly? Much of their success was a result of the military techniques these steppe nomads had practiced for centuries. Mongol expertise in horsemanship and use of the Central Asian bow, which could shoot one-third farther than the bows of their enemies could, made them nearly unstoppable. The only true military rivals to the Mongols were the mamluks, who shared many of the same cultural traditions and were therefore familiar with Mongol weaponry and tactics. The Mongols also adapted the iron weaponry and tactics they encountered in China, and they absorbed many captured peoples into their army, including Persians, Turks, Chinese, and even Europeans.

From 1240 to 1260, the capital of the Mongol Empire was Karakorum, a flourishing city that attracted merchants, missionaries, and scholars from all over Eurasia. During this period, the Great Khan remained in Mongolia and ruled over the khanate of the Golden Horde in Russia, the Jagadai Khanate in Central Asia, and the Il-khan in Persia. After 1265, the Jagadai Khanate continued to control Central Asia and developed and thrived independently from the domain of the Great Khan in the East. Both Turkish nomads and Muslims had a tremendous influence on developments in the Central Asian khanate.

THE GOLDEN HORDE AND THE JAGADAI KHANATE

The Golden Horde, established under Genghis' grandson Batu in 1223, began as a unified khanate but broke apart into smaller khanates, the longest-lasting one surviving up until the eighteenth century. The Mongols ruled Russia from a distance; their capital was just north of the Caspian Sea. This allowed Russia to avoid direct subjugation and kept Russia's principalities in place. Much of the credit for this was due to Prince Alexander Nevskii, who convinced his peers that their best strategy was to cooperate with the Mongols. In appreciation for his help, the Mongols favored Nevskii's territory of Novgorod. Moscow, the town Nevskii's son ruled, eventually became the most important political hub in Russia. The Mongols also recognized and patronized the Orthodox Church, a shrewd political move to win the hearts of the Russian people. Islam was also very influential and became a source of tension among the Mongols of the Golden Horde. Batu's successor declared himself a Muslim, which sparked conflict between Golden Horde leaders and those of the Il-khan, culminating in war in 1260. In 1295, the Il-khan leader declared himself a Muslim, which shifted alliances again.

In securing and controlling Eurasia, the Mongols allowed missionaries, merchants, and diplomats to move freely and exchange ideas and goods. However, the Mongols also unknowingly spread disease, in particular the **bubonic plague**. It began in China under the Tang dynasty. As Mongol troops moved from their stations in China, rats in their cargo spread the disease across Central Asia into Russia and port cities like Kaffa on the

Black Sea, and from there eventually to western Europe. In addition, influenza, typhus, and smallpox were spread. The death and devastation caused by the plague is one of the greatest legacies of the Mongols; peaceful trade allowed for an unforeseeable pandemic. The Mongols brought demographic change in other ways as well. The heavy burden they placed on western Eurasia in terms of taxes and resources led to population loss, drained the local economy, and destroyed rural areas.

As the Il-Khan khanate was declining in the Middle East, new leadership rose in the **Jagadai Khanate** under Timur. (Also known as Tamerlane in the West, he ruled from 1370 to 1405.) Although he was an ambitious military leader, Timur could never be khan because he was not born a Mongol; he was a Turk who had married into the Mongol dynasty. This did not stop him from having incredible success in attacking the Delhi Sultanate and the Ottoman Empire and bringing the Middle East under his control. He then set his sights on East Asia but died before he could attack China. Timur's legacy lived on through his descendants, the Timurids, in the Mughal Empire of the sixteenth century.

Placed strategically between Persia and China, the ends of the Silk Road, Timur's capital at Samarkand became a key trading point on the Silk Road. Timur also patronized great scholars, painters, and historians, helping to preserve and build on the significant contributions of the Muslim world. Astronomy was another field that flourished during this time. Timur's own grandson built an observatory in Samarkand and studied astronomy with great precision and dedication.

THE YUAN EMPIRE

The death of Ögödei caused conflict over who would be the next Great Khan. When Genghis' grandson Khubilai Khan took the title of Great Khan in 1265, Jagadai's descendants refused to recognize Khubilai as the supreme leader. The fighting that ensued destroyed Karakorum, and as a result, Khubilai began to rule from Beijing, where he created an incredible city that was linked to the Grand Canal. In 1271, he created the **Yuan Empire** in China, the new domain of the Great Khan.

One of Khubilai's greatest contributions to Chinese regional identity was his ability to unify the area after the Song's fragmentation. He destroyed the Tanggut and Jin Empires in northern China and conquered the Southern Song dynasty in 1279, thereby laying out the territory of modern China. Eager to establish himself as the rightful ruler of China, he worked to bring together Mongol and Chinese traditions. To that end, Khubilai adopted many of the successful political and cultural practices of the previous dynasties—with a few striking exceptions: he did away with the scholar examination system and placed Mongols in the highest positions of authority in his court. Chinese scholar officials kept their positions but were subordinate to the Mongols. The Confucians were at odds with many of the practices of the Yuan Empire, including the rising status of merchants, whom Confucians did not respect.

Mongol control of the entire Eurasian landmass revitalized the Silk Road. The Yuan Empire stood at one end and the Il-khan at the other, which allowed for the Pax Mongolica, or the Mongol peace. The flow of ideas, religion, technological innovations, and resources brought tremendous wealth and grandeur to the Yuan Empire. Khubilai financed the building of canals and roads to bring the tribute and wealth right to his glorious palace in

Beijing. Because Khubilai valued this exchange so much, he welcomed to his court important men from all parts of the world, including Marco Polo. Polo was a Venetian merchant whose record of his alleged years at the court of Khubilai has given tremendous insight into life in the Yuan dynasty. Muslims furthered astronomical studies, brought new medicinal practices, and left their imprint on language-Mandarin Chinese, a dominant language in China today, has many Mongolian influences that date back to this time.

The Mongols significantly affected Chinese demographics. For various reasons—including warfare, flooding, migration, and bubonic plague—the population under the Mongols declined significantly, perhaps up to 40 percent. By the 1340s, feuding among Mongol princes led to mass rebellion and the eventual rise of a new empire that focused on reestablishing Chinese traditions. The Mongols did not disappear; some were absorbed into Chinese society, and others returned to the Mongol homeland. The Ming would never rule over all the Mongols, who continued to be a serious concern on the northern edge of the Ming Empire.

THE MING EMPIRE

In response to the foreign threat represented by the Mongol's Yuan dynasty, a priority of the first Ming emperor, Hongwu, was to reassert Chinese authority and indigenous cultural practices. He moved the capital from Beijing to Nanjing, on the Yangzi River, and reinstituted the Confucian examination system. The Ming also made many social and economic changes to reflect their desire to take back control from the Mongols. Communication with the rest of Central Asia and the Middle East was scaled back tremendously, and silver replaced paper money as the main currency. Growing staple crops became more important than growing commercial crops because of the large population increase under the Ming. They also completed the Great Wall, which stood as a tangible symbol of imperial desire to keep foreigners out. Despite these efforts, many of the influences of the Mongols remained, including the Mongol calendar.

The second Ming emperor, Yongle, was quite different from Hongwu. He increased ties to the previous empire by moving the capital back to Beijing and added onto Khubilai's royal complex, the Forbidden City. Yongle also reopened trade with the Indian Ocean trade network and reestablished economic relations with the Middle East. To avoid conflicts with the remaining Mongol presence in Central Asia, he sent the eunuch naval admiral Zheng He on maritime voyages to Indian Ocean ports. In the course of seven expeditions between 1405 and 1433, Zheng established trading, mercantile, and diplomatic relationships and added fifty new **tribute states** to China's realm. During this time, Ming cultural achievements blossomed in the areas of literature and painting, and Ming porcelain, known as Ming ware, became the most famous Chinese product throughout Eurasia. The Ming Empire would endure until the mid-seventeenth century.

KOREA

The first written records of Korean history come from Chinese sources, which make clear that the Chinese heavily influenced Korea but that Korea also maintained its own identity. Both Confucianism and Buddhism had a tremendous impact on Korean culture, but political roles were not determined by a civil service examination system as in China. Instead, Korea's landed aristocracy created ruling families who were in power for centuries, and wealth was based on agriculture. One of these families, the Silla, conquered the Korean peninsula with the support of the Tang. The Silla fell in the tenth century, and the **Koryo** family, from which the name Korea derives, took over. Like the Southern Song in China, the Koryo also feared the Liao and Jin Empires, and they established a diplomatic relationship with the Song in light of this threat. The Koryo also had a tense relationship with the Mongols that climaxed when the Mongols attacked in 1231. In 1258, the same year that the Mongols sacked Baghdad, they finally defeated the Koryo and brought Korea under their control. The Mongols demanded economic tribute from the Koreans, and the Koryo family married into the Mongols, which resulted in further exposure to the Yuan culture.

After the Yuan fell, the Yi family rose to power and established a new kingdom focused on reasserting Korean identity. The Yi remained in power until the Japanese takeover in 1910; part of their ability to remain independent as a tributary state to the Qing Empire was their strong naval power—gunpowder technology taken from the Chinese allowed them to mount cannon on ships.

One of the greatest contributions of the Koreans was in printing. Although the earliest woodblock print dates back to Han China and movable type was in place in Korea by the 1300s, it was the invention of metal movable type by the Koreans in the 1400s that allowed for increased accuracy and readability.

JAPAN

The first written records of Japan, like those of Korea, come from the Chinese. Many Chinese influences reached Japan through Korea, among them Confucianism and Buddhism. Indeed, Japan became a center for Mahayana Buddhism in the eighth century. Like Korea, Japan adopted some practices from China but had some key differences in political organization. There was no concept of a Mandate of Heaven in Japan; instead, emperors descended from one continuous lineage. The Fujiwara family assumed protection of the emperor and was in power from 794 to 1185, although civil war plagued the last thirty years. The **Kamakura** family took power in 1185 and established a shogunate that controlled Japan through the military. Japan became a decentralized feudal state that recognized the emperor and shogun but was not unified.

It was the threat of a Mongol invasion that unified feuding Japanese lords and helped create a national identity out of a politically decentralized environment. Every effort went into protecting Japan's economic resources and preparing for attack. Japan's ability to resist a Mongol invasion twice was partly because of weather; both times storms undermined the Mongols' attempts. This fact helped cement the view that Japan was a unique state among her East Asian neighbors. Defending Japan successfully strengthened the power of the warrior elite, or samurai, who developed a culture centered on Zen Buddhism during the period of the Ashikaga Shogunate, established in 1338.

> ## AP® Tip
>
> An important comparison in AP® World History is between Japanese feudalism and European feudalism. These two feudal systems had strikingly similar characteristics.

VIETNAM

During the period 600–1450, Vietnam was divided into two rival kingdoms—Annam, in the north, and Champa, in the south. Sharing an environment similar to southern China's and agriculturally based like its East Asian neighbors, Annam was culturally, politically, and economically tied to China beginning in the Tang period. Because it was part of the Indian Ocean trade network, Champa was heavily influenced by India and Malaya. Both Annam and Champa were tributary states to the Song, and the Champa made a significant tribute gift of Champa rice, which grows fast and allowed Chinese farmers in the Song period to produce more of this staple crop. When the Mongols came, they made both Annam and Champa tribute states. This continued under the Ming, who occupied Annam for a time. Annam regained tribute status, then took Champa, uniting the two kingdoms into one state named Annam by 1500. Annam continued to have Confucian political structures, including the examination system, but women retained property rights.

SOUTH ASIA AND THE INDIAN OCEAN TRADE NETWORK

Since the decline of the Gupta Empire, India was divided into separate states that often fought one another. In the twelfth century, Turkish invaders from Central Asia poured into northern India and established the **Delhi Sultanate**. From 1206 to 1526, this Muslim empire ruled almost the entire subcontinent of India except the south, which Hindu princes held, and did much to centralize India under a strict government bureaucracy. The Turks destroyed temples and massacred thousands. Once the initial conquest was over, the Delhi Sultanate required Hindus to pay a special tax in exchange for protection. This created an ongoing tension between Hindus and Muslims that would ultimately weaken the Delhi Sultanate significantly—in fact, this tension between Hindus and Muslims still goes on today and causes much conflict in the region. The sultanate received a fatal blow in 1398 when Timur sacked and captured Delhi, a defeat that signaled the end of the prominence of Delhi. Despite its difficulty in controlling all of India, the Delhi Sultanate profited tremendously from the Indian Ocean trade network because it held many of the key port cities and regions along the trade routes.

The key to Indian Ocean trade was mastering the monsoon winds and navigating their currents. The typical ship of the Indian Ocean was the **dhow**, a boat fitted with a lateen sail—a triangular sail that caught the winds beautifully. The Chinese junk became known in the Indian Ocean as the best vessel for travel and large transport. The Indian Ocean trade network grew to be the richest trade network during the period 600–1450 and was at its height from 1200 to 1500. So precious was this trade network that gaining control of it would become the quest of European explorers like Christopher Columbus by the end of the period.

The complex trading patterns of the Indian Ocean were not controlled by one central political authority but worked through a series of smaller economic relationships. Gold from Africa flowed through the East African city-states. Goods from the Mediterranean, the Middle East, and Europe were transported across the Arabian peninsula. Port cities like **Malacca** stood as a gateway between Southeast Asia, China, and the Indian Ocean. Islam was the dominant religion of the network and facilitated trading relationships between peoples of all languages and ethnicities who shared this faith, among them Ibn Battuta (1304–1369), a Moroccan Muslim, who chronicled his extensive travels to many of the prominent locations along the Indian Ocean trade route.

Content Review Questions

Iranian Rider on Silk Road Camel from Tang China showing a common stereotype of people from Central Asia with a beard, big nose, no saddle and diminutive size.

From Bulliet et al., *The Earth and Its Peoples*, 7th edition, p. 229.

1. What conclusion could a historian draw about Tang China's view toward foreigners based on the above figurine?
   (A) Tang China tended to view foreigners as less advanced and less civilized.
   (B) Tang China's use of the tribute system led them to revere foreigners for their technological advancements.
   (C) Tang China viewed foreigners as a curiosity to be studied.
   (D) Tang China viewed foreigners as equals and as valuable trading partners.

2. The above figurine can best be used as proof of which of the following trends?
   (A) The intensification of long-distance trade depended on using environmental knowledge and technology to adapt to the local region.
   (B) Imperial cities served as centers of trade.
   (C) Art and architecture reflected the values of religions and belief systems.
   (D) Merchants set up diasporic communities along trade routes where they introduced their own cultural traditions to indigenous cultures.

3. Which of the following was the most significant long-term result of merchants like the one shown above?
   (A) The expansion of Tang China
   (B) Chinese explorers created influential pockets of Chinese culture outside of the Chinese homeland
   (C) Chinese technology transferred west
   (D) Iranian philosophy became dominant in China

The Prince Imperial in person prepared for the first time laws. These were seventeen clauses as follows:

1. Harmony is to be valued, and an avoidance of wanton opposition to be honored. All men are influenced by class-feelings, and there are few who are intelligent. Hence there are some who disobey their lords and fathers, or who maintain feuds with the neighboring villages. But when those above are harmonious and those below are friendly, there is concord in the discussion of business, right views of things spontaneously gain acceptance. Then what is there which cannot be accomplished!

From the Constitution of Prince Shōtoku, as recorded in the *Chronicle of Japan,* c. 720 C.E.

The Human Record: Sources of Global History, 8th edition, volume 1, p. 248.

4. Which philosophy or belief system transferred from China is most evident in the above passage?
   (A) Daoism
   (B) Buddhism
   (C) Confucianism
   (D) Ancestor worship

5. Which indigenous tradition also strongly influenced the development of Imperial Japan in this period?
   (A) Zen Buddhism
   (B) Shintoism
   (C) Kabuki
   (D) Neo-Confucianism

6. Which of the following best explains the similarities between China and Japan as demonstrated in the passage?
   (A) Japan feared the strength of the Chinese imperial state and wished to appease it by paying homage to its customs.
   (B) Japan admired the success of the centralized Chinese government and wished to implement some of its policies.
   (C) Japan retained many Chinese elements from when it was under Chinese control in the Classical period.
   (D) Persecutions of Buddhism during the Tang Dynasty led many Chinese to flee to Japan.

Answers

1. ANSWER: A. The Sui, Tang, and Song Dynasties in China tended to view their culture as superior to that of foreigners—it is part of the reason they eventually banned Buddhism. This image reflects that view. The information in the caption helps explain the reflection by pointing out that the sculpture is an unflattering caricature of an Iranian merchant (*The Earth and Its Peoples*, 6th ed., pp. 226–227/7th ed., p. 229; History Disciplinary Practice—Analyzing Historical Evidence; Learning Objectives CUL-1-4; Key Concept 3.1.III.B).

2. ANSWER: A. Camels and horses were necessary to cross certain parts of the Silk Road. By domesticating the right animals for the environment, merchants were able to increase the volume of trade on the Silk Road (*The Earth and Its Peoples*, 6th ed., pp. 226–227/7th ed., pp. 229–230; History Disciplinary Practice—Analyzing Historical Evidence; Learning Objectives ENV-5; Key Concept 3.1.II.A).

3. ANSWER: C. Although there were some pockets of Chinese merchants outside of China, the question asks the reader to make a judgment call about the *most* significant effect of the trade. The Silk Road brought compasses, printing, and eventually gunpowder out of China and into the west. This allowed for increased Muslim trade in the Indian Ocean and eventually European voyages across the Atlantic, making this the most significant long-term effect (*The Earth and Its Peoples*, 6th ed., pp. 226–227/7th ed., pp. 229–230; History Disciplinary Practice—Analyzing Historical Evidence; Learning Objectives CUL-1-4; Key Concept 3.1.III.B).

4. ANSWER: C. The passage is referring to the five relationships in Confucianism that set up a hierarchical system of society and governing. Japan wanted to adapt this system to help encourage subjects to obey the commands of the new central government (*The Earth and Its Peoples*, 6th ed., pp. 310–313/7th ed., pp. 308–310; History Disciplinary Practice—Analyzing Historical Evidence; Learning Objectives CUL-1-4; Key Concept 3.1.III.B).

5. ANSWER: B. Buddhism and Confucianism both came over from China. While Zen Buddhism was immensely popular among Japanese warriors, its popularity occurred after the downfall of the imperial system. Kabuki also came later, and wasn't a philosophy or belief system. Shintoism, however, was native to Japan and was used to help legitimize the foundation of the first Imperial government (*The Earth and Its Peoples*, 6th ed., pp. 310–313/7th ed., pp. 308–310; History Reasoning Skill—Causation; Learning Objectives CUL-1-4; Key Concept 3.1.III.B).

6. ANSWER: B. Japan had emissaries travel to China to observe the success of the Chinese imperial system, and modeled much of its original constitution and bureaucratic system on one employed in China at the time. Japan made this choice voluntarily—it was never under Chinese rule, and the Chinese state in 618 was not strong enough to pose a serious expansion risk into Japan (*The Earth and Its Peoples*, 6th ed., pp. 310–313/7th ed., pp. 308–310; History Reasoning Skill—Comparison; Learning Objectives CUL-1-4; Key Concept 3.1.III.B).

Marco Polo
1254 CE - 1324 CE
Italian Traveler

Margery Kempe
1373 CE - 1438 CE
CHRISTIAN MYStic/
pilgrim

Prince Henry
1394 CE - 1460 CE
Portuguese Navigator

Gutenberg
1400 CE - 1468 CE
1st European to
use movable type

14

EUROPE: C. 600 C.E. TO C. 1450 C.E.

KEY CONCEPTS

- After the fall of the Roman Empire, the western part of the empire became a decentralized feudal system while the eastern part of the empire continued under imperial rule as the Byzantine Empire.
- Christianity had both a political and a religious impact as the power of the church grew in both western and eastern Europe, and the concept of Christendom took on a territorial context. In particular, the Catholic Church competed for political authority and influence.
- The Crusades sowed the seeds for economic and intellectual changes in late-medieval Europe that would culminate in the Renaissance.
- The Black Death, a horrific pandemic for Europe, was also a major factor in ending feudalism and awakening urban life in western Europe.

KEY TERMS

- Black Death
- Byzantine Empire
- the Crusades
- feudalism
- gothic cathedral
- Great Western Schism
- Hanseatic League
- Holy Roman Empire
- investiture controversy
- Kievan Russia
- Latin West

- manor
- medieval
- monasticism
- pilgrimage
- schism
- scholasticism
- serf
- vassal

serfdom = status of many peasants under feudalism
magna carta = character of rights
100 years War = conflicts from 1337-1453
little Ice Age = period of cooling after Medieval Warm period

Western Europe and the Byzantine Empire are discussed in depth in *The Earth and Its Peoples*, 6th edition, Chapters 10 and 13, and 7th edition, Chapters 11 and 14.

EARLY MEDIEVAL WESTERN EUROPE: 600–1000

The period from the fall of Rome until the beginning of the Renaissance is known as the medieval period, or the Middle Ages, chiefly because it is bracketed by periods of cultural, economic, and political ascendancy—the once-great Roman Empire and the Renaissance. The fall of the Roman Empire, in the fifth century, brought drastic changes to western Europe, which entered a period of economic decline and subsistence living. Local lords and chieftains replaced Roman imperial rule, and the laws of the Roman Empire were supplanted by the Germanic traditions and practices of the tribes in the area. With the absence of centralized imperial authority, safety became the primary concern, and peasants turned to local lords rather than faraway kings to provide safety. This need for protection was the political and cultural context out of which the feudal system emerged in the seventh century.

One exception to the weak kings of the early medieval period was Charlemagne, whose grandfather, Charles Martel, had prevented the Muslims from taking over France (Gaul at the time) at the Battle of Tours in 732. By Martel's time, Muslims controlled all of the Iberian Peninsula, having taken over the Visigoth kingdom and pushed the Christians back. By then, Charlemagne's family, the Carolingians, had created an empire that included all of Gaul and parts of Germany and Italy. Charlemagne brought about a brief period of intellectual revival, but with the death of his son Louis the Pious, the Treaty of Verdun split the empire into three parts, one part for each of Louis's sons, and this brief period of empire in medieval Europe came to an end.

While the Roman Empire had focused on urban life, exemplified by the city of Rome itself, western European cities declined and in some cases became smaller villages. Roman roads also fell into disrepair, as did the great buildings of Rome. The Roman coin became a thing of the past, and local trade was by barter. Contact with the larger world through long-distance trade around the Mediterranean severely declined. With less communication with the larger world and no strong central government, most Europeans relied on their own local resources for both political control and economic survival.

Organization of medieval life thus settled around the institution of the manor, which became the primary source of local agricultural production in both northern and southern Europe. The manor was far more than a single fortified dwelling; life behind its walls sustained a small community of people and included a mill, church, workshops, and a village where serfs lived. Serfs, both men and women, worked the lands of the manor in exchange for protection and were under the complete control of the lord of the manor, the noble whose armed men provided for their safety. Serfs were tied to the land and could not leave. Most peasants across France, England, and western Germany in the tenth and eleventh centuries were serfs.

The rigid system of serfdom did not allow for much personal or political advancement. However, for the noble class, opportunities for political and economic advancement centered on warfare to protect lands from distant enemies like the Vikings as well as other competing lords. This centuries-long tradition of linking land rights to military service was termed feudalism. The feudal society was based on the vassal relationship, in which kings and lords gave land to vassals in exchange for sworn military allegiance. This vassal relationship looked different from region to region, but by the eleventh century the key person in the medieval military was the knight. Land given to a knight by his lord or king allowed him to afford armor and horses, and the land, known as a fief, could be passed down through generations. This allowed knights themselves to become wealthy lords, who could then enter into vassal relationships with other knights. Knights could also be in a vassal relationship with more than one lord at a time.

Noblewomen were also an important part of this system of land ownership and inheritance and were carefully and strategically married. Marriage became a tool to make military alliances or gain more lands, and noble children had very little choice in whom to marry. Likewise, kings used marriage alliances to increase their territorial and political control. Women could own land, however, and while husbands were away on military service, women could manage the estate.

THE CHURCH IN THE WEST

The other central institution of medieval Europe was the Catholic Church, the strongest unifying force in medieval Europe. The church created the moral framework for society, a task it took very seriously. The church also owned and controlled extensive lands throughout medieval Europe on which it placed its monasteries and convents. The Catholic Church wrestled with secular lords and kings to be the dominant authority over all matters, ecclesiastical or not. This tension was not present in the Byzantine Empire; because he appointed the patriarch of Constantinople, the emperor had both political and religious supremacy.

The head of the western Church was the pope, whose authority continued to grow stronger and stronger in the early medieval period. The pope was based in Rome and controlled territory in Rome and central Italy. He exercised authority over all clergy and, through his councils of bishops, drew up the rules and doctrines that priests communicated to lay people—Catholics who were not part of the clergy. He also demanded that secular leadership honor and respect his authority.

Needing political allies, the pope crowned the first Holy Roman Emperor in 962 to serve as the defender of Christendom. The Holy Roman Empire started out as a basic alliance of German princes and held more symbolic than practical power. The creation of the Holy Roman emperor did little to prevent the struggle for control between secular authority and the church from climaxing into what is known as the investiture controversy. Kings and lords had grown used to investing, or handing over authority to, the bishops in their territories. Technically, canon, or church, law assigned responsibility for appointing bishops to the church. But many bishops were also in a vassal relationship to a lord or king. Lords and kings argued that they should be the ones to appoint the bishops in their lands in order to make sure bishops fulfilled their feudal duties. Exacerbated by the proclamations of Pope Gregory VII in 1073, which declared the Catholic Church infallible, capable of removing emperors, and solely responsible for appointing bishops, the controversy came to symbolize the general struggle over who had more political control. The Concordat of Worms finally eased tensions in 1122: the Holy Roman emperor and the pope agreed that the emperor could invest papally appointed bishops with their secular responsibilities and rights.

The tensions between the church and secular monarchs in England, Germany, and France boiled down to competing legal systems. Feudal law, based on Germanic traditions, gave all power to the king; canon law, based on Roman traditions, held that one legal system should govern all of Western Christendom. The Catholic Church would continue to come into conflict with royal control, but as the feudal system and the status of knights declined because of changes in weaponry like the crossbow and firearms, kings began to tighten their control over their territory and the church. In 1302 Pope Boniface asserted papal supremacy, which the French king, Philip, challenged by orchestrating the election of a French pope. The papal seat was moved to Avignon, giving rise to a period of competing papal claimants, which in turn precipitated the Great Western Schism (1378–1415). The papacy was eventually returned to Rome, but these events showed how far monarchs could go in challenging papal authority.

One other unique aspect of medieval European Christian life was monasticism. Monks and nuns separated themselves from daily life and lived in gender-specific communities focused on a celibate life of devotion, religious work, and simple living. Nuns provided a refuge for women who were widowed or sought a spiritual life instead of their traditional obligations to marry. Monks served as missionaries, produced food on their lands, and made their monasteries resting places for weary pilgrims and other travelers. Monks were also the essential link between the past and the future; they were the keepers of literacy and learning. In addition to writing their own books on religious matters, monks conserved the works of the Latin world by painstakingly copying them.

LATE MEDIEVAL WESTERN EUROPE: 1000–1450

Important changes occurred in late medieval Europe between 1000 and 1200. Increases in population and agricultural production allowed for a surplus, which created more opportunities for trade in towns. A surplus of food freed people to focus on other industries in artistry and construction. These changes resulted from technological advances in agriculture. A new plow, the use of the horse collar, and the use of horses instead of oxen all contributed to an increase in the food supply, which in turn helped population growth.

The most dramatic shift in population—a reversal—came to medieval Europe in the fourteenth century because of the bubonic plague. Known as the Black Death, it ravaged Europe from 1347 to 1351, killing one in three Europeans. The plague first hit Mongol armies stationed in Kaffa, a port on the Black Sea; Italian traders brought the disease from Kaffa to Italy, and from there it traveled across the continent and to England. Not until 1500 did Europe's population rebound to its level before the plague.

The Black Death left an impact far more significant than just demographic change. In many ways, the Black Death killed serfdom as well. With so many dead, laborers could charge more for their services, and they rebelled against nobles who initially refused to comply. A demand for the end of serfdom sparked uprisings across Europe. Production rose as free laborers bought land for themselves or became urban workers and could demand higher wages. For those still working the land, technological improvements such as the water wheel and windmill—technologies that had long been in use in the Muslim world—increasingly came into use in western Europe. These devices improved efficiency by powering a number of necessary tasks, from the grinding of grain to papermaking. These technologies were also used for iron production, which brought about the expansion of iron mining.

AP® Tip

In addition to the Muslims, the Scandinavian Vikings were a formidable presence in medieval Europe. The Vikings, who were excellent shipbuilders, raided towns along the coasts of England and France and eventually settled in Normandy. From there they conquered parts of England and took Sicily permanently from the Muslims. The Vikings were among the earliest European explorers, also settling Iceland and Greenland. Around 1000, almost five hundred years before Columbus, they made it to the North American continent without the use of maritime technologies such as the compass and established Vinland, on Newfoundland.

Another important change was a revival of trade, propelled by the politically independent cities in Italy and Flanders that were exclusively focused on seaborne trade. These cities sprang up when individuals banded together to demand freedom from their lord. A lord who allowed this independence was sure to benefit from the economic prosperity the city brought to the region. Laws were passed so that serfs who made their way to these cities were guaranteed their freedom and were able to engage in other forms of industry. These laws would be very important after the Black Death. Walled cities like Pisa, Florence, and Siena had to keep expanding as their population increased. Other Italian cities that rose to tremendous economic importance were Genoa, with its access to the western Mediterranean, and Venice, which would become a trading powerhouse on the Adriatic Sea.

Venice engaged in trade with the Muslim ports of North Africa and the Mediterranean. In this way, western Europe was slowly exposed to the wealth of goods traveling along the Silk Road and circulating in the Indian Ocean trading system. Mongol control of the entire Eurasian landmass further opened trade between Italian ports and the great ports of the East.

Two other vibrant centers of sea trade in Europe were the Hanseatic League, a network of trading cities centered in the Baltic, and the Flanders network, which included cities around the North Sea like Ghent and Bruges that focused on the fishing industry and the growing trade in wool and other textiles. With the increase in trade came increased demand for coined money. Most coinage in the ninth and tenth centuries came from the Muslim world and Byzantium, but with trade reviving in the Mediterranean, gold and silver coinage was no longer a luxury.

As the autonomous trading cities began to flourish, they offered more opportunities for social mobility and individual opportunity. Most of Europe's Jews lived in cities, where they experienced periods of great tolerance, as in Muslim Spain, but also periods of horrific persecution, most often during times of uncertainty and disaster like the Black Death. Cities also became centers of learning as universities specializing in fields such as education, law, and theology sprang up across Europe. Universities allowed for new questions about the relationship between reason and faith, a pursuit that came to be known as scholasticism. Scholars like Thomas Aquinas and other pre-Renaissance thinkers tried to reconcile the Bible with rediscovered Greek works from philosophers like Aristotle. Architecture also flourished; the best example of this is the Gothic cathedral, which first appeared in France in the twelfth century. By trial and error, European architects mastered the mathematical and engineering skills required to construct these huge, soaring buildings.

All of the changes in the late medieval period set the stage for the Renaissance. A rebirth of classical learning and artistry stimulated by urban revival, a growing merchant class, renewed economic contact with the Muslim world, and the rise of new scholarship and artistry in the cities of Europe, the Renaissance began in Italy and spread to northern Europe over the coming centuries.

THE CRUSADES

Economic revival in western Europe occurred alongside of, and contributed to, the Crusades, which had a profound effect on Europe as a whole and on western Europe in particular. The series of military expeditions, spanning more than a hundred years, began with Pope Urban II's call in 1095 for Frankish (a broad term synonymous with *western European*) princes to take back the Holy Land from Muslim control.

Many elements of European culture contributed to the Crusades. In an effort to calm the constant warring characteristic of the feudal system, the church had introduced truces—limits to times of fighting. These truces redirected warring from Christian versus Christian to Christian versus the enemies of Christendom. Because land was inherited only by eldest sons, the Crusades also provided an opportunity for younger sons to gain new lands and titles for themselves. Italian merchants, having reestablished a foothold in Mediterranean trade, encouraged crusades as a way to gain access to ports under the control of Muslims.

By the eleventh century, Muslim leaders had long been in control of the Holy Land; territory sacred to Christians included cities like Jerusalem, Antioch, and Alexandria. Christians had been able to make pilgrimages to these cities, but as Islamic control continued to expand into Byzantine—and therefore Christian—territory, the calls for a crusade quickened. Despite the differences between the Latin Church and the Orthodox Church, the Byzantine emperor requested help—both secular and religious—in securing the land in the name of Christendom. Pope Urban II raised the call to fight in 1095, and the First Crusade resulted in the capture of Jerusalem in 1099 and the establishment of four Crusader kingdoms. The following two Crusades focused on holding these territories, but in 1187, Muslim armies took back Jerusalem. The Fourth Crusade had completely new goals; the capture of Constantinople was driven by economic incentives; it was encouraged by Venetians, who wanted to expand their trading to ports formally under Byzantine and Muslim control.

The Crusades failed in their attempts to take the Holy Land, but they had a tremendous, long-lasting impact on European life. Exposure to the Muslim world sparked the flow of an enormous amount of information, ideas, goods, and resources to Europe. In addition, crusaders brought back discoveries and manufacturing techniques that allowed Europeans to make many of the goods they originally could only import. Demand for these goods from the Middle East stimulated the markets of late medieval Europe and also expanded trade between the Muslim world, western Europe, and the Byzantine Empire. The incredible intellectual contributions of Muslims made their way to Europe in two forms: first, the knowledge of the ancient Greeks, preserved by Muslims; second, scientific and technological understanding, which were more advanced in the Muslim world. Together, they served as the intellectual underpinnings for western Europe's transition from the Middle Ages to the Renaissance.

THE BYZANTINE EMPIRE

After the fall of the Roman Empire, the eastern portion continued as the Byzantine Empire, with Constantinople as its great capital, and the empire would endure until its defeat by the Ottoman Turks in 1453. Geographically centered in Greek and Anatolian areas, the Byzantine Empire, or Byzantium, used Greek as its language, and the empire maintained and built upon many of the traditions of the Roman Empire in terms of both law and economics. Economically, the Byzantine emperors continued to regulate prices, the trading of luxury goods, and grain shipments, which may have slowed technological and economic advancements. Constantinople received the most economic attention, to the detriment of other Byzantine cities and the countryside, where farm tools and practices lagged in efficiency when compared with those used in western Europe. Part of Constantinople's appeal was its ideal location between the Black Sea and the Mediterranean, which made it an ideal center for trade and travel, attracting merchants, aristocrats, and journeying pilgrims. For hundreds of years, this port city—one of the five great patriarchal seats of Europe—would be envied by many.

Constantinople's glory hid the reality that the Byzantine Empire was on a slow and steady decline.

The Byzantine Empire enjoyed many cultural and artistic achievements, all reflecting the Greek Orthodox interpretations of Christianity as opposed to the Latin interpretations used in western Europe. The empire reached its height under the emperor Justinian, who ruled from 527 until 565 and built the Hagia Sophia, the greatest example of Byzantine architecture. Byzantine sacred art had a great influence on pre-Renaissance painting in western Europe.

The Byzantine Empire also had a tremendous impact on the religious and cultural traditions of Slavic Christians. Followers of two Byzantine missionaries sent in the ninth century to preach to the Slavs in their local language developed the Cyrillic writing system, which became the written language of Slavic and Russian Orthodox Christians.

Socially, the Byzantine Empire gradually moved from an urban way of life to a more rural one, although cities, particularly Constantinople, remained important. Local urban elites holding power up through the seventh century gave way to an increase in the power of rural landowners and imperial court aristocrats. This change could in part be the result of the demographic impact of the bubonic plague, which hit the Byzantine Empire in the sixth century—much earlier than in western Europe—as well as the loss of territory to Muslims. Byzantine women also saw a change in their position, moving from a freer status in the public arena during the Roman period to a more secluded existence in the home, marked by wearing the veil in public. Social interactions with men were limited to family members. Despite this, there are strong examples of women ruling with their husbands in the eleventh century. The increasing seclusion of women in the Byzantine Empire can be compared with the seclusion of women in the neighboring Muslim empires.

The rising strength of the Muslim empire always proved to be a formidable challenge for the Byzantine Empire, despite the growing importance of the military, which was the basis of the aristocratic class by the eleventh century. Arab Muslims quickly took territory away from the Byzantine Empire in the seventh century. At the same time, the patriarchal cities Alexandria, Antioch, and Jerusalem came under Muslim control. Other groups, such as the Slavic and Turkic peoples, would also serve as threats to the borders of the Byzantine Empire. The Seljuk Turks in particular would establish a Turkish Muslim state in the early eleventh century; it became the main enemy of the crusaders. The Fourth Crusade in 1204 was a mortal blow for the empire because western European crusaders sacked and destroyed much of Constantinople. After 1200, the Byzantine Empire declined, largely because of a weak military. For the next two hundred years, the empire continued to lose territory. It would limp along until 1453, when Sultan Mehmed II captured Constantinople and ended the Byzantine Empire's reign of more than eleven hundred years.

AP® Tip

Not only did the Roman Empire split politically into East and West; the Christian Church would eventually split as well. A series of doctrinal disputes over issues such as the humanity and divinity of Jesus, the place of icons, and the role of Mary weakened the relationship between the Eastern Orthodox Church and the Roman Catholic Church. At one point, the patriarch in Constantinople also challenged the territorial control that the western church enjoyed. These disagreements eventually resulted in schism in 1054, a formal split in Christendom that has endured through the centuries. This split produced two different cultural expressions of Christianity in the period 600–1450.

KIEVAN RUSSIA

To the north of the Byzantine Empire, a unique society developed in Russia that also followed the traditions of the Orthodox Church. The word *Rus*, from which *Russia* derives, came to refer to Slavic-speaking peoples who were ruled by the Varangians, Swedish Vikings who sailed down into Russia from the Baltic. Varangian princes lived in cities and focused on trade while the Slavs worked the lands. Kiev was one of the key cities for trade with the Byzantine Empire. In 980, Vladimir I made himself grand prince of Russia. He chose Orthodox Christianity as the religion of the region, married an Orthodox princess of the Byzantine imperial family, and let in Orthodox missionaries. Until the arrival of the Mongols in the thirteenth century, Kievan Russia stood as an independent state that spread Orthodox Christianity to eastern Slavs and prevented the spread of Latin Christianity from the west.

Economic prominence in Kiev came from trade, which provided the money to pay soldiers, and artisans were valued above peasants. Churches were built in the Byzantine style, and slowly Christianity obliterated the polytheistic traditions of the Slavs. By the twelfth century, the church had taken over some economic roles such as tax collection and had also assumed political responsibilities. Nonetheless, the large cities of Kiev and Novgorod never matched the population levels or cosmopolitan life found in cities like Constantinople and Baghdad.

Content Review Questions

The comparison between western and eastern Europe appears paradoxical. Byzantium inherited a robust and self-confident late Roman society and economy, while western Europe could not achieve political unity and suffered severe economic decline. Yet by 1200 western Europe was showing renewed vitality and flexing its military muscles, while Byzantium was showing signs of decline and military weakness.

From Bulliet, *The Earth and Its Peoples,* 7th edition, p. 250.

1. Which of the following could best be seen as a cause for the first comparison mentioned in the above passage?
   (A) Constantine relocated the capital of Rome to Constantinople allowing it to be closer to trade routes connecting to Asia.
   (B) The kingdom of Kievan Russia maintained military and economic ties only with the eastern half of Europe.
   (C) Western Europe turned toward Christianity and looked down upon wealth accumulation while eastern Europe remained connected to polytheistic Roman traditions.
   (D) Western Europe suffered a serious population decline as a result of the Bubonic Plague.

2. Which of the following was most responsible for the "renewed vitality" in western Europe referenced in the above passage?
   (A) Re-centralization of political power in France and England following the Hundred Years War
   (B) The imposition of cultural uniformity due to persecutions of Jews and Muslims in Spain
   (C) The decline of urban areas as more people turned to farming and food production
   (D) An increase in agricultural productivity due to technological innovation

3. Which of the following was a significant continuity in both regions throughout the time period 600–1450?
   (A) Both regions remained closely connected to Greco-Roman culture in terms of the art and literature produced.
   (B) Christianity became a significant part of daily life and state politics in both regions.
   (C) Trade drastically declined in both areas due to increasingly violent raids by Germanic peoples.
   (D) Both regions maintained the style of urban life popularized by Greco-Roman states.

What are we saying? Listen and learn! You, girt about with the badge of knighthood, are arrogant with great pride; you rage against your brothers and cut each other in pieces. This is not the [true] soldiery of Christ which rends asunder the sheepfold of the Redeemer. The Holy Church has reserved a soldiery for herself to help her people, but you debase her wickedly to her hurt…

Truly, this is the worst way, for it is utterly removed from God! If you wish to be mindful of your souls, either lay down the belt of such knighthood, or advance boldly, as knights of Christ, and rush as quickly as you can to the defense of the Eastern Church….

Under Jesus Christ, our Leader, may you struggle for your Jerusalem, in Christian battle-line, most invincible line, even more successfully than did the sons of Jacob of old- struggle, that you may assail and drive out the Turks…

From *The Jerusalem History* by Baldric of Dol, a monk who was at the Council of Clermont, c. 1108.

The Human Record: Sources of Global History, 8th edition, volume 1, p. 347.

4. What was the purpose of the speech recounted in the above document?
   (A) To reverse Justinian's conquest of the former Western Roman Empire
   (B) To take Constantinople from the Patriarch after the Roman Catholic Church and Eastern Orthodox Church formally split in the 11th century
   (C) To start the Crusades
   (D) To encourage cross-cultural contacts with peaceful Buddhists in the East

5. What was the historical context most responsible for the description of European knights from the passage above?
   (A) Knights were picking up brutal fighting tactics from engaging with invading Mongol tribes.
   (B) Knights lacked suitable enemies due to a decline in attacks from the Vikings and other nomadic groups which had initially inspired feudalism.
   (C) The behavior of Knights was causing a drastic population drop in Western Europe.
   (D) The Pope wanted to disassociate Christianity with the behavior of knights so he encouraged them to leave kingdoms dominated by Christianity.

6. Which of the following is a long-term effect of the speech described in the above passage?
   (A) Christians regained control of Jerusalem and other strategic sites throughout the Middle East
   (B) The Byzantine Empire was strengthened by an influx of Western soldiers
   (C) The intensification of trade between Western Europe and the East
   (D) A combination of Western European soldiers and Middle Eastern Muslim soldiers was able to repel Mongol advances into Jerusalem

Answers

1. ANSWER: A. The first comparison shows Western Europe weaker than Eastern Europe. Constantine relocated the capital of Rome to the East in the early 4th century. Many of the rich and powerful of Rome followed the new capital, and the new capital was closer to the Silk Road and Indian Ocean trade routes. This hastened the decline of the Western half of the Roman Empire (*The Earth and Its Peoples*, 6th ed., pp. 272–274 and 354–357/7th ed., pp. 270–272 and 348–351; History Reasoning Skill—Causation; Learning Objectives SB-1,2; Key Concept 3.2.I.A).

2. ANSWER: D. Innovations like the horse collar, heavy plow and three field system drastically increased the amount of food produced in Western Europe. This allowed urbanization and trade to intensify, which helped revive Western Europe (*The Earth and Its Peoples*, 6th ed., pp. 287–289 and 351–352; 7th ed., pp. 286–287 and 346–348; History Reasoning Skill—Causation; Learning Objectives ENV-3,4; Key Concept 3.3.I.A).

3. ANSWER: B. Since Constantine legalized Christianity, the significance of the Christian Church on European life drastically increased. Both regions of the former Roman Empire saw mass conversions to Christianity—in the West in part because it offered stability and hope as the Empire declined, and in the East because the Christian church and imperial state kept growing closer together until Christianity became the only legal religion. Even as the Empire fell, Christianity remained a constant in everyone's lives (*The Earth and Its Peoples*, 6th ed., pp. 279–284/7th ed., pp. 279–283; History Reasoning Skill—Continuity and Change Over Time; Learning Objectives SB-1,2; Key Concept 3.2.I.A).

4. ANSWER: C. This is part of a recounting of Pope Urban II's speech starting the Crusades. Clues can be found in the fact that it addresses European knights, and directs them to fight the Turks. The Seljuk Turks held the land around Jerusalem at the time of the Crusades (*The Earth and Its Peoples*, 6th ed., pp. 288–291/7th ed., pp. 288–290; History Disciplinary Practice—Analyzing Historical Evidence; Learning Objectives CUL-3, SB-3,4; Key Concept 3.2.II.A).

5. ANSWER: B. One possible motivating factor behind the Pope's call for the Crusades is the violence knights were doing in Medieval Europe, as referenced in the above passage. One of the original causes of the feudal system and the creation of private armies of knights, Vikings and other invaders, had dissipated by the late eleventh century and knights were left without a dedicated target. Instead, some fought each other or attacked civilians (*The Earth and Its Peoples*, 6th ed., pp. 288–291/7th ed., pp. 288–290; History Disciplinary Practice—Analyzing Historical Evidence; Learning Objectives CUL-3, SB-3,4; Key Concept 3.2.II.A).

6. ANSWER: C. As a result of the Crusades, more contacts were made between Western Europe and the Middle East—a region firmly connected to both Silk Road and Indian Ocean Trade. Western Europeans also began engaging in more trade in part because of the voyages they made to the East during the Crusades (*The Earth and Its Peoples*, 6th ed., pp. 288–291/7th ed., pp. 288–290; History Reasoning Skill—Causation; Learning Objectives CUL-3, SB-3,4; Key Concept 3.2.II.A).

People

Ureachillay
~ BCE 2 CE
Incan Herders'
Llama God

Pachacuti
1418 CE - 1472CE
Inca of the
Incan Empire

Montezuma II
1466 CE - 1520CE
Ruled Aztecs at
their Peak

15

THE AMERICAS:
C. 600 C.E. TO C. 1450 C.E.

KEY CONCEPTS

- Mesoamerica was never a single politically unified region, but its civilizations shared important cultural and religious characteristics and traditions that are continuities throughout the period 600–1450.
- The Aztec of Mesoamerica and the Inca of the Andean region developed complex, sophisticated civilizations with defined social, economic, cultural, and political characteristics that represent important aspects of Amerindian life in the Americas.
- The environment of each society had an important influence on its technological and agricultural development.
- Religion was a central aspect of Amerindian life and shaped many of the cultural rituals and political practices of the Americas.
- The civilizations and empires of the Aztec and Inca built on the earlier civilizations in their respective geographic regions.

KEY TERMS

- Anasazi
- ayllu
- Aztecs
- Inca
- khipus
- mit'a
- Moche
- Tenochtitlan
- Tiwanaku
- Toltecs
- tribute system

Aztlan = ancestral home of the Aztec

Chinampas = a type of MesoAmerican agriculture

Mexica = a Nahuatl speaking indigenous people

Cahokia = site of a Pre-Columbian Native American city

Tawantinsuyu = largest empire in Pre-Columbian America

Chasquis = messengers of the Inca empire

Quipu = recording devices fashioned from strings

Pueblos = Native Americans in the Southwestern United States

233

■ vertical integration
■ Wari

The history of the Americas in the period from c. 600 to c. 1450 is discussed in *The Earth and Its Peoples*, 6th edition, Chapters 7 and 17, and 7th edition, Chapters 8 and 18.

THE POSTCLASSIC PERIOD IN MESOAMERICA: 900–1500

The postclassic period had many continuities with the Mesoamerican classic period in social structure, art, and culture, including religious practices, architecture, and the role of cities. Population growth demanded the management of agricultural resources, and military and political control of various peoples became a priority for the two strongest societies of the postclassic period, the Toltecs and the Aztecs.

THE TOLTECS

A migrating people who eventually settled in central Mexico, the Toltecs built on many of the cultural practices of the people of Teotihuacan to create a sophisticated civilization. Their innovative contributions were mainly political and were based on military conquest that allowed them to create a state reaching from north of Mexico City to Central America. The Toltec capital of Tula, although never as populous as Teotihuacan, was an elaborate architectural achievement in central Mexico. Toltec art depicted and glorified the militaristic aspects of its culture, including scenes of human sacrifice. Political organization was based on two kings who ruled together; at some point after 1000, a struggle between political elites resulted in the expulsion of one of the kings. This was the beginning of the end for the Toltecs, culminating in the destruction of the capital around 1156 when invaders from the north overtook it. As new peoples came into the Toltec region, they built on the ancient Mesoamerican traditions combined with the new Toltec military and political strategies. The strongest group that emerged from the migrating northern peoples in the centuries following the Toltecs were the Mexica, or Aztec people.

THE AZTECS

Organized by clan, the Mexica people, known as the **Aztecs**, were originally serfs and mercenaries for the more powerful groups in the area. As they grew in power, the Aztecs moved to islands off the shore of Lake Texcoco and in 1325 began building the two cities that would become the foundation of modern Mexico City, the twin capitals of **Tenochtitlan** and Tlatelolco.

Aztec society was based on military conquest and looked to the Toltec as models. Continual military success allowed the Aztecs to take good agricultural lands and establish a monarchy in the region. The monarch did not have absolute authority. Selected by a council of aristocrats from among all the males of the ruling family, a new king had to complete a new round of military conquests to validate his rule and the warring class. As these practices continued, social hierarchy tightened. The highest status was assigned to the warrior elite, who enjoyed huge estates that relied on the labor of peasants, who had little say in decision making. Clan-based organization continued to be important in the twin capitals, serving as the method for dividing agricultural labor and civic duties and also for creating military units.

Agricultural laborers provided the food for the Aztecs' large urban population of approximately 150,000. The Aztecs, like the people of Teotihuacan before them, used the chinampa system to grow maize and various fruits and vegetables. They also built an impressive dike to separate freshwater from the salt water in Lake Texcoco so that the land could be used for cultivation. Another vital resource for the Aztecs was the **tribute system**, which allowed the Aztecs to draw on the labor and resources of conquered peoples. This tribute system provided a quarter of the food supplies for the Aztec Empire and also brought a variety of other practical items and luxury goods to the Aztecs. These tribute goods, along with products from long-distance trade, diversified the rich markets of Tenochtitlan.

By 1500, the population of the twin cities and the surrounding lakeshore areas was approximately half a million people. Aztec society was very stratified, and there was great division based on wealth. The rich ate, dressed, and lived well, while commoners had a very basic diet and lived simply. Commoners could have only one spouse, while the elite could have several. One distinct Aztec social group was the merchant class, who managed long-distance trade and also served as valuable sources of political and military information for the elites. Trade, based on barter instead of money or credit, was carried out without the use of beasts of burden or wheels, so the goods needed to be light enough to carry. Merchants grew wealthy as the empire grew, but they could not achieve the same status as the nobility, who watched them with a jealous eye.

Like many other Mesoamerican cultures, religious rule and ceremony were key components of the king's political success and authority. The Aztecs were polytheistic; their most famous religious cult centered on the worship of Huitzilopochtli, a hummingbird from the south. This god was first associated with war, then with the sun. Worship of the sun was a religious continuity throughout Mesoamerican history. The Aztecs believed that Huitzilopochtli needed human hearts to keep the sun shining, thereby sustaining life. As a result, the temple of Tenochtitlan, devoted to Huitzilopochtli and Tlaloc, the rain god, was the site of large-scale rituals involving human sacrifice. This is another continuity from previous Mesoamerican societies, but the Aztecs expanded the ritual significantly, sacrificing war captives, criminals, slaves, and people who were given as tribute. Thousands were sacrificed each year; the very violent and public aspect of the ritual sent a clear message to subject peoples that they must submit to the authority of the empire. The Aztec Empire continued until the arrival of the conquistador Cortés, who captured Tenochtitlan in 1521 before going on to conquer the rest of Mexico.

AP® Tip

The Aztecs created an empire based on tribute and maintained a vibrant urban life. Both of these characteristics can be compared with contemporaneous empires in China. Making this comparison on the AP® exam requires an understanding of the movement of the Aztecs from a nomadic group to a settled people able to create an empire. What other peoples could you compare the Aztecs with in terms of this transition from a migrating group to a settled empire?

THE PEOPLES OF NORTH AMERICA

Around 900, the southwestern desert and the Mississippi River Valley were two areas of high cultural achievement in North America. Building on the economic benefits from long-distance trade, including the introduction of key staples like maize, beans, and squash from Mesoamerica, the peoples of these areas developed societies with defined social structures and political roles unique to each region.

SOUTHWESTERN DESERT CULTURES

The Hohokam people, who lived in what is today Arizona, were heavily influenced by Mesoamerican cultures, particularly Mexican, as is reflected in their architecture, pottery, and ceramics. They in turn influenced other societies in the region, who built on the agricultural technology and the artistic techniques of the Hohokam.

The second group that exemplifies southwestern desert culture is the **Anasazi**, a Navajo word used by archaeologists meaning "ancient ones" to refer to the various desert cultures located in what is now the southwestern United States. By 600, the Anasazi also had an economy based on maize, beans, and squash. They specialized in decorative pottery as well as cotton weaving. Underground buildings called kivas were community centers used for both religious ritual and craftwork. After 900, the Anasazi constructed larger multilevel buildings, which were prominent features in the larger towns.

Chaco Canyon is the site of one of the largest Anasazi societies. Of the eight towns in the canyon, the largest was Pueblo Bonito, which contained large kivas and other residential buildings. Archaeological research of its infrastructure suggests that Pueblo Bonito held religious or political dominance over the region. Merchants engaged in long-distance trade in northern Mexico. Because men hunted, cared for the irrigation works, and traded, they often had to be away. Women specialized in various crafts as well as helped with agriculture and other domestic duties. Chaco Canyon was abandoned in the twelfth century because of drought, but the Anasazi continued to dwell in the larger region of the southwest.

MISSISSIPPIAN CULTURES: 700–1500

The first Amerindians along the Mississippi River were primarily hunter-gatherers. As maize, beans, and squash were introduced, most likely by intermediaries who had contacts with Mesoamerica, a more settled and urban lifestyle emerged. These Amerindians also built mounds for ceremonial and religious use and as dwellings for chiefs. The chief had both religious and political roles and also oversaw long-distance trade, which supplemented food supplies and brought access to luxury goods. Urban communities developed as the food supply became more constant, the bow and arrow was introduced, and trade expanded. With a larger population and larger towns, which served as centers for bartering, class distinctions increased.

Cahokia, the best example of the apogee of Mississippian culture, contained the largest mound—one hundred feet high—in North America. In 1200, with about 20,000 inhabitants, Cahokia was equal in size to many postclassic Maya cities. Cahokia had political dominance over the surrounding agricultural territories and towns, and its long-distance trade, by canoe, brought in tools and goods used for rituals. Cahokia declined after 1250 because of climate changes and population increase, which in turn put pressure on the food supply. Cahokia was eventually abandoned, but other mound cultures continued to thrive in the southeast until the arrival of the Europeans.

ANDEAN CIVILIZATIONS: 600–1500

At the same time that highly sophisticated societies were developing in Mesoamerica, they were also developing in the Andean region. The ability to create and maintain complex civilizations in the difficult environment of the Andes mountains is amazing, and geography played a huge role in how those communities and then larger states were constructed. Andean peoples had to cope with three ecological zones: the high altitudes and harsh weather of the mountainous zone; the arid zone of the coastal region by the Pacific Ocean; and the hot, humid Amazonian tropical zone. Sustaining life in these zones required various technologies, among them terraced hillside farming, irrigation systems, road networks for long-distance exchange, accurate calendars, and plant domestication. In addition, animals like the llama and the alpaca were used as beasts of burden as well as sources of meat and wool. **Khipus**, knotted colored cords that could be used for recordkeeping, were a unique technology that served as an important administrative tool as well.

Productive and efficient use of human labor was also essential in managing the environment. The basic unit that allowed for such labor was the **ayllu**, a clan that worked a piece of land. Families within the ayllu were expected to work together on everyday jobs and were also obligated to supply food and labor to the chief of the ayllu. When larger political organization was placed under the authority of a hereditary king, the mit'a system was created. Every ayllu rotated in and out of the **mit'a** system, which required the ayllu to contribute a specific number of workers every year to do maintenance work for the state—building projects, road maintenance, textile production, and irrigation work. They also cared for the herds and fields that belonged to the royal family, the religious elite, and the aristocracy. The mit'a system was used by Andean societies for more than a thousand years.

Because so many smaller ecological zones existed in the Andean region and each zone produced different goods that were necessary resources, vertical integration was necessary. **Vertical integration** is a term coined by historians to describe the practices of the Andean peoples who purposely exchanged the goods from these differing ecological zones in order to have everything they needed. Colonists were sent out by different ayllus in order to gain access to these goods and the economic benefit they provided.

PRE-INCA SOCIETIES

Although the Inca created an empire that represented the height of Andean civilization, several earlier societies exhibited many of the cultural, social, and political continuities of the Andean peoples.

By 600, the **Moche** were dominant in the northern coastal area of Peru. They relied on the mit'a system to supply laborers for irrigation and depended on the llama and alpaca for trade. The wool of these animals allowed the Moche to create a strong textile industry, and women of all classes had special roles as weavers. The Moche excelled in ceramic work, creating pottery that included vases with detailed portraits, religious imagery, and depictions of daily life. The Moche also developed metal tools for agriculture and military use. A rigid social structure allowed for the clear division of labor, and religion was a central component of society. Priests and military leaders held political control, and their clothing and elaborate gold jewelry demonstrated their wealth and set them apart. The bulk of people, both men and women, focused on agricultural production and other labor requirements. Because we have no written records about the Moche, archaeological evidence alone provides the clues for their decline. Repeated natural disasters seem to be the cause for the weakening of both the economy and the authority of religious and political leaders, who drew their power from the belief that they could control the natural world.

The peoples of **Tiwanaku** and **Wari**, Moche contemporaries, lived in the highlands. Tiwanaku was an urban center located in modern Bolivia next to Lake Titicaca. Once drained, the marshes around the lake provided thousands of acres of land. The lake fish provided protein, as did llamas, which were also used for transport in long-distance trade that brought in a variety of foodstuffs and agricultural goods. Tiwanaku was a grand ceremonial and religious center built out of stone, which was cut and moved many miles to build pyramids and other buildings as well as huge human statues. With limited tools, the labor used to complete the projects was extensive, making the achievement all the more impressive and demonstrating the ability of the people of Tiwanaku to manage a large labor system. Military conquest allowed the Tiwanaku people to establish colonies to ensure food supplies from the different ecological zones of the Andean region. Wari was larger than Tiwanaku, but the relationship between the two centers is unclear even though their peoples had some cultural similarities. Wari contained a walled city that included a huge temple as well as urban and suburban housing. By 1000 both the Wari and Tiwanaku had declined significantly. The stage was set for the Inca, the next great Andean society.

THE INCA

The **Inca** created an amazing empire that stretched up and down the coast of South America and had more than six million people under its control by

1525. Their rise to power began in the 1430s when strong political leaders joined together and began an age of military conquest.

Many of the Andean traditions were fundamental to the life of the Incas. They were pastoralists who depended on the llama and the alpaca for food, clothing, and transport. Caring for these animals was the job of both men and women and was a representation of the obligations of the gods and the ruler to the people. The mit'a system continued as the fundamental building block of the empire. Each ayllu contributed one-seventh of its males for labor to create a food surplus for the elderly and sick. Laborers also built thirteen thousand miles of road, which linked the empire economically and militarily.

In order to rule effectively, local chiefs were kept in place and handled local administrative duties and judicial matters. However, to minimize the risk of rebellion, heirs of defeated territories had to live at the Inca royal court, and images of local deities also had to be brought to Cuzco, the center of government. Inca society was highly stratified; the imperial elite of Cuzco and other urban centers could live a life very removed from the lower class—so much so that a commoner who looked the ruler in the face could be executed. To cement its authority, the royal family also claimed a divine link to the sun, one of the primary gods worshiped by the Inca. Finally, all those who made up the royal bureaucracy had to be kinsmen. As in other American societies, religious ritual reaffirmed the power of the king. Like the Aztec kings, each new Inca king was expected to extend the empire through conquest.

Cuzco was located near the center of the empire and was connected to other cities by the intricate network of Inca roads. Although Cuzco was never as populated as the Aztecs' Tenochtitlan, it was a true imperial city, with massive, detailed stonework as well as elaborate palaces and temples reflecting each ruler's glory. The Temple of the Sun was the most glorious, with gold adorning its inner walls. Sacrifices to the sun included animals, textiles, and, infrequently, humans. As in Mesoamerica, calendars based on astronomical observation were important for religious ritual. Inca textile weaving and metallurgy—continuities handed down from earlier Andean societies—surpassed the Mesoamericans'. Copper and bronze weapons were decorated with gold and silver. Khipus continued to be used for communication and recordkeeping and were especially important because the Inca multiplied their production and economic output with the conquest of peoples in different environments.

The Inca ruled for a century, but in 1525, when the Inca ruler Huayna Capac died, the empire spiraled into a bloody conflict over which son should succeed him. The conflict escalated into a civil war that allowed disgruntled conquered peoples of varying ethnicities and regions to rise up as well. This was the state of the Inca Empire when Europeans arrived in the Andean region in the beginning of the sixteenth century.

AP® Tip

The Aztec and Inca Empires were sophisticated and complex civilizations that flourished for over a century. You should be able to compare the cultural, economic, political, and social aspects of these two great empires.

Content Review Questions

As the basis and foundation of their government, the Incas designed a law by which it seemed to them they could prevent and attack those evils that might spring up in the lands they ruled over. To this end, they mandated that within all towns, large or small, in their empire neighbors were to be registered by tens into *decuries*. One of the ten, called a *Decurion* had charge of the other nine. Five decuries of ten people had a superior Decurion who was responsible for fifty people. Two decuries of fifty had another superior who looked after the one hundred….

The decurions of ten were obligated to perform two duties in regard to the members of their decury, or squad. The first was to be a diligent and caring advocate for assistance in cases of need that arose, bringing notice of the cases to the governor or any other minister who had the responsibility of providing for them…

From *The Royal Commentaries of the Inca* by half-Incan, half-Spanish ethnohistorian Garcilaso de la Vega c. 1609.

The Human Record: Sources of Global History, 8th edition, volume 1, p. 367.

1. Which state's government is least similar to the style of government described in the above passage?
   (A) Maya
   (B) Aztec
   (C) Classical Persia
   (D) Song China

2. Which technological innovation was most important for supporting the growth of the state described above?
   (A) The wheel
   (B) Terracing
   (C) Chinampas
   (D) A written language

3. Which of the following can best be inferred about the Inca after reading the above passage?
   (A) The Empire was larger than a person could reasonably travel and oversee within a week's time.
   (B) The Empire was built using coerced labor.
   (C) The Empire used domesticated animals for transportation and communication.
   (D) The Empire lasted several centuries.

The Aztecs succeeded in developing a remarkable urban landscape. The population of Tenochtitlan and Tlatelolco combined with that of the cities and towns of the surrounding lakeshore was approximately 500,000 by 1500 C.E. Three causeways connected this island capital to the lakeshore. Planners laid out the urban center as a grid where canals and streets intersected at right angles to facilitate the movement of people and goods.

From Bulliet, *The Earth and Its Peoples,* 7th edition, p. 386.

4. Which of the following can be inferred about the Aztecs based on the above passage?
   (A) The Aztecs had a strong centralized government capable or organizing a large labor force.
   (B) The Aztecs had a large number of slaves, and efficient techniques to minimize slave rebellion.
   (C) The Aztecs conquered a pre-existing capital city.
   (D) The Aztecs had contact with urban planners from Eurasia.

5. Which of the following innovations provides the best evidence that the Aztecs used technology to adapt to their environment?
   (A) Construction of rope bridges
   (B) Chinampas
   (C) Domestication of llamas
   (D) The use of a barter system to get crops that were not indigenous to central Mexico

6 Which of the following similarities did the Aztec and Inca NOT share?
   (A) Both relied on public displays of large-scale human sacrifice of war captives.
   (B) Both believed military conquest was a requirement for an incoming political leader.
   (C) Both relied on tribute extracted from conquered regions and peoples.
   (D) Both relied on military control that required large, well-trained armies.

Answers

1. ANSWER: A. The passage describes an imperial bureaucracy. All of the states listed used this system except the Maya. The Maya instead were a collection of smaller city-states (*The Earth and Its Peoples*, 6th ed., pp. 198–201/7th ed., pp. 201–204; History Reasoning Skill—Comparison; Learning Objectives SB-1,2; Key Concept 3.2.I.D).

2. ANSWER: B. The Inca were located in the Andes Mountains of South America. In order to grow a sufficient amount of food to feed a growing empire, they had to learn to farm in the mountains—thus terracing was necessary for the growth of the Empire (*The Earth and Its Peoples*, 6th ed. pp. 198–201/7th ed., pp. 201–204; History Reasoning Skill—Causation; Learning Objectives SB-3, ECON-3; Key Concept 3.2.I.D).

3. ANSWER: A. States set up bureaucracies to manage large amounts of land and subjects. This allowed local matters to be handled by local bureaucrats, instead of everything flowing through the central government. Since the Inca used a bureaucratic system, it can be inferred that they had a state that was too large for the central leader to manage all territories and subjects by himself (*The Earth and Its Peoples*, 6th ed., pp. 198–201/7th ed., pp. 201–204; History Disciplinary Practice—Analyzing Historical Evidence; Learning Objectives SB-2,3; Key Concept 3.2.I.D).

4. ANSWER: A. In order to construct the organized capital cities described above with the technology available to the Aztecs, a large number of people must have been involved. In order for the city to turn out on a grid pattern, the workforce must have been organized. This implies that the government had the ability to mobilize and organize a large amount of people, but does not necessarily mean that the workers were slaves (*The Earth and Its Peoples*, 6th ed., pp. 197–198/7th ed., pp. 199–201; History Disciplinary Practice—Analyzing Historical Evidence; Learning Objectives SB-1,3; Key Concept 3.2.I.D).

5. ANSWER: B. The passage describes the Aztec ability to build cities in a swamp. They used chinampas, or floating islands, in order to reclaim this marshy territory (*The Earth and Its Peoples*, 6th ed., pp. 197–198/7th ed., pp. 199–201; History Disciplinary Practice—Analyzing Historical Evidence; Learning Objectives ECON-2,3; Key Concept 3.2.I.D).

6. ANSWER: A. There is evidence that the Inca practiced textile and animal sacrifice but did not practice human sacrifice on the large scale that the Aztecs did (*The Earth and Its Peoples*, 6th ed., pp. 197–198 and pp. 395–396/7th ed., pp. 199–201; History Reasoning Skill—Comparison; Learning Objectives SB-1-3; Key Concept 3.2.I.D).

AP® FORMAT QUESTIONS FOR PERIOD 3

Multiple-Choice Questions

Questions 1–3 refer to the following map.

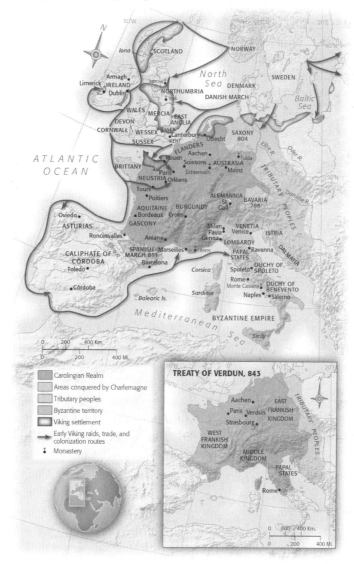

Map of the Carolingian Realms

AP® is a trademark registered by the College Board, which is not affiliated with, and does not endorse, this product.

1. Western Europe displays evidence of which of the following?
   (A) Cross-cultural exchanges
   (B) Migration of Bantu-speaking peoples
   (C) Diffusion of epidemic diseases
   (D) Increased agricultural production due to technological innovations

2. During the time period identified on this map, what was the governing structure of most of western/central Europe?
   (A) Mongol khanates
   (B) Dynastic empires
   (C) Feudalism
   (D) Delhi Sultanates

3. In addition to the territorial divisions shown in the map, which of the following was also a characteristic of western Europe?
   (A) Maritime migrations of the Polynesian peoples
   (B) Diasporic communities
   (C) The cultural transmissions that occurred as a result of the crusades
   (D) The diversification of labor organization

Questions 4–6 refer to the following image.

By Muhammad Mahdi Karim (https://www.google.com/search?q=muhammad+mahdi+Karim+kaba&tbm=
isch&source=iu&ictx=1&fir=OACUjevNf045DM%253A%252CRqFJZmaq63mDFM%252C_&usag=__pm-
8J_cD0U_O1poXQAYzjaGJa2o%3D&sa=X&ved=0ahUKEwjW8Ou5-rTbAhXHo1kKHU-
xBjUQ9QEIOjAC#imgrc=OACUjevNf045DM) via Wikimedia Commons

The Ka'Ba is a small prayer building located within the courtyard of
al-Haram Mosque in Mecca, Saudi Arabia.

4. Which of the following is true of the city which houses the structure in
   the image in the period 600–1450 C.E.?
   (A) As a site of religious pilgrimage, this city did not engage in political
   or economic dealings.
   (B) The religious importance of the city also attracted merchants, making
   it a center of cross-cultural exchange.
   (C) As a sacred site, the city banned practitioners of other monotheistic
   religions from living inside its borders.
   (D) As a site holy to many different religions, this site was devastated by
   constant fighting during the Crusades.

5. The pilgrimage to this place resulted in which of the following?
   (A) Increased cross-cultural interactions that resulted in the diffusion of
   literary, artistic, and cultural traditions
   (B) Decentralized governments in Europe and the Arabian Peninsula
   (C) The flourishing of Mayan city-states
   (D) The peasant revolts in western Europe

6. Which of the following was LEAST responsible for helping to spread the
   religion associated with the given image?
   (A) Military expansion of the caliphates
   (B) Sufi missionaries
   (C) Crusaders retuning to Europe with Islamic books and technology
   (D) The rise of the Mongol khanates

Questions 7–9 refer to the following data.

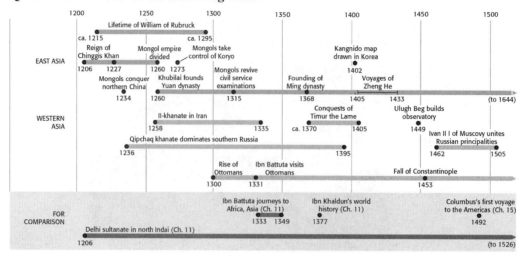

© Cengage Learning

7. Which of the following was the governing system in Asia from 1234 to 1368?
   (A) Khanates
   (B) Chinese dynasties
   (C) Religious theocracies
   (D) Feudal kingdoms

8. Which of the following can be inferred from the chart?
   (A) The Byzantine Empire fell near the end of the period identified on the chart.
   (B) The Mongolian Empire sustained itself during the entire period.
   (C) The Silk Road ceased to be an important trade route.
   (D) The Indian Ocean basin flourished.

9. The trade routes established and continued by the empires identified in the chart were responsible for diffusing which of the following?
   (A) Smallpox
   (B) Hinduism
   (C) The bubonic plague
   (D) Judaism

Questions 10–12 refer to the following passage.

> One lasting product of the Inca labor system was over 25,000 miles of magnificent roads. While some of these routes predated the Inca conquest, the Inca linked them together into an overall system. Since the Inca did not have the wheel, most of the traffic was by foot, and llamas could carry small loads. With no surveying instruments, the Inca constructed these roads across deserts, yawning chasms, and mountains over 16,000 feet high.
>
> *Voyages in World History*, 2nd ed., p. 413

10. Which of the following provides an additional way in which the Inca adapted to their environment?
    (A) The creation of Quipu
    (B) The use of Waru Waru agriculture
    (C) The construction of chinampas
    (D) The integration of rice paddies

11. Which of the following may be inferred about the Incas from this passage?
    (A) Imperial systems were created by the Inca.
    (B) The Incas had a decentralized governing structure.
    (C) The Incas were polytheistic.
    (D) The Incas practiced human sacrifice.

12. Which of the following can be proven using evidence from the given passage?
    (A) The Inca converted conquered peoples.
    (B) The Inca had environmental knowledge and how to adapt technology to the environment.
    (C) The Inca were skilled at diffusing crops.
    (D) The Inca were able to develop new forms of governance.

Questions 13–15 refer to the following passage.

> Likewise, it is more advantageous and more profitable for the merchant's enterprise, if he brings goods from a country that is far away and where there is danger on the road. In such a case, the goods transported will be few and rare, because the place where they come from is far away or because the road over which they come is beset with perils, so that there are few who would bring them, and they are very rare. When goods are rare, their prices go up. Therefore, the merchants who dare to enter the Sudan country are the most prosperous and wealthy of all people.
>
> Ibn Khaldun, *How to Get Rich Quickly*, 1375

13. Which of the following trade routes does Ibn Khaldun reference?
    (A) The Indian Ocean basin
    (B) The Mediterranean Sea
    (C) The Atlantic trade
    (D) Trans-Saharan

14. Which of the following could BEST be used to explain the large presence of Islamic merchants on major Afro-Eurasian Trade Routes?
    (A) The Islamic acceptance of merchants and trade
    (A) The Mongols protection of the Silk Road
    (B) The Chinese rejection of merchants and trade
    (C) The presence of a "dark ages" in Europe

15. Which of the following likely provided the context for the creation of the passage?
    (A) An increasing volume of trade due to the domestication of the camel
    (B) A decrease in the volume of trade due to political instability along the trade route
    (C) A decline in the demand for trade due to the spread of the bubonic plague
    (D) An increase in the dangers to merchants due to the spread of gunpowder

Short-Answer Questions

Question 1 refers to the following map of Africa and the trans-Saharan trade routes (not shown).

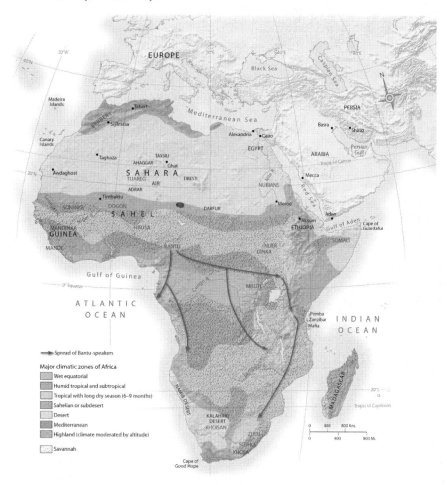

1. Answer Parts A, B, and C.
   A. Identify ONE way trans-Saharan trade contributed to global trade.
   B. Identify ONE nontechnological factor that facilitated trans-Saharan trade.
   C. Explain ONE impact of trans-Saharan trade on sub-Saharan Africa.

2. Answer Parts A, B, and C.
   A. Identify ONE impact of the caliphates on Islam in the Middle East.
   B. Explain ONE impact of Islam on the Southeast Asia.
   C. Explain ONE short-term impact of the Mongols on the Middle East.

3. Answer Parts A, B, and C.
   A. Identify ONE long-term impact of the Mongols on western Europe.
   B. Identify ONE long-term impact of the Mongols on Russia.
   C. Identify and explain ONE way the Ming dynasty reacted to previous Yuan rule.

Question 4 refers to the following passage.

> Western European revival coincided with and contributed to the Crusades, a series of religiously inspired Christian military campaigns against Muslims in the eastern Mediterranean that dominated the politics of Europe from 1095 to 1204. Four great expeditions, the last redirected against the Byzantines and resulting in the Latin capture of Constantinople, constituted the region's largest military undertakings since the fall of Rome. As a result of the Crusades, noble courts and burgeoning cities in western Europe consumed more goods from the east. This set the stage for the later adoption of ideas, artistic styles, and industrial processes from Byzantium and the lands of Islam.
>
> *The Earth and Its Peoples*, 6th ed., p. 289

4. Answer Parts A, B, and C.
   A. Identify ONE reason for the start of the Crusades.
   B. Explain ONE political or economic impact of the Crusades.
   C. Explain ONE artistic or intellectual impact of the Crusades.

5. Answer Parts A, B, and C.
   A. Identify ONE cultural achievement of the Toltecs.
   B. Identify ONE cultural achievement of the Aztecs.
   C. Identify ONE cultural achievement of the Inca.

Long Essay Questions

1. Evaluate the cultural and religious continuities and changes resulting from Islam's presence in Africa during the period c. 600 to c. 1450.

2. Analyze the similarities and differences of the social and economic characteristics between the Muslim caliphates and the Mongols in the Middle East from c. 600 to c. 1450.

3. Analyze the similarities and differences in the role Chinese culture played from c. 600 to c. 1450 in TWO of the following: Japan, Korea, and/or Vietnam.

4. Analyze the political continuities and changes over time in Europe from c. 600 to c. 1450.

5. Evaluate the cultural continuities and changes over time in Mesoamerican society from c. 600 to c. 1450.

Answers

MULTIPLE-CHOICE QUESTIONS

1. ANSWER: A. During the eighth century, the Muslims conquered the Iberian Peninsula (modern day Spain and Portugal); these Muslim inhabitants were called Moors and they ruled the Iberian Peninsula until the late fifteenth century. The Muslims traveled through Northern Africa to reach the Iberian Peninsula; therefore, the map is indicative of cross-cultural exchange (*The Earth and Its Peoples*, 6th ed., p. 275/7th ed., p. 272; History Disciplinary Practice—Analyzing Historical Evidence; Learning Objective SB, CUL; Key Concept 3.1 III D).

2. ANSWER: C. During the post-classical period, most of Europe was governed by decentralized feudal states (*The Earth and Its Peoples*, 6th ed., p. 459/7th ed., pp. 273–278; History Disciplinary Practice—Analyzing Historical Evidence; Learning Objective SB; Key Concept 3.2 I B).

3. ANSWER: B. The term *diaspora* refers to the spread of any people from their original homeland. As shown in the map, the Iberian Peninsula was controlled by a Muslim caliphate. Islam originated in the Arabian Peninsula and quickly spread, with its followers, through North Africa and into the Iberian Peninsula (*The Earth and Its Peoples*, 6th ed., p. 59/7th ed., p. 68; History Disciplinary Practice—Analyzing Historical Evidence; Learning Objective SB; Key Concept 3.1 III B).

4. ANSWER: B. The symbol in the image is the Ka'ba, which is located in modern Saudi Arabia. It is the holy shrine to Muslims around the world. In the period 600–1450, it attracted many pilgrims from all over the Islamic world—thus it became a center of commerce and cross-cultural exchange (*The Earth and Its Peoples*, 6th ed., p. 259/7th ed., pp.248–250; History Disciplinary Practice—Analyzing Historical Evidence; Learning Objective CUL; Key Concept 3.1 III A).

5. ANSWER: A. One of the five pillars of faith in the Muslim faith calls on Muslims to make a pilgrimage to Mecca to pray at the Ka'ba. This hajj will result in the diffusion of culture as thousands of Muslims travel to the Arabian Peninsula (*The Earth and Its Peoples*, 6th ed., p. 251/7th ed., p. 251; History Reasoning Skill—Causation; Learning Objective CUL; Key Concept 3.1 III D).

6. ANSWER: C. Although Crusaders brought many books and tools back with them from the Middle East, Europe remained firmly Christian in the period 600–1450 (*The Earth and Its Peoples*, 6th ed., p. 251/7th ed., p. 251; History Disciplinary Practice—Analyzing Historical Evidence; Learning Objective SB; Key Concept 3.1 I E).

7. ANSWER: A. The Mongols divided their empire into four khanates in order to effectively rule a large amount of territory (*The Earth and Its Peoples*, 6th ed., p. 334/7th ed., p. 323; History Disciplinary Practice—Analyzing Historical Evidence; Learning Objective SB; Key Concept 3.2 I B).

8. ANSWER: A. The Byzantine capital was Constantinople, and the chart shows that in the mid-fifteenth century, the Ottomans were responsible for the fall of Constantinople. The Ottomans then changed the name of the capital to Istanbul and ruled the area for almost 500 years (*The Earth and Its Peoples*, 6th ed., p. 336/7th ed., p. 321; History Disciplinary Practice—Analyzing Historical Evidence; Learning Objective SB; Key Concept 3.2 I A).

9. ANSWER: C. The chart shows Eastern Hemisphere trade routes, which were responsible for the spread of the bubonic plague (*The Earth and Its Peoples*, 6th ed., p. 353/7th ed., pp. 322–325; History Disciplinary Practice—Analyzing Historical Evidence; Learning Objective ECON; Key Concept 3.1 IV).

10. ANSWER: B. The passage describes the Incan achievements in road building. These roads were used to facilitate trade and communication exchanges in the Americas. Similarly, the Inca adapted to their mountainous area by using Waru Waru agriculture to help collect water (*The Earth and Its Peoples*, 6th ed., p. 355/7th ed., p. 212; History Disciplinary Practice—Analyzing Historical Evidence; Learning Objective ECON, CUL; Key Concept 3.1 I B).

11. ANSWER: A. In order for the Incan labor system to create the massive network of roads, the Incas had a powerful governing structure (state) (*The Earth and Its Peoples*, 6th ed., p. 355/7th ed., p. 212; History Disciplinary Practice—Analyzing Historical Evidence; Learning Objective SB; Key Concept 3.2).

12. ANSWER: B. The passage describes the construction of roads through mountainous regions in the Americas, which would have required knowledge of the environment and technology to create the roads (*The Earth and Its Peoples*, 6th ed., p. 197/7th ed., pp. 211–217; History Disciplinary Practice—Analyzing Historical Evidence; Learning Objective ENV; Key Concept 3.1 II A).

13. ANSWER: D. The passage refers to trade in the Sudan that was a part of the trans-Saharan trade routes (*The Earth and Its Peoples*, 6th ed., p. 232/7th ed., p. 235; History Disciplinary Practice—Analyzing Historical Evidence; Learning Objective ECON; Key Concept 3.1 I A).

14. ANSWER: A. Ibn Khaldun was a Muslim traveler who was describing the benefits of trade and clearly supported merchants. Because Muhammad was a merchant, the Islamic faith supported and encouraged trade and merchants (*The Earth and Its Peoples*, 6th ed., p. 332/7th ed., p. 328; History Disciplinary Practice—Analyzing Historical Evidence; Learning Objective ECON; Key Concept 3.1).

15. ANSWER: B. The Mongol Empire just collapsed, ending the protection Mongols had provided for merchants (*The Earth and Its Peoples*, 6th ed., p. 412/7th ed., pp. 331–334; History Disciplinary Practice—Analyzing Evidence: Content and Sourcing; Learning Objective CUL; Key Concept 3.1 III C).

SHORT-ANSWER QUESTIONS

1. In a good response, the student would explain the role salt, kola nuts, or palm oil played in early trans-Saharan trade. The existence of strong states to protect traders facilitated trade. The coming of Islam across the trade routes would be an impact on sub-Saharan Africa (*The Earth and Its Peoples*, 6th ed., pp. 231–235/7th ed., pp. 234–240; History Reasoning Skill—Causation; Learning Objective ECON-7; Key Concept 3.1 I C).

2. A good response by the student would include the caliphates' role in maintaining and spreading a cohesive concept of Islam throughout the Middle East, especially with the Abbasids. The Crusades reinforced unity and allowed them to maintain control of western Asia and Jerusalem. In the Middle East, the Abbasid caliphate ended, leading to the rise of the early Turkic Ottomans (*The Earth and Its Peoples*, 6th ed., pp. 252–258/7th ed., pp. 252–254; History Reasoning Skill—Causation; Learning Objective SB-2; Key Concept 3.1 I E).

3. A good response for the student would be the impact of the bubonic plague on population of social structure or the impact of gunpowder. The Kievan princes started to band together in resistance to the Mongols and formed a unified state. The Ming wanted to recenter China by re-embracing Chinese traditions and culture (*The Earth and Its Peoples*, 6th ed., pp. 324–343/7th ed., pp. 330–339; History Reasoning Skill—Contextualization; Learning Objective SB-2,3; Key Concept 3.1 I E).

4. A good response would include students explaining with some depth or detail a cause such as the religious leaders wanted to slow warfare in Europe or Italian merchants wanting more trade in the Mediterranean. A political/economic impact on Europe would include things such as weakening serfdom or increasing trade. An artistic or intellectual impact would be rediscovery of Greco-Roman learning, the lute, or the concept of "courtly love" espoused by Eleanor of Aquitaine (*The Earth and Its Peoples*, 6th ed., pp. 289–291/7th ed., pp. 286–290; History Reasoning Skill—Causation; Learning Objective SB-3; Key Concept 3.2 II).

5. The Toltecs built off the Teotihuacan cultural achievements and created a sophisticated civilization. Their capital, Tula, displayed their elaborate architecture. The Aztec built off the Mayan cultural achievements but introduced the concept of monarchial empire throughout their empire and tribute. They built organized cities. The Inca worked with metal particularly silver and gold and were known for their khipu system (*The Earth and Its Peoples*, 6th ed., pp. 197–203/7th ed., pp. 385–390; History Reasoning Skill—Contextualization; Learning Objective ECON-3; Key Concept 3.3 I).

Long Essay Questions

1. Your essay should take up both change and continuity as they related to Islam's impact on social interaction, social structure, language, and education. There are numerous examples of cultural changes; some topics include the role of Islam in increasing literacy in both Arabic and local languages, the rise of education centers in great cities like Timbuktu, the religious and social role of mosques, studies in science and medicine, and the increased use of books. Some key social changes occurred in the growth of elite classes and the subsequent increase in slavery. However, there were some social continuity in the roles that women played in various African societies while incorporating the changes brought by Islamic influence. An important continuity throughout the period was the adaptability of Islam to local cultures and traditions and the ability of peoples across Africa to become devout Muslims while maintaining their own cultural identities (*The Earth and Its Peoples*, 6th ed., pp. 380–382, 391–393/7th ed., pp. 372–374; History Reasoning Skill—Continuity and Change over Time; Learning Objective CUL-1,2,3; Key Concept 3.1 III D).

2. For this essay you should include a comparison of treatment of conquered peoples, religious practices, and cultural contributions. Cultural contributions could also be considered in a comparative analysis of the role of trade and cities in both empires as part of economic characteristics. Another economic comparison could also be drawn between the unsuccessful attempts by the Mongol Il-khans to incorporate paper money and tax farming (an economic policy used earlier in the Middle East) and the Abbasid caliphate's economic practices. The use of paper money by the Mongols is in contrast with the Abbasid caliphate's continuation of coinage (*The Earth and Its Peoples*, 6th ed., pp. 330–334/7th ed., pp. 319–326; History Reasoning Skill—Comparison; Learning Objective SB-4; Key Concept 3.1 I E).

3. You begin by addressing how Confucian principles influenced all three areas. Japan, not being on the border of China, would have been somewhat different in how it was influenced, which was primarily by trade. Vietnam and Korea were at times controlled by Chinese dynasties and would have been more directly influenced through provincial rule or as tributary states. The arts such as woodblock printing and silk paintings were common. Chinese writing also influenced development of similar writing systems. The role of women in society in all three was dominated by Confucian principles. The concept of imperial rule and capital cities were also influenced in some way by the Chinese. Chinese steel making also influenced the development of similar technologies in these countries (*The Earth and Its Peoples*, 6th ed., pp. 310–315/7th ed., pp. 302–310; History Reasoning Skill—Comparison; Learning Objective CUL-1, SB-3; Key Concept 3.1 III D).

4. This essay should include a discussion of aspects of both change and continuity as they relate to the change from decentralized feudal systems to stronger monarchies. The political roles of the Catholic Church can

also be analyzed to show how the church and secular authority vied for more political authority. Continuity in political authority would be seen in eastern Europe, where the Byzantine Empire continued under a succession of emperors who served as both emperors and appointers of patriarchs to the Eastern Orthodox Church. The Byzantine Empire's political power waned with its loss of territorial control, but the empire did continue as one fairly stable political organization until the end of this period (*The Earth and Its Peoples*, 6th ed., pp. 272–289/7th ed., pp. 270–283; History Reasoning Skill—Continuity and Change over Time; Learning Objective SB-1,2,5; Key Concept 3.2 I B).

5. The essay should include a discussion of aspects of both change and continuity as they relate to the cultural continuities between the Toltec and the Aztecs in their respective regions of Mesoamerica. The continuity in the role of ritual, religion, urban centers, and architecture can all be discussed. For change, you can address the value placed on military conquest as the Toltec and Aztec came into power. The continuity in cultural and religious traditions is very apparent from 600 to 1450 (*The Earth and Its Peoples*, 6th ed., pp. 197–203/7th ed., pp. 205–207; History Reasoning Skill—Continuity and Change over Time; Learning Objective SB-3,6; Key Concept 3.1 III A).

Period 4: Global Interactions, c. 1450 to c. 1750

Period 4 in the AP® World History framework focuses on the formation of global commercial networks following sustained European contact with the Americas and the consequences of that formation. A major turning point in world history, the colonization/settlement of the Americas by Europeans resulted in profound political, cultural, social, economic, and environmental changes not only in the Americas but also in Europe, Asia, and Africa. Many of these significant changes are tied to the Columbian Exchange, a term for the mass two-way diffusion of plants, animals, and germs between the Americas and the rest of the world. As Europeans extracted resources from their American territories, they also introduced crops and domesticated animals for both personal use and daily life and in order to turn a profit, as with the introduction of plantation agriculture for cash crops. The expansion of the natural resources European nations had access to allowed those nations to develop their own economic activity as well as engage more readily in trade with African and Asian nations.

The desire to maintain a favorable balance of trade as part of a mercantilist economic policy led nations such as England, France, Spain, Portugal, and the Netherlands to establish colonies in the Americas and employ coercive labor to extract resources for use in commerce, particularly with China. The increasing need for American cash crops and silver for use in trade in turn led to an expansion of coercive labor systems, with Europeans trading manufactured goods with African states along the west coast of Africa for slaves to work on plantations and in the mines of the Americas. Of course, Europeans actively sought the conversion of the native peoples, as well as their African captives, to Christianity. Many converted and found ways to practice Christianity that incorporated indigenous traditions. However, the introduction of diverse African cultures into the Americas also led to the development of unique, new practices reflecting the diversity of colonial societies. Thus, social and cultural structures were significantly impacted by European expansion in this period.

As with previous periods, religions and belief systems continued to influence political, economic, and social characteristics of societies. Religions continued to diffuse, through conquest, commerce, and missionary efforts. Commercial networks continued to expand, facilitated by technological developments. Rulers continued to find ways to legitimize and consolidate power over their territories. Some rulers—particularly those in Europe, but also the Ottoman Sultans—found themselves ruling an increasingly diverse population and, therefore, faced the challenge of fostering a sense of unity among peoples of different religions, languages, and cultural traditions.

AP® is a trademark registered by the College Board, which is not affiliated with, and does not endorse, this product.

The following charts outline the learning objectives and topics from the content outline that fit into this period.

Content Review Questions can be found at the end of each chapter. **AP®** **format questions** for Period 4 can be found on page 325. **Document-Based Questions** can be found in the diagnostic test and practice tests.

THEMATIC LEARNING OBJECTIVES FOR PERIOD 4

INTERACTION BETWEEN HUMANS AND THE ENVIRONMENT

Learning Objectives—Students are able to . . .	Relevant Topics in the Concept Outline
ENV-1 Explain how environmental factors, disease, and technology affected patterns of human migration and settlement over time.	4.1. II, III—Maritime technology 4.1. IV—Mixing of cultures 4.2. I—Little Ice Age 4.3. II—Imperial expansion
ENV-2 Evaluate the extent to which migration, population, and urbanization affected the environment over time.	4.1. II, III—Intensification and expansion of maritime trade routes 4.1. V—Colonization; Columbian Exchange 4.I. VI—Spread of Cultures
ENV-3 Evaluate the extent to which the development of diverse technologies, industrialization, transportation methods, and exchange and communication networks have affected the environment over time.	4.1. V—Columbian Exchange 4.1. V—Colonization 4.2. I—Increased agricultural production and forced labor regimes

DEVELOPMENT AND INTERACTION OF CULTURES

Learning Objectives—Students are able to . . .	Relevant Topics in the Concept Outline
CUL-1 Explain how religions, belief systems, philosophies, and ideologies originated, developed, and spread as a result of expanding communication and exchange networks.	4.1. VI—Reformation
CUL-2 Explain how religions, belief systems, philosophies, and ideologies affected political, economic, and social developments over time.	4.1. VI—Syncretic belief systems and practices; spread of these practices 4.3. I—Development of and responses to globalization
CUL-3 Explain how cross-cultural interactions resulted in the diffusion of culture, technologies, and scientific knowledge.	4.1. II—Cartography and navigation 4.1. III—Transoceanic voyages
CUL-4 Explain how the arts are shaped by and reflect innovation, adaptation, and creativity of specific societies over time.	4.1. VII—Spread of literacy; funding and expansion of arts 4.3. I—Courtly literature, rulers
CUL-5 Explain how expanding exchange networks shaped the emergence of various forms of transregional culture, including music, literature, and visual art.	4.1. VII—Spread of literacy; funding and expansion of arts

STATE BUILDING, EXPANSION, AND CONFLICT

Learning Objectives—Students are able to . . .	Relevant Topics in the Concept Outline
SB-1 Explain how different forms of governance have been constructed and maintained over time.	4.1. VII—Taxation 4.3. I—Rulers legitimize power 4.3. II—Trading-post empires
SB-2 Explain how and why different functions and institutions of governance have changed over time.	4.3. I–III—Gunpowder empires, state rivalries
SB-3 Explain how and why economic, social, cultural, and geographical factors have influenced the processes of state building, expansion, and dissolution.	4.1. I—Changes and continuities in social structures, religion 4.1. IV—African, American, and European interactions; mercantilism, joint-stock companies 4.1. V—Effects of globalizing 4.1. VII—Peasant labor, labor systems; Colonial empires 4.3. I—Monumental architecture 4.3. I–III—State consolidation and imperial expansion; land-based and maritime expansion; economic and political rivalries
SB-4 Explain how and why internal and external political factors have influenced the process of state building, expansion, and dissolution.	4.1. I—Globalizing networks and their political and economic effects 4.1. IV—Spread of cultures among states 4.2. II—Colonial Empires 4.3. I—Tributary taxes and expansion; differential treat of groups 4.3. II—Maritime and land-based empires 4.3. III—Competition over trade routes; competition for overland trade routes and local resistance
SB-5 Explain how societies with states and state-less societies interacted over time.	4.1. IV—Globalization 4.3. I—Rulers consolidated power over groups and populations 4.3. III—Competition over trade routes, state rivalries
SB-6 Explain the political and economic interactions between states and non-state actors over time.	4.1. IV—Globalization 4.3. I—Rulers consolidate power over groups and populations 4.3. III—Competition over trade routes; state rivalries

CREATION, EXPANSION, AND INTERACTION OF ECONOMIC
SYSTEMS

Learning Objectives—Students are able to . . .	Relevant Topics in the Concept Outline
ECON-1 Explain how technology shaped economic production and globalization over time.	4.1. III—Cartographic and navigational technology
ECON-2 Explain the causes and effects of economic strategies of different types of communities, states, and empires.	4.1. I—Global economy 4.1. III—State support for maritime voyages and trade 4.1. IV—Mercantilism, joint-stock companies 4.1. V—Columbian Exchange 4.2. I–III—New political and economic elites; Little Ice Age; shifting hierarchies 4.3. I—Techniques of imperial administration 4.3. II—Imperial expansion 4.3. III—Interstate rivalry
ECON-3 Explain how different modes and locations of production and commerce have developed and changed over time.	4.1. I—Global economy 4.1. III—State support for maritime voyages and trade 4.1. IV—Mercantilism, joint-stock companies 4.2. II—New political and economic elites 4.3. I—Techniques of imperial administration 4.3. II—Imperial expansion 4.1. III—Interstate rivalry
ECON-4 Explain how and why labor systems have developed and changed over time.	4.1. IV—Labor regimes in the Atlantic system 4.1. IV, V—Atlantic world 4.2. II—Coerced labor 4.2. II, III—Slavery in Africa; elites' ability to control labor
ECON-5 Explain how economic systems and the development of ideologies, values, and institutions have influenced each other.	4.1. IV—Mercantilism 4.1. VI—Spread of religions and religious syncretism in regional and newly global trade networks 4.3. I—Economic role in the consolidation of imperial power
ECON-6 Explain how local, regional, and global economic systems and exchange networks have influenced and impacted each other over time.	4.1. I, III—Changing and intensification of existing trade routes; new maritime routes 4.1. II—Maritime technology; technological innovations 4.1. III—Royal-chartered companies 4.1. IV—Joint-stock companies; transoceanic shipping; effects on regional markets 4.1. V—Columbian Exchange 4.2. II—Plantation crops 4.3. II—Gunpowder empires and trade

DEVELOPMENT AND TRANSFORMATION OF SOCIAL STRUCTURES

Learning Objectives—Students are able to . . .	Relevant Topics in the Concept Outline
SOC-1 Explain how distinctions based on kinship, ethnicity, class, gender, and race influenced the development and transformations of social hierarchies.	4.1. IV, V—Atlantic world 4.2. II, III—Increased demand for labor; elites 4.2. III—Changing political and economic structures affected gender hierarchies 4.3. I—Legitimizing imperial rule
SOC-2 Evaluate the extent to which different ideologies, philosophies, and religions affected social hierarchies.	4.3. I—Legitimizing imperial rule
SOC-3 Evaluate the extent to which legal systems, colonialism, nationalism, and independence movements have sustained or challenged class, gender, and racial hierarchies over time.	4.1. IV—Merchants 4.1. V—Columbian Exchange 4.2. II, III—Increased demand for labor, elite control of labor in colonies 4.2. III—Restructuring hierarchies 4.3. I—Legitimization and consolidation of imperial rule
SOC-4 Explain how the development of specialized labor systems interacted with the development of social hierarchies.	4.1. IV, V—Atlantic world 4.2. II, III—Increased demand for labor; elites
SOC-5 Explain how social categories, roles, and practices have been maintained or challenged over time.	4.1. IV—Merchants 4.1. V—Columbian Exchange 4.2. II, III—Increased demand for labor, elite control of labor in colonies 4.2. III—Restructuring hierarchies 4.3. I—Confucian rituals; legitimization and consolidation of imperial rule
SOC-6 Explain how political, economic, cultural, and demographic factors have affected social structures over time.	4.1. V—Columbian Exchange 4.2. II—Changes in Atlantic societies affected by slavery 4.2. II, III—Increased demand for labor, elite control of labor in colonies 4.3. I—Legitimization and consolidation of imperial rule

KEY CONCEPTS FOR PERIOD 4

4.1. Globalizing Networks of Communication and Exchange

4.2. New Forms of Social Organization and Modes of Production

4.3. State Consolidation and Imperial Expansion

16

AFRICA: C1450 TO c. 1750

KEY CONCEPTS

- While Africa had long been linked to the Islamic world through trade (and the Muslims' conquest of North Africa), this period saw the first significant European contact with the continent.
- European involvement in Africa began with the Portuguese and initially included a variety of religious, economic, and political motivations. As the period continued, other European powers initiated contact with Africa as well, drawn mainly by the prospect of acquiring slaves to be put to work on New World plantations.
- In general, African interactions with European powers were fairly static, as the Europeans became preoccupied with New World colonization, and were interested in Africa primarily to maintain the slave trade. Most major conflicts that occurred—with the exception of the Portuguese destruction of the East African trading cities in 1505—were among rival groups within Africa itself, such as the Moroccan invasion of the Songhai Empire in 1591.
- The slave trade led to the depopulation of certain areas of sub-Saharan Africa and forced millions of Africans into lives of grueling labor in other parts of the world. However, the economic, political, and social structures of the continent remained largely intact during this period; not until the nineteenth century would European involvement in Africa widen from a focus on the slave trade to true imperialist domination.

KEY TERMS

- Benin
- Cape Colony

- cassava
- Dahomey

261

Caravanserai

Sundiata
Berbers

Bantu Migrations

- Gold Coast
- Hausa
- Kongo
- maize
- manikongo
- Oyo

- Slave Coast
- Songhai Empire
- Swahili Coast
- trans-Saharan trade
- Whydah

The Earth and Its Peoples, Chapters 15 and 18 of the 6th edition, and Chapters 16 and 19 of the 7th edition, describe the impact of the European maritime revolution on coastal sub-Saharan Africa, the subsequent rise of the Atlantic System, and the effects of Africa's slave trade with Europe and the Islamic world.

WEST AND EAST AFRICA: THE EUROPEANS' FIRST CONTACTS

Prince Henry, the Navigator of Portugal, sowed the seeds of tremendous change for Africa in the early to mid-1400s, as he and his men cautiously explored farther and farther south along Africa's west coast. Following their conquest of the Moroccan city of Ceuta in 1415, the Portuguese became intensely curious to discover the origins of the gold and slaves that were brought to North Africa via well-established trade routes from the continent's sub-Saharan interior. They also sought to spread Christianity to any lands they might discover and counteract the expansion of the rising Ottoman Empire. These economic, religious, and political motives combined with European advances in maritime technology during the fifteenth century to spur the Portuguese to reach the southern tip of Africa before the century's end. Along the way, they found many West Africans who were experienced in trade and ready for new contacts that would expand their volume of exports and imports. In 1482, the African king, Caramansa, allowed the Portuguese to open a trading post on what the Europeans would call the **Gold Coast** of West Africa, where vast amounts of African gold were soon traded for goods from Europe, Asia, and other parts of Africa that arrived on Portuguese ships. Soon after, monarchs such as the oba of Benin and the **manikongo** of Kongo sent delegates to Portugal to gather information on the homeland of these foreign men. Satisfied with what they learned, the traders of **Benin** continued to provide the Portuguese with pepper, ivory, and textiles. They also allowed the Portuguese to purchase prisoners of war, who would be taken as slaves to work on the sugar plantations of the previously uninhabited island of São Tomé off the African coast. Africa would soon be forever transformed, and the effects of the European slave trade would be felt in nearly every corner of the world.

The leaders of Benin chose to restrict their contact with the Portuguese by the 1530s, but by then the king of **Kongo** had made Catholicism the official faith of his land and had begun providing the Portuguese with more and more slaves. The Kongolese slave trade soon got out of control, however, with unauthorized traders resorting to kidnapping to meet the growing demand for slaves. The king's plea for help from the Portuguese was met with no response; the Portuguese had already begun to turn their attention to finding a sea route to link with the Indian Ocean trade. The manikongo faced rebellion, and by the 1540s the center of the slave trade moved farther south, to what was dubbed the **Slave Coast**. Sudden social, political, and economic changes such as these would later become the norm for Africa, as the Europeans continued their exploration—and eventual exploitation—of the continent.

Meanwhile, by the end of the fifteenth century, the **Swahili Coast** of East Africa featured a number of prosperous Muslim-ruled trading states. In 1505, nearly all of them were attacked and plundered by the Portuguese, who had just recently rounded the southern tip of Africa in their continuing quest for a sea route to India. Only Ethiopia was spared Portuguese aggression in East Africa—under attack from the Muslim state of Adal, the Christian queen of Ethiopia pleaded for Portuguese aid. The Muslims were held off, but Ethiopian hopes for a permanent alliance with Portugal went unfulfilled as a result of the Ethiopian rulers' refusal to affiliate their church with the pope in Rome rather than the patriarch of Alexandria. More significantly, by the mid-1500s, Portuguese attention had shifted to the Indian Ocean trade as well as to their colonial conquests in the New World. European involvement in Africa would level off temporarily, but as the seventeenth century unfolded, the seeds of change planted by Henry the Navigator would begin to burst forth with dramatic consequences.

THE TRANSATLANTIC SLAVE TRADE EXPLODES

Portugal led the way in bringing change to the Americas as well as to Africa. By the late 1500s, the Portuguese had copied the plantation-style sugar production of their western Atlantic islands, such as Madeira and São Tomé, in their New World colony of Brazil. Initially the Portuguese planters relied on Amerindian slaves to produce their crops, but as epidemics of Old World diseases ravaged the indigenous American population, African slaves were taken across the Atlantic in ever-increasing numbers by the Portuguese, Spanish, British, and other European colonists. By the seventeenth century, the European ships of the so-called Atlantic System were transporting large numbers of young African adults (more males than females) to a life of slavery in the Americas, in exchange for European manufactured goods (including guns) and Indian textiles. African gold, timber, and other products also found their way into the expanding global economic network. It must be noted that the European traders were not the only ones to profit from these transactions: European guidebooks provided detailed information on the preferred trade items of different areas of Africa's Atlantic coast, as African traders were often found to be shrewd bargainers. Indeed, over the eighteenth century, the price demanded for a slave on the Gold Coast more than doubled. The Africans' bargaining advantages resulted in part from their exploitation of the rivalry among several European nations that had established trading "castles" along the West African coast. Traders from the Dutch East India Company and other European concerns found themselves forced to supply the Africans with more and more guns and gunpowder (thus increasing African military strength and preventing European takeover of African territory) in order to compete in trade. The Europeans were also forced to follow African trading rituals and pay customs duties to African leaders.

The European fervor for African slaves fueled the growth of a number of West African kingdoms. The small kingdom of **Whydah**, an early Gold Coast center for the slave trade, was overtaken in 1727 by the neighboring kingdom of **Dahomey**, which had been able to supply its army (of males and females) with firearms furnished by European traders in exchange for slaves. Dahomey was in turn dominated by the inland kingdom of **Oyo** in 1730 and forced to pay tribute to Oyo to remain independent. For Oyo and the adjacent kingdom of Asante, the Atlantic slave trade was merely one element of a thriving economy that also included extensive commercial activity within West Africa and across the Sahara Desert.

AP® Tip

In writing an essay discussing aspects of slavery in this period, it may be useful to mention the varying sources of African slaves. Contrary to the belief of many in Europe at that time, only rarely did parents sell their children into slavery. Instead, prior to the eighteenth century slaves sold to the Europeans by West African traders were usually prisoners of war; however, historical debate continues over just how frequently wars were initiated solely for the purpose of capturing slaves for export. Current theory (bolstered by eighteenth- and nineteenth-century European and African accounts) holds that most wars in the region were fought over territory and other political disputes, and the capture and sale of enemy prisoners was simply a side endeavor. Later, the Europeans moved farther south and east to the Bight of Biafra in search of new sources of slaves. Here there were no large kingdoms, and hence few large-scale wars, so slave traders turned to kidnapping to maintain their supply, which was supplemented by debtors and convicted criminals.

ANGOLA AND THE CAPE COLONY

For the most part, outright European colonization of Africa would not take place until well after 1750. Two exceptions occurred before that time, however. Both the Portuguese and Dutch established African colonies after 1500. The Dutch East India Company's **Cape Colony**, located at the far southern tip of Africa, played a very minor role in African affairs during this period, as the company's economic activities were oriented almost entirely to the Indian Ocean trade and focused very little on commercial ventures within Africa. Even the Cape Colony's slaves were imported primarily from places outside of Africa, such as South Asia and the East Indies.

Angola was a somewhat different story. As the African slave trade moved steadily south and east during the sixteenth century, the Portuguese realized they could profit from maintaining a permanent settlement along Africa's

Atlantic coast. Centered on the ports of Luanda and Benguela, the colony of Angola soon became the primary supplier of African slaves for the Americas. Portuguese settlers in these cities found profitable employment acting as middlemen, transferring slaves brought by caravan from Africa's far interior to ships bound for Brazil. The ships had brought goods from Europe and the Americas, which were taken back to the interior for exchange at huge markets and fairs for more slaves, thus continuing the internal cycle of commerce that fed into the larger Atlantic Circuit.

The Portuguese presence on the Angolan coast was maintained via relationships—partnerships, even—with inland African leaders, many of whom were loosely allied in an enormous federation of kingdoms. Environmental crises in the region actually aided these leaders in boosting their subject populations and maintaining a steady supply of young adults for the slave trade. Severe droughts in Africa's southern grasslands forced refugees to flee to less arid areas. After providing the refugees with food and water, African leaders would then assimilate the children and women of reproductive age (who were also valued as the region's primary food producers), while selling most of the adult males into slavery. The Angolan leaders were thus able to consolidate an ever-growing population (with little threat of rebellion, since few adult males remained); stabilize the land, sometimes by planting new high-yield crops such as **maize** and **cassava** from the Americas; repopulate drought-ravaged territory; and reap substantial profits from the European slave trade. The strong African states that emerged from this process were able to discourage further encroachment and territorial takeover by the Europeans, who—preoccupied with the Indian Ocean trade and colonization in the Americas—remained basically content to trade textiles, metals, and weapons for African slaves until the nineteenth century, when a combination of humanitarian and economic pressures would bring an end to the slave trade and drive the Europeans to formal colonization of African territory.

AFRICA AND ISLAM: NORTH AFRICA, THE SUDAN, AND THE SWAHILI COAST

While the fifteenth century marked the beginning of significant European contact with Africa, the Islamic world had of course long since developed strong ties with the continent, beginning in the century after Muhammad's death. Muslim beliefs and practices had spread from North Africa to the sub-Saharan region via overland trade and to the Swahili Coast of East Africa through the trade ships that plied the Red Sea and Indian Ocean. By the time Henry the Navigator's men were beginning their exploration of West Africa, Islamic legal and governmental structures—as well as the Arabic language—had become firmly entrenched in the African trading cities south of the Sahara and on the southeastern coast. Indeed, the Islamic world would maintain a much stronger influence than Europe over African culture and politics throughout the period of 1450–1750. But while nearly all of North Africa had been engulfed by the Ottoman Empire by the sixteenth century, the kingdoms and states of sub-Saharan Africa remained independent from both Middle Easterners and Europeans, as a result of the region's protective geography and the military skills of its leaders.

One such kingdom was the **Songhai Empire**, which had succeeded Mali as the leading center of **trans-Saharan trade**. As Songhai grew from its base in the western Sudan, its indigenous Muslim leaders began to expand northward into the Sahara. Perhaps fearing an impending territorial rivalry, the kingdom of Morocco sent an expedition of several thousand men and camels across the desert in 1590. Half the men died on the journey, but the remaining two thousand mounted an attack on Songhai's massive military in 1591. Despite a size advantage of nearly twenty times, the Songhai army was no match for the twenty-five hundred muskets of the Moroccans. For the next two hundred years, the Moroccans maintained a tributary dominance over the people of the western Sudan, demanding slaves and goods from them and charging tolls to merchants crossing the territory. Following this decline of the Songhai Empire, those involved in the trans-Saharan trade soon shifted their operations from the western Sudan to the central Sudan, where the **Hausa** trading cities began to provide merchants from North Africa with gold and slaves in exchange for textiles, weapons, and hardware.

AP® Tip

Understanding the impact of religion on various aspects of society can be useful for both multiple-choice and free-response questions. For example, the tenets of Islam played a significant role in many areas of African life, even economics. While the Atlantic Circuit trade brought rum and other alcoholic beverages to coastal Africa, the Muslim merchants of the Hausa trading cities were forbidden by their religion to use alcohol. Conversely, Muslims (as well as Christians) of this period felt free to engage in the trade of slaves—and in fact, Muslims viewed the enslavement of "pagans" to be an act of virtue, as it would bring new followers to their faith.

While the slave trade with the Islamic north played an important role in the economy of the Sudan, what little historical evidence remains indicates that the size of the trans-Saharan slave trade was smaller than that of the transatlantic trade. From the seventeenth to nineteenth centuries, some 1.7 million Africans were marched across the Sahara or shipped over the Red Sea or Indian Ocean to lives of slavery in the Middle East and India. In contrast, between 1550 and 1800 nearly eight million slaves crossed the Atlantic to the Americas.

Their final destination determined the type of work that African slaves were forced to do. Most slaves sent to the Americas ended up performing grueling physical labor on sugar, tobacco, or cotton plantations. Those who wound up in the Islamic world were debatably more fortunate, as they were often placed in employment as soldiers or household servants. The gender balance was different as well: while most African slaves sent to the Americas were men, the majority of African slaves sent to the Middle East or India were women, forced into service as concubines, domestic servants, and entertainers. Many more children were taken to the Islamic world, too—including boys who would have to endure dangerous (often fatal) castrations to be transformed into eunuchs and, thus, considered suitable for serving as harem guards.

By the beginning of the nineteenth century, the slave trade had brought considerable profit to certain African leaders and merchants (and a great deal more, of course, to Europe, the Americas, and the Islamic world). It also decimated the population of young, healthy adults in some parts of sub-Saharan Africa, particularly the inland territory of the Slave Coast. However, the overall population of the region was still quite substantial, and the African artisans and traders who persevered in this era of increasing change were for the most part able to maintain their production and sale of textiles and metal goods, despite the volume of competing products flowing in from Europe and the Islamic world. Thus, a very generalized examination of the slave trade might conclude that, within Africa, its impact was far from devastating. Indeed, it is rather ironic that it was late-nineteenth-century imperialism, initiated after the end of the slave trade, rather than the slave trade itself, that would bring changes of unimaginable consequence to the continent.

Multiple-Choice Questions

Questions 1–3 refer to the quote below.

You should know that the said Lord Infante of Portugal [the crown prince, Henry the Navigator] has leased this island of Argin to Christians [for ten years], so that no one can enter the bay to trade with the Arabs save those who hold the license. These have dwellings on the island and factories where they buy and sell with the said Arabs who come to the coast to trade for merchandise of various kinds, such as woolen cloths, cotton, silver, and "alchezeli," that is, cloaks, carpets, and similar articles and above all, corn, for they are always short of food. They give in exchange slaves whom the Arabs bring from the land of the Blacks, and gold timber. The Lord Infante therefore caused a castle to be built on the island to protect this trade for ever. For this reason, Portuguese caravels are coming and going all the year to this island.

Source: Alvise da Cadamosto, "Description of Capo Bianco and the Islands Nearest to It," in J. H. Parry, *European Reconnaissance: Selected Documents* New York: Walker, 1968, pp. 59–61. The Portuguese in West Africa (1455–1456)

Alvise da Cadamosto
https://college.cengage.com/history/west/resources/students/primary/slavetrade.htm

1. What is the primary type of relationship that develops between the Portuguese and Arabs on the island of Argin in the 15th century?
   (A) The relationship is mostly religious, as exchanges are mostly between Muslims and Christians.
   (B) There is a diplomatic relationship, and Arabs are in control of the goods available on the island.
   (C) The relationship that develops is an economic one in which a variety of goods are exchanged.
   (D) There is a militaristic relationship developing, one in which hostilities between Christians and Muslims are described.

2. The 15th century person most responsible for exploration from Europe in West Africa was
   (A) King Ferdinand of Spain.
   (B) Prince Henry the Navigator.
   (C) Ibn Battuta.
   (D) Marco Polo.

3. After Europeans began their exploration of West Africa, which of the following resulted in the greatest influences in the migration of people?
   (A) Trading food
   (B) Search for gold
   (C) Diplomatic relations in the New World
   (D) Slave trade

Questions 4–6 refer to the quote below.

The trade of the natives consists in gold, slaves, elephants teeth, and bees-wax. The gold is finer than sterling, and is brought in small bars, big in the middle, and turned round into rings, from 10 to 40 s. [shillings] each. The merchants who bring this, and other inland commodities, are blacks of the Mundingo race, called Joncoes, who say, that the gold is not washed out of the sand, but dug out of mines in the mountains, the nearest of which is 20 days journey up the river. In the country where the mines are, they say there are houses built with stone, and covered with terras; and that the short cutlasses and knives of good steel, which they bring with them, are made there. The same merchants bring down elephants teeth, and in some years slaves to the amount of 2000, most of whom they say are prisoners of war; and bought of the different princes by whom they are taken. The way of bringing them is, by tying them by the neck with leather thongs, at about a yard distance from each other, 30 or 40 in a string, having generally a bundle of corn, or an elephant's tooth upon each of their heads.

Source: Printed for J. KNOX, near Southampton-Street, in the Strand. MDCCLXVII. (1767)

TRAVELS Into the Inland Parts of AFRICA, BY FRANCIS MOORE

4. According to the above account, from where does most of the trading between Europeans and Africans emerge?
   (A) Some of the goods come directly from Europe.
   (B) Most of the goods traded come from Northern Africa.
   (C) Almost all of the goods come from the coasts of Africa.
   (D) Much of what is traded comes from the interior of Africa.

5. How do the Europeans value the goods exchanged with the Africans?
   (A) A barter system is set up to supply European goods to the Africans.
   (B) Africans pay the Europeans in gold for the manufactured goods they supply.
   (C) The Europeans compare their currency to the African goods.
   (D) Labor by Africans is exchanged for European goods.

6. What human/environment interaction is used as evidence that Africans had their own system of manufacturing?
   (A) There are steel knives that Africans manufactured, so they must have extracted the steel from the ground.
   (B) African ships were used to transport slaves across vast oceans, so they must have cut down large trees in the area.
   (C) Elephant tusks (tooth) were tied to slaves' heads, and therefore must have been used for transportation from the inland portion of Africa to the coast.
   (D) Stone quarried from the ground was used for tile and other flooring purposes in the African homes found by Europeans at the port cities.

Questions 7–9 refer to the image below.

Source: Punishment of slaves, Muslim custom, engraving from the Description of Africa, by Olfert Dapper (ca 1635–1689), 1686. Africa, 17th century. De Agostini Picture Library/Getty Images https://www.thoughtco.com/the-role-of-islam-in-african-slavery-44532?_ga=2.105441347.1527479866.1500670758-433000754.1500670758

7. When comparing the European (Christian) treatment of African slaves to that of the Muslim treatment of slaves, it can be said that
   (A) Muslims treated African slaves in a much more humane way.
   (B) Christians treated African slaves in a much more humane way.
   (C) Muslims and Christians treated slaves in about the same way.
   (D) Africans punished their own slaves in a harsher way than Christians or Muslims.

8. Most trading of slaves to Muslims occurs
   (A) in West Africa.
   (B) in Central Africa.
   (C) on the Swahili Coast.
   (D) in North Africa, on the Mediterranean coast.

9. What is the purpose of the engraving by Olfert Dapper?
   (A) Dapper wants to show that there is a Christian audience during a punishment administered to an African slave.
   (B) Dapper is showing how Muslims punish slaves in Africa.
   (C) Dapper is proving that Christians treated African slaves differently than Muslims.
   (D) Dapper shows the technology Muslims employed in the engraving.

Answers

1. ANSWER: C. Goods exchanged are economic in nature and include fabrics, metals, foods and slaves (*The Earth and Its Peoples*, 6th ed., pp. 509–517/7th ed., pp. 495–501; History Disciplinary Practice—Analyzing Historical Evidence; Learning Objectives CUL-3, ECON-7; Key Concept 4.1.III.A).

2. ANSWER: B. While all the other people listed were explorers or supported exploring in their own right, it was Prince Henry the Navigator of Portugal who fueled European interest in the western portion of the African continent (*The Earth and Its Peoples*, 6th ed., pp. 410–412/7th ed., pp. 401–403; History Disciplinary Practice—Analyzing Historical Evidence; Learning Objectives CUL-3; Key Concept 4.1.III.C).

3. ANSWER: D. Because of Portuguese contact with West Africa, one of the largest forced migrations in human history emerged with the slave trade between Europeans and Africans (*The Earth and Its Peoples*, 6th ed., pp. 509–517/7th ed., pp. 495–501; History Reasoning Skill—Causation; Learning Objectives ECON-2,5,6; Key Concept 4.1.IV.D).

4. ANSWER: D. While many goods exchanged between Europeans and Africans take place on the coastal ports, most of the goods come from the interior of Africa (*The Earth and Its Peoples*, 6th ed., pp. 509–517/7th ed., pp. 495–506; History Disciplinary Practice—Analyzing Historical Evidence; Learning Objectives ECON-7; Key Concept 4.1.IV.D).

5. ANSWER: C. There is a line in the passage explaining that the goods (especially the line regarding shillings) have value compared to European (British) currency from that time period (*The Earth and Its Peoples*, 6th ed., pp. 509–517/7th ed., pp. 495–506; History Disciplinary Practice—Analyzing Historical Evidence; Learning Objectives ECON-7; Key Concept 4.1.IV.D).

6. ANSWER: A . There were short cutlasses and knives made of steel which they (Africans) made there … in the inland portion of Africa (*The Earth and Its Peoples*, 6th ed., pp. 509–517/7th ed., pp. 495–506; History Disciplinary Practice—Analyzing Historical Evidence; Learning Objective ECON-2,7; Key Concept 4.1.IV.D).

7. ANSWER: C. There are many depictions of Muslims and Christians treating African slaves harshly, as in the seventeenth century engraving provided by Dapper (*The Earth and Its Peoples*, 6th ed., pp. 509–517/7th ed., pp. 495–506; History Disciplinary Practice—Analyzing Historical Evidence; Learning Objectives ECON-2,7; Key Concept 4.1.IV.D).

8. ANSWER: C. Much of the trade between Arabs and Africans had been established on the Swahili coast hundreds of years prior to the arrival of Muslims. Because more Muslims lived in and around the Indian Ocean, most trading of slaves to Muslims occurred from the Swahili Coast (*The Earth and Its Peoples*, 6th ed., pp. 509–517/7th ed., pp. 495–506; History Disciplinary Practice—Analyzing Historical Evidence; Learning Objectives ECON-2,7; Key Concept 4.1.IV.D).

9. ANSWER: B. The answer to the question is given in the 'source' of the engraving. Dapper shows how Muslims punish slaves in Africa (*The Earth and Its Peoples*, 6th ed., pp. 509–517/7th ed., pp. 495–506; History Disciplinary Practice—Analyzing Historical Evidence; Learning Objectives ECON-2,7; Key Concept 4.1.IV.D).

17

THE MIDDLE EAST: C. 1450 TO c. 1750

KEY CONCEPTS

- The central event marking the Ottoman Empire's dominance of the Middle East during this period was its capture of Constantinople from the vanishing Byzantine Empire in 1453.
- Once established, the Ottoman Empire faced growing challenges from the emerging European powers of the period, which had far-ranging (and ultimately detrimental) effects on the empire's social structure, economic prosperity, and political stability.
- Like the Ottoman Empire, the Safavid Empire of Iran emerged during this period as something of a throwback, a land-based empire in an era when power and wealth came increasingly from naval might and sea trade.
- The global inflation caused by the sudden glut of New World silver in the world economy brought crisis to both the Ottomans and the Safavids by the 1700s. The Ottoman Empire would continue struggling to survive-until the early twentieth century, while the Safavid Empire had crumbled completely by 1750.

KEY TERMS

- anderun
- askeri
- devshirme system
- fatwa
- harem
- Isfahan
- Ismail
- Janissary

- mufti
- qizilbash
- raya
- Shari'a
- Sufi

The Ottoman and Safavid Empires are covered in Chapter 19 of *The Earth and Its Peoples*, 6th edition and in Chapter 20 of the 7th edition.

THE OTTOMAN EMPIRE

Although the Turkic warrior Timur had briefly seized power in the region in the early 1400s, his death signaled the dawning of a new era in the Middle East: The formerly nomadic Turks who established the Ottoman Empire would come to dominate territory previously under Mongol and Timurid control, and they would build the largest Islamic empire since the Abbasid Caliphate. And when the Ottomans captured Constantinople in 1453, their influence was extended even farther, toward Europe, in an area once dominated by the Byzantine Empire. This victory was achieved by Sultan Mehmed II, known as "the Conqueror," who combined the strong military skills of Turkish warrior tradition with more innovative tactics. For example, he put gunpowder to use in huge cannon that broke through the walls that ringed Constantinople, hauled his warships over land to circumvent the Byzantine sea forces and reach the vulnerable inner harbor, and then unleashed his troops on the nearly defenseless city. The takeover of Constantinople, soon renamed Istanbul, was crucial for the Ottomans in more ways than one—not only did it solidify Ottoman control over the vital trade link between the Mediterranean and Black Seas (and hence between Europe and Asia) but it also brought about the final demise of the Byzantine Empire and clearly marked the ascendancy of a new regional power.

Having conquered most of southeastern Europe, including Greece, Serbia, and Albania, prior to seizing Constantinople, the Ottomans turned their attention to the east. In the Battle of Chaldiran in 1514, Ottoman ruler Selim I held firm against the expanding Safavid Empire of Persia, establishing a boundary between the two powers that stands more or less intact to this day. A few years later Selim added Egypt and Syria to the Ottoman domain by conquering the Mamluk Sultanate, then continued his expansion when the Muslim rulers of Algeria and Tunisia joined the empire voluntarily.

When Selim's son Suleiman (known to Europeans as "the Magnificent" and to his own people as "the Lawgiver") set his sights on Christian Europe, however, the seemingly invincible Ottoman forces faced a rare setback. Initially victorious—conquering Belgrade and the island of Rhodes in the early 1520s—Suleiman assaulted Vienna in 1529 but was forced to turn back before winter set in. Meanwhile, Ottoman attempts to capture control of the Mediterranean also met with unexpected challenges. From the mid-fifteenth to the mid-seventeenth centuries, various sultans battled the Italian city-state of Venice, which had dominated Mediterranean commerce through control of key territories such as the islands of Crete and Cyprus and certain Greek port cities. The Ottomans never managed to vanquish their Venetian rivals completely; they settled instead for a tribute relationship and allowed the

Venetians and other foreign traders to conduct business in Ottoman ports. Indeed, while Mediterranean trade was seen as an important source of revenue, the Ottomans—perhaps because of their Turkish warrior heritage and lack of any maritime history—always viewed theirs as a land-based, rather than sea-based, empire. They found themselves in control of the Red Sea after their takeover of Egypt, coastal Ethiopia, and the Muslim homeland surrounding Mecca and Medina in Arabia. But they tended to leave the lucrative Indian Ocean trade to the Portuguese and other Europeans, despite controlling outposts at Aden and Oman on the southern Arabian Peninsula.

MILITARY, POLITICAL, AND ECONOMIC STRUCTURES

Ottoman military traditions and practices played a key role in the development of the empire's character. After the Ottoman takeover of the Balkans in eastern Europe, Christian prisoners of war were used to create a corps of new troops called **Janissaries**; supplementing the traditional Turkish archers on horseback, these military slaves fought on foot with guns. After 1400 or so, the Janissary corps began to be replenished through the **devshirme system**, in which young Christian boys from the Balkans (and sometimes other Ottoman-controlled territories) were taught to speak Turkish and given military training. Some were selected to study Islam, liberal arts, and military strategy at the sultan's palace in Istanbul, in effect being groomed to become high-ranking military commanders and government officials. The Ottoman navy, meanwhile, was composed of Greek, Turkish, Algerian, and Tunisian sailors who patrolled the Mediterranean in galleys.

AP® Tip

You should be able to compare characteristics of the Ottoman system of slavery, which allowed non-Muslims to rise to high-ranking positions in the Ottoman military and political systems, with slavery in the European colonies of the New World, which forced Africans into lives of grueling, menial agricultural labor in most cases. Other forms of forced labor also demonstrate characteristics that contrast significantly with Ottoman slavery—for example, Russian serfdom, which tied peasant farmers to land they did not own.

Such calculated incorporation of outsiders into the Ottoman military was typical of an empire that was becoming a virtual mosaic of cultural influences. The court language, Osmanli, blended Turkish with Arabic and Persian; speaking this language was one mark of membership in the **askeri** (military and government bureaucrat) class, whose close ties with the sultan exempted them from paying taxes. The **raya** (flock of sheep) was the name given to the rest of the population, which combined Muslims, Christians, and the Jews who fled to Ottoman territory following their expulsion from Spain in 1492. While Islam—and **Shari'a**, Islamic law—spread steadily into the urban areas of conquered territories in the Balkans, local customs and non-Muslim practices persisted as well, particularly in more rural areas. Most Ottoman subjects, in fact, were influenced more by local officials and religious leaders than by imperial administrators, who were usually Turkish cavalrymen given land grants by the sultan. These provincial officials collected taxes from their subjects and provided order in the region when not off on military campaigns in the summer, but otherwise they maintained a fairly limited involvement in the day-to-day activities of the raya.

URBAN LIFE DURING THE EMPIRE'S PEAK

Istanbul, the Ottoman capital, was also a major crossroads, bridging the European and Asian components of the empire, and it rivaled other major port cities of the time in size, wealth, and cosmopolitan character. The city itself was hilly and crowded, with a mazelike network of narrow streets centered on a busy harbor where Jewish, Hindu, and Christian merchants from Europe and Asia carried out their trading. Dominating the city's skyline was the former Byzantine cathedral Hagia Sophia, converted to a mosque and renamed Aya Sofya after the Ottoman conquest of Constantinople in 1453.

While male citizens frequented the shops and markets run by the guilds of merchants and artisans, most Ottoman women spent their days confined to the **harem**, or "forbidden area," of their homes. Despite such restrictions, women in the Ottoman Empire wielded great influence. Wives were joined in the harem by children, female servants, and in some cases eunuchs (castrated male servants). In addition to running the household, some Ottoman women, taking advantage of the fact that Islamic law allowed females to retain their property after marriage, involved themselves in managing inheritances from their fathers and buying and selling real estate. Because Muslim court systems did not include attorneys, women were also permitted to appear in court and testify on their own behalf on legal matters.

Much of the tone of Ottoman life was set by **fatwas**, or legal opinions issued by urban religious scholars known as **muftis**. A mufti's interpretations of Shari'a theoretically overruled any conflicting policies issued by the sultan, but in practice, the muftis seemed to tailor their opinions to match the views of the sultan, who had appointed them. The fatwas demonstrated not only the religious motivation behind matters as mundane as the ban on drinking coffee but also the Ottoman justification for military campaigns intended to annex territory the empire considered to be under the control of "infidels."

MILITARY REFORMS BRING CRISIS

Such military campaigns gradually became more taxing for the empire to carry out. As the use of gunpowder expanded throughout Asia and Europe, the Ottoman military increased its reliance on the Janissary corps. At the same time, the number of landholding cavalrymen was reduced in order to balance the military budget. The late sixteenth century then saw a period of inflation caused by the influx of New World silver into the economy, which hampered the ability of many of the remaining landholding elites to collect taxes and purchase their military supplies. The sultan's government took this opportunity to further reduce the cavalry, reclaim their lands, expand the

Janissary corps, and hire temporary soldiers—but in order to fund such military expansion, emergency taxes were levied on much of the population.

By 1590, a crisis had developed; displaced landholders, unemployed temporary soldiers, peasants overwhelmed by taxes, and other frustrated citizens joined together in periodic revolts throughout Anatolia and other parts of the empire. The Janissaries emerged from this period with increased leverage, demanding the right to pass corps membership along to their sons. The devshirme system (along with its thorough training) was thus abolished, the size of the corps grew steadily, and the Janissaries' superior military skills began to deteriorate. As a result, Ottoman officials of the early seventeenth century faced serious challenges in maintaining the strength and unity of their empire.

OTTOMAN DECLINE BEGINS

During this period of crisis, one official response had been to confine the sultan's male relatives to the palace in Istanbul to thwart any possible coup attempts. Such confinement bred a new type of Ottoman sultan, no longer a military leader in touch with all corners of his empire, but rather a figurehead remote from involvement in the day-to-day activities of running the government. Grand viziers, or chief administrators, took over the duties of maintaining control in an increasingly fractured empire by the early 1600s. For example, the old system of land grants for high-ranking cavalrymen was finally phased out entirely, replaced with a new program of tax farming that allowed absentee landlords to profit from the taxes they levied on individual farmers, who often resented the arrangement. The sultan was thus forced to shift some of his power to provincial governors to maintain order in many rural areas. Meanwhile, the Janissaries continued to exercise their newfound influence to gain the right to participate in manufacturing and trade activities, further weakening their military skills. Such interest in commerce reflected the global changes of the era, and parts of the empire saw great transformation. Port cities such as Izmir (known in Europe as Smyrna) experienced rapid population growth, in part because of the influx of migrants seeking refuge from the upheaval in other parts of the empire, along with the arrival of European merchants and settlers of Armenian, Greek, and Jewish background. By the late 1500s, the region comprising western Anatolia, the Balkans, and the Mediterranean coast became a key component in the growing world trade network, as farmers there switched from growing grain for subsistence to producing cash crops such as cotton and tobacco.

Tobacco, in fact, was prohibited by the imperial government; its continued cultivation and trade were indicative of the growing weakness of the sultan's central bureaucracy. By the 1700s, European traders had forced the Ottomans to grant them capitulations, or special trade agreements with low duties and fees, in their largely successful quest to dominate the Indian Ocean trade network. The Ottoman economy thus was becoming more and more dependent on Europe at a time when the once-great Ottoman military was steadily weakening—more and more of the Janissaries lacked necessary training, and many of them began sending substitutes on seasonal campaigns. The sultans turned to the provincial governors for assistance in raising temporary armies, yet another step toward a shift in power away from the central government. As the sultan's inner circle in Istanbul distracted itself by throwing lavish parties and indulging in a craze for growing outlandishly expensive tulips, provincial governors, wealthy landowners, and others took advantage of the opportunity to seize power. As a result, various groups came to wrest control—practical if not official—of different parts of the empire from the sultan: mamluks in Egypt, Janissaries in Baghdad, conservative Sunni Muslims in Arabia. In 1730, the power struggle came to Istanbul itself when a conservative Janissary revolt forced Sultan Ahmed III to abdicate. The rebellion itself was short-lived—imperial power was restored after several months—but the fact that the Ottoman Empire had slipped into serious disarray could no longer be ignored.

THE SAFAVIDS OF IRAN

Following the death of Timur in 1405, several tribal chiefs and military leaders battled for dominance in Central and western Asia. In Iran, the eventual victor was **Ismail**, a young boy who was heir to the leadership of a Sufi brotherhood known as the Safaviya; he declared himself shah of Iran in 1502 and ordered that Shi'ite Islam would be the religion of the realm. A tumultuous century of war and persecution followed, as many Iranians resisted abandoning their Sunni beliefs. By the early 1600s, however, Iran had been transformed into a land that was majority Shi'ite, surrounded by Sunni neighbors. Its isolation was heightened by cultural differences as well—centuries of scholarship and writing in Persian rather than Arabic had produced a distinctive Iranian library of legal and theological texts; epic, lyric, and mystic poems; historical volumes; and drama and fiction. Other unique aspects of Safavid society were shaped by mystical **Sufi** traditions and rituals that merged with militant politics aimed at spreading Islam, by force if necessary.

AN INLAND EMPIRE

Under the reign of Shah Abbas I, who ruled from 1587 to 1629, **Isfahan** became the capital of Iran. Located near the center of the realm to give the shah ready access to any frontiers under attack, Isfahan had an economy founded on the trade of silk fabrics and intricately designed wool carpets, facilitated by its location in the centuries-old zone of transport by camel caravan. In many aspects, Isfahan resembled the Ottoman capital of Istanbul: small, crowded streets; houses with interior courtyards and separate women's quarters (known as **anderun**, or "interior," in Iran); and a main bazaar filled with the guild-run shops of artisans and merchants. Its citizens even shared similar styles of dress, with women veiling themselves outside the home, and both sexes covering their hair (scarves for women, turbans for men) and wearing flowing dresses or caftans to conceal their arms and legs. Unlike Istanbul, though, Isfahan could not be described as truly cosmopolitan— colonies of Jews, Hindus, and Armenian Christians were involved in trade ventures, but lacking a harbor, Isfahan rarely received the variety of European, Middle Eastern, and Asian visitors and immigrants that Istanbul did, and its volume of trade was correspondingly lower as well.

> ## AP® Tip
>
> The Ottoman harem and Safavid anderun exemplify the complex, sometimes bewildering role of women in Muslim societies: while women were largely sequestered from the outside world and confined to their separate household quarters, they were allowed to participate in certain business activities independent of their husbands and appear in court to attend to legal matters if necessary. In some ways, this is the direct opposite of the contemporaneous status of European women, who faced fewer restrictions on their participation in public activities but were usually forced to turn over any wages or inheritances to their fathers or husbands.

ECONOMIC CRISIS AND THE SAFAVID DOWNFALL

The manufacture and trade of rugs and silks did not provide Iran with a vital economy. Subsistence farming and herding occupied most of the shah's subjects, and nomadic groups known as **qizilbash** ("redheads," because of their red turbans) were given large sections of land by the shah in exchange for providing mounted soldiers for the military. The chieftains of these groups did not subdivide the land to promote agricultural development, and they often ruled according to their own whims. Thus, the Safavid shah lacked both a solid economy and a firm rule over his territory.

In the late 1500s, pressure from Sunni neighbors such as the Ottomans and the Uzbeks of Central Asia drove Shah Abbas to create a corps of slave soldiers who agreed without resistance to employ modern firearms, unlike the nomadic warriors who insisted on fighting with traditional bows and arrows. Like the Ottoman Janissaries, this new corps (mostly former Christian converts to Islam who had been taken as prisoners of war from the Caucasus region) began to rival the nomadic chiefs for power in the Safavid political and military structure. Shah Abbas's less capable successors faced serious difficulty in keeping these factions under control.

These successors also lacked skill in managing the overland silk trade that had been contributing to the Safavid economy; at the same time, the global inflation caused by the influx of American silver into the world trade market brought on a crisis similar to that faced by the Ottoman Empire: finding the funding to maintain the military and the government. Attempts to force the nomads from their lands in order to increase tax revenues proved futile; the nomads still maintained military capabilities of their own and could successfully elude the shah's forces. Support for the regime dwindled rapidly, and in 1722 invading Afghans seized Isfahan and brought a fairly abrupt end to Safavid rule.

The expense of maintaining a military large and versatile enough to defend a land-based empire such as the Ottoman or Safavid was rapidly becoming untenable. Taxes from agricultural production would fail to generate the wealth necessary to compete with the growing economic might of the European powers. While cultural achievements in poetry, arts, and craft production remained a source of justifiable pride, the Muslim rulers of the Ottoman and Safavid Empires simply did not foresee the vast change that the world economy was about to undergo. Their centuries-old traditions of territorial conquest and expansion as a means of amassing—and displaying—power would become relics in the new era of sea-based trade empires that was set to begin.

Content Review Questions

Questions 1–3 refer to the following image.

Source: Siege of Constantinople, Chronique de Charles VII by Jean Chartier
Artist, Phillippe de Mazerolles.

From https://commons.wikimedia.org/w/index.php?curid=345860
[Public Domain]

1. The siege of Constantinople by Mehmed II in 1453 signifies
    (A) the willingness of the Mughals to suppress other empires.
    (B) the final downfall of the Byzantine Empire.
    (C) a truce between the bordering empires of the Ottomans.
    (D) Mehmed II's abilities in diplomatic solutions.

2. How does the Ottoman passion for growing expensive tulips in the 1720s
    signify a growth in society?
    (A) The growing detachment of the Ottoman sultan from unrest within
        the empire
    (B) An attempt to beautify Istanbul at the expense of taxpayers in rural
        areas
    (C) Ottoman interest in scientific advancement, including botany and
        horticulture
    (D) The efforts of Istanbul's elites to outdo their European rivals

3. Which of the following Ottoman sultans gained the title of "The Lawgiver"?
   (A) Osman
   (B) Mamluk
   (C) Suleiman
   (D) Mehmed I

Questions 4–6 refer to the following quote.

He causes foreigners to sit down beside him and to eat at his table. With that and accompanying all such informality he requires that people shall not [lack] respect toward him and, should anyone fail in this regard, he will punish the individual severely. So the more he demonstrates kindliness toward his subjects and the more familiarly he talks with them, they tremble before him, even the greatest among them, for, while joking, he will have their heads cut off. He is very strict in executing justice and pays no regard to his own favorites in this respect; but rather is the stricter with them in order to serve as an example to others. So he has no private friends, nor anyone who has influence with him . . . . While we were at Court, he caused the bellies of two of his favorites to be ripped open, because they behaved improperly to an ordinary woman. From this it comes about that there are so very few murderers and robbers. In all the time I was at Isfahan, there was never a case of homicide.

Source: Father Simon, a Carmelite friar, writing about Shah Abbas I in the Safavid Empire, 1605.

("Shah Abbas I" is from Robert Simon, *A Chronicle of the Carmelites in Persia and the Papal Mission of the Seventeenth and Eighteenth Centuries* London: Eyre and Spottiswoode, 1939, pp. 158–161.)

4. One of the main points the Carmelite friar is attempting to portray in his account of Shah Abbas I of the Safavid Empire is that
   (A) Safavid rulers are mostly strict followers of their own, written constitutions.
   (B) the Mughal Empire had a great influence on trade in the Safavid Empire.
   (C) the Safavid tend to rule through fear by killing anyone who does not follow their rules.
   (D) crime rates increased under the rule of the Safavids in Isfahan.

5. The form of religion followed by the Safavid was primarily
   (A) Hinduism, influenced heavily by the neighboring Mughal Empire.
   (B) Shi'ite Islam, which separated the Safavids from neighboring Muslim empires.
   (C) Christianity, as the Shah attempted to create stronger trade networks with European countries.
   (D) Sunni Islam, as the Safavids cared deeply about the type of religious practices in the Ottoman Empire.

6. When comparing the primary cities of Isfahan in the Safavid Empire and Istanbul in the Ottoman Empire, both
   (A) seldom allowed women to be seen in public.
   (B) had ports encouraging shipping trade on the Indian Ocean.
   (C) had many wheeled vehicles to transport goods within their city walls.
   (D) had frontiers that allowed for a more cosmopolitan atmosphere.

Answers

1. ANSWER: B. It was one of Mehmed II's life goals to complete the suppression of the final stronghold of the Byzantine Empire. While Mehmed II did attempt to allow for a peaceful solution if Constantine XI would give up Constantinople, Constantine XI would not succumb, and the successful siege by Mehmed II began (*The Earth and Its Peoples*, 6th ed., p. 524/7th ed., pp. 506–511; History Disciplinary Practice— Analyzing Historical Evidence; Learning Objectives ENV-2, SB-3; Key Concept 4.3.II.B).

2. ANSWER: A. The early 1700s saw an Ottoman sultan far removed from, even unaware of, events in outlying territories of his realm. Instead, he and his inner circle busied themselves with growing high-priced tulips and throwing lavish parties in Istanbul while unrest grew in other parts of the empire (*The Earth and Its Peoples*, 6th ed., pp. 524–531/7th ed., pp. 511–515; History Reasoning Skill—Contextualization; Learning Objectives SB-3,4; Key Concept 4.3.III).

3. ANSWER: C. While Suleiman was unsuccessful in attacking Europe at Vienna, he is known for a series of laws developed during his reign. Suleiman also surrounded himself with diplomatic advisors (viziers) who developed strong relationships with neighboring peoples. The time period of his rule is often considered the peak of the Ottoman Empire, as Suleiman did successfully expand the empire, despite turning away from a militarily weakened Vienna (*The Earth and Its Peoples*, 6th ed., pp. 524–531/7th ed., pp. 511–514; History Reasoning Skill— Contextualization; Learning Objectives SB-3,4; Key Concept 4.3.III).

4. ANSWER: C. The passage shows that Shah Abbas I ruled by maintaining authority through fear. Even some of his best friends would be killed if the Shah felt as though his power were undermined in any way (*The Earth and Its Peoples*, 6th ed., pp. 532–536/7th ed., pp. 515–519; History Disciplinary Practice—Analyzing Historical Evidence; Learning Objectives CUL-2, SB-3,4; Key Concept 4.3.I).

5. ANSWER: B. The Safavids were separated from neighboring Muslim empires through the Shah's decision to follow the Shi'ite sect of Islam. In doing so, Iran becomes a separate entity religiously (splitting from its Sunni traditions) (*The Earth and Its Peoples*, 6th ed., pp. 532–536/7th ed., pp. 515-516; History Reasoning Skill— Contextualization; Learning Objectives CUL-2; Key Concept 4.3.I.A).

6. ANSWER: A. Women were relegated to "anderun" in Isfahan and to the "harem" in Istanbul. These were male-dominant societies, and women's areas were frequently separated, even in the homes (*The Earth and Its Peoples*, 6th ed., p. 535/7th ed., p. 517; History Reasoning Skill— Comparison; Learning Objectives SOC-1,3,4; Key Concept 4.2.III.C).

18

ASIA: C. 1450 TO c. 1750

KEY CONCEPTS

- In China, the return of indigenous rule following the Mongol conquest brought about a resurgence of traditional Chinese social, political, and economic practices. However, without the unifying Mongol presence, China retreated from contact with lands to the east and west during the Ming Empire.

- Following the Ming Empire's collapse, the Manchu-ruled Qing Empire expanded China's borders while continuing careful regulation of outside trade and other influences.

- The Tokugawa Shogunate, which emerged after a long period of civil war in Japan, centralized authority over the entire archipelago; like China's emperors, Japan's shoguns maintained strict control over contact with European merchants and missionaries to minimize destabilizing influences in their society.

- While Islam continued to spread around the Indian Ocean, the age of Muslim-dominated trade in the region gave way to European control, with Portuguese, Dutch, British, and French commercial ventures laying the foundation for a coming era of colonial domination.

- On the Indian subcontinent, the Mughal Empire emerged. Under its greatest ruler, Akbar, policies of religious tolerance supported the empire's expansion, but his successors would fail to maintain the centralized authority necessary to withstand European involvement in India.

KEY TERMS

- Canton system
- daimyo
- Dutch East India Company
- Jesuit
- kabuki theater
- Little Ice Age
- Manchu
- Rajputs
- samurai
- shogun
- Sikhs

Asia in this period is discussed in depth in *The Earth and Its Peoples*, 6th edition, Chapters 12, 19, and 20 and 7th edition, Chapters 13, 20, and 21.

CHINA DURING THE MING EMPIRE

Shortly after seizing power and ending the Mongol-ruled Yuan Empire in 1368, the first Ming emperor, Hongwu, moved to isolate China from outside influence and shake off the "foreign" practices of the Mongols. These extreme reactionary policies did not stand very long. Hongwu's successor, Yongle, revived the Yuan provincial government structure, hereditary professions, and the use of the Mongols' Muslim calendar and moved the capital back to Beijing. There, Yongle expanded the Forbidden City begun under Khubilai Khan.

But the Ming Empire retreated from any plans of expansion or increased global contact following Yongle's death in 1424, when China faced growing pressure to defend its borders against Japanese pirate attacks from the east and Mongol raids in the north and west. In fact, the Ming Empire entered a period of stagnation or even decline by the mid-1400s, with shrinking agricultural yields, a lack of innovation in bronze and steel weapons production, and few steps forward in shipbuilding and printing. The return to Confucianism—and its civil-service examination system—begun by Hongwu attracted the most talented young Chinese men to intensive scholarship, pulling them away from commercial ventures. Meanwhile, the pressures of feeding a growing population forced many farmers to focus on staple crops such as wheat and rice; this also reduced the commercial progress associated with crops such as cotton, which had stimulated earlier economic and technological growth in related areas. Population pressures were particularly acute in southern and central China, where heavy deforestation occurred as more and more fields were cleared for growing crops.

The need to defend China's borders led Ming officials to restrict access to technology they feared would get into enemy hands. This had the converse effect of actually stimulating new steelmaking processes in Japan, while Korea emerged as a regional leader in printing, shipbuilding, firearms production, weather prediction, and calendar making. Nevertheless, the bustling cities of Ming China continued to produce masterpieces of literature, opera, poetry, painting, and other artistic pursuits. Novels such as

Romance of the Three Kingdoms reflected the resurgent Chinese national pride following the overthrow of Mongol rule. A similar source of pride was the strong demand for Ming products such as furniture, silk, and especially blue-and-white "Ming ware" porcelain throughout Asia, India, the Middle East, and East Africa. By the mid-1500s, Ming China was awash in silver from Japan and the Spanish and Portuguese colonies in Latin America, thanks to its high volume of exports. This fueled rapid economic expansion as the Ming Empire progressed, but the government's poor monetary policies, along with corruption and mismanagement in the huge government-run ceramics factories, led to inflation and strikes in China's urban areas. Meanwhile, the **Little Ice Age** of the seventeenth century, along with epidemics of disease and stagnant agricultural productivity, led to unrest in the countryside.

THE QING EMPIRE EMERGES

By the late 1500s, the Ming Empire faced both serious internal disorder and a number of external threats. In the southeast, repeated raids by Japanese pirates led many Chinese to migrate to Southeast Asia, where they found opportunities to participate in the growing Indian Ocean trade network. To the north, the Mongols, bonded by their Tibetan Buddhism faith, retained a firm hold on their homeland; Mongolia regained its status as a regional military power by 1600 and competed with China for control of territory along their mutual border. Meanwhile, a group known as the **Manchu** was consolidating power in its homeland northwest of Korea and would soon emerge as a dominant force in the region. For Ming China, a crisis developed in 1592 when the Japanese warlord Hideyoshi attacked Korea, then advanced through Manchuria and into China with a force of 160,000 men. The resulting upheaval created an opportunity for the Manchu, who first allied with Ming troops but then—after Hideyoshi's death in 1598 and the subsequent Japanese withdrawal—proceeded to conquer Korea and set their sights on China itself.

The cost of defending the empire through this period created a severe economic crisis in China; internal rebellions erupted by the 1630s, and a rebel army captured Beijing in 1644. The Ming emperor hanged himself, and in desperation, a Ming general turned to the Manchu for aid in retaking the capital. They did so, but instead of returning control of the empire to Ming officials, the Manchu held on to Beijing and soon established an empire of their own—the Qing—capturing all of China, the island of Taiwan, and even parts of Mongolia and Central Asia.

The Manchu-ruled Qing Empire would retain control of the Chinese government and military until the twentieth century, but most bureaucratic officials, soldiers, merchants, and farmers were ethnic Chinese. As a small minority ruling China, Manchu leaders quickly realized that they would have to adopt many of the practices, customs, and institutions of the land they had conquered. At the same time, an ever-growing European interest in Asian trade brought additional influences into the region.

TRADE AND EXPANSION IN THE MING AND QING ERAS

Ming rulers initially were cautious about regulating contact with European voyagers, who were drawn to China in the sixteenth century by the promise of trade and access to technological information. The Portuguese and Spanish were forced to establish trade outposts in Macao and the Philippines, respectively, thus limiting the volume of commerce they could conduct with the empire. The Dutch, through the Dutch East India Company, were somewhat more successful in gaining the trust of imperial officials, as the company's representatives were willing to perform the rituals of respect and submission asked of them by the emperor himself. The **Dutch East India Company** came to dominate European trade with East Asia for nearly a century. Meanwhile, the Spanish and Portuguese traders who did gain access to China were accompanied by Catholic missionaries; by sharing European scientific and technological advances, **Jesuit** missionaries in particular were able to gain more and more status in the late Ming and early Qing periods. In fact, when the Qing emperor Kangxi, who ruled from 1662 to 1722, contracted malaria in the 1690s, quinine supplied by the Jesuits helped to bring about his recovery—and bolstered the status of Christianity among imperial officials in China at that time.

Kangxi recruited Jesuit advisers to fill key positions in the imperial government; among their duties was the creation of European-style maps of the newly conquered territories of the Qing Empire. Kangxi's Qing predecessors had pursued the restoration of internal order and progress following the chaotic end of the Ming Empire by repairing infrastructure; lowering taxes, rents, and interest rates; and resettling areas disturbed during the peasant rebellions. Upon assuming control of the empire at the age of sixteen, Kangxi found China entering an age of remarkable peace and prosperity, which allowed him to focus much of his attention on continued expansion. China's northern border remained an area of concern, with both the Russians and the Mongols vying for control in the Amur River region. Following several clashes, Russia and the Qing Empire (with the help of Jesuit interpreters) signed the Treaty of Nerchinsk in 1689, which established a firm border and regulated trade between the two empires. Turning his attention to Mongolia, Kangxi himself led troops in defeating the Mongol leader Galdan, adding inner Mongolia to the Qing Empire in 1691.

To maintain continued economic growth through this period of territorial expansion, the Qing happily accepted European silver in exchange for Chinese silk, porcelain, tea, jewelry, and furniture, while continuing to restrict European trade to the port of Canton and placing severe restrictions on the import of European goods. By the late 1700s, however, the British (having displaced the Dutch East India Company as China's dominant trade partner) faced an enormous deficit. Hoping to create a market among China's enormous population and thus restore a balance of trade, Britain would soon lead the other European powers in forcing an end to the Qing Empire's "**Canton system**" of restricting international commerce. The late eighteenth and nineteenth centuries would bring an end to the era of remarkable growth, wealth, and peace of the early Qing era.

JAPAN: CHAOS AND CONTROL

Following the failure of the Mongol invasion and the rise of the Ashikaga Shogunate in 1338, Japan entered a period of decentralized feudalism that lasted for well over two centuries. Elite warlords known as **daimyo**—perhaps forgetting the precepts of peace and simplicity of their Zen Buddhist faith—began competing for territory and power. They soon destroyed themselves, the city of Kyoto, and any real authority the Ashikaga Shogunate may once have had. (Japan's emperor also remained merely a figurehead, the symbolic leader of the native Shinto religion.) New warlords emerged, often basing their wealth on partnerships with local merchants, who traded raw materials, folding fans, and swords for Chinese books and porcelain. Some warlords also affiliated themselves with pirates who plundered trade ships headed to and from China. By the late 1500s, rivalries among the daimyo and their armies of warriors, known as **samurai**, had heated into a civil war. The conflict was resolved only gradually as the most powerful warlords expanded their territorial control to unite the various islands of the Japanese archipelago. Ultimately, one warlord, Hideyoshi, rose above the rest, even attempting to expand beyond Japan and into Korea, Manchuria, and China. Hideyoshi died in 1598, and his successors chose to withdraw their forces from the Asian mainland and focus their energies on stabilizing and centralizing the Japanese government.

The warlord who accomplished this task was Tokugawa Ieyasu, who assumed the title of **shogun**, or supreme military leader, in 1603. The Tokugawa Shogunate, in power until the nineteenth century, saw Japan through that era by balancing the central authority of the shogun with the regional autonomy of the daimyo. The Tokugawa shoguns maintained their power largely through fostering significant economic growth in Japan—they established an administrative capital at Edo (present-day Tokyo) and linked it to the imperial capital of Kyoto with a road that became a key route in the rice trade that sustained the Japanese economy. By 1700, Edo's population had grown to nearly one million, and Japan's urban centers saw major progress in manufacturing and trade, particularly in steelmaking, pottery, lacquer, and porcelain.

JAPANESE ISOLATION DEVELOPS

The Portuguese first arrived in Japan in 1543. The firearms they brought with them were studied with great interest, and by the 1570s, Japanese-made copies were in the hands of the daimyo fighting for control in the civil war. Trade with the Portuguese, Spanish, and Dutch was carefully controlled once the Tokugawa Shogunate assumed power. Porcelain was Japan's chief export, and few European-made goods were of interest to the Japanese.

Christianity, however, was received with great interest by many Japanese, who learned of the religion from the Jesuit missionaries who accompanied the European traders. By the early 1600s three hundred thousand Christian converts were spread throughout Japan. Fear of a destabilizing foreign influence motivated the shogun to issue an edict forbidding the practice of Christianity in 1614. The threat of harsh punishments—including crucifixion and beheading—for those who disobeyed the edict brought an end to the religion's practice as the century progressed. In fact, the government began forcing citizens to acquire certificates from their temples as proof of their adherence to Buddhism and their obedience to the shogunate.

Strict new cutbacks on trade accompanied the Japanese elimination of Christianity. All Europeans except the Dutch were forbidden from trading in Japan in the 1630s; Chinese trade was also curtailed sharply, although some daimyo in remote northern and southern regions ignored official policy and encouraged piracy and trade to promote economic growth in their territories. By the 1700s, it was in these provinces, far from central Japan, where economic progress and innovation were at their highest.

In central Japan, near the imperial and administrative capitals, rapid population growth and economic imbalance began to create problems for the Tokugawa government. In a period of relative peace and centralization, many of the daimyo and especially the samurai found themselves with little function in a society that, despite Confucianism's veneration of agriculture, was moving rapidly toward a basis in manufacturing and trade. In Japan's urban centers, and even in more rural areas, a new merchant class was pushing the nation forward into a period of growth and cultural innovation, with new household conveniences, the rise of **kabuki theater**, artistic experimentation with woodblock prints and silk-screened fabrics, and the opening of new shops and restaurants. These merchants also provided lines of credit to the daimyo and samurai, whose fortunes, based largely on income from the production of rice, were steadily dwindling. As the eighteenth and nineteenth centuries progressed, the Tokugawa Shogunate found itself in the difficult position of having to protect the traditional samurai values that had allowed its rise to power, while upholding the civil laws and policies necessary for continued stability and growth. Not until Westerners renewed their efforts to open the Japanese market to trade in the mid-nineteenth century would this stalemate of tradition versus progress be broken.

EUROPEAN DOMINATION OF INDIAN OCEAN TRADE

While their efforts to establish strong trading relationships with China and Japan met with heavy resistance, the Europeans were much more successful in establishing dominance over the Indian Ocean trade network, which had become the most lucrative in the world by the fifteenth century. Initially, of course, this network was controlled largely by Muslim traders, and their presence continued to grow even after European expansion into much of the region. Muslim communities all around the Indian Ocean, such as the Brunei Sultanate of Borneo and the Acheh Sultanate of Sumatra, expanded as many local non-Muslims joined the faith through intermarriage or to facilitate their participation in commercial activities. Muslims from Southeast Asia began making pilgrimages to Mecca, and their more scholarly understanding of the religion's orthodox practices resulted in the end of a series of women rulers in Acheh in the late 1600s. Shari'a, the Muslim religious law, displaced adat, or custom, in most of the urban centers in the region. The growth of Islam also encouraged the spread of literacy around the Indian Ocean. The Muslims and Europeans would come to clash over trade and territory in Southeast Asia, and in some cases the Muslims prevailed—despite Spain's takeover of most of the Philippines starting in 1565; Muslims in the southern islands held out through several wars to establish the Sulu Empire there. Ultimately, though, the Europeans would transform the Indian Ocean region and its trade network in the centuries to come.

The Portuguese fleets took the lead in displacing many of the local rulers of the Indian Ocean's coastal city-states, establishing control of major trading routes from West Africa to East Asia in the 1500s. The valuable ports of Gujarat, Goa, and Calicut on western India's Malabar Coast fell to Portuguese control in the early part of the century. Malacca, on the Malay Peninsula in the eastern end of the ocean, was seized by a Portuguese force in 1511; this gateway between East Asia and India had become a major distribution center for goods from China, Japan, and India—as well as a cosmopolitan blend of various cultural influences—and was thus seen as a major prize for Portugal.

AP® Tip

It is important to understand the impact of European technological developments on the Indian Ocean trade. The Portuguese took control of the network from Muslim traders because of the Portuguese pursuit of new techniques in shipbuilding, navigation, and the use of firearms. Ironically, many of these innovations were adapted from earlier Muslim technologies that the Portuguese first encountered in the Mediterranean. Two important AP® World History themes—the effects of technology and cultural interactions among societies—are at work here.

Having linked the major port cities of the Indian Ocean, the Portuguese were able to establish a trading monopoly on spices and other goods transported on their routes between Goa and Macao (their outpost in southern China) by forcing merchants to ship their goods on Portuguese vessels. Also, any foreign merchant ships using one of their ports had to maintain a Portuguese license and pay customs fees. Traders and local officials who attempted to defy Portuguese authority faced serious consequences— confiscated cargoes, crews enslaved or put to death, and local economies devastated. Those who agreed to Portuguese terms continued to prosper from the growing European demand for luxury goods from China, Japan, India, and Africa.

Eventually, the Portuguese domination of the Indian Ocean trade was challenged by other European powers. The Dutch, with their well-organized, privately owned Dutch East India Company, finally displaced the Portuguese stronghold in the region by capturing Malacca in 1641. The Dutch also consolidated power by fighting a number of wars against Acheh and other kingdoms, establishing a regional capital at Batavia (now Jakarta) on the island of Java. British, French, Portuguese, and Spanish competition continued, though, as those nations developed their own trading links to Southeast Asia throughout this period. Thus, during the eighteenth century, Dutch economic activity in the region was transformed from the shipping and trade of foreign-produced goods to the production and sale of crops—such as coffee and teak—in the territory they had conquered. It was in essence a transition to true colonial rule, which would set an example for Britain and other European countries in the region during the late eighteenth and nineteenth centuries.

THE MUGHAL EMPIRE OF INDIA

While the Europeans were attempting to gain control of the Indian Ocean, a different group—the Mughals—began establishing their authority over the Indian subcontinent, where centralized rule had not been seen for nearly a thousand years. The Timurids had gravely weakened the Delhi Sultanate of northern India in the late 1300s. A Timurid, Babur, swept into India from Central Asia, displaced the last sultan of Delhi in 1526, founding the Mughal Empire. (While *Mughal* means *Mongol* in Persian, the Timurids, and hence Babur, were primarily of Turkic rather than Mongol descent.) However, it was Babur's grandson Akbar who would establish truly centralized rule over the growing empire. He and his three successors would unite all of India (save the southernmost tip) before the end of the seventeenth century.

Akbar maintained economic growth by trading cotton cloth with European merchants and promoted cultural blending and innovation in the arts, but he demonstrated true genius in creating a well-organized central bureaucracy and strong military. The loyalty of these officials was ensured through the reward of lifetime (but nonhereditary) land grants. Akbar's greatest challenge was in dealing with various Hindu kings, who resented centuries of Muslim domination of their homeland. By incorporating **Rajputs**, Hindu warriors from the north, into the Mughal military and government, Akbar set a tone of religious tolerance that largely freed him and his initial successors from enduring conflict with the Hindus. In fact, Akbar went on to create a new "Divine Faith" that mixed Muslim, Hindu, Christian, and other beliefs. Another, more enduring religion that blended

Muslim and Hindu elements also emerged during the Mughal period: the **Sikhs**. From the Punjab region in northwest India, they initially focused on the peaceful attainment of enlightenment but transformed dramatically into a militant group opposing Mughal rule after Akbar's great-grandson Aurangzeb beheaded their guru for refusing to convert to Islam. Aurangzeb also broke the Mughal policy of religious tolerance by imposing a number of limitations on Hindu rights in the late 1600s. As the 1700s began, the Mughals faced challenges to their authority from both the Sikhs and the now-resentful Hindus. This internal strife combined with the invasion of Nadir Shah of Iran to bring an end to centralized Mughal rule in 1739. The empire disintegrated into a number of regional powers, just as the French, Dutch, and British began turning their attention away from the coastal Indian Ocean trade to seek new opportunities on the subcontinent itself.

Content Review Questions

Questions 1–3 refer to the following passage.

1. The study of literature and the practice of the military arts, archery and horsemanship, must be cultivated diligently. . . . From of old the rule has been to practice "the arts of peace on the left hand, and the arts of war on the right"; both must be mastered. Archery and horsemanship are indispensable to military men. Though arms are called instruments of evil, there are times when they must be resorted to. In peace-time we should not be oblivious to the danger of war. Should we not, then, prepare ourselves for it? **2.** Drinking parties and wanton revelry should be avoided. In the codes that have come down to us this kind of dissipation has been severely proscribed. Sexual indulgence and habitual gambling lead to the downfall of a state. **3.** Offenders against the law should not be harbored or hidden in any domain. Law is the basis of social order. Reason may be violated in the name of the law, but law may not be violated in the name of reason. Those who break the law deserve heavy punishment. **4.** Great lords (daimyo), the lesser lords, and officials should immediately expel from their domains any among their retainers or henchmen who have been charged with treason or murder. Wild and wicked men may become weapons for overturning the state and destroying the people. How can they be allowed to go free? **5.** Henceforth no outsider, none but the inhabitants of a particular domain, shall be permitted to reside in that domain. Each domain has its own ways. If a man discloses the secrets of one's own country to another domain or if the secrets of the other domain are disclosed to one's own, that will sow the seeds of deceit and sycophancy.

Tokugawa Ieyasu's code of behavior, 1615

Primary Source Reader for World History, Elsa Nystrom, Wadsworth Cengage Learning, pp. 306–307.

From Ryusaku Tsunoda, et al., *Sources of Japanese Tradition*, pp. 335–338.
Copyright © 1958 by Columbia University Press. Reprinted by permission.

1. For whom was the above code of behavior probably written?
   (A) The passage was mostly written for women to adhere to high standards.
   (B) The code was written for the samurai elite to show respect for the shogun.
   (C) Farmers were the recipient of such a code to help the Tokugawa Shogunate grow.
   (D) This code was focused primarily on the merchant class.

2. Which group faced the most significant challenges in maintaining its economic status in Tokugawa Japan?
   (A) Shoguns
   (B) Merchants
   (C) Samurai
   (D) Farmers

3. The aforementioned passage is most prominently based upon
   (A) a British economic policy of mercantilism.
   (B) the United States' development of a law abiding, democratic society.
   (C) Russia's centralized system in the use of a tsar.
   (D) China's Confucian-based government.

Questions 4–6 refer to the following passages.

Thoughts on Government

Good government cannot come about if eunuchs are employed as responsible officials. The validity of this statement has been proved in every dynasty of China's past. The harm is even greater if the eunuchs are allowed not only to enjoy power but also to build a larger following who do the eunuchs' bidding. . . . It is for this reason that T'ai-tsu [Taizu] and T'ai-tsung [Taizong],[1] knowing about the eunuchs' abuse of power . . . did not introduce in the imperial court the institution of eunuchs. It was also for this reason that my immediate predecessor [Sunzhi, r. 1638–1661] confined the duties of the eunuchs to those of a servile nature and that when they were entrusted with positions of authority he did not forget that they were evil and conspiratorial. In one of his last decrees he reminded us that the downfall of the Ming dynasty was caused primarily by the employment of eunuchs in positions of power. . . . I shall be most diligent insofar as the observation of eunuchs' behavior is concerned. . . .

The Rural Economy

I was surprised to learn that peasants who volunteer to cultivate abandoned fields can enjoy tax exemption for only a six-year period. . . . the peasants cultivating abandoned fields are among the poorest in the nation. . . . Having to pay taxes that increase their burden, they may decide to abandon the fields and thus become unemployed. About this I am deeply concerned. Let it be known that peasants who volunteer to cultivate abandoned fields will not be taxed for a ten-year period.

[1]Taizu (r. 927–976) was founder of the Song dynasty; he was succeeded by his younger brother Taizong (r. 976–997). Both were considered to be outstanding emperors.

Kangxi, edicts and other writings, 1693–1718

Source: Dun J. Li, *The Civilization of China from the Formative Period to the Coming of the West* New York: Scribner's Sons, 1975, pp. 311, 313, 314.
Andrea Overfield, *The Human Record Documents*, Cengage Learning, 2016.

4. What was a major emphasis during Kangxi's rule in China?
   (A) There was an emphasis on merchant trade in China under Kangxi's rule.
   (B) Kangxi preferred to delegate power to subordinates, such as eunuchs and peasants.
   (C) Foreign diplomacy was crucial to Kangxi's interaction with external powers, not war.
   (D) An emphasis on centralized rules and governance existed under Kangxi.

5. How do we know that the Qing were not too interested in developing diplomatic and economic relationships with other cultures?
   (A) Kangxi was more interested in how to tax farmers during the early rule of the Qing Dynasty.
   (B) The eunuchs were left completely in charge of diplomatic ties with foreign governments under the Qing.
   (C) When the Macartney Mission came to China, Kangxi showed little interest.
   (D) The Qing placed most of their economic interests on the development of paper and different types of pottery.

6. The most desired product by foreigners from early Qing China was which of the following?
   (A) The compass
   (B) Tea
   (C) Opium
   (D) Silk

Answers

1. ANSWER: B. The samurai became more educated and attuned to the elite. The laws were designed, in part, to support the samurai who supported the shogun rise to power. The "rules to live by" were paramount to a civil society under Tokugawa rule (pp. 557–559) (*The Earth and Its Peoples*, 6th ed., pp. 555–559/7th ed., pp. 536–541; History Disciplinary Practice—Analyzing Historical Evidence; Learning Objectives SOC-1,3; Key Concept 4.2.III.B).

2. ANSWER: C. While merchants faced the official disapproval of Japan's Confucian-based society, they continued to profit from contact with the world trade network. Meanwhile, the samurai warriors faced a growing economic crisis as their traditional function declined in an era of centralization (p. 559) (*The Earth and Its Peoples*, 6th ed., pp. 555–559/7th ed., pp. 536–541; History Disciplinary Practice—Analyzing Historical Evidence; Learning Objectives SOC-1,3; Key Concept 4.2.III.B).

3. ANSWER: D. The first point in the code developed in the Tokugawa Shogunate shows an emphasis on education, the military, and behavior. This closely mimics the Chinese Confucian system of government. These rules of behavior are supportive and indicative of how a person should behave in a civilized society. The Chinese had been using this centralized governing technique for centuries (*The Earth and Its Peoples*, 6th ed., pp. 555–559/7th ed., pp. 536–541; History Disciplinary Practice—Analyzing Historical Evidence; Learning Objectives SOC-1,3; Key Concept 4.2.III.B).

4. ANSWER: D. The passage shows that Kangxi did not admire the amount of power given to the eunuchs (during the Ming Dynasty). Under Kangxi's rule, government was centralized and even control of the taxation for peasants was issued by Kangxi's court (*The Earth and Its Peoples*, 6th ed., pp. 563–567/7th ed., pp. 546–549; History Disciplinary Practice—Analyzing Historical Evidence; Learning Objectives SOC-1,3; Key Concept 4.2.III.B).

5. ANSWER: C. The emperor sent a letter to King George explaining that China had no need to increase its foreign trade, had no use for Britain's ingenious devices and manufacturers, and set no value on closer diplomatic ties. (p. 565) (*The Earth and Its Peoples*, 6th ed., pp. 563–567/7th ed., pp. 546–549; History Reasoning Skill—Contextualization; Learning Objectives ECON-2,3,7; Key Concept 4.1.I.A).

6. ANSWER: B. One item of interest to the East India Company was tea. In medieval and early modern times, tea from China had spread overland to Russia, Central Asia, and the Middle East to become a prized import. Consumers knew it by its northern Chinese name, *cha* (p. 564) (*The Earth and Its Peoples*, 6th ed., pp. 563–567/7th ed., pp. 546–549; History Reasoning Skill—Contextualization; Learning Objectives ECON-2,3,7; Key Concept 4.1.I.A).

19

EUROPE: C. 1450 TO c. 1750

KEY CONCEPTS

- Following the Crusades and the Black Death, major changes began to sweep through Europe and bring about the end of the Middle Ages. Towns and cities revived, driven by a growing European interest in trade. This led to important economic changes that soon went hand in hand with an era of world exploration and colonization.
- The humanist worldview of the Renaissance continued to spread throughout Europe. The perfection of the printing press allowed for increasing literacy and a rapid exchange of ideas and technologies; the Scientific Revolution and the Enlightenment emerged as two major results.
- Numerous challenges to the power and influence of the Catholic Church also opened the door to new attitudes regarding science, politics, and society in general.
- Meanwhile, European monarchs began centralizing their authority to create absolutist regimes, which in some cases planted the seeds for their citizens to push for democratic reforms.

KEY TERMS

- Atlantic System
- bourgeoisie
- capitalism
- caravel
- Catholic Counter-Reformation
- Columbian Exchange
- Enlightenment
- guild

- humanist
- indulgence
- joint-stock company
- mercantilism
- Middle Passage
- papacy
- printing press
- Protestant Reformation
- Renaissance
- Scientific Revolution
- serf
- stock exchange
- vernacular

Europe in the period from c. 1450 to c. 1750 is discussed in detail in *The Earth and Its Peoples*, 6th edition, Chapters 13, 15, 16, and 18 and 7th edition, Chapters 14, 16, 17, and 19.

THE END OF THE HUNDRED YEARS WAR AND THE RISE OF EUROPEAN MONARCHS

Several factors drove the changes Europe underwent as the Middle Ages came to a conclusion. The end of the Hundred Years War served as one catalyst for the steadily increasing power of the European monarchs between 1450 and 1750. This in turn allowed for increased European involvement in world exploration and colonization and for the beginnings of a European-dominated world economy. To finance the Hundred Years War (1337–1453), a conflict between the monarchs of England and France over control of the French throne, these monarchs were forced to levy taxes on their vassal subjects' landholdings and merchants' transactions. This had the important effect of elevating the power and status of the English and French monarchies while also nurturing a growing sense of "national" unity among their citizens. While generally supporting their kings in the war, these citizens also began to recognize the collective power of the representative institutions of Parliament in England and the Estates General in France. Throughout this period and beyond—particularly in France—as the monarchs wielded more and more authority, their subjects' sense of nationalist unity would grow at a similar pace. Eventually, these monarchs would be forced to limit their absolutism in favor of more democratic governments.

Meanwhile, other European territories also witnessed important steps toward unification. Spain, as it exists geographically today, came into being following the marriage of Isabella of Castile and Ferdinand of Aragon in 1469. This led to the merger of their respective kingdoms and the retaking of Granada from Muslim control in 1492. Ferdinand and Isabella, of course, would heighten the prestige of their new nation by financing the exploratory voyage of Christopher Columbus. And challenges to the authority of the Catholic Church led to the crumbling of the Holy Roman Empire, as German princes waged war against the empire beginning in 1546. This religious conflict gave the princes an opportunity to reclaim church-held lands in their territories; they also demanded—and won, via the Peace of Augsburg in 1555—the right to choose Catholicism or Lutheranism as the religion of their individual realms. A unified Germany would not emerge until the late nineteenth century, but the Peace of Augsburg was a key early step in the process toward a secular political authority in the region.

The Protestant Reformation, the Catholic Counter Reformation, and European Society

While Christianity served as a major source of unity and hope for European peasants in the Middle Ages, most Roman Catholics were unaware of the growing abuses of power that church leaders were committing in Rome. For centuries the church had supported itself by collecting taxes from its members, renting out church-held lands for farming, and operating businesses such as breweries in its monasteries. Much of this income went toward maintaining the lavish lifestyles of the pope and other high church officials, many of whom had given their lives to church service not out of a sense of devotion to the faith but, rather, out of a desire for wealth and power. By the early 1500s, the church had created a showplace of **Renaissance** art and architecture in Rome, and Pope Leo X began using the sale of **indulgences**—forgiveness of punishment in purgatory for past sins in exchange for a financial donation to the church—to further support church projects. A young German monk, Martin Luther, spoke out against such actions as contrary to the Christian idea of atonement of sins through true faith, not unfeeling action. He held that Christianity should involve a true belief in God's word rather than a blind following of church doctrine or **papal** edicts. After posting a stinging protest, known as the 95 Theses, against the sale of indulgences, Luther was excommunicated by the Catholic Church in 1521 and subsequently broke away from the church entirely. His actions paved the way for other reformers such as John Calvin in France and John Knox in Scotland to join in what became known as the **Protestant Reformation**, which established new branches of Christianity throughout western Europe.

By the mid-1500s, the unified Latin Christendom of the Middle Ages no longer existed, weakened by the challenges to its authority and the loss of followers to Lutheranism and other new Protestant churches, Catholic leaders met at the Council of Trent (1545–1563) to address church abuses. The so-called Catholic Reformation also saw the establishment of a new order, the Jesuits, who would aid in the church's attempts to rebuild its membership by opening educational institutions throughout Europe and, eventually, in the European colonies that were then being established in the Americas.

While both the Protestant and Catholic Reformations had great impact in curbing abuses of religious power and would be linked to key political and economic developments in this period, gender roles in Europe remained largely unchanged. Both Protestants and Catholics continued to promote a male-dominated order in religious leadership, secular authority, and family relationships. For the typical woman, the most common means of preserving her social status upon reaching adulthood was through an advantageous marriage. Noble families frequently arranged marriages among their children to maintain a privileged position in society, while the new and growing bourgeoisie (middle-class townspeople) often created marriage alliances that yielded benefits in business. Marriage in Europe occurred later than in other regions during this period; young adults of the lower classes needed time to save money to live independently from their parents, while bourgeois men delayed marriage to complete vocational training or a professional education. Such delayed marriages played a role in reducing European birthrates and family size in comparison with other regions, where most people married before reaching the age of twenty and thus had more time to have children. Few women were allowed to pursue an advanced education, but bourgeois women often received informal training as bookkeepers to assist their husbands in business. Some European lands allowed women to inherit the throne in royal families that lacked a male heir, but such cases were exceptions to the rule of a social structure dominated by males at every level.

AP® Tip

In spite of the tremendous amount of social change occurring throughout this period, European women remained lower in status than men, but the social status of a woman's family was a critical factor in her life.

THE LATER RENAISSANCE AND THE HUMANIST WORLDVIEW

The spread of Protestant ideas was aided by the movable-type **printing press**, which had been perfected by Johann Gutenberg in the 1450s. Initially used to produce Bibles and other religious materials, the printing press soon proved invaluable in the development of a more secular-oriented **humanist** worldview throughout western Europe. As Europe's feudal system collapsed and the Catholic Church lost its dominance over everyday life, Renaissance writers returned to the works of the ancient Greeks and Romans, translating and printing them in **vernacular** languages for widespread distribution. The increased access to such printed materials was accompanied by a rise in literacy. Exposure to such texts provided inspiration for a new generation of scholars in fields such as history and ethics, who emphasized human potential and achievement. The cumulative effect of this rise of humanism was to move more and more Europeans away from lives dominated by church doctrine; as education spread and literacy rates rose, so too did new, more reason-based ideas in science, technology, and politics. Painting and sculpture of the later Renaissance also reflected the humanist worldview— Biblical figures and scenes no longer dominated European art as they had in the Middle Ages. In addition, artists depicted scenes of everyday life, painted portraits of themselves and their contemporaries, and created works inspired by the history and mythology of classical Greece and Rome.

AP® is a trademark registered by the College Board, which is not affiliated with, and does not endorse, this product.

Merchants, Bankers, Trade, and Capitalism

Many renowned Renaissance artists were supported by patrons, men who had amassed great wealth by tapping into the economic revival of Europe's towns and cities. After the Crusades, European interest in long-distance trading with the Middle East and Asia had continued to grow; the Black Death then cleared the way for lower class Europeans who had survived the epidemic to move to urban areas to work in manufacturing and commerce, where they could demand higher wages. These factors blended to bring about the decline of the agriculturally based feudal system of the Middle Ages and the rise of a new economic system known as **capitalism**. This in turn allowed for the development of a new social order in which the **bourgeoisie** and the upper class were no longer dominated by hereditary nobles.

In the cities, most craftsmen or merchants joined **guilds**, professional associations that promoted good business practices, set prices, and protected their members' interests in interactions with local government leaders. Although some women were allowed to join guilds (occasionally as professionals in their own right, but more often only if they had a family connection to a male member), most guilds excluded women to maintain male control over positions of skilled labor. As a result, Europe's lower-class women remained underpaid, usually working in nonguild jobs in textiles or the food and beverage trade. Jews were also excluded from guild membership; however, because Christianity considered usury—the charging of interest—to be a sin, many Jews found a niche in the banking trade, which grew along with the rest of the European economy during this period.

A strong banking system allowed for more crucial developments in the move toward a capitalist economy. Standardized currencies soon appeared, and enterprising businessmen took advantage of bankers' offers of credit and opportunities to join in shareholding companies. As the era of European exploration and colonization was getting underway at the same time, colonial settlements in the Americas and chartered trading companies such as the Dutch East India Company were often financed by groups of private investors in **joint-stock companies**. Soon, Europe's economy came to be dominated by large banks, chartered companies, and **stock exchanges** that allowed the growing middle and upper classes of the towns and cities to engage in private enterprise. European governments often adopted policies of **mercantilism** to promote such activities for national benefit. Using force if necessary to protect their overseas colonies, the British, French, Portuguese, and Spanish began bringing the natural resources of the Americas back to Europe; manufacturing them into finished goods; and selling many of the goods back to the American colonists, who, to maintain European monopolies, were usually prohibited from manufacturing such products of their own.

World Exploration and the Columbian Exchange

The Europeans' lucrative colonial empires were, of course, the result of one of history's greatest mistakes: Columbus's westward voyage across the Atlantic Ocean in search of a more direct trade route to India. In the Middle Ages, while the world economy was dominated by the Muslim empires of the

Middle East, Italian traders had taken advantage of their Mediterranean location to establish a trade link between northern Europe, the Middle East, Africa, India, and China. By the fifteenth century, Spain and Portugal were determined to break the Italian city-states' virtual monopoly on long-distance trading by finding new, Atlantic-based trade routes to Africa and India. Employing the newly devised **caravel**, a small, maneuverable vessel, along with navigational technologies such as the compass and the astrolabe—brought to Europe via trading contact with the Middle East and China—Prince Henry the Navigator of Portugal explored the west coast of Africa during the mid-1400s. By 1488, Bartolomeu Dias rounded Africa's Cape of Good Hope and reached the Indian Ocean. Ten years later, Vasco da Gama voyaged all the way to India.

Determined not to allow Portugal to monopolize overseas exploration and trade, Ferdinand and Isabella of Spain turned to an Italian named Christopher Columbus, who believed he could sail to India faster than the Portuguese by heading west across the Atlantic—virtually unknown in Europe at the time was the fact that two continents lay in between. Soon, the monarchs of western Europe realized that North and South America were a literal goldmine of opportunity because overpowering the natives and stripping their land of its resources posed little challenge. In what was known as the **Atlantic System**, European ships laden with manufactured goods landed first in Africa, where some of the goods were traded for slaves. The slaves and remaining goods next crossed the Atlantic in what was known as the **Middle Passage**; they were then distributed throughout the Americas. The African slaves were put to work in the fields and mines of the Americas, replacing the Amerindians, who had died in record numbers following exposure to European diseases such as smallpox. Meanwhile, the ships were restocked with American products, most of which served as raw materials for manufacturers back in Europe, and were sent back across the Atlantic to complete the circuit.

This continuous loop of people and products traveling around the Atlantic was an important conduit for the **Columbian Exchange**: the transfer of foods, animals, diseases, technologies, and of course people (accompanied by important elements of their cultures) between the Old World (Europe, Asia, and Africa) and the New (the Americas). In Europe, unlike Africa and the Americas, the impact of the Columbian Exchange was largely positive; in addition to reaping the economic benefits detailed earlier, Europeans found their diet enriched by such exotic additions as tomatoes, peanuts, chilies, and chocolate. More significantly, New World starches such as maize and potatoes began to provide a dependable source of calories that fueled a worldwide population boom after 1700.

> ## AP® Tip
>
> By the end of this period, the various European nations had created a more unified world economy in comparison with the fragmented trading networks such as the Silk Road or the Inca network of roads in previous centuries. With European colonial empires in North and South America, a growing European trade presence in Africa (at least along the coasts, where Europeans linked with overland trade networks of goods and slaves), and European ships sailing the Indian and Pacific Oceans to acquire goods in India and China, an era of European domination of the world economy was set to begin.

THE SCIENTIFIC REVOLUTION AND THE ENLIGHTENMENT

The post-1700 population boom was also a result (in Europe, at least) of contemporaneous advances in science and medicine. The humanist worldview of the early Renaissance inspired not just writers and artists but also astronomers and mathematicians such as Copernicus, who determined that the universe was not centered on the earth (the official doctrine of the Catholic Church) but that the sun was the center of a system of planets, of which the earth was merely one. Kepler and Galileo then built upon his work. Despite condemnation by Catholics and Protestants alike, the publication of such theories soon inspired other scientists, such as Isaac Newton, to adopt and expand upon the new scientific method of careful experimentation developed by these pioneering astronomers. Continuing the period's trend away from an unquestioning worldview dictated by the doctrines of the Catholic Church, logic- and reason-based natural laws and theories in chemistry, physics, mathematics, anatomy, and medicine began to develop.

Rational new theories about political, social, and economic life soon emerged as well, in a movement that became known as the **Enlightenment**. Inspired by the **Scientific Revolution**—along with captivating accounts of lifestyles and governmental structures in the Americas and China—Voltaire, John Locke, and other philosophers promoted religious tolerance, economic opportunity, and political institutions based on the consent and involvement of the governed. This last element of the Enlightenment developed in direct response to the rise of absolute monarchs that had begun after the end of the Hundred Years War. While Germany remained decentralized for another three hundred years, the monarchs of Spain, France, and England steadily increased their nations' unity at the expense of the authority of the church and nobility. Religion remained influential in various ways; however, Philip II of Spain used the Spanish Inquisition to develop a Catholic-based nationalism that promoted his absolute authority, while the Bourbon kings of France reduced the rights of Protestants to appeal to their predominantly Catholic citizenry and created a powerful monarchy that was supported by the church. In England, though, the Catholic Church suffered another blow when Henry VIII convinced Parliament to name the English monarch, not the pope, as the head of the Church of England. Over the ensuing decades,

English monarchs attempted to extend their authority even further; but those attempts sparked the English Civil War when members of Parliament insisted that their rights be respected. By the end of the seventeenth century, the English Bill of Rights and other laws upheld the power of Parliament, transforming England into a constitutional monarchy offering protection of certain political rights and religious freedoms.

RUSSIA

The English, French, and other western and central European monarchs gained power in part by investing in new technologies (mobile cannon, handheld guns) and ever-growing, well-trained armies (or, in England's case, a navy). By the early eighteenth century, a balance of power emerged among England, France, Austria, and the small German kingdom of Prussia. Alliances among these nations (and others of lesser status, such as Sweden, Spain, the Netherlands, and Poland) shifted constantly, preventing any one of them from emerging as dominant. None was particularly large in territory, but their success in world trade allowed their monarchs to increase taxes to finance such military expansion.

In eastern Europe, a different history prevailed. By the late 1400s, the Mongol-ruled Golden Horde had long been in decline; the prince of Moscow, Ivan III, then seized the opportunity to declare himself tsar (Caesar) and ushered in a return of native Russian rule to the region. Ivan IV soon expanded Russia's borders to the south and east, and by the early 1700s, the vast northern region of Siberia had been added to the empire as well. Siberia's wealth of natural resources, particularly animal pelts, provided a link with the vigorous trade economy of western Europe, but otherwise, much of Russia languished in an agriculturally based economy until the reign of Peter the Great, from 1689 to 1725. As tsar, Peter concerned himself with Westernizing Russia by developing industry and trade, reducing the influence of noble boyars in government, modernizing the Russian army and navy, and forcing European fashions and social traditions on the Russian elite. By 1712, his new capital on the Baltic Sea, St. Petersburg, served as a valuable link between Russia and the West, but Peter's vast empire still struggled with issues of religious and ethnic diversity, and its population was dominated by **serfs**, peasant farmers tied almost as slaves to land belonging to a tiny group of landowners. In a sense, much of Russia's land and population retained the feudal structure Europe had shrugged off after the Middle Ages. Not until the early twentieth century would this land-based empire be dramatically transformed.

Content Review Questions

Questions 1–3 refer to the following passage.

In order to have the proper attitude of mind in the Church Militant we should observe the following rules:

1. Putting aside all private judgment, we should keep our minds prepared and ready to obey promptly and in all things the true spouse of Christ our Lord, our Holy Mother, the hierarchical Church.
2. To praise sacramental confession[1] and the reception of the Most Holy Sacrament once a year, and much better once a month, and better still every week, with the requisite and proper dispositions.
3. To praise the frequent hearing of Mass, singing of hymns and psalms, and the recitation of long prayers, both in and out of church; also the hours[2] arranged for fixed times for the whole Divine Office, for prayers of all kinds and for the canonical hours.
4. To praise highly religious life, virginity, and continence; and also matrimony, but not as highly as any of the foregoing.
5. To praise the vows of religion, obedience, poverty, chastity, and other works of perfection.[3] It must be remembered that a vow is made in matters that lead to evangelical perfection. It is therefore improper to make a vow in matters that depart from this perfection; as, for example, to enter business, to get married, and so forth.

Spiritual Exercises, by Ignatius Loyola, 1541

[1]Protestants rejected auricular confession—confessing one's sins to God through a priest, who offers absolution in the name of God.

[2]In his *Table Talk*, Martin Luther denies the merit of such "good works" as prayers, veneration of relics, and pilgrimages, claiming that external actions cannot earn God's grace. He argues that grace is a freely given gift that comes only with a God-instilled faith in Jesus and the promise of salvation.

[3]Arguing that all believers in Jesus are priests, all Protestant groups rejected a special priesthood of celibate ministers.

Source: Nystrom, Wadsworth, *Primary Source Reader for World History,* (Cengage Learning, 2006)

1. The purpose of this document by Loyola in 1541 was to
    (A) ensure the military preparation of the Jesuit order.
    (B) hold Jesuit missionaries accountable for their behaviors.
    (C) show the Chinese that the Jesuit mission is open-minded.
    (D) plead with the Pope that the Jesuits would need plenty of funding for their mission.

2. The major event that is the impetus for Loyola's writing in the sixteenth century is known as the
    (A) Tokugawa Shogunate.
    (B) Enlightenment.
    (C) Colombian Exchange.
    (D) Counter-Reformation.

3. The Protestant Reformation changed Europe by
    (A) contributing to violent wars in areas outside of Europe.
    (B) curtailing the power of the Catholic pope in Europe.
    (C) limiting the power of women in the church.
    (D) making Europe more tolerant of other religions, such as Judaism and Islam.

Questions 4–6 refer to the following passage.

Without a doubt, the king's revenues are derived from a part of the goods and money his subjects accumulate through their labors, by the fruits they harvest from the earth, and by what their industry gains for them. Everything that the people accumulate is divided into three parts: first, what they can set aside for their subsistence and their small savings; second, for their lord who is the owner of the land they cultivate; third, for the king. This is the normal distribution. But when authority is at the level where Your Majesty has put it, it is certain . . . that the people, who fear and respect the royal authority, begin by paying their taxes [to the king] and have little left for their own sustenance, and pay little or nothing to their lords. And since the people need at least something before they think of meeting their tax obligations, and since these taxes must always be proportionate to the amount of money people have, the financial administration . . . must make every effort and [use] all Your Majesty's authority to attract money into the realm, and to distribute the money throughout the provinces so that the people have the ability to live and pay their taxes.

. . . the well-being and economic recovery of the people depend on apportioning what they pay into the public treasury with the amount of money that circulates in commerce. This ratio has always been 150 million livres [in circulation] to 45 million livres.[1] [in taxes and expenditures] . . . But at present it appears that there are no more than 120 million livres in public commerce . . . and that taxes and expenditures are at 70 million livres. As a result, it is in excess by a wide margin, and as would be expected, the people are falling into great misery.

It will be necessary to do one of two things to stop this evil: either lower tax obligations and expenditures, or increase the amount of money in public commerce. For the first, taxes have been lowered already. . . . For the second, it consists of three parts: increase money in public commerce by drawing it away from other countries; by keeping it inside the kingdom and keeping it from leaving; by giving the people the means to make a profit from it.

[1]The livre was the basic unit of the French currency.

Jean-Baptiste Colbert, *Memorandum to the King on Finances*, 1669.

The Human Record (Cengage), p. 143.

Source: Pierre Clément, ed., *Lettres, Instructions, et Mémoires de Colbert*, volume 6, Paris: Imprimerie Impériale, 1869, pp. 264–266, 269, and volume 7, Paris: Imprimerie Impériale, 1869, pp. 237–240, 264, 268, 269. Trans: J. H. Overfield.

4. What is Colbert suggesting to the king of France about finances?
   (A) He suggests that the king should invest profits into France to make even more money.
   (B) Colbert is trying to convince the king that farming is the best way to gain profits.
   (C) He is saying that the best way for France to create revenue is to get income from other countries.
   (D) Colbert is attempting to institute a manufactured-based economy, which would ultimately be owned by the king.

5. The system of gaining revenue for a motherland through raw materials produced or manufactured in a colony is known as
   (A) mercantilism.
   (B) capitalism.
   (C) indentured servitude.
   (D) royalism.

6. How could one describe the relationship between the French, British, and Dutch during the mid-to late seventeenth century?
   (A) The relationship was mostly diplomatic, as these countries held each other in high esteem.
   (B) The relationship was cooperative, as evidenced by the lack of wars during that time period.
   (C) The relationship was improving, as the French, British, and Dutch frequently shared land masses in various colonies.
   (D) The relationship was strained, as economic policies discouraged trade with foreign merchants.

Answers

1. ANSWER: B. Ignatius Loyola is outlining the expectations for the missionaries who would be traveling to distant places in an attempt to convert people into the Catholic Church. The primary goal of Loyola is to make sure the Jesuits are clear about the rules of their mission (*The Earth and Its Peoples*, 6th ed., pp. 436–440/7th ed., pp. 426–430; History Disciplinary Practice—Analyzing Historical Evidence; Learning Objectives CUL-1,2,6; Key Concept 4.1.VI).

2. ANSWER: D. The creation in 1540 of a new religious order, the Society of Jesus, or "Jesuits," by the Spanish nobleman Ignatius of Loyola was among the most important events of the Catholic Reformation, also known as the Counter-Reformation. Well-educated Jesuits helped stem the Protestant tide by their teaching and preaching (p. 438) (*The Earth and Its Peoples*, 6th ed., pp. 436–440/7th ed., pp. 426–430; History Reasoning Skill—Causation; Learning Objectives CUL-1,2,6; Key Concept 4.1.VI).

3. ANSWER: B. The weakening of the pope's power was the only direct result of the Protestant Reformation (p. 438) (*The Earth and Its Peoples*, 6th ed., pp. 436–440/7th ed., pp. 426–430; History Reasoning Skill—Causation; Learning Objectives CUL-1,2,6; Key Concept 4.1.VI).

4. ANSWER: C. Colbert is clearly recommending a mercantilist policy to the king. He wants to the king to benefit from foreign territories as France's own subjects are burdened too heavily with taxes. This foreign revenue would, Colbert suggests, increase the king's coffers (*The Earth and Its Peoples*, 6th ed., pp. 452–457/7th ed., pp. 443–445; History Disciplinary Practice—Analyzing Historical Evidence; Learning Objectives SB-3,6; ECON-2,6; Key Concept 4.1.IV.C).

5. ANSWER: A. European empires sought to monopolize the profits produced in their colonies by controlling trade and accumulating capital in the form of gold and silver, a system called mercantilism (p. 504) (*The Earth and Its Peoples*, 6th ed., pp. 452–457/7th ed., pp. 443–445; History Reasoning Skill—Contextualization; Learning Objectives SB-3,6; ECON-2,6; Key Concept 4.1.IV.C).

6. ANSWER: D. Mercantilist policies strongly discouraged trade with foreign merchants, especially in the colonies, because any balance of trade deficit would be paid in gold or silver. These commercial policies were enforced by customs authorities, navies, and coast guards when necessary to secure exclusive relations (p. 504) (*The Earth and Its Peoples*, 6th ed., pp. 452–457/7th ed., pp. 443–445; History Reasoning Skill—Contextualization; Learning Objectives SB-3,6; ECON-2,6; Key Concept 4.1.IV.C).

20

THE AMERICAS:
C. 1450 TO C. 1750

KEY CONCEPTS

- Prior to European contact, civilizations throughout the Americas continued to rise and fall in relative isolation from one another.
- Once Columbus made Europeans aware of the existence of the "New World," explorers from Spain, Portugal, England, France, the Netherlands, and other European lands rapidly settled throughout the Western Hemisphere.
- Via the Columbian Exchange, European settlement in the Americas drastically reduced Amerindian populations and significantly altered-or even destroyed-indigenous cultures.
- Following the Europeans' economic takeover of the Americas, African slaves were introduced throughout the region, with far-ranging economic, social, and political consequences.
- By 1750, Spain and Portugal remained firmly in control in Mesoamerica and South America; North American territory was shared by several European colonial powers, but the British settlements would soon begin to press for independence from monarchical control.

KEY TERMS

- Algonquin
- Arawak
- Atlantic System
- Aztec
- Carib
- chartered company
- Columbian Exchange

- conquistador
- Dutch West India Company
- encomienda
- Huron
- Iroquois Confederacy
- Inca Empire
- indentured servant
- mit'a
- plantocracy
- Treaty of Tordesillas
- viceroyalty

The Americas in the period from c. 1450 to c. 1750 are discussed in detail in *The Earth and Its Peoples*, 6th edition, Chapters 7, 15, and 18 and 7th edition Chapters 8, 16, and 19.

THE ARRIVAL OF THE SPANISH

For the Americas, the period 1450–1750 was one of profound change. Christopher Columbus's encounter with the Western Hemisphere, a dramatic leap in globalization, sparked intense competition among European powers for dominance in the Americas. By the end of this era, however, the stage was set for a revolt against European hegemony in the region.

In October 1492, Christopher Columbus's ships landed in the Caribbean; within the decade, European explorers realized that he had encountered a "New World," territory previously unknown in what became known as the Old World—Europe, Asia, and Africa. In fact, a mere two years after Columbus's first voyage to the Americas, Spain and Portugal negotiated the **Treaty of Tordesillas**. The agreement divided the world's uncharted territory between the two nations, allowing them to claim lands without competition. The lack of involvement of any indigenous inhabitant of the New World in treaty negotiations set the tone for an era of European domination in the Western Hemisphere; Spain and Portugal were followed by England and France in establishing major colonial settlements in the Americas, in some cases through diplomatic negotiations with the Amerindians, but often through conflict and force.

Early on, the Spanish established a precedent for using force against the Amerindians. When Columbus returned to the Caribbean in 1493, he brought with him hundreds of Spanish settlers hoping either to gain wealth or to convert the natives to Christianity (motives similar to those of the Spanish who had retaken Spain from Muslim control in the preceding centuries). With licenses from the Spanish monarch, **conquistadors**, or conquerors, such as Hernán Cortés soon made their way from the islands of the Caribbean to the Mesoamerican mainland in search of gold, slaves, and converts. Cortés and his men made their way to the **Aztec** capital of Tenochtitlan in 1519, used cavalry charges and steel swords to defeat their opponents easily, and imprisoned the Aztec emperor, Moctezuma II. Many of the Aztecs' subjects willingly assisted the Spanish in hopes of regaining their independence. Instead, the conquistadors swiftly laid claim to much of modern-day Mexico, then set their sights on the **Inca Empire**, which controlled almost three thousand miles of territory along the Pacific coast of South America. With just two cannon, Francisco Pizarro and his small band of 180 men overpowered the Inca, helped themselves to a wealth of gold, silver, and emeralds, and captured the Inca capital of Cuzco in 1533. They also forced the emperor, Atahualpa, to convert to Christianity, then executed him anyway. Their conquest of the entire Inca Empire proceeded quickly, and it encouraged other conquistadors to seek their own fortunes in the Americas as the sixteenth century progressed; by 1600, Spain's colonial empire encompassed much of the Caribbean and a vast expanse of land from southern North America through central South America and territories beyond.

THE COLUMBIAN EXCHANGE

One unforeseen advantage the Spanish had in their rapid takeover of New World territory was the lack of Amerindian resistance to Old World diseases. Centuries of isolation from Europe, Asia, and Africa meant that the indigenous peoples were extraordinarily susceptible to diseases—smallpox, in particular—that the Spanish brought with them. In Mesoamerica, the most conservative estimate puts native population loss at well over 50 percent; the same occurred as the Spanish moved farther into South America. Soon the Portuguese, claiming the territory that became Brazil, devastated the indigenous population there as well. With a few isolated exceptions, those who survived such epidemics found themselves in no position to fight off European control.

As significant as their impact was, however, these diseases were merely one aspect of a much greater phenomenon, called the **Columbian Exchange**, in which plants, animals, technology, religion, and other elements of culture began to make their way across the Atlantic Ocean from the Old World to the New, and vice versa. Very soon after European contact, Old World crops such as wheat, grapes, rice, bananas, citrus fruits, and sugarcane were being successfully cultivated in the Americas and were introduced to the diets of many Amerindians. At the same time, American crops, especially corn and potatoes, found their way to Europe, Africa, and Asia, where they soon provided a steady source of calories that may well have contributed to a boom in world population after 1700. Other New World products such as tomatoes, chocolate, and tobacco became staples in the Eastern Hemisphere as well. The Europeans also introduced livestock such as cattle, horses, and pigs to the Western Hemisphere, causing important changes in the Amerindians' environment and culture. In some areas, grazing cattle and sheep damaged wild grasslands; in others, such as the plains of South America, Mexico, and Texas, herding cattle and sheep provided Amerindians with new sources of food and clothing. Horses also had a great impact, providing indigenous warriors and hunters throughout the Americas with an important new resource.

From the beginning of their conquest of American lands, the Spanish and Portuguese had used a coercive labor system, the **encomienda**, to force the Amerindians to work without pay in the fields and mines taken over by the Europeans. Reforms in the 1500s led to new systems of labor, such as the **mit'a** in Peru, by which adult males worked on rotating basis producing silver or textiles for the Spanish, receiving only token wages in return. However, waves of disease continued to decimate native populations, forcing the Europeans to turn elsewhere for exploitable labor.

It was in the Portuguese colony of Brazil that African slavery first began to take hold. The Portuguese, having profited from slave labor on their sugar plantations on Atlantic islands such as the Azores, recognized that Brazil would be an excellent place to expand their cultivation of the lucrative crop, for which they needed African slaves. The Spanish and, later, the English followed suit, and the trade of European manufactured goods in Africa in exchange for slaves to transport to the Americas soon exploded. Between 1600 and 1750, more than three million Africans were brought to the Americas and forced into slavery (mainly on sugar and tobacco plantations, but also in domestic service) in the **Atlantic System**.

AP® Tip

One of the important cultural legacies of this period is the influence of Africans on American society. African traditions in art, music, and storytelling served as a source of strength and unity through the era of slavery and eventually would be recognized as a vital part of American culture, particularly after the civil rights movement of the twentieth century. Cultural and social history of this kind can be recognized as a reason for continuities and changes within a society.

LATIN AMERICAN GOVERNMENT, SOCIETY, AND ECONOMY

By 1600, Spanish and Portuguese settlement had created a complex new social structure in the New World. The Catholic Church, the colonial governments (or **viceroyalties**, administrative extensions of the Spanish and Brazilian monarchies), and business enterprises in Latin America were usually headed by Peninsulares, or native-born Europeans who had immigrated to the Americas. Creoles—whites of Spanish or Portuguese background born in the New World—often oversaw farming and mining activities; intermarriage between Europeans and creoles was not uncommon. Amerindian elites (descended from Aztec and Inca nobles) and mestizos, or those with a mix of European and Amerindian ancestry, formed a third level of society in certain areas, often functioning as administrators who oversaw the tax and labor obligations of the Amerindians. Indigenous peoples of many cultural and linguistic backgrounds were simply lumped together near the bottom of the social structure as "Indians" by the colonists; those who survived the devastation wrought by the Columbian Exchange faced special taxes and enforced labor, not to mention the significant alteration or destruction of their cultures. Finally, an ever-growing population of African slaves formed the lowest rung of the colonial social ladder in Latin America.

AP® is a trademark registered by the College Board, which is not affiliated with, and does not endorse, this product.

(Eventually, European and African cultures would blend in individuals known as mulattos, who held a social status similar to that of the mestizos.) In Brazil, much the same social structure as that of the Spanish colonies developed, although the Portuguese settlement lacked a class of elite Amerindians. In fact, Brazilian colonial society ultimately would be influenced much more by the culture of its African slaves than by that of its indigenous peoples.

One link, although tenuous, among the various social classes of Latin America was religion. Catholic missionaries had arrived in the New World with some of the first conquistadors. By the middle of the sixteenth century, the Society of Jesus, or Jesuits, had been established by the church in response to the challenges of the Protestant Reformation. Jesuit priests began to open missions, schools, and universities throughout the region to spread Catholicism among the Amerindians, and Christian beliefs and Catholic rituals sometimes blended with the native religious practices of both the Amerindians and the African slaves. However, the church soon looked beyond its missionary role and came to dominate colonial Latin America, with powerful interests in banking and the plantation economy.

Despite church involvement in lucrative business ventures, the Spanish and Portuguese governments continued to maintain strict control over economic activity in Latin America. The monarchs of Spain and Portugal granted monopoly trade rights to certain merchants in their colonies and forced the colonists to buy goods from them. Meanwhile, warships from the royal navies of the two colonial powers protected trading vessels crossing the Atlantic between Europe and Latin America. This system allowed for the safe shipment of goods and the efficient collection of taxes, but it also fostered the growth of a black market for products smuggled into Latin America from England, France, and the Netherlands.

THE WEST INDIAN PLANTATIONS

In the 1500s, the Spanish and Portuguese shifted the focus of much of their colonization to Mesoamerica and South America. As a result, their older colonies in the Caribbean islands, which became known as the West Indies, were largely abandoned. In the next century, however, England and France began to see in these islands an opportunity for the profitable export of tobacco and then—as more tobacco cultivation moved to the North American mainland—sugar. Many of the English and French colonies in the West Indies began as **chartered companies** in which private investors paid the government a fee for exclusive rights to trade. This system, copied from the **Dutch West India Company's** activities in the Caribbean, allowed European governments to maintain a presence in the region without incurring the administrative costs of direct control that Spain and Portugal faced in Latin America. Chartered companies soon became a key component of European mercantilism, which dictated that nations could gain wealth by extracting gold, silver, and valuable agricultural products from other lands.

The production of sugar in the West Indies was at first dependent on the use of **indentured servants**, poor Europeans who were given free passage to the colonies in exchange for several years of unpaid labor. By the 1700s, though, West Indian land had become very expensive, leading most indentured servants to choose to go to North America, where inexpensive land remained available for their purchase after the completion of their labor period. Needing another form of coercive labor, European planters began to bring more and more African slaves to the West Indies, even though the cost of purchasing slaves outright was more expensive than the cost of the transatlantic passage for indentured servants.

Gradually, large sugar plantations emerged in the West Indies as investors took steps to maximize their economic returns. These investors formed a **plantocracy**, a small class of rich Europeans who owned large amounts of land and large numbers of slaves; profits depended on the planters getting as much as possible out of both. For slaves of all ages, this meant long days of work in labor gangs, high production quotas, and severe physical punishments for those who fell behind. A very high mortality rate from overwork and disease soon developed among the slaves, which served only to increase the volume of the Atlantic slave trade. Meanwhile, the land itself began to suffer from deforestation and soil depletion, and the transfer of Old World plants and animals to the Caribbean islands added to the environmental transformation of the region. It was also in the West Indies that European colonization led to the most thorough devastation of the indigenous population—the **Arawak** and **Carib** peoples were driven nearly out of existence as colonial settlement progressed throughout the sixteenth, seventeenth, and eighteenth centuries.

AP® Tip

During this period, silver mined by the Spanish in the Americas played a crucial role in the development of a European-dominated world economy. Mexican and Peruvian silver boosted the supply of money in Europe, which allowed for continued economic expansion there, setting the stage for the Industrial Revolution. In addition, Spanish merchants also took silver to the Philippines (their Pacific island colony) to trade for Asian goods such as tea, silk, and porcelain that were then in high demand in Europe. This flood of American silver also generated severe inflation in Europe in the sixteenth and seventeenth centuries, an economic crisis that spread eastward to the Ottoman Empire—further evidence of the development of a truly global economic system. These important shifts can be emphasized in any essay that asks for analysis of economic changes during this era.

THE COLONIAL SETTLEMENTS OF NORTH AMERICA

Initially, North America's European settlers came mostly from England and France. Their colonies developed differently from those of Spain and Portugal in that neither England nor France chose to institute strong governmental control over their North American territories. Instead, they allowed chartered companies and enterprising individuals to settle and develop their lands independently. The result was a region of much greater political, economic, and cultural diversity than in the Spanish colonies or Brazil.

The earliest English settlements in the New World—in Newfoundland, Canada, and on Roanoke Island off the coast of the Carolinas—met with failure, but in 1607 nearly 150 settlers representing the privately funded Virginia Company established the colony of Jamestown in the Chesapeake Bay region. Facing far greater challenges than they expected in dealing with the Amerindians and in finding wealth in mining, trade, or agriculture, the few colonists who survived began to spread out around the bay and into the interior. Soon these Virginians developed a sustainable economy based on the export of furs, lumber, and tobacco and dependent on the use of indentured servants. Remaining rural in character—again in contrast to the Spanish and Portuguese colonies, which were developing sizable cities and towns through the seventeenth century—Virginia was under the control of a governor appointed by the English monarch. Representatives of the colonists themselves, however, soon began meeting outside of the Crown-approved House of Burgesses and set the English colony on a path toward representative democracy. Meanwhile, English settlement continued to spread into present-day Maryland and North and South Carolina. So too did the population of African slaves, brought to the region by plantation owners who began to consider them a better long-term investment than indentured servants. Many Amerindians initially profited by supplying the English settlers with skins for their fur trade, but the long-term effects of this new opportunity were highly damaging to the environment of the region—and to indigenous cultures. Trade conflicts among the Amerindians and between the Amerindians and the English settlers soon followed; in most cases, the Europeans prevailed and took control of more and more Amerindian land.

To the north, the settlement of New England was directed more by religious influences than economic ones. Following the Reformation in Europe, two groups of English Protestants—the Pilgrims and the Puritans— journeyed to the New World rather than face continued confrontation with the Church of England over religious issues. There they formed what became known as the Massachusetts Bay Colony. The company charter of the colony, granted by the English monarch, dictated the development of political institutions in the region: an elected governor and representatives from each town set the colony on a course of local control with increasingly limited involvement by the Crown. (The indigenous population, meanwhile, was nearly driven out of existence by Old World diseases and military conflicts with the European settlers.) With its harsh climate and relatively poor soil, the region provided limited agricultural opportunities. New England instead became more urbanized than the southern colonies, with an economy based on manufacture, commerce, and shipping services that linked North America and the Caribbean with the Old World. Because it did not rely on large numbers of slaves and indentured servants, New England lacked the rigid, unbalanced social structure of the plantation-based southern colonies; class and economic differences were thus much less pronounced in the northern English colonies.

In between, the so-called Middle Atlantic region developed into a culturally diverse, economically prosperous territory with Dutch—German in Pennsylvania—influences in addition to English ones. For example, New

York, founded by the Dutch West India Company as the colony of New Netherland, capitalized on profitable agreements with the Iroquois Confederacy, creating a large fur-trade network stretching north toward French-controlled Canada. After capturing the colony and renaming it New York in 1664, the English continued to exploit its strategic location between the Atlantic Ocean and the Hudson River to provide a shipping link from the New World to the Old. Pennsylvania, meanwhile, was founded with near-total autonomy when England's king, Charles II, gave an enormous land grant to repay a debt to the Penn family. The Penns, peace-loving Quakers who had come to the New World to escape religious persecution in England, relied more on negotiation than armed conflict in dealing with the region's Amerindians. This factor, in combination with a fairly mild climate and good land, allowed Pennsylvania to prosper rapidly. Its capital, Philadelphia, soon became the largest British colonial city, and it would play a key role when England's North American colonies began to push for independence as the eighteenth century wore on.

NEW FRANCE

Following several sixteenth-century exploratory voyages to Canada, France established its first North American colony at Quebec in 1608. New France's economic development relied heavily on fur-trading alliances with the indigenous **Huron** and **Algonquin** peoples, which in turn drew the French settlers into conflict with the opposing **Iroquois Confederacy** and its allies, the Dutch and English. The widespread use of firearms in these seventeenth-century battles altered the way of life of most Amerindian groups in the region, who adopted the technology for their own hunting and military practices and thus hampered the European takeover of western North America for more than two hundred years. Further, the Amerindians of Canada, recognizing their economic importance to the French, were able to resist much of the territorial loss and cultural destruction brought by earlier European settlers to other parts of the Americas—even the Jesuit missionaries of New France had abandoned most of their conversion efforts by the eighteenth century.

Continuing their quest for territorial expansion in the New World, the French established the territory of Louisiana (which covered much of the middle of the present-day United States) in 1699. French settlement throughout North America remained relatively sparse, however, and France's colonies faced frequent military threats from the wealthier and more populous colonies of English North America. Eventually losing control of Canada and Louisiana to England and Spain, France restricted its New World activities to the Caribbean after the mid-eighteenth century.

Content Review Questions

Questions 1–3 refer to the following passage.

For as much as you, Cristóbal Colón (Christopher Columbus), are going by our command, with some of our ships and with our subjects, to discover and acquire certain islands and mainlands in the ocean, and it is hoped that, by the help of God, some of the said islands and mainlands in the said ocean will be discovered and acquired by your pains and industry; and therefore it is a just and reasonable thing that since you incur the said danger for our service you should be rewarded for it . . . it is our will and pleasure that you, . . . after you have discovered and acquired the said islands and mainlands in the said ocean, or any of them whatsoever, shall be our Admiral of the said islands and mainland and Viceroy and Governor therein, and shall be empowered from that time forward to call and entitle yourself Lord Cristóbal Colón, and that your sons and successors in the said office and charge may likewise entitle and call themselves Lord and Admiral and Viceroy and Governor thereof; and that you may have power to use and exercise the said office of Admiral, together with the said office of Viceroy and Governor of the said islands and mainland . . . and to hear and determine all the suits and causes civil and criminal appertaining to the said office of Admiralty, Viceroy, and Governor according as you shall and by law, . . . and may have power to punish and chastise delinquents, and exercise the said offices . . . in all that concerns and appertains to the said offices . . . and that you shall have and levy the fees and salaries annexed, belonging and appertaining to the said offices and to each of them, according as our High Admiral in the Admiralty of our kingdoms levies and is accustomed to levy them.

Agreement of April 30, 1492 between Spanish Royalty and Christopher Columbus

Human Record (Cengage)

Source: J. B. Thatcher, *Christopher Columbus, His Life and Work* New York and London: Putnam's Sons, 1903, Volume 2, pp. 442–451.

1. What is the purpose of the *Agreement of 1492*?
    (A) The agreement shows that Columbus has the upper hand because he has the navigational skills to make gains for Ferdinand and Isabella.
    (B) The agreement outlines where Columbus is to go and how he might be rewarded.
    (C) The agreement specifically orders what Columbus is to do when he reaches the New World.
    (D) The agreement allows Columbus to practice any religion, as long as he makes some kind of economic gain for Ferdinand and Isabella.

2. Why was Columbus so anxious to gain funding from Ferdinand and Isabella?
    (A) Columbus wanted to explore a potentially new route to Asia.
    (B) Columbus wanted to make a name for himself in the field of navigation.
    (C) Columbus was fleeing from atrocities committed in the New World.
    (D) Columbus was testing the system of capitalism and mercantilism for the king and queen of Spain.

3. In its competition for land with the Portuguese, the Spanish agree to the pope's mediation in the
    (A) *encomienda* system.
    (B) Treaty of Tordesillas.
    (C) *mit'a* system.
    (D) development of an *hacienda* in both countries' territories.

Questions 4–6 refer to the following map.

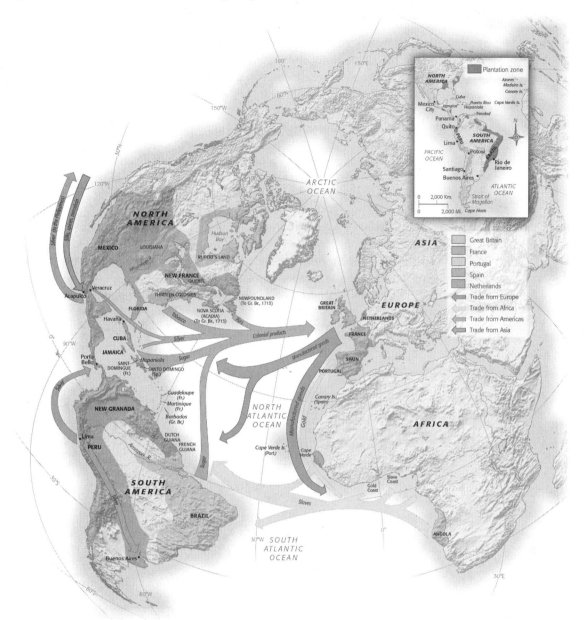

The Atlantic Economy c. 1700
Source: © Cengage Learning.

4. Where were some of the major trading regions of the Atlantic Economy?
   (A) North America, South Asia, and Europe
   (B) South America, Africa, and the Middle East
   (C) North America, South America, Africa, and Europe
   (D) South America, South Asia, Africa, and Europe

5. How did the Atlantic Economy function?
   (A) Colonization allowed indigenous cultures to practice their own farm systems.
   (B) Resources flowed from the Americas to Europe, while European and African resources flowed to the Americas.
   (C) Mercantilism allowed for the European nations to fund resource production throughout the Americas.
   (D) By instituting the system of capitalism, there was support from European royalty to fund various types of farming projects in Africa.

6. How could one describe the relationship between the French, British, and Dutch during the mid-to late seventeenth century?
   (A) The relationship was mostly diplomatic, as countries held each other in high esteem.
   (B) The relationship was cooperative, as evidenced by the lack of wars during that time period.
   (C) The relationship was improving, as the French, British and Dutch frequently share land masses in various colonies.
   (D) The relationship was strained, as economic policies discouraged trade with foreign merchants.

Answers

1. ANSWER: B. Due to the nature of exploration, the agreement between Columbus and Ferdinand and Isabella is somewhat general in nature. There is vague mention of what Columbus might find, how he might govern, and what kinds of consequences he might employ during his "governorship" of any new territories found (*The Earth and Its Peoples*, 6th ed., pp. 412–415/7th ed., pp. 403–406; History Disciplinary Practice—Analyzing Historical Evidence; Learning Objectives ECON-2,3,7; Key Concept 4.1.III.B).

2. ANSWER: A. Columbus wrongly estimated that if Spain were to explore west on the Atlantic, there would be an easier route to get to Asia. He was right, except for the large land mass (the Americas), which prohibited Columbus from gaining access to Asia by traveling in that direction (*The Earth and Its Peoples*, 6th ed., pp. 412–415/7th ed., pp. 403–406; History Disciplinary Practice—Analyzing Historical Evidence, History Reasoning Skill—Contextualization; Learning Objectives ECON-2,3,7; Key Concept 4.1.III.B).

3. ANSWER: B. The Treaty of Tordesillas divided the world's uncharted territory between Spain and Portugal allowing them to claim lands without competition. Territories claimed by Spain were numerous, while territory claimed by Portugal included the Viceroyalty of Brazil. (p. 470) (*The Earth and Its Peoples*, 6th ed., pp. 412–415/7th ed., p. 406; History Reasoning Skill—Contextualization; Learning Objectives ECON-2,3,7; SB-3,6; Key Concept 4.1.III).

4. ANSWER: C. While much of the Atlantic Economy originates from European economic designs to gain wealth, the areas indicated by the map include Africa, Europe, North America, and South America (*The Earth and Its Peoples*, 6th ed., pp. 505–509/7th ed., pp. 491–495; History Disciplinary Practice—Analyzing Historical Evidence; Learning Objectives ECON-6,7; Key Concept 4.1.IV.D).

5. ANSWER: B. There was a system of exchange by which resources needed in the Americas were sent from both Europe and Africa. On return trips, ships would frequently load goods found in the Americas for sale in European markets (*The Earth and Its Peoples*, 6th ed., pp. 505–509/7th ed., pp. 491–495; History Reasoning Skill—Contextualization; Learning Objectives ECON-6,7; Key Concept 4.1.IV.D).

6. ANSWER: D. Mercantilist policies strongly discouraged trade with foreign merchants, especially in the colonies, because any balance of trade deficit would be paid in gold or silver. These commercial policies were enforced by customs authorities, navies, and coast guards when necessary to secure exclusive relations (*The Earth and Its Peoples*, 6th ed., pp. 505–509/7th ed., pp. 491–495; History Reasoning Skill—Contextualization; Learning Objectives ECON-6,7, SB-6; Key Concept 4.1.IV.C).

AP® FORMAT QUESTIONS FOR PERIOD 4

Multiple-Choice Questions

Questions 1–3 refer to the following map.

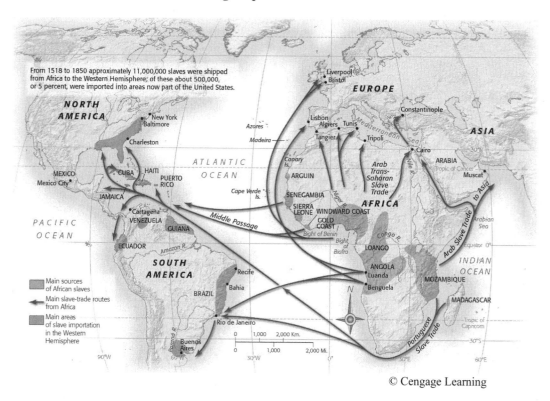

From 1518 to 1850 approximately 11,000,000 slaves were shipped from Africa to the Western Hemisphere; of these about 500,000, or 5 percent, were imported into areas now part of the United States.

© Cengage Learning

1. Which of the following can be inferred from the map?
   (A) African kingdoms controlled the Middle Passage.
   (B) Plantation economies in the Americas fueled the Middle Passage.
   (C) Asian goods made their way to the Americas.
   (D) Regional markets ceased to flourish.

2. Which of the following large economic exchange systems is indicated on this map?
   (A) The Silk Road
   (B) The Neolithic revolution
   (C) The Columbian Exchange
   (D) The Incan Mit'a system

3. As a result of the slave trade shown on the map, which of the following developed in South America?
   (A) A new racial classification system developed in the Americas.
   (B) The European population dramatically decreased due to increased migration to the Americas.
   (C) The global demand for raw materials remained stagnant.
   (D) The Mughal Empire attempted to control the African slave trade.

Questions 4–6 refer to the following image.

NIGRITÆ IN SCRUTANDIS VENIS METALLICIS
ab Hispanis in Insulas ablegantur.

Slaves digging for gold and silver in mines in Hispaniola.
Public Domain, from the British Library's collections, 2013

4. Which of the following can be inferred from the image?
   (A) American Indians refused to participate in plantation work.
   (B) Colonial economies in the Americas depended on a range of coerced labor.
   (C) Gold and silver miners were well paid.
   (D) The Mediterranean region did not participate in global trade.

5. What impact did the product in the image have on the world?
   (A) A global economy was created that was connected to the circulation of silver from the Americas.
   (B) The American foods became staple crops in various parts of Europe.
   (C) Northern Atlantic crossings for fishing continued.
   (D) Populations in Afro-Eurasia increased due to the nutritionally beneficial food.

6. Which of the following European powers controlled the labor system seen in this image?
   (A) English
   (B) French
   (C) Dutch
   (D) Spanish

Questions 7–9 refer to the following chart.

A Sugar Plantation of five hundred Acres of Land requires

A Dwelling-House

Two Windmills

A Boiling-House

A Distilling-House

A Curing-House large enough to contain at least 2500 Pots

A Stable to hold thirty Horses, with a Loft over it for dry Grain

A Rum-House

An House for Servants

A Sick-House

A proper Room to confine disorderly Negroes

A Store-House for Salt Provisions

A Smith-Shop

A Cooper's-Shop

A Trash-House

And a Store for English Goods.

It requires three hundred Slaves

An hundred and fifty head of Cattle

Twenty-five Horses

Fifty head of Sheep

William Belgrove, *A Treatise Upon Husbandry or Planting*, 1750s

7. Where did the sugar that was produced on this plantation from the 1750s most likely end up?
    (A) African markets
    (B) South American markets
    (C) European markets
    (D) Polynesian markets

8. Which of the following can be inferred from the information in the chart?
   - (A) The English were competing with the Spanish to establish a maritime empire.
   - (B) The American Indians provided much of the labor on the plantations.
   - (C) Indentured servants from Europe moved to the Americas to work on plantations.
   - (D) The Ottoman Empire had gained prominence in global trade.

9. Which of the following is evidenced as a "proper Room" in the chart?
   - (A) Slaves could eventually earn their freedom in a similar fashion to indentured servants.
   - (B) Most slaves were household slaves who worked as caregivers for European families who had colonized the Americas.
   - (C) Slaves were practicing peasant agriculture in order to ensure that they could gain freedom.
   - (D) States utilized different ethnic groups for their economic contributions while limiting their ability to challenge the authority of the state.

Questions 10–12 refer to the following passage.

> In the 15th century the Ottomans' military strength had derived from their cavalry, which included soldiers known as *ghazis*, horsemen of nomadic origin who were ambitious to conquer the Christian infidels of Byzantium for Islam. But the increasing scale of Ottoman military operations and the organization necessary to use gunpowder weapons such as muskets and cannon led to greater military professionalism … the Ottomans had begun to rely on Janissaries, slave soldiers who were recruited from conquered Christian lands and trained as professional soldiers.

Voyages in World History, 2nd ed., p. 366

10. The information in the passage demonstrates which of the following differences between the Ottoman and Spanish Empires?
    (A) The Spanish did not use guns to expand.
    (B) The Ottomans were a large land empire, while the Spanish were a maritime empire.
    (C) The Spanish did not attempt to impart their religion on the American Indians, while the Ottomans did want to conquer and convert.
    (D) The Spanish did not use horses.

11. Which of the following is evidenced in the passage?
    (A) Ottoman leaders wanted to maintain centralized control over their populations.
    (B) Ottoman soldiers resisted high taxation.
    (C) The Roman Empire was difficult to conquer.
    (D) The British helped defeat the Byzantines.

12. How is the period 1450–1750 dramatically different from the period 600–1450?
    (A) Trade networks were not important for the diffusion of religion during 600–1450 but were vital for diffusing religion during 1450–1750.
    (B) Imperial expansion during 1450–1750 relied on the increased use of technological diffusion via the Mongols to establish large empires but was not used as much during 600–1450.
    (C) Slaves were not used during 600–1450 but were used during 1450–1750.
    (D) Religious wars did not occur during 600–1450 but did so during 1450–1750.

Questions 13–15 refer to the following passage.

> Whenever barbarians come to present tribute, the inhabitants along the coast communicate and even entice them resulting in trouble. Now it is proper to strictly enact regulations to the following effect:
>
> Upon the coming of the barbarian tributary ships, those people who meet them and trade with them before the examination of the ships, shall be punished;
>
> Those people who trade [and] borrow from them shall be punished;
>
> Those people who have privately purchased contraband goods on behalf of the barbarians shall be punished;
>
> Those people who have buil[t] seagoing vessels for sale to barbarians shall be punished …. For those who are obdurate and irreclaimable, their families shall also be exiled.
>
> Answer to a Memorial by Censor Wang I-chi, from the *Ming Shi lu*, 1524

13. Who were the barbarians that are referenced in the passage?
    (A) The Ottomans
    (B) The Europeans
    (C) The Mughals
    (D) The Koreans

14. How does the information in the passage represent a significant change in Chinese attitudes toward trade?
    (A) The Chinese began to abandon Confucianism during the sixteenth century.
    (B) The Chinese began the Silk Road during the Han dynasty, which means they had somewhat embraced trade in their history.
    (C) The Chinese no longer practiced filial piety during the sixteenth century.
    (D) The Chinese began to compete with the explorers who controlled the Columbian Exchange.

15. The passage was written in response to which of the following?
    (A) The Atlantic slave trade
    (B) The spread of diseases that was endemic in the Eastern Hemisphere
    (C) Indian Ocean region trade
    (D) The daimyo in Japan

Short-Answer Questions

Question 1 refers to the following image.

African slave trade
Public Domain

1. Answer Parts A, B, and C using the image as inspiration.
   A. Identify ONE way in which traditional slavery in Africa continued.
   B. Explain ONE reason for demand for slavery export to the Americas increased.
   C. Explain ONE economic impact of the slave trade on Africa.

2. Answer Parts A and B.
   A. Explain TWO ways in which Islam continued to expand in the Middle East between 1450 and 1750.
   B. Identify ONE way in which the spread of Islam changed between 1450 and 1750.

3. Answer Parts A and B.
   A. Explain TWO belief systems that resulted from increased interactions between newly connected hemispheres and intensification of connections within hemispheres in the period 1450–1750.
   B. Identify the way ONE Asian nation reacted to the spread of a traditional religion (Christianity, Islam, Hinduism, and Buddhism).

4. Answer for Parts A, B, and C.
   A. Identify ONE development facilitating the global circulation of goods in the period 1450–1750.
   B. Explain ONE role of European merchants in Asia in the period 1450–1750.
   C. Explain ONE role of the Americas in global trade in the period 1450–1750.

Question 5 refers to the following passage.

> The term Columbian Exchange refers to the transfer of peoples, animals, plants, and diseases between the New and Old Worlds. The European invasion and settlement of the Western Hemisphere opened a long era of biological and technological transfers that altered American environments. Within a century of the first European settlement, the domesticated livestock and major agricultural crops of the Old World (the known world before Columbus's voyage) had spread over much of the Americas, and the New World's useful staple crops had enriched the agricultures of Europe, Asia, and Africa. Old World diseases that entered the Americas with European immigrants and African slaves devastated indigenous populations. These dramatic population changes weakened native peoples' capacity for resistance and accelerated the transfer of plants, animals, and related technologies. As a result, the colonies of Spain, Portugal, England, and France became vast arenas of cultural and social experimentation.

The Earth and Its Peoples, 6th ed., p. 466

5. Answer Parts A and B.
   A. Identify and explain TWO historical claims about the Columbian Exchange.
   B. Identify ONE limitation of the Columbian Exchange.

Long Essay Questions

1. Compare political and economic aspects in North Africa and West Africa between 1450 and 1750.

2. Using specific examples, analyze continuities and changes in the political structure of the Middle East in the period 1450–1750.

3. Using specific examples, analyze the continuities and changes in the role Confucianism played in both the Ming and Qing Empires in the period 1450–1750.

4. Using specific examples, compare western European economic development with Russian economic development in the period 1450–1750.

5. Analyze major continuities and changes in the political system of North or Latin America during the period 1450–1750.

Answers

MULTIPLE-CHOICE QUESTIONS

1. ANSWER: B. The Middle Passage was the name given to the Atlantic route that transported slaves from Africa to the Americas. Most of the slaves ended up in the Caribbean or Brazil working on cash crop plantations (*The Earth and Its Peoples*, 6th ed., p. 505/7th ed., p. 491; History Disciplinary Practice—Analyzing Historical Evidence; Learning Objective CUL, ECON; Key Concept 4.2 II C).

2. ANSWER: C. The Columbian Exchange was the Atlantic trade system that included the transfer of people, diseases, food, and animals to and from the Old and New Worlds (*The Earth and Its Peoples*, 6th ed., p. 466/7th ed., p. 454; History Disciplinary Practice—Analyzing Historical Evidence; Learning Objective ECON; Key Concept 4.1 V A).

3. ANSWER: A. As a result of the slavery in Latin America and the intermarriage of many Spanish with American Indians, a new racial hierarchy developed in Latin America. The Peninsulares and Creoles were at the top of the hierarchy, and African slaves and American Indians were at the bottom (*The Earth and Its Peoples*, 6th ed., p. 475/7th ed., p. 462; History Reasoning Skill—Causation; Learning Objective CUL; Key Concept 4.2 III).

4. ANSWER: B. The Spanish used slaves and American Indians as coerced labor in the gold and silver mines (*The Earth and Its Peoples*, 6th ed., p. 472/7th ed., p. 459; History Disciplinary Practice—Analyzing Historical Evidence; Learning Objective ECON, CUL; Key Concept 4.2 II D).

5. ANSWER: A. Much of the gold and silver mined in the Americas made its way back to Europe and into China. The Chinese even suffered inflation due to all the silver they had (*The Earth and Its Peoples*, 6th ed., p. 527/7th ed., pp. 510–511; History Reasoning Skill—Causation; Learning Objective ECON; Key Concept 4.2 IV B).

6. ANSWER: D. The Spanish and the Portuguese were the main European powers to colonize South America. The Spanish had a monopoly on the silver mines (*The Earth and Its Peoples*, 6th ed., p. 545/7th ed., p. 445; History Disciplinary Practice—Analyzing Historical Evidence; Learning Objective SB, ECON; Key Concept 4.1 IV).

7. ANSWER: C. Most of the raw materials in the Americas ended up in European markets. Besides sugar, many American foods, such as potatoes and maize, became staple crops in Europe (*The Earth and Its Peoples*, 6th ed., p. 466/7th ed., p. 454; History Disciplinary Practice—Analyzing Historical Evidence; Learning Objective ECON; Key Concept 4.1 V B).

8. ANSWER: A. The chart lists a "store of English goods," which indicates that this is an English plantation. Many of the sugar islands in the Caribbean were initially controlled by the Spanish, but after the 1588 defeat of the Spanish Armada, the English, and the French became involved in American colonization (*The Earth and Its Peoples*, 6th ed., p. 466/7th ed., p. 454; History Disciplinary Practice—Analyzing Historical Evidence; Learning Objective SB; Key Concept 4.3 II C).

9. ANSWER: D. The document references a "house for disorderly negroes," which is indicative of slavery based on race/ethnicity. The need for a house for the slaves who are disorderly shows that the Europeans limited their ability to challenge the authority of the Europeans; and the negroes were utilized for their economic contributions to the sugar plantation (*The Earth and Its Peoples*, 6th ed., pp. 391–392/7th ed., pp.383–384; History Disciplinary Practice—Analyzing Historical Evidence; Learning Objective CUL, SOC; Key Concept 4.3 I B).

10. ANSWER: B. Unlike the Spanish, the Ottomans did not expand their control overseas; they were a large land empire. Both empires used guns and horses to expand and both tried to convert conquered peoples to their religion (*The Earth and Its Peoples*, 6th ed., p. 634/7th ed., pp. 611–612; History Disciplinary Practice—Analyzing Historical Evidence; Comparison; Learning Objective SB; Key Concept 4.3 II B).

11. ANSWER: A. The Sultans of the Ottoman Empire created a large bureaucracy and standing army in an effort to control the conquered populations (*The Earth and Its Peoples*, 6th ed., p. 634/7th ed., pp. 611–612; History Disciplinary Practice—Analyzing Historical Evidence; Learning Objective SB; Key Concept 4.3 C).

12. ANSWER: B. The development of gunpowder and guns is what differentiates expansion from the classical era to the post-classical era (*The Earth and Its Peoples*, 6th ed., p. 341/7th ed., pp. 337, 339; History Reasoning Skill—Continuity and Change over Time; Learning Objective SB; Key Concept 4.3 II).

13. ANSWER: B. The Chinese, under the Ming dynasty, had attempted to explore (Zheng He) but decided it was too expensive and the goods gained from the trade were not valued enough by the Chinese people, so the emperor halted the expeditions of Zheng He. By the mid-sixteenth century, the Portuguese had explored the Indian Ocean and were pressing to get into China (*The Earth and Its Peoples*, 6th ed., p. 339/7th ed., p. 335; History Disciplinary Practice—Analyzing Historical Evidence; Learning Objective CUL; Key Concept 4.2).

14. ANSWER: B. The passage clearly shows that the leaders of China did not want to participate in trade with the Europeans; this is a change from the Han dynasty that created the Silk Road (*The Earth and Its Peoples*, 6th ed., p. 224/7th ed., p. 225; History Disciplinary Practice—Analyzing Historical Evidence; Patterns of Continuity and Change over Time; Learning Objective CUL; Key Concept 2.3 I A).

15. ANSWER: C. The Portuguese and the Dutch dominated Indian Ocean trade in the fifteenth and sixteenth centuries (*The Earth and Its Peoples*, 6th ed., p. 230/7th ed., p. 231; History Disciplinary Practice—Analyzing Historical Evidence; Learning Objective SB; Key Concept 4.1 IV A).

SHORT-ANSWER QUESTIONS

1. A. African traders continued to focus on traditional methods and goods, following a slow transition to slave trade. Slavery in Africa continued both the traditional incorporation of slaves into households and the export of slaves to the Mediterranean and Indian Ocean. Prisoners of war continued to be the most common source of slaves.

   B. The development of the plantation economy in the Caribbean and southern British colonies led to increased demand for African Slaves.

   C. Answers may vary but could include requirements that slave traders pay a substantial customs duty to buy slaves, as well as premium prices for slaves.

   (*The Earth and Its Peoples*, 6th ed., pp. 509–511/7th ed., pp. 495–497; History Reasoning Skill—Contextualization; Learning Objective SB-9, ECON-1,3,5,6,10, SOC-2,7,8; Key Concept 4.2).

2. A. Continuities in the spread of Islam between 1450 and 1750 are many and answers may vary. The continuing importance of Sufi practices contributed to the further spread of Islam as believers adapted to local cultural practices. The rise of the Safavid Empire can also be seen as a continuity of the practice of incorporating non-Muslims into the Muslim world.

   B. Changes in the spread of Islam are also many in this period. Examples may include the Safavids' adoption of Shi'ite Islam (as exemplified in the tomb decoration) and the rising rivalry between the Safavid and Ottoman dynasties (intensifying the Sunni/Shi'a split.)

   (*The Earth and Its Peoples*, 6th ed., pp. 532–536/7th ed., pp. 514–518; History Reasoning Skill—Continuity and Change over Time; Learning Objective CUL-2,4,5, ECON-8; Key Concept 4.1).

3. A. Answers will vary, but could include examples such as the evolution of Sikhism, which developed in South Asia during this period as a result of the interactions between Hinduism and Islam. Similarly, discussion could include the divergence of the practice of Buddhism from Southeast Asia throughout mainland China and Japan (*The Earth and Its Peoples*, 6th ed. pp. 535–536/7th ed., pp. 517–518; History Reasoning Skill—Causation; Learning Objective CUL-2,4,5, ECON-8; Key Concept 4.1).

B. Answers will vary but could include the Tokugawa's ban of Christianity in 1615 as an effort to maintain control (*The Earth and Its Peoples*, 6th ed. p. 554/7th ed., p. 536; History Reasoning Skill—Causation; Learning Objective CUL-2,4,5, ECON-8; Key Concept 4.1).

4. A. Answers may vary. Global circulation of goods was facilitated by technological developments in cartography and navigation, including examples such as the caravel, carrack, and astrolabe.

B. European merchants in Asia focused mainly on transporting goods from one Asian country to another.

C. The Americas functioned mainly to provide silver, which was sold in Asia.

    (*The Earth and Its Peoples*, 6th ed., pp. 410–415/7th ed., pp. 400–405; History Reasoning Skill—Contextualization; Learning Objectives SB-3,4,9,10, ECON-3,5,9,10,11,12,13, SOC-2,7,8, ENV3,6, CUL-6; Key Concept 4.1)

5. A. Answers will vary; the introduction of European livestock such as cattle, pigs, or horses replaced traditional native livestock and changed the environment. The additional introduction of Afro-Eurasian fruit trees, grains, and foods also adapted the landscape and living style of Native Americans.

B. Answers will vary, but a good response must address one of the negative effects (smallpox, measles, influenza, etc.) that led to the decimation of the Amerindian population and had a long-term negative effect.

    (*The Earth and Its Peoples*, 6th ed., pp. 466–468/7th ed., pp. 454–456; History Disciplinary Practices and Reasoning Skills— Argument Development, Analyzing Historical Evidence, Causation; Learning Objective ENV-5,7,8, SB-3, ECON-1,5,10,12, SOC-2,7,8; Key Concept 4.1).

LONG ESSAY QUESTIONS

1. Between 1450 and 1750 Africa was influenced by both Europe and the Islamic world. Thus, a comparative essay in response to this prompt should draw analysis from the larger global context. The Islamic world's influence on Africa was much stronger than Europe's during this period, particularly in North Africa. Politically, of course, nearly all of North Africa was unified under the Muslim-ruled Ottoman Empire in the 1500s, while West Africa remained more independent (due to protective geography and skilled leaders) but less politically cohesive, with various regional kingdoms and empires (such as Benin, Kongo, and Oyo) rising and falling. West Africa also saw the beginning of European imperialism, with the establishment of the Portuguese colony of Angola,

but in general, Islam continued to play a larger role in African affairs in West Africa, too—the Songhai Empire is one example of a Muslim-ruled West African dynasty. Economically, the trans-Saharan gold trade continued to bring wealth to both North and West Africa, with indigenous artisans also producing textiles and metalwork for local consumption and export. West African merchants also began to profit from the transatlantic slave trade, however, which allowed certain regional leaders to acquire European firearms, boost their military strength, and maintain territorial control throughout this period of increased contact with the growing global trade network. (*The Earth and Its Peoples*, 6th ed., pp. 509–516/7th ed., pp. 490–495; History Reasoning Skill—Comparison; Learning Objective SB-10, ECON-3,12,13; Key Concept 4.1).

2. Change in the Middle East during this period began with the death of Timur, whose forces had interrupted the consolidation of the Ottoman Empire. By the mid-1400s, the Ottomans had eliminated the once-mighty Byzantine Empire by capturing its capital of Constantinople, and they continued to add territory around the Mediterranean to their domain for decades to come. Meanwhile, to the east, Timur's death spurred a battle for power among a number of would-be successors; a young Sufi leader named Ismail emerged to establish himself as shah of Iran in 1502. Unlike the Ottomans, the Safavids of Iran battled not to expand beyond their territorial boundaries, but to establish militant Shi'ism as the religion of the realm. The Safavid Empire endured as a regional rival to the larger Ottoman Empire until the mid-1700s, when an economic crisis led to an overthrow of the shah and a period of instability in Iran that would last until the twentieth century. Both the Ottoman Empire and Iran would face growing challenges for control of their territory by the rising powers of Europe as this period came to an end. One continuity of note during this period is the influence of Islam as a source of law and unity in both the Ottoman and Safavid Empires; while the Sunni Ottomans and Shi'ite Safavids were sworn enemies, the leaders of both followed the Shari'a and interpretive fatwas issued by ulama (Muslim scholars) in governing their lands. (*The Earth and Its Peoples*, 6th ed., pp. 534–535/7th ed., pp. 516–518; History Reasoning Skill—Continuity and Change over Time; Learning Objective CUL-4,8, SB-1,2,4,5,7,9,10, ECON-3,8, SOC-3,5,7; Key Concept 4.3).

3. This essay first invites a discussion of the Ming ruler Hongwu's use of a return to Confucian values in reestablishing indigenous control in China following the Mongol rule of the Yuan dynasty. Because Confucianism stressed the value of agriculture as the basis of a strong society, commercial activity in the Ming Empire was somewhat hindered. On the other hand, pride in native Chinese styles in art and literature led to an era of great achievement in poetry, painting, and the production of blue-and-white Ming porcelain that became immensely popular in the Indian Ocean trade. Hongwu's successor, Yongle, broke with the isolationist aspects of Confucian tradition somewhat, reestablishing commercial links with the Middle East and sending the Muslim voyager Zheng He on several voyages of exploration to India, Arabia, and East Africa. When the Manchus invaded

and established the Qing Empire, they recognized the enduring importance of Confucianism in Chinese society and realized that they must embrace its values in order to maintain minority rule over the Chinese people. Confucianism thus remained the basis of the Qing government's civil-service examination system. At the same time, however, persistent European merchants and missionaries started to bring outside commercial and religious influences that would begin to weaken the established dictates of Confucian society in China by the middle of the 1700s (*The Earth and Its Peoples*, 6th ed. pp. 560–568/7th ed., pp. 548–549; Historical Thinking Skill—Continuity and Change over Time; Learning Objective CUL-4,8, SB-1,2,4,5,7,9,10, ECON-3,4,5,6,7,8, SOC-3,5,7; Key Concept 4.3).

4. A good response to this comparative essay will review the rise of a capitalist economy in western Europe, with its emphasis on mercantilist policies: gaining wealth by maintaining a favorable balance of trade, taking possession of other territories, and using their natural resources in the manufacture of trade goods. By 1650, the western European economy had moved away from a dependence on the agricultural output of the feudal system and revolved around the Atlantic System—raw materials from the Americas, slaves from Africa, and trade goods from Europe were circulating in the Atlantic Ocean to generate wealth for European monarchs and their growing bourgeois classes. An important similarity is that after finally shrugging off the rule of the Mongols' Golden Horde, which had drained the region of any wealth it had previously had, Russia also set out to transform its economy in an attempt to link with the wealth of western Europe's manufacturing-based capitalist system. Under Peter the Great, Russia too gained control of new lands—but the annexation of Siberia and other territory to the east created a land-based empire that was forced to struggle with issues of economic stagnation and ethnic and religious diversity. Peter was able to build a modern new capital in St. Petersburg and begin using his newly gained natural resources to move western Russia toward a manufacturing-based economy similar to those of the countries of western Europe, but he and his successors remained saddled with a vast eastern territory that continued to be dominated by a dependence on agricultural output. While Russia also relied on a system of forced labor, Russian serfdom actually resulted in an economy that had more in common with the feudal system of Europe's Middle Ages than with the contemporaneous sea-based empires of western Europe (*The Earth and Its Peoples*, 6th ed., pp. 410–415/7th ed., pp. 400–406; History Reasoning Skill—Comparison; Learning Objectives ENV-3,6, CUL-6, SB-6,9, ECON3,12,13; Key Concept 4.1).

5. A good response to this continuity and change over time question would have to include a discussion of the indigenous political practices of the region chosen, followed by details on the colonial government imposed by the European power that seized control of the territory. In North America, the indigenous political tradition of chiefdom generally gave way to governors appointed by the European powers, although various forms of colonist-led representative government began to develop in the English settlements. The Caribbean islands had seen settlement by the

Arawak and Carib peoples, but their small communities were fairly decentralized and focused mainly on subsistence farming. The Dutch, English, and French eventually established plantation-based colonies throughout the West Indies, with governors who were generally in league with the plantocracy, the small class of wealthy Europeans who owned most of the land and privately governed large populations of African slaves engaged in sugar production. In Mesoamerica and South America, both the Aztec and Inca monarchs had ruled a large and diverse territory, controlling conquered peoples and extracting tribute from them through the threat of invasion; the Spanish and Portuguese then imposed the most elaborate form of colonial government found in the Americas, establishing several viceroyalties that exerted day-to-day administrative control over the economic activities and complex social structure of New Spain, Peru, La Plata, and Brazil. In all regions, the political changes far outweighed the continuities, although hierarchical societies with government oversight of a trade-based economy remained a constant throughout most of the region (*The Earth and Its Peoples*, 6th ed., pp. 432–433/7th ed., pp. 422–423; History Reasoning Skill—Continuity and Change over Time; Learning Objective SB-3,4,9,10, ECON3,5,6,9,11,12,13, SOC-2,7,8; Key Concept 4.1).

Period 5: Industrialization and Global Integration, c. 1750 to c. 1900

Period 5 in the AP® World History framework focuses mainly on the development and spread of industrialization, as well as the transformation of Africa and Asia as a result of European political and economic imperialism. Economic production across the world underwent impressive changes as a result of new industrial technologies and methods in this period. However, it is important to note that not all societies had access to or adopted these techniques. States that did industrialize were often able to subjugate states that did not, as with European imperialism in Africa or Japanese colonization of Korea. The power that industrialization lent conquering nations allowed those nations to extract resources and manpower to further fuel the industrial progress of the mother country. Imperial rulers faced new challenges of not only ruling over diverse populations, but also how to maintain power and stability in far-flung colonial territories.

Apart from industrialization and imperialism, a major pattern of revolution and/or calls for reform mark this period of world history. Enlightenment ideas originating in Europe spread across the Atlantic, inspiring independence movements as well as new forms of political organization. European presence in India and China led to significant rebellions against foreign interference. African states also resisted the increasing encroachment of Europeans, with mixed degrees of success. Rulers of non-Western nations reacted to the growing power of the West (Europe and the United States) in a variety of ways: some nations replicated the advances in technology, economic strategies, political theory, and cultural values of the West; some nations utterly rejected the West and attempted to avoid reform; while still others tried to blend traditional political and cultural traditions with new economic ideas. Even within fully industrialized nations, there were people who called for further reform to allow for expansion of suffrage and political representation, as well as abolition of slavery. Some even desired the elimination of socio-economic classes, rejecting what they viewed as an exploitative capitalist system that had developed in conjunction with industrialization.

The following charts outline the learning objectives and topics from the content outline that fit into this period.

Content Review Questions can be found at the end of each chapter. **AP® format questions** for Period 5 can be found on page 412. **Document-Based Questions** can be found in the diagnostic test and practice tests.

AP® is a trademark registered by the College Board, which is not affiliated with, and does not endorse, this product.

THEMATIC LEARNING OBJECTIVES FOR PERIOD 5

INTERACTION BETWEEN HUMANS AND THE ENVIRONMENT

Learning Objectives—Students are able to . . .	Relevant Topics in the Concept Outline
ENV-1 Explain how environmental factors, disease, and technology affected patterns of human migration and settlement over time.	5.1. IV—Railroads 5.4. I—Urbanization 5.4. I–III—Migration
ENV-2 Evaluate the extent to which migration, population, and urbanization affected the environment over time.	5.1. VI—Unsanitary cities 5.4. I–III—Global migration 5.4. I—Urbanization
ENV-3 Explain how environmental factors have shaped the development of diverse technologies, industrialization, transportation methods, and exchange and communication networks.	5.1. I, II—Rise of industrialization 5.1. II—Natural resource extraction and shifts in commodities production 5.1. VI—Effects of Industrial Revolution 5.2. I—Transoceanic empires
ENV-4 Evaluate the extent to which the development of diverse technologies, industrialization, transportation methods, and exchange and communication networks have affected the environment over time.	5.1. I, II—Industrialization; increased production 5.1. VI—Unsanitary cities 5.2. I—Imperialism 5.4. II—Demographic change and migration; urbanization

DEVELOPMENT AND INTERACTION OF CULTURES

Learning Objectives—Students are able to . . .	Relevant Topics in the Concept Outline
CUL-1 Explain how religions, belief systems, philosophies, and ideologies originated, developed, and spread as a result of expanding communication and exchange networks.	5.1. III—New financial philosophies 5.1. V—Responses to globalization 5.2. II, III—Imperialism; Social Darwinism 5.3. I, II, IV—Enlightenment, reform movements, spread of enlightenment ideas
CUL-2 Explain how religions, belief systems, philosophies, and ideologies affected political, economic, and social developments over time.	5.1. V—Imperialism and state formation 5.2. II—Political rulers 5.2. III—Social Darwinism 5.3. I—Enlightenment 5.3. II—Nationalism 5.3. III—Religious and political rebellions 5.3. IV—Transnational ideologies
CUL-3 Explain how cross-cultural interactions resulted in the diffusion of culture, technologies, and scientific knowledge.	5.1. II—Increased productivity from new technologies
CUL-4 Explain how technological and scientific innovations affected religions, belief systems, philosophies, and ideologies over time.	5.3. I—Enlightenment 5.3. II—Nationalism 5.3. IV—Transnational ideologies
CUL-5 Explain how expanding exchange networks shaped the emergence of various forms of transregional culture, including music, literature, and visual art.	5.4. III—Migrants spread culture

STATE BUILDING, EXPANSION, AND CONFLICT

Learning Objectives—Students are able to . . .	Relevant Topics in the Concept Outline
SB-1 Explain how different forms of governance have been constructed and maintained over time.	5.1. V—Qing and Ottoman empires 5.2. I—Transoceanic empires 5.2. II—Meiji Japan 5.3. III—Revolutions
SB-2 Explain how and why different functions and institutions of governance have changed over time.	5.1. I—Impact of industrialization 5.1. V—Alternate visions of society/government 5.2. I—Transoceanic empires 5.2. II—Imperialism and state formation 5.3. III—Reformist and revolutionary movements 5.4. I—Causes and effects migration
SB-3 Explain how and why economic, social, cultural, and geographical factors have influenced the processes of state building, expansion, and dissolution.	5.1. I—Capitalism; export economies 5.1. II—Industrial production 5.1. V—Alternate visions of capitalist societies, state-sponsored industrialization 5.I. VI—New social classes, communities 5.2. I—Industrialization and imperialism 5.2. II—Imperialism, new states 5.2. III—Social Darwinism 5.3. I—Enlightenment 5.3. II—Nationalism 5.3. III—Decline of empires 5.3. IV—Reformist and revolutionary movements, transnationalism; improved military technology 5.4. I—Spread of European social, political thought
SB-4 Explain how and why internal and external political factors have influenced the process of state building, expansion, and dissolution.	5.1. V—Responses to global capitalism 5.2. I—Imperialism 5.2. III—Social Darwinism 5.3. I—Enlightenment 5.3. III—Imperial discontent, revolutions, transnationalism; eighteenth- and nineteenth-century revolutions
SB-5 Explain how societies with states and state-less societies interacted over time.	5.2. I, II—Imperialism and state formation 5.2. II—New states on edges of empires 5.3. III—Movements against imperialism
SB-6 Explain the political and economic interactions between states and non-state actors over time.	5.1. II—Global economies, merchants and companies 5.2. I, II—Imperialism and state formation 5.3. III—Movements against imperialism
SB-7 Analyze the political and economic interactions between states and non-state actors.	5.2. I, II—Imperialism and state formation

CREATION, EXPANSION, AND INTERACTION OF ECONOMIC SYSTEMS

Learning Objectives—Students are able to . . .	Relevant Topics in the Concept Outline
ECON-1 Explain how technology shaped economic production and globalization over time.	5.1. II—New pattern of global trade 5.1. III—Transnational businesses, transportation 5.2. II—Land-based empire expansion; national reactions to industrialization 5.4. I—Increased global migration
ECON-2 Explain the causes and effects of economic strategies of different types of communities, states, and empires.	5.1. II—Industrialization 5.1. III—Capitalism, financial instruments 5.1. V—Resisting or sponsoring industrialization 5.2. I—Imperialism
ECON-3 Explain how different modes and locations of production and commerce have developed and changed over time.	5.1. I—New machines and methods of industrial production 5.1. II—Industrialization; transnational businesses, transportation 5.1. III—Capitalism, financial instruments 5.1. V—Resisting or sponsoring industrialization 5.2. I—Imperialism 5.2. II—Global conflict; transnational movements 5.4. I— Land-based empire expansion; national reactions to industrialization
ECON-4 Explain the causes and effects of labor reform movements.	5.1. VI—Government reform, socialism 5.3. I—Enlightenment attitudes, abolition of serfdom and slavery 5.3. III—Reform, rebellion, slave resistance, anti-colonial movements 5.3. IV—Transnational ideologies—liberalism, socialism, communism
ECON-5 Explain how and why labor systems have developed and changed over time.	5.1. I, VI—Industrial production 5.4. II—Labor migration; coerced and semicoerced migrant labor
ECON-6 Explain how economic systems and the development of ideologies, values, and institutions have influenced each other.	5.1. I—Legal protection of global capitalism 5.1. III—Classical liberalism 5.1. V, VI—Socialism, Marxism; transformation of social organization 5.2. III—Social Darwinism justified imperialism
ECON-7 Explain how local, regional, and global economic systems and exchange networks have influenced and impacted each other over time.	5.1. II—Raw materials, markets lead to new global trade patterns 5.1. III—Financial institutions; transnational businesses, transportation 5.1. IV—Railroads, steamships, canals, and telegraph 5.4. I—Global migration

DEVELOPMENT AND TRANSFORMATION OF SOCIAL STRUCTURES

Learning Objectives—Students are able to . . .	Relevant Topics in the Concept Outline
SOC-1 Explain how distinctions based on kinship, ethnicity, class, gender, and race influenced the development and transformations of social hierarchies.	5.1. V—Anarchism, utopian socialism, suffrage 5.1. VI—Industrialization affected gender roles, middle class, and industrial working class 5.3. I, IV—Enlightenment ideals 5.4. III—Male migrants, females left in home society
SOC-2 Evaluate the extent to which different ideologies, philosophies, and religions affected social hierarchies.	5.1. I—Industrial specialization 5.1. V—Anarchism, utopian socialism, suffrage 5.1. VI—New social classes and gender roles 5.3. I–IV—Enlightenment ideals
SOC-3 Evaluate the extent to which legal systems, colonialism, nationalism, and independence movements have sustained or challenged class, gender, and racial hierarchies over time.	5.1. I—Private property 5.2. I—Settler colonies 5.3. I—Independence movements 5.3. II—Nationalism 5.3. III—Anticolonial movements 5.3. IV—Suffrage, feminism
SOC-4 Explain how the development of specialized labor systems interacted with the development of social hierarchies.	5.1. I—Industrialization 5.1. VI—Middle class and industrial working class 5.3. I—Abolition of slavery, end of serfdom 5.3. IV—Challenges to social hierarchies, including gender roles 5.4. II—Global migration
SOC-5 Explain how social categories, roles, and practices have been maintained or challenged over time.	5.1. I—Private property 5.2. I—Settler colonies 5.2. II—Anti-imperial resistance 5.2. III—Social Darwinism 5.3. I—Enlightenment ideals; independence movements 5.3. II—Nationalism 5.3. III—Anticolonial movements 5.3. IV—Suffrage, feminism

KEY CONCEPTS FOR PERIOD 5

5.1. Industrialization and Global Capitalism

5.2. Imperialism and Nation-State Formation

5.3. Nationalism, Revolution, and Reform

5.4. Global Migration

21

AFRICA: C. 1750 TO c. 1900

KEY CONCEPTS

- African trading empires continued to control most parts of eastern and western Africa before the 1850s.
- Moral pressure and changes in the global economy led to the end of the transatlantic slave trade by 1867.
- Industrialism and nationalism fed the desire of European nations for increased influence in Africa by the 1870s.
- New Imperialism reshaped the continent of Africa as European countries began exerting political, economic, and cultural control over their African colonies.
- In the "scramble" for Africa, European nations carved up the continent into colonial possessions, with only Ethiopia and Liberia remaining independent.
- European imperialism altered Africans' political, economic, and cultural way of life.

KEY TERMS

- Afrikaners
- Battle of Adowa
- Berlin Conference
- colonialism
- Industrial Revolution
- modernization
- nationalism
- New Imperialism
- palm oil
- "scramble" for Africa

- Sokoto Caliphate
- South African War
- Suez Canal
- transatlantic slave trade
- Zulu

Africa is discussed in depth in *The Earth and Its Peoples*, 6th edition, Chapter 25 and 7th edition, Chapter 26.

THE RISE OF AFRICAN EMPIRES

In the early nineteenth century, changes in trading patterns and population growth, familiar to other parts of Africa, came to the Nguni people of southern Africa. In addition, a severe drought led to increased conflict over grazing and farmlands. The Nguni had traditionally organized themselves in small independent clan groups, but with their society in crisis, a military visionary came forward to reshape southern Africa. In 1818, Shaka created the **Zulu** kingdom. The Zulu were successful because of their powerful military, which included disciplined drills, hand-to-hand combat, and new, advanced technologies—notably the stabbing spear and oxhide shield. In less than a decade, Shaka and the Zulu became a feared force as they seized neighboring grazing and agricultural lands. Areas that were raided lost cattle, and many women and children were enslaved or made homeless, thus creating a large refugee population in southern Africa. Similar to the Mongols' approach, conquered men were integrated into the Zulu army and became fiercely loyal to Shaka. The Zulu did more than any other group in moving central and southern Africa away from clan-based political organization to strong centralized monarchies. In response to the growing Zulu threat, many other clans and displaced people united behind charismatic leaders and adopted Zulu military tactics to control growing populations.

In West Africa, Islam had been an important religion for hundreds of years, though rural people often resisted conversion and continued their traditional religious practices. Because of this, earlier Islamic empires had tolerated local religion. In 1804, Muslim reformers who wanted a more traditional adherence to Islam called for a jihad, or holy war, to enforce shari'a, Islamic religious law, in western Africa. This call for reform was most strongly accepted in the Hausa states (northern Nigeria). The Islamic reformers challenged the Hausa kings, helped to unite Hausa peasants and devout Muslims against traditional West African elites, and established a caliphate based in the city of Sokoto. The **Sokoto Caliphate**, as it came to be known, was the largest Islamic empire in West Africa since the Songhai Empire in the late sixteenth century. Sokoto became a center for Islamic learning, with schools and libraries attracting Muslim scholars from all over West Africa. Non-Muslims were allowed to remain in the caliphate if they paid a tax, but traditional religious ceremonies and festivals were suppressed. Those who resisted were killed or enslaved; many of those slaves were sold through the trans-Saharan slave network. Once power had been consolidated, the Sokoto Caliphate controlled much of western Africa for the remainder of the nineteenth century.

AFRICA AND THE SLAVE TRADE

The effect of the **transatlantic slave trade** on Africa was staggering. It is estimated that more than ten million Africans were enslaved between 1550 and 1800. Eight million of these enslaved African men, women, and children were sent to the Western Hemisphere, while another two million lived in bondage in the Middle East and North Africa. Scholars generally agree that this displacement of people from Africa did not have a dramatic effect on the overall population of sub-Saharan Africa but that some regions, such as parts of western Africa, were greatly affected by the large population losses over many years. They theorize that the ability of some regions to recover from depopulation was directly related to the proportion of women of childbearing age who were enslaved.

In the late eighteenth century, the institution of slavery and the slave trade came under attack. Successful slave revolts in St. Domingue (present-day Haiti) were initially met with brutal repression by European colonial leaders, but the revolts provoked some to question the moral legitimacy of slavery. Several nations banned the inter-national slave trade: Denmark in 1803, Britain in 1807, and the United States in 1808. Abolitionists groups, particularly in Britain, lobbied their governments to outlaw slavery and enforce a ban on slave trading.

AP® Tip

The end of the transatlantic slave trade did not mean that all slavery or slave trade ended. After 1867, thousands of Africans, many from East Africa, would be enslaved over the next several decades. These slaves were shipped to Brazil and Cuba, as well as parts of the Middle East. Ironically, the end of the transatlantic slave trade signaled the growth of slavery in Africa itself. African-led trading companies in West Africa and clove plantations in East Africa enslaved thousands of Africans throughout the nineteenth century. Slavery in Africa increasingly took on the features of the oppressive slave societies that had developed in the Western Hemisphere. Ethiopia did not finally abolish slavery until 1932. This often-overlooked final chapter of slavery and the slave trade provides interesting background information for a free-response essay that deals with slavery or the slave trade.

By the 1840s, with slavery and the international slave trade illegal in most of Europe, the British navy began policing the West African coast. Taking control of Sierra Leone in 1808, the British made that area a colony for liberated slaves. The Royal Navy's aggressive antislavery patrols resulted in the capture of more than 1600 ships and the rescue of 160,000 Africans headed for the slave markets in the Caribbean and South America. As it became more difficult to obtain slaves in West Africa, the slave trade moved farther south and then to East Africa. The transatlantic slave trade joined an already well-established East African slave trade that had existed for decades. A third of the slaves from East Africa were sent to the Americas; the remainder went to North Africa and the Middle East. Because of the high demand for slaves in Cuba and Brazil, the transatlantic slave trade was not completely ended until 1867.

The slave trade accounted for much of the trade with Africa before 1825, but after that, exports like gold, ivory, and palm oil became dominant. The palm oil trade reshaped the Niger River delta of western Africa. **Palm oil**, used in Europe and the United States for industrial machines, soap, and candle making, was in high demand during the nineteenth century. Palm oil companies used many slaves to harvest the oil from the interior of West Africa and transport it to the coast. Leaders of these trading companies were like merchant princes, politically and economically controlling port cities and interior lands as well as thousands of slaves. Slaves owned by these trading companies could work and buy their own freedom, though that rarely happened. King Jaja of Opobo, one slave who purchased his freedom, established an independent trading state from the port of Opobo in 1869. By shifting their trade from slaves to raw materials, Africans were able to keep their access to Western industrial imports.

EGYPT AND ETHIOPIA: MODERNIZATION AND WESTERNIZATION

During the nineteenth century both Egypt and Ethiopia began efforts to adopt European technology in order to compete with and defend themselves from Western power. As **modernization** began, ideas of **nationalism**, which had been on the rise in Europe, arrived in Africa. Egypt was the first African empire to be reshaped by the modernizing influence of western Europe. The power vacuum created when Napoleon's troops were pushed out of Egypt in 1801 was filled by Muhammad Ali. Ali initially led Albanian soldiers to restore Ottoman imperial control in Egypt. Once in control, Ali began a decades-long process to modernize and westernize Egypt. Shocked by the ease with which Napoleon had taken control of Egypt in 1798, Ali moved quickly to begin a political, economic, and military restructuring program. European experts were brought in to train and reorganize the Egyptian military, new weapons were imported, and a European-style military training college was opened. Promising young officers were sent to Europe to be trained in the latest techniques of warfare. In addition, schools were opened to train both army surgeons and military bandleaders. Ali's new army would be built by the conscription of Egyptian peasants. To pay for his modern military, Ali revoked traditional mamluk land privileges and forced Egyptian peasants to grow cotton for export. In other areas, Ali attempted to blend Islamic culture with modernization by starting an Islamic newspaper and printing Islamic classics in Arabic. Though an industrial economy was never fully realized, Ali and his family, who retained control after his death, continued to experiment with modernizing the nation. Egypt was linked by railroads, new irrigation canals increased agricultural production, and a postal service was formed. Ali's grandson Ismail Ali continued Egyptian modernization and westernization efforts in the second half of the nineteenth century, proclaiming, "My country is no longer in Africa; it is in Europe." Egypt's goal of becoming a Western-style power was cut short when the cotton market collapsed after 1870, which led to increasing Egyptian debt and control by European investors.

The ancient kingdom of Ethiopia also began modernizing in the nineteenth century. Partial imperial control was reestablished in the 1830s by Emperor Téwodros II, who began his modernization program with the purchase of European weapons, which he then attempted to manufacture locally, in an effort to update the kingdom's military. When Menelik became emperor in 1889, the integration of his Shoa kingdom created what would constitute modern-day Ethiopia. Under Menelik's rule, Ethiopia continued to industrialize its military and defend against the growing threat of European imperialism. By continually shifting alliances with European powers, Ethiopia was able to import the latest modern weaponry. In 1896 at the **Battle of Adowa**, Menelik and his army routed Italian troops. Ethiopia was one of only two independent African nations at the end of the nineteenth century.

AP® Tip

When students see the term *nationalism*, they often think only about how it affected Western nations. However, the building of national identity can also be seen in the actions taken by African nations like Egypt and Ethiopia during the nineteenth century. The construction of the Suez Canal in Egypt in the 1860s and the military defeat of Italian troops by Ethiopia in the 1890s helped foster nationalistic sentiments among their citizens. If a free-response essay deals with nationalism, mention its importance in Africa.

OLD IMPERIALISM VERSUS NEW IMPERIALISM

As the **Industrial Revolution** emerged in Europe and the United States, Western nations continued expanding their political, economic, and cultural reach. European powers had imperial aspirations before the nineteenth century, and nations like Spain, France, and Britain had built colonial empires in the Americas and Asia over several hundred years. Their goal was to obtain from their colonies the resources for their industries back home.

In the late nineteenth and early twentieth centuries, this **colonialism** was replaced by what historians refer to as **New Imperialism**, by which Europeans used their economic and technological power to reshape Africa politically and culturally. New Imperialism sought to bring Africa more fully into the global economy as both a supplier of raw materials and a purchaser of manufactured goods. To accomplish this, Europeans, who until the 1850s were in Africa primarily as traders on the coasts, invaded and set up colonial governments. These governments reorganized Africa to tap the natural resources of various African regions. A variety of motives pushed Europeans to build new imperialistic empires in Africa. Politically, with nationalism on the rise, creating an empire became important to newly industrial powers. When Britain claimed territory in Africa, its rival France followed suit. By the end of the nineteenth century, even smaller European powers like Belgium had staked claims to parts of Africa. Economically, industrialized countries needed to secure a constant source of raw materials—gold, diamonds, copper, and cotton were among the most significant. Culturally, Europeans wanted to westernize the parts of Africa over which they had influence. Thousands of Christian missionaries came to Africa in the late nineteenth and early twentieth centuries to transfer both religious and cultural ideas. Westerners had begun to equate their advances in technology with the superiority of their cultures. Given this fact, African values were increasingly viewed as a barrier to the development of modern society. As the poet Rudyard Kipling exhorted, Europeans had to embrace the "white man's burden" and "civilize" Africa, assuming political, economic, and cultural control.

Before the 1870s, Europeans had only a few colonial settlements in Africa, such as Britain's Sierra Leone and France's Algeria. But in the last quarter of the nineteenth century, several western European nations invaded and quickly divided up Africa, an example of New Imperialism commonly referred to as the **"scramble" for Africa**.

NORTH AFRICA

Egypt seemed an unlikely victim to be swept up in the quest to control Africa. In 1869, the nation completed the **Suez Canal**, shortening the distance between Europe and Asia and ushering in an age of increased global trade. To many Egyptian elites, the canal symbolized the modernization of Egypt and a source of national pride. But projects like the canal, funded by cotton exports and international loans, increased Egypt's foreign debt. By 1876, more than a third of all export earnings went to pay the debt, and Egypt was forced to sell its shares in the Suez Canal to European investors. As Europeans became more involved in financing the debt, they pressured their governments to protect their investment. In the late 1870s, both Britain and France used their influence to install Europeans as the minister of public works and minister of finance. In 1882, the Ottoman sultan deposed Ismail Ali, setting off a series of revolts. Britain feared the loss of access to India through the canal and stepped in to "stabilize" the country. The British army arrived in Egypt and began a seventy-year occupation, ruling indirectly through a puppet Egyptian government. Development projects—for example, damming the Nile River—did increase agricultural production in the country, but this primarily benefited the traditional elite at the expense of the peasants. European control brought Western customs that challenged traditional Islam. This was the hallmark of the New Imperialism in Egypt.

WESTERN AND EQUATORIAL AFRICA

European nationalism stimulated the competition for colonial territory and exacerbated a potential for armed conflict. In the 1870s, France wanted to increase its access to raw materials in the interior of western Africa by building a railroad. During the same period in equatorial Africa, Belgium's king Leopold II, convinced by explorers that great wealth could be obtained, began his expansion into the Congo River basin. The French were also interested in the vast territory of the Congo.

To avoid increased tension, German chancellor Otto von Bismarck called together European diplomats to help redefine their role in Africa. At the **Berlin Conference** (1884–1885), the nations of Europe agreed to divide up Africa peacefully. The new rules in the "scramble" for Africa, as it was later called, included no slave trading and, most important, no interference in the territory of other European occupiers. From 1885 to 1900, Britain, France, Germany, Italy, Portugal, Belgium, and Spain consolidated their colonial territory in Africa. By the end of the nineteenth century, Ethiopia and Liberia remained the only two independent nations in Africa.

King Leopold II created the Congo Free State after the Berlin Conference, while France and Portugal took control of the remaining territory in equatorial Africa. Unlike western Africa, the Congo region did not have a long history of trade in desirable raw materials. Instead of directly ruling the region, France, Portugal, and Belgium hired private companies to administer their territory and obtain resources that would be profitable. Many of these areas did not have cash crops that could be sold, so Africans were forced to develop new crops to pay the taxes demanded by the private companies. In territories like the Congo Free State, Africans were forced to harvest rubber and transport it out of the jungle themselves. Methods used to coerce people into these new economic activities led to atrocities committed by the private companies to maximize profit. Press coverage of the horrors in the Congo Free State led to the Belgium government taking over King Leopold's private company in 1908.

SOUTHERN AFRICA

Europeans had long been active on the coast of southern Africa. The Dutch East India Company established the Cape Colony in 1652. The British came to control the trading outpost in 1795. **Afrikaners**, descendants of Dutch settlers on the Cape of Good Hope, moved into the interior throughout the next century. The discovery of diamonds in the 1860s brought other European settlers to the region in search of riches. Seeking to control the diamond territory, British troops launched campaigns into the interior of southern Africa. After defeating the Xhosa in 1878, British troops faced off against the most powerful kingdom in southern Africa, the Zulu, led by King Cetshwayo. The large, well-disciplined Zulu military was initially able to hold its own against the outsiders, but in the end superior European weapons led to British victory and the exile of King Cetshwayo. Zulu land was parceled into farms for white ranchers as Britain expanded its imperial rule, founding Southern Rhodesia (now Zimbabwe) and Northern Rhodesia (now Zambia). The British then turned their eyes toward the Afrikaner republics, Transvaal and Orange Free State. The **South African War** (1899–1902) pitted these two early European colonizers, the Afrikaners and the British, against each other. With more than 450,000 troops, the British were able to defeat the Afrikaners and extend their colonial control in southern Africa. Concerned by the increasing costs of their overseas commitments in Africa as well as other parts of the world, the British created the Union of South

Africa, which gave European colonial settlers greater control in administering the empire. Ironically, the recently defeated Afrikaners emerged as the dominant force within the new Union of South Africa. To increase their own power and isolate the indigenous African population, the white South African parliament passed the Native Land Act in 1913. The law placed Africans on reservations and did not allow them to own land in other parts of the nation. Segregation and racial division increasingly became a part of South Africa in the early twentieth century.

THE EFFECTS OF NEW IMPERIALISM ON AFRICA

In the nineteenth and early twentieth centuries, New Imperialism affected all regions of Africa, but not always in the same way. Responses to colonialism took many forms. Some Africans seized on the opportunity to supplant traditional ruling African elites and found jobs in colonial governments or as soldiers in newly developed colonial armies. Others tried desperately to retain their status and their traditional way of life. Groups such as the Zulu in the south and the Asante in the west continued to challenge imperial control. Most Africans tried living the same way they had before colonial power came, but they found this increasingly difficult. Colonial powers disrupted long-established societies by replacing local leaders with new, professional bureaucrats. Challenges to long-held landowning patterns drastically altered the lives of many rural Africans; in parts of Africa where land was held communally, Western ideas of private property reshaped communities. As they put more territory into agricultural production, European powers held that local ideas on land use inhibited progress. The need to pay taxes to colonial governments forced many Africans into new occupations as miners, construction workers, and field hands. Families were split up as men took work in areas away from their homes. Thousands of Christian missionaries came to Africa during this period to open schools and teach Christian doctrine. In southern and central Africa, Christianity found converts, though for many Africans Christianity was tainted by its connection to the European colonial masters who had brought the religion with them. Missionaries had much less success in areas such as northern and eastern Africa, where Islam had a long tradition. Muslims also expanded their reach into sub-Saharan Africa, appealing to Africans in part because Islam was unburdened by the New Imperialism.

Content Review Questions

Questions 1–3 refer to the following map.

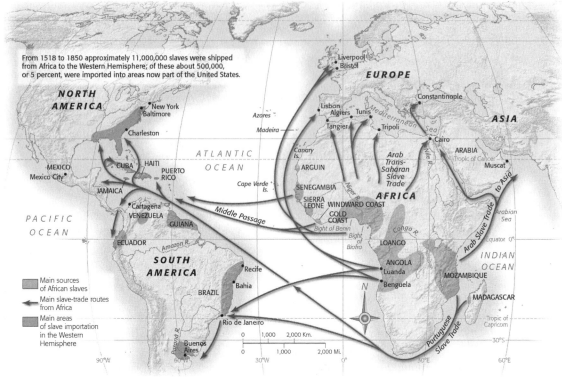

From 1518 to 1850 approximately 11,000,000 slaves were shipped from Africa to the Western Hemisphere; of these about 500,000, or 5 percent, were imported into areas now part of the United States.

Main sources of African slaves

Main slave-trade routes from Africa

Main areas of slave importation in the Western Hemisphere

The African Slave Trade, 1500–1800
Source: © Cengage Learning

1. According to the map, most slaves are transported to which of the following places during this time period?
   (A) The Middle East
   (B) Europe
   (C) South America
   (D) The West Indies

2. Why did planters of colonial Virginia switch from using indentured servants to using African slaves?
   (A) Slaves represented a lower up-front cost than indentured servants.
   (B) Most indentured servants had begun pursuing opportunities in the Caribbean rather than North America.
   (C) Slaves were easier to train.
   (D) Slaves served as a better long-term investment than indentured servants.

3. Most of the slaves held by West Africans in the late 1800s were
   (A) trained for military purposes.
   (B) forced into domestic service.
   (C) sold to the Middle East.
   (D) used to grow food crops.

Questions 4–6 refer to the following passage.

Village plots were set up in each headman's area early in 1902 (September–October). . . . Each headman [village chief] made a plot for his area in the neighborhood of his headquarters. The principle was that every 30–50 men were to cultivate 2½ acres. . . . Where possible, the advice of the natives was obtained as to the crop to be grown. So far as possible, one crop was to be grown on each plot, according to the type of soil. Some 2,000 acres were cleared and cultivated.

What was the labor situation and the supervision? . . . According to returns by the headmen, the number of able-bodied men amounted to:

1902–03 c. 25,000 men
1903–04 c. 26,000 men
1904–05 c. 25,000 men

During the last year, women and children had to be brought in to help, since the men frequently refused to work. . . . Last year (1904–05), following reports from the akidas [native rural officials] and from Sergeant Holzhausen, who was sent to inspect the headmen, numerous headmen were punished by the District Once with imprisonment in chains or solitary confinement for totally neglecting their village plots as a result of the natives' refusal to work. The last, in June, was headman Kibasila, who got one month in chains.

Excerpts from an Interview with a German Official Von Geibler Concerning the Communal Plots
Source: A. Andrea & J. Overfield, *The Human Record*, United States: Cengage, 2015, p. 286.

4. How did the Germans find themselves in Africa during the late nineteenth and early twentieth centuries?
    (A) Africans were attempting to modernize and they employed the help of the Germans in many cases.
    (B) Due to the Berlin Conference many different European nations ruled over African lands.
    (C) After the Boer War it was decided that Europeans had a right to stay in Africa due to the loss of so many European lives.
    (D) As a consequence of the Zulu defense of South Africa, the Germans supported British efforts to seize African lands in that region.

5. After the "scramble" for Africa, which African nations were able to maintain their independence at the end of the nineteenth century?
    (A) Egypt and Liberia
    (B) Congo Free State and Ethiopia
    (C) Union of South Africa and Sierra Leone
    (D) Ethiopia and Liberia

6. What were some of the characteristics of New Imperialism on the African continent?
    (A) A desire to open manufacturing plants in Africa, a need to spread European languages to other parts of the world, and a push for new European education systems in Africa
    (B) A request by European doctors to test new medications in Africa and investors' desires to bring Africa into a more global economy to benefit everyone
    (C) A need for raw materials, a belief that Europeans were culturally superior, and a desire to bring Christianity to Africans
    (D) A problem with overpopulation in Europe made Africa a desirable place to settle, European navies needed more ports during this time and profits from African construction projects were enticing to investors

Answers

1. ANSWER: D. While the amount of slaves transported was staggering, the majority of slaves forced from Africa were taken to the West Indies. Due to the profitable (for the Europeans) plantation system there, slaves were in a higher demand than elsewhere (*The Earth and Its Peoples*, 6th ed., pp. 701–702/7th ed., pp. 677–678; History Disciplinary Practice—Analyzing Historical Evidence; Learning Objectives ECON-2,3; Key Concept 5.2.I.E).

2. ANSWER: D. By the eighteenth century, Virginia's planters had begun to realize that a slave owned for life, although initially expensive to purchase, would provide a much higher rate of return than an indentured servant whose contract would run for only four to seven years (*The Earth and Its Peoples*, 6th ed., pp. 701–702/7th ed., pp. 677–678; History Reasoning Skill—Causation; Learning Objectives ECON-2,3; Key Concept 5.2.I.E).

3. ANSWER: D. Slaves in West Africa, such as those in the Sokoto Kingdom, were mostly used for raising food. By 1865, more slaves were held by West Africans just in the Sokoto Kingdom than in any slave state in the Western Hemisphere (*The Earth and Its Peoples*, 6th ed., pp. 701–702/7th ed., pp. 677–678; History Reasoning Skill—Causation; Learning Objectives ECON-2,3; Key Concept 5.2.I.E).

4. ANSWER: B. After the Berlin Conference, Germany found itself in the midst of the "scramble" for Africa with other European nations. Germany was motivated by resource-rich Africa and gained profit as shown by the system of farming, a form of forced labor, they implemented in the document (*The Earth and Its Peoples*, 6th ed., pp. 698–700/7th ed., pp. 674–676; History Reasoning Skill—Causation; Learning Objectives SB-1,2,3; Key Concept 5.2.I.C).

5. ANSWER: D. The "scramble" for Africa left only Ethiopia and Liberia independent at the end of the nineteenth century (*The Earth and Its Peoples*, 6th ed., pp. 698–700/7th ed., pp. 674–676; History Reasoning Skill—Causation; Learning Objectives SB-1,2,3; Key Concept 5.2.I.C).

6. ANSWER: C. European nations that participated in New Imperialism in the nineteenth century sought to include Africa as part of a global economy; it would supply raw materials and purchase industrial goods made in Europe. This type of imperialism did not require slave labor. However, it is clear that humans and raw materials were exploited by Europeans (*The Earth and Its Peoples*, 6th ed., pp. 698–700/7th ed., pp. 674–676; History Reasoning Skill—Causation; Learning Objectives SB-1,2,3; Key Concept 5.2.I.C).

22

THE MIDDLE EAST: C. 1750 TO C. 1900

KEY CONCEPTS

- During the nineteenth century, the Ottoman Empire was faced with a series of political, economic, and social setbacks that led to a decline in its power.
- Throughout the nineteenth century, attempts at modernization, such as the Tanzimat (reorganization) and Young Ottoman reforms, sought to strengthen the empire.
- Reform did not include women, who were unable to increase their work or educational opportunities, and certain reforms caused them to lose economic powers they previously held.
- Despite these widespread reforms, the Ottomans still lagged behind other more developed nations.
- As the twentieth century approached, the Ottoman Empire was labeled the "sick man of Europe," and European leaders posed the Eastern Question: Should the Ottoman Empire continue to exist; if not, who should take over its territory?
- Nationalistic Turkish reformers called the Young Ottomans gained increasing influence in the empire. They supported a crackdown on ethnic minorities and closer alignment with Germany.

KEY TERMS

- Crimean War
- Eastern Question
- extraterritoriality
- Greek independence
- Janissaries
- "sick man of Europe"

- Tanzimat
- ulama
- Young Ottomans

The Middle East is discussed in depth in *The Earth and Its Peoples*, 6th edition, Chapter 23, and 7th edition, Chapter 24.

THE OTTOMAN EMPIRE AT THE START OF THE NINETEENTH CENTURY

As the nineteenth century began, the Ottoman Empire, which had controlled much of the Middle East since the 1450s, was faced with a series of serious political, economic, and social issues. Economic and technological changes taking place in both Europe and the United States began to have a profound impact on the Middle East. As Western powers continued to modernize, adopting new technology and successfully industrializing, the Ottoman Empire lagged behind. The Ottomans' stagnant economy, lack of financial reserves, and weak governing elites initially made Western-style modernization difficult. In addition, the empire was steeped in centuries of tradition, and powerful political groups within the empire had much to lose if reform was undertaken. Much of the period from 1800 to the start of World War I would be dominated by the Ottomans' struggle to adapt to the powerful changes taking place around them.

By the late eighteenth and early nineteenth centuries, the Ottoman central government had grown weak, and it was increasingly difficult to control an empire that included most of the Middle East and North Africa. Regional power bases had arisen in both Egypt and Arabia, where local ruling elites often ignored the imperial government in Constantinople (modern Istanbul). In Arabia, the Islamic fundamentalist Saud family took control of the sacred cities of Mecca and Medina. This was an embarrassing loss of control for the Ottoman sultan Selim III (1789–1807), who was unable to lead Muslims in the traditional pilgrimage to Mecca, one of the Five Pillars of Islam. In Egypt, Napoleon's French troops had invaded and controlled the region before they were finally forced out in 1801. The Ottomans were unable to reinstate imperial control, which led to the rise of Muhammad Ali. Though Ali did not openly separate himself from the Ottoman Empire in the early part of the nineteenth century, his independence would serve as a constant reminder of the difficulty the Ottomans had in controlling distant territories.

Political divisions in the heart of the empire became more apparent at the start of the nineteenth century. The **Janissaries**—originally young Christian boys taken primarily from the Balkans, converted to Islam, and trained to be the elite military guard of the sultan—resisted the adoption of new, Western ideas. Economic privileges that had been given to these troops strengthened their influence in the empire. Change was viewed as an attack on traditional values and the power of the Janissaries. In addition, the **ulama**, Muslim religious scholars, controlled the Islamic courts within the empire and had great influence over political and cultural policy. Talk of modernization was seen by the ulama as an attack on Islam. Regardless of these opposition forces, Sultan Selim III would be the first of many Ottoman rulers who would try to restore the power of the empire with a program of reform.

MODERNIZATION IN THE OTTOMAN EMPIRE

Sultan Selim III was interested in the technological and military changes that were taking place in western Europe. To strengthen the empire, he devised a modernization plan that included a European-style military, standardized taxation, and reinstitution of Ottoman control over provincial governors. To fund this reform agenda, the Sultan used excise taxes on goods such as tobacco and coffee. These reforms met with strong opposition from both the Janissaries and the ulama. In Serbia, an Ottoman province in which the Janissaries acted as provincial governors, military forces vented their frustration with the reforms on the local Serbian Orthodox Christian population. Unable to put down the military uprising, the Ottoman sultan was forced to seek help from the ruler of Bosnia, and together they were able to defeat the Janissaries. However, because of the threat of Russian intervention, the Ottomans were unable to limit future Bosnian influence in the region, and they could not disarm Serbia's Orthodox Christians. Serbia became effectively independent, another piece of the decaying empire lost from Ottoman control. The resistance of the Janissaries and the ulama forced Sultan Selim III to end his reform program in 1806, but that did not stop a looming rebellion. In a demonstration of the powers arrayed against change, an uprising by traditionalist forces took control of Istanbul; Selim was imprisoned and later killed.

Mahmud II (r. 1808–1839), Selim's cousin, gained the support of the ulama and Janissary forces in Istanbul and became sultan, calming the uprising. Mahmud supported limited reforms but understood that change needed to occur slowly if he hoped to solidify his power. It would be events at the far edge of the empire that would enable him to embark on drastic reform. In Greece, local groups were organizing against Ottoman control throughout the 1820s. European nations, eager to reclaim the Greek and Roman traditions that had been identified as the source of Western civilization, aided **Greek independence** fighters. Volunteers from all over western Europe, among them the English poet Lord Byron, fought and died to liberate Greece from Ottoman control. Mahmud looked to Muhammad Ali's Egyptian forces to help defend the empire from attack. The modernized Egyptian army greatly impressed the sultan as they fought to continue Ottoman control over the region. Still, Egypt's help would not be enough; at the Battle of Navarino, in 1829, the bulk of the Ottoman naval fleet was destroyed by European powers that were determined to see an independent Greece.

After witnessing the effectiveness of the Egyptian troops, Mahmud began an aggressive push to modernize the Ottoman military. In 1830, the sultan's argument to modernize was given added support when his former Egyptian ally attacked Syria and looked to supplant the Ottomans as the dominant power in the Middle East. In response, the sultan reorganized both the empire's military and its financial institutions. A new artillery unit was created, which once again led to revolts by the Janissary forces. Taking more dramatic steps, Mahmud officially dissolved the Janissary corps and turned his new artillery on them to crush the uprising. Mahmud also wanted to limit the power of the ulama, which he saw as a barrier to modernization. Even with these changes, Egyptian troops continued their assault on Ottoman territory. The sultan had trouble retaining the loyalty of his own armed forces, which shocked the empire in 1839 when the rebuilt Ottoman naval force sided with Egyptian troops. In this period of crisis, Mahmud died and was replaced by his sixteen-year-old son, Abdul Mejid (r. 1839–1861). Sensing an opportunity, Egyptian troops attacked in Anatolia (modern Turkey) and headed toward the Ottoman capital, Istanbul. With few alternatives, the new sultan was forced to turn to the British and French, who helped defend the capital and used financial threats to force Egyptian withdrawal from Ottoman territory. Thereafter, the survival of the empire depended on European aid.

The modernizing spirit of Mahmud II would be continued by Abdul Mejid, who announced a series of reforms that would become known as the **Tanzimat** (reorganization). These guaranteed political rights for men—for example, free public trials, a limited right of privacy, and more equitable methods of tax collection. The reforms also attempted to modernize the Ottoman Empire and were supported strongly by its European allies. Military training schools modeled on western European methods were opened. Adopting Muhammad Ali's approach for Egypt, young officers would be trained in Europe, and Westerners were brought in to educate the Ottoman elite. Later, a system of national preparatory schools was established to funnel graduates into military colleges and universities. Increasingly, French became the language of instruction, though most students still learned to read and write using the Quran. Young men educated in these new schools took on the style and fashions of modern Europeans and slowly replaced traditional bureaucratic elites. In Istanbul, a small though prominent elite embraced the Westernization of Ottoman society. They read newspapers in French, traveled to Europe, and supported the importation of military, industrial, and communications technology.

European governments were especially pleased to see reforms concerning religious minorities within the empire. The tax on non-Muslims was abolished, and codes specifying equal legal protection for Muslim, Jewish, and Christian subjects were passed. European powers were increasingly interested in the status of Christians in the empire, and missionaries flowed into Ottoman territories in the second half of the nineteenth century. New tax collection practices ended tax farming, a source of much hardship for the rural population. More secular legal codes began replacing shari'a, Islamic law. As a consequence, the power of the ulama declined, as did the lure of religious education, and fewer students entered religious schools.

Reform dealt exclusively with men. In some ways, it further restricted Ottoman women. Women were not given increased political participation or educational opportunities. Industrial labor and professional occupations, hallmarks of the new process of modernization, were not open to women, who lost more ground as industrialism gripped Ottoman cities and a competitive cash-based economy developed. The Westernization of the court system also led to a loss of power for women, as secularization shifted property and inheritance issues from Islamic courts to state courts, where women had no standing. Despite these widespread reforms, the Ottomans still lagged behind other more developed European nations, a fact that would threaten the empire repeatedly in the second half of the nineteenth century.

AP® Tip

Do industrialism and Westernization give women more rights and opportunities? When students first examine this idea, they think of western Europe and the United States and quickly think yes; more factory jobs open up, women leave home and demand equal treatment and pay, as well as increased access to the political process. Though this did happen in some societies, the process of Westernization narrowed the role of some women in the Ottoman Empire. Industrialization did not lead to new opportunities in either the factories or the professions, which were the exclusive domain of men. In addition, the Westernization of the court system led to women's loss of power over inheritance and property. In Islamic courts, women could continue to control property and wealth by establishing trusts in the name of their sons and acting as executors. However, with no standing in the new secular courts established by the Tanzimat reforms, women lost this power.

THE CRIMEAN WAR: 1853–1856

Throughout the nineteenth century, Russia, looking to expand, had laid claim to Ottoman territory in the northern part of the empire. The tsar had taken over the Georgian region of the Caucasus and supported Serbian independence. The Ottomans' northern neighbors viewed themselves as the protectors of Orthodox Christianity in both Europe and the Middle East. When Egyptian forces invaded Syria, the tsar and his troops came to the defense of the Ottoman sultan, successfully pushing back Muhammad Ali's forces. The treaty that followed officially recognized Russia as "defender of the Orthodox faith" within the Ottoman Empire. But the sultan viewed Russia as a territorial threat in the north, and in the 1840s and 1850s Britain and France were the Ottomans' primary European allies. In 1852, France was named protector of the Holy Sepulcher in Jerusalem, a Christian religious site. Considering this a violation of earlier treaty rights, Russia invaded Ottoman territories in modern-day Romania in 1853, thus beginning the **Crimean War**.

Britain and France quickly came to the aid of their Ottoman allies. Both European nations distrusted Russia and saw its expansion as a threat to their overland access to trade through Central Asia. For the next three years, the Ottoman Empire, Britain, France, and the Italian Kingdom of Sardinia-Piedmont battled the Russians in Romania, the Black Sea, and the Crimean peninsula. The war was fought on both land and sea, with Ottoman troops effectively resisting in Romania, despite reports of incompetence delivered by French and British commanders. In a dramatic naval confrontation on the Black Sea, Tsar Nicholas (r. 1825–1855) was forced to sink the entire Russian naval fleet to protect the approaches to the port city of

Sevastopol. The city was placed under siege and finally taken in 1856. The death of Nicholas in 1855 and repeated military setbacks for Russian troops forced the new tsar, Alexander II (r. 1855–1881), to sue for peace. The peace terms ended Russian expansion and balanced France's and Britain's territorial ambitions in the Ottoman Empire, with both countries agreeing that Ottoman land would not be taken exclusively for their own use. The Crimean War was a clash between traditional and modern methods of warfare, and it altered the world's perception of the Ottoman Empire. Highly trained cavalry troops, the elite of the Ottoman forces, were decimated by new infantry with modern artillery and breech-loading rifles. Ottoman military strength was clearly declining. European powers began to question the legitimacy of its continued existence.

THE "SICK MAN OF EUROPE" AND THE EASTERN QUESTION

Tsar Nicholas had called the Ottoman Empire the "**sick man of Europe**." As the twentieth century approached, it continued to fall behind the European nations militarily, economically, and technologically. As a result, many Western powers asked if the Ottoman Empire should continue to exist, and if not, who should take control of its territory. This idea, known as the **Eastern Question**, was hotly debated during the second part of the nineteenth century.

The Ottomans had serious economic problems that continued to worsen. Declining agricultural revenues, large debts to foreign nations, inflation, widespread corruption—all made reform difficult. Ottoman elites held that the only solution to these systemic problems was to continue reform and tie the empire more closely to Europe. An Ottoman imperial bank was created, the gold coin currency was tied to the British pound, and factories began opening in urban areas. During 1860–1880, a large demographic shift of people from rural villages to large urban areas began to occur in many parts of the empire. Cities such as Istanbul, Damascus, Beirut, and Cairo expanded as an urban professional class was created and industrial wage laborers found work. In addition, Russian expansion in Central Asia, which they would invade and gain control of Azerbaijan, Dagestan, and Chechnya, released a flood of Muslim refugees making their way to the Ottoman Empire and Iran. These new immigrants fueled the growth of cities, and competition for wage labor jobs was intense. Imports into Anatolia far exceeded exports, causing inflation that hit the new arriving urban poor hardest.

Communities of Europeans had increased their presence in the empire, particularly in cities. Bankers, merchants, missionaries, technical experts, and diplomats were just some of these new residents. Europeans lived apart from the rest of Ottoman society, housed in Western enclaves not subject to Ottoman laws. **Extraterritorially**, the exemption from the legal jurisdiction of the country of residence, was granted by some nations to foreign diplomats, but in the Ottoman Empire all Europeans were exempted. For many young reformers this violation of Ottoman sovereignty was unacceptable and demanded action.

AP® Tip

One of the most important skills in AP® World History is the ability to recognize global patterns and processes, such as industrialization, and analyze their effects in various regions. In many ways, attempts at reform and industrialization in the Ottoman Empire were similar to comparable efforts in the Americas, Africa, and Asia. All of these regions were forced to grapple with the issues of modernization and industrialization in the nineteenth century. Western European nations were the first to use the new technology to change and retool their economic system and military power. The Ottoman Empire and other less developed areas were especially interested in gaining new military technology. The creation of a global industrial market turned nations into either manufacturers of consumer goods or suppliers of raw materials for those goods. As suppliers of raw materials, the Ottomans were unable to generate enough wealth to become fully industrialized. Attempts at further industrialism had to be funded from Europe and the United States, leaving many underdeveloped nations in debt and with unwelcome European and American interests managing parts of their economy. The Ottoman Empire's inability to industrialize and the causes of that failure can be compared with the experience of many other areas that went through this global process in the nineteenth and twentieth centuries.

A reform group known as **Young Ottomans** demanded change in the 1860s and 1870s. They were looking to assert Ottoman authority over Europeans living in the empire, who, they held, had been allowed to ignore Ottoman laws and traditions. To that end, they wanted to westernize the empire and thereby make extraterritoriality obsolete. These reformers saw universal male suffrage and the creation of a constitutional monarchy as steps in that direction. A constitution was drafted and accepted by Sultan Abdul Hamid II (r. 1876–1909) in 1876. After that, the Young Ottoman movement lost much of its momentum when the threat of war with Russia arose in 1877, but limited reform continued under the Tanzimat programs.

Content Review Questions

Questions 1–3 refer to the following passage.

Let it be done as herein set forth. . . . All the privileges and spiritual immunities granted by my ancestors from time immemorial, to all Christian communities or other non-Muslim faiths established in my empire shall be confirmed and maintained. Every Christian or other non-Muslim community shall be bound within a fixed period, and with the concurrence of a commission composed of members of its own body, to proceed to examine its actual immunities and privileges, and to discuss and submit to my Sublime Porte the reforms required by the progress of civilization and of the age. . . . In the towns, small boroughs, and villages, where the whole population is of the same religion, no obstacle shall be offered to the repair, according to their original plan, of buildings set apart for religious worship, schools, hospitals, and cemeteries. . . .

As all forms of religion shall be freely professed in my dominions, no subject of my Empire shall be hindered in the exercise of the religion that he professes. No one shall be compelled to change their religion . . . and all the subjects of my Empire, without distinction of nationality, shall be admissible to public employments. . . . All the subjects of my Empire, without distinction, shall be received into the civil and military schools of the government. . . . Moreover, every community is authorized to establish public schools of science, art, and industry. . . .

All commercial and criminal suits between Muslims and Christian or other non-Muslim subjects, or between Christian or other non-Muslims of different sects, shall be referred to Mixed Tribunals [consisting of Muslim and non-Muslim judges]. The proceedings of these Tribunals shall be public; the parties shall be confronted, and shall produce their witnesses, whose testimony shall be received, without distinction, upon an oath taken according to the religious law of each sect. . . . Penal, correctional, and commercial laws, and rules of procedure for the Mixed Tribunals, shall be drawn up as soon as possible, and formed into a code. . . . . Steps shall be taken for the reform of the penitentiary system. . . .

Ottoman Sultan Abdul Mejid, The Islahat Fermani [Reforms] of 1856

Source: E. A. van Dyck, *Report upon the Capitulations of the Ottoman Empire,* Washington D.C.: U.S. Government Printing Office, 1881, 1882, Part I, pp. 106–108.

[1]"Sublime Porte," or "High Gate," refers to the gate in Istanbul giving access to the buildings that house the offices of state officials. It came to refer to the sultan's government in much the same way that the term "the White House" refers to the U.S. presidency.

Human Record Cengage, pp. 289–290.

1. What were the benefits of Sultan Abdul Mejid's proposals?
   (A) The sultan allowed for more religious openness in the Ottoman Empire.
   (B) The sultan wants religions to be treated differently in how taxes are collected in the Ottoman Empire.
   (C) The sultan is attempting to calm recent religious wars in the Ottoman Empire.
   (D) The sultan is creating an environment in the Ottoman Empire that would make Islam the primary religion.

2. This time period in the Ottoman Empire is known as the
   (A) reformation.
   (B) tulip period.
   (C) era of Tanzimat reforms.
   (D) reform of the Ottoman Sultanate.

3. The major reason Janissaries resisted modernization of the military was because
   (A) they did not support the sultan's reforms.
   (B) they had weak leadership within the corps.
   (C) they saw it as a threat to their special privileges.
   (D) Egyptian troops had not had success with a modernized military.

Questions 4–6 refer to the following map.

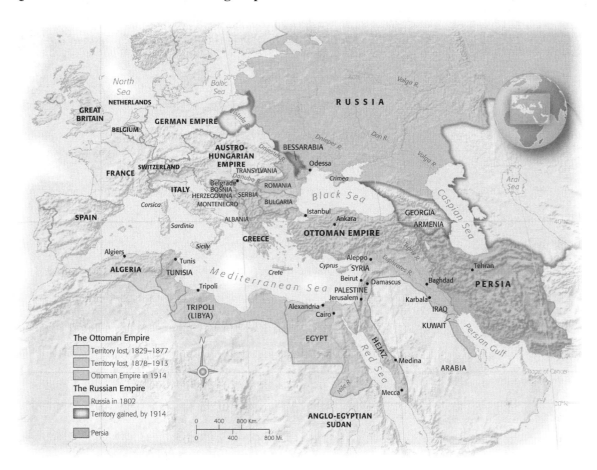

Ottoman and Russian Empires, 1829–1914
Source: © Cengage Learning

4. Where do the Ottomans first begin losing most of their territory in the middle of the nineteenth century?
   (A) The Middle East
   (B) The Arabian Peninsula
   (C) North Africa
   (D) Western Europe

5. Extraterritoriality of the Ottoman Empires was
   (A) the practice of granting special trading privileges to Asians and Europeans.
   (B) exemption from Ottoman laws given to European residents.
   (C) debt restrictions placed by European financiers.
   (D) use of a European monetary system within the empire.

6. Compared to the Russian Empire in the time period given, the Ottoman Empire is
   (A) gaining more territory in western Europe.
   (B) losing some territory, but gaining more than the Russians, especially in eastern Europe.
   (C) gaining territory west of the Black Sea.
   (D) losing more territory as an empire.

Answers

1. ANSWER: A. Sultan Abdul Mejid is proposing what is among the first of a series of reforms for the Ottoman Empire. In his endeavor to create an environment of equality for all religions, the sultan is hoping to attract more people into the Ottoman Empire and realize a gain in taxation revenue as a result (*The Earth and Its Peoples*, 6th ed., pp. 637–639/7th ed., pp. 615–617; History Disciplinary Practice—Analyzing Historical Evidence; Learning Objectives SB-1,2,3,4; ECON-2,3; Key Concept 5.1.V.B).

2. ANSWER: C. After a relatively long decline in the Ottoman Empire, there were a series of reforms, known as the Tanzimat reforms, implemented by a succession of sultans. While the Tanzimat reforms did not allow for a full recovery of the Ottoman Empire's decline, they did allow for a modernization of the Ottoman Empire (*The Earth and Its Peoples*, 6th ed., pp. 637–639/7th ed., pp. 615–617; History Reasoning Skill—Contextualization; Learning Objectives SB-1,2,3,4; ECON-2,3; Key Concept 5.1.V.B).

3. ANSWER: C. The Janissaries rejected Western military technology because they saw it as a rejection of their traditional horse-based warrior culture (*The Earth and Its Peoples*, 6th ed., pp. 637–639/7th ed., pp. 615–617; History Reasoning Skill—Causation; Learning Objectives SB-1,2,3,4; Key Concept 5.1.V.B).

4. ANSWER: C. North Africa, specifically in Algiers, simply transfers military influence from the Ottomans to the French around 1830. There was a great deal of piracy against British, French, and U.S. ships before that time, and the Ottomans lost battles in their attempt to maintain that area of northern Africa (*The Earth and Its Peoples*, 6th ed., pp. 635–639/7th ed., pp. 613–617; History Disciplinary Practice—Analyzing Historical Evidence; Learning Objectives SB-1,2,3,5,6; Key Concept 5.2.II.B).

5. ANSWER: B. Europeans who lived in Ottoman cities created separate enclaves apart from the rest of Ottoman society. In these communities, extraterritoriality made Europeans exempt from the empire's laws (*The Earth and Its Peoples*, 6th ed., pp. 635–639/7th ed., pp. 613–617; History Reasoning Skill—Contextualization; Learning Objectives SB-1,2,3,5,6; Key Concept 5.2.II.B).

6. ANSWER: D. For many reasons, but especially financial decline, the Ottomans consistently lose territory throughout the nineteenth century, into the twentieth century. Most of the territory lost by the Ottomans is in northern Africa and southeastern Europe (*The Earth and Its Peoples*, 6th ed., pp. 635–639/7th ed., pp. 613–617; History Reasoning Skill—Contextualization; Learning Objectives SB-1,2,3,5,6; Key Concept 5.2.II.B).

23

ASIA: C. 1750 TO c. 1900

KEY CONCEPTS

- ■ European colonialism directly and indirectly affected most of Asia during the nineteenth and early twentieth centuries, as nations such as Britain and France enlarged their imperial possessions in the region.
- ■ India came under Great Britain's complete colonial control by the mid-nineteenth century as a large and efficient British bureaucracy reshaped the nation politically, economically, and socially.
- ■ Throughout the nineteenth century, the Qing dynasty's control of much of China was threatened by internal economic crisis and rebellion and by increasing pressure to open up the nation to European colonial powers.
- ■ Unlike most other parts of Asia, Japan was able to limit the influence of the colonial powers and become a strong imperial power as it modernized and industrialized using new ideas and technology from the West.
- ■ By the end of the nineteenth century, nationalist movements that questioned European colonial control began to attract supporters, especially among the educated class.

KEY TERMS

- ■ Aborigines
- ■ Bannermen
- ■ British East India Company (EIC)
- ■ clipper ships
- ■ durbars
- ■ extraterritoriality
- ■ Indian Civil Service
- ■ Maori

364

- Meiji Restoration
- most-favored-nation status
- nawab
- Opium War
- raj
- Russo-Japanese War
- sepoys
- Sepoy Rebellion
- Sino-Japanese War
- Taiping Rebellion
- Treaty of Nanking

Asia is discussed in depth in *The Earth and Its Peoples*, 6th edition, Chapters 21, 23, 25, and 26, and 7th edition, Chapters 22, 24, 26, and 28.

THE BRITISH EMPIRE IN INDIA

By the late eighteenth century, the Mughal Empire was disintegrating. The Maratha Confederation, a group of aligned states in central India, ruled over more territory than the Mughals, and Muslim princes, known as **nawabs**, created powerful states all over India. The Mughals had become just one of the many groups competing for power in South Asia.

South Asia came under the influence of Europeans earlier and more completely than did East Asia or Africa. British, Dutch, and French trading companies pursued access to profitable trade goods, but by the late eighteenth century, Britain was the dominant European power, supplanting the French and Dutch while slowly gaining power over local groups. The British made alliances with various regional powers to strengthen their access to trade and established trading bases in port cities, which they hired Indian troops, known as **sepoys**, to protect. By 1818, the East India Company (EIC) had regional power bases in Bengal, Madras, and Bombay. In some states—such as Bengal—the EIC took complete control of the area, but in other states, they ruled through local princes.

THE RAJ

In 1818, the British Empire's presence in India dwarfed its other colonial possessions, containing more people than all of western Europe. The British **raj** (reign) set out to transform India administratively and economically using a Western model. Like the Mughals before them, the British had to moderate their cultural interference, and long-standing, diverse Indian customs made formulating consistent policies difficult. The British focused on creating a powerful, efficient government that, relying heavily on military power, primarily sepoy regiments, set out to disarm the over two million local warriors. The raj also emphasized private property and attempted to reshape the varied and complex system of land ownership in India. With military control and simplified property ownership, the British maximized taxes to pay for further economic and administrative reform.

While attempting to modernize, the British also supported some Indian traditions, and in the process often increased the power of local princes and religious leaders. Indian and British elites had periods of conflict and harmony, but the common Indian citizens often suffered throughout. Women, members of lower castes, and the poor experienced little benefit from reform or tradition.

British control of the Indian economy spurred trade both within India and with other nations. Opium from Bengal, coffee from Ceylon, and tea from Assam brought needed revenue into South Asia. However, increased competition from British textile mills turned India, once a world leader in textile exports, into an exporter of raw cotton. The new economic order did not provide any protection for the poor or needy, and rebellion was common in the first half of the nineteenth century. Though many of these uprisings were easily suppressed, the EIC was concerned with the loyalty of Indian sepoys, who by the 1850s were well armed and made up more than 80 percent of the British military force in India.

Discontent was growing among the sepoys. Most initially came from the Bengal region, but as the force grew with recruits from other ethnic groups, the Bengali sepoys felt threatened. Hindu and Muslim sepoys encountered service requirements that conflicted with their religious obligations. The British soon changed the requirements, but in 1857 the early protests grew into widespread rebellion by sepoys, peasants, and discontented elites, all joining to challenge the authority of the British. The **Sepoy Rebellion** was put down the next year, but it called for reevaluation of British rule in India.

Political change began immediately with the final removal of Mughal and EIC control. A British viceroy, much like a Mughal emperor, now ruled India from Delhi. Queen Victoria decreed that all Indians would receive equal protection of the law and freedom to practice their religion and traditional customs. Though reform was speeded up, tradition still had its place in a modernizing India. Viceroys continued to grant privileges to local Indian princes as long as they were loyal to the queen, and nurtured that loyalty by inviting the princes to **durbars**, elaborate celebrations similar to the pageants Indian princes had held during the Mughal reign.

India under British control was most notable for an efficient bureaucracy that governed the huge South Asian region. The **Indian Civil Service** (ICS) was open to all applicants, but only those who could afford an elite university education in Britain were eligible for the senior posts. Beyond educational qualifications, the negative racial views of the British kept the number of Indians in the ICS low. The British also spent millions of pounds to modernize Indian infrastructure—harbors, irrigation canals, and other public works—with increased trade in mind. Public and private money poured in as staple crops such as tea and cotton became central to the Indian economy. Railroads, begun in the 1840s, crossed most parts of the country by the 1870s, giving India the fifth-largest railroad network in the world. By 1900, more than one hundred and eighty eight million people used the vast Indian railroad network for business and religious pilgrimage, and to search for work. With the increase in travel came the growth of cities, which, lacking clean water supplies and adequate sewer systems, led to the spread of cholera. In 1869, Calcutta had new water-filtration and sewer systems, which dramatically reduced the number of cholera deaths. Other big cities followed suit, but in small villages, which could not afford the new systems, cholera deaths remained high.

By the end of the nineteenth century, India had become a provider of raw materials and a purchaser of manufactured goods, and through technological change it was becoming economically more profitable. Still, the majority of Indians remained impoverished.

INDIAN NATIONALISM

Indian nationalism had begun to develop in the early part of the nineteenth century. Rammohun Roy, educated in the West and employed by the EIC as an administrator, urged greater Indian control of the nation and argued for Pan-Indian nationalism that would reduce social, economic, and ethnic divisions. Through the Brahmo Samaj (Divine Society), founded in 1818, he attempted to meld both Western nationalism and religious tradition and led an effort to abolish customs such as child marriage, sati (widow burning), and slavery.

AP® Tip

Nationalism, which reshaped much of Europe in the late nineteenth century, was not limited to Europe. As Britain, France, and other colonial powers gained control of parts of Asia and Africa, they introduced a variety of political, economic, and cultural ideas, including nationalism. In India, British control of the education system meant that a new, rising upper middle class was shaped by many of these European values. As you consider comparative, continuity and change over time, causation, periodization or document-based essay questions, expand your discussion of rising nationalism to regions beyond Europe. Many nations and groups in Asia and Africa did not become independent in the late nineteenth century, but the dream of nationalism was providing the basis for movements that would confront colonialism in the twentieth century.

After the Sepoy Rebellion, the Brahmo Samaj became less influential. As Western education spread, Indian intellectuals became more interested in Western secular ideas and nationalism. Many of the new nationalists, members of the rising middle class who sent their children to Western-style schools, felt politically and economically excluded. To push forward new initiatives, the Indian National Congress was founded in 1885. It called for reduced military spending and more government assistance for the poor and needy, and it promoted Pan-Indian unity across the many social, religious, and economic divisions in India. However, because the Indian National Congress presented the views of Indian elites, it lacked the widespread popular support needed to challenge the British Empire's control.

THE DECLINE OF THE QING EMPIRE

By the late eighteenth century, the Qing dynasty in China was experiencing many of the problems common to other Asian land empires—rebellion within the empire among the poor and displaced, corruption of local officials, and failure to recognize the growing threat of European powers. Europeans were starting to complain about China's restrictive trade policy, which allowed Europeans to trade only in Canton. Initially, the Canton system, as Europeans called it, benefited both the Europeans and the Chinese, but by the 1790s Britain was increasingly concerned about its trade deficit with China. Britain had been importing tea from China for centuries, but could find no goods that the Chinese would purchase in return. British silver had to be used to purchase tea. As the **British East India Company (EIC)** drifted closer to bankruptcy, it used its connections in Parliament to press for a diplomatic mission to open the Chinese market. In 1792, Lord George Macartney was sent to meet with the Qing Emperor, but his mission failed; the Chinese were not interested in changing the system. Other Europeans had the same experience with the Qing. Many European leaders concluded that the Chinese were a barrier to modern industrial growth.

China also began to deal with an economic decline that would continue into the next century. Some historians have estimated that the population had exploded to three hundred and fifty million people by the late 1700s. With more people, the demand for food increased as land available for farming decreased. The need for wood for heat and construction led to the deforestation of large parts of China, and the government's inability to maintain dams and dikes led to flooding. Portions of the Grand Canal became impassable, devastating communities that depended on it to transport their crops. Rebellion became common and severe. The Qing, whose empire was twice the size of the Ming Empire, relied on local elites to govern, and corruption became widespread as decline continued. Further, many Han Chinese viewed the Qing as foreign Manchurian conquerors in league with Europeans. The White Lotus Rebellion (1794–1804), a messianic attempt to restore the Ming dynasty and see the return of Buddha to China, set the stage for uprisings throughout the early nineteenth century.

THE OPIUM WAR

During the early 1800s, the Chinese still had little appreciation for the growing power and threat of Europeans. British and American traders were making large profits by importing opium into China as early as the seventeenth century. The first Qing law restricting its importation was enacted in 1729, but opium continued to be smuggled in. Both importers and Chinese merchants benefited as supply rose and addiction increased. By the 1830s, people from all parts of Qing society were using opium, and the government met with European diplomats in Canton to demand a ban on the drug. The British saw any attempt to restrict the importation of opium as a threat to their continued economic success; when negotiations broke off, British naval forces moved into the south China coast and the **Opium War** (1839–1842) began.

The Chinese, like the Ottomans, relied on hereditary soldiers known as the **Bannermen**, many of whom went into battle with swords and knives—

no match for British artillery. With no navy, the Chinese could not counter naval bombardments of their ports, and they could not quickly move troops to protect inland cities when the British began sending naval vessels up the Yangzi River. When Nanjing was threatened, the Qing negotiated for peace. The resulting treaty ended the Canton system. Four more cities were open to foreign traders; the island of Hong Kong became a permanent British colony; the tariff on imports was lowered; **extraterritoriality**—exemption from Qing laws—was given to British citizens living in China; an indemnity of twenty one million ounces of silver was paid to Britain, which was granted **most-favored-nation status**—any privileges the Qing granted to other nations would also be granted to Britain. Most-favored-nation status would prevent colonization of China because land given to one European power would have to be given to Britain as well.

Future treaties would give Europeans more freedom within China, and in 1860, the import of opium would be legalized. By 1900, the number of treaty ports open to Westerners had grown to more than ninety. The treaty ports and extraterritoriality created small, insulated communities of Europeans with little concern for the economic and political conflicts playing out in China. Christian missionaries were moving into rural China to preach the gospel while opening hospitals and social service organizations. Many Chinese saw this new religion as a subversion of traditional Confucian values. Foreigners, who were growing in numbers and privileges, were increasingly resented by the Chinese, who were sinking deeper into poverty.

THE TAIPING REBELLION

The mix of economic crisis, rebellion, and declining Qing power erupted in a civil war. In the southern province of Guangxi, weak agricultural harvests, class conflict, and ethnic divisions gave rise to the Taiping movement. Led by Hong Xiuquan, a Hakka (an ethnic minority long at the bottom of Chinese society), the Taiping ideology was based on the teaching of Christian missionaries. Hong saw himself as the younger brother of Jesus, told by God to build a new kingdom on earth and bring peace by driving the Manchu out of China. As the Taiping movement grew, Hong emphasized the anti-Manchu aspects of his ideology, rallying ethnic Chinese to the movement. As the rebellion expanded, Chinese villages were captured and forced to join the movement, men and women were segregated, and the practice of foot binding was ended because women were required to participate fully in farming and become soldiers. By 1853, the Taiping had taken Nanjing and made it their capital.

This widespread threat forced the Qing to begin to modernize their military under the leadership of provincial governors. With greater knowledge of their terrain and local self-defense forces, provincial governors convinced many Bannermen to serve under civilian military leadership.

In 1856, the Qing were confronted with the **Taiping Rebellion**, the Nian rebellion in northern China, and a renewed threat from European powers, who claimed that all of the provisions of the **Treaty of Nanking** had not been fulfilled. The Arrow War (1856–1860), a series of coastal attacks by French and British forces, culminated in the 1860 invasion of Beijing and the destruction of the Summer Palace. The Qing were forced to agree to a new set of treaties to satisfy European powers; in return, they received European money and weapons, which enabled them to defeat both the Nian and Taiping Rebellions in the 1860s.

The Taiping Rebellion was devastating. Deaths were estimated at twenty million to thirty million. Disease became widespread as bubonic plague, which had been around for centuries, began to infect large numbers again and to spread beyond China. Land lay waste. The government had declining revenue from land taxes.

Recovery took place at the local level as the provincial governors who had come to prominence during the Taiping Rebellion continued to increase their power. Governors began to levy and collect taxes, raise armies, and develop their own bureaucracies. Men like Zeng Guofan instituted reform programs to rebuild agriculture, communications, and the military. An alliance of provincial governors and high-ranking aristocrats, like Cixi, later known as the "Empress Dowager," often supplanted Qing officials by controlling domestic and foreign policy decision making.

THE BOXER REBELLION

The Qing dynasty was a shell of its former self. This was confirmed in 1894 when China went to war against the rising Asian power of Japan over its encroachment into Korea. The **Sino-Japanese War** lasted only six months and forced China to leave Korea, cede Taiwan and the Liaodong Peninsula, and pay a large indemnity. European powers stepped in to help the Qing keep Liaodong, but the dynasty was clearly nearing collapse. China's population had grown to four hundred million. Food production was not keeping pace. Most Chinese peasants survived on a diet of grain and vegetables. Landlords lived off the rents of their tenants, while officials, still chosen by the exam system, had become increasingly corrupt. Young men living in port cities, with few opportunities to get ahead, resented the European elite.

In 1898, the Empress Dowager Cixi seized power in a palace coup. Two years later, she started supporting a secret society known as the Righteous Fists, or Boxers, who attacked foreigners with the goal of forcing them from the country. After attacks on Western missionaries throughout the country, the Boxers turned their sights on the foreign legations in Beijing. Western powers and Japan mobilized a military force and captured the city, ending the Boxer Rebellion and forcing the Chinese to pay reparations.

JAPAN AND MODERNIZATION

Like China, Japan was forced to deal with Western powers in the nineteenth century. But unlike China, Japan used Western industrial and military technology to become an important global power. In the late eighteenth and early nineteenth centuries, the emperor of Japan was revered but had no real power; the country was governed by the Tokugawa Shogunate, headed by a military leader in Edo (present-day Tokyo). Regional lords, or daimyos, controlled large parts of the country with little intervention from the shogunate. The shogunate feared Western influence and in the 1600s had outlawed foreigners from entering Japan. When Russian and British ships were spotted off the Japanese coast in 1792, leading daimyos understood the potential threat and began enlarging their armies.

When American Commodore Matthew C. Perry sailed into Japanese waters in 1853, the potential foreign threat became real. Perry demanded that his steam-powered warships—and U.S. vessels arriving in Japan in the future—be able to enter ports to trade and resupply. Looking to China's defeat in the Opium War and fearing a similar fate, the shogunate accepted the Treaty of Kanagawa, which was modeled on the unequal treaties signed by China and the West. Disappointed with that decision, some provincial governors began secretly plotting the overthrow of the Tokugawa regime. When British and French ships shelled the southwestern coast of Japan in 1864 to protest Japan's treatment of foreigners, provincial leaders—particularly those in Choshu and Satsuma, which had prospered from black-market foreign trade—united against what they viewed as a weak and ineffective shogunate.

THE MEIJI RESTORATION

The civil war that followed was short, but it drastically reshaped Japan. The Tokugawa Shogunate was removed; Emperor Mutsuhito (1868–1912) was declared restored. The new government was referred to as the **"Meiji Restoration,"** after the emperor's reign name. The emperor remained a figurehead. Real power was held by a small group known as "Meiji oligarchs," who wanted to transform the nation into "a rich country with a strong army." To that end, they began a widespread program of modernization and industrialization that would take knowledge from anywhere in the world as long as it would strengthen Japan. Foreign technical help was brought in but always carefully controlled by the state. Reform was funded with deficit financing to avoid the debt that suffocated other developing nations. Meiji leaders modeled their redesigned government on imperial Germany's and their military on Britain's navy and Prussia's army. The new educational system included vocational, technical, and agricultural schools, and a system of universities. State-run industries were started up to produce consumer goods, then later sold off to repay governmental debts to large Japanese investors. Private enterprise and innovation were strongly encouraged.

Japan modernized to protect itself from Western powers, but as it grew stronger, it too turned its eyes to becoming a colonial power. Meiji leaders like Yamagata Aritomo urged that Japan create a sphere of influence that would include Korea, Manchuria, and a portion of China; if Japan did not actively control these areas, others would—a threat to Japan's security. Japan first went to war with China in 1894. The six-month conflict forced China to cede control of Taiwan to Japan and leave Korea. Having sent forces to help China put down the Boxer Rebellion in 1900, Japan pressed for control of the mineral-rich Chinese province of Manchuria. In 1905, to the shock of many around the world, Japan defeated Russia in the **Russo–Japanese War**. By 1910, with control over Korea and southern Manchuria, Japan matched the world's colonial powers.

AP® Tip

Comparing how India, China, and Japan reacted to foreign influence can help you understand the growing impact of the West on this region in the nineteenth and early twentieth centuries. By the early 1800s, India had several regional powers struggling for control, among them the British East India Company, which controlled a large part of the country by the 1850s. After the Sepoy Rebellion, the British Empire took control. India did receive benefits from British colonial rule, but like other colonial possessions India was shaped to benefit Britain commercially, and all significant decisions were made in the mother country. China openly resisted Western influence and first attempted to control European access and trade. By closing themselves off, however, the Qing prevented themselves from learning about and adopting new technology and were ultimately unable to resist repeated demands from Western nations. Only Japan was able to control and shape Western influence. Japan had the luxury of being at the far edge of European influence. With few resources, it was not as desirable as India or China. Using Western ideas and technology, Japan was able to develop an industrial economy and a modern military with which to protect itself—and even defeat Russia, an important European power.

WESTERN DOMINANCE IN SOUTHEAST ASIA AND THE PACIFIC

Britain, France, and the Netherlands competed to become the dominant global power in Asia. By the 1850s, it was becoming clear that Britain was surpassing the others. Several factors resulted in the increasing British presence in Southeast Asia and the Pacific. The aggressive attempts by the British East India Company both to secure new trade routes and centers and to protect its position in India led to its expansion into Singapore in 1824, Burma in 1826, and the port of Rangoon and the remainder of coastal Burma in 1852. However, the EIC was attempting to create a mercantilist network of trade to match the one it had created a century earlier. Tied to the needs of its growing industrial economy, Britain wanted to trade freely with Asia from protected port cities. Raw materials in Asia and other regions were necessary for factories back in Great Britain. Those raw materials would come back to Asia as low-priced manufactured goods for Asian consumers. Both sides benefited, but industrialized nations like Britain dictated the terms of the new trading system. Another major factor propelling British expansion in Southeast Asia was the larger and faster clipper ship. After 1850, **clipper ships** made up the majority of the British commercial fleet. Able to transport more cargo in less time, they further increased Great Britain's commercial dominance.

Captain James Cook mapped and explored New Zealand and the eastern coast of Australia from 1769 to 1778. Increased trade and advanced ship design would lead the British to once-remote parts of the South Pacific. Unlike India, where a limited number of Englishmen controlled a large indigenous population, the South Pacific saw the arrival of many British migrants, who displaced the native residents. Having had few contacts with the outside world, the 650,000 indigenous people in Australia and 250,000 **Maori** in New Zealand had little resistance to diseases brought by the British settlers. The British migration to Australia, originally founded as a penal colony in 1788, proceeded slowly until the discovery of gold in 1851. This brought thousands of European and Chinese migrants to the growing colony. After the gold rush waned, the British pursued an active policy of colonization, which resulted in over a million settlers by 1860. The colonization of New Zealand moved more slowly. The first settlers came to hunt seals and whales. By the late nineteenth century, with the defeat of the Maori resistance, migrants looked to the frontier for profitable agricultural lands. As they had earlier in colonial Canada, the British supported increasing self-government for both Australia and New Zealand. In 1901, six separate colonies united to form a self-governing Australia, and in 1907, New Zealand did the same. These increasingly independent nations did not extend equal rights to the indigenous peoples within their borders. In 1897, Australia legally segregated **Aborigines** onto reservations where they had very few legal rights or protections. A New Zealand law that required that voters be able to read and write English disenfranchised most Maori. On a more progressive note both Australia and New Zealand were among the first nations to allow women the right to vote as early as 1894.

Pressure for new markets and resources led Western powers farther into Southeast Asia in the late nineteenth century. Indochina was occupied and finally controlled by the French in 1895. Britain annexed the last piece of Burma (today Myanmar) in 1885 and extended its control into Malaya (today Malaysia) in waves throughout the 1870s and 1880s. In Southeast Asia, only Siam (today Thailand) would remain independent, although significantly reduced in size. Most of the region contained fertile land and had a history of intensive agriculture. In places where the population was sparse, Europeans imported labor and began profitable agricultural enterprises, growing crops from other parts of the world such as tobacco, manioc, and maize. These political and economic changes reshaped many social elements of Southeast Asian society. As new land was brought under cultivation, people who had traditionally been hunters and gatherers were displaced. Large-scale migration changed the ethnic makeup of many Southeast Asian nations as people from China and India migrated to places like the Malay Peninsula. European missionaries attempted to convert Southeast Asian residents, but it was Islam, which had been in the region for hundreds of years, that became increasingly accepted because it had no ties to foreign occupiers. By the beginning of the twentieth century, nationalist political movements in places like India were starting to have an impact on Southeast Asia's views on colonial occupation. Young people were beginning to question the motives and nature of European imperialism.

Still, Asians recognized the power of industrialism and the increasingly global economy. Beginning in the mid-nineteenth century, thousands of Indians, Chinese, and Pacific Islanders migrated for work overseas. The end of the slave trade and the emancipation of slaves in the British colonial plantation societies created a labor shortage, as many agricultural workers, who were no longer bound to the land, left to seek other opportunities. British plantation owners targeted high poverty areas to recruit field workers. These migrants, initially from India, signed contracts of indenture that bound them to work for a specified amount of time in return for free passage—faster, larger ships made transporting migrants easier and more economical—as well as a salary, housing, clothing, and medical care. As other nations like France and the Netherlands outlawed slavery, the migration of Indians, Chinese, and Japanese to the Caribbean plantations swelled. By the turn of the century, thousands of migrants had left their homes in Asia in search of economic opportunity and a new start.

Content Review Questions

Questions 1–3 refer to the passage below.

It is well known to all that in this age the people of Hindustan [northern India], both Hindus and Muslims, are being ruined under the tyranny and oppression of the infidel and treacherous English.

Section I.—Regarding Zamindars [landholders]—It is evident that the British government, in making settlements with zamindars, have imposed exorbitant taxes, and have disgraced and ruined several zamindars by putting up their estates to public auction for arrears of rent. . . .

Section II.—Regarding Merchants.—It is plain that the infidel and treacherous British government has monopolized the trade of all the fine and valuable merchandise such as indigo, cloth, and other articles, leaving only the trade of trifles to the people, and even in this they are not without their share of the profits, which they secure by means of customs and stamp fees, etc., so that the people have merely a trade in name. . . . When the royal government is established, all these aforesaid fraudulent practices shall be abolished, and the trade of every article, without exception, both by land and water, shall be open to the native merchants of India.

Section IV.—Regarding Artisans.—It is evident that the Europeans, by the introduction of English articles into India, have thrown the weavers, cotton-dressers, carpenters, blacksmiths, and shoemakers out of employ, and have engrossed [taken over] their occupations, so that every description of native artisan has been reduced to beggary. But under the royal government the native artisans will exclusively be employed in the services of the kings, the rajahs, and the rich; and this will no doubt insure their prosperity.

"Great Hero." In this context, a name for the Hindu god Vishnu.

The Azamgarh Proclamation, 1857

Source: Charles Ball, *The History of the Indian Mutiny*, London: London Printing and Publishing, 1858–1859, Volume 2, pp. 630–632.

(*Human Record Documents*, Cengage, p. 344)

1. According to the Azamgarh Proclamation of 1857, what are incentives offered to merchants for a change in India?
   (A) The Proclamation asks the British to sell more goods in India.
   (B) The Proclamation wants merchants to sell their own goods in India.
   (C) The Proclamation encourages Indian merchants to sell more Indian goods to the British.
   (D) The Proclamation asks for more military intervention to allow for the sale of British goods.

2. This Proclamation is a result of the Sepoy Rebellion. The Sepoy Rebellion occurred because
   (A) the British wanted to create a monopoly on opium sales to China.
   (B) the East India Company did not hire enough native Indians to management positions.
   (C) there was no representation by Indians during the British raj.
   (D) Hindu and Muslim sepoys were asked to compromise their religious beliefs.

3. What outcomes are suggested by the Azamgarh Proclamation?
    (A) There should be a royal government set up by Indians, for Indians.
    (B) There should be a war between the British and the Indians.
    (C) Indian Sepoys used by the British army should be for international purposes only.
    (D) Opium sold in China by the British should come exclusively from India.

Questions 4–6 refer to the following passage.

Many people have expressed differing opinions concerning the principles and advantages of engaging foreigners or Japanese in the task of coastal trade. Granted, we may permit a dissenting opinion which suggests that in principle both foreigners and Japanese must be permitted to engage in coastal trade, but once we look into the question of advantages, we know that coastal trade is too important a matter to be given over to the control of foreigners. If we allow the right of coastal navigation to fall into the hands of foreigners in peacetime it means loss of business opportunities and employment for our own people, and in war- time it means yielding the vital right of information to foreigners. In fact, this is not too different from abandoning the rights of our country as an independent nation.

I now propose to do my utmost, and along with my 35 million compatriots, perform my duty as a citizen of this country. That is to recover the right of coastal trade in our hands, and not to delegate that task to foreigners. Unless we propose to do so, it is useless for our government to revise the unequal treaties or to change our entrenched customs. We need people who can respond, otherwise all the endeavors of the government will come to naught. This is the reason why the government protects our company, and I know that our responsibilities are even greater than the full weight of Mt. Fuji thrust upon our shoulders. There have been many who wish to hinder our progress in fulfilling our obligations. However, we have been able to eliminate one of our worst enemies, the Pacific Mail Company of the United States, from contention by application of appropriate means.

I have thought about this problem very carefully and have come to one conclusion. There is no other alternative but to eliminate unnecessary positions and unnecessary expenditures. This is a time-worn solution and no new wisdom is involved. Even though it is a familiar saying, it is much easier said than done, and this indeed has been the root cause of difficulties in the past and present times. Therefore, starting immediately I propose that we engage in this task. By eliminating unnecessary personnel from the payroll, eliminating unnecessary expenditures, and engaging in hard and arduous work, we shall be able to solidify the foundation of our company. If there is a will there is a way. Through our own effort, we shall be able to repay the government for its protection and answer our nation for its confidence shown in us. Let us work together in discharging our responsibilities and not be ashamed of ourselves. Whether we succeed or fail, whether we can gain profit or sustain loss, we cannot anticipate at this time. Hopefully, all of you will join me in a singleness of heart to attain this cherished goal, forbearing and undaunted by setbacks to restore to our own hands the right to our own coastal trade. If we succeed it will not only be an accomplishment for our company alone but also a glorious event for our

Japanese Empire, which shall let its light shine to all four corners of earth. We can succeed or fail, and it depends on your effort or lack of effort. Do your utmost in this endeavor!

IWASAKI YATARO, LETTER TO MITSUBISHI EMPLOYEES, 1871
Source: *Human Record Documents*, Cengage, pp. 320–321.

4. What is Iwasaki asking employees at Mitsubishi to do in 1871?
   (A) He is asking the Japanese workers to take up arms against the British.
   (B) He is asking the Japanese employees to sacrifice for the short term, to gain back control in the future.
   (C) He is asking that British employees allow for the Japanese government to allow for more local control among the Japanese.
   (D) He is asking Japanese employees to go about with business as usual.

5. Influences of Japan's modernization was successful primarily because of
   (A) the adoption of Western technology and ideas and the limitation of foreign influence.
   (B) limits on individual rights and a strong centralized state.
   (C) overseas conquest and the creation of an imperial army and navy.
   (D) the decentralization of the Meiji Restoration.

6. The outcome of responses from Japan to foreign influences by companies like Mitsubishi ultimately
   (A) creates a strong military which is able to defy the United States' and Britain's influence in Japan.
   (B) influences a better economic relationship with Korea and China.
   (C) supports company owners like Yataro to gain more profit for themselves instead of being a part of Japan's collective effort to expel foreign influences.
   (D) allows for a more competitive Japanese business structure and place in the global market.

Answers

1. ANSWER: B. There is a rebellion (the Sepoy Rebellion) taking place, and organized Indians are making an attempt to get the British to leave India and establish an Indian royal government. The Proclamation is attempting to persuade Indian merchants to compete with any items sold in India, whether the goods are from other Indians or not. This is a reaction to the British monopoly on items sold (*The Earth and Its Peoples*, 6th ed., pp. 702–706/7th ed., pp. 679–683; History Disciplinary Practice—Analyzing Historical Evidence; Learning Objectives; Key Concept).

2. ANSWER: D. The Sepoy rebellion is a result of the British asking Indian soldiers, Sepoys, to bite rifle cartridges that were soaked in pig and cow fat for waterproofing. This violates dietary laws for Hindus and Muslims. When the sepoys found out about the cartridges, the rebellion was organized (*The Earth and Its Peoples*, 6th ed., pp. 702–706/7th ed., pp. 679–683; History Reasoning Skill—Causation; Learning Objectives CUL-1, SB-3; Key Concept 5.2.II.C).

3. ANSWER: A. The Proclamation is suggesting that an Indian royal government should replace the British East India Company (and later, the British raj). In this selection, landowners, merchants, and artisans are asked to think about improvements in their areas of interest without British influences (*The Earth and Its Peoples*, 6th ed., pp. 702–706/7th ed., pp. 679–683; History Disciplinary Practice—Analyzing Historical Evidence; Learning Objectives CUL-1, SB-3; Key Concept 5.2.II.C).

4. ANSWER: B. The Mitsubishi factory is asking employees for a sacrifice. Yataro is proposing a cut in staff and a cut in wages. The Japanese government is allowing the Mitsubishi factory to operate despite the British desire to control the entire coast of Japan for its own trading purposes (*The Earth and Its Peoples*, 6th ed. pp., 738–742/7th ed., pp. 714–718; History Disciplinary Practice—Analyzing Historical Evidence; Learning Objectives ENV-4, ECON-1,3,5,6; Key Concept 5.1.I.D).

5. ANSWER: A. Japan used Western ideas and technology to modernize the nation, but it was careful to limit the amount of Western presence in Japan itself (*The Earth and Its Peoples*, 6th ed., pp. 738–742/7th ed., pp. 714–718; History Reasoning Skill—Causation; Learning Objectives ENV-4, ECON-1,3,5,6; Key Concept 5.1.I.D).

6. ANSWER: D. Because Japan considers a competitive and progressive factory structure, Japan begins to compete with other Western companies, especially shipping companies from the United States and Great Britain (*The Earth and Its Peoples*, 6th ed., pp. 738–742/7th ed., pp. 714–718; History Reasoning Skill—Contextualization; Learning Objectives ENV-4, ECON-1,3,5,6, SOC-3; Key Concept 5.1.I.D).

24

EUROPE: C. 1750 TO c. 1900

KEY CONCEPTS

- Revolutionary ideas based on Enlightenment philosophy, dealing with individual liberty and a citizen's right to question the government, swept across Europe in the late eighteenth and early nineteenth centuries.
- The French Revolution produced a conservative reaction throughout Europe, leading traditional elites to actively suppress radical movements.
- The Industrial Revolution transformed European nations in the late eighteenth and nineteenth centuries, as innovation in technology led to massive increases in productivity, creating a new industrial society.
- The Industrial Revolution and Enlightenment ideas combined to create new ideologies that addressed the problems that came with an industrial society.
- By the end of the nineteenth century, European industrialization had linked the global economy as never before, as trade in raw materials and manufactured goods increased in all parts of the world.
- The rise of nationalism in the nineteenth century led to the birth of several new nations in Europe, based on shared language and culture.

KEY TERMS

- Congress of Vienna
- Crimean War
- Declaration of the Rights of Man
- division of labor
- Enlightenment

- Estates General
- Industrial Revolution
- Jacobins
- labor unions
- laissez-faire

- liberalism
- mass production
- mechanization
- National Assembly
- nationalism
- Pan-Slavism
- positivism
- Revolutions of 1848
- "separate spheres"
- Slavophile
- socialism
- steam engine
- Victorian Age

Europe in this period is discussed in depth in *The Earth and Its Peoples*, 6th edition, Chapters 21, 22, 23, and 26, and 7th edition, Chapters 22, 23, 24, and 27.

REVOLUTIONARY IDEAS

In the eighteenth century, the battle over colonial possessions and trade routes to the Americas and Asia would lead to revolutionary changes for much of Europe. The growing sea powers of Great Britain and France had supplanted Spain and Portugal, and Great Britain and France would do battle for dominance over North American colonies and trade outlets. The French and Indian War, part of the Seven Years War in Europe, pitted the French with their Amerindian allies against the British. Britain won, forcing France to relinquish its holdings on the North American continent and withdraw from territory in India. The financial cost of these battles was enormous; traditional tax collections would not cover the war debt.

In addition, **Enlightenment** ideas that attempted to apply scientific method to the study of human society had many intellectuals questioning the actions of their government. Europe's growing middle class read about the new Enlightenment ideas in books and newspapers and were familiar with the ideas of social philosophers like John Locke, who argued that government was created to protect life, liberty, and property, and Jean-Jacques Rousseau, who argued that the power of monarchs depended on the consent of the governed. At the same time, these ideas found their way across the Atlantic and sparked protest against the colonial governments in Europe.

Great Britain was the first to learn the power of new Enlightenment ideas when its demands that its colonial subjects help pay for the French and Indian War sparked popular protest in Britain's North American colonies. New taxes and the Proclamation Line of 1763, which placed limits on colonial expansion, led urban and rural poor to join with colonial leaders in questioning the legitimacy of British rule. Throughout the 1760s repeated British attempts to tax the colonies led to colonists boycotting English goods and attacking royal officials and property. In 1773, the British responded to the Boston Tea Party by closing that port and placing the military in charge of local government. With that, an already active revolutionary leadership was galvanized to break with the colonial master. After an eight-year war, the 1783 Treaty of Paris formalized independence for the new United States of America and a continuing English presence in Canada.

THE FRENCH REVOLUTION

The impact of the American Revolution was felt deeply in France, which had helped the rebelling colonists. An ally of the new United States during the war, France was grappling with its own political and social tensions. French society was made up of three groups, called estates. The First Estate, members of the clergy, accounted for less than 1 percent of the French population; however, the church owned more than 10 percent of all land in France and through ecclesiastical fees and tithes controlled a large amount of the country's wealth. The First Estate was organized from the top down, with most of the powerful positions controlled by hereditary nobility. The Second Estate was made up of nobles—about 300,000 people—who controlled more than 30 percent of the nation's land and held most of the nation's important political, economic, and judicial positions. The rest of French society made up the Third Estate. Peasants made up 80 percent of the Third Estate, but this estate included everyone from the rising middle class, known as the bourgeoisie, to the poorest residents of Paris.

During this period, France, under King Louis XVI, was facing severe economic difficulties. Repeated borrowing to fund military action and support for the colonists during the American Revolution had put the nation deep in debt. France was spending more than half of its national budget to service the debt. In 1788, to deal with this crisis, Louis XVI drew up a series of reforms, which he called on a group of nobles to approve. Instead of rubber-stamping them, the nobles questioned the king's leadership. Unable to gain added tax revenue from the elite, Louis XVI called for a meeting of the **Estates General**, the French national legislature, which had not met since 1614. All three estates came together in 1788 and 1789 to discuss ways to solve the economic crisis, but deeply divided over which direction reform should take, they made little headway. During the stalemate, a new union between members of the First and Third Estates began to form. Called the **National Assembly**, it wanted to create a form of constitutional monarchy. To quash this, the king and his advisers locked the Third Estate out of their meeting place, whereupon the members gathered in an indoor tennis court and vowed to write a constitution. Before Louis had organized military forces for an attack on the National Assembly, the urban poor of Paris rose up on July 14, 1789, and attacked the Bastille, a prison that had come to symbolize the old regime. During the Paris revolt, peasants in the countryside began to attack nobles, seizing land, refusing to pay taxes, and destroying documents that recorded their traditional obligations.

These revolts strengthened the National Assembly and emboldened it to issue the Declaration of the Rights of Man. Modeled in some ways on the American Declaration of Independence, the **Declaration of the Rights of Man** went further in listing the natural rights of man, among them "liberty, property, security, and resistance to oppression." While debate in the National Assembly continued, the economic crisis worsened in Paris. Food became an increasingly volatile issue, as it became more difficult for the poor to feed their families. In October, thousands marched to Versailles to demand action from the National Assembly, and they searched for the royal family, particularly Queen Marie Antoinette, who had become a symbol of the nobility's disregard of the people. Louis XVI and his family were forced back to Paris, and over the next two years the National Assembly, renamed the Legislative Assembly, radically reshaped France. The new constitution limited the power of the king and abolished the nobility. Strong economic reforms were enacted. Church lands were taken to fund a new paper currency, and priests were made employees of the state and had to be elected to their positions.

Neighboring European countries that at first had favored the weakening of the French monarchy began to reconsider. Austria and Prussia threatened to come to the aid of the monarchy; in response, the Legislative Assembly declared war. The threat of foreign intervention stirred French national identity, and large numbers of citizens joined a new volunteer army, which would battle foreign forces to a standstill by 1792. When Louis XVI attempted to escape Paris and find foreign support, he was arrested and sentenced to death by the newly elected National Convention. (Louis XVI was executed by one of the new symbols of the French Revolution, the guillotine.) The National Convention was made up primarily of middleclass people, and most of these members, including the faction known as **Jacobins**, had strongly held democratic values. Factions arose within the Jacobins. The radicals, led by a young lawyer, Maximilien Robespierre, focused in particular on the needs of the Parisian poor and working class. With support in the streets, Robespierre began using the Committee of Public Safety, established to identify domestic threats to the nation, to purge his enemies in the National Convention. Parisian women who had ardently supported the Revolution, at times arming themselves to battle conservative forces, now became targets of the Reign of Terror. This bloodiest period of the French Revolution saw Robespierre and his allies execute 40,000 people and imprison another 300,000. Additional attacks on the church led to forcing priests to marry and changing the calendar to eliminate Sundays. As the threat from outside powers diminished, the Terror continued as Robespierre began to attack former supporters. In July 1794, conservatives in the National Convention took advantage of French military victories to consolidate their power and voted to arrest Robespierre. On July 27, after a two-day trial, Robespierre was executed by the guillotine.

After the fall of Robespierre, the Convention began to abandon many of the Revolution's most radical reforms. Violent uprisings by working-class Parisians were put down, and a more conservative constitution was enacted. A new executive power was created. Named the Directory, it refused to step aside when it lost a popular election in 1797. The republicanism of the French Revolution was being swept away. When the young general Napoleon Bonaparte took control of the nation, a new period in its history had begun.

CONSERVATIVE REACTION IN EUROPE

Napoleon's success had much to do with French society's exhaustion after ten years of revolutionary change. Napoleon became Europe's first popular dictator. He did not turn his back on all of the Revolution's reforms—equality under the law and the protection of personal property were retained and expanded. While the Napoleonic system was committed to personal security, it often restricted individual rights in the name of national security.

Napoleon's run of military victories had stalled by 1812. Looking to boost the French economy, he decided to invade Russia in 1812. His army of 600,000 invaded Russia and occupied Moscow but was forced back by residents who set fire to the city. After more defeats and a difficult winter, only 30,000 troops returned to France. The defeat spurred several European powers to band together to attack France. Unable to defend Paris against the combined forces of Russia, Prussia, Austria, and England, Napoleon was finally forced to abdicate and was sent to exile off the coast of Italy in 1814. In 1815, he escaped and attempted to reestablish his power, but the monarchy had been restored and the age of Napoleon had passed.

The effect of the French Revolution was widely felt throughout Europe. The Revolution had stirred up ideas of nationalism and liberalism that challenged the old aristocratic order and the power of the church. In 1814 and 1815, diplomats from Britain, Russia, Austria, and Prussia met at the **Congress of Vienna**. Counseled by Austrian foreign minister Klemens von Metternich to help reestablish the monarchy in France, these nations desired to create a peaceful Europe that would protect the conservative order. All of the great nations of Europe received some sort of territorial gains as the "Holy Alliance" of Russia, Austria, and Prussia worked to defeat liberal revolutions in Spain and Italy. Through conservative retrenchment, these traditional powers sought to prevent revolutionary ideas from spreading in Europe.

Throughout the next three decades, nationalist and revolutionary movements arose, but more often than not, they were put down, and the conservative order continued in control. In Greece, nationalists attempting to throw off Ottoman control appealed to Europeans for help. Although many conservative leaders like Metternich did not support the idea of a nationalist democratic government in Greece, many intellectuals and artists believed that the cradle of Western culture should be liberated from Ottoman oppression. In 1830 Britain, Russia, and France pressured the Ottoman Empire to grant Greek independence. The Greek example was not typical in this period. In a series of uprisings in Europe known as the **Revolutions of 1848**, urban workers in France, Italy, Austria, and Prussia demanded more democratic rights and economic opportunities. However, the conflicts of 1848 brought little real change, as monarchs continued to retain the support of aristocrats and the military.

THE RISE OF THE WEST: THE INDUSTRIAL REVOLUTION

The economic and social change wrought by the **Industrial Revolution** reshaped every aspect of society from the eighteenth century on. Innovations in manufacturing, transportation, and communication brought massive increases in productivity. New technologies coupled with changing economic and social relationships transformed all regions of the world by the twentieth century. This change was first seen in Britain. Soon after, other parts of western Europe scrambled to create an industrial economy.

Scholars have identified a set of preconditions that explain why Europe was the first region to undergo the Industrial Revolution: population growth, an agricultural revolution, technological experimentation and innovation, and the growth of trade. In the late eighteenth and early nineteenth centuries,

Europe experienced a population explosion as people developed more resistance to disease and new crops from the Americas provided a stable food supply. At the same time, an agricultural revolution resulted from the introduction of crops, like the potato, that doubled or tripled the per-acre yield. In addition, new methods of agriculture such as crop rotation and selective livestock breeding enabled wealthy landowners to "enclose" their land and push many tenant farmers and sharecroppers off the land and into the urban areas to look for work.

An increase in population led to an increase in demand for products. It was in Great Britain that a variety of technological innovations and social conditions came together to push forward the first industrial economy. As demand increased, roads and canals were improved. With transportation strengthened, first local trade but increasingly national and international trade grew. Britain increased its overseas trading networks and soon became the world's leading exporter of manufactured goods. The British were quick to experiment with innovative methods of manufacturing. Continental Europeans were aware of the increasingly industrial British economy, but high transportation costs and governmental regulation delayed their ability to industrialize until the early part of the nineteenth century.

AP® Tip

Although industrialization occurred first in Europe, its impact in the nineteenth century was global. How industrialism affected the relationships among various regions of the world has been a popular topic of both multiple-choice and free-response questions on the AP® World History exam. For example, did the vast wealth and the technological innovation that resulted from the Industrial Revolution alter how industrialized nations viewed nonindustrialized nations? Being able to make global comparisons is an essential skill for this course, and the impact of industrialism makes for an interesting global comparison.

THE TECHNOLOGICAL REVOLUTION

Industrial innovation did not first occur during the Industrial Revolution. Centuries earlier, the Song dynasty in China had used mass production, mechanization, and manufacturing. What made this age of industrial development so remarkable were innovations in the use of energy—steam power and electricity for transportation and communication.

In the eighteenth century, European industries began to use techniques of **mass production**. Men like Josiah Wedgwood divided the process of production—in his case, of pottery—into many small tasks. With the **division of labor** and close monitoring of workers, less time was wasted and

---

the production process was speeded up. This changed age-old methods of craftsmanship but also provided consumers low-cost manufactured goods of high quality.

The growth in **mechanization** was another hallmark of the industrial change. The British textile industry used mechanization to spin thread and weave thread into cloth in a fraction of the time it took a worker. By 1830, cotton that took a worker in India five hundred hours to spin took a machine in England eighty minutes to spin. The economist Adam Smith, who described in glowing terms the increased productivity that mechanization and the division of labor brought, disagreed with the old view that a nation's wealth could be measured in the amount of gold and silver it possessed. Instead, Smith held that a nation's economic health should be measured in the amount of goods and services it created. To Smith, Britain's increase in productivity marked an increase in the country's wealth. What Smith failed to address was the fact that only owners could afford the large amounts of capital needed to innovate and expand. Industrialization was replacing the self-employed craftsman with the wealthy. The other early beneficiaries of the Industrial Revolution were members of the middle class, who formed a new group of entrepreneurs able to invest in the new industrial technology and acquire wealth and influence out of reach to nonaristocratic Europeans in early periods.

Industrialism was advanced by the increasing use of iron. British innovations in iron making during the eighteenth century brought its cost down, and with a greater supply of iron available, the use of interchangeable parts, called the "American system of manufactures," became dominant. Interchangeable parts speeded up the manufacturing process while lowering the price of goods.

The ability to transform fossil fuels into energy distinguished the Industrial Revolution from earlier periods of economic growth and expansion. In 1764 British inventor James Watts developed a **steam engine** powered by coal. In the next decades, the steam engine replaced waterpower and made its way into cotton mills and factories. With a seemingly unlimited supply of coal, innovators looked for every possible use of the new engine. Steamboats that traveled on rivers and canals were built in Europe and the United States, and by 1819, steam engines were powering ships across the Atlantic. By the end of the 1820s, Great Britain and the United States had railroad networks linking cities and factories. The construction of railroads sparked industrialization on the European continent as Belgium, Germany, and France linked regions with rich deposits of coal to urban areas.

Experiments in the use of electrical current in the early nineteenth century culminated in the invention of the electric telegraph in 1837. With the introduction of Samuel Morse's Morse code, the telegraph made instant communication possible. The railroad companies were the first to use the new system to track departures and arrivals and improve safety. By the mid-nineteenth century, telegraph lines were strung over all of western Europe and the United States, and in 1851 the first submarine telegraph cable, placed under the English Channel, linked Britain and France. Unlike other periods of technological growth, in which progress was halted by invasion or natural disaster, the Industrial Revolution never slowed but continued to grow, one technological innovation after another.

THE IMPACT OF THE INDUSTRIAL REVOLUTION

The impact of the Industrial Revolution was not just economic. Daily life was drastically altered as a society industrialized. This was especially true in urban areas. The growth of cities in the eighteenth and nineteenth centuries was unprecedented. In only a century, London doubled in size, and smaller towns, like Manchester, witnessed a twentyfold increase between the mid-eighteenth and nineteenth centuries. Cities were redrawn. The winners in the new industrial age built large homes and funded new churches, museums, and theaters. The poorer sections of cities lacked adequate housing and basic services, which, combined with severe overcrowding, made them breeding grounds for smallpox, dysentery, and tuberculosis.

Most factory jobs were controlled by the clock. Workers performed simple repetitive tasks for long hours under the constant watch of overseers. Unlike the agricultural life that most had left behind, neither the work nor the hours changed over the seasons. Though some more-skilled workers were able to get ahead, most workers toiled day after day, year after year doing physically difficult work. Family life was also changed as women and men rarely worked in the same place and were apart from each other for most of the day. Women who worked in factories generally received significantly less pay than men did and, if married, faced difficult decisions concerning their children—public schools and day care did not exist. Most women chose to work either in domestic service or at home, taking in laundry, sewing, and embroidery. When Europe was beginning to industrialize, children often worked to add to the family income. Many factory owners wanted children as workers because they were inexpensive and easy to manage. Children made up the majority of workers at some textile mills, working between fourteen and sixteen hours a day. The British government enacted laws to restrict child labor in the mid-nineteenth century.

The new industrial era was hardest for traditional workers who did not change their skill-set to keep up. Most workers did not experience the drastic changes that traditional craft workers did, but instead were victims of a new industrial phenomenon: the business cycle. Economic growth and good times could change quickly and without warning into business contraction and bad times. Few workers had savings, and the governments of Europe had yet to adopt the idea of a safety net for their citizens. Downturns in the business cycle were scary for workers. Only after the 1850s were the benefits of industrialization felt by larger numbers of working-class Europeans.

NEW ECONOMIC AND POLITICAL IDEAS

The sweeping changes brought on by the Industrial Revolution led to new political tensions and ideological clashes. As the rich grew richer and the working classes struggled with the new conditions, ideas that both justified and reviled the economic system arose. **Laissez-faire** economics, developed by Adam Smith in his influential book The Wealth of Nations (1776), argued that if people were allowed to seek their fortunes unimpeded by government regulation, all of society would benefit. Directly attacking mercantilism, which supported regulation of trade to protect and build up the nation's supply of gold and silver, Smith theorized that free-market capitalism between nations would increase the wealth of all nations. The British government adopted Smith's laissez-faire principles and lowered import taxes though other European nations retained restrictive tariffs on import goods. German economist Friedrich List argued that free-trade policies kept Britain in a position of power over other less industrialized European nations, which could not compete with well-developed English manufacturers. List proposed that the German states trade freely with one another while raising tariffs against other countries to protect their newly developing industries.

Other political thinkers were more immediately concerned with the plight of the working poor. Two in France were the Count de Saint-Simon and Auguste Comte, who developed a new ideology called **positivism**. Positivists argued that by using the scientific method, enlightened business leaders and artists could come together and fix the problems of industrialism for the working poor. Positivism proved popular with bankers and entrepreneurs, who used it to press for the construction of railroads and canals, which were viewed as symbols of a bright future for workers and owners. Others such as the Frenchman Charles Fourier argued that the workers needed to be protected from industrialists. An ideal worker society would be one where all lived and worked together, sharing the hardships and benefits of their labor. These new ideas, known as utopian socialism, never gained many followers among workers, who viewed them as too dreamy and unrealistic.

The most significant reform ideology of the nineteenth century was known as **socialism**, which questioned the rights of individuals to own private property and supported increased power for industrial workers. The German socialist Karl Marx was one of the earliest and best known socialists. Working with Friedrich Engels, Marx brought together ideas from German philosophy, the French Revolution, and industrial conditions that workers were living under to create a grand theory about historical and economic development. Marx argued that all through history there had been conflicts among social classes. In the industrial age, the conflict was between workers (the proletariat) and owners (the bourgeoisie). What Marx called capitalist exploitation was producing a society composed of a few extremely rich owners and large numbers of increasingly impoverished workers. Ultimately, Marx predicted, workers would rise up against owners and create a new classless communistic society. Marx's ideas resonated with both intellectuals and workers and can be seen most clearly in the creation and development of labor unions.

In the early nineteenth century, workers often ignored the ideas of middle-class thinkers and developed benevolent societies to protect them from the worst conditions of industrial life. Later transformed into trade unions demanding shorter hours and better working conditions, these early labor movements were unsuccessful, but they set the stage for future organizing. In continental Europe, workers erupted violently during the Revolutions of 1848, which led to more acceptance of the idea that trade unions would represent workers' interests.

In the second half of the nineteenth century, **labor unions** linked improved conditions for workers with increased participation in electoral politics. Unlike Marx, who saw revolt by workers as the only way to change the system, labor unions worked to gain influence within the political system. By 1885, universal male suffrage was achieved in France, Germany, and Britain. Labor leaders used their members' voting power to gain additional concessions, and union members began joining socialist-leaning political parties throughout Europe.

WOMEN IN THE INDUSTRIAL AGE

As countries like France, Britain, and Germany become more industrialized, **Victorian** morality, named for Queen Victoria, advanced a new view of the roles of males and females in society. A man's nature was brave, strong, and courageous, while a woman was beautiful, peaceful, and kind. It followed that because men and women were so different, they should be in **"separate spheres,"** men out in the tough world of business and politics, and women at home raising children and building a supportive home environment. This idea of different roles for men and women fit the lifestyles of the growing industrial middle and upper class. It was acceptable for unmarried women to work, but once married, they should leave work and start a family. These women were not encouraged to start careers, and except in education, there were few women professionals before 1914. Education first opened up to women in large part because it fit women's traditional role of working with children. In the mid-nineteenth century, running a household was increasingly time-consuming. Elite women were expected to entertain frequently, and coordinating the activities of many servants could be difficult. Not all middle-class women were content to stay at home; some joined reform organizations fighting prostitution, child labor, or alcohol consumption. At the beginning of the twentieth century, others began to question women's exclusion from the political process. In Britain, Emmeline Pankhurst protested women's lack of voting rights, though not until 1918 would British women finally receive the vote.

AP® Tip

Industrialism had a number of effects on European women in the nineteenth century. Creating separate spheres for men and women, at work and home, and limiting women's economic and political rights are two of the most significant. What was the status of women in other regions during this period? The change in the status of women in Europe over time is another interesting topic. We sometimes assume that because industrialism brought more modern conveniences, the status of women must have improved. Is that true?

Working-class women, toiling long hours for low wages in factories and domestic service, found the new industrial age even more difficult. Sexual abuse was common for women in domestic service. Leadership opportunities were limited, and women were usually paid less than their male counterparts. Married working-class women, pressured by Victorian ideals to stay at home, had to find ways to make money at home if a second income was necessary. Many took in boarders, did sewing piecework, or did laundry.

NEW WORLD ECONOMY

From about 1850 until the beginning of World War I, global trade increased tenfold. Industrialized economies like Britain's needed trade connections to supply the raw materials for manufactured goods. The increased speed of transportation cut the cost of shipping drastically. This new global trade pattern affected both industrialized and nonindustrialized nations. Countries that were becoming more industrialized saw their economies diversify, producing a wide range of consumer products, many at low prices, but they were often victims of the business cycle, which could lead to recession and depression. Suppliers of raw materials, nonindustrial regions were more connected to the world economy than before, but they too could be hurt in an economic downturn. Throughout this period Great Britain, the dominant economic power of the new global market, controlled more than half of the world's shipping and invested heavily in building harbors and railroads in other nations. Nine-tenths of global trade was done in the British pound sterling, which, unlike other national currencies, rarely fluctuated.

THE RUSSIAN EMPIRE

Although Peter the Great had attempted to integrate the massive Russian Empire into the western European economic and cultural orbit, most European powers viewed Russia as backward and underdeveloped. Indeed, Russia in the nineteenth century had almost no middle class and was primarily an agricultural society in which serf labor was controlled by elites. Europe begrudgingly began to notice Russia after its victory over Napoleon in 1812. Tsar Alexander I began to align with other conservative European powers working to keep the old order in power. Alexander I did attempt to begin reform in Russia, but his absolute power remained unchallenged. When his more conservative and anti-Western brother Nicholas I became tsar in 1825, modernization took a backseat to retrenchment.

Russia's limited attempts at industrialization in the nineteenth century were always under the watchful eye of the tsar. Some railroads were built, but a road system linking the immense nation got off to a slow start. Most industrial goods that came to Russia were purchased from the West with profits from agricultural sales.

This lack of interest in modernizing became apparent when Russia entered the **Crimean War** in 1853. Attempting to gain territory from the decaying Ottoman Empire, Russia invaded the Balkan region. Battling the Ottomans' British and French allies, Russians found their weapons no match for their enemies'. Even in defeat, Russia was seen as a power that had to be diplomatically addressed. But Western values and ideals did not appeal to some Russian elites like the **Slavophiles**, who ascribed the nation's strength to its traditions, such as the Orthodox Church, quiet peasant life, and the power of the tsar. After the Crimean defeat, this conservative intellectual group promoted **Pan-Slavism**, the unity of all Slavic peoples, including Slavs living under the Ottoman and Austrian regimes. This view of Russia as a protector of Slavs would shape Russia's relations with western Europe until World War I.

Even though conservative ideology dominated Russia throughout the nineteenth century, reform and change did make headway. The most significant was the emancipation of serfs in 1861. In addition to ending the centuries-old system of forced labor, Tsar Alexander II gave peasants property rights to portions of the land they worked. The practice of monitoring the liberal teachings at Russian universities was continued, but new ideas were increasingly finding their way into Russian society. Writing in the late nineteenth century, Fyodor Dostoyevsky and Leo Tolstoy made the growing debate over reform central to their storytelling. Though not yet industrialized and grappling with reform ideas, Russia remained tied to its authoritarian agricultural past.

NATIONALISM, EMPIRE, AND UNIFICATION

The idea that had the greatest effect on Europe in the nineteenth century was nationalism, which was increasingly viewed as the creation of a national identity through a common language and culture. New nationalistic political leaders attempted to rally people around shared values. In nations like France, where the borders coincided with the use of the French language, nationalism was easily accepted. However, in states with a number of linguistic and ethnic groups, this new concept of **nationalism** was problematic. German speakers, for example, were spread over many nations and empires, each with its own wide variety of languages. Nationalism before 1869 was also associated with **liberalism**, an outgrowth of the French Revolution holding that people should direct their own nations through constitutional governments that protected individual freedoms. Many of the unsuccessful revolutionary movements of 1848 were linked to both nationalism and its supporting liberal ideology. After 1860, many conservative European leaders, sensing the need for some concessions to citizens demanding more say in their governments, used nationalistic ideology to strengthen conservative regimes and maintain the traditional power structure. This can be seen in the unifications of both Italy and Germany.

By mid-century, popular support was growing in Italy for unification. In 1858, Count Camillo Benso di Cavour, Prime Minister of the Kingdom of Piedmont-Sardinia, led a movement, joined by Italian-speaking provinces to the north, that put down a liberal revolutionary movement in the south, and laid the ground for Italy's unification as a constitutional monarchy under King Victor Emmanuel. In Italy, nationalism shifted from a liberal revolutionary movement to a conservative process, which built support for a strong centralized government controlled by a monarch and aristocrats.

German was the most widely spoken language in Europe in the nineteenth century, and political leaders like the authoritarian aristocrat Prussian chancellor Otto von Bismarck looked to unite German-speakers into a nation. After declaring war and defeating Austria, Bismarck created the North German confederation in 1867. Then in 1870, he again went to war, this time with France. The Franco-Prussian War led to territorial gains from France. The new German empire acquired the region of Alsace-Lorraine, which Germans saw as rightly theirs because most people there spoke German. The French, on the other hand, viewed Alsace-Lorraine as theirs because it was part of the nation when it was formed in the revolution. These two different ideas of nationalism would continue to lead to tension between the nations until World War I.

The close of the nineteenth century and beginning of the twentieth century saw a Europe increasingly divided over ideology, borders, trade routes, and colonial ambitions. With its large military force and a powerful, industrialized economy, Germany had become the dominant power on the European continent. When Wilhelm II replaced his father in 1888 and removed Bismarck, Germany also set out to build a colonial empire.

Content Review Questions

Questions 1–3 refer to the image below.

Pit Head of a Coal Mine, with a Newcomen Engine (*Earth and Its Peoples,* Cengage, p. 549) (P. 587 in previous edition).

1. How did expanded interests in coal manifest themselves during the Early Industrial Revolution?
   (A) It was an export material used for preserving and smoking various types of food.
   (B) It was used to soak up rain water on muddy, unpaved roads.
   (C) It was the only source of heating fuel available at the time.
   (D) It was an important fuel source for steam technology.

2. Why did the Industrial Revolution occur first in Britain in the late 1700s?
   (A) Britain had a rising population, good water transportation, and a fluid social structure allowing for contacts between aristocrats and merchants.
   (B) Britain had a slowly growing population, vast amounts of energy resources, a strong monarchy and the ingenuity, and know-how set within its education system.
   (C) Britain had a widespread railroad system set with connections to both larger cities and rural communities.
   (D) Britain had a decentralized political system, small merchant class, and limited access to raw materials.

3. What was the purpose of the Newcomen Engine?
    (A) It allowed for faster and more efficient transportation.
    (B) It pumped water out of mines for better coal extraction.
    (C) It kept workers warm in the cold mines in Great Britain.
    (D) It helped drag coal cars out of mines from a very deep mine.

Questions 4–6 refer to the following passage.

Sebastopol [sic] was built for dominion, and not for commerce. Its palaces were erected by Russian princes who came south for sunshine, or for the military magnates who were there to plot and execute acts of aggression. We must not forget this as we grope among the ruins these bits of torn Berlin wool work—these crushed rose-coloured bonnets—these fluttering fragments of silk and muslin— these playing-cards and dominoes.
George W.Cooke, a Special Correspondent for the *Times* of London in Sevastopol, the Crimean capital

Bulliet, *Earth and Its Peoples*, p. 603.

4. Who were the major opponents in the Crimean War?
    (A) The British and the United States
    (B) The British and the Ottomans
    (C) The Ottomans and the Russians
    (D) The Russians and the United States

5. What would be the importance of correspondence during the time the above article was written?
    (A) Because of the development of steamship technology, reporters were able to keep a safe distance from war, yet still report accurately from afar.
    (B) The correspondence shows that the Russians had little interest in war because they used the Crimean Peninsula primarily as a vacation spot.
    (C) The correspondence displays the lack of knowledge that the Russians had about any impending military conflict.
    (D) By the mid-nineteenth century, communication was faster due to the telegraph, and it brought people at home closer to reports of a war.

6. Which of the following best characterizes Russia's attitude toward western Europe during the nineteenth century?
    (A) Russia slowly recognized the importance of industrialization and modernization, but monitored Western ideas closely.
    (B) Russia ignored industrial advances and closely monitored Western influence.
    (C) Russia embraced industrialization and opened Western-style schools and universities throughout the nation.
    (D) Russia reformed major industries using Western models and competed with other industrial powers by the end of the century.

Answers

1. ANSWER: D. The Early Industrial Revolution saw an increase in the need for coal due to new types of technology. The steam engine, at first stationary, needed coal to heat water at a desirable temperature. It was relatively easy to transport and plentiful (*The Earth and Its Peoples*, 6th ed., pp. 582–589/7th ed., pp. 563–569; History Reasoning Skill—Causation; Learning Objectives ENV-4, ECON-1; Key Concept 5.1.I.B).

2. ANSWER: A. Several important factors made Britain the first nation to begin to fully industrialize, among them a rising population, good water transportation, and a fluid social structure (*The Earth and Its Peoples*, 6th ed., pp. 582–589/7th ed., pp. 563–a569; History Reasoning Skill—Contextualization; Learning Objectives ENV-4, ECON-1; Key Concept 5.1.I.B).

3. ANSWER: B. The Newcomen Engine was important to pump water out of mines during the Early Industrial Revolution. The engine allowed for easier access to the coal in the mines, which would have otherwise been submerged. The Newcomen Engine allowed for more efficient mining to meet increased demands for coal (*The Earth and Its Peoples*, 6th ed., pp. 582–589/7th ed., pp. 563–569; History Reasoning Skill—Causation; Learning Objectives ENV-4, ECON-1; Key Concept 5.1.I.B).

4. ANSWER: C. The Russians were attempting to take the Crimean Peninsula from the Ottomans. As a result, other countries, especially the British and French, attempted to prevent the Russians from their land grab by helping the Ottomans militarily (*The Earth and Its Peoples*, 6th ed. pp., 639–641/7th ed., pp. 617–620; History Reasoning Skill—Contextualization; Learning Objectives CUL-1, SB-3; Key Concept 5.2.II.B).

5. ANSWER: D. The Crimean War was one of the first wars to use the telegraph as an immediate reporting system. People at home (in Great Britain and France) were able to receive reports almost daily about the conflict there. The Crimean War is also the first war to be photographed (*The Earth and Its Peoples*, 6th ed. pp., 639–641/7th ed., pp. 617–620; History Reasoning Skill—Causation; Learning Objectives ENV-2; Key Concept 5.1.IV).

6. ANSWER: A. During the nineteenth century, as Russia viewed the economic success of western Europe, it slowly began a program to modernize. At the same time, ideas of liberal democracy and nationalism were closely monitored and revolutionary movements were quickly suppressed (*The Earth and Its Peoples*, 6th ed., pp. 639–641/7th ed., pp. 617–620; History Reasoning Skill—Causation; Learning Objectives ECON-1,3; Key Concept 5.1.I.D).

25

THE AMERICAS: C. 1750 TO c. 1900

KEY CONCEPTS

- Enlightenment political ideas were adopted by revolutionary thinkers in the Americas and would serve as the ideological basis for their independence movements.
- The American Revolution created the first constitutional democracy and influenced revolutionary movements throughout the world.
- Revolutions in the Americas created limited political democracies in which only a minority of the population participated.
- Independence came to Latin American nations in the nineteenth century, but the creation of stable, successful governments was difficult.
- The process of industrialism transformed the Americas, creating an economically developed North America that produced manufactured goods and an underdeveloped Latin America that supplied raw materials for those consumer goods.
- The impact of industrialism created new economic and social challenges that led to a series of social reform movements during the nineteenth century.
- The United States became the dominant economic and political force in the Americas and began building an empire after its victory in the Spanish–American War.

KEY TERMS

- abolitionists
- American Revolution
- Confederate States of America
- Constitutional Convention

395

- creole
- Declaration of Independence
- Empire of Brazil
- Enlightenment
- free-trade imperialism
- gens de couleur
- Gran Colombia
- Haitian Revolution
- industrialism
- Monroe Doctrine
- Platt Amendment
- Transatlantic slave trade

The Americas are discussed in depth in *The Earth and Its Peoples*, 6th edition, Chapters 22, 24, and 25, and 7th edition, Chapters 23, 25, and 26.

REVOLUTION AND CHANGE

The emergence of revolutionary ideas and action had caused dramatic political, economic, and social changes in the Americas by 1750, which would continue through the end of the nineteenth century. The traditions of Europe's old order, the control of absolute monarchs, widespread church influence, and powerful large landowners were attacked. Hallmarks of this change were new ideas such as increased political participation, a questioning of faith while embracing scientific inquiry, and changes in traditional society as more economic competition gave rise to individual pursuit of wealth.

During the eighteenth century, European powers were involved in several imperial conflicts that would prove costly, as empires battled each other for more power in both Europe and the Americas. Extended conflicts like the War of Spanish Succession (1701–1714), the War of Austrian Succession (1740–1748), and the Seven Years War (1756–1763) left empires in debt and looking for new ways to pay their heavy war expenses. Mercantilism, the dominant imperial economic philosophy, held that wealth equaled power and that colonies existed to benefit the mother country by increasing its wealth. Colonial subjects were asked to share the economic burden of a growing empire. What European powers did not count on was the reaction of their subjects to these economic demands.

Enlightenment ideas had a great impact on colonial elites in the Americas. Thinkers like John Locke and Jean-Jacques Rousseau challenged the political and social order of Europe. Locke argued that government needed to protect citizens' "life, liberty, and property" and that if these natural rights were not protected, people could rebel against their government. Rousseau declared that a social contract existed between a monarch and his people and that a monarch's rule depended on the consent of his people. These Enlightenment ideas were widely accepted and discussed by American intellectuals in the mid-eighteenth century.

THE AMERICAN REVOLUTION

Revolution would first take shape in Great Britain's North American colonies. In 1763, at the conclusion of the Seven Years War (also known as the French and Indian War), the British reigned supreme; they had defeated the French and removed them as an imperial power in North America. However, the British had incurred a large war debt. To deal with it, they called on their colonial subjects to help with repayment of the debt and for the first time directly taxed the colonies. Fueled by Enlightenment ideas and resentment of imperial control, colonial leaders such as Benjamin Franklin began to speak out against the mother country. When the British enacted the Proclamation of 1763 in an attempt to calm frontier conflict with Amerindians by limiting colonial expansion, colonists increasingly questioned whose interests the British government was serving.

Tension rose throughout the 1760s as Great Britain continued to misjudge the colonists' level of dissatisfaction. Groups like the Sons of Liberty responded to what they perceived as attacks on their liberties by organizing boycotts of British goods and intimidating royal officials. In the early 1770s incidents like the Boston Massacre and legislation like the Tea Act of 1773 further convinced colonists that imperial oppression was increasing. Many colonists saw no choice but open rebellion against Great Britain.

By the time colonial leaders met in Philadelphia in 1775 at the Continental Congress, colonists and British troops had already clashed in Massachusetts. The Congress set up a new government and created an army, to be led by George Washington, a veteran of the French and Indian War. Thomas Jefferson's **Declaration of Independence**, summing up the philosophical principles of the new revolutionary age, was approved by Congress on July 4, 1776. Restating the Enlightenment ideals of popular sovereignty and personal liberty, the document would influence revolutionaries throughout the world over the next hundred years.

The underfunded and marginally trained colonial forces found success because of a number of external developments. Military assistance came from France, Britain's traditional enemy. Having focused on the French threat to its more profitable Caribbean colonies, the British government did not commit sufficient forces to the battle for the North American colonies. With the support of French land and naval forces, the colonists defeated the British, who surrendered at Yorktown in 1781. The resulting Treaty of Paris, signed in 1783, gave recognition to American independence. Amerindian tribes, which had fought on both sides, saw their territory ceded to the new United States of America. The Enlightenment ideals of individual freedom and political participation on which the new nation was founded were not applied to the original residents of North America.

Before the war, individual colonies had written constitutions that limited executive power and protected personal liberties. The Articles of Confederation, the nation's postwar government system, was also designed to limit central power. Leaders soon realized that the Articles of Confederation were inadequate for effective government and would have to be revised; the national government needed more power for functions such as public safety, taxation, and payment of postwar debt. Delegates to the **Constitutional Convention**, held in Philadelphia in 1787, determined what powers would be given to the central government, what powers to local governments. They then devised a new form of federal government made up of three branches—executive, legislative, and judicial. The Constitution of the United States laid out the most democratic government of its time, and to this day it serves as a model for codified constitutional governments. Still, only a minority of white males were able participate in it; women and African-Americans, whose help had been crucial to the victory over the British, did not have a voice in the new American constitution.

THE HAITIAN REVOLUTION

News of the revolutionary activity in France in the late 1780s made its way to France's colonial possessions in the Americas. The colony of Saint Domingue (present-day Haiti) was France's richest possession in the Americas. Haiti's large cotton, indigo, coffee, and sugar plantations, which depended on a brutally repressive slave system, accounted for a third of French foreign trade in the eighteenth century. The early stages of the French Revolution had a strong impact on Haiti's mixed-race population, the *gens de couleur*, who pressed their demands for increased political equality. Neither the gens de couleur—some of whom owned slaves—nor their white opponents aimed to end slavery. However, as their conflict turned into open warfare, the colony's slaves seized the opportunity to begin their own revolt. Afro-Haitians turned to a former domestic slave, François Dominique Toussaint L'Ouverture, who assumed leadership of the revolution, creating a well-organized, effective military force. When France's radical National Convention in Paris abolished slavery in all colonial possessions, Toussaint and his followers identified their efforts as part of the struggle for individual freedom for all, begun by the French Revolution.

During the 1790s, Haitian rebels were able to defeat both white slaveholders and invading British troops while liberating slaves in both Haiti and Spanish-held Santo Domingo. Toussaint continually pledged allegiance to France but did not allow the French to play an active role in governing their former colony. As conservative reaction replaced revolution in France, Napoleon consolidated his power and looked to bring Haiti back under French control. In 1802, French troops initially found success with the capture of Toussaint, who would die in a French prison, but they soon met stiff resistance from the Haitian forces, which included armed women. In 1804, after two years of costly struggle, France withdrew, and the free republic of Haiti was established. The toll of the first successful slave rebellion in the Americas was great: tens of thousands dead, a ruined economy, and political violence that would continue throughout the century.

LATIN AMERICAN INDEPENDENCE MOVEMENTS

Spain's and Portugal's Latin American colonies did not ignore the revolutions in the United States and France, but it was the French attack on the Spanish monarchy that spurred change. When Napoleon invaded Spain and Portugal in the early nineteenth century, the Spanish resistance organized a new political body, the Junta Central. Most colonial subjects in the Americas supported the Junta, but a vocal minority, led by Latin American elites, began to challenge royal authority. The early challenges in Venezuela, Mexico, and Alto Peru (now Bolivia) were put down by violent repression, which only strengthened the support for change. In Venezuela, a revolutionary group of **creoles** (colonial-born whites) declared independence in 1811. The group supported the Enlightenment values of political democracy and individual liberty, but it comprised large landowners, who saw little need to liberate slaves or give additional rights to the majority mixed-race population. Loyalists used these facts to rally those groups to defend the crown.

The creoles turned to Simón Bolívar, one of their own, to lead the revolutionary movement. The charismatic Bolívar, a student of the Enlightenment, was able to inspire his troops while building coalitions with other segments of society. To bring additional numbers to his cause, he agreed to support emancipation for slaves. From 1813 through 1820, the battle raged between loyalists and Bolívar's revolutionary army.

Events in Europe again spurred revolutionary changes in the Americas. A military revolt in Spain in 1820 forced King Ferdinand VII to accept new restrictions on his power, which emboldened Bolívar's army to press for definitive military victories. By 1824 revolutionary troops had liberated what today are the nations of Venezuela, Columbia, Ecuador, Peru, and Bolivia, named after the "great liberator" himself. Bolívar and his supporters attempted to build a political confederation from the newly independent regions. Venezuela, Colombia, and Ecuador united to form **Gran Colombia**, and efforts were made to link Peru and Bolivia, but by 1830, unity had failed, and several smaller nations were formed.

A second area of revolutionary activity centered around Buenos Aires, the capital city of Argentina. When news of Ferdinand VII's forced abdication reached Buenos Aires, local elites, military commanders, and ranchers formed a new junta to resist the power of colonial officials. The Argentine Junta claimed loyalty to the ousted monarch, but when Ferdinand regained power, the junta refused to give up control and in 1816 announced the independence of the United Provinces of Rio de la Plata.

Mexico, Spain's richest colony, contained large numbers of Spanish immigrants and owed much of its wealth to the exploitation of the rural poor and Amerindian population. This oppression of the peasants, as well as increasing political conflict and instability in Spain, gave rise to revolutionary action. In 1810 Miguel Hidalgo y Costilla, a priest in the small town of Dolores, urged peasants to rise up and fight oppression from Spanish colonial officials. A disorganized armed force began to attack mines and ranches, striking at both Spanish and creole elites. Though Hidalgo at first appealed to some wealthy Mexicans, the threat of a peasant-led revolution caused them to turn on Hidalgo, who was captured and executed in 1811. The uprising continued throughout the rest of the decade, by the end of which colonial rule seemed to be reestablished. However, the crisis in Spain in 1820 greatly affected Mexico, which declared its independence in 1821. Creole elites replaced their colonial counterparts, demonstrating the conservative nature of the Mexican independence struggle.

The presence of the Portuguese royal family in Brazil, forced to flee Portugal after their defeat by Napoleon in 1808, shaped the colony's independence movement. When King John VI returned to Portugal to protect his power in 1820, he left his son Pedro to act as regent. Pedro, a student of the Enlightenment, supported the independence movement, and in 1822, he separated from Portugal, creating the **Empire of Brazil**. Unlike other newly liberated colonies that established constitutional republics, Brazil had a constitutional monarchy with Pedro as emperor. Often more liberal than Brazil's elites, Pedro advocated the abolition of slavery even though the nation was controlled by a wealthy slaveholding class. Conflict between Brazilians and Portuguese immigrants, whom Pedro protected and supported, led to his abdication in 1831 and the transfer of power to his five-year-old son, Pedro II. After a period of regency, Pedro II ruled Brazil until 1889, when he was finally overthrown and the constitutional monarchy ended.

The newly independent Latin American nations strongly supported constitutional government—even Brazil placed constitutional limits on the emperor's power. However, throughout the nineteenth century political factionalism and threats to constitutional democracy arose. Difficulty in defining the role of the Catholic Church and trouble keeping the military from overthrowing weak constitutional leaders were common problems during this period.

THE INDUSTRIAL REVOLUTION: IMPACT AND CHANGE

The Industrial Revolution transformed economic and social relationships over the late eighteenth and nineteenth centuries. Innovations in manufacturing, mining, transportation, and communications led to changes in both the economic relations of nations and the everyday life of their citizens. Industrializing countries, like the United States, were able to increase production and productivity as they learned to tap the wealth provided by natural resources such as coal, iron ore, and oil. In the Americas, there were both winners and losers; nations that industrialized became rich, while those that did not grew poor.

The development and use of railroads powered by steam engines became the mark of a nation attempting to industrialize in the nineteenth century. By the end of the century, Canada and the United States had developed giant railroad networks that transported raw materials to manufacturing centers and cities. In the early twentieth century, the United States had more than 390,000 miles of track. In non-industrial regions of the Americas, imperial powers and international corporations invested large sums in rail transportation to connect previously isolated areas containing raw materials and agricultural products to densely populated urban areas. Even the railroads in Europe had an impact on the Americas, which experienced a dramatic increase in immigration during this era; as railroads spread deeper into eastern and southern Europe, more people used them to leave their homeland and start a new life in the United States, Argentina, and Canada.

Sea travel became quicker with ships made with steel and the availability of coaling stations throughout the world, making refueling of steam-powered vessels increasingly convenient. Submarine telegraph cables allowed for instant communication between the Western and Eastern Hemispheres. Electricity had a more direct effect on people's lives than any other industrial innovation. With the invention of the incandescent lamp by Thomas Edison and the growth of electrical distribution systems, the rhythm of people's lives was altered. With electric lighting, people got up earlier and stayed up later. **Industrialism** connected the Americas to one another and to the global economy as never before.

While regions like North America became fully industrial, with a diversified economy producing consumer goods for their growing middle class, the nonindustrial nations in Central and South America provided raw materials and a market for manufactured goods. Attempts to industrialize in Latin America were often unsuccessful because of the difficulty in funding these changes from within. Latin American countries that took outside loans for industrial development incurred large debts that impeded additional economic modernization. The need for labor led to large-scale immigration in both North America and South America. In the United States, immigrants from eastern and southern Europe came to work in factories. In Brazil and Argentina, immigrants came to work on coffee plantations.

AP® Tip

Economic and demographic changes are often linked in history. As industrialism occurred in the Americas during the nineteenth and early twentieth centuries, the proliferation of manufacturing centers increased demand for more raw materials—and additional labor—for manufacturing. Immigrants numbering in the millions came to nations like the United States, Canada, Argentina, Chile, and Brazil. Coming primarily from Europe, though a minority were from Asia, immigrants would continue the expansion of industrialism, which led to growing urbanization as they settled in cities. Though immigration brought enormous economic benefits, many immigrants met with hostility from nativists, who believed that foreigners could not be integrated into their new culture. In long-essay questions and document-based questions, look for the links between economic change and demographic movements.

SOCIAL AND ECONOMIC CHALLENGES

Newly independent nations faced social and economic challenges, some left to them by colonialism, others created by industrialism. Slavery and the slave trade, calls for increased political participation, and the economic and social effects of industrialism—all sparked reform movements in the nineteenth century. Though many elites resisted change, by the end of the nineteenth century these reform movements would become popular and produce rapid change.

Under colonial control, Amerindian populations had been both exploited and feared by imperialists. To limit the potential for armed conflict between settlers and indigenous peoples, Spanish, Portuguese, and British colonial governments restricted into what areas settlers could move. With independence, new nations wanted to expand, which often meant confronting powerful native groups. Conflicts with still-independent indigenous populations often resulted in setbacks for frontier settlements and initially hindered expansion. However, throughout the nineteenth century Amerindians were faced with the choice of adapting to the expanding culture or attempting to resist. Resistance inevitably proved futile; by the early twentieth century, indigenous peoples had been defeated.

SLAVERY AND THE SLAVE TRADE

Slavery and the slave trade were discussed as colonies went through their independence struggles. Many revolutionaries in the Americas saw the irony of calling for liberty while denying it to millions of slaves. Slavery as an institution was strongest in places that grew export staple crops such as sugar and coffee on large plantations. These products were in high demand and created large profits for slave owners. People in places like the United States, Brazil, and Cuba who opposed slavery were called **abolitionists**. Using moral pressure, abolitionist groups were able to slow the slave trade when the United States agreed in 1808 to end its importation of slaves. Many slaves were freed during the Latin American revolutions of the 1810s and the 1820s as they fought for the cause of independence.

The slave trade was dealt a serious blow in 1807 when the British outlawed slave trading and became more active in ending what was seen as a moral evil. With slavery abolished in Great Britain in 1833, that nation turned the world's most powerful navy toward stopping the transport of slaves from western Africa to the Americas. That, along with diplomatic pressure, enabled Britain to slow—and in 1867 finally stop—the **transatlantic slave trade**.

In the United States, the struggle to end slavery divided the nation. Northern states increasingly saw slavery as both morally objectionable and a barrier to economic progress. With the 1860 election of Abraham Lincoln, who had pledged to limit the spread of slavery, the country was torn apart when southern states claimed the right to leave the union and formed the **Confederate States of America**. The American Civil War, begun in 1861, saw thousands of slaves flee the South to join Northern troops and fight for their freedom. The Northern victory in 1865 ended slavery, but it was replaced by a system of economic and social segregation that limited African-American liberty over the next century.

In Brazil, slavery would continue for twenty years after the American Civil War. In an 1830 treaty with Britain, Brazil pledged to end its involvement in the slave trade. However, the great demand for slave labor on Brazilian plantations led to the illegal importation of more than 500,000 slaves over the next twenty years. Though Pedro II supported abolition, the powerful slaveholding elite made ending slavery in Brazil difficult. During the 1860s and 1870s, educated Brazilians began to warn that slavery was impeding Brazilian progress, and laws of gradual emancipation were passed. Slavery in Brazil was abolished in 1888.

Cuba and Puerto Rico, Spanish-held Caribbean colonies with valuable sugar plantations, worried about the successful slave revolt in Haiti. Colonial elites expressed little interest in the independence movements that were sweeping the Americas; instead, they counted on the Spanish government to protect their slaveholding property rights. Not until the 1870s did colonial elites begin to question Spanish imperial control and challenge the institution of slavery. Puerto Rican reformers worked to achieve the abolition of slavery in 1873. Cuba waged a decade-long war for independence; although unsuccessful, Cuban pressure forced Spain to end slavery there in 1886. By the end of the century, slavery had been abolished throughout the Americas.

WOMEN'S RIGHTS AND RACIAL EQUALITY

Women were key players in the reform movements of the nineteenth century, particularly in the abolition movement, but women in the Americas faced limits on their own rights and opportunities. At the Women's Rights Convention at Seneca Falls, New York, in 1848, women who had been excluded from an antislavery conference gathered to discuss their treatment as second-class citizens. They demanded the right to vote and greater economic opportunities. During the nineteenth century, women's suffrage (voting rights) was the central demand of the women's rights movement. In South America, women demanded educational opportunities similar to those for men. Argentina and Uruguay were among the first nations in Latin America to educate men and women together. In Chile and Brazil, professional careers in medicine and law opened up to women. In industrialized countries, women also protested the dangerous conditions in factories where many women and children were forced to work. Even with these gains, most women did not attain political equality in the nineteenth century.

Racial inequality and discrimination were also widespread in the Americas. In the southern region of the United States, African-Americans were denied the right to vote, and segregation laws created separate and unequal schools and public accommodations. Those who tried to fight these limits on liberty often found themselves victims of violence; thousands of African-Americans were lynched during the last three decades of the nineteenth century. Though racial discrimination was not codified by law in Latin America, people of color still struggled for equal rights. In all parts of the Americas, groups began organizing to fight the racial stereotypes of the era. In Brazil, Argentina, and the United States, newspapers and magazines publicized the achievements of people of color, and universities were founded to meet the growing demand for advanced education. At the turn of the century, racial discrimination could be seen in all parts of the Americas, but opportunities for people of mixed race were generally greater in Latin America than in the United States.

INDUSTRIAL AND NONINDUSTRIAL REGIONS

By the end of the nineteenth century in the Americas, only North American nations had fully industrialized, but their need for raw materials had linked most of the Americas. Individual income levels rose for everyone during this period, but only in Argentina, Canada, and the United States did individual incomes match those in western Europe. Demand for raw materials such as copper, zinc, and tin led to mining booms in both North and South America, but the expense of mining equipment forced nonindustrialized nations to cede control of these valuable natural resources to foreign corporations. International business interests often intimidated governments that needed their investment capital. Other new forms of industrial technology—for example, railroads and telegraph lines—also needed to be funded by companies from North America and western Europe, increasing their power in Latin America. By 1900, nations had either begun to develop industrial economies or become dependent on those economies, primarily exporting raw materials and creating low-wage jobs. These structural differences would have a long-term impact on economies throughout the Americas.

AP® Tip

Old imperialism, by which European powers played an indirect role, primarily as traders in Africa and Asia, began to change in the late nineteenth century. The industrial nations of Europe began to take political, economic, and cultural control of vast regions in Africa and Asia in what is called New Imperialism or neocolonialism. What about New Imperialism in the Americas? A form of New Imperialism first began in the Americas when Spain and Portugal defeated Amerindian empires such as the Aztec and Inca. These societies were reshaped politically, economically, and culturally, but in the sixteenth and seventeenth centuries, technology had not linked the global market as it would during the growth of industrialism. Although these colonies were profitable, their raw materials would not be essential for industrial production in Europe. By the time industrialism gave nations an economic motive for New Imperialism, the colonies in the Americas had achieved independence, and European imperialists did not have the same opportunity to occupy them as they had in parts of Africa and Asia. At the same time, you could argue that both the United States and international corporations did exert powerful political and economic influence without actually occupying nations. For an essay question that deals with New Imperialism, consider contrasting it with the earlier forms of colonialism in the Americas.

THE UNITED STATES AND NEW IMPERIALISM IN LATIN AMERICA

In 1823, the United States issued the Monroe Doctrine warning European nations, which exerted strong political and economic power over Latin America, to refrain from further expansion in the Americas. The **Monroe Doctrine**, however, did not stop the United States from intervening in the region. In 1846, the United States used a questionable border attack to declare war against Mexico. The short struggle that followed ended when United States troops took the capital, Mexico City; in the Treaty of Guadalupe Hidalgo, a third of Mexico was ceded to the United States. The United States also had long been interested in Cuba, the wealthiest Spanish colony. A revolution led by Cuban nationalist José Martí that erupted in 1895 was supported by the American popular press. When the U.S. battleship

Maine accidentally exploded in the Havana harbor, the United States was quick to implicate Spain. The war that followed brought an end to four hundred years of Spanish colonial rule in the Americas. The Treaty of Paris (1898) ended the Spanish American War, liberated Cuba (though the 1901 **Platt Amendment** granted the United States the right to intervene there if necessary), and gave the United States possession of Puerto Rico, Guam, and the Philippines. The United States had become an imperial power.

By 1900, the United States had the largest economy in the world. Unlike European nations, which had used their economic and technological power to reshape Africa and Asia, the United States was not interested in occupying large parts of the Americas. Instead, New Imperialism was modified to **free-trade imperialism**—though the United States did use military force in the Americas in the early twentieth century when the supply of raw materials needed for their industrial economy was threatened.

Content Review Questions

Questions 1–3 refer to the passage below.

On Territory The entire extent of Saint-Domingue and other adjacent islands form the territory of one colony that is part of the French Empire, but is subject to particular laws.

On its inhabitants There can be no slaves in this territory; servitude has been forever abolished. All men are born, live, and die there free and French. All men can work at all forms of employment, whatever their color. No other distinctions exist than those of virtues and talents, nor any other superiority than that granted by the law in the exercise of a public charge. The law is the same for all, whether it punishes or protects.

On cultivation and commerce The colony, being essentially agricultural, cannot allow the least interruption in its labor and cultivation. Every plantation is a factory that demands a gathering together of cultivators and workers; it shall represent the tranquil haven of an active and constant family, of which the owner of the land or his representative is necessarily the father. Every cultivator and worker is a member of the family and a shareholder in its revenues. The introduction of the cultivators indispensable to the re-establishment and the growth of agriculture will take place in Saint-Domingue. The Constitution charges the governor [L'Ouverture] to take the appropriate measures to encourage and favor this increase in manpower, and to assure and guarantee the carrying out of the respective engagements resulting from this introduction.

On government The administrative reins of the colony are confided to a Governor, who directly corresponds with the government of the metropole [France] in all matters relating to the colony. The Constitution names as governor Citizen Toussaint L'Ouverture, General-in-Chief of the army of Saint-Domingue and, in consideration of the important services that the general has rendered to the colony in the most critical circumstances of the revolution, and per the wishes of the grateful inhabitants, the reins are bonded to him for the rest of his glorious life. If the Governor is informed that there is in the works some conspiracy against the tranquility of the colony, he has arrested the persons presumed to be its authors, executors or accomplices. After having had them submit to an extra-judiciary interrogation if it is called for he has them brought before a competent tribunal.

Haitian Constitution of 1801 Source: Constitution of 1801, from website Marxist Internet Archive http://www.marxists.org/history/haiti/1801/constitution.htm Translated by Mitch Abidor. (Human Records Documents, Cengage, p. 173)

1. What is of major importance when considering the creation of the Haitian Constitution of 1801?
   (A) The Constitution is written after the French Revolution.
   (B) The Constitution directly addresses farming and commerce in the creation of a new country.
   (C) The Constitution is written after a successful slave rebellion.
   (D) The Constitution shows a balance in government, especially in regard to the executive branch.

2. Why is the reference to Toussaint L'Ouverture significant?
    (A) L'Ouverture was a former governor in the French Revolution.
    (B) L'Ouverture was a former slave who led a slave revolt.
    (C) L'Ouverture was a former slave owner who freed all his former slaves after the revolution.
    (D) L'Ouverture was a former marine merchant who guided the economy of Haiti.

3. What were the broader outcomes as a result of the Haitian Revolution?
    (A) The Haitian Revolution led to the development of many other constitutions in the Americas.
    (B) The Haitian Revolution allowed for the emergence of the Mexican Revolution in the twentieth century.
    (C) The Haitian Revolution is successful in allowing more free trade in the Caribbean Sea.
    (D) The Haitian Revolution led to other independence movements in Latin America.

Questions 4–6 refer to the following passage.

Success will crown our efforts, because the destiny of America has been irrevocably decided; the tie that bound her to Spain has been severed. That which formerly bound them now divides them. The hatred that the [Iberian] Peninsula inspired in us is greater than the ocean between us. It would be easier to have the two continents meet than to reconcile the spirits of the two countries. The habit of obedience; a community of interest, of understanding, of religion; mutual goodwill; a tender regard for the birthplace and good name of our forefathers; in short, all that gave rise to our hopes, came to us from Spain. As a result there was born a principle of affinity that seemed eternal. At present the contrary attitude persists: we are threatened with the fear of death, dishonor, and every harm; there is nothing we have not suffered at the hands of that unnatural stepmother—Spain. We have already seen the light, and it is not our desire to be thrust back into darkness.

The role of the inhabitants of the American hemisphere has for centuries been purely passive. Politically they were non-existent. We are still in a position lower than slavery, and therefore it is more difficult for us to rise to the enjoyment of freedom. States are slaves because of either the nature or the misuse of their constitutions; a person is therefore enslaved when the government, by its nature or its vices, infringes on and usurps the rights of the citizen or subject. Applying these principles, we find that America was denied not only its freedom but also an active and effective tyranny.

More than anyone, I desire to see America fashioned into the greatest nation in the world, greatest not so much by virtue of her area and wealth as by her freedom and glory. Although I seek perfection for the government of my country, I cannot persuade myself that the New World can, at the moment, be organized as a great republic. Since it is impossible, I dare not desire it; yet much less do I desire to have all America a monarchy because this plan is not only impracticable but also impossible. Wrongs now existing could not be righted, and our emancipation would be fruitless. The American states need the care of paternal governments to heal the sores and wounds of despotism and war.

From the foregoing, we can draw these conclusions: The American provinces are fighting for their freedom, and they will ultimately succeed. Some provinces as a matter of course will form federal and some central republics; the larger areas will inevitably establish monarchies, some of which will fare so badly that they will disintegrate in either present or future revolutions. To consolidate a great monarchy will be no easy task, but it will be utterly impossible to consolidate a great republic.

SIMÓN BOLÍVAR, THE JAMAICA LETTER
Source: Simón Bolívar, *Selected Writings*, ed., Harold A. Bierck, Jr., Trans. by Lewis Bertrand, New York: Colonial Press, 1951, pp. 103–122.
Human Records Documents, Cengage, p. 175–176.

4. What were Simón Bolívar's goals, according to *The Jamaica Letter*?
    (A) Bolívar had designs to become the leader of most of South America.
    (B) Bolívar aspired to leave South America for good and stay in Jamaica.
    (C) Bolívar wanted to open up more free trade with the people of Central America.
    (D) Bolívar desired South America to become independent from Spain.

5. How did Bolívar propose to follow through with his goals?
    (A) He recommended sending an entourage to Spain to plead with the king for economic independence.
    (B) He wanted the king of Spain to appoint him as the governor of South America for twenty years.
    (C) He suggested that fighting for independence from Spain would be the only solution.
    (D) He applied for a charter, allowing part of South America to become independent.

6. Why did Bolívar reject Spanish policy?
    (A) Bolívar claimed the Spaniards did not recognize basic human freedoms, nor did they recognize autonomy in trade.
    (B) Bolívar's primary desire was to rid the South American continent of Spanish slavery, as the abolitionists there were easier to organize.
    (C) Bolívar refused to recognize the use of Spanish technology in South America, as he believed all technology used should have originated in South America.
    (D) Bolívar politely declined overtures from the king of Spain to create a monarchical system in South America, while Bolívar proposed setting up a gubernatorial system.

Answers

1. ANSWER: C. The slave rebellion that occurred in Haiti is a result of a weakened French monarchy. As France is dealing with a revolution in its homeland, colonial control abroad weakened at the same time. The constitutional government in Haiti replaced the monarchy in Saint-Domingue (which included present-day Haiti and the Dominican Republic) (*The Earth and Its Peoples*, 6th ed. pp., 623–626/7th ed., pp. 604-606; History Disciplinary Practice—Analyzing Historical Evidence; Learning Objectives, SB–3,4, SOC-3; Key Concept 5.3.III.B).

2. ANSWER: B. Toussaint L'Ouverture was a former slave, who by the time the Haitian Revolution occurred was a freed black man. It is significant that he emerges as the ultimate leader of Haiti and is mentioned by name in the Haitian Constitution, showing the success of the rebellion and independence of Haiti (*The Earth and Its Peoples*, 6th ed., pp. 623–626/7th ed., pp. 604–606; History Disciplinary Practice—Analyzing Historical Evidence; Learning Objectives SB-3,4, SOC-3; Key Concept 5.3.III.B).

3. ANSWER: D. The Haitian Revolution shows many other Latin American countries that they have the ability to become independent, most notably from Spain. Leaders such as Jose San Martin and Simón Bolívar follow in the footsteps of Toussaint L'Ouverture in their quest for independent territories (*The Earth and Its Peoples*, 6th ed., pp. 623–626/7th ed., pp. 636–639; History Reasoning Skill—Contextualization; Learning Objectives SB-3,4, SOC-3; Key Concept 5.3.III.B).

4. ANSWER: D. Simón Bolívar tried to show people that Spain would never be successful in maintaining its influence in South America. Bolívar is trying to convince people in *The Jamaican Letter*, that people should rise up against Spain and fight for South American independence (*The Earth and Its Peoples*, 6th ed., pp. 660–662/7th ed., pp. 636–639; History Disciplinary Practice—Analyzing Historical Evidence; Learning Objectives SB-3,4, SOC-3; Key Concept 5.3.III.B).

5. ANSWER: C. After seeing the Venezuelan collapse of Spanish government, Bolívar suggests that the time is ripe for South Americans to organize an independence movement in 1815. After he writes the Jamaican Letter (while he was in exile), Bolívar returns to South America to organize a successful coup against Spanish troops stationed there (*The Earth and Its Peoples*, 6th ed., pp. 660–662/7th ed., pp. 636–639; History Disciplinary Practice—Analyzing Historical Evidence; Learning Objectives SB-3,4, SOC-3; Key Concept 5.3.III.B).

6. ANSWER: A. Bolívar saw South American labor on an equal footing of European serfdom…people bound to the land growing crops for the Spaniards. He wanted South Americans to move away from that policy. Further, human labor was relegated to mining gold for the Spaniards and he explicitly asks for more economic autonomy in trade agreements beyond those with the Spaniards (*The Earth and Its Peoples*, 6th ed., pp. 660–662/7th ed., pp. 634–639; History Disciplinary Practice—Analyzing Historical Evidence; Learning Objectives SOC-3, ECON-4; Key Concept 5.3.III.B).

AP® FORMAT QUESTIONS FOR PERIOD 5

Multiple-Choice Questions

Questions 1–3 refer to the following chart of inventors and their inventions from 1702 to 1843.

Inventor	Date	Invention
Newcomen, Thomas	1702–1712	Steam Engine
Wedgwood, Josiah	1759	Pyrometer (Pottery)
Watt, James	1769	Commercial Steam Engine
Crompton, Samuel	1785	Spinning Mule
Whitney, Eli	1793	Cotton Gin
Volta, Alessandro	1800	Battery
Morse, Samuel	1843	Long Distance Telegraph

Data from: *The Earth and Its Peoples*, 6th ed. p., 579

1. Which of the following is the most direct result of the concept depicted on the chart?
   (A) Increased focus on agriculture and farm life
   (B) Increasing isolation for newly formed nations
   (C) Increasing industrial production
   (D) Decreased reliance on fossil fuels

2. The chart indicates one reason why the European and the U.S. shares of global manufacturing
   (A) stayed below the shares of those in more technically advanced Asia.
   (B) pulled even with Middle Eastern shares of global manufacturing due to increased sharing of technology.
   (C) increased as a result of steam-powered production, while Middle Eastern and Asian shares declined.
   (D) dropped dramatically, due to focus on inventing rather than production.

3. Which of the following is an effect the inventions on the chart had on migration in the period between 1750 and 1900?
   (A) Both internal and external migrants increasingly relocated to cities.
   (B) Internal migrants increasingly relocated to cities, while external migrants relocated to rural areas.
   (C) Lack of transportation prevented migrants from ever returning to their home societies.
   (D) Due to the nature of the labor needed, migrants tended to be unmarried women who were less of an economic loss to their families.

Questions 4–6 refer to the following image.

January 1898 in the Parisian magazine *Le Petit Journal*.
INTERFOTO/Alamy Stock Photo

4. The cartoon above reflects the cause of which of the following?
   (A) Cotton from China being sold at extremely low prices
   (B) Palm oil demand in China leading to British export
   (C) Opium imports to China leading to European involvement
   (D) The development of Chinese steel exports

5. The "claims" on China above were in part a result of European spheres
   of influence living within China. Which of the following was another
   result?
   (A) China gained European land.
   (B) European culture was transplanted into parts of China.
   (C) Many Chinese migrated to Europe.
   (D) The British joined military forces with China.

6. Which of the following could contribute to the reaction of the Chinese
   character in the back of the cartoon?
   (A) Increasing irritation at excessive European exports
   (B) Frustration at a growing number of undocumented European arrivals
   (C) Growing nationalism in China
   (D) Diverse religious ideas causing confusion among young Chinese

Questions 7–10 refer to the following passage.

> I look upon the present state of America as similar to that of Rome after its fall…. But this important difference exists: those dispersed parts later reestablished their ancient nations, subject to the changes imposed by circumstances or events. But we scarcely retain a vestige of what once was; we are, moreover, neither Indian nor European, but a species midway between the legitimate proprietors of this country and the Spanish usurpers. In short, though Americans by birth we derive our rights from Europe, and we have to assert these rights against the rights of the natives, and at the same time we must defend ourselves against the invaders.
>
> We have been harassed by a conduct which has not only deprived us of our rights but has kept us in a sort of permanent infancy with regard to public affairs. If we could at least have managed our domestic affairs and our internal administration, we could have acquainted ourselves with the processes and mechanics of public affairs.
>
> Source: Bolívar, Simón, Jamaica Letter (1815).
> From *Selected Writings of Bolívar*, translated by Lewis Bertrand.
> Copyright © 1951 by The Colonial Press, Inc. All rights reserved.

7. Bolívar's Jamaica Letter reflects the impact of Enlightenment ideas on resistance to political authority in much the same way as
   (A) the French *Declaration of the Rights of Man and Citizen.*
   (B) Benjamin Franklin's *Poor Richard's Almanac.*
   (C) Bartolomé de Las Casas' *New Laws.*
   (D) the English *Magna Carta.*

8. Which of the following is the LEAST likely to be said of imperialism between 1750 and 1900?
   (A) Many European states used both warfare and diplomacy to establish empires.
   (B) Most states with existing colonies intentionally handed control over to their subjects.
   (C) Some European nations established enclaves of European settlers as settler colonies.
   (D) Some states practiced economic imperialism by investing heavily to expand their control.

9. Between 1750 and 1900, Enlightenment ideas succeeded in all of the following reforms EXCEPT
   (A) expansion of suffrage.
   (B) the abolition of slavery.
   (C) the end of serfdom.
   (D) the end of colonization.

10. Bolívar's comment "We are … a species midway between the legitimate proprietors of this country and the Spanish usurpers" could best serve as evidence of which of the following statements?
    (A) Receiving societies did not always embrace immigrants as seen in ethnic and racial prejudice.
    (B) Migrants often created ethnic enclaves that helped transplant their culture.
    (C) Migrants tended to be male, leaving women to take on new roles.
    (D) Large-scale global migrations produced increasingly diverse societies.

Questions 11–13 refer to the following map.

© Cengage Learning

11. The new nations shown on the map reflected a new sense of nationality based on all of the following EXCEPT
    (A) common language.
    (B) common social customs.
    (C) common territory.
    (D) common military.

12. The map would be most similar in argument to a map of which of the following?
    (A) Japan, emphasizing the independent Warrior States
    (B) Europe, emphasizing nationalism
    (C) Africa, emphasizing colonial power
    (D) The United States, emphasizing each independent state

13. Which nation on the map had an increased demand for slaves due to growth in their plantation economy?
    (A) Haiti
    (B) Jamaica
    (C) Gran Colombia
    (D) Puerto Rico

Short-Answer Questions

Question 1 refers to the following image.

Proclamation of the Abolition of Slavery in the French Colonies, 27 April 1848

François-Auguste Biard [Public domain], via Wikimedia Commons

1. Answer Parts A and B.
   A. Identify one example of a negative change that economic imperialism brought to the lives of Africans.
   B. Explain two examples of positive changes economic imperialism brought to the lives of Africans.

Question 2 refers to the following passage.

> We have on our hands a sick man, a very sick man. It will be, I tell
> you frankly, a great misfortune if, one of these days, he should slip
> away from us before all necessary arrangements were made.
>
> Tsar Nicholas of Russia about the Ottoman Empire to George Hamilton,
> British Envoy, 1843.

2. Answer Parts A, B, and C.
   A. Identify ONE change or development between 1750 and 1900 that
      supports Tsar Nicholas' depiction of the Ottoman Empire as a "Sick
      Man."
   B. Explain ONE change or development between 1750 and 1900 that
      challenges Tsar Nicholas' depiction of the Ottoman Empire as a
      "Sick Man."
   C. Explain ONE change that occurred between 1750 and 1900 that
      caused a decline in the Ottoman Empire.

Question 3 refers to the following passage.

> Our nation's emphasis on civil service examinations has sunk deep
> into people's minds for a long time. Intelligent and brilliant scholars
> have exhausted their time and energy in such useless things as the
> stereotyped examination essays, examination papers, and formal
> calligraphy.… We should now order one-half of them to apply
> themselves to the manufacturing of instruments and weapons and to
> the promotion of physical studies.
>
> Feng Guifen, a Chinese official, 1861

3. Answer Parts A, B, and C.
   A. Identify ONE event in China between 1750 and 1900 that supports
      the author's assertion in the passage.
   B. Explain ONE event in an Asian state OTHER than China between
      1750 and 1900 that supports the author's assertion.
   C. Explain ONE event in Asia that challenges the Chinese author's
      assertion to events in the Ottoman Empire

Question 4 refers to the following passage.

> If the spring of popular government in time of peace is virtue, the
> springs of popular government in revolution are at once virtue and
> terror: virtue, without which terror is fatal; terror, without which
> virtue is powerless. Terror is nothing other than justice, prompt,
> severe, inflexible; it is therefore an emanation of virtue.…
>
> Maximillien Robespierre, French Lawyer and leader of the French
> Revolution, 1794

4. Answer Parts A and B.
   A. Identify ONE example of a revolution from the period 1750 to 1900
      that would support the author's assertion in the passage.
   B. Explain TWO examples of a revolution from the period 1750 to 1900
      that would refute the author's assertion in the passage.

5. Many historians argue that economic and demographic changes are often linked and point to the Americas as an example. Answer parts A and B.
   A. Identify TWO pieces of evidence that support this author's argument.
   B. Explain ONE piece of evidence that undermines this argument.

Long Essay Questions

1. Using specific examples, analyze continuities and changes that occurred in the demographics and economy of Africa in the period 1550–1890.

2. Using specific examples, compare the effects of nationalism on both the Ottoman Empire and Europe from 1750 through 1900.

3. Using specific examples, analyze the continuities and changes in British colonialism in Asia in the period 1750–1900.

4. Evaluate the extent to which events changed and stayed the same from the period immediately before through the period of industrialization (1750–1900).

5. Using specific examples, analyze the continuities and changes in the relationship between labor systems and the social and economic structures of the Americas between 1550 and 1900.

Answers

MULTIPLE-CHOICE QUESTIONS

1. ANSWER: C. All of the inventions listed on the chart indicate the growing industrialization of nations and the interconnectedness of the global economy (*The Earth and Its Peoples*, 6th ed., p. 579/7th ed., p. 559; History Disciplinary Practice—Analyzing Historical Evidence; Learning Objective ENV-9, SB-5, ECON-2,4,5,9, SOC-2,3,4; Key Concept 5.1).

2. ANSWER: C. The chart lists a number of inventions that helped increase production and dramatically improved European/U.S. shares of the global market (*The Earth and Its Peoples*, 6th ed., p. 579/7th ed., p. 559; History Disciplinary Practice—Argument Development; Learning Objective ENV-9, CUL-6, SB-9, ECON-3,4,12; Key Concept 5.1).

3. ANSWER: A. Because of the nature of inventions, including new modes of transportation, migrants were more likely to move to the city for jobs and income. This also helped to finance increasingly likely return trips (periodically or sporadically) to their home societies (*The Earth and Its Peoples*, 6th ed., p. 722/7th ed., p. 696; History Reasoning Skill—Causation; Learning Objective ENV-3,4,5,6,7,8, SB-5, ECON-2,4,12, SOC-8; Key Concept 5.4).

4. ANSWER:C. Chinese opium addictions created a favorable balance of trade for European nations, allowing them to get a toehold and leading eventually to the division of China (*The Earth and Its Peoples*, 6th ed., p. 645/7th ed., p. 623; History Reasoning Skill—Causation; Learning Objective ENV-9, CUL-6, SB-9, ECON-3,4,12; Key Concept 5.1).

5. ANSWER: B. European merchants and traders who migrated to China introduced their culture and developed migrant support networks (*The Earth and Its Peoples*, 6th ed., p. 646/7th ed., p. 624; History Disciplinary Practice—Argument Development; Learning Objective ENV-3,4, CUL-9, SOC-1,8; Key Concept 5.3).

6. ANSWER:C. The growing nationalism among the Chinese led to the Boxer Rebellion and continued anger at the terms of the Treaty of Nanking and what was seen as Qing capitulation to Europeans (*The Earth and Its Peoples*, 6th ed., pp. 648–651/7th ed., pp. 626–629; History Reasoning Skill—Analyzing Historical Evidence; Learning Objective CUL-3,5, SB-4,8, ECON-7, SOC-1,2,3,4; Key Concept 5.3).

7. ANSWER: A. The French Declaration of the Rights of Man and Citizen also echoes Enlightenment ideas as foundational to resistance to established political authority (*The Earth and Its Peoples*, 6th ed., pp. 660–662/7th ed., pp. 636–638; History Reasoning Skill—Comparison; Learning Objective CUL-2,3,4,7, SB-4,7, ECON-7, SOC-1,2,3,6,7; Key Concept 5.3).

8. ANSWER: B. Under imperialism during this time, states only relinquished control following revolt or rebellion, never intentionally. Bolívar's excerpt specifically notes the lack of training for filling the holes in political leadership (*The Earth and Its Peoples*, 6th ed., pp. 660–662/7th ed., pp. 636–638; History Disciplinary Practice—Argument Development; Learning Objective CUL-2,3,4,7, SB-4,7, ECON-7, SOC-1,2,3,6,7; Key Concept 5.2).

9. ANSWER: D. Despite the impact of Enlightenment ideas and the number of revolutions throughout the period, imperialism and the process of colonization continued well into the twentieth century (*The Earth and Its Peoples*, 6th ed., pp. 660–662/7th ed., pp. 636–638; History Reasoning Skill—Causation; Learning Objective CUL-2,3,4,7, SB-4,7, ECON-7, SOC-1,2,3,6,7; Key Concept 5.3).

10. ANSWER: D. Bolívar is referring to the development of creole and mixed-race social classes that developed as a result of European colonization of the Americas. Particularly in Spanish and Portuguese colonies in Central and South America and the Caribbean, initial waves of colonization were mostly spearheaded by men seeking fortune and adventure. Many of these men established relationships with indigenous women, resulting in the establishment of new mixed races. In addition, the import of African slaves to the New World resulted in even more interracial relationships. The net result is the creation of a racially, ethnically, and culturally diverse society that was often stratified by place of birth and parentage (*The Earth and Its Peoples*, 6th ed., pp. 660–662/7th ed., pp. 636–638; History Disciplinary Practice—Analyzing Historical Evidence; Learning Objective ENV-3,4, CUL-9, SOC-1,8; Key Concept 5.4).

11. ANSWER: D. Beginning in the eighteenth century, peoples around the world developed a new sense of commonality based on language, religion, social customs, and territory (*The Earth and Its Peoples*, 6th ed., p. 579/7th ed., pp. 559–560; History Disciplinary Practice—Analyzing Historical Evidence; Learning Objective CUL-2,3,4,7, SB-4, SOC-3,7; Key Concept 5.3).

12. ANSWER: B. The map shows newly formed nations embracing nationalism in much the same way a map of Europe would show Italy and Germany as evolutions of nationhood (*The Earth and Its Peoples*, 6th ed., p. 722/7th ed., p. 746; History Reasoning Skill—Comparison; Learning Objective CUL-2,3,4,7, SB-4, SOC-3,7; Key Concept 5.3).

13. ANSWER: A. Haiti used slaves on their plantations and needed more slaves as their plantation economy grew (*The Earth and Its Peoples*, 6th ed., p. 674/7th ed., p. 650; History Reasoning Skill—Comparison; Learning Objective SB-9, ECON-1,3,5,6,10, SOC-2,7,8; Key Concept 4.2).

SHORT-ANSWER QUESTIONS

1. A. Answers may include negative changes such as increased taxation, mistreatment of laborers, European control of government, violence, or loss of traditional culture.

   B. Answers may include positive impacts such as ending slavery, introduction of cash crops, education in Mission schools, or employment in government or European firms.
   (*The Earth and Its Peoples*, 6th ed., pp. 694–702/7th ed., pp. 670–678; History Reasoning Skill and Disciplinary Practice—Contextualization, Analyzing Historical Evidence; Learning Objective ENV-9, CUL-3,4,6, SB-1,2,3,4,9, ECON-3,4,5,8,12, SOC-1,2,3,6,7; Key Concept 5.1, 5.2, 5.4).

2. Answers to this question may vary.
   A. Many signs supported Nicholas' depiction of the Ottoman Empire as the "Sick Man of Europe." Declining agricultural revenue, debt to foreign nations, and inflation were all signs of the empire's weakened state.

   B. Although most signs supported Nicholas' depiction of the Ottoman Empire as a "Sick Man," there were some signs of possible revival. The most positive sign was the growth of the industrial class and the demographic shift to the cities where workers could find jobs. The reforms suggested by the Young Turks also offered some hope, although they died out before their reforms could have significant impact.
   (*The Earth and Its Peoples*, 6th ed., pp. 736–738, 753–755/7th ed., pp. 710–712, 727–729; History Disciplinary Practice and Reasoning Skill—Causation, Analyzing Historical Evidence; Learning Objective ENV3,4,5,6,7,8, CUL-3, SB-1,2,4,5,9, ECON-3,7,9, SOC-3; Key Concept 5.1, 5.4).

3. A. One event in China in this period that would support Guifen's argument that tradition should give way to change would be the Taiping Rebellion. This rebellion, led by Hong Xiuquan, a member of the traditional lower class Hakka, caused massive chaos to society and large-scale death, indicating the Chinese people were not happy with their traditional society.

   B. Answers to this question may vary, but one solid example would be Japanese attempts to fight off Europeans with traditional weapons, before succumbing to modern military power.

   C. Perhaps the best example to challenge Guifen's statement would be the Japanese and the Meiji Restoration. Their ability to meld traditional government while accepting limited modernization allowed the nation to grow in strength and power while maintaining its traditional roots.
   (*The Earth and Its Peoples*, 6th ed., pp. 648, 706, 740–741/7th ed., pp. 714–718; History Disciplinary Practice—Interpretation, Analyzing Evidence: Content and Sourcing; Learning Objective CUL-2,3,4,7, SB-4,7, ECON-7, SOC-1,2,3,6,7; Key Concept 5.3).

4. A. A good response will identify TWO examples of revolutions from this period that included the element of terror and explain how the examples indicate both terror and virtue. Robespierre's position on the Committee of Public Safety could be one good example, as might the storming of the Bastille or the storming of Versailles be. The Revolutions of 1848 or the Belgian Revolution of 1830 could also be used to support Robespierre's argument, as could many other examples of violent revolution.

   B. On the other hand, the Concordat of 1801 or the Industrial Revolution could serve as examples of change achieved without bloodshed or terror.

   (*The Earth and Its Peoples*, 6th ed., Chs. 21–22/7th ed., Ch. 22–23; History Disciplinary Practice and Reasoning Skill—Analyzing Historical Evidence, Continuity, and Change over Time; Learning Objective CUL-2,4, SB-2,3,4,7,9, ECON-7, SOC-3,7; Key Concept 5.3).

5. Answers to this question may vary.

   A. A good response to this question would identify and explain how two specific ways economic change and demographic change were linked. Good examples could include indentured servitude to the British North American colonies, where the economic need for workers as the plantation system flourished led to the arrival of large numbers of indentured servants. Following their indenture, these workers became free citizens desiring land, which led to an additional demographic change. Because indentured servants eventually became free settlers, plantation owners turned instead to African chattel slavery and imported African slaves to allow their economic superiority to continue. Another example could be the influx of Spanish settlers who formed the highest level of the caste system in Spanish Mexico. The economic wealth of these settlers allowed them to arrive and dominate the caste system, and because of their economic superiority, the caste system developed an intricate delineation of social status based on relative proximity to European blood. The higher an individual fell in the caste system, the more access he or she had to economic success.

   B. Answers could include the significant decrease in Native American population due to the introduction of European diseases such as smallpox. This significant demographic change did not affect Native economic status in noticeable ways.

   (*The Earth and Its Peoples*, 6th ed., p. 626/7th ed., pp. 605–606; History Reasoning Skill—Causation; Learning Objective ENV-4, ECON-3,5,6,7,8, SOC-1,2,8; Key Concept 5.3,5.4).

LONG ESSAY QUESTIONS

1. In this question, dates are significant. At the beginning of the period, the African slave trade was just beginning; by the end it was effectively over in the Atlantic. In the sixteenth century, the growing desire for slave labor for sugar plantations in the Caribbean was increasing. You should point out that some regions of Africa were severely affected by the loss in population, while others were relatively untouched; western Africa was the area hardest hit, and the demographic and economic structure of this

region greatly changed. The desire for European manufactured goods and hardware encouraged strong West African empires to meet the growing demand by expanding the taking of prisoners of war to sell to slave traders. As slaves became more difficult to obtain in western Africa, the slave trade moved down the coast to Angola. In the nineteenth century, increasing industrialism, rising moral objections, and the increase in legitimate trade goods, such as palm oil, led to the decrease of the overall number of people enslaved. In a continuity and change over time question, don't forget to address what may remain the same. Throughout the period, both Africans and Europeans worked together to obtain victims who were sold into slavery. By 1890, the slave trade supplying the Americas had ended, but slavery in Africa and the Middle East still remained (*The Earth and Its Peoples*, 6th ed., pp. 694–702/7th ed., pp. 670–678; History Reasoning Skill—Continuity and Change over Time; Learning Objective ENV-9, SB-1,2,3,9,10, ECON-3, SOC-7; Key Concept 5.2).

2. Begin this comparison essay with a definition of nationalism—the identification of people with a nation, often centered on language or religion. The effects of nationalism and the creation of the nation-state were seen first in Europe. Unlike the Ottoman Empire, Europe—the western areas in particular—formed political states often based around a common language or shared culture. Leaders of these new nations used nationalistic sentiment to rally citizens to compete economically, politically, and militarily, fueling the industrial growth of Europe during this period. The European states that suffered the most from nationalism were those that contained many ethnic and religious minorities, such as the Austro-Hungarian Empire, and were not able to create one effective national identity. This was also an issue for the Ottoman Empire. With multiple ethnic, religious, and linguistic minorities in Ottoman territory, creating a shared national identity was difficult, if not impossible. As nationalism grew stronger in the nineteenth century, Ottoman elites worried that outlying provinces would not be loyal to the empire and instead would support a separate state based on local identity. Instead of increasing industrial development to compete with other strong nations, the Ottoman Empire slowly broke apart. By the start of the twentieth century, the reforming Young Turks would begin to give the Ottomans a national identity that was based on ethnic Turks, further alienating minority groups in the empire (*The Earth and Its Peoples*, 6th ed., pp. 736–738, 753–755/7th ed., pp. 709–711; History Reasoning Skill—Comparison; Learning Objective CUL-2,3,4,7, SB-4,7, ECON-7, SOC-1,2,3,6,7; Key Concept 5.3).

3. Britain was a colonial presence in Asia by 1750, with trading settlements led by the British East India Company. Between 1750 and 1900, Britain greatly increased its colonial empire in Asia, adding many possessions throughout this period. The competition with France for power and influence in Asia in the early nineteenth century saw Britain expand into India, Southeast Asia, and the Pacific Islands. Most of these possessions initially had indirect British rule through the East India Company. But after the Sepoy Rebellion in India, Britain began to administer its South Asian possessions more directly. Large numbers of British residents

emigrated to places like Australia and New Zealand, and by the twentieth century, these colonies were encouraged to begin governing themselves. Other parts of the empire, most notably India, were still strongly controlled by the mother country at the start of World War I, though nationalism was on the rise (*The Earth and Its Peoples*, 6th ed., pp. 646–647/7th ed., pp. 624–625; History Reasoning Skill—Continuity and Change over Time; Learning Objective ENV-9, SB-1,2,3,9,10, ECON-3, SOC-7; Key Concept 5.2).

4. Make sure to identify specific nations that the Industrial Revolution impacted; Britain, France, Germany, and Belgium are possible choices. In the first period, only Britain had begun to industrialize. Changes in trading patterns, the growth of urban areas, environmental impacts, and an increase in factory production are some possible topics. In the second period, around 1840, most of western Europe had gone through drastic industrial change. Technological innovations such as railroads, steam engines, and telegraph lines increasingly linked Europe with the rest of the world in a global trading system. Great income gaps began to develop between the very rich and poor, as families were separated by the demands of the factory and radical political ideas like socialism gained supporters. By 1900, nations such as Britain, France, and Germany had begun to see many of the benefits of the Industrial Revolution because the middle class had grown stronger with increased standards of living. Throughout the period, the everyday lives of ordinary citizens were often subject to the boom and bust of the business cycle, and life in a new industrial society could bring great benefits or great hardships (*The Earth and Its Peoples*, 6th ed., Ch. 16–25/7th ed., Ch. 17–26; History Reasoning Skill—Contextualization; Learning Objective ENV-9, SB-5, ECON2,4,5,9, SOC-2,3,4; Key Concept 5.1).

5. Begin by identifying the systems of labor used. Slavery, indentured servitude, the *encomienda* system used in many Spanish colonies, as well as free wage labor—all can be discussed. The English colonies of North America could be used as an effective example because three different systems of labor were used (slavery, indentured servitude, and wage labor) and played a role in shaping the social and economic structures. In the British-held southern colonies, the great demand for labor to work on plantations led to a large population of indentured servants and slaves. This region developed a hierarchal social structure in which economic decisions were most often made by elites who could afford to buy slaves and servants. Great Britain's northern colonies saw a more limited use of indentured servants and slaves with free wage labor dominant. This made for more equitable social and economic structures, though class differences based on wealth still existed. You could also compare a Latin American colony that used the *encomienda* system, a system of forced labor for a predetermined number of days, with one that used slaves. By 1900, slavery, indentured servitude, and the *encomienda* system had been abolished, but the legacy of these labor systems had strongly influenced the social and economic structures that existed (*The Earth and Its Peoples,* 6th ed., p. 662/7th ed., p. 639; History Reasoning Skill—Continuity and Change over Time; Learning Objective ENV-4, ECON-3,5,6,7, SOC-2; Key Concept 5.1,5.2,5.3,5.4).

Period 6: Accelerating Global Change and Realignments, c. 1900 to Present

Period 6 of the AP® World History framework begins by examining how scientific discoveries and technological developments have contributed to the way humans have interacted with and altered the environment. From medical advances such as vaccines and artificial hearts, to new understandings about the size and scope of the universe, our knowledge of science and math expanded exponentially in the twentieth century. Not all human innovations led to positive outcomes, however. Deforestation, soil erosion, desertification, and greenhouse emissions accelerated rapidly. Developments in technology contributed to faster communication and transportation, as well as transforming warfare and entertainment formats.

A major topic for this period is conflict. Students in AP® World History should pay particular attention to the causes and outcomes of the many global conflicts since 1900 that they will study. Patterns emerge that will help you organize the information. One such pattern is the role of nationalism/nationalist ideology (ideas that often developed prior to 1900) as a driving force behind conflict. Another pattern that dominated many conflicts in the second half of the twentieth century was the tension and rivalry between the United States and the Soviet Union. Although not technically an armed conflict, this Cold War between the United States and the USSR frequently directly influenced very violent conflicts in the Americas, Africa, Asia, and the Middle East. It is also important to note the considerable opposition to conflict that emerged throughout the twentieth and twenty-first centuries as you examine the many wars, revolutions, rebellions, and intense rivalries of the period.

The economies of individual nations became increasingly interconnected, as social and cultural trends diffused worldwide as part of the process of globalization occurring in Period 6. We see the rise of international organizations to promote health and welfare, to stimulate economic development, and to mediate international disputes. Advances in communication and transportation technologies facilitated the rapid development of a global community.

The following charts outline the learning objectives and topics from the content outline that fit into this period.

Content Review Questions can be found at the end of each chapter. **AP® format questions** for Period 6 can be found on page 494. **Document-Based Questions** can be found in the diagnostic test and practice tests.

AP® is a trademark registered by the College Board, which is not affiliated with, and does not endorse, this product.

THEMATIC LEARNING OBJECTIVES FOR PERIOD 6

INTERACTION BETWEEN HUMANS AND THE ENVIRONMENT

Learning Objectives—Students are able to . . .	Relevant Topics in the Concept Outline
ENV-1 Explain how environmental factors, disease, and technology affected patterns of human migration and settlement over time.	6.1. II—Deforestation and desertification 6.1. I—Communication and transportation 6.3. II—Consequences of globalization
ENV-2 Evaluate the extent to which migration, population, and urbanization affected the environment over time.	6.1. I—Green Revolution 6.1. II—Global Pollution 6.1. III—Diseases associated with poverty, affluence, and new epidemics 6.3. II—Global governance
ENV-3 Explain how environmental factors have shaped the development of diverse technologies, industrialization, transportation methods, and exchange and communication networks.	6.1. I—Green Revolution 6.1. II—Location of labor and natural resources 6.3. II—Consequences of globalization
ENV-4 Evaluate the extent to which the development of diverse technologies, industrialization, transportation methods, and exchange and communication networks have affected the environment over time.	6.1. I—Green Revolution 6.1. II—Pollution 6.1. III—Diseases associated with poverty, affluence, and new epidemics 6.3. II—Consequences of globalization

DEVELOPMENT AND INTERACTION OF CULTURES

Learning Objectives—Students are able to . . .	Relevant Topics in the Concept Outline
CUL-1 Explain how religions, belief systems, philosophies, and ideologies originated, developed, and spread as a result of expanding communication and exchange networks.	6.2. II—Anti-imperialism 6.2. IV, V—Global conflict; movements against conflict 6.3. I–III—State responses to economic challenges; increasing personal independence; rights-discourse
CUL-2 Explain how religions, belief systems, philosophies, and ideologies affected political, economic, and social developments over time.	6.2. II—Religious and political conflicts 6.3. III—New ideas about race, class, gender, and religion; rights-based discourses, new cultural identities
CUL-3 Explain how cross-cultural interactions resulted in the diffusion of culture, technologies, and scientific knowledge.	6.1. I—Medical innovations
CUL-4 Explain how the arts are shaped by and reflect innovation, adaptation, and creativity of specific societies over time.	6.1. I—Medical innovations 6.2. IV—Government propaganda and public architecture 6.2. V—Cultural critiques of war 6.3. IV—Globalization of popular culture
CUL-5 Explain how expanding exchange networks shaped the emergence of various forms of transregional culture, including music, literature, and visual art.	6.2. II—Cultural critiques of war 6.2. V—People developed new cultural identities 6.3. IV—Globalization of popular culture

STATE BUILDING, EXPANSION, AND CONFLICT

Learning Objectives—Students are able to . . .	Relevant Topics in the Concept Outline
SB-1 Explain how different forms of governance have been constructed and maintained over time.	6.2. II—Colonial independence 6.2. IV—Total wars 6.2. V—Communism, Marxism 6.3. I—State-controlled economies
SB-2 Explain how and why different functions and institutions of governance have changed over time.	6.2. I—End of European dominance, independence movements 6.2. II—Transnationalism 6.2. IV—Total war, global conflicts 6.2. V—Intensified conflict 6.3. I—Governments and economic control 6.3. II—Global governance
SB-3 Explain how and why economic, social, cultural, and geographical factors have influenced the processes of state building, expansion, and dissolution.	6.1. II, III—Global migration 6.2. I—Competition over environmental resources 6.2. II—Anti-imperialist movements 6.2. III—Restructuring of states 6.2. IV—Ideologies of expansion; total war, Cold War, neocolonial dominance 6.2. V—Global conflict 6.3. I–III—New conceptualization of global society and culture
SB-4 Explain how and why internal and external political factors have influenced the process of state building, expansion, and dissolution.	6.1. III—Improved military technologies 6.2. I–V—Global conflicts and their consequences 6.2. I—Collapses, internal issues 6.2. II—Anti-imperialism 6.2. III—Ethnic violence 6.2. I–V—Individuals and groups 6.3. I—Responses to global capitalism 6.3. II—Global interdependence
SB-5 Explain how societies with states and state-less societies interacted over time.	6.2. I–V—Global conflicts and their consequences 6.3. III—Global interdependency
SB-6 Explain the political and economic interactions between states and non-state actors over time.	6.1. III—Improved military technologies 6.2. I–V—Global conflicts and their consequences 6.3. II—Global interdependency

CREATION, EXPANSION, AND INTERACTION OF ECONOMIC
SYSTEMS

Learning Objectives—Students are able to . . .	Relevant Topics in the Concept Outline
ECON-1 Explain how technology shaped economic production and globalization over time.	6.1. II—Global problems 6.2. I, IV—Global conflicts, transnational movements 6.3. I, II—Global economies and institutions 6.3. III—New technologies and spread of ideas 6.3. IV—Global popular culture; new machines and methods of industrial production
ECON-2 Explain the causes and effects of economic strategies of different types of communities, states, and empires.	6.1. I—Rapid spread of innovation 6.2. IV—Global conflict; fascism 6.2. V—Non-Aligned Movement 6.3. I—State-controlled economies 6.3. II—New economic institutions
ECON-3 Explain how different modes and locations of production and commerce have developed and changed over time.	6.1. I—Increasing global migration 6.2. I—Global problems 6.2. IV—Global conflict; fascism 6.2. V—Non-Aligned Movement 6.3. I—State-controlled economies; global economics and institutions 6.3. II—New economic institutions 6.3. III—New technologies and spread of ideas 6.3. IV—Global popular culture
ECON-4 Explain the causes and effects of labor reform movements.	6.2. II—Land redistribution
ECON-5 Explain how economic systems and the development of ideologies, values, and institutions have influenced each other.	6.2. II—Land redistribution 6.2. IV—Cold War 6.3. I, II—Free market economics, regional trade agreements, protest movements
ECON-6 Explain how local, regional, and global economic systems and exchange networks have influenced and impacted each other over time.	6.1. I—Oil and nuclear power 6.3. II—Changing economic institutions; global economic institutions

DEVELOPMENT AND TRANSFORMATION OF SOCIAL STRUCTURES

Learning Objectives—Students are able to . . .	Relevant Topics in the Concept Outline
SOC-1 Explain how distinctions based on kinship, ethnicity, class, gender, and race influenced the development and transformations of social hierarchies.	6.2. II—Redistribution of land, migrants in metropoles 6.2. V—Nonviolence 6.3. III—Changing ideas about rights-based discourses; new conceptualization of society and culture
SOC-2 Evaluate the extent to which different ideologies, philosophies, and religions affected social hierarchies.	6.2. II—Redistribution of land, migrants in metropoles 6.2. V—Nonviolence 6.3. III—New conceptualizations of society and culture
SOC-3 Evaluate the extent to which legal systems, colonialism, nationalism, and independence movements have sustained or challenged class, gender, and racial hierarchies over time.	6.2. II—Postcolonial independence, migration 6.2. IV—Global conflict 6.2. V—Popular protests 6.3. II—Protesting inequalities
SOC-4 Explain how social categories, roles, and practices have been maintained or challenged over time.	6.1. III—Demographic shifts, including birth control 6.2. II—Global conflict 6.2. V—Popular protests 6.3. II—Protesting inequalities 6.3. III—Challenges to old assumptions about religion; rights-based discourses
SOC-5 Explain how political, economic, cultural, and demographic factors have affected social structures over time.	6.2. II—Postcolonial independence, migration 6.2. III—Migrants to metropoles 6.2. IV—Global conflict

KEY CONCEPTS FOR PERIOD 6

6.1. Science and the Environment

6.2. Global Conflicts and Their Consequences

6.3. New Conceptualizations of Global Economy, Society, and Culture

26

AFRICA: C. 1900 TO THE PRESENT

KEY CONCEPTS

- During the first half of the twentieth century, much of Africa was under colonial rule by European powers, which resulted in the exploitation of labor, creation of cash crop systems, and extraction of raw materials for the benefit of colonial powers.
- Soldiers returning from fighting in World War II played a key role in demanding equality and an end to colonization.
- The era in which African nations gained political independence from European colonial powers was from 1957 to 1991. The fight for freedom and independence became most violent in areas with large populations of white settlers unwilling to relinquish privileges or political control.
- During the Cold War, some African nations attempted to resist aligning with either superpower unless they could benefit from the superpower economically or politically.

KEY TERMS

- African National Congress (ANC)
- apartheid
- Bandung Conference
- colonialism
- El Alamein
- League of Nations
- mandate system
- proxy wars
- United Nations

Africa from 1900 to the present is discussed in *The Earth and Its Peoples*, 6th edition, Chapters 25, 28, 30, 31, and 32, and 7th edition, Chapters 26, 29, 31, and 33.

WORLD WAR I

At first glance, the First World War seems to have little to do with the continent of Africa. However, a closer look reveals that while Africans themselves had little say in the events surrounding World War I, the destiny of Africans was intrinsically tied to the desires and aspirations of the European powers. By 1914, much of the African continent was under colonial rule by various European powers as a result of the 1884–1885 Berlin Conference. European powers, interested largely in African labor to extract resources for their industries, used various methods, such as the "Hut" tax or "Head" tax to force Africans into the colonial economies. In order to pay the taxes, Africans were forced to accept low-wage jobs—on plantations, in mines, on railroads, and the like—within the European colonial system.

Despite the agreements made at the Berlin Conference, the imperialistic ambitions of the European powers were not satiated, and they began competing for new territory and new resources to fuel industrialization within their own nations. The crumbling Ottoman Empire, which had outlying territories in North Africa, was at the center of this new scramble for territory and resources. In 1912, Italy conquered Libya, the Ottomans' last remaining territory in Africa. Imperialism proved a way to bolster both industrialization and nationalistic fervor, and nationalism offered the same reinforcement to colonization. So when the Great War began in 1914, Africans and their land were drawn into the conflict.

Only a few battles were fought on the African continent, but resources and manpower were greatly coveted. World War I exacerbated colonial hardships. The colonial powers forced Africans throughout the continent to grow export crops and sell them at low prices, imposed heavy taxes, and demanded foodstuffs in order to support European military forces. More than two million Africans served in colonial armies fighting side by side with Europeans. An even greater number of Africans was used as porters to carry military equipment. Many were badly fed and mistreated. African involvement in the war as well as the heavy demands and burdens placed on them provided an opportunity to demand equal rights, but even though Africans played a major role in the Allied victory, only a few demands for equality were met. At the beginning of the war, French and British forces attacked German ports in present-day Togo, Cameroon, and Tanganylka. The Allied forces took over the German colony of Togo in West Africa. By 1915, they had conquered German Southwest Africa and German Cameroon. The British and the French were on their way to an even greater foothold on the continent than even they had expected.

THE INTERWAR PERIOD

The end of World War I brought little consolation for people throughout the African continent. Despite the idealistic and democratic rhetoric of self-determination, it became clear that none of these ideals were meant for the people of the colonies. Colonies previously run by Germany saw one colonizing force merely replaced by another. Tanganyika, a German colony in East Africa, for instance, became a British colony at the end of World War I. South Africa, a nation independent from Britain but run by a minority composed of Afrikaners and British settlers, replaced Germany as the new colonizers of Southwest Africa. According to the Treaty of Versailles, these former German colonies would be administered as class C mandates. Under the **mandate system**, the colonies were to be run by their new European rulers for "the material and moral well-being and social progress of the inhabitants." The rulers were also to be accountable to the newly formed **League of Nations**. However, while the League of Nations was a world organization designed to foster world peace and cooperation, colonized people were excluded from decision making and all other forms of involvement. In that respect, the League was set up with a decidedly European and imperial bent. As such, autonomy for the colonies/mandates was a theoretical goal for some unspecified time in the future. Thus, like their counterparts in the Middle East and Asia, Africans yearned for still-elusive independence—equality as well as the promised material well-being.

Even after World War I, few Africans benefited from colonial rule. The colonial system was set up to benefit the European powers. Railroads and other forms of infrastructure were built merely to transport raw materials to the coast so that they might be shipped off to Europe for manufacturing. Colonial governments even stripped Africans of land to sell or lease to European companies or settlers. While colonial governments eagerly developed resources within the colonies, they refused to pay high wages to African workers. Sometimes their only means of acquiring workers was by forcing Africans to work for little or no pay, under harsh conditions. The French colonial government of Equatorial Africa, for example, forced 127,000 men to build a railroad from Brazzaville to the Atlantic coast during the 1920s; lacking food, clothing, and medicine, 20,000 workers—an average of sixty-four men per mile of track—died. Even hospitals and modern health care benefited few Africans. In fact, the colonial system often worsened public health. Diseases spread rapidly among migrant workers and soldiers; in Central Africa, sleeping sickness and smallpox ravaged entire villages. The need to pay colonial taxes forced many men into migrant work, causing severe problems for their wives, who were left in rural areas to farm and raise the children on their own. To feed so many migrant laborers, many colonial officials requisitioned food from rural areas, leaving people in rural areas undernourished and vulnerable to disease.

There were a few economic exceptions to the colonial rule. Cocoa farmers in Ghana and palm oil producers in Nigeria, for instance, profited from high prices. Coffee farmers in East Africa experienced similar benefits. In most of these cases, economic success was a result of colonial policies that divided land into small farms. Likewise, African merchant women, allowed to continue as they had before **colonialism**, maintained a degree of economic independence at home as well as within society. But when the Depression hit in the 1930s, some Africans were severely affected—France and Great Britain forced their colonies to purchase their products. The economy in southern Africa, on the other hand, boomed during the Depression, as a result of the rising value of gold and the cheaper cost of mining copper in Rhodesia and the Belgian Congo as compared to Chile. However, the wealth was enjoyed only by the small number of Europeans and white South Africans. While mining jobs and cash wages remained steady for many southern Africans, they gained little of the profits.

The most severe experiences of colonial rule occurred in the white settler colonies such as Algeria, Kenya, Rhodesia, and South Africa. While all cities built during the time of colonization had segregated housing, clubs, restaurants, and hospitals, racial discrimination was at its utmost in the settler colonies. Colonization also meant the spread of Christianity, especially in areas where European influences were the strongest. Mission schools were established across the continent as a way to encourage what was seen as a European religion. Few Europeans imagined that Africans would use Christianity in the fight to end colonization. Mission schools taught in colonial languages, thus helping Africans to work within the colonial economy. The schools created a new educated elite familiar with Western ways. Although only a few Africans gained a secondary education and even fewer were able to travel to Europe or the United States to attend a university, those few were exposed to liberal Western ideas that contradicted the racial prejudice and colonialism Africans faced every day. Many of the Western-educated elite returned home with a strong desire to work for freedom and equality. Senegalese Blaise Diagne, for example, fought for African political participation and equal treatment within the French army. Similarly, J. E. Casely Hayford struggled for African autonomy in British West Africa. In South Africa, Western-educated lawyers and journalists used the **African National Congress** (ANC), established in 1909, as a means to fight for the rights of Africans. Africans who received a university education overseas, seeing that people of African descent around the world were facing similar conditions, were drawn to Pan-Africanism. Popularized by the African-American W. E. B. Du Bois and the Jamaican Marcus Garvey, Pan-Africanism advocated the unity of all African peoples in the global struggle against white supremacy and colonialism. In many ways, it combined European ideas of liberalism and nationalism neatly transformed into a weapon against Western colonial powers.

AP® Tip

While colonial hardships increased during World War I and World War II, the nature of colonialism within Africa remained constant. You should be able to compare Africans' experiences of colonialism with those of South and Southeast Asians. You should also be able to compare Africans' experiences of the world wars with those of Asians, Europeans, and people of the Americas.

World War II and Independence Movements

World War II had an even greater impact on the continent of Africa than the First World War. There were more Africans fighting, more battles within Africa, and more ramifications at the end of the war. For the continent of Africa, the Second World War perhaps began with the Italian conquest of Ethiopia in 1935, then one of only two independent African states. The invasion of Ethiopia was met by a very weak response from the European powers and the United States. The League of Nations protested but did little else to aid Ethiopia, one of its members. The international community failed to impose punishments, and it allowed Italian ships continued use of the Suez Canal. For many Africans, this showed a lack of respect for an independent African nation and symbolized European unwillingness to support African independence, despite the promises outlined during the post–World War I Paris Peace Conference.

The Italian invasion also emboldened Hitler, who concluded that German aggression would face little resistance. It was not until Italy joined forces with Germany as part of the Axis powers and Italian forces invaded British Somaliland in 1940 that the British offered support to exiled Ethiopian emperor Haile Selassie. In the meantime, Italian forces marched north and invaded Egypt. During 1941, British forces fought the Italians in Somaliland, and Haile Selassie led his troops into the Ethiopian capital, Addis Ababa, and reclaimed his title by ousting the Italians. During that same year, the British also overtook the Italians in Libya, and at the end of 1942 defeated the Germans at **El Alamein**, Egypt.

For Africans, the effects of the Second World War were similar to those of the first but on a far broader scale. European colonial rulers increasingly forced Africans to labor in mines and on plantations. Raw materials were once again requisitioned, and as a result, mining companies opened new mines and towns in Central Africa. Inflation afflicted most regions of the continent. As in World War I, millions of Africans served as soldiers and porters. Serving alongside Europeans in North Africa, Europe, and Asia, Africans became well aware of Allied propaganda lambasting Nazi aggression and racism and promoting European liberation efforts. They returned to their countries emboldened to demand liberty from the very colonizers with whom they fought against the Nazis.

Decolonization

The greatest impact of World War II was the impetus it gave anticolonial independence movements throughout Africa and Asia. For the people of Africa, India's independence in 1947 provided a model as well as extra motivation to demand independence for their respective nations. At the same time, support for colonialism was ebbing among the British, who were less willing to spend money to maintain colonial territories. The year of Indian independence was also the year of Kwame Nkrumah's return to the Gold Coast. Released from a British prison by public pressure, Nkrumah was appointed prime minister in 1951, but it took until 1957 for Ghana to gain full independence. Other British West African colonies soon became independent as well. The large and diverse nation of Nigeria gained independence in 1960. On the whole, French colonies were slower in gaining independence. But under the dynamic leadership of Sékou Touré, Guinea gained independence in 1958. Two years later in 1960, other French West African colonies followed.

Despite being severely weakened by the Second World War, European powers often struggled to hold on to their colonies. This frequently led to contentious and bloody fights, especially in areas with a large population of white settlers, who strongly resisted majority rule. The struggle for Algerian independence was just such a case. Not only was there a sizable French population within Algeria, the French economy was dependent on Algerian oil and gas fields. Even Algerian vineyards were the source of large quantities of French wine. The fight, therefore, was both bloody and brutal. French colonists considered Algeria rightfully a part of France, and they swore to fight to the bitter end. Leading the independence movement was the Front de Liberation National (FLN), which received support from Egypt and other Arab and African countries. Algeria finally won independence in 1962, more than fifteen years after the end of World War II. At the end of the Algerian war for independence, many French colonists hastily returned to France. However, their departure caused severe problems for the Algerian economy because few Algerians were trained for any of the technical and management positions. Economic problems also led many Algerians fleeing unemployment to seek opportunities in France. Nonetheless, despite the bloody war, France and Algeria managed to retain close, albeit shaky, ties.

The East African nation of Kenya faced a similar struggle to gain freedom. Though not as large as Algeria, it too had a white settler population that had gained wealth and influence as coffee planters in the colonial economy. Intent on retaining power in Kenya, the coffee planters characterized Kenyans as unequipped for self-government, referring to a Kikuyu protest movement as Mau Mau to suggest primitive savagery. The Kenyan rebels referred to themselves as Muingi, meaning "the movement," or the Kikuyu Central Association—the vast majority of the rebels belonged to the Kikuyu, an ethnic group that had been displaced by the settlers from the lush agricultural highlands. When violence between the settlers and the freedom fighters escalated in the early 1950s, British troops managed to capture the leaders and resettle them in fortified villages—essentially concentration camps—to prevent contact with other rebel fighters. The British then banned all political protest and activity, declared a state of emergency, and imprisoned Jomo Kenyatta and other nationalist leaders. Released in 1961 after eight years of imprisonment, Kenyatta negotiated with the British for independence and in 1964 was elected the first president of the Republic of Kenya.

No region had more white settlers than southern Africa, which made the fight for independence there longer and more intense. Throughout southern Africa, the settlers defended white supremacy and white rule at all costs, provoking armed struggle. During the 1960s, an armed guerrilla struggle began against Portuguese rule in Angola and Mozambique. Ironically, war in the Portuguese colonies became increasingly unpopular in Portugal, causing the Portuguese army to overthrow the government of Portugal in 1974. In 1975, the new Portuguese government granted independence to both Angola and Mozambique. White settlers in Southern Rhodesia finally accepted African majority rule in 1980, after ten years of fighting. The new government changed the name of the nation to Zimbabwe, in honor of the ancient kingdom that predated European colonization.

The fight for independence proved hardest in South Africa and Namibia. In South Africa, the white minority-rule government was based on a system of racial separation and subjugation called **apartheid**. Though minority-ruled, South Africa had existed as an independent nation since 1910. Thus, the struggle in South Africa was against apartheid, and the ANC was at the forefront of this antiapartheid struggle. As in other regions with settler populations, armed struggle became inevitable. In 1960, South African police fired on hundreds of demonstrators in the town of Sharpeville. The government banned all forms of protest, and Nelson Mandela, the ANC leader, was captured and sentenced to life in prison in 1964. The ANC, banned in South Africa, was forced to operate armed resistance from neighboring countries, such as Mozambique and Tanzania, that had recently gained independence. The struggle against apartheid continued until 1990 when the government officially ended the practice.

THE COLD WAR

One cannot look at decolonization in Africa without looking at Cold War politics. Both the United States and the USSR were attempting to influence the newly independent states. As a result of this pressure and in hope of gaining allies in the fight against colonialism, various African leaders— among them Kwame Nkrumah and Egypt's Nasir—attended the **Bandung Conference** in 1955. The conference proclaimed the solidarity of all people fighting against colonial rule. Despite claiming to be nonaligned, African leaders were drawn, willingly or not, into the struggle of the two superpowers. African liberation movements often gained assistance from Cuba and the Soviets because no Western democracies supported African independence. The decision to accept aid from communist nations thrust them deep into the Cold War. In the Belgian Congo, competing political and ethnic groups received aid from Cuba and the Soviets on the one hand, while others received assistance from the West. Cold War struggles and the stubbornness of Belgian colonial authorities led to violence, property destruction, and heavy loss of life. In 1965, the first democratically elected prime minister, Patrice Lumumba, was assassinated after serving in office for only sixty-seven days. From the onset, Lumumba was surrounded by Cold War pressures. He received support from the Soviets, which angered U.S. President Eisenhower. Evidence has also revealed that the coup that removed Lumumba from office was CIA sponsored.

In somewhat similar fashion, Ghanaian independence was also entrenched in Cold War politics. A year after Lumumba's assassination, Nkrumah was overthrown in a CIA-backed military coup while he was away on a state visit to Vietnam in 1966. Throughout the independence/anti-apartheid struggle, the South African government attempted to discredit the ANC by highlighting ties and support from Cuba and the Soviets. What is clear is that upon independence, African nations became prime battlegrounds for conflicts in which the United States and the USSR provoked, financed, and armed competing factions or parties. These **proxy wars**, as they were called, led to decades of violence and military struggle. They often resembled wars in which small newly independent nations were fighting at the bidding of the two superpowers, which were hoping to gain strategic advantages. Proxy wars also inflamed ethnic rivalries and hatreds that had been lying dormant during colonial rule. When the European colonial powers created artificial national boundaries during the Berlin Conference, they did so without regard to ethnic and religious makeup. The result was ethnic groups such as the Wolof, were split among four different countries: Senegal, Gambia, Mali, and the Ivory Coast. Upon independence, feelings of ethno-nationalistic pride were stirred and encouraged by Africans and the superpowers alike.

AP® Tip

Decolonization was a long and haphazard process in Africa. You should be able to identify the key factors that helped bring about independence and compare the nature of the independence struggle in various nations throughout Africa, as well as around the world.

THE POST–COLD WAR WORLD

The post–Cold War era has been stoked with both optimism and disappointment. Many viewed the fall of the Soviet Union as an opportunity for wealth and democracy to spread to the nations of Africa. Wealth and democracy, however, have been slow in coming. Military coups, often stemming from Cold War battles and frustrations, have been frequent in sub-Saharan Africa. Many leaders have also used their offices to limit the power of opponents and for personal enrichment. Conflicts over resources such as diamonds and other minerals have proliferated. The year 1994 witnessed a massive case of ethnic cleansing in the Central African nation of Rwanda. When political leaders incited the Hutu majority to massacre their Tutsi neighbors on claims of discrimination and favoritism stemming from the colonial period, the result was more than 750,000 dead and millions of refugees flooding into the neighboring nations of Congo, Tanzania, and Burundi. As the international community was slow to respond, violence spilled over into Congo, causing greater conflict and destabilization.

Nonetheless, post–Cold War Africa has witnessed many success stories, among them the ending of apartheid in South Africa and the 1994 election victory of former political prisoner Nelson Mandela and the African National Congress. The ANC victory marked the first time in which the black majority could participate equally. The 1990s also witnessed the election of Olusegun Obasanjo as president of Nigeria after years of military rule. Likewise, in 1992, the **United Nations**, with the help of various African nations, helped to end the civil war in Mozambique. For Angola, peace was not realized until 2002, and the civil war in Liberia did not end until 2003. Two years later, Liberians elected their first female head of state, Dr. Ellen Johnson-Sirleaf.

Peace and political stability, however, have not meant wealth. In fact, since 1945, the gap between rich nations and poor nations has only grown wider and has concentrated poverty in the former colonies of Africa, Asia, and Latin America. Many have struggled to diversify their economies from the cash crop systems established during the colonial period. Poverty in African nations has coincided with high mortality rates and low life-expectancy rates. And with the contemporary onset of AIDS, African nations are suffering some of the highest incidences around the world. In fact, 70 percent of the forty million people infected with AIDS worldwide live in sub-Saharan Africa. Such drastic numbers are causing serious problems in food production and job staffing. The problem of AIDS, and its high mortality rate in Africa, is closely related to poverty. Hence, AIDS has become one of the greatest threats to contemporary Africa. Because treatment for AIDS is so expensive, recent global efforts have been made to provide drugs at lower costs.

Poverty has also caused large-scale migrations. Numerous migrants from rural areas of Nigeria, for instance, have moved to the city of Lagos in order to find jobs. Migrations were not without reason. Urban residents throughout sub-Saharan Africa, for instance, are six times more likely to have potable water than their rural counterparts. Unfortunately, few nations have been able to expand basic services at the same rate as the rapid population growth. Many Africans have also sought better lives by emigrating to western Europe and the United States. A growing number of Moroccans and Algerians have found their way to Spain, France, and Belgium. A large population of Ghanaians and Nigerians have made new homes in Houston, Texas; Atlanta, Georgia; and Washington, D.C. Migration and emigration are fueled by exploding population growth that is far outpacing the rate in developed nations. Nonetheless, despite much progress since independence, the hope for national wealth has eluded most African nations, as well as their citizens.

Content Review Questions

Questions 1–3 refer to the passage below.

The foreign policy of the United States, which reflects the imperialist tendencies of American monopolistic capital, is characterized in the post-war period by a striving for world supremacy. This is the real meaning of the many statements by President Truman and other representatives of American ruling circles: that the United States has the right to lead the world. All the forces of American diplomacy—the army, the air force, the navy, industry, and science—are enlisted in the service of this foreign policy. For this purpose broad plans for expansion have been developed and are being implemented through diplomacy and the establishment of a system of naval and air bases stretching far beyond the boundaries of the United States, through the arms race, and through the creation of ever newer types of weapons.

In this regard, it was thought that the main competitors of the United States would be crushed or greatly weakened in the war, and the United States by virtue of this circumstance would assume the role of the most powerful factor in resolving the fundamental question of the postwar world. These calculations were also based on the assumption that the Soviet Union, which had been subjected to the attacks of German Fascism in June 1941, would also be exhausted or even completely destroyed as a result of the war.

Obvious indications of the U.S. effort to establish world dominance are to be found in the increase in military potential in peacetime and in the establishment of a large number of naval and air bases both in the United States and beyond its borders.

All of these facts show clearly that a decisive role in the realization of plans for world dominance by the United States is played by its armed forces.

NIKOLAS NOVIKOV, TELEGRAM, SEPTEMBER 27, 1946
Source: Nikolai Novikov, "Telegram, September 27, 1946," in Kenneth Jensen, ed., *Origins of the Cold War: The Novikov, Kennan, and Roberts Long Telegrams of 1946* Washington, D.C.: United States Institute of Peace, 1993. (*Human Records Documents*, Cengage, pp. 414–418.)

1. What were the Soviet perceptions of ambitions in the United States after the Second World War?
    A. Following World War II, there was potential for good diplomatic relations between the Soviet Union and the United States.
    B. The Soviet Union was convinced that the United States was poising itself for world domination.
    C. The Soviet Union saw the United States as more of an economic power than anything else after World War II.
    D. The United States was trying to connect more territory to itself, starting with Canada and Mexico.

2. Why did the alliances formed between the Soviet Union and the United States deteriorate after World War II?
   A. Both countries agreed that they would not get along, as it would be perceived as weakness to the citizens of the Soviet Union and the United States.
   B. Both countries have a different governmental hierarchy, whereby the elected officials of the Soviet Union do not have to respond to the Politburo, or legislative branch.
   C. Both countries embrace different religions, and do not have any common ground socially.
   D. Both countries have different views on how government and economic systems should operate.

3. How did the Cold War between the Soviet Union and the United States influence the rest of the world?
   A. The Cold War allowed for smaller countries to be divided evenly to be influenced by the United States and the Soviet Union.
   B. The Cold War improved economies throughout the world by offering more competitive pricing for consumers.
   C. The Cold War divided countries as much as the United States and the Soviet Union could control their "spheres of influence."
   D. The rest of the world started to organize against the United States and the Soviet Union, forming their own military and governmental influences.

Questions 4–6 refer to the following passage.

George Washington was not God Almighty. He was a man like any Negro in this building, and if he and his associates were able to make a free America, we too can make a free Africa. Hampden, Gladstone, Pitt, and Disraeli were not the representatives of God in the person of Jesus Christ. They were but men, but in their time they worked for the expansion of the British Empire, and today they boast of a British Empire upon which "the sun never sets." As Pitt and Gladstone were able to work for the expansion of the British Empire, so you and I can work for the expansion of a great African Empire. Voltaire and Mirabeau were not Jesus Christ; they were but men like ourselves. They worked and overturned the French Monarchy. They worked for the Democracy, which France now enjoys, and if they were able to do that, we are able to work for a democracy in Africa. Lenin and Trotsky were not Jesus Christs, but they were able to overthrow the despotism of Russia, and today they have given to the world a Social Republic, the first of its kind. If Lenin and Trotsky were able to do that for Russia, you and I can do that for Africa. Therefore, let no man, let no power on earth, turn you from this sacred cause of liberty. I prefer to die at this moment rather than not to work for the freedom of Africa. If liberty is good for certain sets of humanity it is good for all. Black men, colored men, Negroes have as much right to be free as any other race that God Almighty ever created, and we desire freedom that is unfettered, freedom that is unlimited, freedom that will give us a chance and opportunity to rise to the fullest of our ambition and that we cannot get in countries where other men rule and dominate.

It falls to our lot to tear off the shackles that bind Mother Africa. Can you do it? You did it in the Revolutionary War. You did it in the civil war; you did it at the Battles of the Marne and Verdun; you did it in Mesopotamia. You can do it marching up the battle heights of Africa. Let the world know that 400,000,000 Negroes are prepared to die or live as free men. Despise us as much as you care. Ignore us as much as you care. We are coming 400,000,000 strong. We are coming with our woes behind us, with the memory of suffering behind us—woes and suffering of three hundred years—they shall be our inspiration. My bulwark of strength, in the conflict of freedom in Africa, will be the three hundred years of persecution, and hardship left behind in this Western Hemisphere. The more I remember the suffering of my forefathers, the more I remember the lynchings and burnings in the Southern States of America, the more I will fight on even though the battle seems doubtful. Tell me that I must turn back, and I laugh you to scorn. Go on! Go on! Climb ye the heights of liberty and cease not in well doing until you have planted the banner of the Red, the Black, and the Green on the hilltops of Africa.

MARCUS GARVEY PREACHES AFRICAN REVOLUTION, 1923
Primary Source Reader for World History (Cengage, pp. 533–534) From
Marcus Garvey, "Redeeming the African Motherland," in *Philosophy and
Opinions of Marcus Garvey*, Vol. I, ed. by Amy Jacques Garvey, New York:
University Publishing House, 1923.

4. Who is the audience for Marcus Garvey's speech from 1923?
   (A) The United States government
   (B) The Soviet Union
   (C) People of African descent
   (D) Citizens outside of the influence of either the United States or the Soviet Union

5. African nations became prime battlegrounds for proxy wars because
   (A) they had little experience in self-rule and were thus unable to govern successfully.
   (B) the United States and USSR supported competing factions in order to gain influence within newly independent nations.
   (C) they were willing to sacrifice stability in exchange for the promise of profit from the two superpowers.
   (D) Soviet and American intentions to colonize African nations forced many Africans to form armed resistance.

6. How did French sub-Saharan African colonies differ from British sub-Saharan African colonies?
   (A) French colonies were more Christianized.
   (B) Independence movements in French colonies were more violent.
   (C) French colonial farmers were less dependent on cash crops.
   (D) Independence was achieved through a more gradual process in French colonies.

Answers

1. ANSWER: B. After the Second World War, the Soviets saw Harry Truman and the United States as attempting to flex its imperialist muscle. The Soviets were fearful of U.S. world domination, according to the document from Novikov (*The Earth and Its Peoples*, 6th ed., pp. 840–846/7th ed., pp. 810–816; History Disciplinary Practice—Analyzing Historical Evidence; Learning Objectives ECON-2; Key Concept 6.2.IV.C).

2. ANSWER: D. The differences between the United States and the Soviet Union are striking, both economically and in government. While the Soviet leadership used a totalitarian, communist form of operation, the United States furthered a democratic, capitalist government and economy (*The Earth and Its Peoples*, 6th ed., pp. 840–846/7th ed., pp. 811–814; History Reasoning Skill—Contextualization; Learning Objectives ECON-6; Key Concept 6.2.IV.C).

3. ANSWER: C. The Soviet Union and the United States were attempting to gain as much geographical and economic influences in the world as possible. Both countries would offer trade and military incentives if countries would align themselves with either the Soviet Union or the United States (*The Earth and Its Peoples*, 6th ed., pp. 840–846/7th ed., pp. 811–814; History Reasoning Skill—Causation; Learning Objectives ECON-6; Key Concept 6.2.IV.C).

4. ANSWER: C. While Marcus Garvey is famous for his "back to Africa" movement, in this speech, he is primarily targeting Africans and African-Americans. Garvey is attempting to motivate people to influence governments and citizens to allow for a more independent African continent (*The Earth and Its Peoples*, 6th ed., pp. 850–853/7th ed., pp. 821–823; History Disciplinary Practice—Analyzing Historical Evidence; Learning Objectives CUL-2, SB-1; Key Concept 6.2.II.A).

5. ANSWER: B. Proxy wars were conflicts in which the rival superpowers financed and armed competing factions or parties to gain greater influence. As newly independent nations or those on the verge of independence, African countries were seen by the United States and the USSR as being open to influence. Proxy wars occurred in Angola, Congo, Mozambique, and other nations (*The Earth and Its Peoples*, 6th ed., pp. 850–853/7th ed., pp. 821–822; History Reasoning Skill—Causation; Learning Objectives ECON-6, SB-3, CUL-1; Key Concept 6.2.IV.C).

6. ANSWER: D. The French, with their policies of assimilation of colonial people, had colonies that wanted independence but in a more gradual manner. African leaders of these French colonies saw some advantages with maintaining connections to France ((*The Earth and Its Peoples*, 6th ed., pp. 850–853/7th ed., pp. 822–823; History Reasoning Skill—Contextualization; Learning Objectives SB-1,2,3; Key Concept 5.2.1.C).

27

THE MIDDLE EAST: C. 1900 TO THE PRESENT

KEY CONCEPTS

- The mandate system divided German colonies and the Ottoman Empire among the victorious Allies of World War I—France, Great Britain, Italy, and Japan.
- Mandates were to be administered with the goal of their eventual independence, but in fact they experienced recolonization.
- Tension between Zionism and Arab nationalism remains a constant source of conflict in the Middle East today.
- Despite gaining independence from European powers in the 1950s, and despite the rise of oil wealth in the region, most Middle Easterners have remained poor, and no Middle Eastern nation has become a major industrial or geopolitical power.
- Islamic terrorist groups that emerged during the Cold War and the post–Cold War era have aimed much of their anger at the State of Israel and at the United States, the lone superpower wielding influence in the Middle East.

KEY TERMS

- al Qaeda
- Balfour Declaration
- El Alamein
- League of Nations
- mandate system
- militant Islam
- Organization of Petroleum Exporting Countries (OPEC)
- Palestinian Liberation Organization (PLO)
- terrorism

- ◼ United Nations
- ◼ Zionism

The Middle East during the twentieth century is discussed in *The Earth and Its Peoples*, 6th edition, Chapters 27, 30, 31, and 32, and 7th edition, Chapters 28, 31, 32, and 33.

NATIONALISM AND THE DECLINE OF THE OTTOMAN EMPIRE

By the beginning of the twentieth century, the weakness of the Ottoman Empire had created a power vacuum in the Middle East. The rise of nationalism—the identification of people with a nation often centered on language or religion—had spread over much of Europe and by the turn of the century was affecting the Ottoman territories. The empire comprised dozens of ethnic, religious, and language groups, and officials were concerned about the impact of nationalistic sentiment. Would these minority groups remain loyal to the empire, or would they identify with others that proposed a new national identity?

The "sick man of Europe" began to receive its answer in the first decade of the twentieth century. In 1902, Macedonia rebelled and achieved independence a year later; in 1908, Austria-Hungary annexed the predominantly Muslim Bosnia. Italy conquered Libya in 1912, ending the Ottoman presence in North Africa. With the Balkan Wars (1912–1913), the Ottomans finally lost all control of Serbia, Bulgaria, and Romania. By 1913, all of the Ottoman European territories were either independent or under the control of a European power. Only Istanbul would remain within the empire.

Further demonstrating the weakening of the Ottoman Empire, European powers were meddling in various aspects of Ottoman affairs. To fund Ottoman modernization, loans from European nations were necessary, but these loans came at a price: European financiers had a controlling influence in tax collection, railroad construction, mine development, and public utilities. European nations also exerted their influence as they claimed to be protectors of different ethnic and religious minorities within the empire. In response to this outside control, the Young Turks, a nationalistic reform group, began to gain supporters. The Young Turks blamed Sultan Abdul Hamid for the empire's troubles and used their growing influence to have him replaced in 1909 by his brother Muhammad V Rashid (1909–1918). Reformers wanted to create a constitutional monarchy, and they helped reshape the bureaucracy, educational system, and law enforcement in an attempt to limit European influence. Because of the influence of nationalism, the empire increasingly saw itself as dominated by ethnic Turks, not as being multiethnic. With the support of the Young Turks, Ottoman officials began to crack down on ethnic minorities, such as Armenians and Greeks. These new reforms also came with a shift in European allies. The Young Turks, resenting French and British influence, began to align themselves more closely with Germany, which had been least involved in Ottoman internal affairs. As the world drifted toward World War I, this shift would lead the decaying Ottoman Empire to support the Central Powers during the war.

WORLD WAR I

The Middle East was central to the development of World War I. The vast majority of the region was under the control of the Ottoman Empire, which by the turn of the twentieth century had grown weak and was beginning to tear at the seams. Rebellions and loss of territory began in the provinces closest to Europe, such as Macedonia, Crete, and Albania. The internal problems of the Ottoman Empire provided a prime opportunity for the imperialistic-minded European powers to intervene and gain territory. It is at this particular time, long before the start of World War I, that alliances began taking shape. Each European power either coveted the territory of or sided with the ethnic minorities fighting for independence from the Turks. The Austro-Hungarian Empire, for example, sought the Slavic-populated regions of the Ottoman Empire, much to the annoyance of the Russians, who supported the Slavs. There was in essence both an internal and external tug of war.

The Ottoman Turks began to impose more restrictions on ethnic minorities, who were intent on pulling away and gaining independence. A group known as the Young Turks began a campaign for changes, among them the Turkification of ethnic minorities. This crackdown on minorities led to hundreds of thousands of Armenians being forcibly evacuated and massacred in what has recently become known as the Armenian holocaust. At the same time, Great Britain, Austria-Hungary, Russia, France, and Germany intervened as allies or rivals over Ottoman territory.

The spark for a world war came when the Archduke Franz Ferdinand of the Austro-Hungarian Empire was assassinated by ethnic Serbian nationalists angered by the presence of Austria-Hungary in the Balkans, which had recently gained independence from the Ottomans. The Russians supported the Slavic Serbians. The Germans supported the Austro-Hungarians. The British and French supported the Russians. The Ottoman Turks formed a secret alliance with Germany in hopes of gaining territory from the Russians. By the end of 1914, the Ottomans were heavily involved in the war; the following year the British unsuccessfully attempted to attack the Ottomans at Gallipoli, near Istanbul.

The British, however, did succeed in undermining the Ottomans by allying with disenchanted groups within the Ottoman Empire. In 1916, the British promised independence to Arabs who revolted against their Ottoman rulers. Hussein Ibn Ali and his son Faisal led the Arab armies against the Turks, which contributed to the defeat of the Ottoman Empire. The British also made promises to Jewish minorities in eastern and central Europe who were calling for the creation of a Jewish state in the Jewish ancestral homeland of Palestine. This nationalist movement, known as **Zionism**, appealed to many European Jews as a solution to the problem of anti-Semitism in Europe. Just before the British armies gained control of Palestine in 1917, Foreign Secretary Sir Arthur Balfour wrote a statement, later known as the Balfour Declaration, which simultaneously gave sanction to Zionism while promising not to infringe on the rights of current Palestinian residents.

At the end of World War I, much to the dismay of many, independence did not come to the Middle East. Instead, the Allied Powers claimed the former Ottoman territories as mandates. The mandate system, essentially a compromise made at the Paris Peace Conference, stipulated that the former German colonies and the Ottoman Empire would be divided among the Allied victors of World War I—namely, France, Great Britain, Italy, and Japan. All mandates were to be overseen by the **League of Nations**, and they were to be administered with the goal of eventual independence for the territory. In regard to the Middle East, the mandate system called for temporary British and French control. The British took control of Palestine, Iraq, and Trans-Jordan. The French took control of Syria and Lebanon.

AP® Tip

You should be able to discuss the changes and continuities from colonialism under the Ottoman Empire to the mandate system under the British and French. You will have to draw upon some of your knowledge of the previous period when discussing the Ottoman Empire. However, you will be expected to detail changes and continuities regarding political leadership and power, as well as the economic and social impact on the people of the Middle East.

THE INTERWAR PERIOD

World War I proved the death knell for the once-powerful Ottoman Empire. But instead of independence, the people of the Middle East found themselves recolonized by the very group that claimed to fight for their freedom, the Allied Powers. Recolonization, which the Allied Powers accomplished by means of the mandate system, gave rise to various revolutionary nationalist movements throughout the region. One of the first nationalist uprisings erupted at the heart of the former Ottoman Empire. In 1919, Mustafa Kemal formed a nationalist government for Turkey and by 1922 had regained the territory of Anatolia and Constantinople. Like the Young Turks who had preceded him, Kemal began to modernize Turkey, creating a secular state with a constitution modeled after those of the Western powers. He later took as his family name Atatürk—"father of the Turks."

A similar trend occurred in Persia when resentment toward British domination came to a head in 1921. The nationalist movement, led by army officer Reza Khan, overthrew the Qajar dynasty and kicked out the British. Once in control, Reza Khan became known as Reza Shah Pahlavi, and Persia became known as Iran. Like Mustafa Kemal Atatürk of Turkey, Reza Shah proceeded to modernize Iran by creating a secular state based on Western ideals.

Most nationalist movements in the Middle East, however, did not find success. The French crushed nationalist uprisings in Lebanon and Syria, and while Iraq and Egypt were declared independent, Britain maintained

---

AP® is a trademark registered by the College Board, which is not affiliated with, and does not endorse, this product.

economic and military control. There was one state, however, that managed to attain full independence. In 1932, Prince Ibn Saud united the many Arabian tribes and founded the Kingdom of Saudi Arabia. When oil reserves were discovered in 1938, Saudi Arabia gained global importance.

Despite the lack of independence, massive changes occurred in the Middle East during the interwar period. Encouraged by Zionism and the **Balfour Declaration**, thousands of European Jews emigrated to Palestine in hopes of creating a Jewish state.

The British, however, attempted to limit immigration so as not to alienate the Arabs. In the end, both Arabs and Jews were angered by British rule. Jewish immigration was only one of many changes occurring in the region. Numerous people moved to the cities during the interwar years, causing many cities to double in size. While population in the Middle East doubled, nomads were becoming a dying breed, and Western ideals were becoming quite popular.

WORLD WAR II AND INDEPENDENCE MOVEMENTS

The Second World War would have tremendous consequences for the Middle East. Because much of the region was under the mandate of either France or Great Britain, its fate was inextricably tied to the Allied Powers. Unlike the First World War, fighting in the Second World War was widespread around the globe. As the imperial ambitions of Germany and Italy grew, fighting eventually spread to the Middle East and North Africa. Italy attacked Egypt from Somaliland in hopes of gaining territory, but British forces eventually overpowered the Italians, then proceeded to conquer the Italian colonies of Somaliland and Libya. Despite being tied up fighting the Soviets on the eastern front, Germany sent troops to help the Italians. With better intelligence in the region and a greater supply of material, the British eventually defeated the Germans at **El Alamein**, Egypt, and expelled the Nazis from North Africa. German losses on the eastern front in Stalingrad and in Egypt at El Alamein weakened the Nazis and precipitated the end of Nazi expansion and the eventual downfall of their regime. World War II also signaled the downfall of European colonial power, even in the form of the **mandate system**. The Middle East, however, would struggle to define independence in the wake of the emergence of the United States and the Soviet Union as the two global superpowers.

THE COLD WAR AND DECOLONIZATION

After World War II, Syria and Lebanon gained independence, and by the 1950s, Egypt, Iraq, and Jordan began removing British military presence and control. However, countries such as Jordan often depended on their former colonial ruler for financial assistance. Many leaders in the Middle East attempted both to break from colonial dependency and to extract money by playing the two superpowers against each other. This was most certainly the case in Egypt, as both Presidents Nasir and Sadat gained assistance from the superpowers. In order to increase its industrial potential, Nasir sought assistance from the United States to build a dam at Aswan; at the same time, he courted the Soviet Union for weapons. This infuriated the United States, which then reneged on the dam project. In response, the Soviet Union offered to complete the project. In many ways, Egypt exemplifies the Cold War in the Middle East. Both superpowers offered financial and military assistance in order to gain favor and influence in the region. However, regional leaders also attempted to gain power and assistance from the two superpowers by aligning sometimes with one, sometimes with the other.

While the Cold War did spill into the Middle East, affecting all areas of military and political life, the post–World War II Middle East was primarily dominated by two phenomena: the creation of Israel and the realization of Middle East oil capacity. After the fall of the Nazi regime in Germany, intense pressure to resettle more European Jewish refugees in Palestine grew. Tension between Palestinian Arabs and Jewish immigrants grew more intense as the **United Nations** deliberated on splitting Palestine into two nations: one Jewish and one Arab. In 1947, the United Nations voted in favor of partitioning Palestine into the two states. This attempt to solve a crisis created a larger one. Many Arabs believed the division of land was unfair, and they took up arms to fight the Jewish State of Israel, which declared its independence in May 1948. More than 700,000 Palestinian refugees fled to United Nations refugee camps in the neighboring countries of Jordan, Syria, Lebanon, and Egypt. Israel often had the assistance of two global powers, the United States and Great Britain, and thus usually prevailed. However, Israel constantly feared attack from neighboring Arab nations. In 1967, this fear resulted in Israel preemptively attacking Egyptian and Syrian air bases. The conflict, known as the Six-Day War, ended with Israel taking control of Arab territory in the West Bank, the Golan Heights, the Gaza Strip, and the Sinai Peninsula. Israel also won control of all of Jerusalem, which had previously been split with Jordan and Palestinians in the West Bank. The war produced an even greater number of Palestinian refugees and deeper conflicts over the Jewish and Muslim holy city of Jerusalem. The war also resulted in acts of **terrorism** against Israel and guerilla warfare by the **Palestinian Liberation Organization (PLO)**, led by Yasir Arafat, and by Israeli attacks on Palestinians in Gaza and the West Bank. Fighting between Israelis and the Palestinians continues to this day.

The end of World War II coincided with the full realization of oil wealth in the Persian Gulf states. As the global demand for oil rose, the Persian Gulf states of Bahrain, Iran, Iraq, Kuwait, Saudi Arabia, Qatar, and United Arab Emirates joined other oil-producing nations in 1960 to form the **Organization of Petroleum Exporting Countries (OPEC)**. The purpose of OPEC was to promote the collective interests of the oil producers, one of which was the support of the Palestinian Arabs in their struggle against Israel. Thus in 1973 OPEC placed an embargo on the United States and the Netherlands for their support of Israel. In 1974, OPEC vastly increased its oil prices. Oil became a weapon in the Cold War politics of the Middle East. It also allowed for nations in the Middle East to gain wealth and positions of power in global politics.

Oil clearly made the Middle East a region of interest for both the United States and the Soviet Union. Both superpowers became directly involved in military action within the region. In 1979, revolution erupted in Iran, at least in part because of covert American intervention to help the Shah of Iran retain his throne despite popular discontent. American backing of the corrupt and inefficient ruler led to his eventual overthrow. In the Shah's place,

Ayatollah Khomeini, a Shi'ite cleric, rose to power. He established an anti-Western, conservative Islamic republic. Like other Middle Eastern nations moving away from Westernization, Iran scaled back many political and social gains and compelled women to wear modest Islamic dress. Iran vehemently opposed Israel and its perceived backer, the United States. Bordering the Soviet Union and with enormous oil reserves, Iran was of great strategic and economic importance to the United States. Thus, the Iranian revolution proved to be a black eye for the United States. The final blow to American prestige came when Iranian radicals held fifty-two American diplomats as hostages for more than a year.

The Iranian revolution also led to war. Its neighbor, Iraq, invaded Iran in 1980 in hopes of toppling the Islamic regime. A secular nation based on Arab nationalism, Iraq was controlled by Saddam Hussein, a Sunni. Hussein feared that Iran's Shi'ite rulers would influence Iraq's Shi'ites, who formed a majority of the Iraqi population. By 1986, the United States was lending its support to Hussein. The Iraq–Iran conflict, lasting eight long years, featured covert American and Soviet action as well as weapons supplied by the superpowers.

AP® Tip

You should be able to analyze the reasons for the rise of Islamic regimes and Islamic fundamentalism in the Middle East during the Cold War era. Be prepared to discuss poverty and the sense of global powerlessness as an impetus for social reform. You will also be expected to explain how religion was used as a unifying factor within Middle Eastern nations.

While the situation in Iran embarrassed the United States, Afghanistan was even more disastrous for the Soviet Union. Like Iran, Afghanistan bordered the Soviet Union. In 1979, the Soviets sent troops into Afghanistan to support a young communist regime that was fighting a small band of local guerillas. The guerrillas, backed by the United States, proved unbelievably resilient. The war was both costly and embarrassing for the Soviet Union, as fighting dragged on for more than ten years. In 1989, Soviet leaders withdrew their troops because the war in Afghanistan was causing domestic discontent in the Soviet Union.

THE POST–COLD WAR WORLD

The end of the Cold War did not bring peace to the Middle East. Nor did it bring stability. Despite the accumulation of oil wealth, many Middle Easterners remained poor. Moreover, conflicts that arose or existed at the end of World War II remained unsolved by the dawn of the new millennium. As in other parts of the world, some political groups in the Middle East used terrorism to proclaim and advance their political objectives. The premise of terrorism is that a government loses its legitimacy when it cannot protect its citizens from horrible acts of violence. Superpowers might have the technological ability to wage war with minimal casualties to themselves, but terrorism can be effective in the hands of those who are unable to match the might of stronger nations.

Because it is hard to combat, terrorism became a popular strategy by the end of the twentieth century. The most prominent groups using terrorist strategies were Palestinian groups angry at the existence of Israel. In 1968, Palestinian groups were involved in airplane hijackings; in 1972, their capture and murder of eleven Israeli athletes at the Munich Olympic Games generated global news coverage and struck fear around the world. Terrorist attacks on Israel and Israeli incursions into the West Bank and Gaza to kill suspected terrorists have become the pattern that continues to the present day. The controversy over the existence of Israel remains the paramount issue within the Middle East.

The first major post–Cold War conflict in the Middle East, however, was the Persian Gulf War of 1990–1991. Like most conflicts in the region, what began as a local problem quickly took on global implications. During the summer of 1990, Iraq invaded Kuwait in hopes of gaining control of Kuwaiti oil fields. Saddam Hussein was angered by the Kuwaitis' refusal to reduce Iraq's debt. Hussein believed that Iraq, being much larger and more powerful than Kuwait, would quickly and easily defeat the Kuwaitis. However, Saudi Arabia, another neighboring oil power, felt threatened by the actions of Iraq. Saudi Arabia appealed to the United States, its ally and the sole superpower, to intervene. The United States gathered a coalition of nations, amassed a large military force with sophisticated weapons, and had the approval of the United Nations, as well as various Islamic nations within the region. In early 1991, President George H. W. Bush ordered the attack on Iraq. The victory was quick and decisive, as the American-led forces drove Iraq out of Kuwait. The United States enforced a no-fly zone, which restricted Iraqi military movements, but it did not remain as occupiers, and Saddam Hussein was allowed to remain in power. Nonetheless, the coalition victory in the Persian Gulf War restored American military confidence after Vietnam and signaled to the world that the United States was the unrivaled global superpower.

Despite its efforts to "win the hearts and minds" of the people in the Middle East, the United States has often been viewed as an unwelcome intruder within the region. For instance, **al Qaeda**, the terrorist network formerly led by Usama bin Laden, has claimed responsibility for attacks on various American embassies and military targets throughout the Islamic world. Through al Qaeda, bin Laden used **militant Islam** as a rallying cry for Muslims around the world, which many desperate and disenchanted Muslims have heeded. This globalized terrorism has struck fear in the United States and other Western powers. Bin Laden has successfully united people beyond traditional nation-state boundaries and beyond Arab identity. In September 2001, terrorists sponsored by al Qaeda attacked within the United States. In response, American and NATO forces joined with Afghan opposition groups to overthrow the Islamic fundamentalist regime of the Taliban, which had been providing refuge for bin Laden in Afghanistan. This, the first effort in what President George W. Bush has called the War on Terror, overthrew the Taliban but bin Laden eluded capture until 2011 when he was killed by American forces in Pakistan.

The War on Terror spilled into Iraq when the United States, claiming that Saddam Hussein was supporting terrorists and harboring weapons of mass destruction, invaded Iraq and overthrew Saddam Hussein in the spring of 2003. This attack on Iraq has become known as the Second Persian Gulf War. This time, however, American forces remained. Many Middle Easterners regard the Second Persian Gulf War as another example of American aggression in the region. Iraq remains an unstable nation with constant fighting and frequent attacks by Iraqi insurgents against both American forces and Iraqi civilians. Like Israel and oil, Iraq has become a central issue in the Middle East.

Content Review Questions

Questions 1–3 refer to the following passage.

It is obvious that the need for implementing laws was not exclusive to the prophet's age and that this need continues because Islam is not limited by time or place. Because Islam is immortal, it must be implemented and observed forever. If what was permissible by Muhammad is permissible until the day of resurrection [the end of time] and what was forbidden by Muhammad is forbidden to the day of resurrection, then Muhammad's restrictions must not be suspended, his teachings must not be neglected, punishment must not be abandoned, tax collection must not be stopped and defense of the nation of the Muslims and of their lands must not be abandoned. The beliefs that Islam came for a limited period and for a certain place violates the essentials of the Islamic beliefs. Considering that the implementation forever of laws after the venerable prophet, . . . one of the essentials of life, then it is necessary for government to assist and for this government to have the qualities of an executive and administrative authority. Without this, social chaos, corruption and ideological and moral deviation would prevail. This can be prevented only through the formation of a just government that runs all aspects of life.

The Timelessness of Islamic Law, Ayatollah Ruhollah Khomeini, 1970

Source: Ruhollah Khomeini, *Islamic Government*. U.S. Government Publication, *Translations on the Near East and Northern Africa*, no. 1897, Joint Publications Research Service, no. 72663, Arlington, VA: 1979, pp. 3–5, 15, 18, 52, 53, 55–57, 61.

(*Human Records Documents*, Cengage, pp. 445–446)

1. How did Ayatollah Ruhollah Khomeini come to power?
   (A) He participated in a free election that included the people of Iran.
   (B) He led a revolution to oust the Shah of Iran.
   (C) He claimed to be in a dynastic line to succeed the previous ruler.
   (D) He managed large businesses, influencing the political climate of Iran.

2. How did U.S. foreign policy toward Iran differ from Soviet policy in Afghanistan during the 1980s?
   (A) The United States used military force more than the Soviets.
   (B) The United States had more restraint than the Soviets.
   (C) The United States depended more on treaty agreements than the Soviets.
   (D) The United States used economic aid more than the Soviets.

3. It is clear from the document that the Ayatollah Ruhollah Khomeini would
   (A) support Islamic law.
   (B) be ready for diplomatic relations with the United States.
   (C) prefer to have a society open to all religions.
   (D) like to implement a government that is governed by representatives.

Questions 4–6 refer to the following passage.

. . . Among the Ottoman rulers there were some who endeavored to form a gigantic empire by seizing Germany and Western Europe. One of these rulers hoped to unite the whole Islamic world in one body, to lead it and govern it. For this purpose he obtained control of Syria and Egypt and assumed the title of Caliph. Another Sultan pursued the twofold aim, on the one hand of gaining the mastery over Europe, and on the other of subjecting the Islamic world to his authority and government. The continuous counterattacks from the West, the discontent and insurrections in the Muslim world, as well as the dissensions between the various elements which this policy had artificially brought together had the ultimate result of burying the Ottoman Empire, in the same way as many others, under the pall of history. . . .

To unite different nations under one common name, to give these different elements equal rights, subject them to the same conditions and thus to found a mighty State is a brilliant and attractive political ideal; but it is a misleading one. It is an unrealizable aim to attempt to unite in one tribe the various races existing on the earth, thereby abolishing all boundaries. Herein lies a truth which past centuries . . . have clearly shown in dark and sanguinary events.

In order that our nation should be able to live a happy, strenuous, and permanent life, it is necessary that the State should pursue an exclusively national policy and that this policy should be in perfect agreement with our internal organization and be based on it. When I speak of national policy, I mean it in this sense: To work within our national boundaries for the real happiness and welfare of the nation and the country by relying on our own strength in order to retain our existence. But not to lead the people to follow fictitious aims, of whatever nature, which could only bring them misfortune, and expect from the civilized world civilized human treatment, friendship based on mutuality. . . .

Nationalism and Empire, Mustafa Kemal Atatürk, 1929

Source: Mustafa Kemal, *A Speech Delivered by Ghazi Mustapha Kemal*, Leipzig: F. F. Koehler, 1929, pp. 376–379, 589–594, 717, 721–722. (*Human Records Documents*, Cengage, pp. 378–379)

4. The Turkish leader, Mustafa Kemal Atatürk, a modernizer, did which of the following?
    (A) Expelled the British and reintroduced Islamic Shari'a
    (B) Declared Turkey a secular republic and introduced European laws
    (C) Supported modernist architectural styles and imported American literature
    (D) Established Islamic schools throughout Turkey and redistributed money to the peasantry

5. What allowed Atatürk to come to power in Turkey in 1923?
    (A) The Soviet Union supported Atatürk militarily.
    (B) The United States supported Atatürk economically to rebuild the infrastructure of Turkey.
    (C) The fall of the Ottoman Empire left a possibility for Atatürk to gain power.
    (D) Atatürk was able to seize control of all businesses owned by Muslims.

6. All of the following were reforms instituted by Atatürk EXCEPT
   (A) a new alphabet.
   (B) abolition of the Sultanate.
   (C) a drive toward literacy.
   (D) a codification of Islamic law.

Answers

1. ANSWER: B. The Ayatollah Ruhollah Khomeini led a successful revolution to oust the U.S.-backed Shah of Iran in 1979. The Ayatollah was appointed by an Assembly of Experts, though he did promise free elections without interference from clergy when he was leader (*The Earth and Its Peoples*, 6th ed., pp. 871-873/7th ed., pp. 839–841; History Reasoning Skill—Causation; Learning Objectives CUL-1, SB-3; Key Concept 6.2.II.B).

2. ANSWER: B. After the Iranian Revolution in 1979 and the hostage crisis, the United States pursued a lengthy process of restrained responses. The Soviets invaded Afghanistan (*The Earth and Its Peoples*, 6th ed., pp. 871–873/7th ed., pp. 839–841; History Reasoning Skill—Comparison; Learning Objective CUL-1, SB-3; Key Concept 6.2.II.B).

3. ANSWER: A. The document states that the government of Iran should run all aspects of people's daily lives in Iran. The Ayatollah would only be open to a government that is controlled by Shari'a law (*The Earth and Its Peoples*, 6th ed., pp. 871–873/7th ed., pp. 839–841; History Disciplinary Practice—Analyzing Historical Evidence; Learning Objectives CUL-1, SB-3; Key Concept 6.2.II.B).

4. ANSWER: B. Mustafa Kemal Atatürk was among a growing number of leaders who were pushing to westernize their nation in order to usher in a modern era and compete with the Western powers (*The Earth and Its Peoples*, 6th ed., pp. 768–769/7th ed., pp. 744–747; History Disciplinary Practice—Analyzing Historical Evidence; Learning Objectives SB-4; Key Concept 6.2.I.A).s

5. ANSWER: C. After the fall of the Ottoman Empire, Atatürk was able to successfully organize military operations and consolidate power to unite Turkey. Once in power, Atatürk instituted many reforms (*The Earth and Its Peoples*, 6th ed., pp. 768-769/7th ed., pp. 744–747; History Reasoning Skill—Contextualization; Learning Objective SB-4; Key Concept 6.2.I.A).

6. ANSWER: D. Atatürk preferred a more westernized, modern Turkish society. As a result, he instituted the implementation of a new alphabet, a drive toward literacy, and the abolition of the Sultanate, which was the governance system widely accepted in the Ottoman Empire (*The Earth and Its Peoples*, 6th ed., pp. 768–769/7th ed., pp. 744–747; History Reasoning Skill—Causation; Learning Objective SB-4; Key Concept 6.2.I.A).

28

ASIA:
C. 1900 TO THE PRESENT

KEY CONCEPTS

- Despite many similarities in culture and civilization, Japan's and China's modern history took completely different paths; Japan quickly rose to become a modern industrial power, whereas China experienced foreign control and revolution.
- The Chinese revolution led to the fall of the Qing and the end of the dynastic system in 1911, but the country was unable to unite under a single national government as regional powers competed for control.
- The Nanjing massacre is often referred to as the "Hidden Holocaust" because of its similarities to the Holocaust in Europe.
- The surrender of Japan at the end of World War II thrust China into a civil war that had been brewing for decades. With greater popular support and seized Japanese weapons, the Communists overpowered the Guomindang. In 1949, Mao announced the founding of the People's Republic of China.
- Despite increased violence and partition into the two states of India and Pakistan, Indian independence in 1947 served as a model for other anticolonial movements around the world.
- While the Cold War caused massive deaths in Korea and Indochina, it also served as a catalyst in transforming numerous Asian economies.
- Japan, South Korea, Hong Kong, and Singapore all experienced rapid economic growth on the heels of the Cold War.

KEY TERMS

- Asian Tigers
- Bandung Conference
- Battle of Midway
- Boxer Rebellion
- Cultural Revolution
- Great Leap Forward
- Guomindang
- Indian National Congress
- Kashmir
- keiretsu
- Korean War
- Long March
- newly industrialized economies (NIEs)
- nonaligned nations
- Tiananmen Square
- Third World
- Twenty-One Demands
- Viet Cong
- Viet Minh
- Vietnam War

Asia during the twentieth century is covered in *The Earth and Its Peoples*, 6th edition, Chapters 25, 27–32, and 7th edition, Chapters 26, 28–33.

THE COLLAPSE OF THE QING DYNASTY

For many people in China, the **Boxer Rebellion** was final evidence of the need to get rid of the Qing dynasty and modernize their country. When Cixi died in 1908, a growing nationalist political movement, the Revolutionary Alliance, led by Sun Yat-sen, prepared to overthrow the Qing. Sun's thinking, combining nationalism, socialism, and traditional Confucian philosophy, appealed to many, but Sun also had to deal with the regional military warlords, who had modernized their armies and were not inclined to give up power to a new central government. In 1911 when one of these regional militias rebelled, the most powerful warlord, Yuan Shikai, refused to defend the Qing; the boy-emperor Puyi was forced to abdicate, finally ending the Qing dynasty. A revolutionary assembly elected Sun president of the new Chinese republic in 1911, but with no military force to defend his position, Sun stepped down in favor of Yuan, who became president. Sun's nationalist supporters formed the Guomindang (National People's Party), which Yuan, resistant to Western-style reform, repressed. The great dynastic system in China had come to an end, but as World War I approached, China remained a nation controlled by regional powers, both internal and external.

WORLD WAR I

The twentieth century proved quite different for Japan and China. Japan became an industrialized power facing little intervention from the European imperial powers. China, on the other hand, began the new millennium militarily defeated by a coalition of various Western powers and Japan—all bent on staking claims on the Chinese mainland. This event, known as the Boxer Rebellion, caused many Chinese to demand revolutionary change, overthrow of the Qing dynasty, and modernization. In 1908, Sun Yat-sen formed the Revolutionary Alliance, or **Guomindang**, which by 1911 had overthrown the last Qing ruler. To unify the country, Sun shared power with Yuan Shikai, a brilliant military leader and the most powerful regional general. But instead of peace, a struggle ensued between the military, led by Yuan, and the Guomindang, led by Sun.

The struggle in Japan was quite different. Industrialization programs implemented by the Meiji rulers were continued at the turn of the twentieth century. The Japanese economy, in fact, was growing faster than that of any of the Western powers. Sudden prosperity caused tensions within Japanese society. Many young urbanites who adopted Western ways and lifestyles clashed with traditionalists. Industrialization also caused tensions between the rising industrial conglomerates, which controlled most of Japan's industry and commerce, and poor farmers, who made up more than half of the population. Nonetheless, Japan's prosperity largely depended on foreign trade, so like the Western powers, Japan depended on its ability to colonize resource-rich territories.

In that regard, World War I worked in Japan's favor. Having joined the war on the side of the Allies, Japan enjoyed rising demand for its products. More important, the war was an opportunity to gain territory. The Japanese quickly conquered the German colonies in the northern Pacific and on the coast of China. By 1915, Japan had extended its influence to the rest of China by imposing the **Twenty-One Demands**, which guaranteed Japanese control and access to resource-rich territories in China. In response, boycotts and anti-Japanese riots erupted throughout China.

India provides another example of the struggle against foreign influence in Asia. India had been under British colonial rule since 1857. By the turn of the century, many Indians had learned English and adopted British ideals and ways. Nonetheless, they confronted racial quotas and other methods used to bar Indians from jobs and even social clubs. Despite appeals from the Hindu-dominated Indian National Congress, founded in 1885, and the All-India Muslim League, founded in 1906, British colonial rule continued to favor British citizens. Nonetheless, Indians supported British efforts during World War I. More than a million Indians volunteered for the British Army, and millions of others contributed money and other resources. Still the British made only vague references to eventual independence of India.

> ## AP® Tip
>
> Japan and China had vastly different experiences in the
> modern era. The former rose quickly as an industrial power,
> while the latter suffered chaos, foreign control, and
> revolution. Be prepared to compare the modern experiences
> of both nations, including their various responses to
> Western influence and their roles in the world wars.

THE INTERWAR PERIOD

China's hope for reclaiming its territory rested in the hands of the Allies,
most of whom had played a part in forcing foreign influence on China at the
turn of the twentieth century. But at the end of the war, it was decided at the
Paris Peace Conference to give Japan continued control over the German
holdings in northern parts of China. Protests led by students began in Beijing
on May 4, 1919, then spread across China to become the May Fourth
Movement. A new generation was no longer willing to tolerate foreign
control and influence within their nation, and it was tired of the Chinese
regional leadership. Perhaps sensing the growing disdain within Chinese
society, Sun Yat-sen restructured the Guomindang along Leninist ideals. Sun
was succeeded by Jiang Jieshi (Chiang Kai-shek) in 1925. A skilled military
leader, Jiang crushed the regional lords and united the nation. Jiang's goal
was modernization, but after crushing the Communist party and banning
labor unions, his government was left with corrupt opportunists and
incompetent administrators. As a result, modernization did not come to
China.

China, because it was not dependent on foreign trade, was not much
affected by the Depression, but it did face numerous political challenges. In
1927, Jiang Jieshi's government began arresting and executing members of
the Communist party and labor unions. Remaining Communists fled to the
remote mountain region of Jiangxi to join Mao Zedong, a leader in the
Chinese Communist party who had gained favor among peasants with his
calls for social reform. The Chinese government, concerned about the
growing popularity of Mao, pursued the Communists. In 1934, the
Guomindang army surrounded the Communists, who escaped and began a
one-year journey, the so-called **Long March**. At its end, in the remote
northwest province of Shaanxi, only four thousand of the original one
hundred thousand remained.

Dependent on exports to pay for food and fuel, Japan suffered greatly
during the Depression. Hardest hit were farmers and fishermen, who saw
their incomes steadily drop. The economic struggles created a reaction that in
many ways mirrored that in Germany. Japanese ultranationalists believed
that Japan could end its dependence on foreign trade by creating a colonial
empire much like those of Great Britain and France. But much of Asia was
already colonized by Europeans and Americans. Japan's colonial ambitions
would inevitably conflict with the desires of its World War I partners. The

---

AP® is a trademark registered by the College Board, which is not affiliated with, and does not endorse, this product.

colonial conquest of the entire resource-rich province of Manchuria, the first step in Japan's quest to dominate Asia, was condemned by the League of Nations; in response, Japan simply withdrew from the League. The conquest fortified the Japanese military, which began to encroach on the civilian-controlled government.

While the Guomindang fought the Communists, it tried to deal with external pressures. In 1937, Japanese troops attacked Beijing and within four months held Beijing, as well as Shanghai and other coastal cities. The fighting grew increasingly violent during the winter of 1937–1938 when the Japanese took over Nanjing, killing more than two hundred thousand Chinese civilians and prisoners, raping upward of twenty thousand Chinese women, and looting and burning much of the city. Both Jiang Jieshi's government troops and Mao's Communist troops had little success in fighting the Japanese. The government forces retreated to the central mountains of Sichuan. Jiang resorted to drafting men for the military and raising taxes despite a famine. In Shaanxi, Mao set up a Communist government and built up his military while the majority of China was under Japanese control. The Sino-Japanese War would last eight years, 1937–1945.

As the Chinese fought against the Japanese in Manchuria, Indians struggled against British colonial rule. In 1919, a British colonial officer ordered his troops to fire on a peaceful crowd of ten thousand demonstrators, killing 379 Indians and wounding 1,200. Demonstrations spread across the nation in response, but it was six months before the British appointed someone to investigate the massacre. In the years following the massacre, the British gradually and reluctantly admitted Indians to the Civil Service and the officer corps. The demands of the Indian National Congress and the Muslim League were finally coming to realization. Areas such as national education and public works were slowly placed under Indian control. Indians also fought for the right to erect tariff barriers to protect budding local industries, which in turn helped ward off the Depression. However, it was Mohandas Gandhi who provided the moral leadership for independence. Gandhi's insistence on nonviolence and his affinity for the poor won him admirers worldwide. During the 1930s, Gandhi led numerous fasts and marches to protest colonial rule, and he was frequently arrested and jailed. Much to the dismay of the British, jailing Gandhi only made him more popular, both at home and abroad. Gandhi would eventually pass leadership to Jawaharlal Nehru, who is credited with leading India into independence and modernity.

WORLD WAR II AND INDEPENDENCE MOVEMENTS

On the eve of World War II, Indians still had little true power. Indeed, in 1939, the British viceroy declared war on behalf of India without consulting any Indians. A wave of protests ensued as Gandhi and other leaders demanded full independence immediately. The Indian National Congress opposed the war, and many of its members resigned from positions within the regional governments. A small number of Indians even joined the Japanese in order to fight against their colonizers. Still, as in World War I, Indians made an enormous contribution to the Allied war effort. More than two million Indians fought for the British, while large amounts of Indian raw materials were used to aid the Allied war machine. In the province of Bengal, more than two million Indians starved to death in a war-related famine.

At the end of the war, Britain began preparing India for independence. However, tensions between Hindus and Muslims were growing; Muslims feared that the Hindu-dominated **Indian National Congress** would not share power with the Muslim League. Despite Gandhi's appeals for tolerance, violent rioting broke out between Hindus and Muslims. In 1947, the Indian National Congress and the Muslim League agreed to partition the nation into two states: Hindu-dominated India and the Muslim nation of Pakistan. The split, however, came with continued violence between Hindus and Muslims. In protest, Gandhi refused to attend the independence day celebrations. The split also resulted in waves of refugees, as Hindus fled Muslim areas and Muslims fled Hindu areas. India did, however, annex the province of Kashmir, a resource-rich region in the north dominated by Muslims. While World War II helped usher in Indian independence, it came at a high cost in lives, violence, and sectarianism.

World War II provided Japan the opportunity to expand its colonial ambitions beyond China. While European nations were embroiled in conflict, Japan took aim at the European colonies in Southeast Asia. Like Britain, France, and the Netherlands, Japan coveted the rubber, oil, and other vital resources of Southeast Asia. When France fell in 1940, Japan moved in to occupy Indochina. Dismayed by Japan's increasing power, the United States and Great Britain responded by halting shipments of steel, iron, oil, and other products that Japan urgently needed. The Japanese chose to retaliate in December 1941 with a surprise attack on Pearl Harbor, an American naval base in Hawaii. They then proceeded to attack various European colonies in Southeast Asia. By March 1942, Japan occupied Thailand, the Philippines, Malaya, and all of the Dutch East Indies. While Asians initially viewed the Japanese as heroes who had liberated them from white colonialism, Japanese rule grew harsh, and Asians came to despise Japanese rule.

Japanese victories in Asia were geographically more extensive than those of the Nazis in Europe. The United States joined Britain in battling the Japanese in Asia, and by the spring of 1942, the United States had bombed Tokyo and defeated the Japanese in the Coral Sea. Months later, in June, the Japanese suffered one of their largest defeats at the **Battle of Midway**. Allied bombing and submarine warfare cut Japan off from vital shipments of oil and other raw materials, severely damaging the economy and military. In August 1945, the United States dropped an atomic bomb on the Japanese city of Hiroshima. Three days later, a second bomb was dropped on Nagasaki. More than 200,000 Japanese civilians died as a result of the bombings. The massive civilian death toll convinced the Japanese emperor to surrender, signaling the official end of World War II.

Japanese surrender sparked a struggle for power in China. The Guomindang and the Communist forces began a civil war that would last four years. Although the Guomindang had more troops, weapons, and the support of the United States, it continued its harsh and corrupt practices. In certain regions, the Guomindang looted, confiscated supplies, and taxed the Chinese people more heavily than the Japanese had. The Communists, on the other hand, worked for the support of the people—in Manchuria, for example, the Communists redistributed land to the peasants—and the widespread support of the citizenry proved far more valuable than the Guomindang's superior weaponry. In 1947, Communist forces surrounded Nanjing, and by 1949 the Guomindang armies were collapsing and in full retreat. High-ranking members of the Guomindang fled to Taiwan, where they remained, protected by the U.S. Navy. On October 1, 1949, the Communist forces, led by Mao, announced the founding of the People's Republic of China.

THE COLD WAR AND DECOLONIZATION

Despite defeat in World War II, Japan served as an inspiration to many in Southeast Asia for the numerous, albeit temporary, defeats it inflicted on the British, French, and Dutch. Anticolonial movements gained plenty of steam after the war, leading to the independence of the Philippines in 1946, Burma and the Malay Federation in 1948, and Indonesia in 1949. However, many anticolonial leaders, attracted to communism, found themselves caught in the Cold War conflicts of the United States and the Soviet Union.

The end of World War II left the Soviet Union in control of the northern portion of Korea and the United States in control of the southern portion. No agreement could be made on nationwide elections, so in 1948 two nations were established: communist North Korea and capitalist South Korea. Two years later, North Korean troops invaded South Korea, sparking the **Korean War**. Almost immediately American troops came to the aid of South Korea, while North Korea received assistance from communist China. The struggle remained a deadlock after three years. Finally, a truce agreed on in 1953 fixed the boundary at the thirty-eighth parallel—the line established by the Americans and the Soviets in 1948. No one benefited from the war except, ironically, the Japanese, whose economy was stimulated by American military supply purchases and the purchases of American servicemen in Japan while on leave from Korea.

The Cold War also allowed Japan to concentrate on developing industry, trade, and new markets throughout Asia. The government gave assistance to the electrical, steel, and shipbuilding industries, all of which would help make Japan a global economic superpower by 1975.

The Cold War conflict in **Vietnam**, then part of French Indochina, proved far different from that of Korea. The struggle began at the end of World War II when the French refused to relinquish their colony. Led by Ho Chi Minh and helped by the Chinese, revolutionaries known as the **Viet Minh** eventually overthrew the French. The Viet Minh gained control in the north while a noncommunist government was in control of the south. The split led to a civil war. The United States, which had initially supported the French, gave support to the South Vietnamese government of Ngo Dinh Diem and, intent on stopping the spread of communism, increased its involvement in Vietnam. However, the Viet Minh and the communist guerilla group in South Vietnam, known as the **Viet Cong**, were unstoppable. In 1973, after massive casualties on both sides, the United States ended its military involvement in Vietnam. Two years later, Vietnam was united when South Vietnam was taken over by the communist forces of the Viet Cong and the Viet Minh government of the North.

While the Soviet Union was the global symbol and propagator of communism, China was the primary communist player in Asia, involved in both Vietnam and Korea. Indeed China received aid and support from the Soviet Union, even though it defined communism in a slightly different manner. While communism in China focused largely on the peasantry, communism in the Soviet Union ignored peasants and favored the urban working class. In 1958, Mao introduced his **Great Leap Forward**, an attempt to make China an industrial power by means of collectivizing agriculture and village-level industries. The Great Leap Forward, however, resulted not in industrialization but in more than thirty million deaths, mainly from famine. In 1966, Mao introduced the **Cultural Revolution** in an attempt to mobilize youth and rekindle revolutionary spirit, but this program led to factionalism, violence, incarcerations, and executions. By 1971, half a million Chinese had died as a result of the Cultural Revolution. Nonetheless, China continued on a path different from that of the Soviet Union, a path that led to reestablishing ties with the United States in 1971 and occupying a permanent seat in the United Nations Security Council.

While the conflict between capitalists and Communists ensnared most of Asia, partition and religious sectarianism afflicted South Asia. Even after independence, tensions between Hindus and Muslims in India and Pakistan resumed. Matters were made worse when the Hindu ruler of Kashmir chose to join India without consulting Kashmiri citizens, who were overwhelmingly Muslim. The annexation of Kashmir by India led to war with Pakistan, which also coveted the resource-rich territory. Over the years, tensions have flared in Kashmir, but an uneasy truce remains. Still, Pakistan, which defines itself by Islam, believes that it has a religious connection to the region of Kashmir. In 1971, however, the connection with its Bengali-speaking people of the east eroded. The region seceded from Pakistan and formed the independent nation of Bangladesh. India, meanwhile, formed a secular democracy based on socialism. Despite struggles, Indians have successfully managed to maintain unity in a nation of extreme linguistic diversity.

Despite Cold War politics, most Asians were primarily concerned with decolonization. In fact, most of the Cold War battles were intertwined with Asians' desires to rid themselves of colonial rule. Like other non-Europeans, they sought to define their own destinies. Both capitalism, pushed by the United States, and communism, pushed by the Soviets, looked too much like new forms of colonialism. In 1955, therefore, Indonesian President Achmed Sukarno called a meeting in Bandung, Indonesia, of twenty-nine Asian and African nations. The **Bandung Conference** produced an alliance of **nonaligned nations** that declared solidarity among non-European nations fighting colonialism. In direct reference to Cold War politics, these nations were often referred to as the **Third World**, representing countries that were not a part of either the capitalist bloc or the communist bloc. But despite the show of solidarity and their efforts at nonalignment, many of the nations were still sucked into the global conflicts of the Cold War.

AP® Tip

India served as a model for other nations struggling to free themselves from European colonial rule. Indian independence in 1947 set off a wave of anticolonial momentum around the world. Be sure you can both compare various anticolonial efforts and explain how India changed over time during the twentieth century.

THE POST–COLD WAR WORLD

The Cold War helped propel Japan forward as a global economic superpower. During the 1970s and 1980s, Japan's economic growth was faster than that of any industrialized nation. By the 1990s, average income in Japan surpassed even that in the United States. Much of the economic success was a result of the industrial alliances, known as **keiretsu**, which received government assistance in the form of tariffs and import regulations, which protected them from foreign competition. Six major Japanese keiretsu formed. Alliances of banks, commerce, industry, and construction, the keiretsu developed some of the best manufactured goods in the world. As a result, Japan built up a huge trade surplus with other nations around the world. The United States and the European Community attempted to break the economic power of Japan by negotiating to force open Japan's markets.

This effort did not succeed, but Japan's economy was not as strong as it appeared. Japan's housing and stock markets became overvalued, and corruption and overspeculation took its toll on the Japanese economy. Still, other nations in Asia adopted the Japanese model. South Korea used keiretsu to spark rapid economic growth. In fact, the four giant Korean corporations—among them Hyundai, which produces a broad range of manufactured goods—account for nearly half of South Korea's gross domestic product. Taiwan, Hong Kong, and Singapore also modeled themselves after Japan, creating modern industrial and commercial economies. Along with South Korea, these **newly industrialized economies** (NIEs) were often referred to as the **Asian Tigers**. Certain characteristics help explain their rapid ascent: all invested in education, had high rates of personal savings, emphasized exports, used government sponsorship and protection, relied heavily on current technology, and had hard-working, disciplined labor forces. The Asian Tigers also share another feature: all of their economies were stimulated by American purchases of supplies during the Korean and Vietnam Wars. In this regard, the Cold War was central to the economic restructuring of East Asia.

China also experienced economic growth. After the death of Mao in 1976, the new leader, Deng Xiaoping, implemented numerous economic reforms. Limited private enterprise and foreign investment was allowed, and individuals were allowed to contract land for personal use. By 1993, China's per capita output had grown at a rate eight times faster than the global average. Despite the growth, China remained a poor nation, and economic reform did not translate into political reform. In 1989, Chinese students led a series of protests demanding democratic changes and an end to inflation and corruption. The protestors convened in **Tiananmen Square**, sparking a standoff that lasted for weeks. The Chinese government sent in tanks to crush the protest; hundreds of Chinese students were killed, and thousands were arrested. Like other Asian nations, China's Communist government has struggled to balance rapid economic growth, population growth, inequality, unemployment, and large-scale migrations to the cities. Since Deng's death in 1997, China has allowed greater free expression.

Democracy is not a foregone conclusion in Asia. Whereas Indonesia moved from authoritarian rule to more open political institutions, India seemed to regress toward ethnic nationalism. In 1998, the Bharatiya Janata

Party gained control through blatant appeals to Hindu nationalism. Violence against Muslims was often condoned, and social and economic progress by Untouchables was opposed. Likewise, the struggle between India and Pakistan over **Kashmir** grew more intense when both nations successfully tested nuclear bombs in 1998.

Despite the political swings throughout Asia, rapid economic growth has allowed many Asian nations to become transmitters, not just receivers, of culture. East Asian manufactured goods have become household names around the world. The Indian and Chinese film industries have carved an increasingly strong niche in the global film market. The growing global strength in Asia is unquestioned. In fact, by population alone, India and China are both superpowers. Those two nations currently account for one-third of the world's population. However, it remains to be seen whether China or India can translate their dominance in population to the wealth and industrial muscle of a true global superpower.

Content Review Questions

Questions 1–3 refer to the passage below.

The chief enemies in China's revolutionary war are imperialism and the feudal forces. Although the Chinese bourgeoisie may take part in the revolutionary war on certain historical occasions, yet owing to its selfish character and its lack of political and economic independence, it is neither willing nor able to lead China's revolutionary war to complete victory. The masses of the Chinese peasantry and of the urban petty bourgeoisie are willing to take part actively in the revolutionary war and to bring about its complete victory. They are the main forces in the revolutionary war, yet small-scale production, which is their characteristic and limits their political outlook, renders them unable to give correct leadership in the war. Thus, in an era when the proletariat has already appeared on the political stage, the responsibility of leadership in China's revolutionary war inevitably falls on the shoulders of the Chinese Communist Party. At such a time any revolutionary war will certainly end in defeat if the leadership of the proletariat and the Communist Party is lacking or is forsaken. For of all the social strata and political groups in semi-colonial China only the proletariat and the Communist Party are the most open-minded and unselfish, possess the most farsighted political outlook and the highest organizational quality, and are also the readiest to learn with an open mind from the experiences of the advanced proletariat of the world and its parties as well as to apply what they have learned in their own undertakings. . . .

Mao Zedong, 1936
From Mao Zedong, Selected Works,
New York: International Publishers, volume I, 1954.
(Primary Source Reader for World History, Cengage... p. 540)

1. What circumstances precipitated Mao's Long March?
   (A) Mao and the Communists, having gained control of southern China, set out to gain control of the North.
   (B) Mao and the Communists, pursued by the Japanese, were forced to flee from the Japanese.
   (C) Mao and the Communist forces needed food and shelter after a severe drought.
   (D) Mao and the Communists were nearly surrounded, forcing them to escape Nationalist forces.

2. According to Mao, what is one of the Communist Party's major goals in 1936?
   (A) Mao prefers to see China continue with current (1936) economic and political conditions to avoid any kind of war.
   (B) Mao is making a plea for military operations to organize among the workers of China.
   (C) Mao would like to reduce the class stratification in China between rich and poor.
   (D) Mao wants to lead China into a more industrialized future to compete with capitalist nations.

3. How did Chinese communism differ from Soviet communism?
   (A) Chinese communism focused on the rural peasantry, whereas the Soviet version focused on the urban working class.
   (B) Chinese communism focused on creating a worldwide communist revolution, whereas Soviet communism concentrated on national affairs.
   (C) Chinese communism focused on the urban working class, whereas Soviet communism focused on rural peasantry.
   (D) Chinese communism focused on large-scale industries, whereas Soviet communism focused on small, village-level industries.

Questions 4–6 refer to the following passage.

Long years ago we made a tryst with destiny, and now the time comes when we shall redeem our pledge, not wholly or in full measure, but very substantially. At the stroke of the midnight hour, when the world sleeps, India will awake to life and freedom. A moment comes, which comes but rarely in history, when we step out from the old to the new, when an age ends, and when the soul of a nation, long suppressed, finds utterance. It is fitting that at this solemn moment we take the pledge of dedication to the service of India and her people and to the still larger cause of humanity.

Jawaharal Nehru, Speech on India's Independence, 1947
(*The Earth and Its Peoples*, Cengage, ... p. 775.)

4. By the 1920s, the demands of the Indian National Congress and the All-Indian Muslim League resulted in which of the following?
   (A) Higher tariffs to protect local industries and greater Indian control in education and public works
   (B) Independence and the expulsion of the British
   (C) The partitioning of India into three nations: India, Pakistan and Bangladesh
   (D) The British viceroy to India answering to an Indian Civil Service under the control of Indians

5. When Nehru speaks about India being "long suppressed," to what does he refer?
   (A) Nehru is referring to the internal strife between Hindus and Muslims and their respective political organizations.
   (B) Nehru is referring to the British Raj.
   (C) Nehru is talking about the kinds of internalized oppression that occurs when an oppressed people finally find their freedom.
   (D) Nehru is eluding to the upcoming partition between India and Pakistan, ultimately separating most of the country's Hindus and Muslims.

6. Which of the following accurately depicts events right after Indian independence?
   (A) Violence erupted between Hindus and Muslims, resulting in the partition of the country.
   (B) The British remained in order to create a smooth transition from colonial status to independence.
   (C) A treaty united the Indian National Congress and the All-Indian Muslim League.
   (D) Gandhi became the first elected president of an independent India.

Answers

1. ANSWER: D. The Guomindang army pursued Mao and his Communist forces into the mountains. The Communists responded with guerilla warfare until the Guomindang forces nearly surrounded them. Despite support from the peasants, Mao decided to lead his troops on an escape out of the mountains. The Long March began in 1934; after one year and 6,000 miles, Mao and only 4,000 of his original troops arrived in Shaanxi (*The Earth and Its Peoples*, 6th ed., pp. 791–796/7th ed., pp. 761–763; History Reasoning Skill—Causation; Learning Objectives CUL-2; Key Concept 6.2.II.D).

2. ANSWER: C. Mao is attempting to win the hearts and minds of the Chinese peasantry and working class in his 1936 speech. The goal is to have workers and peasants (farmers) take a leadership role in the future of China. Mao would like to rid China of what he believes is the oppressive Guomindang ruling class (*The Earth and Its Peoples*, 6th ed., pp. 817–819/7th ed., pp. 761–763; History Disciplinary Practice—Analyzing Historical Evidence; Learning Objectives; Key Concept 6.2.II.D).

3. ANSWER: A. Despite the fact that the Soviet Union remained a source of arms and support for China, when Mao Zedong took over and established the People's Republic of China, his form of communism diverged from that of the Soviets. Mao focused on the rural peasantry, with whom Chinese Communists had formed an intimate bond. The Soviets, intent on rapid industrialization, neglected the rural peasantry in favor of the urban working class (*The Earth and Its Peoples*, 6th ed., pp. 858–859/7th ed., p. 829; History Reasoning Skill—Comparison; Learning Objectives ECON-2; Key Concept 6.3.I.A).

4. ANSWER: A. During the 1920s the British began to give in to the pressures of the Indian National Congress and the All-Indian Muslim League, gradually admitting Indians to the Civil Service and allowing them to control areas of education, economy, and public works. Indians then began to erect high tariff barriers to protect local industries from foreign, including British, imports (*The Earth and Its Peoples*, 6th ed., pp. 790–796/7th ed., pp. 787–794; History Reasoning Skill—Causation; Learning Objectives CUL-2, SB-3; Key Concept 6.2.I.A).

5. ANSWER: B. While the British East India Company controlled much of India in the eighteenth century, there was a transition of power to the British Raj, or the British crown. When the British government takes over control of India from the British East India Company, it becomes an oppressive regime, rarely allowing Indians to become a part of decision-making in its own country (*The Earth and Its Peoples*, 6th ed., p. 791/7th ed., pp. 789–790; History Disciplinary Practice—Analyzing Historical Evidence; Learning Objectives ECON-2, SB-3; Key Concept 5.1.II.B).

6. ANSWER: A. On the eve of independence, talks between the Indian National Congress and the All-Muslim League broke down. Violent rioting broke out between Hindus and Muslims, despite Gandhi's protests and appeals. On August 15, 1947, India gained independence and was partitioned into two states: India and Pakistan. In protest, Gandhi refused to attend any independence day celebrations (*The Earth and Its Peoples*, 6th ed., p. 796/7th ed., p. 794; History Reasoning Skill—Causation; Learning Objectives SB-3,4; Key Concept 6.2.III.A).

29

EUROPE: C. 1900 TO THE PRESENT

KEY CONCEPTS

- European imperialism came to an end during the twentieth century, but not before Europeans had exploited nearly every corner of the globe.
- World Wars I and II, the Depression, and the Cold War not only resulted in the interaction of numerous nations; they ultimately led to the creation of technology such as the satellite and the Internet that would allow people around the world to communicate with one another in a matter of seconds.
- The United States and the Soviet Union arose as competing superpowers after World War II. For more than forty years, they would attempt to influence other nations around the world to adopt capitalism or communism, respectively.

KEY TERMS

- Cold War
- European Union
- fascist
- globalization
- Great Depression
- Helsinki Accords
- Holocaust
- imperialism
- iron curtain
- Marshall Plan
- militarism
- multinational corporations

- nationalism
- Nazis
- nongovernmental organizations
- North Atlantic Treaty Organization (NATO)
- Treaty of Versailles
- Warsaw Pact

Europe during the twentieth century is discussed in depth in *The Earth and Its Peoples*, 6th edition, Chapters 27–32, and 7th edition, Chapters 28–33.

WORLD WAR I

The industrialization of the late nineteenth century, which increased the power of Europeans and North Americans, resulted in a race to conquer or control other peoples and other lands. By the beginning of the twentieth century, young imperial powers such as the United States and Germany were on the rise. Technological superiority gave all of these powers great success in expanding their empires; however, that expansion led to a severe crisis when the imperial powers found themselves competing over the same territory. The decline of the Ottoman Empire meant that territory and resources would be up for grabs. As a consequence, the European powers began meddling in its affairs. **Imperialism** had clearly reached a boiling point.

The flames of imperialism, however, were also fueled by intense **nationalism**. Nationalism not only united nations under a common language and culture, it also engendered a deep hatred of those viewed as enemies. Moreover, in the name of nationalism, ethnic minorities attempted to break away from empires such as the Ottoman and the Austro-Hungarian.

To protect and expand their territories, European nations began to seek other nations as military allies. Two major systems of alliances developed: the Triple Alliance (Germany, Austria-Hungary, and Italy) and the Entente (Britain, France, and Russia). Such was the state of Europe when the Archduke Franz Ferdinand of the Austro-Hungarian Empire was assassinated by ethnic Serbian nationalists. Because of imperialistic desires, nationalistic fervor, military alliances, and maneuverings, this seemingly isolated incident blew into an enormous war that involved all of Europe and many colonies of the imperial powers. On July 28, 1914, Austria-Hungary declared war on Serbia, thus beginning the First World War.

World War I lasted for four years. It was the most destructive war in the history of the world up until that time, mainly because of technological advances that produced such deadly weapons as the machine gun and poison gas. At war's end, many of the traditional imperial powers, such as France and Britain, were weakened. The Austro-Hungarian and Ottoman Empires, meanwhile, were dissolved and divided into smaller, weak nations. World War I also caused the destruction of Russia's old regime and aristocracy and led to civil war, revolution, and the adoption of communism. Instead of creating a lasting peace, the League of Nations proved inefficient, serving primarily the interests of the victorious nations of France and Great Britain, both of which gained territory and colonies from Germany and the Ottoman Empire. Despite fighting alongside the Allies, Russia had no role in creating the **Treaty of Versailles**. Its exclusion would sow Russian bitterness. Moreover, the Treaty of Versailles humiliated Germany and laid the ground for the Second World War. The one nation that emerged unscathed was the United States, which became the wealthiest power in the world.

The Great Depression and the Rise of Totalitarianism

While many people spoke of World War I as the "war to end all wars," imperialistic tendencies and the desire to attain national wealth did not abate. Indeed, the effects of World War I created greater problems than anyone could have anticipated. First and foremost, the astronomical cost of the war proved devastating to the economies of the European nations. Germany found it difficult to pay reparations to the Allies, so Great Britain and France were unable to repay their debts to the United States. The economic crisis in Europe became clear when banks began to fail and unemployment rose. France and Great Britain attempted to resolve the economic crisis by forcing their colonies to purchase their products. But as a whole, most European countries became insular in an attempt to protect domestic industries. Such protectionist efforts only crippled global trade and industry. Many governments thereupon intervened with social welfare and economic stimulus programs. All countries around the world were seeking radical answers to the economic crisis.

AP® Tip

World War I and World War II caused a major shift in global power. They led to the decline of the European imperial powers, gave rise to independence movements throughout Africa and Asia, and set the stage for the emergence of the United States and the Soviet Union as the new superpowers. Be sure you can identify and analyze this change over time in global power.

Those nations that were young, had political institutions that lacked popular support, or were embittered by the results of World War I witnessed the rise of totalitarian regimes. Italy under Mussolini, Germany under Hitler, and Russia under Stalin—all experienced violent repression as the price for the reduction of unemployment and economic malaise. At the heart of these totalitarian regimes were the same long-term tendencies that led to World War I. Nationalist fervor was used to drum up support for taking over territories and dominating people and resources outside national boundaries. Germany blamed its economic depression directly on the Treaty of Versailles, which stripped it of colonial territories, restricted its

AP® is a trademark registered by the College Board, which is not affiliated with, and does not endorse, this product.

access to resource-rich border lands, and handcuffed its ability to further industrialize. The anger fanned by Hitler caused Germans to scapegoat German Jews and rebuild their military for the purpose of satisfying their imperial desires.

WORLD WAR II AND INDEPENDENCE MOVEMENTS

Japan's imperialistic successes in Asia during the early 1930s encouraged Nazi Germany in its hopes to expand German territory. Similarly, Mussolini's **fascist** regime in Italy was emboldened to invade Ethiopia. Both Germany and Italy supported the fascist regime of Francisco Franco in Spain. Despite the clear acts of **militarism** and the aggressive positioning of these authoritarian regimes, Britain and France, old imperial powers, attempted to avoid conflict and the prohibitive costs of war. By the end of the 1930s, however, Britain and France found themselves unable to avoid the conflicts for fear of German and Italian domination of Europe. As with the First World War, European nations began forming alliances to protect their own interests. Once again, Britain and France formed an alliance (the Allied powers) in competition with the rising authoritarian regimes of Germany and Italy (the Axis powers). Just before the start of the war, in 1939, the **Nazis** made a pact with the Soviets. Later, when the Germans broke that pact, the Soviets joined the side of the Allied powers. Japan, having common interests with Germany and Italy, would later join the Axis powers. Both the Allied and Axis alliances dragged numerous other nations into the conflict, which encompassed two-thirds of the entire planet and included sixty-one nations. As with World War I, the cost of World War II—estimated at five trillion dollars—was astronomical. So too was the human cost. Nazi Germany's crackdown on its minority populations, resulting in the genocide of six million Jews and millions of others considered inferior to the "Aryan" race, shocked the entire world. The **Holocaust**, as this extermination became known, was fashioned after the crackdown on minority populations in the Ottoman Empire at the time of World War I, in which Armenians and other minorities faced eradication.

The Axis powers seemed assured of victory until the United States entered the war in 1941 on the side of the Allies. This too had a hint of déjà vu. The United States, arguably the world's most powerful nation at the end of World War I, turned the tide in favor of the Allies. Allied victory in Europe came in 1945 following the suicide of Hitler. By the end of the war, thirty-five million people had lost their lives. The European imperial powers, with colonies around the world, finally lost their position of global dominance. People in the colonial territories who had fought and died on the side of the European powers began demanding independence, sparking decolonization throughout Africa and Asia. After two world wars, the European nations no longer had the means to maintain colonial territories. The mantle of global power shifted to two new superpowers, the United States and the Soviet Union. Even the Yalta and Potsdam Conferences of 1945 were dominated by the two new superpowers. And as was the case after World War I, peace proved only a façade.

THE COLD WAR AND DECOLONIZATION

On the surface, the **Cold War** was a battle of West versus East, democracy versus communism. In reality, the Cold War was an attempt by the United States and the Soviet Union to influence other people and territories, promoting their economic ideologies of capitalism and communism, respectively, all at a time when the downfall of the old imperial powers, crippled by the end of World War II, left a vacuum for the emergence of a new world order. Colonial territories throughout Africa and Asia broke free. Both the United States and the Soviet Union actively promoted their ideologies in these newly independent nations as well as throughout Europe.

The Western capitalist nations, led by the United States, created an international monetary system with prices determined by supply and demand. A system of exchange rates was also created. The Communist nations, led by the Soviet Union, constructed a system in which the state allocated goods and fixed prices. Both sides were suspicious of each other and perceived the success of one as the failure of the other. Nothing symbolized this suspicion more than Winston Churchill's reference to an **"iron curtain"** dividing eastern and western Europe. Western European nations recovered from the devastation of World War II with the aid of the United States' **Marshall Plan**. Eastern European nations also saw rapid—though only temporary—recovery with the aid of the Soviet Union.

On both sides of the iron curtain, the superpowers responded to each other both politically and militarily. When, for instance, the westerners established the **North Atlantic Treaty Organization (NATO)** as a military alliance, the easterners established the **Warsaw Pact**. Tensions along this east–west divide grew to enormous proportions, and many feared the onset of a third world war. Ironically, Germany proved the tensest battleground. During the post–World War II peace conferences, Germany, and its capital Berlin, were split into four parts. Berlin, however, was located deep in the territory controlled by the Soviet Union. When the Soviets blockaded West Berlin in 1948, the United States airlifted supplies to West Berlin.

Incidents such as these filled the Cold War period, but the stakes were raised in 1949 when the Soviets successfully tested their first nuclear device. The whole of Europe seemed to watch as the two superpowers engaged in an arms race for nuclear supremacy. But rather than take part in the type of militarization that led to the world wars, the European nations, clearly exhausted from war, sought to ease tensions between the east and west. Take, for example, the **Helsinki Accords**, signed in 1975, which affirmed that boundaries within Europe were fixed and could not be altered by military force and called for increased contact and cooperation across the iron-curtain divide.

The fall of the Berlin Wall, in 1989, marks the end of the Cold War. During the 1980s, economic troubles caused social unrest in the eastern European nations. Despite many efforts to restructure the communist economies, citizens were demanding change. A flood of protest and rebellion swept through Poland, Hungary, Czechoslovakia, and Bulgaria. After the fall of the Berlin Wall, large numbers of East Germans began to cross into the western portion. These events in Europe precipitated many changes in the Soviet Union and led eventually to its breakup in 1991, as Lithuania, Estonia,

Latvia, and other small Soviet states declared their independence. After forty-six years, the United States emerged from the Cold War as the lone superpower.

AP® Tip

After World War II, the United States and the Soviet Union arose as the world's two superpowers. Vying to fill the void left by the decline of the traditional imperial powers, each nation sought to influence countries around the world to adopt capitalism and communism, respectively. Some wars and proxy wars developed, but not once did the two superpowers engage in direct conflict with each other. You must be able to compare the economic and political philosophies of the two Cold War superpowers, as well as their efforts to influence nations around the world.

THE POST–COLD WAR WORLD

The post–Cold War era is perhaps still without a true definition, but a New World Order that did not include a European superpower had clearly arisen by the early 1990s. Whether that new world order would finally bring about peace was still a matter of debate. And whether the United States as the lone superpower would impose and/or export its influence and create a true global community was also unclear.

Post–Cold War Europe was not free of conflict. Old tensions caused Yugoslavia to erupt into religious and ethnic factionalism. The struggle among Muslims, Catholics, Orthodox Christians, Serbs, Croats, and Albanians led to the disintegration of Yugoslavia and the creation, once again, of new nations. And once again, the world saw the rise of ethnic cleansing, as the Serbs of Bosnia, who are Orthodox Christians, attempted to rid the state of Muslims. Yugoslavia became a prime example of the failure of the nation-state and of a united global community.

However, the New World Order did bring about a new level of cooperation in Europe. In 1973, Great Britain joined the European Economic Community, which was established both to ensure economic cooperation and growth and to counteract the powerful economic influence of the United States. By the turn of the twenty-first century, most European nations had come together to form the **European Union** and had adopted a common currency, the euro. Moreover, efforts to eliminate ethnic cleansing and other types of oppression and abuse led to the proliferation of **nongovernmental organizations** (NGOs). NGOs such as Amnesty International and Médecins Sans Frontières (Doctors Without Borders), in attempting to eliminate or at least reduce global suffering, were also effectively nullifying the traditional nation-state boundaries.

Nation-state boundaries were further eroded by **multinational corporations**—corporations with ownership and management teams from more than one nation. It was multinational corporations based in the United States that led the way, transmitting not only technological developments but also American culture around the world. McDonald's, CNN, and Coca-Cola became prime symbols of vehicles of American culture. Critics argued that powerful multinational corporations used sophisticated marketing techniques to promote consumption.

Despite the efforts to prevent American global dominance, most European nations joined the United States in efforts to stem terrorism and nuclear proliferation. Terrorism in the twenty-first century is largely associated with Islamic groups in the Middle East angered by the creation of Israel following World War II. Much of that anger is aimed at western European nations, which along with the United States are seen as staunch supporters of Israel.

Immigrant populations throughout Europe are growing rapidly, and fertility rates among immigrants are far outpacing those of native-born Europeans. As a result, many western European nations have implemented regulations to slow immigration. Thus, **globalization** has not created a unified global culture. In fact, many social scientists marvel at the endurance of cultural diversity in the face of globalization. People around the world use technology such as the Internet and satellites to export and maintain their own ethnic and cultural values, even as the traditional nation-state weakens.

Multiple-Choice Questions

Questions 1–3 refer to the following image.

British Ministry of Munitions Poster, 1917
World War I (Europe).
(*Human Record Documents,* Cengage, p. 337)

1. Why was there more inclusion in the work force in Great Britain during
    World War I?
    (A) There was a push for more inclusion in the work force in Great
         Britain because the French were looking for more jobs in
         manufacturing.
    (B) Women were asked to take on more political leadership prior to
         World War I, as many women were teachers at the time.
    (C) The largest inclusion in the work force in Great Britain during
         World War I was with child labor, as laws were relaxed to allow
         children into manufacturing positions.
    (D) Men were traditionally involved in manufacturing, but with an
         increase in the military assignments, more women were needed in
         manufacturing.

2. In which of the following ways did World War I affect Russia?
   (A) Russia gained stability and wealth through war reparations.
   (B) Russia split into independent republics.
   (C) Russia was devastated by revolution and civil war.
   (D) Russia created an expanded empire.

3. Which region of Europe had its territorial boundaries changed most dramatically as a result of the peace treaties that ended World War I?
   (A) Eastern Europe
   (B) Central Europe
   (C) Mediterranean Europe
   (D) Northern Europe

Questions 4–6 refer to the following passage.

As a fanatical National Socialist, I was thoroughly convinced that our ideas gradually would take hold and would come to be dominant in all countries. This would then break the dominance of the Jews. Anti-Semitism in the whole world really was nothing new. It always reappears when the Jews had forced themselves into positions of power and when their evil doings become visible to the general public. . . . I want to emphasize here that I myself have never hated the Jews. To me they were considered to be the enemy of our people. However, that was exactly the reason to treat them the same way as any other prisoners. I never made a distinction concerning this. Furthermore, the feeling of hatred is not characteristic of me. But I know what hate is, and how it manifests itself. I have seen it and I have recognized it. . . .

> Rudolf Höss, Commander of Auschwitz Concentration Camp,
> written after capture, 1947.
> (*Human Record Documents,* Cengage, p. 360)

Source: Rudolf Höss, *Kommandant in Auschwitz: Autobiographische Aufzeichen von Rudolf Höss*, Martin Broszat, ed., *Quellen und Darstellung zur Zeitgeschichte*, Volume, Stuttgart: Deutsche Verlags-Anstalt, 1958, pp. 120–125, 127, 129, 130. Trans. J. H. Overeld.

4. How can Höss's views toward Jews in the world best be described?
   (A) Höss is complacent (uncritical) in his views toward Jewish people.
   (B) Höss views the Jews as too dominant in positions of power.
   (C) Höss offers that the National Socialists should totally annihilate the Jews.
   (D) Höss prefers a continued role in anti-Semitism, even after his capture.

5. All of the following statements are accurate about the Holocaust EXCEPT
   (A) the Nazis especially targeted Jews.
   (B) Nazis killed the disabled, Gypsies, homosexuals, Jehovah's Witnesses, and Polish Catholics.
   (C) many German Jews were forcibly evacuated and sent to Israel.
   (D) ordinary citizens were involved in supporting the genocide.

6. Which of the following economic policies did western Europe follow in the years after World War II?
   (A) Laissez-faire capitalism
   (B) Government nationalization of major segments of the population
   (C) Collectivization of agriculture
   (D) Economically helping devastated eastern Europe

Answers

1. ANSWER: D. There was a large increase in military recruitment at the outset of World War I in Great Britain. Because men traditionally worked in manufacturing jobs, the decrease in male labor forced Great Britain to look elsewhere for people to manufacture weapons and support the war effort. Women fulfilled that role by taking manufacturing jobs once occupied by men (*The Earth and Its Peoples*, 6th ed., p. 757/7th ed., p. 732; History Reasoning Skill—Causation; Learning Objectives SOC-2,5; Key Concept 6.2.IV.A; 6.3.III).

2. ANSWER: C. On top of the enormous numbers of deaths, World War I was a destructive force on Russian society, paving the way for both communism and industrialization (*The Earth and Its Peoples*, 6th ed., pp. 755–757/7th ed., pp. 729–732; History Reasoning Skill—Causation; Learning Objectives SOC-2,5; Key Concept 6.2.IV.A).

3. ANSWER: A. New countries of Yugoslavia, Czechoslovakia, Poland, Lithuania, Latvia, and Estonia were all created in eastern Europe as a result of the treaties that ended World War I (*The Earth and Its Peoples*, 6th ed., p. 763/7th ed., p. 734; History Reasoning Skill—Causation; Learning Objectives SB-3,4; Key Concept 6.2.I).

4. ANSWER: B. Höss offers his response after his capture in 1947. During World War II, however, Höss was known to have overseen the deaths of almost 1 million people in the concentration camp Auschwitz, most of whom were Jews. Höss is trying to downplay his role in the extermination in his statement (*The Earth and Its Peoples*, 6th ed., pp. 814–815/7th ed., pp. 758–759; History Disciplinary Practice—Analyzing Historical Evidence; Learning Objectives SOC-6; Key Concept 6.2.III.C).

5. ANSWER: C. Along with 6 million Jews, the Nazis exterminated homosexuals, Jehovah's Witnesses, Gypsies, the disabled, and the mentally ill. They also killed 3 million Polish Catholics. The Holocaust resulted in torture, medical experimentation, and mass extermination, all in an effort to create a "pure race" (*The Earth and Its Peoples*, 6th ed., pp. 825–828/7th ed., p. 771; History Disciplinary Practice—Analyzing Historical Evidence; Learning Objectives SOC-6; Key Concept 6.2.III.C).

6 ANSWER: B. Britain, France, and other western European countries nationalized major portions of their economy, such as coal, steel, and medical care following World War II (*The Earth and Its Peoples*, 6th ed., pp. 825–828/7th ed., p. 771; History Reasoning Skill—Causation; Learning Objectives SOC-6; Key Concept 6.2.III.C).

30

THE AMERICAS: C. 1900 TO THE PRESENT

KEY CONCEPTS

- Most nations in the Americas suffered from foreign economic control and a drastic degree of social inequality during the twentieth century.
- The United States became a wealthy global power after World War I and one of the two global superpowers following World War II.
- Throughout North and South America, the Depression caused unemployment, homelessness, and protectionist policies.
- Its foreign policy of containment during the Cold War led the United States to sponsor coups and proxy wars throughout Latin America.
- The emergence of the United States as the lone superpower at the end of the Cold War resulted in the globalization of culture, a more interconnected global economy, and the spread of democracy. It has also caused new conflicts in response to U.S. domination.

KEY TERMS

- Contras
- Dirty War
- import-substitution industrialization
- North American Free Trade Agreement (NAFTA)
- North Atlantic Treaty Organization (NATO)
- oligarquía
- Pearl Harbor
- proxy wars
- Sandinistas
- Truman Doctrine

The Americas during the twentieth century are discussed in *The Earth and Its Peoples*, 6th edition, Chapters 27–32, and 7th edition, Chapters 28–33.

WORLD WAR I

On the eve of World War I, most countries in the Americas could be defined by two common characteristics. First, most had sharp social divides between a small, very wealthy class and a large population of poor. Second, most were victims of foreign intervention or some sort of foreign economic control. Despite the success of the revolutions that rid them of colonial rule, Western Hemisphere nations had difficulty shrugging off the economic hold of European nations. The United States had proved one of the few exceptions to the second rule. It not only gained economic independence, but also became an imperial power itself, strategically positioned to exert economic influence over its neighbors in the Americas. Nonetheless, the social divide and foreign control caused simmering tensions in most American societies. In many cases, it was as if the revolutions of the nineteenth century were not yet complete.

Consider Mexico. Close to 1 percent of the population owned 85 percent of the land. These few wealthy families were mostly of direct Spanish origin and lived on huge estates. In contrast, the vast majority of the population consisted of poor peasants of Native American or mixed ancestry (commonly referred to as mestizos). Industry in Mexico was dominated by companies from the United States and Great Britain—both imperial and industrial powers—that controlled most of Mexico's railroads, mines, plantations, and other major industries. Wealthy Mexicans were often closely tied to the foreign companies, and together they forced the peasants to endure harsh working and living conditions. Thus, popular resentment was high, military coups were frequent, and revolutionary sentiment was rife. In southern Mexico, Emiliano Zapata led peasant revolts to wrest land from wealthy hacienda owners and return it to the Amerindian villages to which it had once belonged. Similarly, Pancho Villa organized peasant revolts in northern Mexico, where 95 percent of the people had no land at all. They also seized haciendas in an effort to redistribute wealth. Neither Zapata nor Villa was able to gain support outside their own locales, but their demands were heard. By 1920, a group of middle-class leaders known as the Constitutionalists had defeated all their adversaries, including Zapata and Villa, to gain control of Mexico. They did, however, restore communal lands to Amerindians and establish social programs for the poor. In an effort to chip away at foreign economic control, they also placed restrictions on foreign ownership of property.

Argentina and Brazil faced circumstances similar to those of Mexico. The governments of both nations represented the interests of a few wealthy landowners. In Argentina, this elite, known as the **oligarquía**, controlled vast tracts of farmland and made Argentina, like the United States, one of the world's largest producers of meat and wheat. As a result of its tremendous agricultural success, the oligarquía was quite content to let foreign companies control other industries, such as public utilities and railroads. Likewise, Brazil's elite focused on coffee, cacao, and rubber exports, and let foreigners control industries. Railroads, harbors, public utilities, and other forms of infrastructure were controlled by Great Britain. While Argentina and Brazil exported agricultural goods, they imported almost all manufactured goods. During World War I, European nations slowed the importation of crops, which weakened the landowning classes in both Argentina and Brazil. The urban middle class was able to gain power during this time. However, little was done for the masses of poor, landless peasants, many of whom were of Native American and/or African ancestry.

World War I had a very different effect on the United States. A young yet growing industrial and imperial nation, the United States was catapulted into the position of a global power by the war. In the United States, as in other nations in the Americas, wealth was fairly restricted, and much of it was secured for those of European descent. However, the United States had extensive and varied industries, a growing middle class, and a number of colonial territories from which to extract resources. At the start of World War I, the United States, seemingly content with its status, maintained an official position of neutrality. However, the neutrality was only technical. While no military was involved in fighting, U.S. businesses were providing supplies to France and Great Britain. German submarines, therefore, began attacking all ships heading to Great Britain, resulting in numerous American civilian casualties. In 1917, President Woodrow Wilson asked Congress to declare war on Germany. That proved costly for the Central Powers. The arrival of fresh, healthy troops from the United States turned the tide in favor of the Allies. The Germans were soon in retreat. They signed an armistice to end the war in November 1918.

Most surprising, however, was the social and economic impact on the United States. To help the war effort, civilians were encouraged to invest in war bonds. As soldiers left their jobs and went off to war, employment opportunities opened up for women and African-Americans. Job openings in cities in the north led to large-scale migrations of African-Americans from the rural south. Social equality was by no means achieved, but the progress provided an impetus for groups that were discriminated against to fight for greater freedoms and opportunities. Businesses prospered too, especially if they were engaged in war production. All in all, the United States was the one nation that grew rich from the war.

AP® Tip

The effect of World War I was drastically different on the United States than on other nations in the Americas. The United States thrived economically. Most nations in the Americas, however, suffered economically. You will need to be able to analyze the reasons for such differences.

THE INTERWAR PERIOD

The first event that symbolized U.S. ascendancy as a world power was the Paris Peace Conference. U.S. President Woodrow Wilson, along with British Prime Minister David Lloyd George and French Premier Georges Clemenceau, laid out the framework for the Treaty of Versailles. In addition, Wilson proposed a League of Nations to help safeguard peace and foster international cooperation—ironically, the United States, in an effort to return to isolationism, refused to join. Many in the United States were comfortable with the newfound prosperity that the war had provided. A steady economic boom, the result of European nations borrowing American money and repaying wartime loans, brought an air of optimism to the United States in the 1920s. Many who had been marginalized increased their demands for equality and greater participation in American society—demand for social change seemed to accompany the economic growth. Having joined the labor force during the war, women pressed for the right to vote, which they got in 1920 with the Nineteenth Amendment. For most African-Americans, on the other hand, the right to vote was merely theoretical. Increasingly, organizations such as the National Association for the Advancement of Colored People (NAACP) and the United Negro Improvement Association (UNIA) pushed the nation to grant first-class citizenship to African-Americans.

South American countries also experienced growing prosperity during the 1920s. Trade with European nations, curtailed by the war, resumed, and agricultural exports once again commanded high prices. Both Argentina and Brazil used their profits to industrialize and improve their transportation and public utilities systems—a goal helped by Great Britain's need to sell many of its transportation holdings and industrial companies to Argentina and Brazil in order to pay its war debt. Still, with the introduction of new technologies, South American nations remained dependent on foreign companies. British, French, Germans, and Americans formed a cartel to control all radio communication in Latin America. The cartel set up a national radio company in each nation, held all the stock and received all the profits. European and American companies also controlled aviation technology in Latin America. Aeropostale and Pan American Airways introduced airmail services throughout the continent and were linked to cities in the United States and Europe.

Economic prosperity in Latin America also led to social changes. However, the more stratified societies of Argentina and Brazil witnessed various levels of turmoil as workers and middle-class professionals demanded social changes and a greater say in politics. Junior military officers in Brazil rose up to demand universal suffrage and freedom for labor unions, among other social reforms. In Argentina, demonstrations were crushed. However, they not only laid the groundwork for later change but also opened a space for the middle class to share power with the wealthy elite. Throughout both North and South America, the middle class was growing, but the growth was often at the expense of poor, landless peasants and urban workers. Social progress was perhaps greatest in Mexico, where the revolution ensured that representatives of rural communities, unionized workers, and public employees gained a greater voice in society. In 1928, President Plutarco Elías Calles established the National Revolutionary Party (PNR) to provide a forum in which businessmen, peasants, laborers, landowners, the military, and members of other interest groups could reach compromises for the good of the nation.

Throughout the Americas, prosperity and access to technology were spreading beyond the realms of the elite. In the United States, the economic boom gave rise to an overconfidence that foreshadowed the impending crisis.

Few had anticipated the fall of the New York stock market, but sure enough, on October 24, 1929, the market plunged; the downward spiral would last for three years. Investors lost money, people lost their savings, and banks collapsed. The crisis grew circular, as consumers purchased less, so businesses produced less, so companies were forced to lay off workers, and laid-off workers could purchase less. In 1930, to protect U.S. businesses from foreign competition, Congress passed the Smoot-Hawley tariff, the highest import duty in U.S. history. Other nations around the world retaliated by raising their tariffs. World trade was crippled, dropping by 62 percent. Three years after the stock market crash, the U.S. economy was cut in half, and unemployment had reached a record high of 25 percent of the workforce.

The Depression devastated Latin America as well. Most Latin American countries depended on exports and were thus hit hard, as most industrial nations imposed high tariffs and reduced their imports. Sugar exports from the Caribbean fell. Coffee exports from Brazil and Colombia dropped, as did tin exports from Bolivia and beef exports from Argentina. Exports from Latin America fell by two-thirds from 1929 to 1932. Again, the devastation was circular. Nations could no longer import manufactured goods. Industrialization efforts within nations were set back. Unemployment and homelessness increased dramatically.

In many nations, military officers seized power, and governments began imposing authoritarian rule. Getulio Vargas of Brazil, one such authoritarian ruler, staged a coup and came to power in 1930. He initially made some socially progressive changes—for example, broadening the franchise, allowing labor unions, and installing pension plans—but his reforms were largely geared to urban workers. He did little to help the millions of landless peasants for fear of provoking the ire of the powerful landowners. Vargas was, however, successful in helping Brazil recover from the Depression. His policy of **import-substitution industrialization**, which aimed at building the nation's industry by restricting foreign trade, became a model emulated by other Latin American nations. By 1938, however, Vargas had abolished his own constitution, banned political parties, and jailed opposition leaders. Argentina followed a path similar to Brazil's. In 1930, General José Uriburu overthrew the popularly elected President Hipólito Irigoyen. The new government protected the interests of the oligarquía and big business. Tension among the poor and the working class continued to build.

Mexico, however, proved different from the others. The revitalized revolution saw Lázaro Cárdenas come to power, renaming the PNR the Mexican Revolutionary Party (PRM). Cárdenas removed generals from government positions and redistributed more than forty four million acres of land to peasant communes. In an effort to break the foreign economic stranglehold, Cárdenas nationalized railroads and foreign-owned oil companies. The revitalized revolution under Cárdenas brought some of the most widespread changes of any nation in the Americas, but Mexico remained stubbornly poor, with little industrialization. Like Mexico, the United States did not fall to an authoritarian regime and had to use dramatic intervention to overcome the Depression. When Franklin D. Roosevelt became president in 1932, he implemented his New Deal program to stimulate and revitalize the economy. Despite the many critics who complained that the New Deal resembled socialism and communism, it was extremely successful, but it would take the Second World War to fully push the United States out of the Depression.

WORLD WAR II

When war erupted in Europe and Asia during the latter half of the 1930s, the United States once again adopted an official policy of isolationism. But as in the First World War, it began profiting from the war by making loans and selling supplies to France and Great Britain. The guise of neutrality remained thin when the United States, along with Britain, stopped shipments of steel, oil, and other materials that the Japanese needed for their war and industrial efforts. That action led the Japanese to attack the United States by bombing **Pearl Harbor** in 1941. The bombing of the naval base put an end to the nation's isolationist stance, as the United States joined Britain, the Soviet Union, and other nations in an alliance commonly known as the Allies. Once again, U.S. involvement in the war was crucial in turning the tide in favor of the Allies. The Americans played an essential role in forcing Italy to surrender and in storming the Normandy Coast, which pushed the Germans into retreat. In May 1945, Germany surrendered. Turning its attention to Japan, the United States dropped atomic bombs on Hiroshima and Nagasaki in August. Japan surrendered a week later.

World War II clearly helped the United States escape from the Depression. The economy flourished during the war. The United States alone produced more weapons and supplies than all of the Axis Powers combined. Such demand and production capacity led to plentiful jobs and opportunities. The war effort was boosted by the sale of bonds and rationing, which resulted in a tremendous growth in personal savings. Like the First World War, the Second built up national and individual wealth. And once again, it gave strength to the efforts of minorities and women in fighting for democracy and equality. As job opportunities opened up during the war, employers hired women, African-Americans, Latinos, and other minorities. The many minorities who fought and died on the battlefield alongside white Americans, in a war billed as a fight for freedom and democracy, returned home demanding the same freedom and democracy in the United States. The demands of soldiers and laborers were a huge impetus for the impending Civil Rights movement.

Despite turning Brazil into a fascist state, Vargas's regime allied itself with the United States during World War II. Argentina, on the other hand, remained officially neutral. However, the military rulers of Argentina were clearly inspired by Nazi Germany. In 1943, under the leadership of Colonel Juan Perón, Argentina hoped to conquer South America just as the Nazis were conquering Europe. But as the Nazis began losing ground, the popularity of Argentina's military officers began to wane as well. In an effort to regain the trust of the populace, Perón departed from his previous military stance. He and his charismatic wife, Eva Duarte Perón, began appealing to urban workers, pushing for social benefits for women, children, and the poor. With his wife's help, Juan Perón become a popular leader and won the presidency in 1946. Under him, Argentina was essentially a populist dictatorship, much like Brazil under Vargas. Like Brazil, Argentina also industrialized rapidly. However, industrialization only masked internal social and economic problems. When Eva Perón died in 1952, her husband lost his popular appeal and was overthrown in a military coup later that year.

THE COLD WAR

Devastation throughout Europe at the end of World War II, combined with the tremendous wealth amassed by the United States during the war, resulted in the further ascendancy of the United States as a world superpower. The Soviet Union also emerged from the war a global superpower as it too had witnessed stunning industrial growth. However, the United States distrusted the USSR and its communist economic system, which ran counter to American capitalism. Suspicion grew between both new superpowers. In 1947, the United States issued the **Truman Doctrine**, which promised military aid to any nation that was fighting communist or socialist insurrections. In 1949, the United States and various Western European nations established the **North Atlantic Treaty Organization (NATO),** a military alliance. In response, the Soviet Union and Eastern European countries formed the Warsaw Pact. Measures meant to quell the tensions only exacerbated them. Even the United Nations, which had been established to maintain world peace, became just another arena in which the Cold War would be played out.

Early Cold War conflicts all took place on the back of post–World War II settlements. When the Soviets blockaded Berlin, Germany, in 1948, the United States orchestrated an airlift to get supplies to the people of West Berlin. In Asia during that same year, Korea split into a communist North Korea and a capitalist South Korea. When North Korea invaded South Korea in 1950, the United States came to the aid of the South Koreans, while communist China sent troops to assist the North Koreans. Fighting lasted for three years before a truce was signed that fixed the border at its original post–World War II line, the thirty-eighth parallel. The Korean War convinced many Americans that the USSR was fomenting communist revolutions worldwide. Fear of communism even spilled onto the domestic scene when the government, as well as private individuals, began blacklisting, harassing, and discriminating against people thought to be members of the Communist Party in the United States. Thousands of Americans lost their jobs, many as a result of the vaguest unsubstantiated accusations.

In the same vein, the government adopted a foreign policy, known as containment, that communism should be stopped at all costs anywhere in the world. When the Cold War reached Vietnam, the containment policy took on greater urgency. Some Americans began to cite the domino theory—that if Vietnam became communist, the rest of Southeast Asia, nation by nation, would fall to communism. The United States supported the noncommunist government of South Vietnam against North Vietnam and the Viet Cong, the communist rebels in the south. The United States supported South Vietnam despite the fact that the government was corrupt, unpopular, and undemocratic. Nonetheless, the United States was so committed to containment that it spent more than a decade fighting a war to defeat the Viet Cong and the North Vietnamese. The United States finally withdrew in 1973. The Vietnam War had profound domestic consequences. A huge antiwar movement developed during the war that questioned not only the handling of the war but also its validity. At times the antiwar movement meshed with the civil rights movement, which highlighted the contradiction of fighting a war overseas in the name of freedom and democracy when those were not realities at home. Nonetheless, the obsession with fighting communism worldwide continued to affect both foreign and domestic policy.

The U.S. desire to contain communism often came into direct conflict with the ideals of the people and nations of Latin America. In seeking economic freedom, Latin Americans were essentially challenging the supremacy of the United States. Even after World War II, U.S. corporations controlled large portions of industry there—communication networks throughout Latin America, sugar in Cuba, coffee in Colombia, bananas in Guatemala, and copper in Chile. Efforts by Latin Americans to rid their nations of foreign control were often perceived by the United States as communist insurrections, financed and fueled by its archnemesis, the Soviet Union. In fact, Soviet involvement was minimal. Latin American nations had been attempting to reclaim their economic power for over a century. Even their attraction to communist ideals was less about the Soviet Union and more about efforts to address the vast economic and social disparities within their own nations. Nonetheless, Latin American nations were effectively dragged into the middle of the Cold War. During the 1950s, Guatemalan president Jacobo Arbenz Guzmán attempted to nationalize various industries, including the U.S.-controlled United Fruit Company. Perceiving this as a move toward communism, the U.S. Central Intelligence Agency (CIA) sponsored a military coup that resulted in the removal of Arbenz from power and decades of civil war and instability in Guatemala.

In Cuba, however, the CIA did not experience the same success. U.S. economic control in Cuba was even more extensive and overwhelming than in Guatemala. Public utilities, banking, transportation, and sugar, Cuba's most important industry, were all controlled by U.S. companies. Wealth was held by foreigners and the small Cuban elite. Moreover, President Fulgencio Batista's regime was undemocratic, corrupt, and repressive. Still, the United States gave Batista wide support. In 1959, Fidel Castro led a popular rebellion that forced Batista from power. The Cuban Revolution under Castro was a huge blow to U.S. power in Cuba. Castro redistributed land, lowered urban rents, raised wages, and nationalized foreign-controlled corporations. Within a year, Castro had effectively transferred 15 percent of the national income from the rich to the poor. In response to the Revolution, the CIA hoped to overthrow Castro, just as it had over-thrown Arbenz in Guatemala. However, the CIA-sponsored Bay of Pigs invasion failed. His reputation bolstered, Castro asked the Soviet Union for assistance to help prevent a U.S. takeover. The Soviets were more than willing to oblige by placing nuclear missiles in Cuba—U.S. missiles were already deployed in Turkey. A crisis ensued. Eventually, Soviet president Nikita Khrushchev backed down and withdrew the missiles from Cuba. The 1962 Cuban missile crisis was perhaps the closest that the United States and the USSR came to direct military confrontation. However, Castro had proved that U.S. economic domination could be challenged and that economic and social reform could be achieved. Cuba would serve as a model for revolutionary change even in the post–Cold War era.

A conservative response to the Cuban Revolution erupted in Brazil as military officers, claiming that civilian leaders could not protect the nation from communist rebellion, staged a coup. The constitution was suspended, and paramilitary organizations known as death squads were sanctioned by the government in order to eliminate opposition leaders. Thousands of civilians were detained, tortured, and executed. Brazil's mix of military dictatorship, violent repression, and industrialization through import-substitution, known as the Brazilian solution, was adopted by other Latin American nations. In 1973, Chile's democratically elected president Salvador Allende was overthrown in a CIA-backed coup as he attempted to nationalize U.S.-owned copper mines. Coup leader Augusto Pinochet took control of the nation and, with the backing of the United States, implemented various aspects of the Brazilian solution. Civilians were imprisoned, tortured, and executed. Socialist reforms in Argentina also resulted in the rise of military dictatorship. Between 1976 and 1983, Argentineans would experience what was known as the **Dirty War**, in which thousands of civilians were tortured and executed.

Revolutionary movements in Central America found a bit more success than those in South America. In 1979, revolutionaries known as the **Sandinistas** overthrew the U.S.-backed Nicaraguan dictator, Anastasio Somoza. With support from Cuba, they then fought off the **Contras**, rebels supported by the United States. In El Salvador, the United States intervened to prevent Salvadoran revolutionaries from overthrowing the U.S.-allied military dictatorship. As a result, a decade-long civil war ensued.

AP® Tip

The quest for economic independence in Latin America often ran counter to the Cold War ambitions of the United States. As such, proxy wars erupted throughout the Americas. Be sure you can analyze U.S. involvement in various Latin American nations and compare the causes and effects of these interventions.

THE POST–COLD WAR WORLD

In many ways, the Cold War contributed to the transformation of Latin America into a region of revolution, counterrevolution, violence, and repression. In search of economic independence and social equality, nations unwittingly became arenas for **proxy wars**, in which the United States and the Soviet Union armed and financed the warring parties. However, U.S. military interventions in Grenada and Panama, in 1983 and 1989, respectively, sent a powerful message that the United States was to be the dominant force in the region. The 1990s, therefore, ushered in a new era throughout the Americas. The military dictatorships of Brazil, Chile, and Argentina all came to an end after being undermined by reports of corruption, torture, and violence. Civil war came to an end in Nicaragua as the Sandinistas called for free elections in 1990; the election of a moderate coalition led by Violeta Chamorro clearly signified that Nicaraguans were tired of decades of violence and civil war. The end to civil war in neighboring El Salvador was also negotiated during the 1990s.

Economically, Latin American nations found themselves in debt at the end of the Cold War. Many nations had borrowed heavily during the Cold War era, and the rise of oil prices during the 1980s forced many nations to build up greater debt. This escalation of Latin American debt, along with the collapse of the Soviet Union, provided even greater opportunity for the United States to gain more influence in the area. Latin American nations introduced economic reforms that were advocated by the United States. Industries that earlier had been nationalized were sold to foreign-owned companies, and free-market policies that reduced protectionism were implemented. By 1994, the **North American Free Trade Agreement (NAFTA),** which eliminated tariffs among the United States, Canada, and Mexico, governed the largest free trade zone in the world. With the United States leading the way, free market capitalism was taking hold and connecting economies around the world. Although democracy has become almost universal in Latin America, poverty has continued. The people of the Americas, like those elsewhere, are still primarily driven by the hope of economic stability.

Technological advances were also helping to spread U.S. culture around the world. American organizations like CNN ensured the airing of television programs and viewpoints from the United States.

In 2001, a group known as Al Qaeda successfully organized attacks on the World Trade Center in New York City and on the Pentagon in Washington, D.C. In response, the United States began a global war against terror.

Content Review Questions

Questions 1–3 refer to the painting below.

José Clemente Orozco, Hispano-America—The Rebel and His International Enemies—General John Pershing to the right.
(*Human Record Documents*, Cengage, p. 400)

1. Why would José Clemente Orozco, a Mexican Revolution painter and muralist, include the United States general, John Pershing, in his work?
   (A) Pershing was a friend of Orozco, as he provided military protection while Orozco created his murals.
   (B) Pershing was seen as a threat against the Mexican Revolution, leading forces against Pancho Villa, who attacked New Mexico.
   (C) Pershing defected from the United States military and joined forces with the Mexican revolutionaries.
   (D) Orozco was to use Pershing as a symbol of Mexico's friendship with the United States during the Mexican Revolution.

2. How did the Mexican Revolution of 1910 compare to the independence movement in India?
   (A) For both, the greatest changes were achieved nonviolently.
   (B) For both, religious diversity created divisions.
   (C) For both, freedom from European imperialism motivated change.
   (D) Mexican revolutionaries had a more fragmented set of goals and leadership.

3. Which of the following best describes one of the more immediate outcomes of the Mexican Revolution?
   (A) Mexico prefers to follow a communist form of government.
   (B) There is more religious diversity allowed in Mexico after the revolution.
   (C) The newly elected Mexican government almost immediately approves a new constitution.
   (D) Mexico allows for more foreign investments immediately following the revolution.

Questions 4–6 refer to the following passage.

The nation [the United States] which was peopled by nine millions of men in 1820 now numbers eighty millions—an immense demographic power; in the space of ten years, from 1890 to 1900, this population increased by one-fifth. By virtue of its iron, wheat, oil, and cotton, and its victorious industrialism, the democracy aspires to a world-wide significance. . . . Yankee pride increases with the endless multiplication of wealth and population, and the patriotic sentiment has reached such intensity that it has become transformed into imperialism. . . .

Since the very beginnings of independence the Latin democracies, lacking financial reserves, have had need of European gold. . . . the necessities of the war [of independence] with Spain and the always difficult task of building up a new society demanded the assistance of foreign gold; loans accumulated. The lamentable history of these bankrupt democracies dates from this period.

To sum up, the new continent, politically free, is economically a vassal. This dependence is inevitable; without European capital there would have been no railways, no ports, and no stable government in [Latin] America. But the disorder which prevails in the finances of the country changes into a real servitude what might otherwise have been a beneficial relation.

Francisco García Calderón, Peruvian Author and Diplomat, 1912
Source: From Francisco García Calderón, *Latin America: Its Rise and Progress.* Charles Scribner's Sons and T. Fisher Unwin, Ltd., 1913, pp. 298, 301–303, 306, 311, 378–382. Trans by Bernard Miall.

4. Why does García Calderón view Latin America as so much different than the United States?
   (A) García Calderón makes the claim that Latin America, and Peru in particular, are not necessarily too different from the United States.
   (B) García Calderón shows that the social background of the United States is emphasized by more European migration.
   (C) García Calderón says that Latin America was led by more economic progress earlier in its history than the United States.
   (D) García Calderón argues that the United States could ultimately never be as powerful as Latin America because it simply does not have adequate land mass.

5. How did the global Depression affect nations in Latin America?
   (A) Revolutions spread throughout the continent as the poor demanded a redistribution of wealth.
   (B) Democracy spread and citizens demanded a greater voice in government.
   (C) Exports fell, and unemployment and homelessness increased.
   (D) The cost of goods dropped dramatically, giving consumers a higher standard of living.

6. Which of the following is an accurate comparison of the dictatorships of Brazil, Chile, and Argentina during the 1970s and 1980s?
   (A) They were supported by the Soviet Union.
   (B) The promoted policies of corruption, torture and violence.
   (C) Their economies flourished under military rule.
   (D) All expelled foreign-owned companies and implemented state control over the economy.

Answers

1. ANSWER: B. During the Mexican Revolution, Pancho Villa was accused of rustling cattle in Columbus, New Mexico in 1916. General Pershing was charged to lead an expeditionary force against the paramilitary troops organized by Villa. Pershing was unsuccessful in his attempts to capture and arrest Villa, further adding to Villa's appeal to Mexicans during the revolutionary years (*The Earth and Its Peoples*, 6th ed., pp. 711–714/7th ed., pp. 686–690; History Reasoning Skill—Contextualization; Learning Objectives CUL-2, SB-1; Key Concept 6.2.II.D).

2. ANSWER: D. The Mexican Revolution against the conservative and elite Mexican government was primarily a social movement, not a movement of independence. Many leaders emerged with different agendas in Mexico, but most of the issues were related to the huge social divisions that fragmented Mexican society (*The Earth and Its Peoples*, 6th ed., pp. 711–714/7th ed., 687–690; History Reasoning Skill—Comparison; Learning Objectives SOC-1,3,5; Key Concept 6.2.II.D).

3. ANSWER: C. While Mexico approves a new constitution almost immediately after the revolution in 1917, Mexico is not without its problems. Francisco Madero, a constitutionalist, was elected president during the revolution (in 1911), but was assassinated. Also, Mexico goes through other transformations, but much later… nationalizing businesses and discouraging foreign investments (*The Earth and Its Peoples*, 6th ed., pp. 796–797/7th ed., pp. 687–690; History Reasoning Skill—Contextualization; Learning Objectives SB-1,2,3,4; Key Concept 6.2.II.D).

4. ANSWER: B. García Calderón is arguing that there are many social differences in Latin America than there are in the United States. Many of those differences are founded in the way Latin America was colonized and subjected to foreign economic dependency (*The Earth and Its Peoples*, 6th ed., p. 797/7th ed., 794–797; History Disciplinary Practice—Analyzing Historical Evidence; Learning Objectives SB-1,2,3,4,6; Key Concept 6.2.II.D).

5. ANSWER: C. Most Latin American nations depended upon exports. Sugar was the main export from Cuba, coffee from Brazil and Colombia, tin from Bolivia, and beef from Argentina. The Depression caused the industrial nations to curb imports. Latin Americans were thus hit hard. In many cases, the Depression prompted military coups and takeovers (*The Earth and Its Peoples*, 6th ed., p. 796–799/7th ed., 794–797; History Reasoning Skill—Causation; Learning Objectives SB-1,2,3,4,6; Key Concept 6.2.II.D).

6. ANSWER: B. Brazil, Chile, and Argentina had military dictatorships that promoted industrialization while implementing methods of violent repression of its citizenry. All three dictatorships came to an end between 1983 and 1990, undermined by credible reports of kidnappings, torture and corruption (*The Earth and Its Peoples*, 6th ed., pp. 796–799/7th ed., 794–797; History Reasoning Skill—Comparison; Learning Objectives SB-1,2,3,4,6; Key Concept 6.2.II.D).

AP® FORMAT QUESTIONS FOR PERIOD 6

Multiple-Choice Questions

Questions 1–3 refer to the following passage.

> It is impossible even to compare the present state of the family with that which obtained before the Soviet regime—so great has been the improvement towards greater stability and above all, greater humanity and goodness. The single fact that millions of women have become economically independent and are no longer at the mercy of men's whims speaks volumes.
>
> Alexandra Kollontai, an outspoken member of the Bolshevik party, addressing the concept of Women's Rights at a lecture at Sverdlov University in 1921.

1. The views expressed in the excerpt are best seen as evidence of which of the following characteristics of the twentieth century?
   (A) Growth of popular and consumer culture
   (B) Rights-based discourse challenging old assumptions of race, class, and gender
   (C) Global protests of the inequality of environmental consequences of global integration
   (D) Changing economic institutions

2. Kollontai attributes the cause of the improved role of women to which of the following?
   (A) Communist state control
   (B) Minimal governmental interference
   (C) Economic liberalization of the society
   (D) International organizations formed to maintain world peace

3. Following World War II, Americans might have been hesitant to believe Kollontai's statements because of
   (A) ideological struggles against communism.
   (B) promotion of the practice of nonviolence rather than verbal attack.
   (C) intensified conflict in militarized states.
   (D) U.S. military alliances in NATO.

Questions 4–6 refer to the following graph.

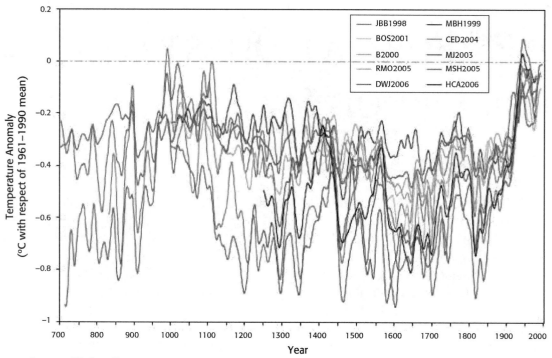

Source: "Paleoclimate temperature reconstruction of past 1300 years." Ross McKitrick. February 1, 2007. Wikicommons. https://commons.wikimedia.org/wiki/File:Temperatures_700-2000.png

4. Which of the following can be associated with the changes in temperature seen in the graph?
   (A) Rapid population growth occurred between 1900 and 2000
   (B) Shifting of the Earth's axis as discovered by Soviet scientists
   (C) Decreasing population of earth allowing more heat to be reflected
   (D) The release of Green Revolution into the atmosphere

5. Which of the following is true about the argument made by the image?
   (A) The nature and cause of climate change are unimportant to world history.
   (B) The nature and causes of climate change are based on data provided.
   (C) The nature and causes of climate change continue to be debated.
   (D) The nature and causes of climate change are only important to developed societies.

6. Which of the following is the LEAST likely to have been a main contributor to the information visible on the graph?
   (A) Greenhouse gasses
   (B) Atmospheric pollutants
   (C) Use of petroleum
   (D) Increasing disease in developing nations

Questions 7–9 refer to the following image.

7. This political cartoon could be used to support which of the following arguments about disease in Africa in the twentieth century?
   (A) Diseases associated with poverty persisted despite the improvement of the African economy.
   (B) Africa saw overwhelming improvement in disease treatment leading to demographic shifts.
   (C) Most diseases associated with poverty were overcome as the African economy improved.
   (D) No epidemic diseases continued in developing nations.

8. Which of the following is true of the area emphasized in the cartoon during the period c. 1900 to the present?
   (A) Nationalist leaders challenged imperial rule.
   (B) Imperialism continued unchallenged.
   (C) African nations were able to control their own colonies for the first time.
   (D) Regional movements always left colonial rule unchallenged.

9. Which of the following contributed the LEAST to the growth of institutions of global governance designed to address issues such as those listed in the cartoon?
   (A) International organizations such as the Red Cross
   (B) Economic institutions such as the World Bank funding local economic initiatives
   (C) Protest movements challenging government corruption
   (D) Nationalist movements fighting to expel specific ethnic groups

Questions 10–12 refer to the following passage.

In modern industrialized nations fast food has come to cater to changing needs. Women and men in modern industrial societies marry later or not at all, and families have fewer meals together because of intense school and work schedules. As a result, fast food outlets have appeared everywhere to meet the needs of this busy, mobile population. In 2006 alone the world market for fast food grew by just under 7 percent, reaching sales of $155 billion.

Increased immigration and travel, as well as greater cultural connectivity promoted by films, television, and the Web, have combined to globalize ideas about food preparation and delivery. McDonald's now operates more than 31,000 restaurants in 119 countries. When a new franchise opened in Kuwait City, the drive-through line was over 10 kilometers (6.2 miles) long. Generally fast food meals cost the same in every cultural setting. In the United States, one of the richest countries in the world, McDonald's provides low-cost food to the masses, while in Pakistan, one of the poorest, these meals are luxuries. For many in the developing world, the fast food cuisines, restaurant designs, and styles of preparation represent the world of modernity and sophistication, not unlike the enthusiasm in the developed world for Mexican, Thai, or Ethiopian restaurants and cuisines.

The Earth and Its Peoples, 6th ed., p. 890

10. Based on this excerpt, which of the following was true of the period c. 1900 to the present?
    (A) Popular and consumer culture has become more global.
    (B) Nationalism has resulted in increasingly dissimilar identities across the globe.
    (C) Food production has become the most important aspect of a nation's identity.
    (D) Increasing availability of cheap food has made culture less valuable.

11. Which of the following could best be argued as a cause of the migrations due to cultural and economic ties from a former colony, even after the dissolution of an empire, as discussed in the excerpt?
    (A) New modes of communication and transportation reduced the problem of geographic distance.
    (B) Medical innovations increased the ability of humans to survive and live longer lives.
    (C) Energy technologies including the use of petroleum and nuclear power raised productivity.
    (D) The Green Revolution decreased the amount of food available per person agriculturally.

12. The fact that cultural and economic ties between a former colony and its metropoles continued to be maintained could best be exemplified by which of the following?
    (A) McDonald's in Korea serving traditional Korean Bulgogi (meat)
    (B) Increasing prevalence of Ethiopian restaurants in America
    (C) McDonald's in England serving Indian curries and chutney
    (D) China refusing to allow McDonald's franchises to be built

Questions 13–15 refer to the following map.

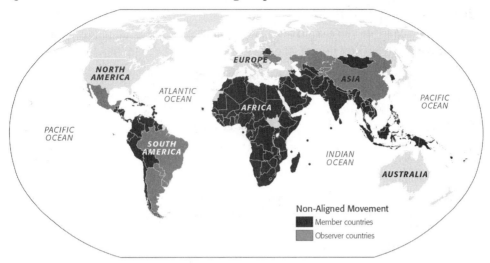

© Cengage Learning

13. Which of the following is the best explanation of the function of the Nonaligned Movement?
    (A) Oppose and promote alternatives to existing economic, political, and social orders.
    (B) Fight for increased economic accommodations for developing nations.
    (C) Expand military response to small-scale crises around the globe.
    (D) Divide the globe based on Cold War military alignments.

14. Which of the following is the LEAST likely way that individuals and groups (like the Nonaligned Movement) responded to conflict distinguished in the twenty-first century?
    (A) Used violence against civilians to achieve political aims
    (B) Promoted nonviolence
    (C) Further intensified conflict
    (D) Eliminated conflict in favor of UN discussion

15. Which of the following was an essential part of the foundation and growth of the Nonaligned Movement?
    (A) The emergence of the United States and the Soviet Union as superpowers
    (B) A lack of military alliances for countries in the Eastern Hemisphere
    (C) A desire to promote growing "Black Power" movements
    (D) A recognition of the impact of greenhouse gasses on the environment near the equator

Short-Answer Questions

Question 1 refers to the following passage.

> One does not need to plan for or actively encourage real integration. Once the various groups within a given community have asserted themselves to the point that mutual respect has to be shown then you have the ingredients for a true and meaningful integration.
>
> Stephen Biko, I Write What I Like

1. Answer Parts A and B.
   A. Identify ONE change or development in twentieth-century Africa that would support the author's assertion in the passage.
   B. Explain TWO changes or developments in twentieth-century Africa that would challenge the author's assertion in the passage.

Question 2 refers to the following passage.

> We do not acknowledge any right claimed by the French Government in any part whatever of our Syrian country and refuse that she should assist us or have a hand in our country under any circumstances and in any place.
>
> Memorandum of the General Syrian Congress, called in 1919 to consider the role of an independent Syria following expulsion of the Ottoman Empire. July 2, 1919.

2. Answer Parts A and B.
   A. Identify ONE example that would support the author's view of post-Imperial nationalism.
   B. Explain TWO examples of post-Imperial nationalism that would challenge the author's view of post-Imperial nationalism in the passage.

Question 3 refers to the following image.

Photo of The Bund in Shanghai, c. 1900. The Bund was the most important street in Shanghai, containing banks, corporate headquarters, and luxury hotels facing the waterfront where ships from around the world docked.

Bettmann/Corbis

3. Answer Parts A and B.
   A. Identify ONE historical claim about early twentieth-century China that can be supported by the image.
   B. Explain TWO limitations of the image as a source of information about early twentieth-century China.

Question 4 refers to the following image.

Nuclear warhead stockpiles of the United States and the USSR/Russia, 1945–2014. These numbers are total stockpiles, including warheads that are not actively deployed (that is, including those on reserve status, but not those that are scheduled for dismantlement).

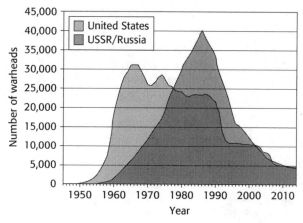

Source: Wikimedia Commons. Data from: Robert S. Norris and Hans M. Kristensen, "Global nuclear stockpiles, 1945–2006." *Bulletin of the Atomic Scientists* 62, no.4 (July/August 2006). 64–66. Online. https://commons.wikimedia.org/wiki/File:US_and_USSR_nuclear_stockpiles.svg

4.   Answer Parts A and B.

A.   Identify TWO historical claims about the Cold War that can be supported by the graph.

B. Explain ONE effect of the Cold War on a nation NOT mentioned in the graph.

5. Answer Parts A, B, and C.
   A. Identify ONE military alliance produced by the Cold War.
   B. Explain ONE example of a pro-Communist government in Latin America.
   C. Explain ONE example of a pro-Democracy government in Latin America.

LONG ESSAY QUESTIONS

1. Compare the extent of struggle for negotiated independence and the armed struggle for independence in the twentieth century.

2. Compare the extent of influence of the Islamic revolutions in Iran and Afghanistan in the twentieth century.

3. Analyze the political continuities and changes experienced in ONE of the following nations between World War I and the present.
   ▨ India
   ▨ China
   ▨ Japan

4. Using specific examples, analyze continuities and changes in the political and economic structures of European nation-states during the second half of the twentieth century.

5. Compare the extent of causes of the Mexican Revolution in the early twentieth century with that of the Cuban Revolution in the 1950s and 1960s.

Answers

MULTIPLE-CHOICE QUESTIONS

1. ANSWER: B. Kollontai's comments highlighted the changes in family structure, and emphasized the changes in women's roles that took place in the Soviet Union. This reflects the fact that rights-based discourses challenged old assumptions of gender (*The Earth and Its Peoples*, 6th ed., pp. 836–837/7th ed., pp. 806–807; History Reasoning Skill—Continuity and Change over Time; Learning Objective CUL-2,3,4,5,9, SB-4, ECON-4, SOC-1,3,5,6; Key Concept 6.3.III).

2. ANSWER: **A.** Kollontai indicated that the catalyst for the changes that she identified was the rise of the Soviet Regime, and thereby the rise of Communist state control (*The Earth and Its Peoples*, 6th ed., pp. 836–837/7th ed., pp. 806–807; History Reasoning Skill—Causation; Learning Objective CUL-3,8, SB-1,2,3,4,8,9,10, ECON-3,4, SOC-7; Key Concept 6.2.IV).

3. ANSWER: A. Statements such as those Kollontai put forth would have been difficult for U.S. citizens to accept following World War II because of the intense suspicion of communism. Kollontai's praise of the Soviet state would have been highly questionable in that environment (*The Earth and Its Peoples*, 6th ed., pp. 836–837/7th ed., pp. 806–807; History Reasoning Skill—Causation; Learning Objective CUL-3,8, SB1,2,3,4,8,9,10, ECON-3,4, SOC-7; Key Concept 6.2.IV).

4. ANSWER: A. Rapid advances in science throughout the Industrial Revolution and the twentieth century led to an increase in population, which is argued to be one cause of generalized global temperature increase (*The Earth and Its Peoples*, 6th ed., p. 914/7th ed., p. 875; History Reasoning Skill—Contextualization; Learning Objective ENV-6,8,9, CUL-6,7, ECON-1,12; Key Concept 6.1.I,II).

5. ANSWER:C. The image indicates a rise in general temperatures but gives no specific cause. In addition, the graph indicates repeated increases and decreases in temperature over time, indicating that the cause of these temperature increases could be variable. This leaves them open to debate (*The Earth and Its Peoples*, 6th ed., p. 914/7th ed., p. 875; History Disciplinary Practice—Argument Development; Learning Objective ENV-6,8,9, CUL-6,7, ECON-1,12; Key Concept 6.1.I,II).

6. ANSWER: D. Increasing disease lowers population and decreases overall use of fossil fuels. It cannot be argued as a cause for increasing temperatures (*The Earth and Its Peoples*, 6th ed., p. 914/7th ed., p. 875; History Disciplinary Practice—Argument Development; Learning Objective ENV-6,8,9, CUL-6,7, ECON-1,12; Key Concept 6.1.II,III).

7. ANSWER: A. The location of "AIDS" alongside the word "Poverty" on the ball and chain still attached to the individual indicates that disease continued to persist and cause difficulty for individuals in countries of Africa, while the ball and chain of debt was broken (*The Earth and Its Peoples*, 6th ed., pp. 880–883/7th ed., pp. 848–851; History Disciplinary Practice—Argument Development; Learning Objective ENV-7, CUL-7, SB-9,10, SOC-6; Key Concept 6.1.II).

8. ANSWER: A. Africa in the twentieth century experienced significant upheaval as imperial policy dissipated. Nationalist leaders in many African nations began to challenge and overthrow their imperial rulers (*The Earth and Its Peoples*, 6th ed., pp. 880–883/7th ed., pp. 848–851; History Reasoning Skill—Contextualization; Learning Objective CUL-3,4,9, SB-1,2,4,7,9,10, ECON-7,8,9, SOC-3,4,7; Key Concept 6.2.II).

9. ANSWER: D. Each of the listed organizations was designed to facilitate solutions to the problems listed in the cartoon except for nationalist movements that were designed to enforce ethnic cleansing. By definition, nationalist movements are not multinational (*The Earth and Its Peoples*, 6th ed., pp. 880–883/7th ed., pp. 848–851; History Reasoning Skill—Contextualization; Learning Objective ENV-3,9, CUL-3, SB2,4,9,10, ECON-3,4,9,11,13, SOC-4; Key Concept 6.3.II).

10. ANSWER: A. The excerpt focuses on McDonald's. The spread of this American chain restaurant and comments regarding access to popular culture indicate the globalization of culture (*The Earth and Its Peoples*, 6th ed., p. 890/7th ed., p. 890; History Reasoning Skill—Continuity and Change over Time; Learning Objective CUL-2,3,4,5,9, SB-4, ECON-4, SOC-1,3,5,6; Key Concept 6.3.III).

11. ANSWER: A. The facilitation of a global culture is tied intricately to the ease with which ideas, goods, and technology can spread across the globe. As more people are able to live and travel in multiple areas, they bring with them elements of global culture. This is echoed in the passage with the reference to U.S. fascination with ethnic restaurants (in comparison to global fascination with McDonald's) (*The Earth and Its Peoples*, 6th ed., p. 890/7th ed., p. 890; History Reasoning Skill—Causation; Learning Objective ENV-6,8,9, CUL-6,7, ECON-1,12; Key Concept 6.1.I).

12. ANSWER: C. McDonald's in England serving Indian curries and chutney is a reflection of the long-term impact that England's colonization of India continues to have. Indian citizens who have moved to England have continued to build a market for traditional Indian culture in the center of a former colonial power (*The Earth and Its Peoples*, 6th ed., p. 890/7th ed., p. 890; History Reasoning Skill—Causation; Learning Objective SB-4,7,9,10, ECON-2, SOC-8; Key Concept 6.2.III).

13. **ANSWER: A.** The purpose of the Nonaligned Movement was specifically to give power to those countries outside of traditional aligned nations by promoting alternatives to existing political, economic, and social orders (*The Earth and Its Peoples*, 6th ed., pp. 856–857/7th ed., pp. 827–828; History Reasoning Skill—Contextualization; Learning Objective CUL-3,9, SB-1,2,7,8,9,10, ECON-3, SOC-3,4; Key Concept 6.2.V).

14. **ANSWER: C.** The Nonaligned Movement was created specifically to decrease and end violence and conflict among nations. Nonaligned nations such as those in the map responded to conflict in many ways designed to end conflict. They did not promote or intensify conflict (*The Earth and Its Peoples*, 6th ed., pp. 856–857/7th ed., pp. 827–828; History Reasoning Skill—Comparison; Learning Objective CUL3,9, SB-1,2,7,8,9,10, ECON-3, SOC-3,4; Key Concept 6.2.V).

15. **ANSWER: A.** The Nonaligned Movement was initiated as a method of gaining support from both the United States and the Soviet Union during the Cold War. The emergence of these two nations as superpowers led to the creation of the movement (*The Earth and Its Peoples*, 6th ed., pp. 856–857/7th ed., pp. 827–828; History Reasoning Skill—Causation; Learning Objective CUL-3,9, SB-1,2,7,8,9,10, ECON-3, SOC-3,4; Key Concept 6.2.V).

SHORT-ANSWER QUESTIONS

1. Answers will vary. A variety of examples could successfully respond to this prompt. Most appropriate examples refuting the author's assertion would include references to Apartheid policies (limited voting, inability to hold office, etc.), which indicated that integration required far more than simply assertive groups. Evidence to support Biko's position could include an explanation of Biko's position and actions as a member of the Black Consciousness Movement, or may address Nelson Mandela's role in ending Apartheid (*The Earth and Its Peoples*, 6th ed., pp. 854–855/7th ed., pp. 824–825; History Disciplinary Practice—Argument Development; Learning Objective CUL-2,3,4,5,9, SB-4, ECON-4, SOC-1,3,5,6; Key Concept 6.3).

2. This question asks for analysis of the role of imperial nations in the emerging nationalism of the post-imperial world. Answers will vary. For Part A, examples may show some level of violence and complete requirement of the imperial power's removal (see French from Vietnam, Portuguese being removed from Angola, French from Syria, etc.). Part B requires a recognition of nations requiring or requesting continued support from imperial nations. The best example of this in the Middle East might be Israel's reliance on British power following the Balfour Declaration for the creation of the State of Israel (*The Earth and Its Peoples*, 6th ed., p. 771/7th ed., p. 745; History Disciplinary Practices—Argument Development, Analyzing Historical Evidence; Learning Objective CUL-3,4,9, SB-1,2,4,7,9,10, ECON 7,8,9, SOC-3,4,7; Key Concept 6.2).

3. A good response would identify and explain TWO characteristics of China that can be specifically evidenced from the photo presented. The mix of pedestrian and rickshaw could be used to support discussion of China's conflict between tradition and modernity. Supporting details could include Empress Cixi's reign, the Righteous Fists, or Boxer Rebellion. Similarly, references to the European buildings and the modern waterfront could be supported with details about European involvement, spheres of influence, or the eventual May Fourth Movement and the growing tension between the Chinese and the Europeans.

A good response must also address one limitation of the document as a source of information. One example of a limitation could be a lack of information about the photographer or the person paying for the photograph. This could lead to questions about the purpose of the photograph or the veracity of the image (*The Earth and Its Peoples*, 6th ed., p. 765/7th ed., p. 740; History Disciplinary Practices—Argument Development, Analyzing Historical Evidence; Learning Objectives SB-2,7,8,9,10, ECON-4; Key Concept 6.2).

4. A. A good response would identify the fact that the global balance of economic and political power shifted after the end of World War II, and the United States and the Soviet Union emerged as superpowers. These arguments could be developed with specific examples such as treaties, presidential meetings, the Berlin Wall, the Berlin Airlift, and so on.

   B. The effects of the Cold War on non-superpower nations could be adequately argued with reference to any of the Soviet satellite nations or the war in Afghanistan. In addition, reference to Vietnam or Korea as proxy wars could also be sufficient.

   (*The Earth and Its Peoples*, 6th ed., pp. 838–893/7th ed., pp. 806–833; History Reasoning Skill—Causation; Learning Objective CUL-3,8, SB-1,2,3,4,8,9,10, ECON-3,4,9, SOC-7; Key Concept 6.2).

5. A. The most common examples for Part A are likely to be NATO and the Warsaw Pact. Additional answers might include the OAS (Organization of American States) established in 1948.

B. Common answers may include Cuba, Chile, Costa Rica, and Guatemala (pre-1954).

C. Answers will vary but may include Nicaragua, Mexico, and Brazil post-1963 coup.

(*The Earth and Its Peoples*, 6th ed., pp. 853–857/7th ed., pp. 823–828; History Disciplinary Practice—Argument Development; Learning Objective SB-2,7,8,9,10, ECON-4; Key Concept 6.2)

LONG ESSAY QUESTIONS

1. Five key factors explain the independence struggle throughout Africa—World War II, the role of Western-educated African elites, the independence of India, Pan-Africanism, and the weakening of Europe as a result of the two world wars. A good response should compare/contrast at least two of the factors. It should include the role of white settler populations and their effect on the independence struggle. For example, both Kwame Nkrumah of Ghana and Jomo Kenyatta of Kenya studied abroad, in the United States and Great Britain, respectively. There they witnessed the hypocrisy of Western democratic ideals while absorbing notions of black pride and Pan-Africanism. South Africa, Algeria, and Kenya were all areas with a significant population of white settlers. Whereas Africans in some places were eventually able to negotiate freedom after the success of Indian independence, the settlers fiercely resisted majority rule. Thus, Africans in Algeria, Kenya, and South Africa were forced to use armed struggle in order to gain independence (*The Earth and Its Peoples*, 6th ed., pp. 820–821/7th ed., pp. 764–765; History Reasoning Skill—Comparison, Argumentation; Learning Objective SB-2,7,8,9,10, ECON-4; Key Concept 6.2).

2. A good response should discuss the Cold War strategic importance of both nations—both were located on the border of the Soviet Union. Both the United States and the Soviet Union were attempting to gain influence and allies. The response should also mention that Iran became an American war and Afghanistan became a Soviet war. The United States resorted to covert involvement, while the Soviets' involvement was more direct. In regard to effects, mention that both nations shunned Westernization for conservative Islam. It should also make clear that while the outcomes for both the United States and the Soviet Union would be considered failures, the Soviet Union suffered greater loss because of its greater sense of urgency and involvement (*The Earth and Its Peoples*, 6th ed., p. 871/7th ed., pp. 839–840; History Reasoning Skill—Comparison; Learning Objective CUL-3,9, SB-1,2,7,8,9,10, ECON-3, SOC-3,4; Key Concept 6.2).

3. All three nations had very different experiences during the twentieth century. Japan and China overlapped and directly related to each another. Nonetheless, all three regions faced various degrees of foreign involvement and colonization. A good response will illustrate this struggle, as well as the role played by the two world wars and the Cold War. It should also describe the economic growth that positioned all three nations on the cusp of global power (*The Earth and Its Peoples*, 6th ed., p. 765/7th ed., p. 740; History Reasoning Skill—Continuity and Change over Time; Learning Objectives SB-2,7,8,9,10, ECON-4; Key Concept 6.2).

4. A good response could begin with an explanation of the traditional European nation-state. It should then show how the Cold War created ideological blocks/alliances that were manifested within the United Nations, an organization that by its very nature is often asked to intrude

in the affairs of sovereign nations. Nongovernmental organizations, multinational corporations, and the European Union have all chipped away at the role of the nation-state. The essay should chart this increase in globalization to demonstrate how the nation-state was becoming more fluid and less bound by physical borders. Continuities could include the continuing use of transnational groups, such as alliances before World War I and groups like the League of Nations, the United Nations, and the European Union (*The Earth and Its Peoples*, 6th ed., pp. 838–893/7th ed., pp. 808–813; History Reasoning Skill—Continuity and Change over Time; Learning Objective SB-2,7,8,9,10, ECON-4; Key Concept 6.2).

5. Despite the difference in period, both revolutions were responses to two fundamental issues that plagued nations in the Americas during the twentieth century: foreign economic domination and social inequality. Mexicans were dismayed by the fact that the largest industries in Mexico, such as oil, mining, and transportation, were controlled by companies from the United States and other foreign nations. Similarly, Cuba's largest industries, sugar production, banking, and transportation, were controlled by Americans. Thus, in both Mexico and Cuba, wealth was accumulated and held by foreigners and the small domestic elite. The vast majority of people in both Mexico and Cuba were poor. The Mexican Revolution was more gradual and experienced a period of very moderate progress. In Cuba, on the other hand, Fidel Castro succeeded in transferring 15 percent of the national income from the rich to the poor in the first year. While both nations witnessed drastic social transformations, Cuba faced harsh and consistent pressure from the United States to alter the effects of the Revolution (*The Earth and Its Peoples*, 6th ed., pp. 712–714, 854–855/7th ed., pp. 687–690, 823–824; History Reasoning Skill—Comparison; Learning Objective SB-2,7,8,9,10, ECON-4; Key Concept 6.2).

Part III

Practice Tests

Practice Test 1

AP® WORLD HISTORY EXAMINATION
Section I
Part A: Multiple-Choice Questions
Time: 55 minutes
Number of questions: 55
Percent of examination score: 40%

Note: This examination uses the chronological designations B.C.E. (before the Common Era) and C.E. (Common Era). These correspond to B.C. (before Christ) and A.D. (anno Domini), which are used in some world history textbooks.

DIRECTIONS: The multiple-choice section consists of question sets organized around a stimulus—a primary or secondary source, a historian's argument, or a historical problem. For each question, select the best response.

Questions 1–2 refer to the following passage.

> If a man came forward with false testimony in a case, and has not proved the word which he spoke, if that case was a case involving life, that man shall be put to death. If a man stole the property of church or state, that man shall be put to death; also the one who received the stolen goods from his hand shall be put to death. If a man has struck the cheek of a man who is superior to him, he shall be beaten sixty times with an oxtail whip in the assembly.
>
> Code of Hammurabi, 1750 B.C.E.

1. The Code of Hammurabi demonstrates which of the following?
   (A) The development of regional and interregional trade
   (B) The development of legal codes to facilitate the rule of governments over people
   (C) The development of new weapons
   (D) The development of urban planning

2. What is demonstrated with the punishment described in the passage?
   (A) New religious beliefs developed, such as Hebrew monotheism.
   (B) The existence of intensified social hierarchies as states expanded.
   (C) Systems of record keeping developed in early civilizations.
   (D) Plants and animals had been domesticated.

Questions 3–4 refer to the following passage.

> When the head of a household arrives at his estate . . . he must go round his farm on a tour of inspection on the very same day. If the work doesn't seem to him to be sufficient, and the manager starts to say how hard he tried, but the slaves weren't any good, and the slaves ran away . . . you must draw his attention to your calculation of the labor employed and time taken.
>
> Cato the Elder, Roman, Concerning Agriculture, second century B.C.E.

3. Which of the following could best be used to provide context for the focus of the above passage?
   (A) The growth of trade and urbanization in Rome threatened to make farming obsolete, making farmers fear for the success of their businesses.
   (B) Roman social structure was based on land ownership and the elite saw successful management of agriculture as a key to Rome's prosperity.
   (C) Rome was reaching the limits of its expansion, and new slaves were becoming scarce in the Empire.
   (D) Rome's transition to Empire made retaining tradition and social order extremely important.

AP® is a trademark registered by the College Board, which is not affiliated with, and does not endorse, this product.

GO ON TO NEXT PAGE

4. The above passage could best be used as evidence of which of the following broader historical trends?
   (A) Patriarchy continued to shape gender and family relationships.
   (B) Classical societies relied on a range of methods to maintain the production of food and provide rewards for the elites.
   (C) New technology was utilized to improve agricultural production and produce population growth.
   (D) The spread of crops from South Asia to the Middle East and Europe encouraged changes in farming techniques.

Questions 5–7 refer to the following passage.

Let a woman retire late to bed, but rise early to duties; let her not dread tasks by day or by night. Let her not refuse to perform domestic duties whether easy or difficult. That which must be done, let her finish completely, tidily, and systematically. Let a woman be correct in manner and upright in character in order to serve her husband. The Way of the husband and wife is intimately connected with Yin and Yang and relates the individual to gods and ancestors.

Ban Zhao, *Lessons for Women*, China 80 C.E.

5. This excerpt by Ban Zhao most closely represents which of the following belief systems?
   (A) Buddhism
   (B) Confucianism
   (C) Vedic beliefs
   (D) Hinduism

6. The *Lessons for Women* reinforced which of the following gender systems?
   (A) Strict obedience to the rulers
   (B) A bureaucracy
   (C) Caste system
   (D) Patriarchy

7. Which of the following represents a significant challenge to the ideas represented in Ban Zhao's *Lessons for Women*?
   (A) Demands for women's suffrage during the nineteenth century
   (B) Growing nationalism during the nineteenth century
   (C) The spread of the second agricultural revolution in the nineteenth century
   (D) The global economy of the nineteenth century

Questions 8–10 refer to the following map.

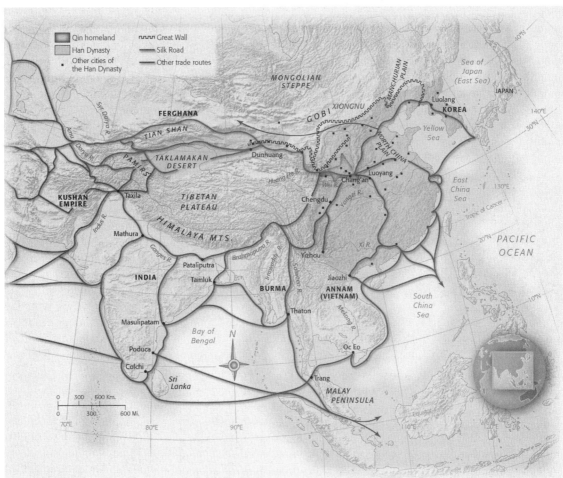

© Cengage Learning

8. Which of the following belief systems diffused to East Asia via the roads in the image?
   (A) Shintoism
   (B) Hinduism
   (C) Zoroastrianism
   (D) Buddhism

9. During the Classical era, all of the following were true of imperial governments. Which of the following methods of projecting military power over large areas can best be proved by the above map?
   (A) They issued currency to develop a consistent monetary system.

(B) They drew new groups of soldiers from conquered populations.
(C) The built defensive walls and roads.
(D) They mobilized resources and concentrated too much wealth in the hands of elites.

10. Which of the following developments during the fifteenth and sixteenth centuries had a similar trans-regional impact (as that shown on the map)?
   (A) The Columbian Exchange
   (B) The expansion of the Mughal Empire
   (C) The collection of Tribute
   (D) The restructuring of families in Africa

Questions 11–12 refer to the following map.

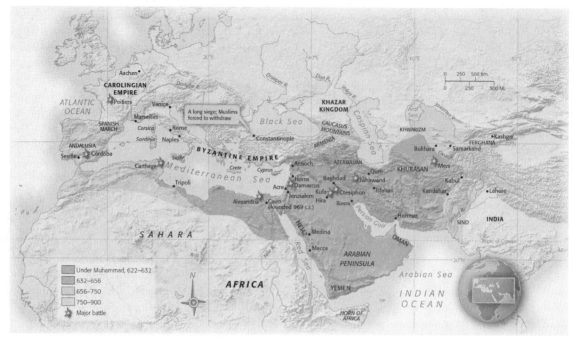

11. Which of the following most directly led to the conquests seen in the map?
    (A) The expansion of the Silk Road
    (B) The Bantu migrations
    (C) The maritime migrations of the Polynesian peoples
    (D) The spread of Islam

12. Which of the following challenged and changed the governing structures in the Middle East during the thirteenth century?
    (A) The Mongol Khanates
    (B) The Byzantine Empire
    (C) The Tang Dynasty
    (D) The Feudal Kingdoms in Japan

Questions 13–15 refer to the following passage.

The pope can be judged by no one; The Roman church has never erred and never will err till the end of time; the pope alone can depose and restore bishops; he can depose emperors; all princes should kiss his feet.

Pope Gregory VII, 1073 C.E.

13. The ideas expressed in the above passage most closely resemble which of the following governing structures?
    (A) The decentralized government in Japan
    (B) The Caliphate
    (C) The Imperial system of the Aztecs
    (D) The mit'a system of the Inca Empire

14. Which of the following led to changes in the belief system espoused in the quote by Pope Gregory VII?
    (A) Populations in Afro-Eurasia that benefited from increased diversity of American food crops
    (B) The growth of the Ottoman Empire

    (C) The spread of new technology like the printing press and the subsequent spread of new political, philosophical, and scientific ideas throughout Europe
    (D) The growth of the trans-Saharan trade route, which led to new powerful trading cities

15. Which of the following was Pope Gregory most trying to influence with the above passage?
    (A) The Byzantine Empire
    (B) The Hanseatic League
    (C) Imperial Rome
    (D) Feudal Western Europe

Questions 16–18 refer to the following passage.

Hereditary class distinctions meant less than they had in Tang times, when noble lineages played a greater role in the structure of power. The new system recruited the most talented men, whatever their origin. Yet men from wealthy families enjoyed an advantage. Preparation for the tests consumed so much time that peasant boys could rarely compete.

Success in the examinations brought good marriage prospects, the chance for a high salary, and enormous prestige. This put great pressure on candidates, who spent days writing essays in tiny, dim, airless examination cells.

The Earth and Its Peoples, 6th ed., p. 307

16. The young men referenced in the passage hoped to get what type of job?
    (A) A military leader
    (B) A job in an administrative institution (bureaucracy)
    (C) A merchant
    (D) A sponsor of commercial infrastructures, such as the Grand Canal

17. The social mobility discussed in the quote above is most similar to the social mobility to which of the following?
    (A) The class system that developed in response to the Industrial Revolution during the eighteenth and nineteenth centuries
    (B) The Nationalist leaders in Africa who challenged imperial rule during the twentieth century
    (C) The caste system of India
    (D) The tributary system of the Mongol Khanates

18. Which of the following brought a drastic change to the Chinese examination system?
    (A) The communist revolution in China
    (B) The expansion of the Silk Road
    (C) The growth of Daoism
    (D) The spread of Buddhism to China

Questions 19–20 refer to the following image of the Great Plaza at Tikal, in Guatemala.

By Dennis Jarvis from Halifax, Canada [CC BY-SA 2.0 (http://creativecommons.org/licenses/by-sa/2.0)], via Wikimedia Commons

19. Which of the following can be inferred from this image?
    (A) The Mayans had synthesized their local traditions with foreign traditions.
    (B) The Mayans had a city-state with monumental architecture.
    (C) The Mayans were heavily influenced by Afro-Eurasian trade networks.
    (D) The Mayans utilized the astrolabe to encourage trade.

20. Which of the following was most likely the cause of the demise of the people who built the structures seen in the image?
    (A) European colonization of the Americas
    (B) Intertribal warfare combined with climate changes
    (C) The introduction of Afro-Eurasian fruit trees, grains, and sugar, which changed the geography of the region
    (D) The importation of African slaves

Questions 21–22 refer to the following image.

The Metropolitan Museum of Art/Image source/
Art Resource, NY

Mongolian passport, thirteenth century C.E.

21. The image supports which of the following assumptions regarding the Mongols?
(A) The Mongols followed the teachings of the prophet Muhammad.
(B) The Mongols stimulated new labor practices due to their expansion.
(C) The Mongols controlled the Indian Ocean basin.
(D) The Mongols facilitated and protected trade networks.

22. Which of the following technological developments would most likely be used in conjunction with the passport seen in the image?
(A) Compass
(B) Astrolabe
(C) Caravanserai
(D) Larger ship designs

Questions 23–25 refer to the following image of people burying victims of the Black Death.

Snark/Art Resource, NY

23. Which of the following was the primary cause of the scene in the above image?
    (A) The diffusion of pathogens along Eastern Hemispheric trade routes
    (B) The increase of cross-cultural interactions that resulted in the diffusion of scientific innovations
    (C) The pastoral peoples of Eurasia migrated to the east
    (D) The strained environmental resources that caused dramatic demographic swings

24. Which of the following causes of mass casualties throughout history can best be compared to the situation depicted in the above image?
    (A) The release of greenhouse gases and other pollutants during the twentieth century
    (B) Wartime deaths caused by improved military technology and tactics
    (C) Twentieth-century genocides carried out in Germany, Rwanda and Cambodia
    (D) The spread of smallpox to the Americas during the sixteenth century

25. Which of the following was a direct result of what is depicted in the image?
    (A) The elimination of the patriarchy in Europe
    (B) The decline of urban areas
    (C) Western Europeans turned away from religion as their prayers appeared to go unanswered
    (D) The increased reliance on Buddhism in order to eliminate suffering

Questions 26–29 refer to the following passage.

In 1545, shortly after silver deposits were found in Mexico, the greatest discovery in world history was made high in the Andes at Potosi where Spanish found a whole mountain of silver. Andean silver enabled European trade with Asia, and much of the silver extracted from Potosi ended up in China. The exploitation of American silver and Amerindian labor therefore stimulated the development of a more integrated early modern world economy.

Voyages in World History, 3rd ed., p. 535

26. Which of the following occurred as an immediate result of the discovery described in the above system?
    (A) The Incan Empire went to war with Spain.
    (B) China sent Zheng He to secure direct access to silver.
    (C) South American states fought over control of the silver deposits.
    (D) Spain adopted the Mit'a system.

27. Which of the following was a direct result of the development described in the passage?
    (A) The Atlantic system developed that led to the mixing of African, American, and European cultures.
    (B) The silver mining led to the Little Ice Age that lasted until the nineteenth century.
    (C) Religious art was used in the new world in order for the ruling elite to legitimize their rule.
    (D) Land empires, such as the Manchu, Mughal, and Ottomans, responded to the growth of the Spanish Empire by decreasing in size.

28. Which of the following could best be used to refute the argument made in the above passage?
    (A) The silver trade caused mass inflation in China, which destabilized and contributed to the collapse of the Qing Dynasty.
    (B) Spain's influence in global politics declined in part from poor management of wealth in the sixteenth and seventeenth centuries.
    (C) Medical innovations and vaccines were spread throughout the world in the nineteenth and twentieth centuries in part due to the existence of an interconnected global society.
    (D) The agricultural revolution caused a drastic increase in food supply and demographics in the pre-classical age

29. Which of the following led directly to the conditions described in the excerpt?
    (A) An Islamic monopoly on Asian goods
    (B) The increase of travelers within Afro-Eurasia who wrote about their travels, thus inspiring the West
    (C) The European search for multiple routes to Asia
    (D) The emergence of Neo Confucianism in China which led to an increase in demand for Chinese goods

Questions 30–32 refer to the following passage.

The first object which saluted my eyes when I arrived on the coast was the sea, and a slaveship. . . . These filled me with astonishment, which was soon converted into terror. . . . I was now persuaded that I had gotten into a world of bad spirits, and that they were going to kill me . . . They made ready with many fearful noises, and we were all put under deck. The closeness of the place, and the heat of the climate, added to the number in the ship, which was so crowded that each had scarcely room to turn himself, almost suffocated us. The shrieks of the women, and the groans of the dying, rendered the whole scene of horror almost inconceivable.

Olaudah Equiano, The Interesting Narrative of the Life of Olaudah Equiano, eighteenth century

30. Which of the following was a direct result of the situation that Equiano described in the passage above?
    (A) There was a formation of new political and economic elites in the Caribbean.
    (B) There were demographic changes in Africa.
    (C) The Second Industrial Revolution in the Americas was made possible by slave labor from Africa.
    (D) Steamships were developed in order to alleviate the hardships described in the passage.

31. Which of the following philosophical or political developments fostered a sense of outrage at what Equiano described?

    (A) Emerging feminism that developed during the nineteenth century
    (B) Enlightenment ideas that developed during the eighteenth and nineteenth centuries
    (C) Capitalist ideas that were spreading in the nineteenth century
    (D) Monarchist ideals that encompass the social contract

32. Which of the following revolutions does Equiano seem to foreshadow?
    (A) The American Revolution
    (B) The Haitian Revolution
    (C) The Latin American independence movements
    (D) The French Revolution

GO ON TO NEXT PAGE

Questions 33–35 refer to the following map.

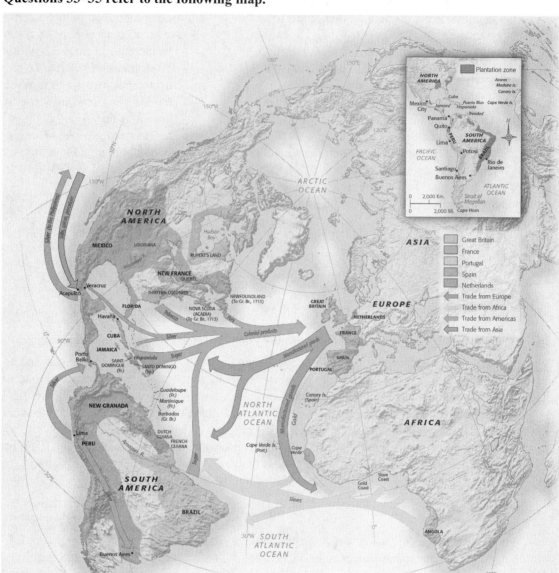

33. According to this map, why do historians consider 1450–1750 a turning point in world history?
    (A) It marks the first time silver was used as a monetized currency system.
    (B) It marks the beginning of African dominance in oceanic trade.
    (C) It marks the beginning of the diffusion of multiple languages.
    (D) It marks the beginning of globalizing networks of communication and exchange.

34. What was the impact of the trade routes shown in the map?
    (A) Populations increased in Europe due to the nutrition in the American food crops.
    (B) Populations decreased in Europe and Africa due to increased migration to the Americas.
    (C) New ethnic and racial classifications arose in Europe and Africa.
    (D) The Amerindians benefited economically from the interregional trade.

35. Which of the following trends during the twentieth century was similar to the trends shown in the map?
(A) Global markets of the twentieth century were similar in that they practiced free market economics.
(B) Regions became increasingly interdependent during the twentieth century.
(C) Western Europe lost global economic power during the latter half of the twentieth century.
(D) Human interaction with the environment during the twentieth century did not change from the interaction during the eighteenth century.

Questions 36–38 refer to the following passage.

The hour was already advanced, the day was declining and near evening, and the sun was at the Ottomans' backs but shining in the faces of their enemies. To begin, the archers and slingers and those in charge of the cannon and the muskets, in accord with the commands given them, advanced against the wall slowly. All of it had been destroyed by cannon. Sultan Mehmed, who happened to be fighting quite near by, saw that the palisade and the other part of the wall had been destroyed were now empty of men and deserted by the defenders.

Greek official, The Fall of Constantinople, 1453

36. Which of the following occurred as a result of the event described in the passage?
(A) Eastern Orthodox Christians fled west and joined the Catholic Church.
(B) Byzantine Christians fled to Russia to convert the Kievan princes to Orthodoxy.
(C) The Eastern Orthodox Church collapsed and ceased to exist.
(D) Eastern Orthodox Byzantines continued practicing their religion under the new Ottoman state, provided they pay a special tax.

37. What other Muslim land empire also utilized gunpowder technology to expand?
(A) The Mughal Empire
(B) The Manchu Empire
(C) The Russian Empire
(D) The Mongolian Empire

38. The empire described in the passage collapsed due to a combination of internal and external factors. What century did this empire collapse?
(A) Seventeenth century
(B) Eighteenth century
(C) Nineteenth century
(D) Twentieth century

Questions 39 and 40 refer to the following passage.

Supposing that a man born fifty years ago returned to Japan after a wandering life in a foreign country without any news from his fatherland, how many of the scenes before him would resemble those of his childhood? Very few indeed. To commence with: he would find no trace of the Shogun, and no daimyo. The castles of the daimyo would now show themselves to him as a mass of crumbling ruins; the spears, swords, and other implements of warfare, which he regarded with awe as a child, he would only find preserved by amateurs as objects of historic interest.

Sakutaro Fujioka, Fifty Years of New Japan, 1909

39. What was the cause of this drastic change in Japan that Fujioka is describing in this passage?
(A) The expansion of the United States and European influence in Tokugawa Japan
(B) The continued Portuguese dominance of maritime technology
(C) The rivalry between Qing China and Japan for dominance in overseas trade
(D) The influence of European Enlightenment thinkers

GO ON TO NEXT PAGE

40. Which of the following empires resisted the changes that Fujioka is describing?
(A) The Russian Empire
(B) The Qing Empire
(C) The British Empire
(D) The United States

Questions 41–43 refer to the following labor cartoon drawn by John Leech in 1843.

CAPITAL AND LABOUR.

Scanned by Philip V. Allingham for The Victorian Web, www.victorianweb.org

41. The author of this cartoon would most likely support which of the following?
(A) Free market capitalism
(B) Imperialism
(C) The development of the factory system
(D) Workers organizations

42. The image depicts which of the following results of the Industrial Revolution?
(A) State-sponsored industrialization
(B) Unsanitary living conditions
(C) New social classes, including the middle class and the industrial working class
(D) The development of machines to initiate industrialization

43. Which of the following was LEAST likely a cause of the situation depicted in the image?
(A) The Industrial Revolution
(B) The increased exchanges of raw materials and finished goods in most parts of the world
(C) The decline of the world's silver market
(D) The proliferation of large-scale transnational businesses

Questions 44–46 refer to the following passage.

Everything was on a military basis, but so far as I could see, the one and only reason for it all was rubber. It was the theme of every conversation, and it was evident that the only way to please one's superiors was to increase the output somehow. I heard from the white men and some of the soldiers some most gruesome stories. The former white man would stand at the door of the store to receive the rubber from the poor trembling wretches, . . . a man bringing rather under the proper amount, the white man flies into a rage, and seizing a rifle from one of the guards, shoots him dead on the spot.

A. E. Scrivener, *Private Company Rule in the Congo*, 1903

44. Scrivener's passage describes which of the following developments?
   (A) Imperialism
   (B) Mercantilism
   (C) Marxism
   (D) Communism

45. Which of the following philosophies would be used to justify the actions described in the passage?
   (A) The argument for classical liberalism by John Stuart Mill
   (B) Social Darwinism
   (C) The need for new methods of production of steel, chemicals, and electricity
   (D) The global market for finished goods

46. Which of the following was the long-term consequence of the situation described in the passage?
   (A) The economic crisis engendered by the Great Depression
   (B) The Cold War
   (C) Nationalist leaders challenged imperial rule
   (D) Large-scale migrations of Africans to the Americas

Questions 47–48 refer to the following image.

Aunt Emily's Visit, 1845

47. According to this image, how did industrialization impact Victorian England?
    - (A) Gender roles changed for middle class women and they were expected to join the work force.
    - (B) The specialization of labor led to a rising middle class and that changed family dynamics.
    - (C) Enlightenment ideas led to a women's suffrage movement.
    - (D) Feminists challenged traditional gender hierarchies.

48. Which of the following represents a significant change from this image that occurred during the twentieth century?
    - (A) Due to access to education in much of the world, participation in new political and professional roles became more inclusive in terms of gender.
    - (B) Consumer culture became more global.
    - (C) More effective forms of birth control gave women greater control over fertility.
    - (D) Movements to redistribute land and resources occurred.

Questions 49–50 refer to the following passage.

Dear Lord Rothschild: I have much pleasure in conveying to you, on behalf of His Majesty's Government, the following declaration of sympathy with Jewish Zionist aspirations which have been submitted to and approved by, the Cabinet: His Majesty's Government view with favor the establishment in Palestine of a national home for the Jewish people, and will use their best endeavors to facilitate the achievement of this object, it being clearly understood that nothing shall be done which may prejudice the civil and religious rights of existing non-Jewish communities in Palestine, or the rights and political status enjoyed by Jews in any other country. Yours, Arthur James Balfour

The Balfour Declaration of 1917

49. Which of the following was a long-term result of the Balfour Declarations?
    - (A) World War II and genocide
    - (B) The migration of former colonial subjects to imperial metropoles
    - (C) The redrawing of old colonial boundaries led to population displacement and resettlements
    - (D) Transnational movements sought to unite people across national boundaries

50. Balfour expresses his desire to protect the religious rights of which of the following?
    - (A) Muslim Arabs
    - (B) Zoroastrians
    - (C) Hindus
    - (D) East Asian Buddhists

Questions 51–52 refer to the following map.

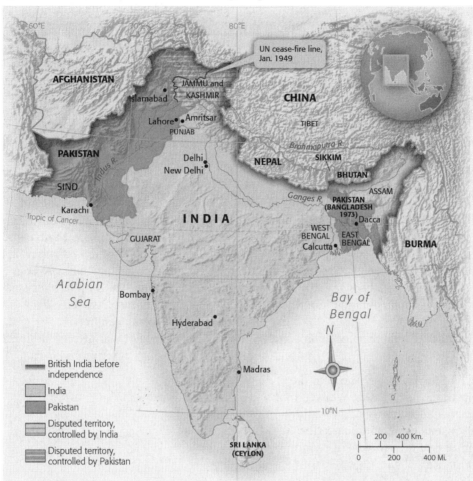

© Cengage Learning

51. Which of the following led to the new boundaries shown in the map above?
   (A) NATO and the Warsaw Pact produced new military alliances which worked on behalf of Non-Aligned states.
   (B) Colonies achieved independence through armed struggles.
   (C) The practice of nonviolence brought about the political change seen in the map.
   (D) The proliferation of ethnic violence.

52. The remnants of which of the following empires populates the northwestern portion of the map?
   (A) The Ottoman Empire
   (B) The German Empire
   (C) The Mughal Empire
   (D) The Dutch Empire

Questions 53–55 refer to the following passage.

I have always thought, in modern history the Chinese people are like a dish of sand, never really close together. But today I think a dish of sand is a good metaphor because now we have the Internet. We don't have to be physically united. You can be an individual and have your own set of values but join others in certain struggles. There is nothing more powerful than that. On the Internet, people do not know each other, they don't have common leaders, sometimes not even a common political goal. But they come together on certain issues. I think that is a miracle.

Ai Weiwei, 2011

53. How is Ai Weiwei's view of modern China a change from China during the Classical period?
(A) Classical China viewed the Silk Road as a vehicle to bring the Chinese people together.
(B) Classical China emphasized filial piety and not individualism.
(C) Classical China did not promote social harmony.
(D) Classical China remained completely isolated.

54. Which of the following is one of the results of the miracle that Weiwei described in the passage?
(A) New modes of communication increased the problem of geographic distance.
(B) The world has become less global.
(C) Popular culture remained distinctly isolated.
(D) Popular culture became more global.

55. Which of the following can be similarly compared to the internet?
(A) The creation of syncretic belief systems and practices during the sixteenth and seventeenth centuries.
(B) The growth of feudalism in Japan during the Post-Classical era.
(C) The Ottoman Empire's resistance to economic change during the nineteenth century.
(D) The use of warfare and diplomacy to establish empires in Africa.

STOP
END OF SECTION I, PART A

IF YOU FINISH BEFORE TIME IS CALLED, YOU MAY CHECK YOU R WORK ON THIS SECTION. DO NOT GO ON TO SECTION I, PART B UNTIL YOU ARE TOLD TO DO SO.

AP® WORLD HISTORY EXAMINATION
Section I
Part B: Short-Answer Questions
Time: 40 minutes
Number of questions: 3
Percent of examination score: 20%

DIRECTIONS: Answer Question 1 **and** Question 2. Answer **either** Question 3 **or** Question 4.
In your responses, be sure to address all parts of the questions you answer. Use complete
sentences; an outline or bulleted list alone is not acceptable.

Question 1 refers to the following passage.

> By the mid-seventeenth century, however, the world war far different. By then, the output of
> silver mines in Mexico and South America affected silk prices in China; the growing taste of
> Europeans for sweets led to the enslavement of Africans on sugar plantations in Brazil and
> the West Indies; statesmen in Lisbon, Madrid, and other European capitals controlled
> political affairs in North and South America; political disorders in seventeenth-century China
> stimulated the porcelain industry in the Netherlands and England; policies adopted by
> Japanese shoguns and Chinese emperors drew the attention of papal officials in Rome;
> wealthy Europeans kept warm by wearing coats and hats made from the furs of animals
> trapped in North America or Siberia; and Native Americans died from epidemics caused by
> pathogens imported from Europe and Africa
>
> From *The Human Record: Sources of Global History, 8th edition, Volume 2*, p. 3.

1. Answer all parts of the question that follows.
    A. Identify ONE additional piece of evidence that could be used to prove change was
        occurring in the mid-seventeenth century.
    B. Identify ONE continuity that could be used to refute the claim "By the mid-seventeenth
        century, however, the world was far different."
    C. Explain ONE reason that explains the author's claim that the world was different by the
        mid-seventeenth century.

2. From Edict of the Collection of Swords, issued in Japan by Toyotomi Hideyoshi in 1588.

1. The farmers of all provinces are strictly forbidden to have in their possession any swords,
    bows, spears, firearms or other types of weapons. If unnecessary implements of war are kept,
    the collection of annual rent may become more difficult, and without provocation uprisings
    can be fomented. Therefore those who perpetrate improper acts against samurai . . . must be
    brought to trial and punished . . .

2. The swords and short swords collected . . . will not be wasted. They will be used as nails and
    bolts in the construction of the Great Image of Buddha. In this way, the farmers will benefit
    not only in this life but also in lives to come.

3. If farmers possess only agricultural implements and devote themselves exclusively to
    cultivating the fields, they and their descendants will prosper. This compassionate concern for
    well-being of the farmers is the reason for issuance of this edict, and such a concern is the
    foundation for the peace and security of the country and the joy and happiness of all the
    people . . .

From *The Human Record: Sources of Global History, 8th edition, Volume 2* page 119

A. Identify one additional method deployed by Japanese leaders to recentralize the government.
B. Identify a similar method of social control used by a ruler outside of Japan in the period 1450–present.
C. Explain one similarity between the effects of the methods of social control used during Japanese unification and methods of social control used by European monarchs in the period 1450–1900.

3. Answer all parts of the question that follows.

Many historians argue that Hellenism (the spread of Greek culture through colonization and conquest) led to greater networks and exchanges from about 300 B.C.E. to around 600 C.E.
A. Provide ONE piece of evidence that support this argument
B. Provide an ADDITIONAL piece of evidence to support this argument.
C. Provide ONE piece of evidence that refutes this argument and explain how it undermines the argument.

4. Answer all parts of the question that follows.
A. Identify one way in which the interconnection of the Eastern and Western Hemispheres transformed religion in the period 1450–1750.
B. Identify one way in which the interconnection of the Eastern and Western Hemispheres transformed demographics in the period 1450–1750.
C. Identify one way in which the interconnection of the Eastern and Western Hemispheres transformed social structure in the period 1450–1750.

STOP
END OF SECTION I

IF YOU FINISH BEFORE TIME IS CALLED, YOU MAY CHECK YOUR WORK ON THIS SECTION. DO NOT GO ON TO SECTION II UNTIL YOU ARE TOLD TO DO SO.

AP® WORLD HISTORY EXAMINATION
Section II: Free-Response Essays
Part A: Document-Based Question (DBQ)
Suggested writing time: 60 minutes
Percent of examination score: 25%

It is suggested that you spend 15 minutes reading the documents and 45 minutes writing your response. **Note:** You may begin writing your response before the reading period is over.

DIRECTIONS: Question 1 is based on the accompanying documents. The documents have been edited for the purpose of this exercise.

In your response you should do the following.

- Respond to the prompt with a historically defensible thesis or claim that establishes a line of reasoning
- Describe a broader historical context relevant to the prompt
- Support an argument in response to the prompt using at least six documents
- Use at least one additional piece of specific historical evidence (beyond that found in the documents) relevant to an argument about the prompt
- For at least three documents, explain how or why the document's point of view, purpose, historical situation, and/or audience is relevant to an argument
- Use evidence to corroborate, qualify, or modify an argument that addresses the prompt

QUESTION 1. Using the following documents, analyze the extent to which technology has led to the formation of the global marketplace in the period 1750–1900.

Document 1

Document 1 from *The Human Record: Sources of Global History, 8th edition, Volume 2,* p140Source: From *Sketch of the Progress of the Human Mind*, written by the Marquis de Condorcet in 1793. The Marquis de Condorcet was a mathematician, philosopher, and educational reformer in France.

If we were to limit ourselves to showing the benefits derived from the immediate applications of the sciences, or in their application to man-made devices for the well-being of individuals and the prosperity of nations, we would be making known only a slim part of their benefits. The most important, perhaps, is having destroyed prejudices and re-established human intelligence, which until then had been forced to bend down to false instructions instilled in it by absurd beliefs passed down to the children of each generation by terrors of superstition and the fear of tyranny . . .

Document 2

Document 2 from *The Human Record: Sources of Global History, 8th edition, Volume 2* p195

Source: From Joseph Dupleix, Memorandum to the Directors of the French East India Company, written in 1753

All the Company's commerce in India is shared with the English, Dutch, Portuguese and Danes. The division of trade, or rather this rivalry, has served to raise considerably the price of merchandise here and has contributed quite a little toward cheapening the quality – two unfortunate circumstances which further reduce the price and profits in Europe . . . Our Company can hope for no monopoly in the Indian trade.

Document 3

Document 3 from *The Human Record: Sources of Global History, 8th edition, Volume 2* p232

Source: From Richard Guest, A Compendious History of the Cotton Manufactory, published in 1823

The present age is distinguished beyond all others by the rapid progress of human discovery . . . One, however, which would seem to merit the attention of the Englishman from its having brought an immense increase of wealth and population to his territory, has obtained comparatively little attention. While admiration has been unboundedly lavish on other triumphs of the mind, the successive inventions and improvements of the Machinery employed in the Cotton Manufacture have [not] obtained the notice . . . their national importance required . . .

Under the influence of the manufacture of which they have been the promoters, the town of Manchester has, from an unimportant provincial town, become the second in extent and population in England, and Liverpool has become in opulence, magnitude, elegance and commerce, the second Seaport in Europe . . .

Document 4

Document 4 from *The Human Record: Sources of Global History, 8th edition, Volume 2* p236

Source: From a booklet published by the Liverpool and Manchester Railway Company to publicize the opening of its railroad in 1830.

During the last fifty years, the transit of goods between Liverpool and Manchester has taken place on the Mersey and Irwell Navigation or the Duke of Bridgewater's canal. These in their day, were great works . . . but they cease to be adequate to the conveyance of goods . . . it was recommended I 1832 to diminish the distance between these two great towns by the means of a Rail-road . . .

Speed – despatch – distance – are still relative terms, but their meaning has been totally changed within a few months, what was quick is not slow, what was distant is now near, and this change in our ideas will not be limited to the environs of Liverpool and Manchester – it will pervade society at large . . .

Document 5

Document 5 from *The Human Record: Sources of Global History, 8th edition, Volume 2,* p265

Source: Advertisement for Lipton Teas, published in the *Illustrated London News*, 1890s

The Earth and Its Peoples, 7th edition, p658.

Document 6

Source: Map of the expansion of the United States, 1850–1920

Document 7 from *The Human Record: Sources of Global History, 8th edition, Volume 2* p320

Document 7

Source: From a letter by Iwasaki Mitsubishi to his employees in 1876

Many people have expressed differing opinions concerning the principles and advantages of engaging foreigners or Japanese in the task of coastal trade . . . Looking back into the past . . . when we abandoned the policy of seclusion and entered into an era of friendly commerce with foreign nations, we should have been prepared for this very task. However, due to the fact that our people lack knowledge and wealth, we have yet to assemble a fleet sufficient to engage in coastal navigation. Furthermore, we have neither the necessary skills for navigation nor a plan for developing maritime transportation industry. This condition is the cause of attracting foreign shipping companies to occupy our major maritime transportation lines . . . I now propose . . . to recover the right of coastal trade in our hands.

AP® WORLD HISTORY EXAMINATION
Section II: Free-Response Essays
Part B: Long Essay Questions
Suggested planning and writing time: 40 minutes
Percent of examination score: 15%

DIRECTIONS: You are to choose ONE question from the three questions below. Make your selection carefully, choosing the question that you are best prepared to answer thoroughly in the time permitted. You should spend 5 minutes organizing or outlining your answer. Write your answer to the question on the lined pages of the Section II free-response booklet, making sure to indicate the question you are answering by writing the appropriate question number on the top of each page.

Write an essay that
- Respond to the prompt with a historically defensible thesis or claim that establishes a line of reasoning
- Describe a broader historical context relevant to the prompt
- Support an argument in response to the prompt using specific and relevant examples of evidence
- Use historical reasoning (e.g., comparison, causation, continuity or change over time) to frame or structure an argument that addresses the prompt
- Use evidence to corroborate, qualify, or modify an argument that addresses the prompt

QUESTION 1. Analyze changes and continuities in social structure and gender roles in the period 8000 B.C.E. to 600 C.E.

QUESTION 2. Analyze the continuities and changes in the Islamic world between 622 and 1750.

QUESTION 3. Analyze major changes and continuities of world political systems and the rebellious outcomes toward those political systems from 1750 to 1900.

END OF EXAMINATION

ANSWERS FOR SECTION I, PART A: MULTIPLE-CHOICE QUESTIONS

ANSWER KEY FOR PART A: MULTIPLE-CHOICE QUESTIONS

1. B	12. A	23. A	34. A	45. B
2. B	13. B	24. D	35. B	46. C
3. A	14. C	25. B	36. D	47. B
4. D	15. D	26. C	37. A	48. A
5. B	16. B	27. A	38. D	49. C
6. D	17. C	28. D	39. A	50. A
7. A	18. A	29. C	40. B	51. C
8. D	19. B	30. B	41. D	52. C
9. C	20. A	31. B	42. B	53. B
10. A	21. D	32. B	43. C	54. D
11. D	22. C	33. D	44. A	55. A

EXPLANATIONS FOR THE MULTIPLE-CHOICE ANSWERS

1. ANSWER: B. Hammurabi's law code is from Babylonia (ancient Mesopotamia) and was written around 1754 B.C.E. The code is one of the earliest law codes in world history and is an example of Hammurabi's desire to govern his people (*The Earth and Its Peoples*, 6th ed., p. 18/7th ed., pp. 31–32; History Disciplinary Practice—Analyzing Historical Evidence; Learning Objective SB; Key Concept 1.3.III C).

2. ANSWER: B. Hammurabi's law code contains different consequences based on social hierarchies (*The Earth and Its Peoples*, 6th ed., p. 18/7th ed., pp. 31–32; History Disciplinary Practice—Analyzing Historical Evidence; Learning Objective SOC; Key Concept 1.3 III F).

3. ANSWER: B. Cato the Elder was from the elite Roman social class—this can also be seen from references in the passage to owning an estate, and having both managers and slaves. Cato's attention to proper management of an estate is influenced by the Roman elite's view that success was tied to land ownership. (*The Earth and Its Peoples*, 6th ed., pp. 138, 146, 151/7th ed., pp. 150–152; History Disciplinary Practice—Analyzing Historical Evidence; Learning Objective SOC; Key Concept 2.2 IV A).

4. ANSWER: B. The passage mentions various styles of labor used on Roman agricultural estates, from slaves to paid managers. This shows that the Romans used a range of methods to produce food (*The Earth and Its Peoples*, 6th ed., p. 138/7th ed., pp. 150–152; History Disciplinary Practice—Analyzing Historical Evidence; Learning Objective ECON; Key Concept 2.2 IV A).

5. ANSWER: B. Ban Zhao wrote *Lessons for Women* during the Han Dynasty which was heavily influenced by Confucianism. Confucianism emphasizes obedience and proper social relationships for all people (*The Earth and Its Peoples*, 6th ed., p. 153/7th ed., pp. 162–163; History Disciplinary Practice—Analyzing Historical Evidence; Learning Objectives SOC, CUL; Key Concept 2.1 II B).

6. ANSWER: D. A patriarchy is a system in which men hold the economic and political power in a society (*The Earth and Its Peoples*, 6th ed., p. 84/7th ed., pp. 162–163; History Disciplinary Practice—Analyzing Historical Evidence; Learning Objective SOC; Key Concept 2.2 III D).

7. ANSWER: A. The passage offers a very traditional view of patriarchy and separate spheres for men and women. During the late nineteenth century, women countered this traditional view by pushing for voting rights. As these rights were gradually realized throughout the twentieth century, women began to enter the traditionally male sphere of politics and governance. (*The Earth and Its Peoples*, 5th ed., p. 646/6th ed., p. 595; Historical Thinking Skill—Patterns of Continuity and Change Over Time; Learning Objective SOC; Key Concept 5.3 IV B).

8. ANSWER: D. Buddhism began in India and quickly spread into East Asia along trade routes, such as the Silk Road. Missionaries and merchants helped spread Buddhism to the East (*The Earth and Its Peoples*, 6th ed., p. 158/7th ed., pp. 164–165; History Disciplinary Practice and Reasoning Skill—Analyzing Historical Evidence, Causation; Learning Objective CUL; Key Concept 2.1 II A).

9. ANSWER: C. The map shows the Great Wall of China that was started by the Qin dynasty in an effort to protect and defend China from outside invaders (*The Earth and Its Peoples*, 6th ed., p. 158/7th ed., pp. 158–160; History Disciplinary Practice—Analyzing Historical Evidence; Learning Objective SB; Key Concept 2.2 II B).

10. ANSWER: A. The map shows numerous trades routes that linked many regions and facilitated the exchange of goods, people, technology, religious beliefs, food crops, and disease. During the sixteenth and seventeenth centuries the Columbian Exchange connected the Eastern and Western hemispheres and also facilitated the exchange of food, people, disease, and culture (*The Earth and Its Peoples*, 6th ed., p. 466/7th ed., p. 159; History Reasoning Skill—Comparison; Learning Objectives ECON, ENV; Key Concept 4.1 V A).

11. ANSWER: D. The development of and spread of Islam due to military expansion is depicted on the map (*The Earth and Its Peoples*, 6th ed., p. 252/7th ed., 252–253; History Disciplinary Practice and Reasoning Skill—Analyzing Historical Evidence, Causation; Learning Objective SB; Key Concept 3.1 III A).

12. ANSWER: A. The Mongols captured Baghdad and much of the Middle East during the Siege of Baghdad in 1258, effectively ending the Abbasid Caliphate (*The Earth and Its Peoples*, 6th ed., p. 533/7th ed., pp. 257–259; History Disciplinary Practice and Reasoning Skill—Analyzing Historical Evidence, Causation; Learning Objective SB; Key Concept 3.2 I B).

13. ANSWER: B. The passage by Pope Gregory VII clearly demonstrates the power of the Papacy and the Roman Catholic Church. The pope often exercised political power as well religious power. This was very similar to the role of the Islamic Caliphate. The Caliph is a religious and political leader (*The Earth and Its Peoples*, 6th ed., p. 436/7th ed., pp. 278–281; History Disciplinary Practice—Analyzing Historical Evidence; Learning Objectives SB, CUL; Key Concept 3.2).

14. ANSWER: C. The passage refers to a belief in papal infallibility which became part of Western European Christian beliefs during the post-classical period. This idea was strongly challenged by the Reformation, and Martin Luther's idea that salvation comes from faith alone. The printing press helped spread the ideas of Luther and other religious reformers who challenged the authority of the Pope in the fifteenth, sixteenth, and seventeenth centuries. (*The Earth and Its Peoples*, 6th ed., pp. 436–438/7th ed., pp. 426–428; History Reasoning Skill—Causation; Learning Objective SOC; Key Concept 4.1 VI).

15. ANSWER: D. The Byzantine Empire broke away from the Roman Catholic Church during The Great Schism that occurred in 1053–1054. The Hanseatic League did not exist until 1400. Imperial Rome was long dead (*The Earth and Its Peoples*, 6th ed., p. 279/7th ed., p. 270; History Reasoning Skill—Contextualization; Learning Objective SB; Key Concept 3.2 I A).

16. ANSWER: B. The Chinese developed an extensive bureaucracy that helped the emperor run the government. These administrative positions were highly sought after and required the passing of a civil service exam (*The Earth and Its Peoples*, 6th ed., p. 339/7th ed., pp. 303–306; History Disciplinary Practice—Analyzing Historical Evidence; Learning Objective SB; Key Concept 2.2 II A).

17. ANSWER: C. The author points out that peasants could rarely compete with the men from wealthy families with regard to performance on the civil service exams. Therefore, this system perpetuated a very rigid class and social hierarchies much like the Hindu caste system that developed in India (*The Earth and Its Peoples*, 6th ed., p. 704/7th ed., p. 385; History Reasoning Skill—Comparison; Learning Objective SOC; Key Concept 2.2 III B).

18. ANSWER: A. In the early twentieth century, a communist revolution began in China; Communist China attempted to equalize land distribution and the Chinese economy, thereby ending the civil service exams in the mainland of China (*The Earth and Its Peoples*, 6th ed., p. 817/7th ed., pp. 768–769; History Reasoning Skill—Continuity and Change Over Time; Learning Objective SB; Key Concept 6.3 I A).

19. ANSWER: B. The Mayans had developed complex city-states as evidenced by the structures in the picture (*The Earth and Its Peoples*, 6th ed., p. 201/7th ed., pp. 205–207; History Disciplinary Practice—Analyzing Historical Evidence; Learning Objective SB; Key Concept 3.2 I D).

20. ANSWER: A. When the Spanish colonized what is now called Latin America, they spread smallpox to the American Indians which resulted in a radical demographic change in the Americas as millions of American Indians died of the disease. The Mayans also fell victim to the superior weapons that the Spanish had (*The Earth and Its Peoples*, 6th ed., p. 422/7th ed., pp. 454–458; History Reasoning Skill—Causation; Learning Objective ENV; Key Concept 4.1 V A).

21. ANSWER: D. The Mongols controlled a very large land empire across Asia during the thirteenth and fourteenth centuries. The Mongols protected the trade routes that had previously been established, particularly the Silk Road. The passport represents the Mongolian movement among different regions (*The Earth and Its Peoples*, 6th ed., p. 328/7th ed., p. 323; History Disciplinary Practice—Analyzing Historical Evidence; Learning Objective ECON; Key Concept 3.1 I E).

22. ANSWER: C. A Caravanserai was a place where travelers could rest and recover from a journey along the Silk Road; its Persian name is Khan (*The Earth and Its Peoples*, 6th ed., p. 224/7th ed., pp. 229–230; History Disciplinary Practice—Analyzing Historical Evidence; Learning Objective ECON; Key Concept 3.1 I C).

23. ANSWER: A. The bubonic plague, also known as the black death, spread along trade routes in the Eastern Hemisphere (*The Earth and Its Peoples*, 6th ed., p. 353/7th ed., pp. 345–348; History Reasoning Skill—Causation; Learning Objective ENV; Key Concept 3.1 IV).

24. ANSWER: D. During the sixteenth and seventeenth centuries, millions of American Indians died due to the transmission of smallpox, brought to the Americas by the Europeans who were immune to the disease (*The Earth and Its Peoples*, 6th ed., p. 422/7th ed., p. 466; History Reasoning Skill—Comparison; Learning Objective ENV; Key Concept 4.1 V A).

25. ANSWER: B. As a result of the black death being spread along trade routes many urban areas declined (*The Earth and Its Peoples*, 6th ed., p. 353/7th ed., pp. 345–348; History Reasoning Skill—Causation; Learning Objective ECON; Key Concept 3.3 II A).

26. ANSWER: D. In order to get silver out of the mines and into the newly created global market, Spain needed a local source of labor. They turned to the Native Americans, forcing them to mine for silver. The Spanish saw the labor system already implemented by the Incan Empire that required people to work for the state, and attempted to adopt this system to their needs (*The Earth and Its Peoples*, 6th ed., p. 475/7th ed., pp. 460–462; History Reasoning Skill—Continuity and Change Over Time; Learning Objective ECON; Key Concept 4.2 II D).

27. ANSWER: A. The discovery of silver in the Americas by the Spanish led to the rapid colonization of Spanish people to the Americas. The Spanish (along with other European countries) also cultivated sugar on large plantations and used African slaves as their labor force. Eventually, this led to the mixing of African, American, and European cultures and peoples (*The Earth and Its Peoples*, 6th ed., p. 475/7th ed., pp. 460–462; History Reasoning Skill—Causation; Learning Objective CUL; Key Concept 4.1 IV D).

28. Answer:D. The passage argues that the discovery of silver deposits in the Americas and the subsequent development of a global trading network was the greatest discovery in world history. However, the discovery of how to farm and the subsequent development of permanent civilizations could be used to refute this statement, as an event that caused a greater amount of change and development. For the other options—the spread of medical innovations required the existence of the global trade network described in the passage, and A and B are both effects of the change mentioned in the passage (*The Earth and Its Peoples*, 6th ed., p. /7th ed., pp. 460–462; History Reasoning Skill—Continuity and Change Over Time; Learning Objective ECON; Key Concept 4.2 II D).

29. Answer: C. The desire for access to spices from South Asia (India) led European countries and merchants to begin sea exploration. As a result, the Spanish crown sponsored Christopher Columbus's voyage, and he thought he had landed in India (*The Earth and Its Peoples*, 6th ed., p. 412/7th ed., pp. 401–402; History Reasoning Skill—Causation; Learning Objective ECON; Key Concept 4.1 IV A).

30. Answer: B. The Atlantic slave trade led to a loss of young African men from the continent of Africa, especially West Africa (*The Earth and Its Peoples*, 6th ed., p. 495/7th ed., pp. 481–488; History Reasoning Skill—Causation; Learning Objective SOC; Key Concept 4.2 III C).

31. Answer: B. Enlightenment thinkers challenged the existing notions of social relations and many Enlightenment philosophers were abolitionists (*The Earth and Its Peoples*, 6th ed., p. 674/7th ed., pp. 650–652; History Disciplinary Practice—Analyzing Historical Evidence; Learning Objective SOC; Key Concept 5.3 I C).

32. Answer: B. The Haitian Revolution is considered a slave revolution. The island of Haiti had been colonized by the French and utilized for sugar plantations. Around 90 percent of the population of Haiti were African slaves and in the early nineteenth century, these slaves successfully rebelled against the French and won their independence (*The Earth and Its Peoples*, 6th ed., p. 623/7th ed., pp. 604–606; History Reasoning Skill—Continuity and Change Over Time; Learning Objectives SOC, SB; Key Concept 5.3 I A).

33. Answer: D. The period of 1450–1750 is defined by the creation of global trade networks that connected the Eastern and Western hemispheres. Transoceanic voyages marked a key transformation of this period (*The Earth and Its Peoples*, 6th ed., p. 466/7th ed., pp. 394–400; History Reasoning Skill—Contextualization; Learning Objectives ECON, SB. Key Concept 4.1).

34. Answer: A. Due to the Columbian Exchange new, more nutritious foods were introduced into Europe (specifically the potato) and the population of Europe increased (*The Earth and Its Peoples*, 6th ed., p. 466/7th ed., pp. 454–456; History Reasoning Skill—Causation; Learning Objective ENV; Key Concept 4.1 V D).

35. Answer: B. The latter half of the twentieth century is largely defined as a global society. Globalization means that states became increasingly interdependent, especially financially. The World Bank, The World Trade Organization, and the International Monetary Fund are examples of the economic institutions created during the twentieth century in an effort to ensure a global market (*The Earth and Its Peoples*, 6th ed., p. 900/7th ed., pp. 877–878; History Reasoning Skill—Comparison; Learning Objective ECON; Key Concept 6.3 II).

36. Answer: D. The passage describes the fall of Constantinople. After conquering the Byzantine Empire, the Ottomans practiced religious tolerance of other monotheistic religions, and set up a separate legal system to allow Jews and Christians to continue practicing their religions—they just had to pay an extra tax to the Ottoman Empire. Russia was converted much earlier in part due to the influence of Cyril, Eastern Orthodoxy continues to exist, and while some Byzantines did flee to Italy, most kept their religion (*The Earth and Its Peoples*, 6th ed., p./7th ed., pp. 270–272; History Reasoning Skill—Comparison; Learning Objective SB; Key Concept 3.3.II).

37. Answer: A. The Mughal Empire was also a Muslim Gunpowder Empire that conquered India (*The Earth and Its Peoples*, 6th ed., p. 536/7th ed., 519–522; History Disciplinary Practice—Analyzing Historical Evidence; Learning Objective SB; Key Concept 4.3 II B).

38. Answer: D. The Ottoman Empire had long been considered the "Sick Man of Europe" due to inept leaders, heavy taxation, and nationalist movements within its borders, and its unwillingness to industrialize. By the end of World War I, the Ottoman Empire was gone and the nation of Turkey was created (*The Earth and Its Peoples*, 6th ed., p. 759/7th ed., pp. 744–746; History Reasoning Skill—Causation; Learning Objective SB; Key Concept 6.2 I A).

39. Answer: A. In the 1850s the United States forced Japan to open up to the West, which ushered in the Meiji Restoration. The Japanese restored the power to the Emperor and began to industrialize in order to compete with the West (*The Earth and Its Peoples*, 6th ed., p. 740/7th ed., pp. 714–723; History Reasoning Skill—Causation; Learning Objectives ECON, SB; Key Concept 5.2 II A).

40. Answer: B. The Chinese resisted European Imperialism. The Qing dynasty did not choose to industrialize and they also rebelled against the Europeans (The Boxer Rebellion) (*The Earth and Its Peoples*, 6th ed., p. 563/7th ed., pp. 625–629, 723; History Reasoning Skill—Comparison; Learning Objective SB; Key Concept 5.1 V B).

41. Answer: D. The cartoon portrays the class divisions that occurred in Western Europe during the Second Industrial Revolution. The image shows the lavish lifestyle of the capitalists and the poverty of the laborer. The cartoonist is sympathetic to the laborers and would therefore support the formation of labor unions (*The Earth and Its Peoples*, 6th ed., p. 746/7th ed., p. 722; History Disciplinary Practice—Analyzing Historical Evidence; Learning Objectives ECON, SOC; Key Concept 5.1 V A).

42. Answer: B. As a result of the Second Industrial Revolution, new social classes developed. A new middle class arose, made up of bankers, managers, etc. The conditions of the poor were often unhealthy and unsanitary (*The Earth and Its Peoples*, 6th ed., p. 885/7th ed., pp. 571–576; History Reasoning Skill—Causation; Learning Objective SOC; Key Concept 5.1 VI A).

43. Answer: C. The demand for silver did not decline during the late nineteenth century and there was the development of extensive mining centers during this period. The Second Industrial Revolution and the need for raw materials and the financing of large businesses led to the development of the factory system which led to the class distinction shown in the image (*The Earth and Its Peoples*, 6th ed., p. 889/7th ed., p. 859; History Reasoning Skill—Causation, Contextualization; Learning Objective ECON; Key Concepts 5.1 II B,C,D).

44. Answer: A. Imperialism is a policy of extending a country's power and influence through diplomacy or military force. Late nineteenth century imperialism was spurred by the desire for resources and markets required during the Second Industrial Revolution. Much of Africa was carved up during the 1880s by European powers (this occurred at the Berlin Conference). Belgium controlled the Congo and used the area for rubber production (*The Earth and Its Peoples*, 6th ed., p. 803/7th ed., p. 801; History Reasoning Skill—Causation, Contextualization; Learning Objectives SB, ECON; Key Concept 5.2 I B,C).

45. Answer: B. Social Darwinism is a social theory that was inspired by Darwinism, by which the social and economic order of people is a product of "survival of the fittest." Under this theory, the wealthiest or most powerful in society must be biologically superior (*The Earth and Its Peoples*, 6th ed., pp. 742–743/7th ed., p. 718; History Disciplinary Practice—Analyzing Historical Evidence; Learning Objectives SB, SOC; Key Concept 5.2 III).

46. Answer: C. World War II resulted in the loss of power for Western European nations and therefore nationalist leaders in Asia and Africa began the process of de-colonization. By the 1970s, most of Africa was independent (*The Earth and Its Peoples*, 6th ed., p. 843/7th ed., pp. 819–827; History Reasoning Skill—Causation; Learning Objective SB; Key Concept 6.2 II A).

47. Answer: B. The Second Industrial Revolution created a new middle class during the nineteenth century and therefore changed the dynamics of the family. The idea of the "Cult of Domesticity" advocated that the most important duty of a middle-class woman was raising the children. The image shows the division of men at work and women at home (*The Earth and Its Peoples*, 6th ed., p. 885/7th ed., p. 655; History Disciplinary Practice—Analyzing Historical Evidence; Learning Objective SOC; Key Concept 5.1 VI A).

48. Answer: A. In developed nations, the education and political systems became much more inclusive during the twentieth century, especially for women. Although there were new forms of birth control that did give women more control over their fertility, the image depicts a woman's

place in society (*The Earth and Its Peoples*, 6th ed., p. 828/7th ed.,
p. 849; History Reasoning Skill—Continuity and Change Over Time;
Learning Objective SOC; Key Concept 6.3 III).

49. ANSWER: C. The Balfour Declaration was a part of the Zionist movement
that had started during the late nineteenth century and culminated in the
creation of the Jewish state of Israel after World War II. The creation of
Israel took place in Palestine and led to the displacement of thousands of
Arab Palestinians (*The Earth and Its Peoples*, 6th ed., p. 859/7th ed.,
p. 748; History Reasoning Skill—Causation; Learning Objectives SB,
CUL; Key Concept 6.2 III A).

50. ANSWER: A. In the document, Balfour expresses that he wishes to protect
the rights of the Palestinians, who were predominately Muslim Arabs
(*The Earth and Its Peoples*, 6th ed., p. 859/7th ed., pp. 744–745; History
Disciplinary Practice—Analyzing Historical Evidence; Learning
Objectives SB, CUL; Key Concept 6.2 III A).

51. ANSWER: C. In the early twentieth century, Mahatma Gandhi used the
tactic of nonviolence to free India from British control. After World War
II, Britain granted India independence and the predominately Muslim
state of Pakistan was also created (*The Earth and Its Peoples*, 6th ed.,
p. 793/7th ed., p. 794; History Reasoning Skill—Causation; Learning
Objectives SB, CUL; Key Concept 6.2 V A).

52. ANSWER: C. The Mughal Empire was a Gunpowder Empire that
controlled India during the sixteenth century. The Mughal Empire was a
Muslim Empire and Pakistan was created to ease the tension between the
Muslim and the Hindus (*The Earth and Its Peoples*, 6th ed., p. 537/7th
ed., pp. 519–522; History Reasoning Skill—Continuity and Change Over
Time; Learning Objective SB; Key Concept 4.3 II B).

53. ANSWER: B. The quote by Weiwei emphasizes the power of the individual
which is the antithesis of Classical China which emphasized filial piety
and obedience (*The Earth and Its Peoples*, 6th ed., p. 156/7th ed., pp.
161–162; History Reasoning Skill—Continuity and Change Over Time;
Learning Objective CUL; Key Concept 2.1 III).

54. ANSWER: D. The latter half of the twentieth century and the beginning of
the twenty-first century are defined as a more global society. The
increased speed and availability to communicate ideas through the
television and the internet has helped popular and consumer culture
become more global (*The Earth and Its Peoples*, 6th ed., p. 900/7th ed.,
pp. 877–878; History Reasoning Skill—Causation; Learning Objectives
CUL, ECON; Key Concept 6.3 IV).

55. ANSWER: A. The key to this question is knowing the definition of
syncretic. Syncretism is the combining of different beliefs; it commonly
occurs in arts and culture. During the fifteenth century, the world became
truly global when the Americas were "discovered" by the Europeans,
which created syncretic belief systems (*The Earth and Its Peoples*, 6th
ed., p. 410/7th ed., pp. 400–401; History Reasoning Skills—Comparison;
Learning Objectives CUL, SOC; Key Concept 4.1 VI).

Answers for Section I, Part B: Short-Answer Questions

Question 1

This passage explains many changes that are connected to exploration and global trading systems. Part A asks students to identify a change that isn't mentioned in the passage. Students could bring up other topics, such as the end of religious warfare in Europe following the conclusion of the 30 Years War, or scientific advancements connected to the Scientific Revolution, such as a turn towards using hypothesis and experimentation. Part B asks students to find something that did not change leading into the seventeenth century—students could bring up China's continual role as a manufacturer of luxury goods into the seventeenth century, which inspired merchants to seek routes to China throughout world history. Part C asks students to explain why there are so many historical facts that support the idea of a changing world. Students could mention that Atlantic trade routes connected two previously disconnected areas in World History—both of which had developed substantially independently. By the seventeenth century, there was a high volume of travel on these routes, which led the impact of this new exchange to be heavily felt by this period.

(*The Earth and Its Peoples*, 6th ed., Chapters 13, 15, and 20 /7th ed., Chapters 14, 16, and 21)

Question 2

This passage is from the time period when Japan transitioned from decentralized feudalism back to the centralized rule of a shogun. It shows that Japanese leaders wanted to freeze social mobility to maintain order. To answer part A, students could also mention the Tokugawa hostage system at Edo used to control rebellious Daimyo. To answer part B, students may want to bring up that Louis XIV had a very similar hostage system at Versailles in France. For the third part, students may want to mention that as leaders in both Europe and Japan repressed the growth of the middle class, it encouraged ideas of rebellion. In both places, the middle class pushed for a new government that would offer them more political and economic participation.

(*The Earth and Its Peoples*, 6th ed., pp. 555–558/7th ed., pp. 537–539; Key Concept 4.3.I.C)

Question 3

To answer parts A and B, students may want to consider that many historians argue that Hellenism (the spread of Greek culture through colonization) led to greater networks and exchanges from about 300 B.C.E. to around 600 C.E. Hellenism spread Greek culture from southern Europe to northeastern Africa through the Middle East to the western portion of South Asia. Greeks colonized the area but allowed for some local control. Populations in these areas outside of Greece learned the Greek language and adopted elements of Greek lifestyle. There was a synthesis of local cultures and Greek civilization. To answer part C, students should realize that there were frequent clashes with the spread of Greek culture. In Persia, the conquests of Alexander the Great left many with a desire to reclaim territory lost to the Greeks. In particular, the Achaemenid Persian Empire fell, and Alexander would marry Iranian women to gain peace through royal connections. Force was used frequently in gaining territory and power as Hellenism spreads toward Western India.

(*The Earth and Its Peoples*, 6th ed., Chapter 4 /7th ed., Chapter 5; Key Concept 2.1 II D)

QUESTION 4

A. This question asks students to consider the impact of exploration and colonization. To answer part A, students might talk about syncretic blends between Catholicism and Native American customs, or they might want to talk about syncretic blends between Christianity and West African customs. To answer part B, students will probably bring up either the massive population decline in the Americas that resulted from the spread of smallpox, the drain on men from Africa as part of the slave trade, or the population boom in Europe and Asia from the Columbian Exchange. For part C, students may want to talk about the new class structures created in South America due to new mixed-race children.

(*The Earth and Its Peoples*, 6th ed., Chapter 17 /7th ed., Chapter 18; Key Concept 4.1 VI)

ANSWER FOR SECTION II, PART A: DOCUMENT-BASED QUESTION (DBQ)

THE DOCUMENTS

Below are short analyses of the documents. The italicized words suggest what your margin notes might include.

DOCUMENT 1. *Human intellect should be praised over technology.* While technology can lead to national prosperity, it is the human ingenuity behind the technology that is really responsible for success. Technology alone did not create the global marketplace.

DOCUMENT 2. *National rivalries drove the need for new technology.* Competition to produce goods the cheapest and transport them the cheapest were prominent in the minds of European businessmen. Nationalism fueled the desire for better technology to get a competitive edge in the global marketplace.

DOCUMENT 3. *Technological advancements in cotton allowed English cities to become prominent in global trade.* Technological advancements in cotton deserve more recognition because they have allowed both Manchester and Liverpool to become significant participants in the global market through increased production speed and volume.

DOCUMENT 4. *Railroads increase the speed and volume of trade.* Technological advancements in the form of rail travel made trade easier and faster. This allows for more long distance trade, and helps more areas get connected to the global market.

DOCUMENT 5. *Technology allowed easier access to raw materials.* European countries exploited labor markets around the world to get raw materials. Technology (like the boat and train on the left and right of the picture) allowed them to ship these raw materials back to European markets. Technology-fueled factories like the one in the middle sped up production, increasing the need for more sources of raw materials.

DOCUMENT 6. *Technology increased participation in the global marketplace.* Initially, only the east coast of the United States could easily participate in long distance trade, but the expansion of rail lines into the interior connected more people to trade ports on the Atlantic and Pacific coastlines.

DOCUMENT 7. *Nationalism fueled technological development.* Japan realized it was falling behind technologically, which led it to fall behind economically. Japanese businessmen began making changes to advance Japan technologically to give it a better position in the global market.

A potential thesis for this essay would argue that, while technology improved the speed, volume, and number of participants in the global marketplace, other factors were also at work. Competition between states was also a driving force behind developing the global marketplace between 1750 and 1900. Your thesis does not have to sound like this word for word, but should communicate similar ideas. Make sure your thesis makes an argument that clearly answers the prompt and addresses all parts of the question.

You are then ready to prove your thesis, using the documents one by one to address the question and provide evidence. Remember your essay needs to cover a lot of bases in addition to addressing the question—document analysis and sourcing, the use of evidence, contextualization, and argumentation.

For contextualization, the industrial revolution and imperialism provide a perfect backdrop to this essay. Although a global market preceded the technological advancements of industrialization, the industrial revolution vastly expanded the reach of the market. England first went through an agricultural revolution, a burgeoning factory system, and rapid urbanization. England was able to produce things quickly and cheaply because of the new technology invented like steam power. This led to England's quest to create colonies through imperialism for raw materials and markets. It also led to competitiveness as continental Europe struggled to catch up after the Napoleonic Wars. As Europe stepped forward, modernization programs started in other parts of the world as well including the Tanzimat Reforms of the Ottoman Empire and the Meiji Restoration in Japan—all aimed at technological and subsequent economic improvements.

Thinking about sourcing, several documents are especially useful. When considering the audience for Document 2, remember it is addressing directors of the French East India Company. The Memorandum plays to the desires of the French joint-stock company to remain competitive in business in India, and for the need to have technology that can cut the costs of production.

Considering the purpose of document 4, a railroad company would make a brochure touting the marvels of their company's product. They want more investors to see railroads as the best way to increase England's footing in the global marketplace. The historical context for Document 7 is that of America's arrival in Japan and the subsequent Meiji Restoration. Japan realized it had fallen behind technologically and enacted a massive reform to regain a competitive status—this document is one example of the type of reforms Japan carried out to import technology and increase its role in the global market.

When searching for outside evidence, consider technology that improved global trade that isn't included in the documents. Perhaps you should bring up steamships. While railroads increased trade over land, steamships made sea travel much faster. Workers could and did commute long distances by sea (like China to California), providing cheap labor pools in areas of industrial development.

To get the second analysis and reasoning point, continue to refer to the multiple variables you brought up in your thesis. Yes, technology caused an increase in speed, volume, and participation in global trade, but it was often nationalism that fueled the development and adoption of new technology. Or, as Document 1 states, pride in human achievement. Also, while technology connected all these areas, in many imperialized regions, the raw materials were still collected in old-fashioned ways (as shown in Document 5) and technology was only used to get them to the factories and markets.

(*The Earth and Its Peoples*, 6th ed., Chapters 21, 22/7th ed., Chapters 22, 23; History Reasoning Skill—Causation; Learning Objectives ECON, CUL, SB; Key Concept 5.1)

SCORING: 1 point for thesis. For 1 point, the thesis makes a historically defensible claim that establishes a line of reasoning. 1 point can be earned for contextualization—describing a broader historical context that is relevant to the prompt. Up to 2 points may be earned for evidence from the documents. 1 point if a student utilizes the content of at least three of the documents to support the stated thesis or a relevant argument. 2 points if they support the argument with at least six documents. The response must accurately describe, rather than simply quote, the contents and use them to support the argument in response to the prompt. For a third evidence point, students must use at least one piece of specific historical evidence beyond that found in the documents that is relevant to an argument about the prompt. If a student explains the significance of the author's point of view, author's purpose, historical context, and/or audience for at least four documents they may earn a point in analysis and reasoning. The second analysis and reasoning point can be earned by demonstrating a complex understanding of the historical development that is the focus of the prompt, using evidence to corroborate, qualify, or modify an argument that addresses the question.

ANSWER FOR SECTION II, PART B: LONG ESSAY QUESTION

LONG ESSAY FOR QUESTION OPTION 3

This essay asks students to address major changes and continuities in connection with political systems and rebellious outcomes toward those political systems from 1750 to 1900. Students will most likely be drawn to rebellions including the American, French, and Haitian revolutions. However, they may include rebellions in Latin America and elsewhere in this broad time frame. Further, students may address the institute of slavery in the Americas and its eventual demise.

Beginning with the thesis, students need to be sure to address both changes and continuity. The essay should take the reader through much of the period, citing specific pieces of evidence of change and continuity and providing thorough analysis. Remember to address all parts of the question, even in the thesis. Therefore, attention to world political systems is necessary to gain credit in the thesis category.

What kinds of information should students discuss? In the beginning of the period, students may point out European colonial systems in Africa, the Americas, and Asia. With mercantilist-driven kingships, the politics of the "mother" country often was reflected in territories through governorships or viceroys. In North America, students may point out that colonists felt disengaged and unfairly treated by the policies set forth by the British government. Similar activity was occurring in Spanish Latin America, but the reaction to perceived oppressive governments was led by the Catholic church. In French colonies, lucrative sugar plantations offered the French government riches but slaves and *gens de couleur* rebelled when royalty was weakened by unrest in France. Rebellions in Europe may be addressed using such evidence as the Congress of Vienna as a reaction to widespread European unrest.

While systemic slavery was a continuity through much of the period, especially in Brazil, there was a great deal of emerging rebellious activity (which depending upon how it is written, may offer a separate continuity as well). Slave rebellions were numerous, but mostly put down before any large movements took place. The aforementioned French rebellions did allow for the successful Haitian slaves to complete a wholesale revolution and government. Plantocracy continued from the beginning of the period through the middle of the nineteenth century.

As rebellions emerged as a reaction to political systems in the Americas and Europe, Asia was not immune to changes and continuities of its own. The Qing Dynasty, for example, was accused of relationships that were too close to foreigners, so the White Lotus Rebellion made an attempt to restore China's "independence" from foreign influences. Later, a different kind of rebellion in China developed in the Opium War. The populations in the Americas were more successful in breaking from the imperialistic systems coming from Europe, but the rebellions in East Asia were not successful in expelling foreign influences.

Scoring The Long Essay is worth a possible 6 points. 0–1 point is awarded for the thesis. 0–2 points are awarded for "argument development: using the targeted history reasoning skill." 0–2 points are awarded for "argument development: using evidence." Finally, 0–1 point is awarded for "contextualization."

(*The Earth and Its Peoples*, 6th ed., pp. 610, 614; History Disciplinary Practice—Analyzing Historical Evidence; Learning Objectives CUL, SB; Key Concept 5.3, 6.3)

Practice Test 2

AP® WORLD HISTORY EXAMINATION
Section I
Part A: Multiple-Choice Questions
Time: 55 minutes
Number of questions: 55
Percent of examination score: 40%

Note: This examination uses the chronological designations B.C.E. (before the Common Era) and C.E. (Common Era). These correspond to B.C. (before Christ) and A.D. (anno Domini), which are used in some world history textbooks.

DIRECTIONS: The multiple-choice section consists of question sets organized around a stimulus—a primary or secondary source, a historian's argument, or a historical problem. For each question, select the best response.

Questions 1–4 refer to the following image.

By Unknown artist [Public domain], via Wikimedia Commons

Soviet propaganda poster, 1920. Translation, "What the October revolution gave to female workers and peasants." The buildings' names are "library," "kindergarten," "adult education center," "community food hall," "shelter for mothers and children," and so on.

1. A historian researching the social history of the twentieth century would find this art most useful as a source of information about
   (A) the spread of literacy among the elite classes.
   (B) men gaining more control over women's reproductive rights.
   (C) challenges to traditional notions about class and gender.
   (D) the rapid industrialization that occurred immediately after political revolutions.

2. When this poster was published, what had become the focus of feminist movements in the industrial nations in Europe and North America?
   (A) Economic equality in the work force
   (B) Equality in domestic affairs
   (C) Expanded participation in politics
   (D) More effective forms of birth control

3. The propagandists who produced this poster would argue that the changes it depicts were
   (A) anti-colonial independence movements.
   (B) Imperial Russia's success in the Great War.
   (C) classic capitalism.
   (D) an economic alternative to the status **quo.**

*4. The social changes praised in this poster were part of a new vision of production and wealth. Which of the following developments in the twentieth century was an indirect result of that vision?
(A) A global conflict between opposing economic ideologies
(B) The rapid decolonization of most of Africa and Asia
(C) A decline in totalitarian states
(D) Intense industrialization in much of the undeveloped world

Questions 5–7 refer to the following two passages.

Nature has four seasons and five elements. To grant long life, these seasons and elements must store up the power of creation in cold, heat, dryness, moisture, and wind. Man has five viscera in which these five climates are transformed into joy, anger, sympathy, grief, and fear. The emotions of joy and anger are injurious to the spirit just as cold and heat are injurious to the body. Violent anger depletes Yin; violent joy depletes Yang.

The Yellow Emperor's Classic of Medicine (China), 1000–300 B.C.E.

It is thus with regard to the disease called Sacred: it appears to me to be nowise more divine nor more sacred than other diseases, but has a natural cause from which it originates like other afflictions. Men regard its nature and cause as divine from ignorance and wonder, because it is not at all like the other diseases. And this notion of its divinity is kept up by their inability to comprehend it, and the simplicity of the mode by which it is cured, for men are freed from it by purifications and incantations.

Hippocrates (Greek physician), *On the Sacred Disease*, 400 B.C.E.

Alfred J. Andrea and James H. Overfield, *The Human Record: Sources of Global History, Vol. 1: To 1700* (Boston), pp. 100–101, 104–105

5. The most significant difference between the two views represented above is
(A) the first one emphasized the healthy functioning of the state above that of the individual.
(B) the second one led to an easing of patriarchy.
(C) the first one emphasized rigid formalities of class and government.
(D) the second placed a higher emphasis on empirical observation.

6. What belief system of the classical age inspired the first text about medicine?
(A) Daoism
(B) Shamanism
(C) Buddhism
(D) Confucianism

7. In what way are the political attitudes associated with these beliefs systems most different?
(A) The second belief system was more open to cultural borrowing to ease political tensions.
(B) The first belief system held that rigid formalities and hierarchies were the key to political stability.
(C) The first belief system held that politics would be transformed indirectly.
(D) The second belief system advocated a decentralized system resting on equality.

Questions 8–10 refer to the following passage.

Considering the circumstances of British Kaffraria, a country peopled as yet by uncivilized heathen tribes who therefore are unable to comprehend our laws and usages. Also the dangerous state the country is now in and the necessity of putting down crime quickly and effectively. . . . It seems expedient and not unjust to omit the forms usual among the civilized people of Europe in criminal cases and trials and to precede in the simplest and most natural manner. The supreme power should be satisfied of the guilt of the prisoners and the punishment ordained should be sharp and severe.

> J. B. Peires, *The Dead Will Arise: Nongqawuse and the Great Xhosa Cattle-Killing Movement of 1856–1857* (Indiana University Press), 1989, p. 224

British colonial officer in southeastern Africa, in response to a cattle killing rampage ordered by a local Xhosa prophetess (1857)

8. What nineteenth-century practice best explains the presence of the British in Africa?
   (A) Nationalism
   (B) Mercantilism
   (C) Religious evangelicalism
   (D) Imperialism

9. The change of colonial administrative policies evident from the passage occurred across much of Africa and Asia at this time. Which of the following best explains this?
   (A) The racial and cultural tenets of Social Darwinism
   (B) Increasing geographic limits on transportation and communication
   (C) Competition from Catholic Jesuits in the race to convert natives to Christianity
   (D) The strengthened African nationalism after the Berlin Conference

10. What generalization about nineteenth-century anti-colonialism can be inferred by the passage above?
    (A) Organized resistance and individual leadership had not yet emerged.
    (B) Some anti-colonial rebellions were influenced by religious ideas.
    (C) Anti-colonial movements often adopted the ideologies of the colonizers.
    (D) Anti-colonial rebellions were not yet directed at the colonizing nations.

Questions 11–13 refer to the following passage.

Accordingly the [Buddha] possessed every quality required in [a ship's captain]. Knowing the course of the celestial luminaries, he was never at a loss with respect to the regions of the sky . . . by means of manifold marks, observing the fishes, the color of the water, the species of the ground, birds, rocks, and so on, he knew how to ascertain rightly the part of the sea . . . . So being skilled in the art of taking a ship out and bringing her home, he exercised the profession of one who conducts the merchants by sea to their destination.

http://www.ancient-buddhist-texts.net/English-Texts/Garland-of-Birth-Stories/14-The-Story-of-Suparaga.htm

Jātakamālā (A birth story about an earlier incarnation of the Buddha, first-century C.E.)

11. What conclusion can be drawn about trade based on the passage?
    (A) Maritime trade had exceeded land-based trade by the first-century C.E.
    (B) Maritime trade was hindered by a general lack of navigational knowledge.
    (C) It decreased after imperial support of religion declined.
    (D) It diffused religions and could influence their original practices.

12. What best explains the increase in the form of trade between 600 B.C.E. and 600 C.E. as described by the passage?
    (A) The diffusion of maritime technology
    (B) Islamic laws that provided protection for merchants
    (C) Alexander the Great's Hellenistic Empire connecting northern India and Egypt under a single ruler
    (D) The Indian Ocean region falling under control of a single religious culture

13. The nature of trade implied in the passage led to which of the following developments after 600 C.E.?
    (A) The creation of religious diasporic merchant communities intensified
    (B) The conversion of most of the Indian Ocean region to Theravada Buddhism
    (C) Conflicts between Chinese and Buddhist merchants
    (D) European domination of the spice trade

Questions 14–16 refer to the following passage.

You can't spread the doctrines of Marx among people who drink Coca-Cola. It's just that simple. The dark principles of revolution and a rising proletariat may be expounded over a bottle of vodka on a scarred table, or even a bottle of brandy; but it is utterly fantastic to imagine two men stepping up to a soda fountain and ordering a couple of Cokes in which to toast the downfall of their capitalist oppressors.

J. C. Louis and Harvey Yazijan, *The Cola Wars* (Everest House), 1980, p. 78

A French newspaper commenting on Coca-Cola's decision to build bottling plants in France after World War II

14. What reality of the last half of the twentieth century is evident in this newspaper editorial?
   (A) American consumer products were accepted in communist states.
   (B) Western Europe had a general distaste for the American way of life.
   (C) France was on the verge of a Marxist revolution.
   (D) Transnational products had come to represent free market economics.

15. The widespread availability of American consumer goods in Europe after World War II was mostly the result of
   (A) the power and force of American labor unions.
   (B) the mercantilistic policies of multinational corporations.
   (C) governments promoting free market liberalism.
   (D) the impact of advertising in post–war Europe.

16. What twentieth-century development caused the increase in global corporations such as Coca-Cola, Sony, and Nestlé?
   (A) Economic nationalism was practiced to keep jobs from going overseas.
   (B) International economic organizations arose.
   (C) Classic liberalism became discredited in most of the world.
   (D) The Cold War intensified and almost led to nuclear war.

GO ON TO NEXT PAGE

Questions 17–19 refer to the following map.

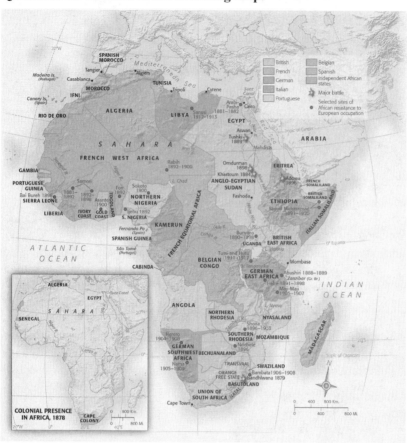

Africa in 1878 and 1914.
© Cengage Learning

17. What was the primary motivation for the pattern of imperialism evident in this map?
    (A) To find markets for consumer products
    (B) The needs of industrialized Western Europe
    (C) The need for indentured servants
    (D) To bring European education and infrastructure to Africa

18. Which statement best describes the change in Europe's relationship with Africa between 1600 and the era represented by the map?
    (A) In the later period, European nations were more likely to employ indigenous South Asians in the administration of their colonies.
    (B) In the previous period, Europe was not as concerned with labor needs as in the period shown in the map.

    (C) In the earlier period, colonization was led mainly by Protestant nations, while Catholics were more involved in nineteenth-century imperialism.
    (D) In the earlier period, Europe controlled mainly coastal areas as part of several trading post empires.

19. The inability of African civilizations to resist European imperialism in the nineteenth century was most similar to events in
    (A) South and East Asia between 1830 and 1900.
    (B) Latin America between 1800 and 1900.
    (C) Indian Ocean trade entrepôts between 1350 and 1450.
    (D) East Asia between 1450 and 1750.

Questions 20–22 refer to the following image of a Portuguese caravel circa 1460.

https://commons.wikimedia.org/wiki/File:Bras_de_Oliveira_Caravel_with_oars.png.

20. Based on the array of multiple maritime technologies displayed on the Portuguese ship in the image, of which of the following processes is this most likely an example?
(A) Cultural diffusion
(B) Independent innovation
(C) Cultural isolationism
(D) Metallurgic advancement

21. Which culture did the Portuguese probably have contact with that increased their maritime knowledge and technology?
(A) Vikings
(B) Muslims
(C) Baltic states
(D) Atlantic states

22. Prominently featured in the image are the Portuguese caravel's lateen sails, which would have been most necessary in navigating which maritime basin?
(A) The North Sea
(B) The Baltic Sea
(C) The Mediterranean Sea
(D) The Indian Ocean

GO ON TO NEXT PAGE

Questions 23–25 refer to the following passage.

Instead of bemoaning the rural exodus, the Welsh patriot should sing the praises of industrial development. In that tremendous half century before the World War I, economic growth in Wales was so vigorous that her net loss of people through emigration was a mere four per cent of the bountiful increase over that period. Few countries in Europe came anywhere near to that. The unrighteous Mammon [money] in opening up the coalfields at such a pace unwittingly gave the Welsh language a new lease on life and Welsh Nonconformity a glorious high noon.

T7homas Brinley (Welsh economist), *The Industrial Revolution and the Atlantic Economy*, 1959

23. As evident in the passage, what basic change in migration did industrialization bring about that was different from previous centuries?
    (A) It was economically motivated.
    (B) It became truly interregional.
    (C) It was motivated by the need for more farmers.
    (D) It targeted urban destinations.

24. Which of the following economic conditions were necessary for industrialization to occur?
    (A) A strong aristocracy to fund industrial development
    (B) An increase in agricultural production
    (C) A state to limit the movement of raw materials across national borders
    (D) The control and movement of capital by the government

25. Which of the following is the best explanation for the author's motive in praising industrialization?
    (A) Nationalism
    (B) Liberalism
    (C) Maritime gain
    (D) Demographic concerns

Questions 26–28 refer to the following image of Native Americans suffering from smallpox circa sixteenth century.

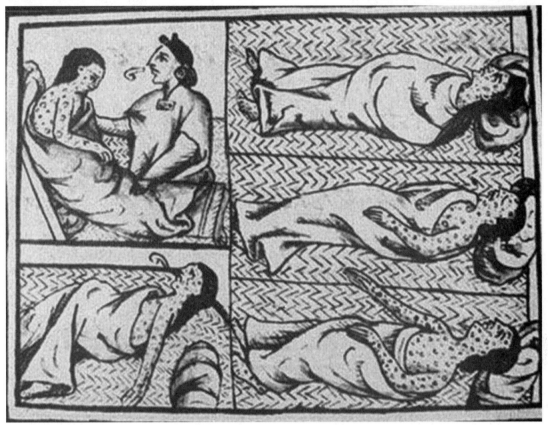

Source: Illustration from Sahagún, *Historia general de las cosas de Nueva España*, c. 1575–1580
http://nationalhumanitiescenter.org/tserve/nattrans/ntecoindian/essays/columbianb.htm.

26. The event illustrated in the image would have been part of what major movement during 1450–1750?
    (A) The Africa Diaspora
    (B) The Columbian Exchange
    (C) The Black Death
    (D) The Spanish Inquisition

27. The event illustrated in the image was possibly due to which of the following?
    (A) Lack of animal domestication in the Western Hemisphere
    (B) Localized natural outbreak
    (C) Poor hygiene and sanitation
    (D) Lack of proper nutrition

28. Which of the following caused the events depicted in the illustration?
    (A) Internal migrations in the Western Hemisphere
    (B) Introduction of llamas
    (C) Internal tributary conquests by native empires
    (D) New global connections to the Eastern Hemisphere

Questions 29–31 refer to the following passage.

The examination system became instrumental to the spread of Confucianism in Chinese society. Thus, the entire imperial bureaucracy was tutored in Confucian thinking. . . . The connection between Confucius and government service made knowledge of Confucianism the best route to career advancement. Confucius may have believed in learning for learning's sake, but in imperial China, the Confucian classic became equated with material betterment and social status. Families everywhere threw their sons into Confucian studies in the hopes of getting them into the imperial bureaucracy and enhancing the family's wealth and prestige.

Michael Schuman, *Confucius and the World He Created*, 2015

29. How was the imperial bureaucracy described in the passage an asset to centralized state-building in the Han Dynasty?
 (A) It decreased the influence of powerful aristocratic families.
 (B) It brought peace by bringing acceptance to a wide array of beliefs, such as Buddhism.
 (C) It widened the pool of talent by allowing people of any education level access to government positions.
 (D) Confucianism emphasized the primary role of merchants and the military.

30. In addition to the Chinese empire, in what other state did a codified ethical code give political legitimacy to the government?
 (A) Egypt under Akhenaton
 (B) The Hellenistic Empire of Alexander the Great
 (C) The Roman Empire after Constantine
 (D) Sumer after Sargon

31. In which of the following classical civilizations was social mobility least easily achieved?
 (A) The Persian Empire
 (B) The Roman Republic
 (C) The city-state of Athens
 (D) Gupta India

Questions 32–34 refer to the following image.

Turkish soldier carrying a musket, common in eighteenth and early nineteenth centuries

32. The military technology revealed in the image was made possible in the Muslim empires of 1450–1750 by which of the following processes?
    (A) Increased cross-cultural interactions
    (B) Contact with Europeans during the Crusades
    (C) Friendly economic competition among land empires in the period
    (D) Independent innovation during the Abbasid Caliphate

33. Based on the use of the illustrated technology, which of the following postclassical Islamic empires in India expanded most in size during 1450–1750?
    (A) Abbasid Caliphate
    (B) Safavid Empire
    (C) Mughal Empire
    (D) Umayyad Caliphate

34. The use of this military technology allowed the Ottoman Turks to do which of the following during 1450–1750?
    (A) Conquer sub-Saharan Africa
    (B) Reconquer all the lands of the Abbasid Caliphate
    (C) Invade Eastern Europe
    (D) Conquer the Holy Roman Empire

Questions 35–37 refer to the following passage.

Here I am anxious to add certain details concerning these military undertakings, which are due to divine rather than human inspiration. After Pope Urban had aroused the spirits of all the promise of forgiveness to those who undertook the expedition with single-hearted devotion . . . it was truly an army of "crusaders," for they bore the sign of the cross on their garments as a reminder that they should mortify the flesh, and in the hope that they would in this way triumph over the enemies of the cross of Christ.

Ekkehard, 1102 B.C.E.

35. Which of the following was the cause of what Ekkehard described?
    (A) The migration of the Bantu-speaking people into the Holy Land
    (B) The collapse of the Byzantine Empire
    (C) The development and spread of Islam
    (D) The invention of the compass and the astrolabe

36. Which of the following was the result of the Crusades?
    (A) Technological and cultural transfers occurred.
    (B) The Roman Catholic Church permanently reclaimed Jerusalem.
    (C) Pope Urban lost all power.
    (D) Trade along the Silk Road was halted.

37. The conflict that was the cause of Pope Urban's desire to send men to fight is similar to which of the following cultural clashes?
    (A) The Europeans and the Amerindians
    (B) The Daoists and the Confucianists
    (C) The Enlightenment philosophers and scientists
    (D) The hunters and foragers and the agriculturalists

Questions 38–40 refer to the following maps of the Spanish maritime empire.

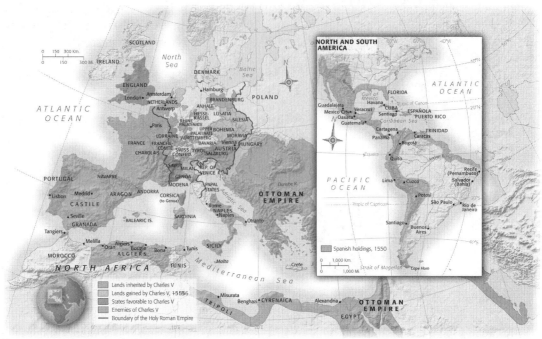

From page 421, *The Earth and Its Peoples,* Cengage 2017

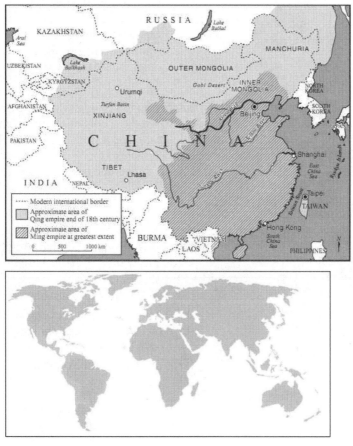

Wikispaces and Wikimedia public domain.
Spain in Europe, Africa, and the Americas under Charles V.

The Spanish Empire at its greatest extent (1790).

Source: Public Domain
https://www.reddit.com/r/MapPorn/comments/74jzqd/spanish_empire_at_its_greatest_extent_1790/

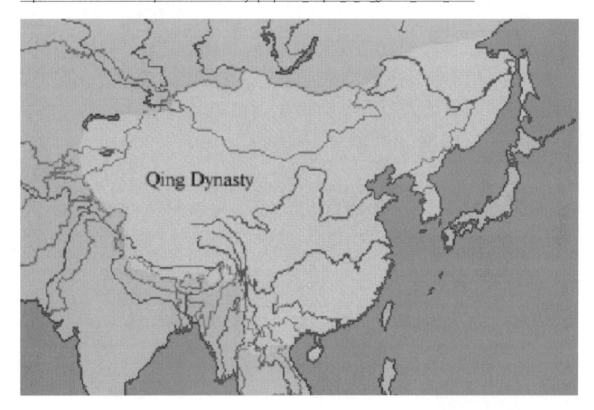

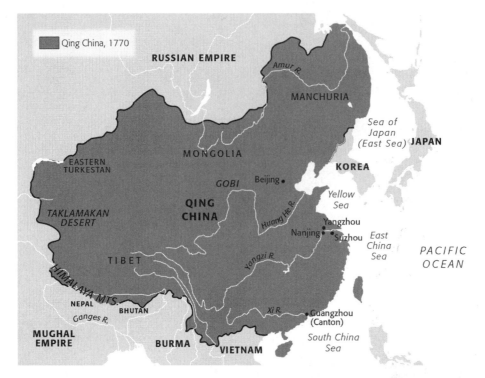

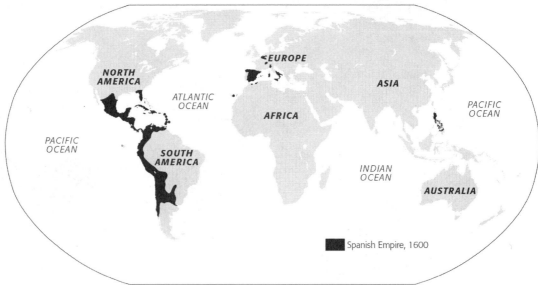

Qing Dynasty, 1644–1911

Source: http://www.empires-tv-series.net/gallery/maps/qing_empire_map.html

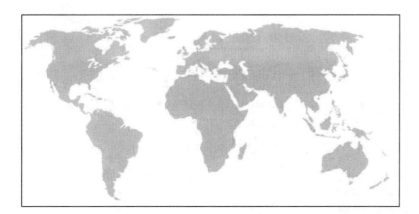

38. Based on the maps, which of the following would explain the widespread nature of Spain's empire relative to Qing China?
(A) Better global knowledge
(B) Less ability for resistance by native populations
(C) Better centralized government
(D) Larger economic influence globally

39. Which of the following is the LEAST possible explanation of China's relative seclusion compared to Spain's?
(A) Stronger central government through dynastic rule
(B) Fear of foreign invasion, especially from its frontier
(C) China's view of all other cultures as "barbarians"
(D) China's poor economy relative to other empires

40. Spain's desire for additional long-range territories can best be explained by which of the following?
(A) Conditions in the mother country required a mass migration of Spaniards to save their culture.
(B) Strong, controlling monarchs wanted to extend their imperial domain.
(C) Individual explorers' desires to continue maritime expansion were stronger than the Spanish monarchs' ability to expand their territories.
(D) Spain had an overwhelming desire to spread Christianity above all else.

Questions 41–43 refer to the following passage.

(As a result of the plague) the people fasted for three successive days. . . . (Afterward they) assembled in the Great mosque until it was filled to overflowing . . . and spent the night there in prayers . . . . Then, after performing the dawn prayer, they all went out together carrying Korans in their hands. The entire population of the city (of Damascus) joined. . . . The Jews went out with their book of the law and the Christians with the gospel, . . . (all) of them in tears . . . imploring the favor of God through His Books and His Prophets.

Ibn Battuta, *Travels in Asia and Africa*, 1325–1354

41. Which of the following contributed to the plague described by Ibn Battuta?
    (A) The increased demand for slaves for both military and domestic purposes in Eurasia
    (B) The increased activity in trade routes throughout the Eastern Hemisphere
    (C) The diffusion of classic Greek texts
    (D) The creation of the Grand Canal in China

42. The event described by Ibn Battuta was most similar to which of the following events?
    (A) The imperialist efforts of the late nineteenth century
    (B) The growth of an industrial economy
    (C) European colonization of the Americas, which led to the spread of smallpox
    (D) The Chinese communist revolution

43. Who of the following would have criticized the responses to the plague that Battuta described in the passage?
    (A) Hindus
    (B) Caliphs
    (C) Enlightenment philosophers
    (D) The pope

Questions 44–46 refer to the following map of the origin and spread of agricultural practices, 8000 B.C.E. to 500 C.E.

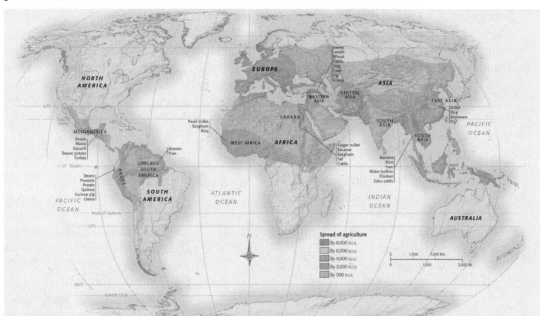

© Cengage Learning

44. According to the map, which of the following conclusions is true of the Agricultural Revolution?
    (A) The practice of agriculture created religious emphasis on nature and fertility gods.
    (B) Pastoral societies naturally developed into farming communities.
    (C) Agricultural practices diffused outward from a single locale to the rest of the world.
    (D) The adoption of agriculture was gradual from several points of origin.

45. Which of the following is the best explanation as to why the map above is also useful for locating the first large-scale permanent settlements?
    (A) Agriculture developed only in close proximity to major river systems.
    (B) Permanent settlements require surpluses of agriculture.
    (C) Agriculture thrived best where elements of nature were personified as deities.
    (D) Trade routes were a precondition for the creation of large permanent settlements.

46. A significant long-term social result of the economic changes shown on the map is
    (A) a relaxing of rigid, male-dominated societies.
    (B) the end of foraging and hunting societies.
    (C) the specialization of labor.
    (D) a decrease of violence between societies.

GO ON TO NEXT PAGE

Questions 47–49 refer to the following passage.

This locality is a mart of the country of the African Muslims, to which merchants come to sell their goods: gold is carried hither, and bought by those who come up from the coast. There are many rich men here. The states which are under their rule border upon the land of the Blacks. I shall speak of those known to men here, and which have inhabitants of the faith of Muhammad. These adhere to the law of Muhammad. The wares for which there is a demand here are many: but the principal articles are copper, and salt in slabs, bars, and cakes. The copper of Romania, which is obtained through Alexandria, is always in great demand throughout the land of the Blacks . . . other merchants come hither from the land of the Blacks bringing gold.

Antonius Malfante, Letter to a Colleague in Genoa, 1447

47. About which of the following trade routes was Malfante most likely writing about in this passage?
   (A) Silk Road
   (B) Trans-Saharan
   (C) Indian Ocean basin
   (D) Mediterranean Sea

48. Which of the following is an example of cultural diffusion that is evident in the passage?
   (A) The spread of Islam outside of the Arabian Peninsula
   (B) The spread of new technologies
   (C) The spread of agriculture
   (D) The spread of new forms of labor systems

49. The writings by Malfante evidenced which of the following phenomena?
   (A) The influence of Hinduism and Buddhism in Southeast Asia
   (B) An increase in the number of travelers within Afro-Eurasia
   (C) The influence of Greek and Indian mathematics on Muslim scholars
   (D) The disdain for outsiders in Afro-Eurasia

Questions 50–52 refer to the following map of South Asia, 1947.

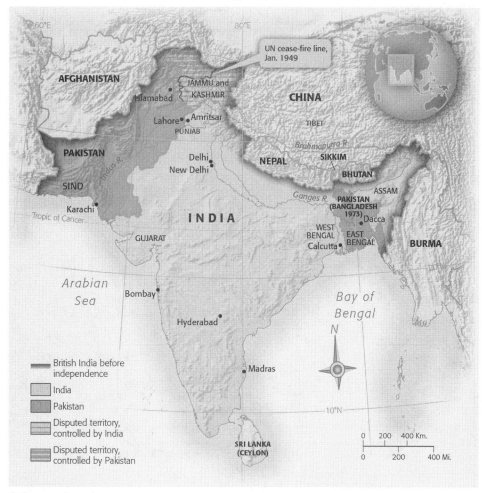

© Cengage Learning

50. What was a result of the redrawing of boundaries in the former colony shown in the map?
    (A) The formation of an economic trading bloc
    (B) A blending of religious cultures
    (C) Population resettlement
    (D) Detente in the Cold War

51. Unlike independence in Algeria and Southeast Asia, the decolonization pictured in the map took place through a process of
    (A) playing the Cold War superpowers off against each other.
    (B) a violent anti-colonial rebellion.
    (C) negotiations with the former colonizer.
    (D) allying with the colonizer's enemies in World War II.

52. After World War II, newly independent nations such as India and Algeria kept close economic and even cultural ties to their former colonizers. What best explains this?
    (A) Newly independent nations attempted industrialization and depended on materials and technology from their former colonizers.
    (B) Newly independent nations forgot about their heritage and instead adopted the culture of their former colonizers.
    (C) Imperial nations continued to treat the newly independent nations as if they were suppliers of raw material.
    (D) Many migrated from newly independent nations to the cities of their former colonizing countries.

GO ON TO NEXT PAGE

Questions 53–55 refer to the following image.

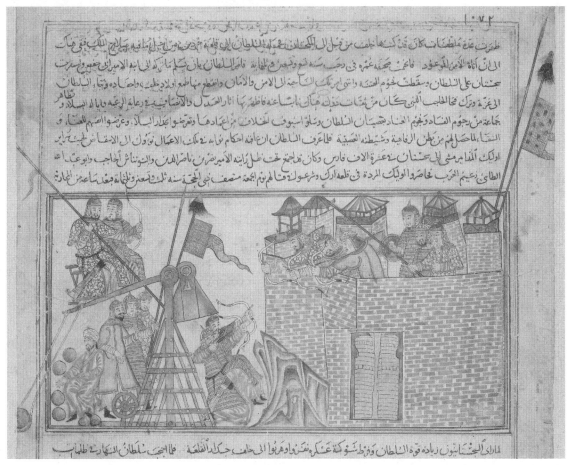

Persian Miniature illustration, attack on a Persian city, about 1307.

53. The image depicts which of the following land empires?
   (A) Russia
   (B) Japan
   (C) Mongols
   (D) Aztecs

54. Which of the following was a consequence of what is shown in the image?
   (A) Cultural transfers
   (B) The practice of foot binding in Song China began
   (C) The Crusades
   (D) The institution of serfdom took root in Western Europe

55. Which of the following was the new form of government that emerged as a result of the conquest shown in the image?
   (A) Feudalism
   (B) City-states
   (C) Islamic states
   (D) Khanates

STOP
END OF SECTION I, PART A
IF YOU FINISH BEFORE TIME IS CALLED, YOU MAY CHECK YOUR WORK ON THIS SECTION. DO NOT GO ON TO SECTION I, PART B UNTIL YOU ARE TOLD TO DO SO.

AP® WORLD HISTORY EXAMINATION
Section I
Part B: Short-Answer Questions
Time: 40 minutes
Number of questions: 3
Percent of examination score: 20%

DIRECTIONS: Answer Question 1 **and** Question 2. Answer **either** Question 3 **or** Question 4. In your responses, be sure to address all parts of the questions you answer. Use complete sentences; an outline or bulleted list alone is not acceptable.

Question 1 refers to the following two passages.

The Taiping Rebellion led by a Christian convert named Hong Xiuquan (1814–1864) was a widespread civil war that started in southern China from 1850 to 1864. Hong claimed to have received visions in a dream and announced that he was the younger brother of Jesus Christ. He believed that his mission was to fight against the Qing (1644–1912) government ruled by the Manchus. About 20 million people, mainly civilians, died in this military conflict.

In 1853, Karl Marx argued in the *New York Daily Tribune* that the origins of [the] Taiping rebellion were entirely based on external factors, mainly the opium war and European intrusion, and that the movement came forth with the Han peasant masses against the Manchu rule. Understandably, Marx's views have been widely accepted in mainland China where the Communist Party still treats Marx as one of its patriarchs in both the theory and practice of revolution. Yet these two views seem to be too simplistic, as Marx overlooked the social causes that led many to become part of the movement and did not notice the key role played by the Hakka, a minority within the Han population, in the early development of the rebellion. Actually, the Taiping rebellion was considerably endogenous [having an internal cause] in origin, and was a result of the mobilization of the Hakka through Hong Xiuquan's God-worshippers.

Janice Y. Leung, *Journal of History*, University of Washington, 2014

1. Use the passage above to answer all parts of the question that follow.
    A. Provide one piece of historical evidence (not specifically mentioned in the passage) about the Taiping Rebellion that would support Leung's interpretation of the event.
    B. Provide one piece of historical evidence (not specifically mentioned in the passage) that would support Leung's use of Karl Marx's interpretation.
    C. Explain another interpretation of the Taiping Rebellion not mentioned by the author that would refute the author's causes of the rebellion.

GO ON TO NEXT PAGE

Question 2 refers to the following image.

© Cengage Learning

Expanding trade drew much of Africa into global networks, but foreign colonies in 1870 were largely confined to Algeria and southern Africa. Growing trade, Islamic reform movements, and other internal forces created important new states throughout the continent

2. Using the map answer Parts A, B, and C.
    A. Describe one piece of evidence beyond the map that would show growing trade that created new states throughout Africa.
    B. Explain one way in which the map shows growing Islamic reform movements or other internal forces that created new states throughout Africa.
    C. Explain one economic limitation of the map in its description of the African continent in the nineteenth century.

3. Answer Parts A, B, and C.
   A. Identify ONE cause of regional and interregional interactions in the period 600–1450.
   B. Explain ONE effect of a new trade network during 600–1450 in Africa.
   C. Explain ONE effect of a new trade network during 600–1450 in Asia.

4. Answer Parts A, B, and C.
   Many historians argue that the Industrial Revolution from 1750 to 1900 was a major turning point in world history.
   A. Identify ONE piece of evidence that would support the argument.
   B. Explain ONE way in which the argument about the Industrial Revolution may be refuted.
   C. Explain ONE way in which a comparison could be made with the Industrial Revolution to another time period in history.

STOP
END OF SECTION I, PART B
IF YOU FINISH BEFORE TIME IS CALLED, YOU MAY CHECK YOUR WORK ON THIS SECTION. DO NOT GO ON TO SECTION II UNTIL YOU ARE TOLD TO DO SO.

AP® WORLD HISTORY EXAMINATION
Section II: Free-Response Essays
Part A: Document-Based Question (DBQ)
Suggested writing time: 60 minutes
Percent of examination score: 25%

It is suggested that you spend 15 minutes reading the documents and 45 minutes writing your response. Note: You may begin writing your response before the reading period is over.

DIRECTIONS: Question 1 is based on the accompanying documents. The documents have been edited for the purpose of this exercise.

In your response you should do the following.

■ Respond to the prompt with a historically defensible thesis or claim that establishes a line of reasoning

■ Describe a broader historical context relevant to the prompt

■ Support an argument in response to the prompt using at least six documents

■ Use at least one additional piece of specific historical evidence (beyond that found in the documents) relevant to an argument about the prompt

■ For at least three documents, explain how or why the document's point of view, purpose, historical situation, and/or audience is relevant to an argument

■ Use evidence to corroborate, qualify, or modify an argument that addresses the prompt

QUESTION 1. Using the documents, analyze the roles of women in twentieth-century political movements.

Document 1

Source: Petition by Ellen Leeuw and 122 South African black women to the Mayor of Johannesburg, 1910.
It is well known that our husbands are getting low wages and cannot afford to discharge their liabilities unless they get our assistance. All classes of work formerly performed by women are now in the hands of men, such as kitchen or general servants work, washing and ironing, eating houses for natives, nursing in native hospitals.

Document 2

Source: H. N. Brailsford, British socialist, from his book *Rebel India*, describing Indian women's efforts to keep shoppers from buying British goods during the boycott, 1931.
In ones and twos women were resting themselves on chairs at the doors of certain shops. . . . If anyone attempted to enter, the lady joined her hands in supplication; she pleaded, she reasoned, and if all else failed, she would throw herself across the threshold and dared him to walk over her body.

Document 3

Source: Josie Mpama, commenting on a law that further restricted the mobility of South African black women, 1937.
We women can no longer remain in the background or concern ourselves only with domestic and sports affairs. The time has arrived for women to enter the political field and stand shoulder to shoulder with their men in the struggle.

Document 4

Source: Draft Constitution for the African National Congress, a group founded to promote the rights of South African blacks, 1945.
In the Congress women members shall enjoy the same status as men, and shall be entitled to elect and be elected to any position including the highest office. Notwithstanding this fact, however, and without in any way diminishing the rights of women members, the Congress may, recognizing the special disabilities and differences to which African women are subjected and because of the peculiar problems facing them, and in order to arouse their interest and facilitate their organization, create a Women's Section within its machinery, to be known as the ANC Women's Section.

GO ON TO NEXT PAGE

Document 5

Source: Photograph of Haydee Santamaria and Celia Sanchez, female guerrilla rebel leaders, with Fidel Castro, the leader of the Cuban Revolution, 1950s.

Document 6

Source: Women's Charter, adopted at the founding conference of the Federation of South African Women, 1954.

Preamble: We, the women of South Africa, wives and mothers, working women and housewives, African, Indians, European and Coloured, hereby declare our aim of striving for the removal of all laws, regulations, conventions and customs that discriminate against us as women, and that deprive us in any way of our inherent right to the advantages, responsibilities and opportunities that society offers to any one section of the population.

Women's Lot: We women share with our menfolk the cares and anxieties imposed by poverty and its evils. As wives and mothers, it falls upon us to make small wages stretch a long way. It is we who feel the cries of our children when they are hungry and sick. It is our lot to keep and care for the homes that are too small, broken and dirty to be kept clean. We know the burden of looking after children and land when our husbands are away in the mines, on the farms, and in the towns earning our daily bread.

Document 7

Source: Edict from Empress Dowager, 1901.

We have now received Her Majesty's decree to devote ourselves fully to China's revitalization, to suppress vigorously the use of the terms new and old, and to blend together the best of what is Chinese and what is foreign. The root of China's weakness lies in harmful habits too firmly entrenched, in rules and regulations too minutely drawn, in the overabundance of inept and mediocre officials and in the paucity of truly outstanding ones, in petty bureaucrats who hide behind the written word and in clerks and yamen runners who use the written word as talismans to acquire personal fortunes, in the mountains of correspondence between government offices that have no relationship to reality, and in the seniority system and associated practices that block the way of men of real talent . . .

Source: www.istianjinelearning.org/michaelconway/files/.../Late-Qing-Writing-26126dr.pdf

END OF DOCUMENTS FOR PART A.
GO ON TO THE NEXT PAGE.

AP® WORLD HISTORY EXAMINATION
Section II: Free-Response Essays
Part B: Long Essay Questions
Suggested planning and writing time: 40 minutes
Percent of examination score: 15%

DIRECTIONS: You are to choose ONE question from the three questions below. Make your selection carefully, choosing the question that you are best prepared to answer thoroughly in the time permitted. You should spend 5 minutes organizing or outlining your answer. Write your answer to the question on the lined pages of the Section II free-response booklet, making sure to indicate the question you are answering by writing the appropriate question number on the top of each page.

In your response you should do the following.

- In your response you should do the following. Respond to the prompt with a historically defensible thesis or claim that establishes a line of reasoning

- Describe a broader historical context relevant to the prompt

- Support an argument in response to the prompt using specific and relevant examples of evidence

- Use historical reasoning (e.g., comparison, causation, continuity or change over time) to frame or structure an argument that addresses the prompt

- Use evidence to corroborate, qualify, or modify an argument that addresses the prompt

QUESTION 1. Evaluate the extent to which connections between religion and politics in Rome can be compared to the connections between religion and politics in one of the following from 600 BCE – 600 CE.

- China
- India

QUESTION 2. Evaluate the extent to which China's response to the West (Europe and the United States) from 1600 to 1800 compares to the response of ONE of the following countries to the interaction with the West from 1600 to 1800.

- Russia
- Japan

QUESTION 3. Evaluate the extent to which changes in Latin American politics can be compared to changes in politics in one of the following from 1750 to Present.

- The Middle East
- Sub-Saharan Africa

END OF EXAMINATION

Answers for Section I, Part A: Multiple-Choice Questions

Answer Key for Part A: Multiple-Choice Questions

1. C	12. A	23. D	34. C	45. C
2. C	13. A	24. B	35. C	46. C
3. D	14. D	25. A	36. A	47. B
4. A	15. C	26. B	37. A	48. A
5. D	16. B	27. A	38. B	49. B
6. D	17. B	28. D	39. D	50. C
7. A	18. D	29. A	40. C	51. C
8. D	19. A	30. C	41. B	52. D
9. A	20. A	31. D	42. C	53. C
10. B	21. B	32. A	43. C	54. A
11. D	22. D	33. C	44. D	55. D

Explanations for the Multiple-Choice Answers

1. ANSWER: C. The twentieth century saw many attempts to understand basic human rights in a universal way. Attempts to emancipate women from traditional roles and alleviate differences between classes were part of that trend (*The Earth and Its Peoples*, 6th ed., pp. 785, 909–916/7th ed., pp. 782–783, 873–877; History Disciplinary Practice—Analyzing Historical Evidence; Learning Objectives SOC-1,2,5; Key Concept 6.3 III).

2. ANSWER: C. About the time the poster was published, women in the United States and Great Britain gained wider political participation, through the right to vote, after a long struggle that began in the nineteenth century (*The Earth and Its Peoples*, 6th ed., p. 785/7th ed., pp. 782–783; History Reasoning Skill—Continuity and Change Over Time; Learning Objectives SOC-5, CUL-2; Key Concept 5.3 IV B, 6.3 III).

3. ANSWER: D. The communism of the Bolsheviks represented a break from the economics of industrial capitalism as well as a redefining of the society they claimed was connected to capitalistic production (*The Earth and Its Peoples*, 6th ed., pp. 760–761/7th ed., pp. 735–740; History Disciplinary Practice—Argument Development; Learning Objectives SOC-3, ECON-2; Key Concept 6.2 V B).

4. ANSWER: A. The Bolshevik Revolution created the Soviet Union. After World War II, the Cold War was a conflict between the Soviet Union and its communist states on one hand, and the United States and its allies determined to keep markets open on the other (*The Earth and Its Peoples*, 6th ed., pp. 841–844/7th ed., pp. 810–813; History Reasoning Skill—Causation; Learning Objectives ECON-2,3,6; Key Concept 6.2 IV C).

5. ANSWER: D. The Greek text clearly emphasizes a rational and empirical mode of inquiry, which was a hallmark of Hellenism (*The Earth and Its Peoples*, 6th ed., pp. 81, 84, 128–132/7th ed., 88–92, 135–139; History Disciplinary Practice and Reasoning Skill—Analyzing Historical Evidence, Comparison; Learning Objective CUL-2; Key Concept 2.1 II C, 2.1 II E).

6. ANSWER: D. Although Daoism did not form a specific political response to the downfall of the Zhou, it did have a profound influence on Chinese civilization. The values of Yin and Yang and the relationship to the currents of nature are clearly evident in the first text about medical practices (*The Earth and Its Peoples*, 6th ed., p. 81/7th ed., pp. 91–92; History Disciplinary Practice—Analyzing Historical Evidence; Learning Objective CUL-5; Key Concept 2.1 II C).

7. ANSWER: A. Daoists rejected formal rituals and rigid social hierarchies. Their emphasis on inaction presumed that political problems would resolve when individuals had found proper balance with nature (*The Earth and Its Peoples*, 6th ed., p. 81/7th ed., pp. 91–92; History Disciplinary Practice and Reasoning Skill—Analyzing Historical Evidence, Comparison; Learning Objective CUL-5; Key Concept 2.1 II B).

8. ANSWER: D. As industrialization took place in Western Europe, these nations became more imperialistic and turned to Africa and Asia for resources (*The Earth and Its Peoples*, 6th ed., pp. 694–698/7th ed., pp. 670–679; History Disciplinary Practice and Reasoning Skill—Contextualization, Analyzing Historical Evidence; Learning Objectives ECON-6, SOC-5; Key Concept 5.2 III).

9. ANSWER: A. Some people in the nineteenth century applied the evolutionary ideas of Charles Darwin to society. Social Darwinism, as it was called, altered European perceptions of non-whites, thus altering their colonial relations with them (*The Earth and Its Peoples*, 6th ed., pp. 694–698/7th ed., pp. 670–679; History Disciplinary Practice and Reasoning Skill—Contextualization, Analyzing Historical Evidence; Learning Objectives ECON-2, SOC-6; Key Concept 5.2 I E).

10. ANSWER: B. Many anti-colonial rebellions in the nineteenth century were motivated by diverse religious beliefs. The nature of the African actions—in addition to the fact that these were ordered by a religious figure—connects the Xhosa cattle killing incident with more familiar rebellions aided by religion (*The Earth and Its Peoples*, 6th ed., pp. 648–650/7th ed., pp. 623–629; History Disciplinary Practice and Reasoning Skill—Analyzing Historical Evidence, Comparison; Learning Objective SB-3; Key Concept 5.3 III E).

11. ANSWER: D. All major belief systems were transformed as they spread during this period. The passage makes it clear that Buddhism, which originally had high demands on an individual in terms of material possessions, later recast the Buddha as one who cares about accumulating wealth through trade (*The Earth and Its Peoples*, 6th ed., pp. 171, 175–176/7th ed., pp. 173–175; History Disciplinary Practice—Analyzing Historical Evidence; Learning Objectives CUL-1, ECON-6; Key Concept 2.3 III C).

12. ANSWER: A. Indian Ocean trade was facilitated by distinctive maritime technologies during this period, such as the lateen sail (*The Earth and Its Peoples*, 6th ed., pp. 229–230/7th ed., pp. 230–232; History Reasoning Skills—Causation, Contextualization; Learning Objectives ENV-2, ECON-7; Key Concept 2.3 II A).

13. ANSWER: A. As trade and religion diffused simultaneously, merchants established Jewish, Christian, and Chinese merchant communities across major routes (*The Earth and Its Peoples*, 6th ed., pp. 240, 228, 390/ 7th ed., pp. 225–226, 380–382; History Reasoning Skills—Causation; Learning Objectives CUL-1,2,3, ECON-7; Key Concept 3.1 III B).

14. ANSWER: D. Multinational corporations, with the ability to marshal cheap labor, raw materials, and capital across the globe, proliferated in the late twentieth century and embodied the principles of free market capitalism (*The Earth and Its Peoples*, 6th ed., p. 888/7th ed., pp. 857–859; History Reasoning Skill—Contextualization; Learning Objectives ECON-1,2, SB-3; Key Concept 6.3 II B).

15. ANSWER: C. Having just been liberated from imperialism after World War II, many newly independent nations were tempted by communism rather than the economic system of their former colonizers. During the Cold War, the United States implemented many programs to draw newly independent nations into its sphere of influence, including Marshall Plan funds and the promotion of its affluent lifestyle (*The Earth and Its Peoples*, 6th ed., pp. 841–844/7th ed., pp. 810–814; History Disciplinary Practice—Argument Development; Learning Objectives ECON-2,3,6, SB-4; Key Concept 6.2 IV C).

16. ANSWER: B. Individual nations found it harder to regulate corporations whose business transcended so many national boundaries. As a result, policies of institutions such as the World Trade Organization and the International Monetary Fund often had greater relevance for multinational corporations than for national governments (*The Earth and Its Peoples*, 6th ed., pp. 888–889/7th ed., pp. 857–859; History Reasoning Skill—Causation; Learning Objectives SB-6, CUL-1; Key Concept 6.3 II A, B).

17. ANSWER: B. The industrialization of Europe in the late eighteenth and early nineteenth centuries stimulated a second surge of imperialism. As opposed to the previous wave of colonization, which sought gold and had religious conversion as its goal, the second wave sought raw materials for industrial production and markets for mass produced goods (*The Earth and Its Peoples*, 6th ed., p. 718/7th ed., p. 694; History Reasoning Skill—Contextualization; Learning Objectives ECON-1,2,3,7, SB-3; Key Concept 5.1 II C, D).

18. ANSWER: D. In the time between Columbus and the Industrial Revolution, Europeans did not project power over the interior of Africa as they did in the nineteenth century after the Berlin Conference. Instead, they controlled ports along the east or Swahili coast of Africa and slaving fortresses on the western side (*The Earth and Its Peoples*, 6th ed., pp. 509–510/7th ed., pp. 495–497; History Reasoning Skill—Continuity and Change Over Time; Learning Objectives ECON-2, SB-3; Key Concept 4.3 II A).

19. ANSWER: A. Qing and Mughal India were able to resist European direct control between 1450 and 1800, unlike Latin America during this same time. However, in the nineteenth century, the Sepoy Rebellion in India and the Opium Wars in China made it clear that these states were no

longer able to resist the powerful and industrialized British Empire (*The Earth and Its Peoples*, 6th ed., pp. 645–646, 703–704/7th ed., pp. 626–629, 680–682; History Reasoning Skill—Comparison; Learning Objectives ECON-2, SB-3; Key Concept 5.2 I B).

20. ANSWER: A. The mixing and blending of knowledge and technologies occurs when cultures come into contact with each other. The lateen sails are Indian Ocean, the oars Mediterranean, and the rudder is East Asian. The Portuguese probably gained knowledge of these technologies through Islamic contacts because Muslims controlled North African and West African trading (*The Earth and Its Peoples*, 6th ed., pp. 404–407, 411–412/7th ed., pp. 394–403; Historical Thinking Skill—Contextualization; Learning Objectives ENV-2, CUL-3; Key Concept 4.1 II).

21. ANSWER: B. All the technologies displayed in the image were used in the Indian Ocean, especially prior to 1460. The oars were old Mediterranean technology that was probably on its way out as Portuguese sailors learned how to use rudders and lateen sails to their advantage (*The Earth and Its Peoples*, 6th ed., pp. 227–230, 404–407, 411–412/7th ed., pp. 400–403, 405–409; History Reasoning Skill—Causation; Learning Objectives ENV-2, CUL-3; Key Concept 4.1 II).

22. ANSWER: D. The Portuguese were highly interested in the spice trade of the Indian Ocean and would have needed lateen sails to maneuver with the monsoon winds (*The Earth and Its Peoples*, 6th ed., pp. 410–412/7th ed., pp. 400–403; History Reasoning Skill—Contextualization; Learning Objectives ENV-2, CUL-3; Key Concept 4.1 II).

23. ANSWER: D. Migrations in the industrial age represented continuities as well as changes with previous migrations. Many were interregional and, like migrations in the previous eras, were driven by the need for labor. However, a significant change in migration patterns was the shift from rural to urban movements of people that was greatly accelerated by the growth of large factories around cities (*The Earth and Its Peoples*, 6th ed., p. 578/7th ed., p. 558; History Reasoning Skill—Continuity and Change Over Time; Learning Objectives ENV-5, SB-2, ECON-3; Key Concept 5.4 I B).

24. ANSWER: B. The millions of workers crowding into factories were not involved in the production of food. Thus, industrialization required enormous surpluses of agriculture to free up rural labor. A revolution in agricultural productivity is one reason England was the first to industrialize (*The Earth and Its Peoples*, 6th ed., p. 578/7th ed., p. 558; History Reasoning Skill—Causation, Contextualization; Learning Objectives ENV-5, ECON-3; Key Concept 5.1 I A).

25. ANSWER: A. Nationalism was one of the most powerful new ideologies emerging out of the nineteenth century. The author's references to the strengthening of the Welsh language, Welsh patriotism, and Nonconformity are clearly elements of national identity (*The Earth and Its Peoples*, 6th ed., p. 736/7th ed., p. 710; History Disciplinary Practice—Analyzing Evidence: Content and Sourcing; Learning Objective SB-3; Key Concept: 5.3 III).

26. ANSWER: B. The Columbian Exchange is responsible for what is known as the Great Dying in the Americas, due to exposure to new diseases like smallpox, which came from animal domestication. Some exchanges between cultures had negative impacts (*The Earth and Its Peoples*, 6th ed., p. 466/7th ed., pp. 454–456; History Reasoning Skill—Periodization; Learning Objectives ENV-3,5; Key Concept 4.1 V A).

27. ANSWER: A. The new diseases introduced by the Europeans, such as measles and smallpox, all came from contact with domesticated animals. The Western Hemisphere only had one domesticated large animal, the llama (*The Earth and Its Peoples*, 6th ed., p. 466/7th ed., pp. 454–456; History Reasoning Skill—Periodization; Learning Objective ENV-3; Key Concept 4.1 V A).

28. ANSWER: D. Disease was one of the negative exchanges brought to the new world. Columbus's men infected an island with the flu, the African slave trade brought smallpox, and British traders traded smallpox-infected blankets to North Amerindian tribes (*The Earth and Its Peoples*, 6th ed., p. 466/7th ed., pp. 454–456; History Reasoning Skill—Periodization; Learning Objective ENV-3; Key Concept 4.1 V A).

29. ANSWER: A. A key task in centralizing China under the Qin was reining in the power of local aristocrats and relying upon bureaucrats to carry out the functions of the government. One innovation of the Han Dynasty was to recruit civil servants educated in Confucian schools, thus opening the government to officials based on merit. Although aristocrats gained back some of the rights taken by the Qin, the Han imperial order was highly centralized through its Confucian bureaucracy (*The Earth and Its Peoples*, 6th ed., pp. 152, 155–156/7th ed., pp. 157–161; Historical Thinking Skill—Contextualization; Learning Objectives SB-1,2,3; Key Concept 2.2 II A).

30. ANSWER: C. Historians debate whether Constantine's conversion was genuine or whether he was simply an opportunist. Nevertheless, his conversion to Christianity, and the subsequent establishing of it as the empire's official religion, gave his rule enormous power and reinforced its authority and laws (*The Earth and Its Peoples*, 6th ed., pp. 151–152/7th ed., pp. 156–157; History Reasoning Skill—Comparison; Learning Objective SB-4; Key Concept 2.1 II D).

31. ANSWER: D. The Gupta Empire saw a waning of Buddhism and a return to Hinduism. In this belief system, one accepts his or her birth into a varna, or caste, and carries out the duties therein. Social mobility is virtually impossible (*The Earth and Its Peoples*, 6th ed., p. 179/7th ed., pp.180–181; History Reasoning Skill—Comparison; Learning Objective SOC-2; Key Concept 2.1 I B).

32. ANSWER: A. Mongols invading the Middle East in the thirteenth and fourteenth centuries brought gunpowder with them. It was also traded on the newly opened Silk Road (*The Earth and Its Peoples*, 6th ed., pp. 306, 526–527/7th ed., pp. 337–340; History Reasoning Skill—Causation; Learning Objective SB-3; Key Concept 3.1 III D).

33. ANSWER: C. The Turks under Babur used gunpowder weapons to invade and secure northern India. They were Muslim (*The Earth and Its Peoples*, 6th ed., pp. 536–538/7th ed., pp. 519–522; History Reasoning Skill—Contextualization; Learning Objective SB-3; Key Concept 4.3 II B).

34. ANSWER: C. Memed II of the Ottoman Turks captured the city of Constantinople in 1453, using cannons to end the long reign of the eastern Roman Empire (Byzantine). Without this technology, the Turks had been unable to take the city during the preceding century but now could invade Eastern Europe, laying siege to Vienna and conquering the Balkans region of Europe (*The Earth and Its Peoples*, 6th ed., pp. 524–526/7th ed., pp. 508–511; History Reasoning Skill—Causation; Learning Objective SB-3; Key Concept 4.3 II B).

35. ANSWER: C. The Crusades were a series of Holy Wars waged by the pope in an effort to reclaim the Holy Land (Jerusalem) from the Abbasid Empire. The Abbasid Empire was a Muslim empire; therefore, the development of Islam that began in the seventh century was the long-term cause of the Crusades (*The Earth and Its Peoples*, 6th ed., p. 289/7th ed., pp. 288–289; History Reasoning Skill—Causation; Learning Objectives CUL, SB; Key Concept 3.1 III A).

36. ANSWER: A. The Abbasid Empire was the Golden Age of Islam and was far more advanced than Western Europe was during the post-Classical period. The Muslims made advances in mathematics, adopted numerals from India, perfected the astrolabe, and translated Greek classics of philosophy and science. Muslim doctors stressed observation and experimentation and developed surgical techniques. This knowledge was brought back to Western Europe by the crusading knights (*The Earth and Its Peoples*, 6th ed., p. 330/7th ed., pp. 253–254; Historical Thinking Skill—Causation; Learning Objectives CUL, ECON; Key Concept 3.2 II).

37. ANSWER: A. The colonization of the Americas by the Europeans led to cultural and religious clashes similar to the Crusades (*The Earth and Its Peoples*, 6th ed., p. 481/7th ed., pp. 464–465; History Reasoning Skill—Comparison; Learning Objectives CUL, SB; Key Concept 4.1).

38. ANSWER: B. Local native populations of the Americas and Pacific lacked sufficient technology and any natural resistance to European diseases. China was surrounded by cultures that did have these abilities (*The Earth and Its Peoples*, 6th ed., pp. 466–479/7th ed., pp. 454–456; Historical Thinking Skill—Contextualization; Learning Objective SB-9; Key Concept 4.3 II C).

39. ANSWER: D. China had the world's most powerful economy up to the nineteenth century. Chinese products were the reason that the Silk Road and Indian Ocean maritime trades were so successful (*The Earth and Its Peoples*, 6th ed., pp. 526–527/7th ed., p. 542; History Reasoning Skill—Contextualization; Learning Objective SB-4; Key Concept 4.3 II B).

40. ANSWER: C. The Spanish monarchs were fresh off reunifying the Iberian Peninsula and were in no position to consider expansion. Spanish maritime expansion was driven by the desires of explorers and

PRACTICE TEST 2 ❖ 577

conquistadors (*The Earth and Its Peoples*, 6th ed., pp. 410–415/7th ed., pp. 401–406; History Reasoning Skill—Contextualization; Learning Objective SB-4; Key Concept 4.3 II C).

41. ANSWER: B. The diffusion of the bubonic plague occurred along trade routes throughout the Eastern Hemisphere (*The Earth and Its Peoples*, 6th ed., pp. 273, 330/7th ed., pp. 322–326; History Reasoning Skill—Causation; Learning Objective ENV; Key Concept 3.1 IV).

42. ANSWER: C. Just as the bubonic plague spread along trade routes, smallpox spread to the Americas through the Columbian Exchange (*The Earth and Its Peoples*, 6th ed., p. 328/7th ed., pp. 453–454; History Reasoning Skill—Comparison; Learning Objective ENV; Key Concept 4.1 V A).

43. ANSWER: C. Enlightenment philosophers critiqued the role that religion played in public life, insisting on the importance of reason as opposed to revelation. The Enlightenment philosophers would have turned to science, not religion, during the bubonic plague (*The Earth and Its Peoples*, 6th ed., p. 443/7th ed., p. 434; History Reasoning Skill—Continuity and Change Over Time; Learning Objective CUL; Key Concept 5.3 I A).

44. ANSWER: D. Although agriculture first appeared in North Africa and the Middle East, it later developed independently in South America and East Asia. It diffused from these points of origin to wider areas (*The Earth and Its Peoples*, 6th ed., pp. 10–11/7th ed., pp. 16–20; History Reasoning Skill—Interpretation; Learning Objective ENV-2; Key Concept 1.2 I A).

45. ANSWER: B. After 10,000 B.C.E., an ice age gave way to global warming. Current theory holds that the formation of deserts put pressure on human populations. In addition, warmer and wetter climates turned grassland, on which many hunted animals depended, into forests that could not support them. This drove people to pastoralism and agriculture (*The Earth and Its Peoples*, 6th ed., p. 12/7th ed., pp. 16–20; History Reasoning Skill—Causation; Learning Objectives ENV-4, ECON-1; Key Concept: 1.2 I A, 1.2 II A).

46. ANSWER: C. Agriculture produced surpluses of food, which in turn allowed populations to grow larger than possible in foraging and hunting societies. With people freed from the necessities of producing food, large agricultural communities could support many craftsmen and artisans (*The Earth and Its Peoples*, 6th ed., p. 14/7th ed., pp. 16–20; History Disciplinary Practice and Reasoning Skill—Argument Development, Comparison; Learning Objectives SOC-2, ECON-5; Key Concept: 1.2 II A).

47. ANSWER: B. Malfante was describing Africa; therefore, he was describing the trans-Saharan trade route. He wrote approximately 100 years after Mansa Musa made his pilgrimage to Mecca, which increased interest in West Africa. The vast amounts of gold in Africa drew merchants from Eurasia (*The Earth and Its Peoples*, 6th ed., p. 512/7th ed., pp. 495–497; History Disciplinary Practice—Analyzing Historical Evidence; Learning Objective ECON; Key Concept 3.1 A).

© 2019 Cengage Learning, Inc. May not be scanned, copied or duplicated, or posted to a publicly accessible website, in whole or in part.

48. ANSWER: A. Malfante pointed out that the country had many African Muslims, which provides evidence of cultural diffusion. Islam began during the seventh century in the Arabian Peninsula and quickly spread throughout the Middle East, Africa, and to the Iberian Peninsula (*The Earth and Its Peoples*, 6th ed., p. 391/7th ed., p. 383; History Disciplinary Practice—Analyzing Historical Evidence; Learning Objective CUL; Key Concept 3.1 III A).

49. ANSWER: B. As a result of the increase of exchange networks, an increasing number of travelers within Afro-Eurasia wrote about their travels (*The Earth and Its Peoples*, 6th ed., p. 386/7th ed., p. 378; History Disciplinary Practice—Analyzing Historical Evidence; Learning Objective CUL; Key Concept 3.1 III C).

50. ANSWER: C. There were several instances in the twentieth century when populations were partitioned. After World War I, Palestine and part of the Middle East were divided into mandates. In India, independence from Britain led to deep religious divisions. Hence the former colony was divided into Pakistan and India (*The Earth and Its Peoples*, 6th ed., pp. 848–849/7th ed., pp. 819–820; History Reasoning Skill—Causation; Learning Objectives SB-4,7; Key Concept 6.2 III A).

51. ANSWER: C. After World War II, a wave of independence movements swept across Africa and Asia. Some, such as Algeria and Indo-China, were bloody struggles against their colonizers. Although India would be wracked by religious violence immediately after independence, the separation from Britain was a mostly peaceful process of negotiations (*The Earth and Its Peoples*, 6th ed., pp. 793–796/7th ed., pp. 791–794; History Reasoning Skill—Contextualization, Comparison; Learning Objectives SB-7,10, SOC-7; Key Concept 5.2 I E).

52. ANSWER: D. A new pattern of migration in the last half of the twentieth century involved people moving from their newly independent nations into large cities of their former colonizers. In London and Paris, for example, large cultural enclaves of South Asian and Algerian immigrants formed. These communities retained ties to their former nations (*The Earth and Its Peoples*, 6th ed., p. 850/7th ed., p. 821; History Reasoning Skill—Causation, Comparison; Learning Objectives SOC-8, ECON-2; Key Concept 6.2 III B).

53. ANSWER: C. During the eleventh and twelfth centuries, the Mongols took over most of Asia through superior military strategy. The image depicts the use of catapults, which was a Mongol specialty (*The Earth and Its Peoples*, 6th ed., p. 324/7th ed., pp. 320–322; History Disciplinary Practice—Analyzing Historical Evidence; Learning Objective SB; Key Concept 3.1 I E).

54. ANSWER: A. As a result of the Mongolian Empire, significant technological and cultural transfers took place. Many Mongols converted to Islam and adapted to the culture of those whom they conquered (*The Earth and Its Peoples*, 6th ed., p. 330/7th ed., pp. 322–324; History Disciplinary Practice—Analyzing Historical Evidence; Learning Objective CUL; Key Concept 3.3 II).

55. ANSWER: D. The Mongols had the largest empire in world history and divided it into four khanates (*The Earth and Its Peoples*, 6th ed., p. 334/7th ed., p. 328; History Disciplinary Practice—Analyzing Historical Evidence; Learning Objective SB; Key Concept 3.2 I B).

ANSWERS FOR SECTION I, PART B: SHORT-ANSWER QUESTIONS

QUESTION 1

A. This question asks students to interpret an author's evaluation of Marx's interpretation of the Taiping Rebellion. The first portion of the question asks students to consider why the author disagrees with Karl Marx's view that the Taiping Rebellion was based on external factors. This requires the student to closely read, interpret, and understand the argument made by the author. If a student knows that Marx was an anti-imperialist, it will help support the idea that he was more fixed in his viewpoint that external forces were the cause behind the Taiping Rebellion. The author counters Marx by pointing out that there were factors inside China that supported the event.

B. The second portion of the question asks students to explain two reasons that would support the author's assertion about the Taiping Rebellion. It is clear the author argues that internal forces, such as the oppressed Hakka and the leadership of Hong Xiuquan, were factors beyond the external reasons supported by Marx. Students may add that the persecution of the Manchus (Qing) was considered to be oppressive to much of the Chinese population. This oppressive submission at least partially led to the rebellious reactions during the Taiping Rebellion.

(*The Earth and Its Peoples*, 6th ed., p. 747/7th ed., pp. 626–629; History Disciplinary Practice—Argument Development; Learning Objectives CUL-2,4, SB-1,2,4,7,9, ECON-7, SOC-3.7; Key Concept 5.3 III A).

QUESTION 2

A. This question refers to the map of Africa in the nineteenth century. The first portion of the question asks students to provide two pieces of evidence beyond the map that would show growing trade, Islamic reform movements, or other internal forces that created new states throughout Africa. Multiple responses could be given, including types of goods traded or extracted, such as gold mining, slaves, and diamond mining. The map does not show the number of whites introduced into the continent, especially in southern Africa.

B. The map neglects the sophisticated network of trade and political systems already in place in Africa. This network allowed for better initial trade, especially on the coasts of Africa. Although some states are shown in the map, the technological advantage (weaponry) of the Europeans in defeating those African states is lacking. Perhaps major areas of African resistance to the European influx could be shown as well.

(*The Earth and Its Peoples*, 6th ed., p. 694/7th ed., pp. 670–671; History Disciplinary Practice and Reasoning Skill—Analyzing Historical Evidence, Causation; Learning Objectives ENV-9, SB-5, ECON-2,4,5,9, SOC-2,3,4; Key Concept 5.1).

QUESTION 3

A. This question refers to regional and interregional interactions from 600 to 1450. Students may answer that one cause for the interactions includes the Silk Road, the Mediterranean Sea, the trans-Saharan routes, and the Indian Ocean maritime trade system. Goods (such as silk, porcelain, spices, metals, and gems), slaves, and the spread of language and religion were the impetus and led to the need for more regional and interregional interactions during the period.

B. One effect of a new trade network in Africa during the period included the development of cities such as Timbuktu and Swahili city-states. The Bantu language mixed with Arabic to form a Swahili culture on the east coast of Africa. Muslim merchant communities populated that east coast of the continent. Crops such as bananas are known to have diffused to other regions during this time.

C. An effect of new trade in Asia during the time would include the emergence of cities such as Hangzhou, Calicut, Baghdad, and Melaka. More trade empires emerged, and the Mongols facilitated trade along the Silk Road. Major works of infrastructure, such as the Grand Canal in China, were also built during this time. The use of paper money began in China during this time. Horses were used more widely for trade and interaction in Central Asia.

(*The Earth and Its Peoples*, 6th ed., p. 331/7th ed., p. 327; History Reasoning Skill—Causation, Contextualization; Learning Objectives ENV-3,6,8, CUL-6, SB-1,2,5,6,9, ECON-2,3,5,6,10,11,12, SOC-3,5,8; Key Concept 3.1).

QUESTION 4

A. This question refers to the Industrial Revolution beginning in the eighteenth century as a major turning point in world history. Students have choices of evidence that are almost too numerous to write about for the first portion of the essay. For each piece of evidence given, students must not merely list items that were produced in the period, but show how each might be considered as a support for the idea that the Industrial Revolution is a major turning point. Cotton, rubber, palm oil, sugar, wheat, meat, guano, and metals are a few of the items that fueled the change and influenced better shipbuilding, more ironworks, and increased textile production.

B. Students are asked to think about other periods that may be more of a turning point in world history, or they may choose to refute the notion that the Industrial Revolution was a major turning point at all. On the environmental side, students may show the negative influence of the Industrial Revolution through coal mining and subsequent air pollution in cities. Factories drew more people into urban areas, spreading various diseases and providing poor working conditions.

(*The Earth and Its Peoples*, 6th ed., p. 575/7th ed., pp. 571–575; History Reasoning Skill—Periodization; Learning Objectives ENV-9, SB-5, ECON-2,4,5,9, SOC-2,3,4; Key Concept 5.1).

ANSWER FOR SECTION II, PART A: DOCUMENT-BASED QUESTION (DBQ)

THE DOCUMENTS

Following are short analyses of the documents. The italicized words suggest what your margin notes might include.

DOCUMENT 1. This document shows some of the issues women faced in terms of working and supporting their families. *This document also shows women carrying out political roles by petitioning the government.*

DOCUMENT 2. *This document shows the lengths Indian women went to in order to fight against British colonial rule in India. This boycott tactic was a powerful strategy that would be used by other groups in history.*

DOCUMENT 3. This document is *a call for women to act and to be involved politically with what was happening to women and in the larger struggle for equal treatment.*

DOCUMENT 4. This document shows the African National Congress responding to women's call for equal political representation in one of the key organizations fighting for African rights in southern Africa. *This document is an example of women's goals of having equal status while at the same time acknowledging women's particular concerns.*

DOCUMENT 5. Both women are noted revolutionary leaders in the Cuban Revolution. You see them both armed here and in that way *they carried out roles that are stereotypically thought of as men's roles in revolution.*

DOCUMENT 6. This document is similar to Document 3 in that it *describes the ongoing struggles of both men and women living under an oppressive regime in South Africa. It called for particular rights for women as well as the general fight against poverty. This is another example of women organizing politically.*

The documents can be grouped several ways; you could group by location—Africa, Latin America, and India—by time, by the types of roles, or by the types of goals addressed in the documents.

DBQ ESSAY

For this DBQ, you need to be sure your thesis makes an analytical argument for the differing roles women played as described in the documents. The analysis of the documents should provide enough evidence to support the thesis clearly. Attempt to use evidence from all documents. Avoid simply listing one document after another. Instead, make connections between or among documents in responding to the question. There are some good opportunities for point of view to earn the second document analysis point.

For your analysis, it is important to remember the historical context. A discussion of what was happening in India, South Africa, and Latin America at the time is an important component of your essay. Both India and South Africa were experiencing the inequalities of imperial rule firsthand, and women suffered in particular ways because of those inequalities. Latin America was not experiencing direct colonial rule; the Cuban Revolution was affected by global conflict. Argentina, under Perón, may be a good example to use that was not provided in the given documents. The notion that Eva Perón was a recognizable, popular personality in Argentina allowed her husband, President Juan Perón, to maintain a more popular public persona. Frieda Kahlo's art in Mexico is yet another Latin American example of women's roles in political movements. A well-known communist sympathizer, Kahlo and her famous artist husband, Diego Rivera, housed Leon Trotsky to give him asylum from an oppressive Soviet Union regime.

The documents give good insight into the global issues. You should also devote some attention to an analysis and synthesize many issues faced by women as caregivers and political activists. What were women's roles at home? What were women's roles in the nation?

SCORING 0 (zero) to 2 points may be awarded for thesis. For 1 point, the thesis makes a historically defensible claim. Another point may be earned if a student develops and supports a cohesive argument that recognizes and accounts for historical complexity by explicitly illustrating relationships among historical evidence, such as contradiction, corroboration, and/or qualification. Up to 2 points may be earned for document analysis. 1 point if a student utilizes the content of at least five of the documents to support the stated thesis or a relevant argument. The student must explain the significance of the author's point of view, author's purpose, historical context, and/or audience for at least four documents in order to earn another point in document analysis. For using evidence beyond the documents, students may earn the first point by situating (contextualization) the argument by explaining the broader historical events, developments, or processes immediately relevant to the question. To earn the second point, students must provide an example or additional piece of specific evidence beyond those found in the documents to support or qualify the argument. A last point may be earned for synthesis. The argument may be extended by explaining the connections between the argument and ONE of the following: (a) a development in a different historical period, situation, era, or geographical area; (b) a course theme and/or approach to history that is not the focus of the essay (such as political, economic, social, cultural, or intellectual history); or (c) a different discipline or field of inquiry (such as economics, government and politics, art history, or anthropology).

(*The Earth and Its Peoples*, 6th ed., pp. 660, 794–797; History Reasoning Skill—Causation; Learning Objectives CUL-2,3,4,5,9, SB-4, ECON-4, SOC-1,3,5,6; Key Concept 6.3).

ANSWER FOR SECTION II, PART B: LONG ESSAY QUESTION

LONG ESSAY FOR QUESTION OPTION 2

This essay asks students to compare the policy of China to one out of two countries in terms of their interaction with the West from 1600 to 1800. Be sure to include both similarities and differences in order to get the full points for addressing the question using argumentation.

Of the three, Russia was unique in that it made some radical changes in an effort to embrace Western ideals under the leadership of autocrats such as Peter the Great. China took a more cautious approach, limiting trade using the Canton system in order to keep careful control over economic interactions with foreigners; one specific example of this might be the failure of the British Macartney mission in the late eighteenth century, which did not succeed in getting China to increase foreign trade. Japan took an even stronger approach, severely limiting interaction through trade and basically cutting off interaction with the West under the Tokugawa Shogunate, which lasted until 1868. Here the essay should analyze why each country made its particular choice regarding interaction with the West, comparing and contrasting their reasons. All three regions were protective of their domestic traditions and cultural identities. Remember, China must be compared to either Russia OR Japan. There are also opportunities to go beyond the examples given (for synthesis). For example, the colonial period in Latin America showed similarities in the European and later U.S. dominance in that region. The West dominated indigenous peoples in Latin America, and it controlled Latin America's resources, setting the stage for later desires to become independent. The Atlantic Trade System between the African continent and the West show some differences in the way trade was controlled by African kings and merchants.

Again, be sure to discuss similarities and differences, and take the time to analyze why you are claiming certain similarities and differences. Use good evidence to support your comparisons in order to earn a high score.

SCORING The Long Essay is worth a possible 6 points. 0–1 point is awarded for the thesis. 0–2 points are awarded for "argument development: using the targeted history reasoning skill." 0–2 points are awarded for "argument development: using evidence." Finally, 0–1 point is awarded for "contextualization."

(*The Earth and Its Peoples*, 6th ed., p. 645/7th ed., Chapter 24; History Reasoning Skill—Continuity and Change Over Time, Comparison; Learning Objectives CUL-2,4,5, ECON-8; Key Concept 4.1).